Conformity and Conflict

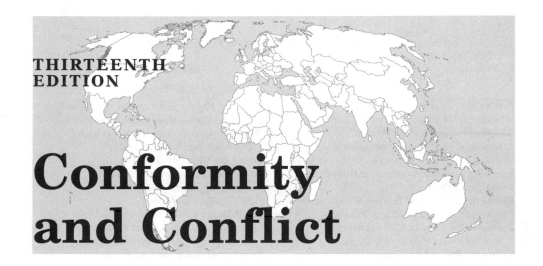

**THIRTEENTH
EDITION**

Conformity and Conflict

Readings in Cultural Anthropology

JAMES SPRADLEY

DAVID W. MCCURDY
Macalester College

PEARSON

Prentice
Hall

Upper Saddle River, New Jersey 07458

Library of Congress Cataloging-in-Publication Data

Conformity and conflict : readings in cultural anthropology / [edited by]
James Spradley, David W. McCurdy.—13th ed.
   p. cm.
  Includes index.
  ISBN-13: 978-0-205-64585-5
  ISBN-10: 0-205-64585-2
  1. Ethnology. 2. Anthropology. I. Spradley, James P. II. McCurdy, David W.
  GN325.C69 2009
  305.8—dc22   2008030815

Editorial Director: Leah Jewell
Director of Marketing: Brandy Dawson
AVP, Publisher: Nancy Roberts
Editor-in-Chief: Dickson Musslewhite
Senior Operations Supervisor: Sherry Lewis
Prepress and Manufacturing Buyer:
  Maura Zaldivar
Marketing Manager: Lindsey Prudhomme
Marketing Assistant: Craig Deming
Full-Service Project Management:
  Bruce Hobart/Pine Tree Composition, Inc.
Editorial Project Manager:
  Vanessa Gennarelli
Production Liaison: Joanne Hakim
Editorial Assitant: Nart Varoqua

Manager, Rights and Permissions: Zina Arabia
Manager, Visual Research: Beth Brenzel
**Manager, Cover Visual Research and
  Permissions:** Karen Sanatar
Cover Art Director: Jayne Conte
Cover Design: Bruce Kenselaar
Image Permission Coordinator:
  Angelique Sharps
Front Cover Art: Johnny Bivers/AFP/Getty
  Images, Inc. and Andres Hemandez/
  Getty Images News/Getty Images, Inc.
Supplements Editor: Mayda Bosco
Composition: Pine Tree Composition, Inc.
Printer, Binder, and Cover Printer:
  R. R. Donnelley & Sons

For permission to use copyrighted material, grateful acknowledgment is made to the copyright holders listed on appropriate page within text.

Pearson Education LTD. London
Pearson Education Singapore, Pte. Ltd
Pearson Education, Canada, Ltd
Pearson Education–Japan
Pearson Education Australia PTY, Limited

Pearson Education North Asia Ltd
Pearson Educación de Mexico, S.A. de C.V.
Pearson Education Malaysia, Pte. Ltd
Pearson Education, Upper Saddle River,
  New Jersey

10 9 8 7 6 5 4 3 2 1

Student ISBN-13:   978-0-205-64585-5
Student ISBN-10:   0-205-64585-2
Exam Copy ISBN-13: 978-0-205-65957-9
Exam Copy ISBN-10:   0-205-65957-8

To Barbara Spradley and Carolyn McCurdy

Contents

Preface   XV

ONE ━━━━━━━━━━━━━━━━━━━━━━━━━━━━━

Culture and Ethnography   1

1 Ethnography and Culture   7

JAMES SPRADLEY

To discover culture, the ethnographer must learn from the informant as a student.

2 Eating Christmas in the Kalahari   15

RICHARD BORSHAY LEE

The "generous" gift of a Christmas ox involves the anthropologist in a classic case of cross-cultural misunderstanding.

3 Shakespeare in the Bush   23

LAURA BOHANNAN

Cross-cultural communication breaks down when the anthropologist attempts to translate the meaning of *Hamlet* to the Tiv.

4 Fieldwork on Prostitution in the Era of AIDS   33

CLAIRE E. STERK

Fieldwork among urban prostitutes means doing ethnography under difficult but, in the end, manageable circumstances.

5 Nice Girls Don't Talk to Rastas   46

GEORGE GMELCH

Interaction between a U.S. student and a Rastafarian illustrates the destructive power of naïve realism in the fieldwork setting.

TWO

Language and Communication   52

6 Manipulating Meaning: The Military Name Game   56

SARAH BOXER

Public perception can be affected by one's choice of words, a fact embraced by the U.S. armed forces as they try to name military operations without offending anyone.

7 Conversation Style: Talking on the Job   61

DEBORAH TANNEN

On the job, men and women use distinctive conversation styles to ask for help, leading them to evaluate performance and character differently.

8 Kinds of Talk: *Juicing* Clients in Tattoo World   69

JENNIFER BOEHLKE

Tattoo artists use a kind of talk, *juicing,* to persuade clients to have tattoos, reduce their fear, reinforce their decisions, and spend more money.

9 Anthropologists Investigate Communication Technology   79

BELLE MELLOR

Anthropologists study how people use and carry cell phones, the Internet, land lines, and other channels of communication.

THREE

Ecology and Subsistence   83

 10 The Hunters: Scarce Resources in the Kalahari   88

RICHARD BORSHAY LEE

!Kung and other foragers traditionally worked less and ate better than many other people with more "advanced" food producing techniques. Today, however, their survival depends more on drilling wells and keeping cattle than on collecting wild foods.

 11 Adaptive Failure: Easter's End   104

JARED DIAMOND

Polynesian settlers on Easter Island prospered and multiplied until they eventually destroyed their island habitat and, with it, their civilization. Is this a harbinger of things to come for all humankind?

12 Subsistence and Market: When the Turtle Collapses   114

BERNARD NIETSCHMANN

World demand for green sea turtles disrupts the traditional lives of Miskito Indians.

13 Forest Development the Indian Way   124

RICHARD K. REED

South American governments could learn much about tropical forest development from the Amazonian Indians who live there.

FOUR

Economic Systems   135

 14 Reciprocity and the Power of Giving   139

LEE CRONK

Gifts not only function to tie people together but may also be used to "flatten" an opponent and control the behavior of others.

15   Global Women in the New Economy   146

BARBARA EHRENREICH AND ARLIE RUSSELL HOCHSCHILD

Millions of women migrate from poor to wealthy
nations serving as nannies, maids, and sex workers.
They send money home but find it hard to separate
from their countries and families.

16   Cocaine and the Economic Deterioration
of Bolivia   156

JACK WEATHERFORD

The world market for cocaine robs Bolivian villages
of their men and causes problems for health, nutrition,
transportation, and family.

17   Malawi Versus the World Bank   167

SONIA PATTEN

Malawi government's successful state-subsidized
fertilizer program challenges the World Bank and IMF's
insistence on market-driven agricultural programs.

FIVE

Kinship and Family   172

18   Mother's Love: Death without Weeping   176

NANCY SCHEPER-HUGHES

Close mother–child bonds suffer in the presence of
high infant mortality in a Brazilian shantytown.

19   Family and Kinship in Village India   187

DAVID W. MCCURDY

Kinship still organizes the lives of Bhil villagers despite
economic opportunities that draw people away from
the community and dependence on relatives.

20   Polyandry: When Brothers Take a Wife   195

MELVYN C. GOLDSTEIN

By jointly marrying one woman, Tibetan brothers
preserve family resources and the "good life."

21 Uterine Families and the Women's Community   203

Margery Wolf

To succeed in a traditional patrilineal family, a Chinese woman must create her own informal uterine family inside her husband's household.

SIX

Identity, Roles, and Groups   210

22 Heading Home: Women, Work, and Identity in America   215

Dianna Shandy and Karine Moe

Why are young, educated, professional women leaving high-paying jobs for a life at home?

23 Poverty at Work: Office Employment and the Crack Alternative   227

Philippe Bourgois

Poor, uneducated Puerto Rican men living in Spanish Harlem feel that the risks they run selling drugs are preferable to the disrespect they encounter as low-wage employees in New York's financial and service companies.

24 Symbolizing Roles: Behind the Veil   240

Elizabeth W. Fernea and Robert A. Fernea

The women's veil stands for everything from personal protection to female honor in Mediterranean societies.

25 Mixed Blood   248

Jeffrey M. Fish

A woman can change her race from black to "brunette" by taking a plane from New York to Brazil.

SEVEN

Law and Politics   259

26 Cross-Cultural Law: The Case of the Gypsy
Offender   263

ANNE SUTHERLAND

Legal cultures clash when a young Gypsy is convicted
of using someone else's social security number to apply
for a car loan.

27 Life without Chiefs   272

MARVIN HARRIS

Small societies based on reciprocal and redistributive
economic exchange can do without officials.

28 The Founding Indian Fathers   281

JACK WEATHERFORD

Although their contribution goes unrecognized, Indian,
especially Iroquoian, political structure served as a
model that helped to produce the United States federal
government.

29 The Kindness of Strangers: The U.S. and Iraq   291

ROBIN FOX

Like missionaries of the past, the U.S. government
believes people everywhere crave democracy, even in
Iraq where loyalty cleaves to tribes, sects, and ethnic
backgrounds, not the state.

EIGHT

Religion, Magic, and Worldview   298

30 Taraka's Ghost   303

STANLEY A. FREED AND RUTH S. FREED

A woman relieves her anxiety and gains family support
when she is possessed by a friend's ghost.

31 Baseball Magic   310

GEORGE GMELCH

American baseball players employ magical practices as they try to deal with the uncertainty of their game.

32 Run for the Wall: An American Pilgrimage   320

JILL DUBISCH

An annual ritual motorcycle pilgrimage from Los Angeles to Washington, D.C., transforms the Vietnam veterans and other participants.

33 Body Ritual among the Nacirema   334

HORACE MINER

The Nacirema display a complex array of body rituals aimed at achieving health and beauty.

NINE

Globalization   340

34 The Road to Refugee Resettlement   344

DIANNA SHANDY

Nuer refugees must develop the skill and determination to pass through a series of bureaucratic hurdles to reach and adjust to life in the United States.

35 Why Tourism Matters   354

SHARON BOHN GMELCH

Although many people associate it with vacations and viewing exotic natives, tourism is a central globalizing agent worth anthropological study.

36 Japanese Hip-Hop and the Globalization of Popular Culture   365

IAN CONDRY

Using the ethnographic approach in hip-hop clubs to understand a transnational trend, an anthropologist discovers that a form of pop culture invented in the United States can be hybridized to take on a Japanese flavor in Tokyo.

TEN

Culture Change and Applied Anthropology   380

37 The Kayapo Resistance   385

TERENCE TURNER

Using everything from airplanes to the world environmental movement, the Kayapo Indians of Brazil manage to prevent the building of a dam that would have flooded their Amazonian habitat.

38 Medical Anthropology: Improving Nutrition in Malawi   403

SONIA PATTEN

A medical anthropologist is part of a team that introduces milk goats to Malawi villagers to counter a high rate of infant mortality among toddlers.

39 Using Anthropology   415

DAVID W. MCCURDY

Professional anthropologists do everything from ethnographies of automobile production lines to famine relief, but even the neophyte may be able to use the ideas of culture and ethnography to understand the workplace.

40 Career Advice for Anthropology Undergraduates   428

JOHN T. OMOHUNDRO

The ability to translate useful anthropological skills into "résumé speak" is one way for anthropology graduates to find employment.

Glossary   439

Index   445

Preface

Cultural anthropology has a twofold mission: to understand other cultures and to communicate that understanding. Thirty-five years ago, in preparing the first edition of this book, Jim Spradley and I sought to make communication easier and more enjoyable for teachers and students alike. We focused on the twin themes stated in the title—conformity (order) and conflict (change)—while organizing selections into sections based on traditional topics. We balanced the coverage of cultures between non-Western and Western (including North American) societies so students could make their own cultural comparisons and see the relation between anthropology and their own lives. We chose articles that reflected interesting topics in anthropology, but we also looked for selections that illustrated important concepts and theories, because we believed that anthropology provides a unique and powerful way to look at human experience. We searched extensively for scholarly articles written with insight and clarity, and where suitable material was absent, encouraged anthropologists to send us original material. Students and instructors in hundreds of colleges and universities responded enthusiastically to our efforts and a pattern was set that carried through twelve editions.

This thirteenth edition retains the features of earlier ones: the focus on stability and change, the coverage of a broad range of societies, the combination of professionalism and readability in selections, the view that anthropology provides a perspective on experience, and carefully integrated organization. As in previous editions, I have revamped topics and added and subtracted selections in response to the suggestions of instructors and students across the country. Anthropology and the world it seeks to understand have changed since the first edition of *Conformity and Conflict*. New articles have been chosen to reflect these changes. Most new selections have been written within the last few years; ten articles were created especially for this volume, and eight are revised and updated versions of previous selections. In all, of forty articles, ten are new and four are revised and updated.

I have also continued the expanded special features that have appeared in past editions. Part introductions include discussion of many basic anthropological definitions for instructors who do not want to use a standard textbook but find it useful to provide students with a terminological foundation. Article introductions seek to tie selections to anthropological concepts and explanations in a coherent and systematic way.

Several student aids are retained in the thirteenth edition. Lists of key terms accompany each part introduction. Each article is followed by several review questions. Maps locating societies discussed in articles accompany each selection. There is also a glossary and subject index at the end of the book.

A complimentary instructor's manual and test bank are available from the publisher. The manual contains a summary of each article along with a large selection of true–false and multiple-choice questions for articles and part introductions.

It has always been my aim to provide a book that meets the needs of students and instructors. To help with this goal, I encourage you to send your comments and ideas for improving *Conformity and Conflict* to me at dcmccurdy@comcast.net.

Many people have made suggestions that guided this revision of *Conformity and Conflict*. I am especially grateful to George and Sharon Gmelch, Union College; Sonia Patten and Dianna Shandy, Macalester College; and the reviewers for this edition: Craig Bacino, Maria Chavez, Western Washington University; Dorothy L. Hodgson, Rutgers University; Barbara K. Jones, Brookdale Community College; David Minderhout, Bloomsburg University; Bhavani Sitaraman, University of Alabama-Huntsville; and Mary R. Vermilion, Washington University. I would also like to thank my editor, Dickson Musslewhite, for his guidance and work on this volume.

Conformity and Conflict

ONE

CULTURE AND ETHNOGRAPHY

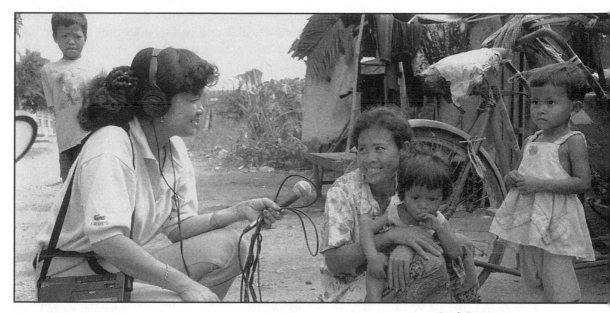

Stock Boston

READINGS IN THIS SECTION

Ethnography and Culture   7
James P. Spradley

Eating Christmas in the Kalahari   15
Richard Borshay Lee

Shakespeare in the Bush   23
Laura Bohannan

Fieldwork on Prostitution in the Era of AIDS   33
Claire E. Sterk

Nice Girls Don't Talk to Rastas   46
George Gmelch

Culture, as its name suggests, lies at the heart of cultural anthropology. And the concept of **culture,** along with ethnography, sets anthropology apart from other social and behavioral sciences. Let us look more closely at these concepts.

To understand what anthropologists mean by *culture,* imagine yourself in a foreign setting, such as a market town in India, forgetting what you might already know about that country. You step off a bus onto a dusty street where you are immediately confronted by strange sights, sounds, and smells. Men dress in Western clothes, but of a different style. Some women drape them-selves in long shawls that entirely cover their bodies. They peer at you through a small gap in this garment as they walk by. Buildings are one- or two-story affairs, open at the front so you can see inside. Near you some people sit on wicker chairs eating strange foods. Most unusual is how people talk. They utter vocalizations unlike any you have ever heard, and you wonder how they can pos-sibly understand each other. But obviously they do, since their behavior seems organized and purposeful.

Scenes such as this confronted early explorers, missionaries, and anthro-pologists, and from their observations an obvious point emerged. People living in various parts of the world looked and behaved in dramatically different ways. And these differences correlated with groups. The people of India had customs different from those of the Papuans; the British did not act and dress like the Iroquois.

Two possible explanations for group differences came to mind. Some argued that group behavior was inherited. Dahomeans of the African Gold Coast, for example, were characterized as particularly "clever and adaptive" by one British colonial official, while, according to the same authority, another African group was "happy-go-lucky and improvident." Usually implied in such statements was the idea that group members were born that way. Such think-ing persists to the present and in its most malignant extreme takes the form of racism.

But a second explanation also emerged. Perhaps, rather than a product of inheritance, the behavior characteristic of a group was learned. The way people dressed, what they ate, how they talked—all these could more easily be explained as acquisitions. Thus a baby born on the African Gold Coast would, if imme-diately transported to China and raised like other children there, grow up to dress, eat, and talk like a Chinese. Cultural anthropologists focus on the expla-nation of learned behavior.

The idea of learning, and a need to label the lifestyles associated with par-ticular groups, led to the definition of culture. In 1871, British anthropologist Sir Edward Burnet Tylor argued that "Culture . . . is that complex whole which includes knowledge, belief, art, law, morals, custom, and any other capabilities and habits acquired by man as a member of society."[1] The definition we present

[1]Edward Burnet Tylor, *Primitive Culture* (New York: Harper Torchbooks, Harper & Row, 1958; originally published by John Murray, London, 1871), p. 1.

here places more emphasis on the importance of knowledge than does Tylor's. We will say that *culture is the learned and shared knowledge that people use to generate behavior and interpret experience.*

Important to this definition is the idea that culture is a kind of knowledge, not behavior. It is in people's heads. It reflects the mental categories they learn from others as they grow up. It helps them *generate* behavior and *interpret* what they experience. At the moment of birth, we lack a culture. We don't yet have a system of beliefs, knowledge, and patterns of customary behavior. But from that moment until we die, each of us participates in a kind of universal schooling that teaches us our native culture. Laughing and smiling are genetic responses, but as infants we soon learn when to smile, when to laugh, and even how to laugh. We also inherit the potential to cry, but we must learn our cultural rules for when crying is appropriate.

As we learn our culture, we acquire a way to interpret experience. For example, Americans learn that dogs are like little people in furry suits. Dogs live in our houses, eat our food, share our beds. They hold a place in our hearts; their loss causes us to grieve. Villagers in India, on the other hand, often view dogs as pests that are useful only for hunting (in those few parts of the country where one still can hunt) and as watchdogs. Quiet days in Indian villages are often punctuated by the yelp of a dog that has been threatened or actually hurt by its master or a bystander.

Clearly, it is not the dogs that are different in these two societies. Rather, it is the meaning that dogs have for people that varies. And such meaning is cultural; it is learned as part of growing up in each group.

There are two basic kinds of culture, explicit and tacit. **Explicit culture** is cultural knowledge that people can talk about. As you grow up, for example, you learn that there are words for many things you encounter. There are items such as *clothes,* actions such as *playing,* emotional states such as *sadness,* ways to talk such as *yelling,* and people such as *mother.* Recognizing that culture may be explicit is important to the ethnographic process discussed below. If people have words for cultural categories, anthropologists can use interviews or observations of people talking to uncover them. Because so much culture is explicit, words—both spoken and written—become essential to the discovery and understanding of a culture.

Tacit culture is cultural knowledge that people lack words for. For example, as we grow up we learn to recognize and use a limited number of sound categories such as /d/, /e/, and /f/. Although anthropological linguists have given sound categories a name *(phonemes),* nonlinguists lack such a term. Instead, we learn our sound categories by hearing and replicating them and we use them unconsciously. No parent said, "Now let's work on our phonemes tonight, dear," to us when we were little.

Anthropologist Edward Hall pioneered the study of tacit culture. He noted, for example, that middle-class North Americans observe four speaking distances—intimate, personal, social, and public—without naming them. (Hall, not his informants, invented the terms above.) Hall also noticed that people from other societies observed different tacit speaking distances, so that a Latin American's closer (than North American) personal speaking distance made North Americans uncomfortable because it seemed intimate. Because it is unspoken, tacit culture can be discovered only through behavioral observation.

Ethnography is the process of discovering and describing a particular culture. It involves anthropologists in an intimate and personal activity as they attempt to learn how the members of a particular group see their worlds.

But which groups qualify as culture-bearing units? How does the anthropologist identify the existence of a culture to study? This was not a difficult question when anthropology was a new science. As Tylor's definition notes, culture was the whole way of life of a people. To find it, one sought out distinctive ethnic units, such as Bhil tribals in India or Apaches in the American Southwest. Anything one learned from such people would be part of their culture.

But discrete cultures of this sort are becoming more difficult to find. The world is increasingly divided into large national societies, each subdivided into a myriad of subgroups. Anthropologists are finding it increasingly attractive to study such subgroups, because they form the arena for most of life in complex society. And this is where the concept of the microculture enters the scene.

Microcultures are systems of cultural knowledge characteristic of subgroups within larger societies. Members of a microculture will usually share much of what they know with everyone in the greater society but will possess a special cultural knowledge that is unique to the subgroup. For example, a college fraternity has a microculture within the context of a university and a nation. Its members have special daily routines, jokes, and meanings for events. It is this shared knowledge that makes up their microculture and that can serve as the basis for ethnographic study. More and more, anthropologists are turning to the study of microcultures, using the same ethnographic techniques they employ when they investigate the broader culture of an ethnic or national group.

More than anything else, it is ethnography that is anthropology's unique contribution to social science. Most scientists, including many who view people in social context, approach their research as **detached observers.** As social scientists, they observe the human subjects of their study, categorize what they see, and generate theory to account for their findings. They work from the outside, creating a system of knowledge to account for other people's behavior. Although this is a legitimate and often useful way to conduct research, it is not the main task of ethnography.

Ethnographers seek out the insider's viewpoint. Because culture is the knowledge people use to generate behavior and interpret experience, the ethnographer seeks to understand group members' behavior from the inside, or cultural, perspective. Instead of looking for a **subject** to observe, ethnographers look for an **informant** to teach them the culture. Just as a child learns its native culture from parents and other people in its social environment, the ethnographer learns another culture by inferring folk categories from the observation of behavior and by asking informants what things mean.

Anthropologists employ many strategies during field research to understand another culture better. But all strategies and all research ultimately rest on the cooperation of informants. An informant is neither a subject in a scientific experiment nor a **respondent** who answers the investigator's questions. An informant is a teacher who has a special kind of pupil: a professional anthropologist. In this unique relationship a transformation occurs in the anthropologist's understanding of an alien culture. It is the informant who transforms the anthropologist from a tourist into an ethnographer. The informant may be a child who explains how to play hopscotch, a cocktail waitress who teaches the anthropologist to serve drinks and to encourage customers to leave tips, an elderly man who teaches the anthropologist to build an igloo, or a grandmother who explains the intricacies of Zapotec kinship. Almost any individual who has acquired a repertoire of cultural behavior can become an informant.

Ethnography is not as easy to do as we might think. For one thing, North Americans are not taught to be good listeners. We prefer to observe and draw our own conclusions. We like a sense of control in social contexts; passive listening is a sign of weakness in our culture. But listening and learning from others is at the heart of ethnography, and we must put aside our discomfort with the student role.

It is also not easy for informants to teach us about their cultures. Culture often lies below a conscious level. A major ethnographic task is to help informants remember their culture.

Naive realism may also impede ethnography. **Naive realism** is the belief that people everywhere see the world in the same way. It may, for example, lead the unwary ethnographer to assume that beauty is the same for all people everywhere or, to use our previous example, that dogs should mean the same thing in India as they do in the United States. If an ethnographer fails to control his or her own naive realism, inside cultural meanings will surely be overlooked.

Culture shock and ethnocentrism may also stand in the way of ethnographers. **Culture shock** is a state of anxiety that results from cross-cultural misunderstanding. Immersed alone in another society, the ethnographer understands few of the culturally defined rules for behavior and interpretation used by his or her hosts. The result is anxiety about proper action and an inability to interact appropriately in the new context.

Ethnocentrism can be just as much of a liability. **Ethnocentrism** is the belief and feeling that one's own culture is best. It reflects our tendency to judge other people's beliefs and behavior using values of our own native culture. Thus if we come from a society that abhors painful treatment of animals, we are likely to react with anger when an Indian villager hits a dog with a rock. Our feeling is ethnocentric.

It is impossible to rid ourselves entirely of the cultural values that make us ethnocentric when we do ethnography. But it is important to control our ethnocentric feeling in the field if we are to learn from informants. Informants resent negative judgment.

Finally, the role assigned to ethnographers by informants affects the quality of what can be learned. Ethnography is a personal enterprise, as all the articles in this section illustrate. Unlike survey research using questionnaires or short interviews, ethnography requires prolonged social contact. Informants will assign the ethnographer some kind of role and what that turns out to be will affect research.

The selections in Part One illustrate several points about culture and ethnography. The first piece, by the late James Spradley, takes a close look at the concept of culture and its role in ethnographic research. The second, by Richard Lee, illustrates how a simple act of giving can have a dramatically different cultural meaning in two societies, leading to cross-cultural misunderstanding. Laura Bohannan's article deals with the concept of naive realism and its role in cross-cultural misunderstanding. When she tells the classic story of *Hamlet* to African Tiv elders, the plot takes on an entirely different meaning as they use their own cultural knowledge in its interpretation. In the fourth selection, Claire Sterk describes how she conducted ethnographic field research under difficult circumstances. She sought to learn the culture of prostitutes working in New York City and Atlanta as part of a broader research interest in the spread and control of AIDS. The fifth article, by George Gmelch, explores how naive realism nearly ended a student's field research in Barbados.

Key Terms

culture p. 2	informant p. 4
culture shock p. 5	microcultures p. 4
detached observer p. 4	naive realism p. 5
ethnocentrism p. 5	respondent p. 5
ethnography p. 4	subject p. 4
explicit culture p. 3	tacit culture p. 3

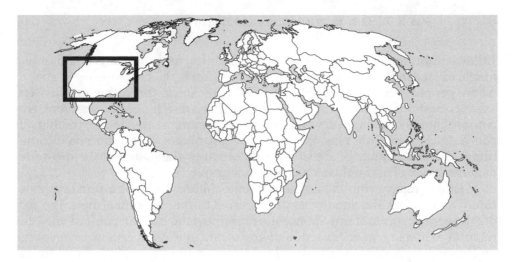

1

Ethnography and Culture

James P. Spradley

Most Americans associate science with detached observation; we learn to observe whatever we wish to understand, introduce our own classification of what is going on, and explain what we see in our own terms. In this selection, James Spradley argues that cultural anthropologists work differently. Ethnography is the work of discovering and describing a particular culture; culture is the learned, shared knowledge that people use to generate behavior and interpret experience. To get at culture, ethnographers must learn the meanings of action and experience from the insider's or informant's point of view. Many of the examples used by Spradley also show the relevance of anthropology to the study of culture in the United States.

Ethnographic fieldwork is the hallmark of cultural anthropology. Whether in a jungle village in Peru or on the streets of New York, the anthropologist goes to where people live and "does fieldwork." This means participating in activities, asking questions, eating strange foods, learning a new language, watching ceremonies, taking field notes, washing clothes, writing letters home, tracing out genealogies, observing play, interviewing informants, and hundreds of other things. This vast range of activities often obscures the nature of the most fundamental task of all fieldwork: doing ethnography.

Ethnography is the work of describing a culture. The central aim of ethnography is to understand another way of life from the native point of view. The goal of ethnography, as Malinowski put it, is "to grasp the native's point of view, his relation to life, to realize *his* vision of *his* world."[1] Fieldwork, then, involves the disciplined study of what the world is like to people who have learned to see, hear, speak, think, and act in ways that are different. Rather than *studying people*, ethnography means *learning from people*. Consider the following illustration.

George Hicks set out, in 1965, to learn about another way of life, that of the mountain people in an Appalachian valley.[2] His goal was to discover their culture, to learn to see the world from their perspective. With his family he moved into Little Laurel Valley, his daughter attended the local school, and his wife became one of the local Girl Scout leaders. Hicks soon discovered that stores and storekeepers were at the center of the valley's communication system, providing the most important social arena for the entire valley. He learned this by watching what other people did, by following their example, and slowly becoming part of the groups that congregated daily in the stores. He writes:

> At least once each day I would visit several stores in the valley, and sit in on the groups of gossiping men or, if the storekeeper happened to be alone, perhaps attempt to clear up puzzling points about kinship obligations. I found these hours, particularly those spent in the presence of the two or three excellent storytellers in the Little Laurel, thoroughly enjoyable. . . . At other times, I helped a number of local men gather corn or hay, build sheds, cut trees, pull and pack galax, and search for rich stands of huckleberries. When I needed aid in, for example, repairing frozen water pipes, it was readily and cheerfully provided.[3]

In order to discover the hidden principles of another way of life, the researcher must become a *student*. Storekeepers and storytellers and local farmers become *teachers*. Instead of studying the "climate," the "flora," and the "fauna" that made up the environment of this Appalachian valley, Hicks tried to discover how these mountain people defined and evaluated trees and galax and huckleberries. He did not attempt to describe social life in terms of what most Americans know about "marriage," "family," and "friendship"; instead he

[1]Bronislaw Malinowski, *Argonauts of the Western Pacific* (London: Routledge, 1922), p. 22.

[2]George Hicks, *Appalachian Valley* (New York: Holt, Rinehart, and Winston, 1976).

[3]Hicks, p. 3.

sought to discover how these mountain people identified relatives and friends. He tried to learn the obligations they felt toward kinsmen and discover how they felt about friends. Discovering the *insider's view* is a different species of knowledge from one that rests mainly on the outsider's view, even when the outsider is a trained social scientist.

Consider another example, this time from the perspective of a non-Western ethnographer. Imagine an Inuit woman setting out to learn the culture of Macalester College. What would she, so well schooled in the rich heritage of Inuit culture, have to do in order to understand the culture of Macalester College students, faculty, and staff? How would she discover the patterns that made up their lives? How would she avoid imposing Inuit ideas, categories, and values on everything she saw?

First, and perhaps most difficult, she would have to set aside her belief in *naive realism*, the almost universal belief that all people define the *real* world of objects, events, and living creatures in pretty much the same way. Human languages may differ from one society to the next, but behind the strange words and sentences, all people are talking about the same things. The naive realist assumes that love, snow, marriage, worship, animals, death, food, and hundreds of other things have essentially the same meaning to all human beings. Although few of us would admit to such ethnocentrism, the assumption may unconsciously influence our research. Ethnography starts with a conscious attitude of almost complete ignorance: "I don't know how the people at Macalester College understand their world. That remains to be discovered."

This Inuit woman would have to begin by learning the language spoken by students, faculty, and staff. She could stroll the campus paths, sit in classes, and attend special events, but only if she consciously tried to see things from the native point of view would she grasp their perspective. She would need to observe and listen to first-year students during their week-long orientation program. She would have to stand in line during registration, listen to students discuss the classes they hoped to get, and visit departments to watch faculty advising students on course selection. She would want to observe secretaries typing, janitors sweeping, and maintenance personnel plowing snow from walks. She would watch the more than 1,600 students crowd into the post office area to open their tiny mailboxes, and she would listen to their comments about junk mail and letters from home or no mail at all. She would attend faculty meetings to watch what went on, recording what professors and administrators said and how they behaved. She would sample various courses, attend "keggers" on weekends, read the *Mac Weekly*, and listen by the hour to students discussing things like their "relationships," the "football team," and "work study." She would want to learn the *meanings* of all these things. She would have to listen to the members of this college community, watch what they did, and participate in their activities to learn such meanings.

The essential core of ethnography is this concern with the meaning of actions and events to the people we seek to understand. Some of these meanings are directly expressed in language; many are taken for granted and communicated only indirectly through word and action. But in every society people make constant use of these complex meaning systems to organize their behavior, to understand themselves and others, and to make sense out of the world in which they live. These systems of meaning constitute their culture; ethnography always implies a theory of culture.

Culture

When ethnographers study other cultures, they must deal with three fundamental aspects of human experience: what people do, what people know, and the things people make and use. When each of these is learned and shared by members of some group, we speak of them as *cultural behavior, cultural knowledge*, and *cultural artifacts*. Whenever you do ethnographic fieldwork, you will want to distinguish among these three, although in most situations they are usually mixed together. Let's try to unravel them.

Recently I took a commuter train from a western suburb to downtown Chicago. It was late in the day, and when I boarded the train, only a handful of people were scattered about the car. Each was engaged in a common form of *cultural behavior: reading.* Across the aisle a man held the *Chicago Tribune* out in front of him, looking intently at the small print and every now and then turning the pages noisily. In front of him a young woman held a paperback book about twelve inches from her face. I could see her head shift slightly as her eyes moved from the bottom of one page to the top of the next. Near the front of the car a student was reading a large textbook and using a pen to underline words and sentences. Directly in front of me I noticed a man looking at the ticket he had purchased and reading it. It took me an instant to survey this scene, and then I settled back, looked out the window, and read a billboard advertisement for a plumbing service proclaiming it would open any plugged drains. All of us were engaged in the same kind of cultural behavior: reading.

This common activity depended on a great many *cultural artifacts*, the things people shape or make from natural resources. I could see artifacts like books and tickets and newspapers and billboards, all of which contained tiny black marks arranged into intricate patterns called "letters." And these tiny artifacts were arranged into larger patterns of words, sentences, and paragraphs. Those of us on that commuter train could read, in part, because of still other artifacts: the bark of trees made into paper; steel made into printing presses; dyes of various colors made into ink; glue used to hold book pages together; large wooden frames to hold billboards. If an ethnographer wanted to understand the full cultural meaning in our society, it would involve a careful study of these and many other cultural artifacts.

Although we can easily see behavior and artifacts, they represent only the thin surface of a deep lake. Beneath the surface, hidden from view, lies a vast reservoir of *cultural knowledge*. Think for a moment what the people on that train needed to know in order to read. First, they had to know the grammatical rules for at least one language. Then they had to learn what the little marks on paper represented. They also had to know the meaning of space and lines and pages. They had learned cultural rules like "move your eyes from left to right, from the top of the page to the bottom." They had to know that a sentence at the bottom of a page continues on the top of the next page. The man reading a newspaper had to know a great deal about columns and the spaces between columns and what headlines mean. All of us needed to know what kinds of messages were intended by whoever wrote what we read. If a person cannot distinguish the importance of a message on a billboard from one that comes in a letter from a spouse or child, problems would develop. I knew how to recognize when other people were reading. We all knew it was impolite to read aloud on a train. We all knew how to feel when reading things like jokes or calamitous news in the paper. Our culture has a large body of shared knowledge that people learn and use to engage in this behavior called *reading* and make proper use of the artifacts connected with it.

Although cultural knowledge is hidden from view, it is of fundamental importance because we all use it constantly to generate behavior and interpret our experience. Cultural knowledge is so important that I will frequently use the broader term *culture* when speaking about it. Indeed, I will define culture as *the acquired knowledge people use to interpret experience and generate behavior.* Let's consider another example to see how people use their culture to interpret experience and do things.

One afternoon in 1973 I came across the following news item in the *Minneapolis Tribune:*

> **Crowd Mistakes Rescue Attempt, Attacks Police**
> *Nov. 23, 1973. Hartford, Connecticut.* Three policemen giving a heart massage and oxygen to a heart attack victim Friday were attacked by a crowd of 75 to 100 persons who apparently did not realize what the policemen were doing.
>
> Other policemen fended off the crowd of mostly Spanish-speaking residents until an ambulance arrived. Police said they tried to explain to the crowd what they were doing, but the crowd apparently thought they were beating the woman.
>
> Despite the policemen's efforts the victim, Evangelica Echevacria, 59, died.

Here we see people using their culture. Members of two different groups observed the same event, but their *interpretations* were drastically different. The crowd used their cultural knowledge (a) to interpret the behavior of the policemen as cruel and (b) to act on the woman's behalf to put a stop to what they perceived as brutality. They had acquired the cultural principles for acting and interpreting things in this way through a particular shared experience.

The policemen, on the other hand, used their cultural knowledge (a) to interpret the woman's condition as heart failure and their own behavior as a life-saving effort and (b) to give her cardiac massage and oxygen. They used artifacts like an oxygen mask and an ambulance. Furthermore, they interpreted the actions of the crowd in an entirely different manner from how

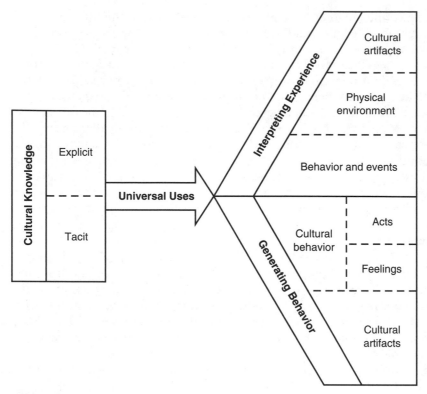

FIGURE 1

the crowd saw their own behavior. The two groups of people each had elaborate cultural rules for interpreting their experience and for acting in emergency situations, and the conflict arose, at least in part, because these cultural rules were so different.

We can now diagram this definition of culture and see more clearly the relationships among knowledge, behavior, and artifacts (Figure 1). By identifying cultural knowledge as fundamental, we have merely shifted the emphasis from behavior and artifacts to their *meaning*. The ethnographer observes behavior but goes beyond it to inquire about the meaning of that behavior. The ethnographer sees artifacts and natural objects but goes beyond them to discover what meanings people assign to these objects. The ethnographer observes and records emotional states but goes beyond them to discover the meaning of fear, anxiety, anger, and other feelings.

As represented in Figure 1, cultural knowledge exists at two levels of consciousness. *Explicit culture* makes up part of what we know, a level of knowledge people can communicate about with relative ease. When George Hicks asked storekeepers and others in Little Laurel Valley about their relatives, he discovered that any adult over fifty could tell him the genealogical connections among large numbers of people. They knew how to trace kin relationships and the cultural rules for appropriate behavior among kins. All of us have acquired large areas of cultural knowledge such as this which we can talk about and make explicit.

At the same time, a large portion of our cultural knowledge remains *tacit*, outside our awareness. Edward Hall has done much to elucidate the nature of tacit cultural knowledge in his books *The Silent Language* and *The Hidden Dimension*.[4] The way each culture defines space often occurs at the level of tacit knowledge. Hall points out that all of us have acquired thousands of spatial cues about how close to stand to others, how to arrange furniture, when to touch others, and when to feel cramped inside a room. Without realizing that our tacit culture is operating, we begin to feel uneasy when someone from another culture stands too close, breathes on us when talking, touches us, or when we find furniture arranged in the center of the room rather than around the edges. Ethnography is the study of both explicit and tacit cultural knowledge. . . .

The concept of culture as acquired knowledge has much in common with symbolic interactionism, a theory that seeks to explain human behavior in terms of meanings. Symbolic interactionism has its roots in the work of sociologists like Cooley, Mead, and Thomas. Blumer has identified three premises on which this theory rests.

The first premise is that "human beings act toward things on the basis of the meanings that the things have for them."[5] The policemen and the crowd in our earlier example interacted on the basis of the meanings things had for them. The geographic location, the types of people, the police car, the policemen's movements, the sick woman's behavior, and the activities of the onlookers—all were *symbols* with special meanings. People did not act toward the things themselves, but to their meanings.

The second premise underlying symbolic interactionism is that the "meaning of such things is derived from, or arises out of, the social interaction that one has with one's fellows."[6] Culture, as a shared system of meanings, is learned, revised, maintained, and defined in the context of people interacting. The crowd came to share their definitions of police behavior through interacting with one another and through past associations with the police. The police officers acquired the cultural meanings they used through interacting with other officers and members of the community. The culture of each group was inextricably bound up with the social life of their particular communities.

The third premise of symbolic interactionism is that "meanings are handled in, and modified through, an interpretive process used by the person dealing

---

[4]Edward T. Hall, *The Silent Language* (Garden City, NY: Doubleday, 1959); *The Hidden Dimension* (Garden City, NY: Doubleday, 1966).

[5]Herbert Blumer, *Symbolic Interactionism* (Englewood Cliffs, NJ: Prentice-Hall, 1969), p. 2.

[6]Blumer, p. 2.

with the things he encounters."[7] Neither the crowd nor the policemen were automatons, driven by their culture to act in the way they did. Rather, they used their cultural knowledge to interpret and evaluate the situation. At any moment, a member of the crowd might have interpreted the behavior of the policemen in a slightly different way, leading to a different reaction.

We may see this interpretive aspect more clearly if we think of culture as a cognitive map. In the recurrent activities that make up everyday life, we refer to this map. It serves as a guide for acting and for interpreting our experience; it does not compel us to follow a particular course. Like this brief drama between the policemen, a dying woman, and the crowd, much of life is a series of unanticipated social occasions. Although our culture may not include a detailed map for such occasions, it does provide principles for interpreting and responding to them. Rather than a rigid map that people must follow, culture is best thought of as

> a set of principles for creating dramas, for writing script, and of course, for recruiting players and audiences. ... Culture is not simply a cognitive map that people acquire, in whole or in part, more or less accurately, and then learn to read. People are not just map-readers; they are map-makers. People are cast out into imperfectly charted, continually revised sketch maps. Culture does not provide a cognitive map, but rather a set of principles for map making and navigation. Different cultures are like different schools of navigation to cope with different terrains and seas.[8]

If we take *meaning* seriously, as symbolic interactionists argue we must, it becomes necessary to study meaning carefully. We need a theory of meaning and a specific methodology designed for the investigation of it.

Review Questions

1. What is the definition of *culture?* How is this definition related to the way anthropologists do ethnographic fieldwork?

2. What is the relationship among cultural behavior, cultural artifacts, and cultural knowledge?

3. What is the difference between tacit and explicit culture? How can anthropologists discover these two kinds of culture?

4. What are some examples of naive realism in the way Americans think about people in other societies?

[7]Blumer, p. 2.

[8]Charles O. Frake, "Plying Frames Can Be Dangerous: Some Reflections on Methodology in Cognitive Anthropology," *Quarterly Newsletter of the Institute for Comparative Human Development* 3 (1977): 6–7.

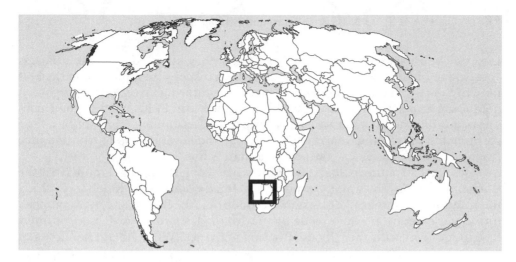

2

Eating Christmas in the Kalahari

Richard Borshay Lee

What happens when an anthropologist living among the !Kung of Africa decides to be generous and to share a large animal with everyone at Christmastime? This compelling account of the misunderstanding and confusion that resulted takes the reader deeper into the nature of culture. Richard Lee carefully traces how the !Kung perceived his generosity and taught the anthropologist something about his own culture.

The !Kung Bushmen's knowledge of Christmas is thirdhand. The London Missionary Society brought the holiday to the southern Tswana tribes in the early nineteenth century. Later, native catechists spread the idea far and wide among the Bantu-speaking pastoralists, even in the remotest corners of the Kalahari

From Richard Borshay Lee, "Eating Christmas in the Kalahari," *Natural History*, December 1969, pp. 14–22, 60–64. Reprinted from *Natural History* December 1969; copyright © Natural History Magazine, Inc., 1969.

Desert. The Bushmen's idea of the Christmas story, stripped to its essentials, is "praise the birth of white man's god-chief"; what keeps their interest in the holiday high is the Tswana-Herero custom of slaughtering an ox for his Bushmen neighbors as an annual goodwill gesture. Since the 1930s, part of the Bushmen's annual round of activities has included a December congregation at the cattle posts for trading, marriage brokering, and several days of trance dance feasting at which the local Tswana headman is host.

As a social anthropologist working with !Kung Bushmen, I found that the Christmas ox custom suited my purposes. I had come to the Kalahari to study the hunting and gathering subsistence economy of the !Kung, and to accomplish this it was essential not to provide them with food, share my own food, or interfere in any way with their food-gathering activities. While liberal handouts of tobacco and medical supplies were appreciated, they were scarcely adequate to erase the glaring disparity in wealth between the anthropologist, who maintained a two-month inventory of canned goods, and the Bushmen, who rarely had a day's supply of food on hand. My approach, while paying off in terms of data, left me open to frequent accusations of stinginess and hardheartedness. By their lights, I was a miser.

The Christmas ox was to be my way of saying thank you for the cooperation of the past year; and since it was to be our last Christmas in the field, I was determined to slaughter the largest, meatiest ox that money could buy, insuring that the feast and trance dance would be a success.

Through December I kept my eyes open at the wells as the cattle were brought down for watering. Several animals were offered, but none had quite the grossness that I had in mind. Then, ten days before the holiday, a Herero friend led an ox of astonishing size and mass up to our camp. It was solid black, stood five feet high at the shoulder, had a five-foot span of horns, and must have weighed 1,200 pounds on the hoof. Food consumption calculations are my specialty, and I quickly figured that bones and viscera aside, there was enough meat—at least four pounds—for every man, woman, and child of the 150 Bushmen in the vicinity of /ai/ai who were expected at the feast.

Having found the right animal at last, I paid the Herero £20 ($56) and asked him to keep the beast with his herd until Christmas day. The next morning word spread among the people that the big solid black one was the ox chosen by /ontah (my Bushman name; it means, roughly, "whitey") for the Christmas feast. That afternoon I received the first delegation. Ben!a, an outspoken sixty-year-old mother of five, came to the point slowly.

"Where were you planning to eat Christmas?"

"Right here at /ai/ai," I replied.

"Alone or with others?"

"I expect to invite all the people to eat Christmas with me."

"Eat what?"

"I have purchased Yehave's black ox, and I am going to slaughter and cook it."

"That's what we were told at the well but refused to believe it until we heard it from yourself."

"Well, it's the black one," I replied expansively, although wondering what she was driving at.

"Oh, no!" Ben!a groaned, turning to her group. "They were right." Turning back to me she asked, "Do you expect us to eat that bag of bones?"

"Bag of bones! It's the biggest ox at /ai/ai."

"Big, yes, but old. And thin. Everybody knows there's no meat on that old ox. What did you expect us to eat off it, the horns?"

Everybody chuckled at Ben!a's one-liner as they walked away, but all I could manage was a weak grin.

That evening it was the turn of the young men. They came to sit at our evening fire. /gaugo, about my age, spoke to me man-to-man.

"/ontah, you have always been square with us," he lied. "What has happened to change your heart? That sack of guts and bones of Yehave's will hardly feed one camp, let alone all the Bushmen around /ai/ai." And he proceeded to enumerate the seven camps in the /ai/ai vicinity, family by family. "Perhaps you have forgotten that we are not few, but many. Or are you too blind to tell the difference between a proper cow and an old wreck? That ox is thin to the point of death."

"Look, you guys," I retorted, "that is a beautiful animal, and I'm sure you will eat it with pleasure at Christmas."

"Of course we will eat it; it's food. But it won't fill us up to the point where we will have enough strength to dance. We will eat and go home to bed with stomachs rumbling."

That night as we turned in, I asked my wife, Nancy, "What did you think of the black ox?"

"It looked enormous to me. Why?"

"Well, about eight different people have told me I got gypped; that the ox is nothing but bones."

"What's the angle?" Nancy asked. "Did they have a better one to sell?"

"No, they just said that it was going to be a grim Christmas because there won't be enough meat to go around. Maybe I'll get an independent judge to look at the beast in the morning."

Bright and early, Halingisi, a Tswana cattle owner, appeared at our camp. But before I could ask him to give me his opinion on Yehave's black ox, he gave me the eye signal that indicated a confidential chat. We left the camp and sat down.

"/ontah, I'm surprised at you; you've lived here for three years and still haven't learned anything about cattle."

"But what else can a person do but choose the biggest, strongest animal one can find?" I retorted.

"Look, just because an animal is big doesn't mean that it has plenty of meat on it. The black one was a beauty when it was younger, but now it is thin to the point of death."

"Well, I've already bought it. What can I do at this stage?"

"Bought it already? I thought you were just considering it. Well, you'll have to kill it and serve it, I suppose. But don't expect much of a dance to follow."

My spirits dropped rapidly. I could believe that Ben!a and /gaugo just might be putting me on about the black ox, but Halingisi seemed to be an impartial critic. I went around that day feeling as though I had bought a lemon of a used car.

In the afternoon it was Tomazo's turn. Tomazo is a fine hunter, a top trance performer . . . and one of my most reliable informants. He approached the subject of the Christmas cow as part of my continuing Bushman education.

"My friend, the way it is with us Bushmen," he began, "is that we love meat. And even more than that, we love fat. When we hunt we always search for the fat ones, the ones dripping with layers of white fat: fat that turns into a clear, thick oil in the cooking pot, fat that slides down your gullet, fills your stomach and gives you a roaring diarrhea," he rhapsodized.

"So, feeling as we do," he continued, "it gives us pain to be served such a scrawny thing as Yehave's black ox. It is big, yes, and no doubt its giant bones are good for soup, but fat is what we really crave, and so we will eat Christmas this year with a heavy heart."

The prospect of a gloomy Christmas now had me worried, so I asked Tomazo what I could do about it.

"Look for a fat one, a young one . . . smaller, but fat. Fat enough to make us //gom (evacuate the bowels), then we will be happy."

My suspicions were aroused when Tomazo said that he happened to know a young, fat, barren cow that the owner was willing to part with. Was Tomazo working on commission, I wondered? But I dispelled this unworthy thought when we approached the Herero owner of the cow in question and found that he had decided not to sell.

The scrawny wreck of a Christmas ox now became the talk of the /ai/ai water hole and was the first news told to the outlying groups as they began to come in from the bush for the feast. What finally convinced me that real trouble might be brewing was the visit from u!au, an old conservative with a reputation for fierceness. His nickname meant spear and referred to an incident thirty years ago in which he had speared a man to death. He had an intense manner; fixing me with his eyes, he said in clipped tones:

"I have only just heard about the black ox today, or else I would have come here earlier. /ontah, do you honestly think you can serve meat like that to people and avoid a fight?" He paused, letting the implications sink in. "I don't mean fight you, /ontah; you are a white man. I mean a fight between Bushmen. There are many fierce ones here, and with such a small quantity of meat to distribute, how can you give everybody a fair share? Someone is sure to accuse another of taking too much or hogging all the choice pieces. Then you will see what happens when some go hungry while others eat."

The possibility of at least a serious argument struck me as all too real. I had witnessed the tension that surrounds the distribution of meat from a kudu or gemsbok kill, and had documented many arguments that sprang up from a real or imagined slight in meat distribution. The owners of a kill may spend up to two hours arranging and rearranging the piles of meat under the gaze of a circle of recipients before handing them out. And I knew that the Christmas feast at /ai/ai would be bringing together groups that had feuded in the past.

Convinced now of the gravity of the situation, I went in earnest to search for a second cow; but all my inquiries failed to turn one up.

The Christmas feast was evidently going to be a disaster, and the incessant complaints about the meagerness of the ox had already taken the fun out of it for me. Moreover, I was getting bored with the wisecracks, and after losing my temper a few times, I resolved to serve the beast anyway. If the meat fell short, the hell with it. In the Bushmen idiom, I announced to all who would listen:

"I am a poor man and blind. If I have chosen one that is too old and too thin, we will eat it anyway and see if there is enough meat there to quiet the rumbling of our stomachs."

On hearing this speech, Ben!a offered me a rare word of comfort. "It's thin," she said philosophically, "but the bones will make a good soup."

At dawn Christmas morning, instinct told me to turn over the butchering and cooking to a friend and take off with Nancy to spend Christmas alone in the bush. But curiosity kept me from retreating. I wanted to see what such a scrawny ox looked like on butchering, and if there *was* going to be a fight, I wanted to catch every word of it. Anthropologists are incurable that way.

The great beast was driven up to our dancing ground, and a shot in the forehead dropped it in its tracks. Then, freshly cut branches were heaped around the fallen carcass to receive the meat. Ten men volunteered to help with the cutting. I asked /gaugo to make the breast bone cut. This cut, which begins the butchering process for most large game, offers easy access for removal of the viscera. But it also allows the hunter to spot-check the amount of fat on an animal. A fat game animal carries a white layer up to an inch thick on the chest, while in a thin one, the knife will quickly cut to bone. All eyes fixed on his hand as /gaugo, dwarfed by the great carcass, knelt to the breast. The first cut opened a pool of solid white in the black skin. The second and third cut widened and deepened the creamy white. Still no bone. It was pure fat; it must have been two inches thick.

"Hey /gau," I burst out, "that ox is loaded with fat. What's this about the ox being too thin to bother eating? Are you out of your mind?"

"Fat?" /gau shot back. "You call that fat? This wreck is thin, sick, dead!" And he broke out laughing. So did everyone else. They rolled on the ground, paralyzed with laughter. Everybody laughed except me; I was thinking.

I ran back to the tent and burst in just as Nancy was getting up. "Hey, the black ox. It's fat as hell! They were kidding about it being too thin to eat. It was a joke or something. A put-on. Everyone is really delighted with it."

"Some joke," my wife replied. "It was so funny that you were ready to pack up and leave /ai/ai."

If it had indeed been a joke, it had been an extraordinarily convincing one, and tinged, I thought, with more than a touch of malice, as many jokes are. Nevertheless, that it was a joke lifted my spirits considerably, and I returned to the butchering site where the shape of the ox was rapidly disappearing under the axes and knives of the butchers. The atmosphere had become festive. Grinning broadly, their arms covered with blood well past the elbow, men packed chunks of meat into the big cast-iron cooking pots, fifty pounds to the load, and muttered and chuckled all the while about the thinness and worthlessness of the animal and /ontah's poor judgment.

We danced and ate that ox two days and two nights; we cooked and distributed fourteen potfuls of meat and no one went home hungry and no fights broke out.

But the "joke" stayed in my mind. I had a growing feeling that something important had happened in my relationship with the Bushmen and that the clue lay in the meaning of the joke. Several days later, when most of the people had dispersed back to the bush camps, I raised the question with Hakekgose, a Tswana man who had grown up among the !Kung, married a !Kung girl, and who probably knew their culture better than any other non-Bushman.

"With us whites," I began, "Christmas is supposed to be the day of friendship and brotherly love. What I can't figure out is why the Bushmen went to such lengths to criticize and belittle the ox I had bought for the feast. The animal was perfectly good and their jokes and wisecracks practically ruined the holiday for me."

"So it really did bother you," said Hakekgose. "Well, that's the way they always talk. When I take my rifle and go hunting with them, if I miss, they laugh at me for the rest of the day. But even if I hit and bring one down, it's no better. To them, the kill is always too small or too old or too thin; and as we sit down on the kill site to cook and eat the liver, they keep grumbling, even with their mouths full of meat. They say things like, 'Oh, this is awful! What a worthless animal! Whatever made me think that this Tswana rascal could hunt!'"

"Is this the way outsiders are treated?" I asked.

"No, it is their custom; they talk that way to each other, too. Go and ask them."

/gaugo had been one of the most enthusiastic in making me feel bad about the merit of the Christmas ox. I sought him out first.

"Why did you tell me the black ox was worthless, when you could see that it was loaded with fat and meat?"

"It is our way," he said, smiling. "We always like to fool people about that. Say there is a Bushman who has been hunting. He must not come home and announce like a braggart, 'I have killed a big one in the bush!' He must first sit down in silence until I or someone else comes up to his fire and asks, 'What did you see today?' He replies quietly, 'Ah, I'm no good for hunting. I saw nothing at all [pause] just a little tiny one.' Then I smile to myself," /gaugo continued, "because I know he has killed something big.

"In the morning we make up a party of four or five people to cut up and carry the meat back to the camp. When we arrive at the kill we examine it and cry out, 'You mean to say you have dragged us all the way out here in order to make us cart home your pile of bones? Oh, if I had known it was this thin I wouldn't have come.' Another one pipes up, 'People, to think I gave up a nice day in the shade for this. At home we may be hungry, but at least we have nice cool water to drink.' If the horns are big, someone says, 'Did you think that somehow you were going to boil down the horns for soup?'

"To all this you must respond in kind. 'I agree,' you say, 'this one is not worth the effort; let's just cook the liver for strength and leave the rest for the hyenas. It is not too late to hunt today and even a duiker or a steenbok would be better than this mess.'

"Then you set to work nevertheless; butcher the animal, carry the meat back to the camp and everyone eats," /gaugo concluded.

Things were beginning to make sense. Next, I went to Tomazo. He corroborated /gaugo's story of the obligatory insults over a kill and added a few details of his own.

"But," I asked, "why insult a man after he has gone to all that trouble to track and kill an animal and when he is going to share the meat with you so that your children will have something to eat?"

"Arrogance," was his cryptic answer.

"Arrogance?"

"Yes, when a young man kills much meat he comes to think of himself as a chief or a big man, and he thinks of the rest of us as his servants or inferiors. We can't accept this. We refuse one who boasts, for someday his pride will make him kill somebody. So we always speak of his meat as worthless. This way we cool his heart and make him gentle."

"But why didn't you tell me this before?" I asked Tomazo with some heat.

"Because you never asked me," said Tomazo, echoing the refrain that has come to haunt every field ethnographer.

The pieces now fell into place. I had known for a long time that in situations of social conflict with Bushmen I held all the cards. I was the only source of tobacco in a thousand square miles, and I was not incapable of cutting an individual off for noncooperation. Though my boycott never lasted longer than a few days, it was an indication of my strength. People resented my presence at the water hole, yet simultaneously dreaded my leaving. In short I was a perfect target for the charge of arrogance and for the Bushman tactic of enforcing humility.

I had been taught an object lesson by the Bushmen; it had come from an unexpected corner and had hurt me in a vulnerable area. For the big black ox was to be the one totally generous, unstinting act of my year at /ai/ai and I was quite unprepared for the reaction I received.

As I read it, their message was this: There are no totally generous acts. All "acts" have an element of calculation. One black ox slaughtered at Christmas does not wipe out a year of careful manipulation of gifts given to serve your own ends. After all, to kill an animal and share the meat with people is really no more than the Bushmen do for each other every day and with far less fanfare.

In the end, I had to admire how the Bushmen had played out the farce—collectively straight-faced to the end. Curiously, the episode reminded me of the *Good Soldier Schweik* and his marvelous encounters with authority. Like Schweik, the Bushmen had retained a thoroughgoing skepticism of good intentions. Was it this independence of spirit, I wondered, that had kept them culturally viable in the face of generations of contact with more powerful societies, both black and white? The thought that the Bushmen were alive and well in the Kalahari was strangely comforting. Perhaps, armed with that independence and with their superb knowledge of their environment, they might yet survive the future.

Review Questions

1. What was the basis of the misunderstanding experienced by Lee when he gave an ox for the Christmas feast held by the !Kung?

2. Construct a model of cross-cultural misunderstanding, using the information presented by Lee in this article.

3. Why do you think the !Kung ridicule and denigrate people who have been successful hunters or who have provided them with a Christmas ox? Why do Americans expect people to be grateful to receive gifts?

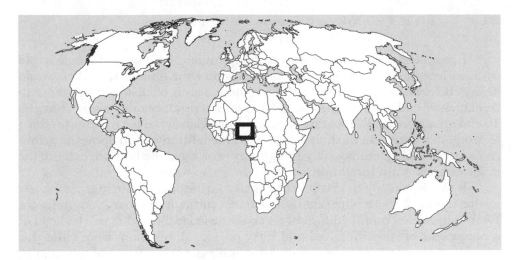

3

Shakespeare in the Bush

Laura Bohannan

All of us use the cultural knowledge we acquire as members of our own society to organize our perception and behavior. Most of us are also naive realists: we tend to believe our culture mirrors a reality shared by everyone. But cultures are different, and other people rarely behave or interpret experience according to our cultural plan. In this article, Laura Bohannan describes her attempt to tell the classic story of Hamlet to Tiv elders in West Africa. At each turn in the story, the Tiv interpret the events and motives in Hamlet using their own cultural knowledge. The result is a very different version of the classic play.

Just before I left Oxford for the Tiv in West Africa, conversation turned to the season at Stratford. "You Americans," said a friend, "often have difficulty with Shakespeare. He was, after all, a very English poet, and one can easily misinterpret the universal by misunderstanding the particular."

From Laura Bohannan, "Shakespeare in the Bush." Used by permission.

I protested that human nature is pretty much the same the whole world over; at least the general plot and motivation of the greater tragedies would always be clear—everywhere—although some details of custom might have to be explained and difficulties of translation might produce other slight changes. To end an argument we could not conclude, my friend gave me a copy of *Hamlet* to study in the African bush: it would, he hoped, lift my mind above its primitive surroundings, and possibly I might, by prolonged meditation, achieve the grace of correct interpretation.

It was my second field trip to that African tribe, and I thought myself ready to live in one of its remote sections—an area difficult to cross even on foot. I eventually settled on the hillock of a very knowledgeable old man, the head of a homestead of some hundred and forty people, all of whom were either his close relatives or their wives and children. Like the other elders of the vicinity, the old man spent most of his time performing ceremonies seldom seen these days in the more accessible parts of the tribe. I was delighted. Soon there would be three months of enforced isolation and leisure, between the harvest that takes place just before the rising of the swamps and the clearing of new farms when the water goes down. Then, I thought, they would have even more time to perform ceremonies and explain them to me.

I was quite mistaken. Most of the ceremonies demanded the presence of elders from several homesteads. As the swamps rose, the old men found it too difficult to walk from one homestead to the next, and the ceremonies gradually ceased. As the swamps rose even higher, all activities but one came to an end. The women brewed beer from maize and millet. Men, women, and children sat on their hillocks and drank it.

People began to drink at dawn. By midmorning the whole homestead was singing, dancing, and drumming. When it rained, people had to sit inside their huts: there they drank and sang or they drank and told stories. In any case, by noon or before, I either had to join the party or retire to my own hut and my books. "One does not discuss serious matters when there is beer. Come, drink with us." Since I lacked their capacity for the thick native beer, I spent more and more time with *Hamlet*. Before the end of the second month, grace descended on me. I was quite sure that *Hamlet* had only one possible interpretation, and that one universally obvious.

Early every morning, in the hope of having some serious talk before the beer party, I used to call on the old man at his reception hut—a circle of posts supporting a thatched roof above a low mud wall to keep out wind and rain. One day I crawled through the low doorway and found most of the men of the homestead sitting huddled in their ragged cloths on stools, low plank beds, and reclining chairs, warming themselves against the chill of the rain around a smoky fire. In the center were three pots of beer. The party had started.

The old man greeted me cordially. "Sit down and drink." I accepted a large calabash full of beer, poured some into a small drinking gourd, and tossed it down. Then I poured some more into the same gourd for the man second in seniority to my host before I handed my calabash over to a young man for further distribution. Important people shouldn't ladle beer themselves.

"It is better like this," the old man said, looking at me approvingly and plucking at the thatch that had caught in my hair. "You should sit and drink with us more often. Your servants tell me that when you are not with us, you sit inside your hut looking at a paper."

The old man was acquainted with four kinds of "papers": tax receipts, bride price receipts, court fee receipts, and letters. The messenger who brought him letters from the chief used them mainly as a badge of office, for he always knew what was in them and told the old man. Personal letters for the few who had relatives in the government or mission stations were kept until someone went to a large market where there was a letter writer and reader. Since my arrival, letters were brought to me to be read. A few men also brought me bride price receipts, privately, with requests to change the figures to a higher sum. I found moral arguments were of no avail, since in-laws are fair game, and the technical hazards of forgery difficult to explain to an illiterate people. I did not wish them to think me silly enough to look at any such papers for days on end, and I hastily explained that my "paper" was one of the "things of long ago" of my country.

"Ah," said the old men. "Tell us."

I protested that I was not a storyteller. Storytelling is a skilled art among them; their standards are high, and the audiences critical—and vocal in their criticism. I protested in vain. This morning they wanted to hear a story while they drank. They threatened to tell me no more stories until I told them one of mine. Finally, the old man promised that no one would criticize my style "for we know you are struggling with our language." "But," put in one of the elders, "you must explain what we do not understand, as we do when we tell you our stories." Realizing that here was my chance to prove *Hamlet* universally intelligible, I agreed.

The old man handed me some more beer to help me on with my storytelling. Men filled their long wooden pipes and knocked coals from the fire to place in the pipe bowls; then, puffing contentedly, they sat back to listen. I began in the proper style, "Not yesterday, not yesterday, but long ago, a thing occurred. One night three men were keeping watch outside the homestead of the great chief, when suddenly they saw the former chief approach them."

"Why was he no longer their chief?"

"He was dead," I explained. "That is why they were troubled and afraid when they saw him."

"Impossible," began one of the elders, handing his pipe on to his neighbor, who interrupted, "Of course it wasn't the dead chief. It was an omen sent by a witch. Go on."

Slightly shaken, I continued. "One of these three was a man who knew things"—the closest translation for scholar, but unfortunately it also meant witch. The second elder looked triumphantly at the first. "So he spoke to the dead chief, saying, 'Tell us what we must do so you may rest in your grave,' but the dead chief did not answer. He vanished, and they could see him no more. Then the man who knew things—his name was Horatio—said this event was the affair of the dead chief's son, Hamlet."

There was a general shaking of heads around the circle. "Had the dead chief no living brothers? Or was this son the chief?" "No," I replied. "That is, he had one living brother who became the chief when the elder brother died."

The old men muttered: such omens were matters for chiefs and elders, not for youngsters; no good could come of being behind a chief's back; clearly Horatio was not a man who knew things.

"Yes, he was," I insisted, shooing a chicken away from my beer. "In our country the son is next to the father. The dead chief's younger brother had become the great chief. He had also married his elder brother's widow only about a month after the funeral."

"He did well," the old man beamed and announced to the others, "I told you that if we knew more about Europeans, we would find they really were very like us. In our country also," he added to me, "the younger brother marries the elder brother's widow and becomes the father of his children. Now, if your uncle, who married your widowed mother, is your father's full brother, then he will be a real father to you. Did Hamlet's father and uncle have one mother?"

His question barely penetrated my mind; I was too upset and thrown too far off balance by having one of the most important elements of *Hamlet* knocked straight out of the picture. Rather uncertainly I said that I thought they had the same mother, but I wasn't sure—the story didn't say. The old man told me severely that these genealogical details made all the difference and that when I got home I must ask the elders about it. He shouted out the door to one of his younger wives to bring his goatskin bag.

Determined to save what I could of the mother motif, I took a deep breath and began again. "The son Hamlet was very sad because his mother had married again so quickly. There was no need for her to do so, and it is our custom for a widow not to go to her next husband until she has mourned for two years."

"Two years is too long," objected the wife, who had appeared with the old man's battered goatskin bag. "Who will hoe your farms for you while you have no husband?"

"Hamlet," I retorted without thinking, "was old enough to hoe his mother's farms himself. There was no need for her to remarry." No one looked convinced. I gave up. "His mother and the great chief told Hamlet not to be sad, for the great chief himself would be a father to Hamlet. Furthermore, Hamlet would be the next chief: therefore he must stay to learn the things of a chief. Hamlet agreed to remain, and all the rest went off to drink beer."

While I paused, perplexed at how to render Hamlet's disgusted soliloquy to an audience convinced that Claudius and Gertrude had behaved in the best possible manner, one of the younger men asked me who had married the other wives of the dead chief.

"He had no other wives," I told him.

"But a chief must have many wives! How else can he brew beer and prepare food for all his guests?"

I said firmly that in our country even chiefs had only one wife, that they had servants to do their work, and that they paid them from tax money.

It was better, they returned, for a chief to have many wives and sons who would help him hoe his farms and feed his people; then everyone loved the chief who gave much and took nothing—taxes were a bad thing.

I agreed with the last comment, but for the rest fell back on their favorite way of fobbing off my questions: "That is the way it is done, so that is how we do it."

I decided to skip the soliloquy. Even if Claudius was here thought quite right to marry his brother's widow, there remained the poison motif, and I knew they would disapprove of fratricide. More hopefully I resumed, "That night Hamlet kept watch with the three who had seen his dead father. The dead chief again appeared, and although the others were afraid, Hamlet followed his dead father off to one side. When they were alone, Hamlet's dead father spoke."

"Omens can't talk!" The old man was emphatic.

"Hamlet's dead father wasn't an omen. Seeing him might have been an omen, but he was not." My audience looked as confused as I sounded. "It *was* Hamlet's dead father. It was a thing we call a 'ghost.'" I had to use the English word, for unlike many of the neighboring tribes, these people didn't believe in the survival after death of any individuating part of the personality.

"What is a 'ghost'? An omen?"

"No, a 'ghost' is someone who is dead but who walks around and can talk, and people can hear him and see him but not touch him."

They objected. "One can touch zombis."

"No, no! It was not a dead body the witches had animated to sacrifice and eat. No one else made Hamlet's dead father walk. He did it himself."

"Dead men can't walk," protested my audience as one man.

I was quite willing to compromise. "A 'ghost' is a dead man's shadow."

But again they objected. "Dead men cast no shadows."

"They do in my country," I snapped.

The old man quelled the babble of disbelief that rose immediately and told me with that insincere, but courteous, agreement one extends to the fancies of the young, ignorant, and superstitious, "No doubt in your country the dead can also walk without being zombis." From the depths of his bag he produced a withered fragment of kola nut, bit off one end to show it wasn't poisoned, and handed me the rest as a peace offering.

"Anyhow," I resumed, "Hamlet's dead father said that his own brother, the one who became chief, had poisoned him. He wanted Hamlet to avenge him. Hamlet believed this in his heart, for he did not like his father's brother." I took another swallow of beer. "In the country of the great chief, living in the same homestead, for it was a very large one, was an important elder who was often with the chief to advise and help him. His name was Polonius. Hamlet was courting his daughter, but her father and her brother . . . [I cast hastily about for some tribal analogy] warned her not to let Hamlet visit her when she was alone on her farm, for he would be a great chief and so could not marry her."

"Why not?" asked the wife, who had settled down on the edge of the old man's chair. He frowned at her for asking stupid questions and growled, "They lived in the same homestead."

"That was not the reason," I informed them. "Polonius was a stranger who lived in the homestead because he helped the chief, not because he was a relative."

"Then why couldn't Hamlet marry her?"

"He could have," I explained, "but Polonius didn't think he would. After all, Hamlet was a man of great importance who ought to marry a chief's daughter, for in his country a man could have only one wife. Polonius was afraid that if Hamlet made love to his daughter, then no one else would give a high price for her."

"That might be true," remarked one of the shrewder elders, "but a chief's son would give his mistress's father enough presents and patronage to more than make up the difference. Polonius sounds like a fool to me."

"Many people think he was," I agreed. "Meanwhile Polonius sent his son Laertes off to Paris to learn the things of that country, for it was the homestead of a very great chief indeed. Because he was afraid that Laertes might waste a lot of money on beer and women and gambling, or get into trouble by fighting, he sent one of his servants to Paris secretly, to spy out what Laertes was doing. One day Hamlet came upon Polonius's daughter Ophelia. He behaved so oddly he frightened her. Indeed"—I was fumbling for words to express the dubious quality of Hamlet's madness—"the chief and many others had also noticed that when Hamlet talked one could understand the words but not what they meant. Many people thought that he had become mad." My audience suddenly became much more attentive. "The great chief wanted to know what was wrong with Hamlet, so he sent for two of Hamlet's age mates [school friends would have taken long explanation] to talk to Hamlet and find out what troubled his heart. Hamlet, seeing that they had been bribed by the chief to betray him, told them nothing. Polonius, however, insisted that Hamlet was mad because he had been forbidden to see Ophelia, whom he loved."

"Why," inquired a bewildered voice, "should anyone bewitch Hamlet on that account?"

"Bewitch him?"

"Yes, only witchcraft can make anyone mad, unless, of course, one sees the beings that lurk in the forest."

I stopped being a storyteller, took out my notebook and demanded to be told more about these two causes of madness. Even while they spoke and I jotted notes, I tried to calculate the effect of this new factor on the plot. Hamlet had not been exposed to the beings that lurk in the forest. Only his relatives in the male line could bewitch him. Barring relatives not mentioned by Shakespeare, it had to be Claudius who was attempting to harm him. And, of course, it was.

For the moment I staved off questions by saying that the great chief also refused to believe that Hamlet was mad for the love of Ophelia and nothing else. "He was sure that something much more important was troubling Hamlet's heart."

"Now Hamlet's age mates," I continued, "had brought with them a famous storyteller. Hamlet decided to have this man tell the chief and all his homestead a story about the man who had poisoned his brother because he desired his brother's wife and wished to be chief himself. Hamlet was sure the great chief could not hear the story without making a sign if he was indeed guilty, and then he would discover whether his dead father had told him the truth."

The old man interrupted, with deep cunning. "Why should a father lie to his son?" he asked.

I hedged: "Hamlet wasn't sure that it really was his dead father." It was impossible to say anything, in that language, about devil-inspired visions.

"You mean," he said, "it actually was an omen, and he knew witches sometimes send false ones. Hamlet was a fool not to go to one skilled in reading omens and divining the truth in the first place. A man-who-sees-the-truth could have told him how his father died, if he really had been poisoned, and if there was witchcraft in it; then Hamlet could have called the elders to settle the matter."

The shrewd elder ventured to disagree. "Because his father's brother was a great chief, one-who-sees-the-truth might therefore have been afraid to tell it. I think it was for that reason that a friend of Hamlet's father—a witch and an elder—sent an omen so his friend's son would know. Was the omen true?"

"Yes," I said, abandoning ghosts and the devil; a witch-sent omen it would have to be. "It was true, for when the storyteller was telling his tale before all the homestead, the great chief rose in fear. Afraid that Hamlet knew his secret, he planned to have him killed."

The stage set of the next bit presented some difficulties of translation. I began cautiously. "The great chief told Hamlet's mother to find out from her son what he knew. But because a woman's children are always first in her heart, he had the important elder Polonius hide behind a cloth that hung against the wall of Hamlet's mother's sleeping hut. Hamlet started to scold his mother for what she had done."

There was a shocked murmur from everyone. A man should never scold his mother.

"She called out in fear, and Polonius moved behind the cloth. Shouting 'A rat!' Hamlet took his machete and slashed through the cloth." I paused for a dramatic effect. "He had killed Polonius!"

The old men looked at each other in supreme disgust. "That Polonius truly was a fool and a man who knew nothing! What child would not know enough to shout, 'It's me!'" With a pang, I remembered that these people are ardent hunters, always armed with bow, arrow, and machete; at the first rustle in the grass an arrow is aimed and ready, and the hunter shouts "Game!" If no human voice answers immediately, the arrow speeds on its way. Like a good hunter Hamlet had shouted, "A rat!"

I rushed in to save Polonius's reputation. "Polonius did speak. Hamlet heard him. But he thought it was the chief and wished to kill him to avenge his father. He had meant to kill him earlier that evening. . . ." I broke down, unable to describe to these pagans, who had no belief in individual afterlife, the difference between dying at one's prayers and dying "unhousell'd, disappointed, unaneled."

This time I had shocked my audience seriously. "For a man to raise his hands against his father's brother and the one who has become his father—that is a terrible thing. The elders ought to let such a man be bewitched."

I nibbled at my kola nut in some perplexity, then pointed out that after all the man had killed Hamlet's father.

"No," pronounced the old man, speaking less to me than to the young men sitting behind the elders. "If your father's brother has killed your father, you must appeal to your father's age mates; *they* may avenge him. No man may use violence against his senior relatives." Another thought struck him. "But if his father's brother had indeed been wicked enough to bewitch Hamlet and make him mad, that would be a good story indeed, for it would be his fault that Hamlet, being mad, no longer had any sense and thus was ready to kill his father's brother."

There was a murmur of applause. *Hamlet* was again a good story to them, but it no longer seemed quite the same story to me. As I thought over the coming complications of plot and motive, I lost courage and decided to skim over dangerous ground quickly.

"The great chief," I went on, "was not sorry that Hamlet had killed Polonius. It gave him a reason to send Hamlet away, with his two treacherous age mates, with letters to a chief of a far country, saying that Hamlet should be killed. But Hamlet changed the writing on their papers, so that the chief killed his age mates instead." I encountered a reproachful glare from one of the men whom I had told undetectable forgery was not merely immoral but beyond human skill. I looked the other way.

"Before Hamlet could return, Laertes came back for his father's funeral. The great chief told him Hamlet had killed Polonius. Laertes swore to kill Hamlet because of this; and because his sister Ophelia, hearing her father had been killed by the man she loved, went mad and drowned in the river."

"Have you already forgotten what we told you?" The old man was reproachful. "One cannot take vengeance on a madman; Hamlet killed Polonius in his madness. As for the girl, she not only went mad, she was drowned. Only witches can make people drown. Water itself can't hurt anything. It is merely something one drinks and bathes in."

I began to get cross. "If you don't like the story, I'll stop."

The old man made soothing noises and himself poured me some more beer. "You tell the story well, and we are listening. But it is clear that the elders of your country have never told you what the story really means. No, don't interrupt! We believe you when you say your marriage customs are different, or your clothes and weapons. But people are the same everywhere; therefore, there are always witches and it is we, the elders, who know how witches work. We told you it was the great chief who wished to kill Hamlet, and now your own words have proved us right. Who were Ophelia's male relatives?"

"There were only her father and her brother." Hamlet was clearly out of my hands.

"There must have been many more; this also you must ask of your elders when you get back to your country. From what you tell us, since Polonius was dead, it must have been Laertes who killed Ophelia, although I do not see the reason for it."

We had emptied one pot of beer, and the old men argued the point with slightly tipsy interest. Finally one of them demanded of me, "What did the servant of Polonius say on his return?"

With difficulty I recollected Reynaldo and his mission. "I don't think he did return before Polonius was killed."

"Listen," said the elder, "and I will tell you how it was and how your story will go, then you may tell me if I am right. Polonius knew his son would get into trouble, and so he did. He had many fines to pay for fighting, and debts from gambling. But he had only two ways of getting money quickly. One was to marry off his sister at once, but it is difficult to find a man who will marry a woman desired by the son of a chief. For if the chief's heir commits adultery with your wife, what can you do? Only a fool calls a case against a man who will someday be his judge. Therefore Laertes had to take the second way: he killed his sister by witchcraft, drowning her so he could secretly sell her body to the witches."

I raised an objection. "They found her body and buried it. Indeed Laertes jumped into the grave to see his sister once more—so, you see, the body was truly there. Hamlet, who had just come back, jumped in after him."

"What did I tell you?" The elder appealed to the others. "Laertes was up to no good with his sister's body. Hamlet prevented him, because the chief's heir, like a chief, does not wish any other man to grow rich and powerful. Laertes would be angry, because he would have killed his sister without benefit to himself. In our country he would try to kill Hamlet for that reason. Is this not what happened?"

"More or less," I admitted. "When the great chief found Hamlet was still alive, he encouraged Laertes to try to kill Hamlet and arranged a fight with machetes between them. In the fight both the young men were wounded to death. Hamlet's mother drank the poisoned beer that the chief meant for Hamlet in case he won the fight. When he saw his mother die of poison, Hamlet, dying, managed to kill his father's brother with his machete."

"You see, I was right!" exclaimed the elder.

"That was a very good story," added the old man, "and you told it with very few mistakes. There was just one more error, at the very end. The poison Hamlet's mother drank was obviously meant for the survivor of the fight, whichever it was. If Laertes had won, the great chief would have poisoned him, for no one would know that he arranged Hamlet's death. Then, too, he need not fear Laertes's witchcraft; it takes a strong heart to kill one's only sister by witchcraft.

"Sometime," concluded the old man, gathering his ragged toga about him, "you must tell us some more stories of your country. We, who are elders, will instruct you in their true meaning, so that when you return to your own land your elders will see that you have not been sitting in the bush, but among those who know things and who have taught you wisdom."

Review Questions

1. In what ways does Bohannan's attempt to tell the story of Hamlet to the Tiv illustrate the concept of naive realism?

2. Using Bohannan's experience of telling the story of *Hamlet* to the Tiv and the response of the Tiv elders to her words, illustrate cross-cultural misunderstanding.

3. What are the most important parts of *Hamlet* that the Tiv found it necessary to reinterpret?

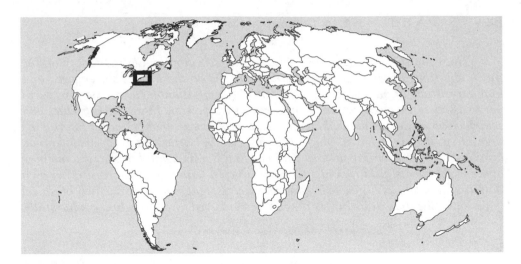

4

Fieldwork on Prostitution in the Era of AIDS

Claire E. Sterk

Many Americans associate social research with questionnaires, structured interviews, word association tests, and psychological experiments. They expect investigators to control the research setting and ask for specific information, such as age, income, place of residence, and opinions about work or national events. But ethnographic field-work is different. Cultural anthropologists may administer formal research instruments such as questionnaires, but largely their goal is to discover culture, to view the actions and knowledge of a group through the eyes of its members. In this sense, ethnographers are more like students; cultural informants are more like teachers. To implement ethnographic research, anthropologists must often become part of the worlds they seek to understand. They arrive as strangers, seek entrance into a group, meet and develop relationships of trust with informants, and wrestle with the ethical dilemmas that naturally occur when someone wants to delve into the lives of others.

From *Tricking and Tripping* by Claire E. Sterk (Putnam Valley, NY: Social Change Press, 2000), pp. 14–20. Reprinted by permission.

These are the challenges discussed in this selection by Claire Sterk. Working inside the United States, as many anthropologists do these days, she engaged in a long-term study of prostitutes in New York City and Atlanta. Her research required her to discover the places where her informants worked and hung out, introduce herself, develop rapport, and conduct open-ended interviews that permitted informants to teach her about their lives. During this process, she learned not to depend too much on contacts (gatekeepers) she met initially, that it was helpful to know something about respondents but to avoid an "expert" role, to refrain from expressing her own opinions about the culture and lives of her subjects, and to manage a variety of ethical questions. She ends by listing six themes that emerged from her ethnographic study.

Prostitution is a way of life. IT IS THE LIFE.

We make money for pimps who promise us
love and more,

but if we don't produce, they shove us out the door.

We turn tricks who have sex-for-pay.

They don't care how many times we serve
every day.

The Life is rough. The Life is tough.

We are put down, beaten up, and left for dead.

It hurts body and soul and messes with
a person's head.

Many of us get high. Don't you understand it is
a way of getting by?

The Life is rough. The Life is tough.

We are easy to blame because we are lame.

—Piper, 1987[1]

One night in March of 1987 business was slow. I was hanging out on a stroll with a group of street prostitutes. After a few hours in a nearby diner/coffee shop, we were kicked out. The waitress felt bad, but she needed our table for some new customers. Four of us decided to sit in my car until the rain stopped. While three of us chatted about life, Piper wrote this poem. As soon as she read it to us, the conversation shifted to more serious topics—pimps, customers, cops, the many hassles of being a prostitute, to name a few. We decided that if I ever finished a book about prostitution, the book would start with her poem.

---

[1]The names of the women who were interviewed for this study, as well as those of their pimps and customers, have been replaced by pseudonyms to protect their privacy.

This book is about the women who work in the lower echelons of the prostitution world. They worked in the streets and other public settings as well as crack houses. Some of these women viewed themselves primarily as prostitutes, and a number of them used drugs to cope with the pressures of the life. Others identified themselves more as drug users, and their main reason for having sex for money or other goods was to support their own drug use and often the habit of their male partner. A small group of women interviewed for this book had left prostitution, and most of them were still struggling to integrate their past experiences as prostitutes in their current lives.

The stories told by the women who participated in this project revealed how pimps, customers, and others such as police officers and social and health service providers treated them as "fallen" women. However, their accounts also showed their strengths and the many strategies they developed to challenge these others. Circumstances, including their drug use, often forced them to sell sex, but they all resisted the notion that they might be selling themselves. Because they engaged in an illegal profession, these women had little status: their working conditions were poor, and their work was physically and mentally exhausting. Nevertheless, many women described the ways in which they gained a sense of control over their lives. For instance, they learned how to manipulate pimps, how to control the types of services and length of time bought by their customers, and how to select customers. While none of these schemes explicitly enhanced their working conditions, they did make the women feel stronger and better about themselves.

In this [article], I present prostitution from the point of view of the women themselves. To understand their current lives, it was necessary to learn how they got started in the life, the various processes involved in their continued prostitution careers, the link between prostitution and drug use, the women's interactions with their pimps and customers, and the impact of the AIDS epidemic and increasing violence on their experiences. I also examined the implications for women. Although my goal was to present the women's thoughts, feelings, and actions in their own words, the final text is a sociological monograph compiled by me as the researcher. . . .

The Sample

. . . The research was conducted during the last ten years in the New York City and Atlanta metropolitan areas. One main data source was participant observation on streets, in hotels and other settings known for prostitution activity, and in drug-use settings, especially those that allowed sex-for-drug exchanges. Another data source was in-depth, life-history interviews with 180 women ranging in age from 18 to 59 years, with an average age of 34. One in two women was African-American and one in three white; the remaining women were Latina. Three in four had completed high school, and among them almost two-thirds had one or more years of additional educational training. Thirty women had graduated from college.

Forty women worked as street prostitutes and did not use drugs. On average, they had been prostitutes for 11 years. Forty women began using drugs an average of three years after they began working as prostitutes, and the average time they had worked as prostitutes was nine years. Forty women used drugs an average of five years before they became prostitutes, and on the average they had worked as prostitutes for eight years. Another forty women began smoking crack and exchanging sex for crack almost simultaneously, with an average of four years in the life. Twenty women who were interviewed were ex-prostitutes.

Comments on Methodology

When I tell people about my research, the most frequent question I am asked is how I gained access to the women rather than what I learned from the research. For many, prostitution is an unusual topic of conversation, and many people have expressed surprise that I, as a woman, conducted the research. During my research some customers indeed thought I was a working woman, a fact that almost always amuses those who hear about my work. However, few people want to hear stories about the women's struggles and sadness. Sometimes they ask questions about the reasons why women become prostitutes. Most of the time, they are surprised when I tell them that the prostitutes as well as their customers represent all layers of society. Before presenting the findings, it seems important to discuss the research process, including gaining access to the women, developing relationships, interviewing, and then leaving the field.

Locating Prostitutes and Gaining Entree

One of the first challenges I faced was to identify locations where street prostitution took place. Many of these women worked on strolls, streets where prostitution activity is concentrated, or in hotels known for prostitution activity. Others, such as the crack prostitutes, worked in less public settings such as a crack house that might be someone's apartment.

I often learned of well-known public places from professional experts, such as law enforcement officials and health care providers at emergency rooms and sexually transmitted disease clinics. I gained other insights from lay experts, including taxi drivers, bartenders, and community representatives such as members of neighborhood associations. The contacts universally mentioned some strolls as the places where many women worked, where the local police focused attention, or where residents had organized protests against prostitution in their neighborhoods.

As I began visiting various locales, I continued to learn about new settings. In one sense, I was developing ethnographic maps of street prostitution. After several visits to a specific area, I also was able to expand these maps by adding information about the general atmosphere on the stroll, general characteristics of the various people present, the ways in which the women and customers connected, and the overall flow of action. In addition, my visits allowed the regular actors to notice me.

I soon learned that being an unknown woman in an area known for prostitution may cause many people to notice you, even stare at you, but it fails to yield many verbal interactions. Most of the time when I tried to make eye contact with one of the women, she quickly averted her eyes. Pimps, on the other hand, would stare at me straight on and I ended up being the one to look away. Customers would stop, blow their horn, or wave me over, frequently yelling obscenities when I ignored them. I realized that gaining entree into the prostitution world was not going to be as easy as I imagined it. Although I lacked such training in any of my qualitative methods classes, I decided to move slowly and not force any interaction. The most I said during the initial weeks in a new area was limited to "How are you" or "Hi." This strategy paid off during my first visits to one of the strolls in Brooklyn, New York. After several appearances, one of the women walked up to me and sarcastically asked if I was looking for something. She caught me off guard, and all the answers I had practiced did not seem to make sense. I mumbled something about just wanting to walk around. She did not like my answer, but she did like my accent. We ended up talking about the latter and she was especially excited when I told her I came from Amsterdam. One of her friends had gone to Europe with her boyfriend, who was in the military. She understood from her that prostitution and drugs were legal in the Netherlands. While explaining to her that some of her friend's impressions were incorrect, I was able to show off some of my knowledge about prostitution. I mentioned that I was interested in prostitution and wanted to write a book about it.

Despite the fascination with my background and intentions, the prostitute immediately put me through a Streetwalker 101 test, and apparently I passed. She told me to make sure to come back. By the time I left, I not only had my first conversation but also my first connection to the scene. Variations of this entry process occurred on the other strolls. The main lesson I learned in these early efforts was the importance of having some knowledge of the lives of the people I wanted to study, while at the same time refraining from presenting myself as an expert.

Qualitative researchers often refer to their initial connections as gatekeepers and key respondents. Throughout my fieldwork I learned that some key respondents are important in providing initial access, but they become less central as the research evolves. For example, one of the women who introduced me to her lover, who was also her pimp, was arrested and disappeared for months. Another entered drug treatment soon after she facilitated my access. Other key respondents provided access to only a segment of the players on a scene. For example, if a woman worked for a pimp, [she] was unlikely . . . to introduce me to women working for another pimp. On one stroll my initial contact was with a pimp whom nobody liked. By associating with him, I almost lost the opportunity to meet other pimps. Some key respondents were less connected than promised—for example, some of the women who worked the street to support their drug habit. Often their connections were more frequently with drug users and less so with prostitutes.

Key respondents tend to be individuals central to the local scene, such as, in this case, pimps and the more senior prostitutes. Their function as gatekeepers often is to protect the scene and to screen outsiders. Many times I had to prove that I was not an undercover police officer or a woman with ambitions to become a streetwalker. While I thought I had gained entree, I quickly learned that many insiders subsequently wondered about my motives and approached me with suspicion and distrust.

Another lesson involved the need to proceed cautiously with self-nominated key respondents. For example, one of the women presented herself as knowing everyone on the stroll. While she did know everyone, she was not a central figure. On the contrary, the other prostitutes viewed her as a failed streetwalker whose drug use caused her to act unprofessionally. By associating with me, she hoped to regain some of her status. For me, however, it meant limited access to the other women because I affiliated myself with a woman who was marginal to the scene. On another occasion, my main key respondent was a man who claimed to own three crack houses in the neighborhood. However, he had a negative reputation, and people accused him of cheating on others. My initial alliance with him delayed, and almost blocked, my access to others in the neighborhood. He intentionally tried to keep me from others on the scene, not because he would gain something from that transaction but because it made him feel powerful. When I told him I was going to hang out with some of the other people, he threatened me until one of the other dealers stepped in and told him to stay away. The two of them argued back and forth, and finally I was free to go. Fortunately, the dealer who had spoken up for me was much more central and positively associated with the local scene. Finally, I am unsure if I would have had success in gaining entrance to the scene had I not been a woman.

Developing Relationships and Trust

The processes involved in developing relationships in research situations amplify those involved in developing relationships in general. Both parties need to get to know each other, become aware and accepting of each other's roles, and engage in a reciprocal relationship. Being supportive and providing practical assistance were the most visible and direct ways for me as the researcher to develop a relationship. Throughout the years, I have given countless rides, provided child care on numerous occasions, bought groceries, and listened for hours to stories that were unrelated to my initial research questions. Gradually, my role allowed me to become part of these women's lives and to build rapport with many of them.

Over time, many women also realized that I was uninterested in being a prostitute and that I genuinely was interested in learning as much as possible about their lives. Many felt flattered that someone wanted to learn from them and that they had knowledge to offer. Allowing women to tell their stories and engaging in a dialogue with them probably were the single most important techniques that allowed me to develop relationships with them. Had I only wanted to focus on the questions I had in mind, developing such relationships might have been more difficult.

At times, I was able to get to know a woman only after her pimp endorsed our contact. One of my scariest experiences occurred before I knew to work through the pimps, and one such man had some of his friends follow me on my way home one night. I will never know what plans they had in mind for me because I fortunately was able to escape with only a few bruises. Over a year later, the woman acknowledged that her pimp had gotten upset and told her he was going to teach me a lesson.

On other occasions, I first needed to be screened by owners and managers of crack houses before the research could continue. Interestingly, screenings always were done by a man even if the person who vouched for me was a man himself. While the women also were cautious, the ways in which they checked me out tended to be much more subtle. For example, one of them would tell me a story, indicating that it was a secret about another person on the stroll. Although I failed to realize this at the time, my field notes revealed that frequently after such a conversation, others would ask me questions about related topics. One woman later acknowledged that putting out such stories was a test to see if I would keep information confidential.

Learning more about the women and gaining a better understanding of their lives also raised many ethical questions. No textbook told me how to handle situations in which a pimp abused a woman, a customer forced a woman to engage in unwanted sex acts, a customer requested unprotected sex from a woman who knew she was HIV infected, or a boyfriend had unrealistic expectations regarding a woman's earnings to support his drug habit. I failed to know the proper response when asked to engage in illegal activities such as holding drugs or money a woman had stolen from a customer. In general, my response was to explain that I was there as a researcher. During those occasions when pressures became too severe, I decided to leave a scene. For example, I never returned to certain crack houses because pimps there continued to ask me to consider working for them.

Over time, I was fortunate to develop relationships with people who "watched my back." One pimp in particular intervened if he perceived other pimps, customers, or passersby harassing me. He also was the one who gave me my street name: Whitie (indicating my racial background) or Ms. Whitie for those who disrespected me. While this was my first street name, I subsequently had others. Being given a street name was a symbolic gesture of acceptance. Gradually, I developed an identity that allowed me to be both an insider and an outsider. While hanging out on the strolls and other gathering places, including crack houses, I had to deal with some of the same uncomfortable conditions as the prostitutes, such as cold or warm weather, lack of access to a rest room, refusals from owners for me to patronize a restaurant, and of course, harassment by customers and the police.

I participated in many informal conversations. Unless pushed to do so, I seldom divulged my opinions. I was more open with my feelings about situations and showed empathy. I learned quickly that providing an opinion can backfire. I agreed that one of the women was struggling a lot and stated that I felt sorry for her. While I meant to indicate my genuine concern for her, she heard that I felt sorry for her because she was a failure. When she finally, after several weeks, talked with me again, I was able to explain to her that I was not judging her, but rather felt concerned for her. She remained cynical and many times asked me for favors to make up for my mistake. It took me months before I felt comfortable telling her that I felt I had done enough and that it was time to let go. However, if she was not ready, she needed to know that I would no longer go along. This was one of many occasions when I learned that although I wanted to facilitate my work as a researcher, that I wanted people to like and trust me, I also needed to set boundaries.

Rainy and slow nights often provided good opportunities for me to participate in conversations with groups of women. Popular topics included how to work safely, what to do about condom use, how to make more money. I often served as a health educator and a supplier of condoms, gels, vaginal douches, and other feminine products. Many women were very worried about the AIDS epidemic. However, they also were worried about how to use a condom when a customer refused to do so. They worried particularly about condom use when they needed money badly and, consequently, did not want to propose that the customer use one for fear of rejection. While some women became experts at "making" their customers use a condom—for example, by hiding it in their mouth prior to beginning oral sex—others would carry condoms to please me but never pull one out. If a woman was HIV positive and I knew she failed to use a condom, I faced the ethical dilemma of challenging her or staying out of it.

Developing trusting relationships with crack prostitutes was more difficult. Crack houses were not the right environment for informal conversations. Typically, the atmosphere was tense and everyone was suspicious of each other. The best times to talk with these women were when we bought groceries together, when I helped them clean their homes, or when we shared a meal. Often the women were very different when they were not high than they were when they were high or craving crack. In my conversations with them, I learned that while I might have observed their actions the night before, they themselves might not remember them. Once I realized this, I would be very careful to omit any detail unless I knew that the woman herself did remember the event.

In-Depth Interviews

All interviews were conducted in a private setting, including women's residences, my car or my office, a restaurant of the women's choice, or any other setting the women selected. I did not begin conducting official interviews until I developed relationships with the women. Acquiring written informed consent prior to the interview was problematic. It made me feel awkward. Here I was asking the women to sign a form after they had begun to trust me. However, often I felt more upset about this technicality than the women themselves. As soon as they realized that the form was something the university required, they seemed to understand. Often they laughed about the official statements, and some asked if I was sure the form was to protect them and not the school. None of the women refused to sign the consent form, although some refused to sign it right away and asked to be interviewed later.

In some instances the consent procedures caused the women to expect a formal interview. Some of them were disappointed when they saw I only had a few structured questions about demographic characteristics, followed by a long list of open-ended questions. When this disappointment occurred, I reminded the women that I wanted to learn from them and that the best way to do so was by engaging in a dialogue rather than interrogating them. Only by letting the women identify their salient issues and the topics they wanted to address was I able to gain an insider's perspective. By being a careful listener and probing for additional information and explanation, I as the interviewer, together with the women, was able to uncover the complexities of their lives. In addition, the nature of the interview allowed me to ask questions about contradictions in a woman's story. For example, sometimes a woman would say that she always used a condom. However, later on in the conversation she would indicate that if she needed drugs she would never use one. By asking her to elaborate on this, I was able to begin developing insights into condom use by type of partner, type of sex acts, and social context.

The interviewer becomes much more a part of the interview when the conversations are in-depth than when a structured questionnaire is used. Because I was so integral to the process, the way the women viewed me may have biased their answers. On the one hand, this bias might be reduced because of the extent to which both parties already knew each other; on the other, a woman might fail to give her true opinion and reveal her actions if she knew that these went against the interviewer's opinion. I suspected that some women played down the ways in which their pimps manipulated them once they knew that I was not too fond of these men. However, some might have taken more time to explain the relationship with their pimp in order to "correct" my image.

My background, so different from that of these women, most likely affected the nature of the interviews. I occupied a higher socioeconomic status. I had a place to live and a job. In contrast to the nonwhite women, I came from a different racial background. While I don't know to what extent these differences played a role, I acknowledge that they must have had some effect on this research.

Leaving the Field

Leaving the field was not something that occurred after completion of the fieldwork, but an event that took place daily. Although I sometimes stayed on the strolls all night or hung out for several days, I always had a home to return to.

I had a house with electricity, a warm shower, a comfortable bed, and a kitchen. My house sat on a street where I had no fear of being shot on my way there and where I did not find condoms or syringes on my doorstep.

During several stages of the study, I had access to a car, which I used to give the women rides or to run errands together. However, I will never forget the cold night when everyone on the street was freezing, and I left to go home. I turned up the heat in my car, and tears streamed down my cheeks. I appreciated the heat, but I felt more guilty about that luxury than ever before. I truly felt like an outsider, or maybe even more appropriate, a betrayer.

Throughout the years of fieldwork, there were a number of times when I left the scene temporarily. For example, when so many people were dying from AIDS, I was unable to ignore the devastating impact of this disease. I needed an emotional break.

Physically removing myself from the scene was common when I experienced difficulty remaining objective. Once I became too involved in a woman's life and almost adopted her and her family. Another time I felt a true hatred for a crack house owner and was unable to adhere to the rules of courteous interactions. Still another time, I got angry with a woman whose steady partner was HIV positive when she failed to ask him to use a condom when they had sex.

I also took temporary breaks from a particular scene by shifting settings and neighborhoods. For example, I would invest most of my time in women from a particular crack house for several weeks. Then I would shift to spending more time on one of the strolls, while making shorter and less frequent visits to the crack house. By shifting scenes, I was able to tell people why I was leaving and to remind all of us of my researcher role.

While I focused on leaving the field, I became interested in women who had left the life. It seemed important to have an understanding of their past and current circumstances. I knew some of them from the days when they were working, but identifying others was a challenge. There was no gathering place for ex-prostitutes. Informal networking, advertisements in local newspapers, and local clinics and community settings allowed me to reach twenty of these women. Conducting interviews with them later in the data collection process prepared me to ask specific questions. I realized that I had learned enough about the life to know what to ask. Interviewing ex-prostitutes also prepared me for moving from the fieldwork to writing.

It is hard to determine exactly when I left the field. It seems like a process that never ends. Although I was more physically removed from the scene, I continued to be involved while analyzing the data and writing this book. I also created opportunities to go back, for example, by asking women to give me feedback on parts of the manuscript or at times when I experienced writer's block and my car seemed to automatically steer itself to one of the strolls. I also have developed other research projects in some of the same communities. For example, both a project on intergenerational drug use and a gender-specific intervention project to help women remain HIV negative have brought me back to the same population. Some of the women have become key respondents in these new projects, while others now are members of a research team. For example, Beth, one of the women who has left prostitution, works as an outreach worker on another project.

Six Themes in the Ethnography of Prostitution

The main intention of my work is to provide the reader with a perspective on street prostitution from the point of view of the women themselves. There are six fundamental aspects of the women's lives as prostitutes that must be considered. The first concerns the women's own explanations for their involvement in prostitution and their descriptions of the various circumstances that led them to become prostitutes. Their stories include justifications such as traumatic past experiences, especially sexual abuse, the lack of love they experienced as children, pressures by friends and pimps, the need for drugs, and most prominently, the economic forces that pushed them into the life. A number of women describe these justifications as excuses, as reflective explanations they have developed after becoming a prostitute.

The women describe the nature of their initial experiences, which often involved alienation from those outside the life. They also show the differences in the processes between women who work as prostitutes and use drugs and women who do not use drugs.

Although all these women work either on the street or in drug-use settings, their lives do differ. My second theme is a typology that captures these differences, looking at the women's prostitution versus drug-use identities. The typology distinguishes among (a) streetwalkers, women who work strolls and who do not use drugs; (b) hooked prostitutes, women who identify themselves mainly as prostitutes but who upon their entrance into the life also began using drugs; (c) prostituting addicts, women who view themselves mainly as drug users and who became prostitutes to support their drug habit; and (d) crack prostitutes, women who trade sex for crack.

This typology explains the differences in the women's strategies for soliciting customers, their screening of customers, pricing of sex acts, and bargaining for services. For example, the street-walkers have the most bargaining power, while such power appears to be lacking among the crack prostitutes.

Few prostitutes work in a vacuum. The third theme is the role of pimps, a label that most women dislike and for which they prefer to substitute "old man" or "boyfriend." Among the pimps, one finds entrepreneur lovers, men who mainly employ street-walkers and hooked prostitutes and sometimes prostituting addicts. Entrepreneur lovers engage in the life for business reasons. They treat the women as their employees or their property and view them primarily as an economic commodity. The more successful a woman is in earning them money, the more difficult it is for that woman to leave her entrepreneur pimp.

Most prostituting addicts and some hooked prostitutes work for a lover pimp, a man who is their steady partner but who also lives off their earnings. Typically, such pimps employ only one woman. The dynamics in the relationship

between a prostitute and her lover pimp become more complex when both partners use drugs. Drugs often become the glue of the relationship.

For many crack prostitutes, their crack addiction serves as a pimp. Few
plan to exchange sex for crack when they first begin using; often several weeks
or months pass before a woman who barters sex for crack realizes that she is
a prostitute.

Historically, society has blamed prostitutes for introducing sexually transmitted diseases into the general population. Similarly, it makes them scape-
goats for the spread of HIV/AIDS. Yet their pimps and customers are not held
accountable. The fourth theme in the anthropological study of prostitution is
the impact of the AIDS epidemic on the women's lives. Although most are knowledgeable about HIV risk behaviors and the ways to reduce their risk, many mis-
conceptions exist. The women describe the complexities of condom use,
especially with steady partners but also with paying customers. Many women
have mixed feelings about HIV testing, wondering how to cope with a positive
test result while no cure is available. A few of the women already knew their HIV-
infected status, and the discussion touches on their dilemmas as well.

The fifth theme is the violence and abuse that make common appearances
in the women's lives. An ethnography of prostitution must allow the women to
describe violence in their neighborhoods as well as violence in prostitution and
drug-use settings. The most common violence they encounter is from customers.
These men often assume that because they pay for sex they buy a woman. Apparently, casual customers pose more of a danger than those who are regulars. The
types of abuse the women encounter are emotional, physical, and sexual. In
addition to customers, pimps and boyfriends abuse the women. Finally, the
women discuss harassment by law enforcement officers.

When I talked with the women, it often seemed that there were no opportunities to escape from the life. Yet the sixth and final theme must be the escape
from prostitution. Women who have left prostitution can describe the process
of their exit from prostitution. As ex-prostitutes they struggle with the stigma
of their past, the challenges of developing a new identity, and the impact of
their past on current intimate relationships. Those who were also drug users
often view themselves as ex-prostitutes and recovering addicts, a perspective
that seems to create a role conflict. Overall, most ex-prostitutes find that their
past follows them like a bad hangover.

Review Questions

   1. Based on reading this selection, how is ethnographic research different
      from other social science approaches to research?

   2. What can ethnographic research reveal that other forms of research can-
      not? What can the use of questionnaires and observational experiments
      reveal about people that ethnographic research might miss?

3. What were some of the techniques used by Sterk to enter the field, conduct her research, and leave the field? What problems did she face?

4. What advice does Sterk have for aspiring ethnographers?

5. What are some of the ethical issues faced by anthropologists when they conduct ethnographic research?

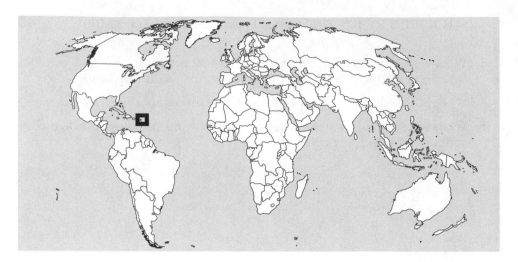

5

Nice Girls Don't Talk to Rastas

George Gmelch

We all are subject to naive realism. It's only natural that the cultural knowledge we learn as we grow up and live in our society shapes the way we see the world and behave in it. It is normal for us to accept our cultural perspective as an accurate portrayal of the way the world really is. Although our naive realism usually goes unnoticed as we function inside our own society, it becomes more obvious when we attempt to communicate with outsiders who possess a different cultural view of reality. Anthropologists attempt to consciously control their own naive realism, but even they sometimes must learn about their own naivete by making mistakes when they do fieldwork in foreign settings.

This article by George Gmelch describes a case of cross-cultural misunderstanding involving an American student living in a Barbadian village as part of a study abroad program. She unwittingly assumes that villagers are

From George Gmelch, "Nice Girls Don't Talk to Rastas." Used by permission of George Gmelch.

46

a homogeneous group of which Rastafarians (a religious sect) are members. By interacting with them, she finds herself shunned by everyone. Her American vision of equality causes her to assume that villagers accepted everyone as equal. She overlooks the existence of class distinctions in this small community characterized by face-to-face relationships.

———

For the past thirty years I have been taking American undergraduates to the field on anthropology training programs in Ireland, Tasmania, and Barbados. It's been no surprise that when my students—young and inexperienced—venture into cultures different from their own they sometimes violate local norms. Professional anthropologists are not immune from making such mistakes; in fact there is a small but lively literature about fieldwork in which anthropologists recount their cultural blunders and the revealing consequences that followed.[1]

In this essay I describe the predicament of a female American student, Johanna, living in a rural village in Barbados. The trouble, which stems from her associating with people—Rastafarians—her community regards as undesirables, speaks to a common shortcoming of American students living abroad for the first time, namely, their failure to understand social class and the workings of small-scale, face-to-face societies. I will return to this point later, first the story.

"George, telephoooone," called out my Barbadian neighbor from the house next door early one morning. "It's Johanna, your student, she say it important." Johanna's voice was full of emotion. "I'm in trouble and I really need to talk to you." I told her to start walking toward Josey Hill and that I would set out toward her village, and that we would meet at the pasture where many families grazed cattle and sheep and boys played cricket and soccer.

When I arrived Johanna—tall, green eyed, and pretty was already there. "They've turned against me. When I walk by, they turn their heads the other way. Someone in the rum shop called me the 'devil's child.'"

Johanna, from a college town in upstate New York where her father taught theater and her mother taught English, had made many friends in her village. In fact, she was enjoying her time in Freeman Hill so much that she fantasized about settling there and teaching school at St. Margaret's, the small elementary school where she had been doing research.[2]

---

[1]See, for example, Barbara Anderson, First Fieldwork: The Misadventures of an Anthropologist, Long Grove, IL: Waveland Press, 1990; and Philip DeVita, The Naked Anthropologist: Tales from Around the World, Belmont, CA: Wadsworth, 1992.

[2]The name of the student, Johanna, and the Rasta, Joseph, are real; the names of all other persons and places are pseudonyms.

Slowly, the story emerged. Johanna revealed that she had been seeing a Rastafarian named Joseph, and that some villagers had seen her walking with him into the hills beyond the village. In a rugged area an hour's walk down the coast from Freeman Hill a small group of Rastas—orthodox Rastas who wore no clothes and subsisted off the land—lived in caves. That morning Johanna's homestay mother, Thelma, had entered the bedroom, shut the door tightly, and breathing very hard told Johanna that people in the village were saying that she was smoking marijuana and bathing naked with the Rastas. Some thought she must be a drug addict.

"I had no idea people would react this way," said Johanna defensively. "Joseph said he was a 'bush doctor.' I mean what is the harm? He's a nice guy, he wouldn't harm anyone. Aren't anthropologists supposed to be interested in everyone? Anthropologists don't ignore people just because some people don't like them. Right?"

Johanna assured me that she hadn't gone naked with the Rastas or become sexually involved. I thought this an unnecessary declaration, but then I recalled the talk my anthropologist wife, Sharon, had with the female students about the problems created by romantic involvements with local men. In the past, such liaisons had upset the students' homestay families and damaged the students' reputations and rapport, as often the men involved had been considered disreputable characters—beach bums—who were beneath the social status of the host families.

With much anguish, Johanna recounted that Thelma wanted her to move out, to leave the village. Johanna had only few weeks left in Barbados. There wasn't time for her to start over somewhere else, nor did I know of another family who had space to take her in. I told her to go back to the village and that I would call on her that evening. When I got home I looked through my copy of Johanna's field notes (the students turned in a copy of their notes every week). A reference to Rastas took on new meaning:

> [February 21] I went to Janice's primary school today and on the way out I started talking to a Rastaish looking dude with a leather Crocodile Dundee hat on just standing on the roadside. I was aware that I could be seen by the children on the playground. When Janice got home, she reprimanded me for talking to him. Janice: "We don't live the way Rastas do. It's not right just to go and talk to anyone you feel like. That man is a killer. Once you left all the children said, 'Look, he is going to carry her away into the hills and kill her.' I am serious. Even teacher told me to tell you not to talk to him. And teachers know about these things."

Later, Johanna described her encounters with the Rastas in more detail. After walking home from the school yard with Joseph, she had agreed to meet him the following week at the small village shop. It wasn't a good choice, as the shop is located where the village's three roads meet, and its veranda is a social gathering place. There wasn't a more conspicuous place in all of Freeman Hill. Johanna described what happened in her journal:

When I saw Joseph coming down the road, I hopped off the porch to go meet him, and every person within the viewing distance did a double take. On the days that I've spent with Joseph, we meet at ten, arrive at his place in the later morning, and usually begin cooking right away. His single meal a day usually takes three hours to prepare, so he likes to get it started as soon as possible so he can relax once it gets dark. His place is so simple and relaxing. It's set up on a ridge, and well hidden. You ascend a steep rock incline and step onto a ledge with a panoramic view of the Atlantic. On one side is a looming two-story rock with an opening in the center; this is Joseph's bedroom. You step down in a dark, cool, homey cave, about 10 by 20 feet with smooth rocks on the floor, a slender little bed on one side, and a natural stone bench coming out of the wall. Joseph's "dresser" is a jutting piece of rock where he rests his Bible, a broken fragment of a mirror, and his shell necklace. He said he took three months process of burning and chipping away at the floor and walls of his cave to make the place livable. "Yeah, it was rough," he said, "but I want my place to be just right when I have a wife come live with me. Because no woman is going to want to come live in a cave she can't stand up in, right?" He grinned.

My usual response to the problems that students unwittingly create is to visit the parties involved first, to better understand the problem and then to try to resolve the misunderstanding by explaining each side's custom to the other. I hoped Johanna's situation would be no different, although it involved a large number of people and I didn't know much about the villagers' relationship with the local Rastas. I was friendly with two respected elders in Freeman Hill, so I decided to go to them for advice. I went first to Ezra Cumberbatch a Pentecostal preacher whose daughters had befriended Johanna; and then to Randall Trotman, a return migrant who had recently resettled in Barbados after a dozen years in England—he was wise and had the perspective that comes with having lived in another society.

    Reverend Cumberbatch told me that the Rastas Johanna had been visiting were well known to the village, and that most people, especially the old ones, viewed them as lazy layabouts, who smoked marijuana and stole fruit and vegetables from their gardens. I remembered that one of my neighbors in Josey Hill had cut down his banana tree after Rastas had repeatedly taken the fruit, or so he claimed. He said he'd rather not have the tree than have Rastas around his house.

    Randall Trotman had a more balanced view. "Some are good and some are bad. Some of them steal your coconuts and aloe, but others are school teachers and craftsman and good citizens." He recognized that in rural places like Freeman Hill all Rastas were tarred with the same brush. Before I left the Trotman home, I asked about a rumored crime that I had heard earlier but had found villagers unwilling to say much about. Apparently, a villager several years before had become furious about the theft of his crops (which could have been taken by monkeys as easily as Rastas) and had put poison in some cucumbers. Randall said two Rastas had died and that the police investigation was inconclusive. In the end, both preacher and returnee were sympathetic to Johanna's plight, but neither had any practical advice on what she could do to repair her reputation and save her fieldwork.

Thinking I should meet the Rastas themselves, I set out to visit them. With the vaguest of directions, I hiked down the steep and rugged coastline looking for the area the Rastas called "Creation." I lost the trail and worked my way through the dense brush on a steep hillside that rose directly from the sea. Remembering Johanna's account, I climbed up several steep inclines to the openings in the rock wall looking for the Rasta caves. The erosion caused by water trickling down through the coral capstone which overlays nearly all of Barbados had created dozens of large caves. The view was magnificent, down the green cliffs and out across the blue Atlantic.

I called out several times but nothing came back. The place was eerily quiet, and I began to question what I was doing there. What was I going to say if I did find them? That I was here to check them out for the safety of my student? Feeling that I was intruding in their living space, I turned and trekked for home, and then to Johanna's homestay.

Thelma, Johanna's homestay mother, listened patiently to my explanations of what anthropologists do and of Johanna's naivete. (Actually, I entertained some doubts about Johanna's innocence for I now knew that she had spent several days in "Creation" and had learned a good deal about the Rastas that had not shown up in fieldnotes.) I told Thelma that students sometimes innocently violate local norms but that these misunderstandings were usually easily cleared up, that in the end no one is the worse for it. She responded that my students would all be returning to the United States, leaving behind whatever ill will they created, and that she was the one that would be living in Freeman Hill for the rest of her life. "I don't want my children exposed to these Rastas," she said, adding that she would be implicated in the minds of many villagers if Johanna's Rastas brought harm to anyone.

After sincere assurances from Johanna that she would stay away from the Rastas, Thelma finally agreed to let her stay. Although Johanna remained, the villagers had little to do with her during her last weeks there. "It's like I have something contagious and they don't want to get too close to me," she wrote. "The road workers who verbally harassed me at the beginning of my stay but finally stopped after I made friends in the village, have now begun to treat me, once again, as a sexual object." In an assessment of her field experience, Johanna concluded, "I learned the power of a societal norm. Nice girls don't talk to Rastas. Exceptions: none."

As I began to reflect on Johanna's experience, it became clear that she had not fully appreciated social class distinctions in Barbadian society or the communal nature of village life. Compared to their European counterparts, American students generally have little understanding of social class. Even after weeks in the field, my students typically view the inhabitants of their villages as being fairly homogeneous. They are not. The students only gradually become aware of social class from comments by their homestay families about other villagers. It takes time for them to understand the workings of life in a small-scale, face-to-face society where people pay close attention to the actions of neighbors, where gossip is recreation, and where, with the slightest provocation, rumor can affect a family's reputation. And like Johanna, sometimes they also learn about class and status by making mistakes—by violating norms concerning relationships between different categories of people. I doubted that the English university students I once taught, steeped in the meaning of class, would have made the same mistake as Johanna.

But it was not just a lack of awareness of status and class. American students often operate on an assumption of *personal autonomy*. That is, if they can see "the truth" in a situation (or view their actions as harmless) then they feel entitled to act without regard for what others might think. Such an attitude sometimes stems more from what anthropologists call *naive realism*, the mistaken view that deep down everyone perceives the world in basically the same way. And why shouldn't they think this way. Most were raised in fairly homogeneous suburbs and on college campuses where they typically have little contact with the international students who might challenge their assumptions. For students like Johanna, Barbados is the first time they have ever lived in another culture, and they arrive with their naive realism fairly intact. The words Johanna used in defense of her actions were revealing, "Joseph wouldn't harm anyone. [The Rastas] are just spiritual people, they don't want anything to do with modern society, they just want to be left alone to do their own thing. Why can't they [the villagers] see that?" Typically it takes my students some weeks before they begin to appreciate that they, like the Rastas, simply cannot always "do their own thing" without repercussions.

I now use Johanna's story as a lesson for other field school students: communities are never as homogeneous as they seem; be sensitive to class and status differences; think about how your actions and relationships could be viewed by others; not everybody perceives the world the way you do.[3]

Review Questions

1. What does the term *naive realism* mean? Give some examples from your own experience.

2. What behavior by an American study abroad student offended the Barbadian villagers she lived with? Why was she surprised by their reaction?

3. What did George Gmelch do to mediate the cross-cultural misunderstanding? How successful was it?

4. What part does social class play in this event?

5. Why is this story a good example of naive realism?

---

[3]Thelma, Johanna's homestay mother, has since housed several other students. Johanna went on to graduate school and is now teaching theater at a small college in New England.

TWO

LANGUAGE
AND COMMUNICATION

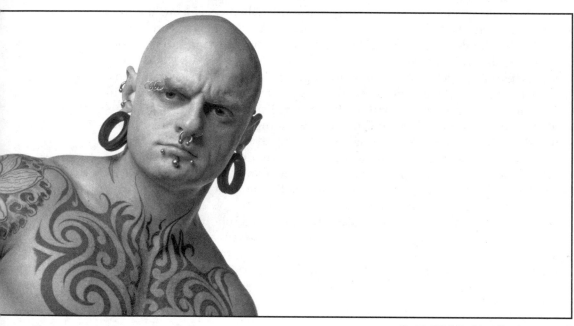

READINGS IN THIS SECTION

Manipulating Meaning: The Military Name Game   56
Sarah Boxer

Conversation Style: Talking on the Job   61
Deborah Tannen

Kinds of Talk: Juicing Clients in Tattoo World   69
Jennifer Boehlke

Anthropologists Investigate Communication Technology   79
Belle Mellor

Culture is a system of symbols that allows us to represent and communicate our experience. We are surrounded by symbols: the flag, a new automobile, a diamond ring, billboard pictures, and, of course, spoken words.

A **symbol** is anything that we can perceive with our senses that stands for something else. Almost anything we experience can come to have symbolic meaning. Every symbol has a referent that it calls to our attention. The term *lawn*, for example, refers to a field of grass plants. When we communicate with symbols, we call attention not only to the referent but also to numerous connotations of the symbol. In U.S. culture we associate lawns with places such as homes and golf courses; actions such as mowing, fertilizing, and raking; and activities such as backyard games and barbeques. Human beings have the capacity to assign meaning to anything they experience in an arbitrary fashion, which allows limitless possibilities for communication.

Symbols greatly simplify the task of communication. Once we learn that a word such as *barn*, for example, stands for a certain type of building, we can communicate about a whole range of specific buildings that fit into the category. And we can communicate about barns in their absence; we can even invent flying barns and dream about barns. Symbols make it possible to communicate the immense variety of human experience, whether past or present, tangible or intangible, good or bad.

Many channels are available to human beings for symbolic communication: sound, sight, touch, and smell. Language, our most highly developed communication system, uses the channel of sound (or, for some deaf people, sight). **Language** is a system of cultural knowledge used to generate and interpret speech. It is a feature of every culture and a distinctive characteristic of the human animal. **Speech** refers to the behavior that produces vocal sounds. Our distinction between language and speech is like the one made between culture and behavior. Language is part of culture, the system of knowledge that generates behavior. Speech is the behavior generated and interpreted by language.

Every language is composed of three subsystems for dealing with vocal symbols: phonology, grammar, and semantics. Let's look briefly at each of these.

Phonology consists of the categories and rules for forming vocal symbols. It is concerned not directly with meaning but with the formation and recognition of the vocal sounds to which we assign meaning. For example, if you utter the word *bat*, you have followed a special set of rules for producing and ordering sound categories characteristic of the English language.

A basic element defined by phonological rules for every language is the phoneme. **Phonemes** are the minimal categories of speech sounds that serve to keep utterances apart. For example, speakers of English know that the words *bat, cat, mat, hat, rat,* and *fat* are different utterances because they hear the sounds /b/, /c/, /m/, /h/, /r/, and /f/ as different categories of sounds. In English, each of these is a phoneme. Our language contains a limited number of phonemes from which we construct all our vocal symbols.

Phonemes are arbitrarily constructed, however. Each phoneme actually classifies slightly different sounds as though they were the same. Different languages may divide up the same range of speech sounds into different sound categories. For example, speakers of English treat the sound /t/ as a single phoneme. Hindi speakers take the same general range and divide it into four phonemes: /t/, /t^h/, /T/, and /T^h/. (The lowercase *t*'s are made with the tongue against the front teeth, while the uppercase *T*'s are made by touching the tongue to the roof of the mouth further back than would be normal for an English speaker. The *h* indicates a puff of air, called *aspiration*, associated with the *t* sound.) Americans are likely to miss important distinctions among Hindi words because they hear these four different phonemes as a single one. Hindi speakers, on the other hand, tend to hear more than one sound category as they listen to English speakers pronounce *t*'s. The situation is reversed for /w/ and /v/. We treat these as two phonemes, whereas Hindi speakers hear them as one. For them, the English words *wine* and *vine* sound the same.

Phonology also includes rules for ordering different sounds. Even when we try to talk nonsense, we usually create words that follow English phonological rules. It would be unlikely, for example, for us ever to begin a word with the phoneme /ng/—usually written in English as "ing." It must come at the end or in the middle of words.

Grammar is the second subsystem of language. **Grammar** refers to the categories and rules for combining vocal symbols. No grammar contains rules for combining every word or element of meaning in the language. If this were the case, grammar would be so unwieldy that no one could learn all the rules in a lifetime. Every grammar deals with *categories* of symbols, such as the ones we call *nouns* and *verbs*. Once you know the rules covering a particular category, you can use it in appropriate combinations.

Morphemes are the categories in any language that carry meaning. They are minimal units of meaning that cannot be subdivided. Morphemes occur in more complex patterns than you may think. The term *bats*, for example, is actually two morphemes, /bat/ meaning a flying mammal and /s/ meaning plural. Even more confusing, two different morphemes may have the same sound shape. /Bat/ can refer to a wooden club used in baseball as well as a flying mammal.

The third subsystem of every language is semantics. **Semantics** refers to the categories and rules for relating vocal symbols to their referents. Like the rules of grammar, semantic rules are simple instructions for combining things; they instruct us to combine words with what they refer to. A symbol can be said to *refer* because it focuses our attention and makes us take account of something. For example, /bat/ refers to a family of flying mammals, as we have already noted.

Language regularly occurs in a social context, and to understand its use fully it is important to recognize its relation to sociolinguistic rules. **Sociolinguistic rules** combine meaningful utterances with social situations into appropriate messages.

Although language is the most important human vehicle for communication, almost anything we can sense may represent a **nonlinguistic symbol** that conveys meaning. The way we sit, how we use our eyes, how we dress, the car we own, the number of bathrooms in our house—all these things carry symbolic meaning. We learn what they mean as we acquire culture. Indeed, a major reason we feel so uncomfortable when we enter a group from a strange culture is our inability to decode our host's symbolic world.

The articles in Part Two illustrate several important aspects of language and communication. The first, by Sarah Boxer, describes the way the U.S. armed forces (and by extension people in general) use words to influence how listeners will define events. To do so, she traces the history of how military operations receive their names and points out that today, names such as "Just Cause" may actually create negative as well as positive images in an audience. Article 7, by Deborah Tannen, looks at another aspect of language—conversation styles. Focusing on the different speaking styles of men and women in the workplace, she describes and analyzes how conversational styles themselves carry meaning and unwittingly lead to misunderstanding. In the third selection, Jennifer Boehlke illustrates the concept of speech acts, which are ways to talk. Based on her ethnography of tattooists at a tattoo and piercing parlor, she describes the speech act called *juicing*, which is used by tattooists to persuade clients to get tattoos, reduce their fear, reinforce their decisions, and spend more money. The final article, by Belle Mellor, describes how anthropologists have been hired to discover the ways people use technical communication devices, such as cell phones, computers, and landlines.

Key Terms

grammar　p. 54
language　p. 53
morphemes　p. 54
nonlinguistic symbol　p. 55
phonemes　p. 53

phonology　p. 53
semantics　p. 54
sociolinguistic rules　p. 54
speech　p. 53
symbol　p. 53

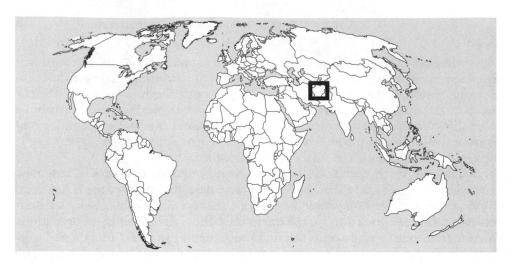

6

Manipulating Meaning: The Military Name Game

Sarah Boxer

In the 1930s, a young man named Benjamin Lee Whorf argued that words did more than label things; they could also shape peoples' perception of and actions toward them. Whorf was a largely self-taught linguist but also a successful insurance executive. To make his point about words, he often cited the case of a warehouse employee who set off an explosion by throwing a hot match into an empty gasoline barrel, thinking that since it was marked "empty," it was safe to do so. Since fumes remained in the barrel, it exploded. Whorf, along with anthropological linguist Edward Sapir, went on to expand observations such as this into what became known as the Sapir-Whorf Hypothesis.*

Critics of the hypothesis have challenged the notion that words and grammar can limit the human ability to physically perceive their environments.

Most agree, however, that words do carry attributional meaning and speakers and writers regularly choose words to convey a particular view of a situation. Hence, we reserve parking spaces for the "handicapped," not "cripples," for example.

The choice of words is especially important in politics. For example, in an effort to repeal a tax on the estates of wealthy Americans, Republicans have renamed the "estate tax" the "death tax," which seems to imply that the government is taxing dead people, not their heirs. President Lyndon Johnson instituted a "war" on poverty, and several presidents who followed him established and continued a "war" on drugs. They used the word war, *which was usually defined as an armed conflict between states or nations, to give extra emphasis to these efforts. More recently, however, the use of "war" in the phrase the* war on terror *has come to have legal consequences that define presidential power. Despite the fact that the war on terror does not name a conflict between states, it has been treated as one, giving the president extended authority over a wide range of policy and action.*

Especially articulate individuals can create word images on their feet, but corporations and government agencies often institutionalize the process. This selection, by Sarah Boxer, traces the history of one such bureaucratic process— the naming of military operations by members of the U.S. armed forces. Challenged by the need to generate public support for military actions, the naming process has taken on grand proportions. First used by the Germans in World War II, operations naming changed from a secret code to a positive statement designed to generate public support by 2001. At first, commanders chose the military operations' names. When these names were later revealed to the public, naming came to be seen as a form of public relations. By the Vietnam War, the U.S. military had created a computer program called "Code Word, Nickname, and Exercise Term System" or "NICKA" for short. Today each major military command has rights to certain letter combinations from which to create names for operations, but higher authorities may discard these names. Boxer concludes by noting that an unanticipated pitfall of the process is the potential for almost any word to offend some members of the national audience. For that reason, some of the best names may be those that have no meaning at all.

For a few days in September [2001] it looked as if the United States would be fighting a war named Infinite Justice. By late September the name was gone. The Council on American-Islamic Relations had found the name offensive because it sounded too much like Eternal Retribution. In other words the United States seemed to be assuming God's role. On Sept. 25 Defense Secretary Donald H. Rumsfeld announced that the military operation would be called Enduring Freedom.

Never mind that Enduring Freedom presented its own troubling ambiguities: Is "enduring" supposed to be taken as an adjective, like long-lasting? Or as a present participle, as in "How long are we going to be enduring this freedom?"

This is not the first time that the name of a military operation has been floated then grounded. The history of naming such operations shows how an art that was once covert has slowly become bureaucratic propaganda.

As Lt. Col. Gregory C. Sieminski points out in his classic short history, "The Art of Naming Operations," published in 1995 in *Parameters*, the quarterly of the United States Army War College, the name of the 1989 United States invasion of Panama, Just Cause, was originally Blue Spoon, until the commander of the Special Operations Command, Gen. James Lindsay, asked an operations officer on the Joint Staff, Lt. Gen. Thomas Kelly, "Do you want your grandchildren to say you were in Blue Spoon?"

So who does create nicknames for military operations these days? There are 24 Defense Department entities, each of which is assigned "a series of two-letter alphabetic sequences," Colonel Sieminski explains. For example, AG-AL, ES-EZ, JG-JL, QA-QF, SM-SR, and UM-UR belong to the Atlantic Command. In order to name the invasion of Granada in 1983, the Atlantic Command started with the letters UR and came up with Urgent Fury. Once the name was generated, it was sent to the Joint Chiefs of Staff, who sent it to the Defense Secretary for the ultimate decision.

But all this can be overridden if the naming seems important enough. And that seems to be happening more and more. "Since 1989 U.S. military operations have been nicknamed with an eye toward shaping domestic and international perceptions," Colonel Sieminski notes.

A huge effort, for example, went into choosing the right name for the operation to defend Kuwait from Iraq. Gen. H. Norman Schwarzkopf wanted the name Peninsula Shield, even though the letters PE were not assigned to his command. Then Crescent Shield was proposed, with an eye to local sentiment. Finally it became Desert Shield. And then the word "desert" bloomed and multiplied: Desert Storm, Desert Saber, Desert Farewell, Desert Share.

The naming game began with the Germans. In World War II they seem to have been the first to give military operations code names, Colonel Sieminski writes. They ransacked mythology and religion for ideas: Archangel, St. Michael, St. George, Roland, Mars, Achilles, Castor, Pollux, and Valkyrie. Hitler himself named the invasion of the Soviet Union Barbarossa for the "12th-century Holy Roman Emperor Frederick I, who had extended German authority over the Slavs in the east," Colonel Sieminski writes.

Churchill, like Hitler, was partial to names that came from "heroes of antiquity, figures from Greek and Roman mythology, the constellations and stars, famous racehorses, names of British and American war heroes," Colonel Sieminski writes. And he set naming etiquette. Names should not "imply a boastful or overconfident sentiment," Churchill said; they should not have "an air of despondency"; they should not be frivolous or ordinary; and they should not be a target for fun. No widow or mother, Churchill said, should have "to say that her son was killed in an operation called 'Bunnyhug' or 'Ballyhoo.'"

For all of Churchill's pains with nomenclature, the names of British and American operations were originally designed to be secret, not meant for public ears until the war or operation was finished.

The United States named its first operations after colors. When the colors began to run out, the War Department drew up a list of "10,000 common nouns and adjectives," avoiding "proper nouns, geographical terms, and names of ships" that might give military clues away to the enemy, Colonel Sieminski writes. And each theater had its own blocks of code words; "the European Theater got such names as Market and Garden, while the Pacific Theater got names like Olympic and Flintlock."

Soon after World War II ended, the Pentagon began creating operation names that were especially designed for public ears. The first nickname was Operation Crossroads, for the 1946 atomic bomb tests conducted on Bikini Atoll. And then things opened up more. During the Korean War Gen. Douglas MacArthur "permitted code names to be declassified and disseminated to the press once operations had begun, rather than waiting until the end of the war," Colonel Sieminski writes.

What followed were some very "aggressive nicknames" for counteroffensives in China: Thunderbolt, Roundup, Killer, Ripper, Courageous, Audacious, and Dauntless.

The bloody names kept flowing in Vietnam, but public relations concerns soon stemmed the tide. The most controversial name, Colonel Sieminski notes, was Masher, the nickname for a "sweep operation through the Bong Son Plain." President Lyndon B. Johnson "angrily protested that it did not reflect 'pacification emphasis.'" In other words Masher somehow did not say "peace" to the world, Colonel Sieminski writes. Masher was reborn as White Wing. After 1966, operations tended to be named for towns and figures: Junction City, Bastogne, Nathan Hale. To rouse the troops at the Khe Sanh garrison, a "round-the-clock bombing attack" was called Operation Niagara, "to invoke an image of cascading shells and bombs," Colonel Sieminski notes.

By the end of the Vietnam War the process of naming had grown baroque. So in 1975 the Joint Chiefs of Staff created a computer system, the Code Word, Nickname, and Exercise Term System. "The NICKA system is not, as some assume, a random word generator for nicknames," Colonel Sieminski writes; "it is in fact merely an automated means for submitting, validating and storing them."

There is plenty of room for drama. But the fashion now, he writes, is "to make the names sound like mission statements by using a verb-noun sequence: Promote Liberty, Restore Hope, Uphold Democracy, Provide Promise." They are boring, unmemorable names.

Despite the monotonous trend, names are more important than they have ever been. With "the shrinking scale of military action," Colonel Sieminski writes, the nickname of an operation now may well become the name for the whole war and its rationale. Maybe that is the problem.

Robin Tolmach Lakoff, a professor of linguistics at the University of California, Berkeley, and the author of *The Language War*, a book about the unintentional overtones of language, said, "Whoever gives the name has control over it." Naming an operation is like naming a baby, she added. "Your creation is opaque, but the name suggests what you hope it will be." What then was the hope with Infinite Justice and then with Enduring Freedom?

The nouns in the name of the operation, she said, were no problem: freedom and justice. It was the adjectives that presented problems. The name had to please so many different kinds of people that every adjective seemed fraught with offensive overtones. "It is a virtue in times of peril," Ms. Lakoff said, "to find words without meaning."

Review Questions

1. Why do military commanders and public officials take the naming of military actions so seriously?

2. How has the procedure for naming military actions changed since campaigns were first given names in World War II?

3. What pitfalls are there in choosing names for military actions in the United States today? Are there solutions to such problems?

4. What evidence supports or challenges the belief held by many in authority that the way something is portrayed in words does actually affect how people will understand it?

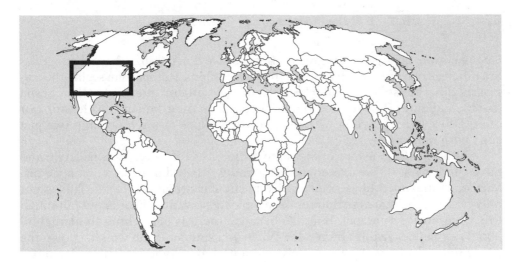

7

Conversation Style:
Talking on the Job

Deborah Tannen

*In this piece excerpted from her book about conversation in the workplace,
Deborah Tannen discusses a tacit dimension of communication, conversation style. Looking at the different ways men and women approach or
avoid asking for help on the job, she argues that gender differences in conversation style are responsible not only for miscommunication but also for
misguided evaluations and moral judgments about the performance and
character of co-workers.*

People have different conversational styles, influenced by the part of the country they grew up in, their ethnic backgrounds and those of their parents, their
age, class, and gender. But conversational style is invisible. Unaware that these
and other aspects of our backgrounds influence our ways of talking, we think

we are simply saying what we mean. Because we don't realize that others' styles are different, we are often frustrated in conversations. Rather than seeing the culprit as differing styles, we attribute troubles to others' intentions (she doesn't like me), abilities (he's stupid), or character (she's rude, he's inconsiderate), our own failure (what's wrong with me?), or the failure of a relationship (we just can't communicate). . . .

Although I am aware of the many influences on conversational style and have spent most of my career studying and writing about them . . . style differences influenced by gender receive particular attention [here]. This is not only because these are the differences people most want to hear about (although this is so and is a factor), but also because there is something fundamental about our categorization by gender. When you spot a person walking down the street toward you, you immediately and automatically identify that person as male or female. You will not necessarily try to determine which state they are from, what their class background is, or what country their grandparents came from. A secondary identification, in some places and times, may be about race. But, while we may envision a day when a director will be able to cast actors for a play without reference to race, can we imagine a time when actors can be cast without reference to their sex?

Few elements of our identities come as close to our sense of who we are as gender. If you mistake people's cultural background—you thought they were Greek, but they turn out to be Italian; you assumed they'd grown up in Texas, but it turns out they're from Kentucky; you say "Merry Christmas" and they say, "we don't celebrate Christmas; we're Muslim"—it catches you off guard and you rearrange the mental frame through which you view them. But if someone you thought was male turns out to be female—like the jazz musician Billy Tipton, whose own adopted sons never suspected that their father was a woman until the coroner broke the news to them after his (her) death—the required adjustment is staggering. Even infants discriminate between males and females and react differently depending on which they confront.

Perhaps it is because our sense of gender is so deeply rooted that people are inclined to hear descriptions of gender patterns as statements about gender *identity*—in other words, as absolute differences rather than a matter of degree and percentages, and as universal rather than culturally mediated. The patterns I describe are based on observations of particular speakers in a particular place and time: mostly (but not exclusively) middle-class Americans of European background working in offices at the present time. Other cultures evince very different patterns of talk associated with gender—and correspondingly different assumptions about the "natures" of women and men. I don't put a lot of store in talk about "natures" or what is "natural." People in every culture will tell you that the behaviors common in their own culture are "natural." I also don't put a lot of store in people's explanations that their way of talking is a natural response to their environment, as there is always an equally natural and opposite way of responding to the same environment. We all tend to regard the way things are as the way things have to be—as only natural.

The reason ways of talking, like other ways of conducting our daily lives, come to seem natural is that the behaviors that make up our lives are ritualized. Indeed, the "ritual" character of interaction is at the heart of this book. Having grown up in a particular culture, we learn to do things as the people we encounter do them, so the vast majority of our decisions about how to speak become automatic. You see someone you know, you ask "How are you?," chat, then take your leave, never pausing to ponder the many ways you could handle this interaction differently—and would, if you lived in a different culture. Just as an American automatically extends a hand for a handshake while a Japanese automatically bows, what the American and Japanese find it natural to say is a matter of convention learned over a lifetime.

No one understood the ritual nature of everyday life better than sociologist Erving Goffman, who also understood the fundamental role played by gender in organizing our daily rituals. In his article "The Arrangement Between the Sexes," Goffman pointed out that we tend to say "sex-linked" when what we mean is "sex-class-linked." When hearing that a behavior is "sex-linked," people often conclude that the behavior is to be found in every individual of that group, and that it is somehow inherent in their sex, as if it came hooked to a chromosome. Goffman suggests the term "genderism" (on the model, I assume, of "mannerism," not of "sexism") for "a sex-class linked individual behavioral practice." This is the spirit in which I intend references to gendered patterns of behavior: not to imply that there is anything inherently male or female about particular ways of talking, nor to claim that every individual man or woman adheres to the pattern, but rather to observe that a larger percentage of women or men *as a group* talk in a particular way, or individual women and men *are more likely* to talk one way or the other.

That individuals do not always fit the pattern associated with their gender does not mean that the pattern is not typical. Because more women or men speak in a particular way, that way of speaking becomes associated with women or men—or, rather, it is the other way around: More women or men learn to speak particular ways *because* those ways are associated with their own gender. And individual men or women who speak in ways associated with the other gender will pay a price for departing from cultural expectations.

If my concept of how gender displays itself in everyday life has been influenced by Goffman, the focus of my research—talk—and my method for studying it grow directly out of my own discipline, linguistics. My understanding of what goes on when people talk to each other is based on observing and listening as well as tape-recording, transcribing, and analyzing conversation. In response to my book *You Just Don't Understand,* I was contacted by people at many companies who asked whether I could help them apply the insights in that book to the problem of "the glass ceiling": Why weren't women advancing as quickly as the men who were hired at the same time? And more generally, they wanted to understand how to integrate women as well as others who were historically not "typical" employees into the increasingly diverse workforce. I realized that in order to offer insight, I needed to observe what was really going on in the workplace. . . .

Women and Men Talking on the Job

Amy was a manager with a problem: She had just read a final report written by Donald, and she felt it was woefully inadequate. She faced the unsavory task of telling him to do it over. When she met with Donald, she made sure to soften the blow by beginning with praise, telling him everything about his report that was good. Then she went on to explain what was lacking and what needed to be done to make it acceptable. She was pleased with the diplomatic way she had managed to deliver the bad news. Thanks to her thoughtfulness in starting with praise, Donald was able to listen to the criticism and seemed to understand what was needed. But when the revised report appeared on her desk, Amy was shocked. Donald had made only minor, superficial changes, and none of the necessary ones. The next meeting with him did not go well. He was incensed that she was now telling him his report was not acceptable and accused her of having misled him. "You told me before it was fine," he protested.

Amy thought she had been diplomatic; Donald thought she had been dishonest. The praise she intended to soften the message "This is unacceptable" sounded to him like the message itself: "This is fine." So what she regarded as the main point—the needed changes—came across to him as optional suggestions, because he had already registered her praise as the main point. She felt he hadn't listened to her. He thought she had changed her mind and was making him pay the price.

Work days are filled with conversations about getting the job done. Most of these conversations succeed, but too many end in impasses like this. It could be that Amy is a capricious boss whose wishes are whims, and it could be that Donald is a temperamental employee who can't hear criticism no matter how it is phrased. But I don't think either was the case in this instance. I believe this was one of innumerable misunderstandings caused by differences in conversational style. Amy delivered the criticism in a way that seemed to her self-evidently considerate, a way she would have preferred to receive criticism herself: taking into account the other person's feelings, making sure he knew that her ultimate negative assessment of his report didn't mean she had no appreciation of his abilities. She offered the praise as a sweetener to help the nasty-tasting news go down. But Donald didn't expect criticism to be delivered in that way, so he mistook the praise as her overall assessment rather than a preamble to it.

This conversation could have taken place between two women or two men. But I do not think it is a coincidence that it occurred between a man and a woman. . . . Conversational rituals common among men often involve using opposition such as banter, joking, teasing, and playful put-downs, and expending effort to avoid the one-down position in the interaction. Conversational rituals common among women are often ways of maintaining an appearance of equality, taking into account the effect of the exchange on the other person, and expending effort to downplay the speakers' authority so they can get the job done without flexing their muscles in an obvious way.

When everyone present is familiar with these conventions, they work well. But when ways of speaking are not recognized as conventions, they are taken literally, with negative results on both sides. Men whose oppositional strategies are interpreted literally may be seen as hostile when they are not, and their efforts to ensure that they avoid appearing one-down may be taken as arrogance. When women use conversational strategies designed to avoid appearing boastful and to take the other person's feelings into account, they may be seen as less confident and competent than they really are. As a result, both women and men often feel they are not getting sufficient credit for what they have done, are not being listened to, are not getting ahead as fast as they should.

When I talk about women's and men's characteristic ways of speaking, I always emphasize that both styles make sense and are equally valid in themselves, though the difference in styles may cause trouble in interaction. In a sense, when two people form a private relationship of love or friendship, the bubble of their interaction is a world unto itself, even though they both come with the prior experience of their families, their community, and a lifetime of conversations. But someone who takes a job is entering a world that is already functioning, with its own characteristic style already in place. Although there are many influences such as regional background, the type of industry involved, whether it is a family business or a large corporation, in general, workplaces that have previously had men in positions of power have already established male-style interaction as the norm. In that sense, women, and others whose styles are different, are not starting out equal, but are at a disadvantage. Though talking at work is quite similar to talking in private, it is a very different enterprise in many ways.

When Not Asking Directions
Is Dangerous to Your Health

If conversational-style differences lead to troublesome outcomes in work as well as private settings, there are some work settings where the outcomes of style are a matter of life and death. Healthcare professionals are often in such situations. So are airline pilots.

Of all the examples of women's and men's characteristic styles that I discussed in *You Just Don't Understand,* the one that (to my surprise) attracted the most attention was the question "Why don't men like to stop and ask for directions?" Again and again, in the responses of audiences, talk-show hosts, letter writers, journalists, and conversationalists, this question seemed to crystallize the frustration many people had experienced in their own lives. And my explanation seems to have rung true: that men are more likely to be aware that asking for directions, or for any kind of help, puts them in a one-down position.

With regard to asking directions, women and men are keenly aware of the advantages of their own style. Women frequently observe how much time they would save if their husbands simply stopped and asked someone instead of driving around trying in vain to find a destination themselves. But I have also been told by men that it makes sense not to ask directions because you learn a lot about a neighborhood, as well as about navigation, by driving around and finding your own way.

But some situations are more risky than others. A Hollywood talk-show producer told me that she had been flying with her father in his private airplane when he was running out of gas and uncertain about the precise location of the local landing strip he was heading for. Beginning to panic, the woman said, "Daddy! Why don't you radio the control tower and ask them where to land?" He answered, "I don't want them to think I'm lost." This story had a happy ending, else the woman would not have been alive to tell it to me.

Some time later, I repeated this anecdote to a man at a cocktail party—a man who had just told me that the bit about directions was his favorite part of my book, and who, it turned out, was also an amateur pilot. He then went on to tell me that he had had a similar experience. When learning to fly, he got lost on his first solo flight. He did not want to humiliate himself by tuning his radio to the FAA emergency frequency and asking for help, so he flew around looking for a place to land. He spotted an open area that looked like a landing field, headed for it—and found himself deplaning in what seemed like a deliberately hidden landing strip that was mercifully deserted at the time. Fearing he had stumbled upon an enterprise he was not supposed to be aware of, let alone poking around in, he climbed back into the plane, relieved that he had not gotten into trouble. He managed to find his way back to his home airport as well, before he ran out of gas. He maintained, however, that he was certain that more than a few small-plane crashes have occurred because other amateur pilots who did not want to admit they were lost were less lucky. In light of this, the amusing question of why men prefer not to stop and ask for directions stops being funny.

The moral of the story is not that men should immediately change and train themselves to ask directions when they're in doubt, any more than women should immediately stop asking directions and start honing their navigational skills by finding their way on their own. The moral is flexibility: Sticking to habit in the face of all challenges is not so smart if it ends up getting you killed. If we all understood our own styles and knew their limits and their alternatives, we'd be better off—especially at work, where the results of what we do have repercussions for co-workers and the company, as well as for our own futures.

To Ask or Not to Ask

An intern on duty at a hospital had a decision to make. A patient had been admitted with a condition he recognized, and he recalled the appropriate medication. But that medication was recommended for a number of conditions, in different dosages. He wasn't quite sure what dose was right for this condition. He had to make a quick decision: Would he interrupt the supervising resident during a meeting to check the dose, or would he make his best guess and go for it?

What was at stake? First and foremost, the welfare, and maybe even the life, of the patient. But something else was at stake too—the reputation, and eventually the career, of the intern. If he interrupted the resident to ask about the dosage, he was making a public statement about what he didn't know, as well as making himself something of a nuisance. In this case, he went with his guess, and there were no negative effects. But, as with small-plane crashes, one wonders how many medical errors have resulted from decisions to guess rather than ask.

It is clear that not asking questions can have disastrous consequences in medical settings, but asking questions can also have negative consequences. A physician wrote to me about a related experience that occurred during her medical training. She received a low grade from her supervising physician. It took her by surprise because she knew that she was one of the best interns in her group. She asked her supervisor for an explanation, and he replied that she didn't know as much as the others. She knew from her day-to-day dealings with her peers that she was one of the most knowledgeable, not the least. So she asked what evidence had led him to his conclusion. And he told her, "You ask more questions."

There is evidence that men are less likely to ask questions in a public situation, where asking will reveal their lack of knowledge. One such piece of evidence is a study done in a university classroom, where sociolinguist Kate Remlinger noticed that women students asked the professor more questions than men students did. As part of her study, Remlinger interviewed six students at length, three men and three women. All three men told her that they would not ask questions in class if there was something they did not understand. Instead, they said they would try to find the answer later by reading the textbook, asking a friend, or, as a last resort, asking the professor in private during office hours. As one young man put it, "If it's vague to me, I usually don't ask. I'd rather go home and look it up."

Of course, this does not mean that no men will ask questions when they are in doubt, nor that all women will; the differences, as always, are a matter of likelihood and degree. As always, cultural differences play a role too. It is not unusual for American professors to admit their own ignorance when they do not know the answer to a student's question, but there are many cultures in which professors would not, and students from those cultures may judge American professors by those standards. A student from the Middle East told a professor at a California university that she had just lost all respect for one of his colleagues. The reason: She had asked a question in class, and the offending professor had replied, "I don't know offhand, but I'll find out for you."

The physician who asked her supervisor why he gave her a negative evaluation may be unusual in having been told directly what behavior led to the misjudgment of her skill. But in talking to doctors and doctors-in-training around the country, I have learned that there is nothing exceptional about her experience, that it is common for interns and residents to conceal their ignorance by not asking questions, since those who do ask are judged less capable. Yet it seems that many women who are more likely than men to ask questions (just as women are more likely to stop and ask for directions when they're lost) are unaware that they may make a negative impression at the same time that they get information. Their antennae have not been attuned to making sure they don't appear one-down.

This pattern runs counter to two stereotypes about male and female styles: that men are more focused on information and that women are more sensitive. In regard to classroom behavior, it seems that the women who ask questions are more focused on information, whereas the men who refrain from doing so are more focused on interaction—the impression their asking will make on others. In this situation, it is the men who are more sensitive to the impression made on others by their behavior, although their concern is, ultimately, the effect on themselves rather than on others. And this sensitivity is likely to make them look better in the world of work. Realizing this puts the intern's decision in a troubling perspective. He had to choose between putting his career at risk and putting the patient's health at risk.

It is easy to see benefits of both styles: Someone willing to ask questions has ready access to a great deal of information—all that is known by the people she can ask. But just as men have told me that asking directions is useless since the person you ask may not know and may give you the wrong answer, some people feel they are more certain to get the right information if they read it in a book, and they are learning more by finding it themselves. On the other hand, energy may be wasted looking up information someone else has at hand, and I have heard complaints from people who feel they were sent on wild-goose chases by colleagues who didn't want to admit they really were not sure of what they pretended to know.

The reluctance to say "I don't know" can have serious consequences for an entire company—and did: On Friday, June 17, 1994, a computer problem prevented Fidelity Investments from calculating the value of 166 mutual funds. Rather than report that the values for these funds were not available, a manager decided to report to the National Association of Securities Dealers that the values of these funds had not changed from the day before. Unfortunately, June 17 turned out to be a bad day in the financial markets, so the values of Fidelity's funds that were published in newspapers around the country stood out as noticeably higher than those of other funds. Besides the cost and inconvenience to brokerage firms who had to re-compute their customers' accounts, and the injustice to investors who made decisions to buy or sell based on inaccurate information, the company was mightily embarrassed and forced to apologize publicly. Clearly this was an instance in which it would have been preferable to say, "We don't know."

Flexibility, again, is key. There are many situations in which it serves one well to be self-reliant and discreet about revealing doubt or ignorance, and others in which it is wise to admit what you don't know.

Review Questions

1. What does Tannen mean by *conversational style?*

2. What is the important style difference in the way men and women ask for directions or help, according to Tannen?

3. What is Tannen's hypothesis about why males avoid asking other people for directions?

4. In Tannen's perspective, what conclusions do men and women draw about each other when they display typically different approaches to asking directions?

("Asking for Drink" = better)

8

Kinds of Talk: Juicing Clients in Tattoo World

Jennifer Boehlke

In the introduction to Part One of this book, we argued that there are two basic kinds of culture, tacit and explicit, and that the difference between the two involves language. There are no words for tacit cultural categories, so behavioral observation is the only way to discover them. But words name explicit cultural categories. We can discover them by listening to people talk and by interviewing informants. There are words for many kinds of cultural things—people, material items, geographical features, actions, feelings, and times, for example. But it may come as a surprise that there are also words for ways to talk. When you attend class at your college or university, you might listen to a lecture or participate in a discussion. After class you might tease, joke, flirt, greet, or call out to someone. Each requires special verbal content and styles of speaking.

In this article, Jennifer Boehlke describes one way that tattoo artists and piercers talk to prospective or actual customers. Called juicing *inside tattoo shop culture, this kind of talk is designed to persuade clients to have tattoos, reduce fears they have about getting a tattoo or piercing, make them feel good about their new body art, and encourage them to spend more money.*

I talked to a friend on my cellular phone as he guided me through one of the seediest streets in the city. He had been delayed at *the shop* and was not going to be able to meet me at his house as we had planned. Instead, he invited me to eat take-out food with him at the shop. After passing rows of used furniture stores, fast food restaurants, ethnic grocery markets, and pawnshops, I finally spotted his car parked in front of a tattoo shop with a bright neon sign saying "Damascus." (All names of people, organizations, and places are fictitious.) Inside the shop, I am greeted by a group of about seven men. Some of them are friends whom I originally met in a bar. Most of them are heavily tattooed and bear several body piercings. I am instantly offered a seat at a large round black table located at the front of the shop, where they are eating "authentic" Mexican food, prepared by two "grandmas" in the store next to the tattoo shop. One friend, Chris, passes me the tamales and apologizes for not having silverware, while another, Adam, is busy creating a makeshift spoon for me out of a Styrofoam cup. Chris is the owner of the store; he does tattoos and body piercings. Adam is Chris's best friend who works at the shop as a body piercer.

As my eyes wander, I notice that the shop is divided into four main sections: the front area contains a round table, a couple of leather sofas, and a display case containing body jewelry, several custom-made knives, and advertisements for a local night club. A blocked-off area, which I later learn is the "office," is located to the right of the front area, while the tattoo area—which takes up the majority of the shop—is to the left. The tattoo area contains three tattoo stations and an artist table. Each station has a chair, a power source, a tattoo gun, bright lighting, and a table covered with plastic sandwich bags, a container of Vaseline jelly, and large glass jars holding plastic gloves, tongue depressors, ink caps, and razor blades. I notice that a large red curtain sections off the back right corner of the tattoo area. Adam explains to me that this area is his "Elvis shrine," where most piercings and some "strategically" placed tattoos are given. The walls of the entire shop are covered with giant, colorful paintings that have a "trippy" feel about them.

There is a strong scent of incense mixed with cigarette smoke wafting through the shop. Our dinner is accompanied by the blaring music of Stone

Temple Pilots playing on the stereo and the constant hum of the *tattoo gun*. One of the tattooists is working on an Asian woman and her boyfriend. I recognize her boyfriend as one of the waiters who works at a popular downtown restaurant. Some of the guys with whom I am eating get up at various intervals to see how the tattooing is going. "That shit is dope" or "It's looking really good" they would say, as the couple smiles and agrees.

Throughout the meal, the conversation revolves around music, plans for a diner that several of the guys are opening, and general occurrences that took place in the shop that day. Several people had come and gone. One man had stopped in to let the guys know that he had obtained some sawed-off guns for sale. He was a shaggy, older man who seemed incredibly wired and paranoid. The guys simply humored him by listening to his pitch about the latest "weapons" he had to offer and then declared him as "whacked" when he left. Another man covered in heavy gold jewelry stopped by in search of a lost bracelet. The handful of potential customers who wandered in were greeted with a "What can we do for you?" or "What do you have to work with?" followed by "Do you want to look at some tattoo books?" A couple of people settled into the leather couches and perused the tattoo books for about an hour as we ate.

The quick one-hour dinner I had planned at the tattoo shop turned into a four-hour hanging-out adventure. I had seen and interacted with a larger variety of people in one evening than I had during the entire previous month. What caught my attention was the fact that the men who worked at the shop not only made me feel comfortable enough to stay so long, they related to *everyone* who walked through the door with the same charm and ease. A tattoo shop can be very intimidating, but they make it a pleasant place to be. They could relate to a club-owner, a biker, a businessman, a young couple, and even an anthropology student! Adam comments,

> I'm a fucking chameleon to society. I could sit down at a stool at the bar and talk intellectually with a guy in a suit; talk with you about a Cuban writer, or walk out the door and talk to a fucking bum on the corner about drinking whiskey. Any of those formats, I will become a chameleon to that situation because of the fact that I work in a tattoo shop.

I realized that these men were incredibly talented and knowledgeable about dealing with people and that this seemed to be a special feature of tattoo shop culture. The emphasis on social ability interested me and I wanted to learn more about it. I spent the next three months conducting interviews, spending time at the shop, and even getting a tattoo myself in order to understand exactly how this microculture works. I wanted to determine how they manage to attract customers, make them feel comfortable in an atmosphere that is often intimidating and associated with pain, and even encourage them to return for repeated visits.

Things people worry about when getting pierced or tattooed	Permanence of the tattoo/piercing
	Cost of service
	Infection of tattoo or piercing
	Quality of art
	Privacy
	Pain of the procedure

FIGURE 1　　Taxonomy of things people worry about when getting pierced or tattooed

Chris and Adam worked together as my main informants. They were able to "play off" each other in a way that was extremely effective in the interview process. During the first interview they revealed a "catch term" that expressed how they relate to customers: juicing. Chris explains, "*Juicing* is like going to see what's up, good cop/bad cop, the high-low game, under the table . . . all things that can be included as talking to the customer and getting them to get tattooed."

I soon discover that juicing not only includes ways to get someone to get a tattoo, but also how to make them feel good about doing it and make them want to come back for more. Chris and Adam also informed me of the various concerns or reservations that people have regarding the tattoo process. They highlighted six main issues that seem to be a source of anxiety for their customers: permanence of the tattoo, cost of the tattoo, disease and infection, quality of art, privacy, and pain. This ethnography is an attempt to organize and explain how these men help to overcome several of these concerns through their technique of juicing. What follows is an abbreviated version of the original ethnography in which these concerns and the cultural strategies tattoo artists use to deal with them are addressed.

The Art of Juicing

The first step in building a relationship with tattoo or body piercing customers is to meet them and to get them to stop by the shop. This is where the technique of juicing is indispensable. Chris and Adam spend a considerable amount of time in bars, putting two variations of juicing to use: the *flirt juice* and the *"we'll take care of you" juice.*

The "we'll take care of you" juice may be performed by either one of the shop employees, friends, or previous customers and may take place anywhere. It consists of catching someone's eye (usually by revealing your own tattoo), talking to them, and then encouraging them to go to the shop by insisting that "we'll take care of you." If it is a friend, they might say, "Tell them I sent you. They'll take care of you."

The flirt juice, a technique used mostly on women, is performed by shop employees. It may be used in a bar or social situation in order to get someone to stop by the shop for the first time, or it may be used in the shop in order to get customers to return. Chris explains how this is done.

> You are having a few drinks, having a good time. You see a good looking female, she's got a navel piercing, she's attractive, you look at yourself and you say, "I'm not an ugly man. I work at the tattoo shop. I could go over and juice her." It's nothing intimate. It's just you walk over, you compliment her, you say, "How are you doing?" Then you flip out a card and say, "By the way, that's a nice navel piercing you have there. You should come down and get some work done by me." That's called the flirt juice, when you use appearance or looks to win the young lady over, or young man, whatever. What it comes down to is you can be a little extra nice to them and they think they are special and they'll come down (to the shop) to see you.

One problem that my informants have is that they may not remember someone whom they juiced while they were drinking at a bar. "They'll come down to the shop and be like 'don't you remember me?' and we'll be like, 'NO, but don't feel bad.' But at the same time, it worked out pretty well because they came down, they were *juiced*."

Flirting with customers has also led to another phenomenon—groupies. Adam and Chris explained: "For a certain period of time you'll get a pack of young girls who are kind of 'in lust' with us. It is kind of funny because they will come in and they will bring all their friends. They will be like, 'Come see who works here, they are really nice (or they're really cute).'"

Once the customers are lured into the shop, the next step is convincing them to get a tattoo. This requires the tattoo artist or body-piercer to be able to offer plenty of reassurance regarding the customer's decision. They have to be able to counteract years of negative connotations regarding tattoos and pacify the customer's fear of applying a permanent mark on their body.

Show Me the Money!

Once a customer has decided to get a tattoo or piercing, the next step is arranging payment. Tattoo shops have a general up-front payment policy. This is due to the fact that customers have been known to run off without paying, or simply do not have enough money on them.

Since many customers are concerned about the expense of having a tattoo applied, the shop has developed many juicing techniques that allow them to charge the most money possible, while making the customers feel as though they got a good deal. These *juice mechanisms* include the *high-low game, good cop/bad cop, under-the-table, add-on juice, come back juice*, and *"What do you have to work with?" juice.*

The classic juice mechanism is the *"What do you have to work with?" juice.* I saw this used many times during my first visit to the tattoo shop. It involves one of the men in the shop asking the customer, "What are you looking to spend today?" or "What are you working with today?" as soon as they walk through the door. This allows the tattoo artist or body piercer to determine how much money the customers have with them that tattooists can get them to spend. They try to make their service affordable while making a profit at the same time.

However, since tattoo customers have become quite adept at bargaining for a good price, my informants don't always rely on what the customer claims he or she is willing to spend. They often try to determine how much people will spend before they even walk through the door. All of the artists at the shop play a game called the *"who's coming and what are they coming for?" game.* Since the shop has big windows, the artists often see the customers as they approach the door and they try to guess what the customers want and how much they can get them to spend.

> One of us will be like, "No, they're coming in for a tongue piercing." "No way man, that girl is getting a tat on her arm, that's why her mom is with, you know." So we have this guessing game of what is going on and what they are going to get. To be honest with you . . . we are usually right.

Once the tattoo artists have determined how much they can probably get the customer to spend, they agree on a price. This may involve further juicing mechanisms such as the high-low game, good cop/bad cop, or under-the-table.

> We have good cop/bad cop. What that [consists of] is one of the people will be the good cop, which is the person who is going to do the tattoo and, the other, like myself, would be the bad cop and he [the good cop] would be like, "Well, I could probably do it for $200," and then [I] would be like, "No, no, no, you have to do it for fucking $300, $200 is way too low!" And then [we] would compromise with like $250. So I take the bad rap. The [artist performing the tattoo] takes the good rap, but the customer is still getting a good deal. It's just like used car salesman shit. Sometimes people get more than their value, sometimes they get less than their value. It just depends on certain circumstances.

Good cop/bad cop and the high-low game both require the participation of two artists. High-low game is very similar to good cop/bad cop. The main difference that separates the two is that *good cop/bad cop* requires "one person to be the dick and the other person to be the good guy, and the *high-low* is simply a price game."

Permanence of Tattoo

While body piercing seems to be a fairly recent phenomenon in the U.S., tattoos have been a source of controversy for many years. People bearing tattoos have long been identified as "freaks" by mainstream society. They have been associated with

Juice Mechanism	No. of Workers Needed	Where Mostly Used	Purpose	Unique Features	Phrases Used
High-low game	2	The shop	Charge more	A price game	1. "Well, I could probably do it for $200." 2. "No, no you have to do it for fucking $300, $200 is way too low." (Compromise for $250.)
Good cop/bad cop	2	The shop	Charge more	One person is a dick, the other is a nice guy	—
Under-the-table	1	The shop	Exchange "tax-free" services	Service is not recorded for tax purposes	"Oh, you're a painter, we need our walls painted. . . . Oh cool, you want a tattoo?"
Add-on juice	1	The shop	Get customer to come back/apply bigger, more expensive tattoo	—	"Well God, you know since you're already here and stuff, why don't we go ahead and touch up this one; it's small and you could just tip me like $20."
Come-back juice	1	The shop	Get customer to come back	—	"God, that's a really nice tattoo. I know you don't have the money right now, but you should think about getting roses around it, cause it would look really good."
"We'll take care of you" juice	1	Bars	Get customer into the shop	May be done by friends of people who work at the shop	"Hey, go to this shop . . . tell them I sent you, and they'll take care of you."
"What do you have to work with?" juice	1	The shop	Charge the most possible	Called "the classic" juice	"So, what do you have to work with today?"/"How much are you looking to spend?"
During tattoo juice	1–2	The shop	Make customer feel good/come back	Helps reduce pain of the tattoo	"That shit is dope."/"That's clean, very clean."
Flirt juice	1	Bars and the shop	Get customer into shop/come back	Used mostly on women and leads to having "groupies"	"How are you doing?" (flip out a card) "By the way, that's a nice navel piercing you have there, you should come down and get some work by me."

FIGURE 2   Paradigm of Juicing Mechanisms

rebels, bikers, and broken hearts. Even as tattoos are becoming increasingly main-stream and fashionable, stereotypes are difficult to overcome. Strong negative associations that often surround tattoos are especially intimidating for a potential tattoo customer considering the fact that they are permanent. People who get a tattoo are often making a statement about themselves that will be carried for the rest of their life. Of course, one may opt to have a tattoo removed surgically by laser, but this is an extremely expensive procedure that is financially feasible for very few people and leaves scars. Therefore, the permanence of a tattoo is a large source of anxiety for many people. Chris noted, "People are scared. It's a scary thing for one to put something on your body for the rest of your life. It's scary [deciding] where you're going to put it, it's scary [wondering] how it's going to be done."

There is also a great deal of pressure placed on the tattooist due to the permanent nature of their job.

> It's a fucking weird job. You wake up and you apply something permanent on someone's body for the rest of their life. You're not selling them a bottle of beer, or you're not giving them a fucking omelet on a platter. You're selling them something that is going to be on them forever. It's a hard thing to do and you have to be convincing. Not that you are trying to convince them into something that they don't want to do, you just have to be reassuring. Working in that kind of environment is more psychological than it is anything else.

Since getting a tattoo or body piercing is often seen as making a permanent statement about oneself, the artists want to make sure that customers get exactly what they want. In order to help customers choose what kind of statement they would like to make about themselves, the shop has a large reference library of books.

> Over the two and a half years that we have been open, we went and found all the different topics of things that people are generally really into, as far as tattoos go. We have books on human anatomy, pose books which have thousands of different figure poses, cartoon books, horse books, lettering books, Japanese and Chinese character books, dragon books. It's an essential tool in tattooing. You've got to have reference material.

The shop also has portfolios of piercings and tattoos that they have done on previous customers. These artists are especially talented at creating the perfect tattoo for each individual because they specialize in *custom work*. Custom work is anything that is uniquely tailored to the taste of each customer, not simply something copied out of a book.

> We do mainly custom work, so what we really promote at the shop is totally getting people in there, and when they do walk through the door, preferably drawing something out of their imagination. It's not like a lot of places where you just walk in and pick something off the wall.

Custom work is also a term that may be applied to piercings. This would include anything that is not the "norm."

One final way that my informants may pacify a customer's concern regarding the permanence of a tattoo is through a version of the flirt juice. They might say to a black woman, "You have a really nice complexion, a gold tattoo would really compliment your skin tone." When customers are reassured that a tattoo would look good on them, they are not as concerned about its permanence.

When people have decided to make a permanent alteration on their bodies and they are paying a substantial amount of money to have it done, quality of art becomes a major concern. This is not an occupation that allows room for mistakes. My informants made it very clear that their job is mostly "psychological."

> It's an easy job as far as time is concerned and being physical about it, but it is a very mental job, you can't forget anything, you DON'T fuck up. You don't poke somebody through their tongue and say "OOPS!" . . . they don't want to hear it, you don't have time to fuck up . . . so that is the biggest thing on your mind, you want to get them in there, make them feel comfortable, and get them out.

The artists reassure customers that they will receive a high-quality service by ensuring them that they are licensed tattoo artists and body piercers, that they are knowledgeable about their job and human anatomy, and that they have had many satisfied customers. They may also use the *during tattoo/piercing juice* to make the customer feel good about the art.

Although my informants convinced me of their ability to offer quality art to their customers, we all know that no one is perfect. So the question arises, "What happens if they do make a mistake?" This is where the during tattoo juice comes into play. The *during tattoo juice* consists of one of the guys in the shop walking over to someone else's tattoo station while the artist is working on a customer and commenting on how good the tattoo looks. I noticed this technique during the first evening I spent in the shop. While a couple was getting tattooed, my friends would get up from eating and say "Hey, that looks really good," or "That shit is tight!" The couple was being juiced. Adam explained how his friends juiced him when he got an eagle tattooed on his chest.

> Last night I got tattooed on my chest, and my first question when I opened my eyes—cause I was like trying to relax because of the pain factor—I open my eyes to the guys standing above me and I say, "Does it look tight?" and they looked at me and they's like, "That shit is dope," which means they are juicing me, making me feel better about getting a tattoo which you can do to customers as well. You like walk over to another artist's station and be like, "Hey, that tattoo looks really good," and the customer is like, "Yeah, you're right." Or we'll say, "That's clean, very clean." Clean is a good juice. It means not crispy or flaky.

The during tattoo juice can be a helpful way to cover up mistakes or flaws in a tattoo that is being given. The artists may compliment each other in front of a customer even if they don't especially like the tattoo. They may also help to reassure customers. For example, if a tattoo is a bit crooked and the customer notices, the other artists may say, "It gives it character" or "I think it looks better that way." They are using *juicing mechanisms* to cover up any minor flaws.

Conclusion

From the interviews and careful observation it became clear that tattoo artists and body piercers have to deal with a plethora of customer concerns on a daily basis. My informants highlighted six main issues that seem to be a source of anxiety for customers: permanence of the tattoo, cost of the tattoo or piercing, transmission of disease or infection, quality of art, privacy, and pain. They proved to be extremely adept at pacifying these concerns through techniques of *juicing,* creating a clean and comfortable environment, and by simply being knowledgeable about their job. It was also obvious that Chris and Adam have learned to be "chameleons." They can relate to just about anybody: a biker, a businessman, a stripper, a club-owner, a bum on the street, and even an anthropology student. Good communication and people skills are talents that will allow them to be successful wherever they go in life. Their techniques of juicing may also be applied to a wide variety of sales jobs.

The bottom line is this: people like to be comfortable. Whether they are having their hair cut, eating at a restaurant, buying a house, or piercing their tongue, they want to be relaxed and assured that they are making the right decision.

Review Questions

1. What are the six things people worry about when they consider whether or not to get a tattoo or piercing?

2. What *juices* do tattooists use to persuade people to visit their shop and get a tattoo? Give examples of each.

3. What *juices* do tattooists use to negotiate the price of a tattoo or piercing? How do these strategies compare with what salespeople say in other commercial settings?

4. In what other circumstances do tattooists use *juices?* Give examples.

5. Based on reading this article, assess the importance of studying kinds of talk for successful ethnographic research.

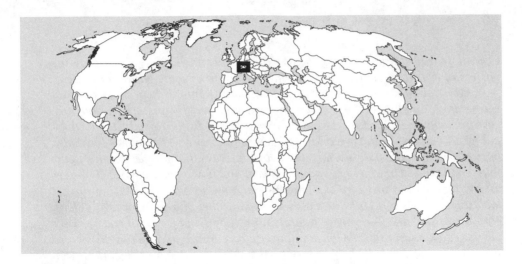

9

Anthropologists Investigate Communication Technology

Belle Mellor

A young woman's fingers fly over her cell phone keys as she "texts" someone while standing in her college dining hall salad bar line. An airline passenger flips open his cell phone and calls his wife the minute his plane lands and an announcement is made that he can do so. A construction company book-keeper checks her e-mail every half hour as she enters invoices in a spreadsheet.

From Belle Mellor, "Technology and Society: Anthropologists Investigate the Use of Communications Technology and Reach Some Surprising Conclusions," *The Economist* (print ed.) June 7, 2007. Reprinted by permission.

Countless times a day, people all over the world increasingly use a growing variety of technical devices and channels to communicate with each other.

Most often, anthropological linguists have focused their study of communication on verbal (talking) and nonverbal (speaking distances, body art, gestures) channels. But as Belle Mellor points out in this article, the anthropologists—especially those working for companies or governments—have also begun to investigate the new, largely electronic, ways that people communicate with each other. They have researched where and how people carry cell phones and what they use them for (i.e., texting, taking photographs, playing music, locating themselves). They have also looked at other channels—e-mail, blogs, chat lines, land lines—trying to establish how often and for what reasons people use each. As an example, Mellor notes that an anthropologist has discovered that for Europe at least, the most sophisticated users of communication technology are immigrants. Immigrants can't afford to travel home, so they communicate by using everything from webcams to texting.

SUCH is the social significance of mobile phones that when it comes to evaluating their use and planning new products and services, mobile operators and handset-makers cannot rely on the technology-driven, engineering mindset that has traditionally dominated the telecoms industry. Most famously, industry leaders expected people to embrace videotelephony, which flopped, but failed to anticipate the success of text-messaging. So they are turning to social scientists, and in particular to anthropologists, the better to understand how telephones are used.

One of Nokia's in-house anthropologists, Jan Chipchase, recently investigated how people carry their phones, for example. He and his colleagues carried out street-level surveys in 11 cities on four continents. They found that 60% of men carried their phones in their trouser pockets, whereas 61% of women carried their phones in handbags. (The difficulty of finding a mobile phone in a cluttered handbag meant that half of women reported missing calls as a result.) Belt pouches were particularly popular in China: 19% of men used them in Beijing, and 38% in Ji Lin City. But they were less popular in fashion-conscious Milan, where only 4% of men used them, and belt pouches were non-existent in Tokyo. Adding covers to phones was most widespread in Seoul and Kampala, and the use of decorative phone straps was most popular in Seoul and Tokyo. Findings like these can help handset-makers design new products and accessories that are appropriate to particular markets.

Meanwhile, Stefana Broadbent, an anthropologist who leads the User Adoption Lab at Swisscom, Switzerland's largest telecoms operator, has been looking at usage patterns associated with different communications technologies. She and her team based their research on observation, interviews, surveys of users' homes and asking people to keep logbooks of their communications usage in several European countries. Some of their findings are quite unexpected. Although mobile phones make it easier to keep in regular touch with a wide group of friends, for example, it turns out that a typical user spends 80% of his or her time communicating with just four other people.

Next, despite much talk of "convergence" within the industry, people are in fact using different communications technologies in distinct and divergent ways. The fixed-line phone "is the collective channel, a shared organizational tool, with most calls made 'in public' because they are relevant to the other members of the household," she says. Mobile calls are for last-minute planning or to co-ordinate travel and meetings. Texting is for "intimacy, emotions and efficiency." E-mail is for administration and to exchange pictures, documents and music. Instant-messaging (IM) and voice-over-internet calls are "continuous channels," open in the background while people do other things. "Each communication channel is performing an increasingly different function," says Ms Broadbent.

Another finding is that despite the plunging cost of voice calls, and the rise of free internet-calling services such as Skype, people seem to prefer typing. "The most fascinating discovery I've made this year is a flattening in voice communication and an increase in written channels," says Ms Broadbent. Her research in Switzerland and France found that even when people are given unlimited cheap or free calls, the number and length of calls does not increase significantly. This may be because there is only so much time you can spend talking; and when you are on the phone it is harder to do other things. Written channels such as e-mail, text-messaging and IM, by contrast, are discreet and allow contact to be continuous during the day. "Users are showing a growing preference for semi-synchronous writing over synchronous voice," says Ms Broadbent.

And although the rise of the BlackBerry has prompted concern about work invading private life, the opposite actually seems to be true: private communications are invading the workplace. Workers expect to be plugged into their social networks while at work, whether by e-mail, IM or mobile phone. Last year at a food-processing factory near Geneva, the workers revolted when the director tried to ban mobile phones from the factory floor, and he was forced to relent. Their argument was that they wanted to be reachable during the day, just as people who sit at desks are.

Of course, improvements to mobile networks and the spread of third-generation (3G) and Wi-Fi networks mean that you no longer need to be at your desk to get things done. But Ms Broadbent found that there is not, in fact, much appetite for working while on the move. Indeed, she calls this "the hypermobility myth." After studying workers who spend more than half their time out of the office—salesmen, consultants, pilots, journalists and photographers— she found that they generally stick to communications while on the move, gathering information that they then work on when they get back to their desks. Hotel rooms and airports are, she says, "not seen as an appropriate environment for substantive work" and are mainly used for e-mail.

Finally, Ms Broadbent found that migrants are the most advanced users of communications technology. A family of immigrant workers from Kosovo living in Switzerland has installed a big computer screen in their living room, for example, and almost every morning they have breakfast with their grandmother back home, via a webcam. It is migrants, rather than geeks, who have emerged as the "most aggressive" adopters of new communications tools, says Ms Broadbent. Dispersed families with strong ties and limited resources have taken to voice-over-internet services, IM and webcams, all of which are cheap or free. They also go online to get news or to download music from home. In the case of a Spanish family living in Switzerland, the daughter often does her homework with her aunt—but over a free Skype video-link, since the aunt lives in Spain.

Review Questions

1. According to Mellor, anthropologists have discovered that most men and women carry their cell phones where?

2. How many people on average do most individuals communicate with using technical channels?

3. What means of communication—talking or texting on cell phones, using e-mail, talking on wired phone lines—do people use for different communication purposes?

4. Where do employees prefer to communicate with each other about business matters?

5. In Europe, what kind of people are most sophisticated in their use of technical communication devices? Why?

THREE

ECOLOGY
AND SUBSISTENCE

READINGS IN THIS SECTION

The Hunters: Scarce Resources in the Kalahari   88

Richard Borshay Lee, with an update by *Richard Borshay Lee and Megan Biesele*

Adaptive Failure: Easter's End   104

Jared Diamond

Subsistence and Market: When the Turtle Collapses   114

Bernard Nietschmann

Forest Development the Indian Way   124

Richard K. Reed

Ecology is the relationship of an organism to other elements within its environmental sphere. Every species, no matter how simple or complex, fits into a larger complex ecological system; each adapts to its ecological niche unless rapid environmental alterations outstrip the organism's ability and potential to adapt successfully. An important aim of ecological studies is to show how organisms fit within particular environments. Such studies also look at the effect environments have on the shape and behavior of life forms.

Every species has adapted biologically through genetically produced variation and natural selection. For example, the bipedal (two-footed) locomotion characteristic of humans is one possible adaptation to walking on the ground. It also permitted our ancestors to carry food, tools, weapons, and almost anything else they desired, enabling them to range out from a home base and bring things back for others to share.

Biological processes have led to another important human characteristic, the development of a large and complex brain. The human brain is capable of holding an enormous inventory of information. With it, we can classify the parts of our environment and retain instructions for complex ways to deal with the things in our world. Because we can communicate our knowledge symbolically through language, we are able to teach one another. Instead of a genetic code that directs behavior automatically, we operate with a learned cultural code. Culture gives us the ability to behave in a much wider variety of ways and to change rapidly in new situations. With culture, people have been able to live successfully in almost every part of the world.

Cultural ecology is the way people use their culture to adapt to particular environments. All people live in a **physical environment,** the world they can experience through their senses, but they will conceive of it in terms that seem most important to their adaptive needs and cultural perspective. We call this perspective the **cultural environment.**

All human societies must provide for the material needs of their members. People everywhere have to eat, clothe themselves, provide shelter against the elements, and take care of social requirements such as hospitality, gift giving, and proper dress.

Societies employ several different strategies to meet their material needs, strategies that affect their complexity and internal organization as well as relationships to the natural environment and to other human groups. Anthropologists often use these **subsistence strategies** to classify different groups into five types: hunter-gatherers, horticulturalists, pastoralists, agriculturalists, and industrialists. Let us look briefly at each of these.

People who rely on **hunting and gathering** depend on wild plants and animals for subsistence. Hunter-gatherers forage for food, moving to different parts of their territories as supplies of plants, animals, and water grow scarce. They live in small bands of from 10 to 50 people and are typically egalitarian, leading a life marked by sharing and cooperation. Because hunter-gatherer bands are so small, they tend to lack formal political, legal, and religious structure, although members have regular ways to make group decisions, settle disputes, and deal ritually with the questions of death, adversity, social value, and world identification.

Hunter-gatherers tend to see themselves as part of the environment, not masters of it. This view shapes a religious ritual aimed at the maintenance and restoration of environmental harmony. All people lived as hunter-gatherers until about 10,000 years ago, when the first human groups began to farm and dwell in more permanent settlements. Today few hunter-gatherers survive. Most have lost their habitats to more powerful groups bent on economic and political exploitation.

Horticulture represents the earliest farming strategy, one that continues on a diminishing basis among many groups today. Horticulturalists garden. They often use a technique called **slash-and-burn agriculture,** which requires them to clear and burn over wild land and, with the aid of a digging stick, sow seeds in the ashes. When fields lose their fertility after a few years, they are abandoned and new land is cleared. Although horticulturalists farm, they often continue to forage for wild foods and still feel closely related to the natural environment.

Horticulture requires a substantial amount of undeveloped land, so overall population densities must remain fairly low. But the strategy permits higher population densities than hunting and gathering, so horticulturalists tend to live in larger permanent settlements numbering from 50 to 250 individuals. (Some horticultural societies have produced chiefdomships with much larger administrative and religious town centers.) Although they are still small by our standards, horticultural communities are large enough to require more complex organizational strategies. They often display more elaborate kinship systems based on descent, political structures that include headmen or chiefs, political alliances, religions characterized by belief in a variety of supernatural beings, and the beginnings of social inequality. Many of today's so-called tribal peoples are horticulturalists.

Pastoralism is a subsistence strategy based on the herding of domesticated animals such as cattle, goats, sheep, and camels. Although herding strategies vary from one environment to another, pastoralists share some general attributes. They move on a regular basis during the year to take advantage of fresh sources of water and fodder for their animals. They usually congregate in large encampments for part of the year when food and water are plentiful, then divide into smaller groups when these resources become scarce. Pastoralists often display a strong sense of group identity and pride, a fierce independence, and skill at war and raiding. Despite attempts by modern governments to place them in permanent settlements, many pastoral groups in Africa and Asia continue their nomadic lifestyle.

Agriculture is still a common subsistence strategy in many parts of the world. *Agriculture* refers to a kind of farming based on the intensive cultivation of permanent land holdings. Agriculturalists usually use plows and organic fertilizers and may irrigate their fields in dry conditions.

Agrarian societies are marked by a high degree of social complexity. They are often organized as nation-states with armies and bureaucracies, social stratification, markets, extended families and kin groups, and some occupational specialization. Religion takes on a formal structure and is organized as a separate institution.

The term **industrialism** labels the final kind of subsistence strategy. Ours is an industrial society, as is much of the Western, and more recently, the Asian world. Industrial nations are highly complex; they display an extensive variety of subgroups and social statuses. Industrial societies tend to be dominated by market economies in which goods and services are exchanged on the basis of price, supply, and demand. There is a high degree of economic specialization, and mass marketing may lead to a depersonalization of human relations. Religious, legal, political, and economic systems find expression as separate institutions in a way that might look disjointed to hunter-gatherers or others from smaller, more integrated societies.

The study of cultural ecology involves more than an understanding of people's basic subsistence strategies. Each society exists in a distinctive environment. Although a group may share many subsistence methods with other societies, there are always special environmental needs that shape productive techniques. Andean farmers, for example, have developed approximately 3,000 varieties of potatoes to meet the demands of growing conditions at different elevations in their mountain habitat. Bhil farmers in India have learned to create fields by damming up small streams in their rugged Aravalli hill villages. Otherwise, they would find it difficult to cultivate there at all. American farmers learned to "contour-plow" parallel to slopes in response to water erosion and now increasingly use plowless (no-till) farming to prevent the wind from carrying away precious topsoil.

No matter how successful their microenvironmental adjustments are, most groups in the world now face more serious adaptive challenges. One difficulty is the exploitation of their lands by outsiders, who are often unconstrained by adaptive necessity. A second is the need to overexploit the environment to meet market demand. (See Part Four for articles on market pressures.) In either case, many local peoples find that their traditional subsistence techniques no longer work. They have lost control of their own environmental adjustment and must struggle to adapt to outsiders and what is left of their habitat.

Finally, just as humans adapt culturally to their environments, altering them in the process, environments may biologically adapt to humans. For example, intensive agriculture in the United States provides greater food sources for deer. In response, the number of deer has risen by as much as 400 percent. Animals domesticated by humans, such as cows, pigs, chickens, sheep, goats, dogs, and cats, have also experienced both genetic modification and increased numbers from their association with people. Less obviously, microbes have evolved to take advantage of the growing human presence. Some subsist on human wastes; others, including many that cause epidemic diseases, have evolved to subsist on people themselves.

The !Kung, described by Richard Lee in the first selection, provide an excellent example of a traditional foraging lifestyle. The update to this article by Richard Lee and Megan Biesele show that the same bands of people who once lived on wild foods in the Kalahari now find themselves confined to small government-mandated settlements. Cattle herders tend their animals on the desert lands once occupied by the !Kung. The second article, by Jared Diamond, describes the fate of Easter Islanders who overexploited their small island ecosystem. The example serves as a warning to people everywhere as populations grow and resources diminish. The third article, by Bernard Nietschmann, details the impact of the international market system on a local subsistence economy. Motivated by money, Miskito Indians came to be dependent on outsiders for food and found themselves unable to meet their traditional reciprocal obligations. Readers should note that most Miskito Indians were displaced from their traditional communities and occupations by the Sandinista government of Nicaragua after this article was written. Many have not returned to their former homes. The fourth selection, by Richard Reed, is a sobering reminder of what can happen to a horticultural people who once subsisted in harmony with their tropical forest habitat, but who now find themselves being displaced by colonists. These outsiders have stripped the forest bare. Nevertheless, the horticultural model is emerging as the most economical solution for sustained use of the forest in today's world.

Key Terms

agriculture   p. 85
cultural ecology   p. 84
cultural environment   p. 84
ecology   p. 84
horticulture   p. 85
hunting and gathering   p. 84

industrialism   p. 86
pastoralism   p. 85
physical environment   p. 84
slash-and-burn agriculture   p. 85
subsistence strategies   p. 84

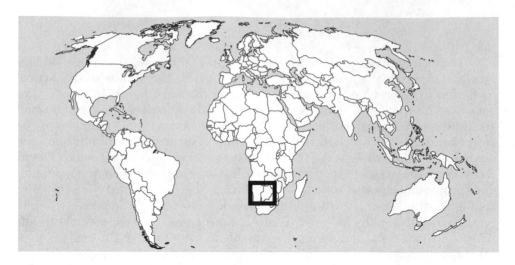

10

The Hunters: Scarce Resources in the Kalahari

Richard Borshay Lee

Until about 10,000 years ago, everyone in the world survived by hunting and gathering wild foods. They lived in intimate association with their natural environments and employed a complex variety of strategies to forage for food and other necessities of life. Agriculture displaced foraging as the main subsistence technique over the next few thousand years, but some hunter-gatherers lived on in the more remote parts of the world. This study by Richard Lee was done

From "The Hunters: Scarce Resources in the Kalahari," by Richard Borshay Lee, from *Man the Hunter*, edited by Richard Lee and Irven DeVore, 1968, with update from "A Local Culture in the Global System: The Ju/Hoansi-!Kung Today" by Richard B. Lee and Megan Biesele, *General Anthropology*, Vol. 1, No. 1, Fall 1994, pp. 1, 3–5.

*in the early 1960s and describes the important features of one of the last forag-
ing groups, the Ju/'hoansi-!Kung living in the Kalahari Desert. It argues against
the idea, held by many anthropologists at that time, that hunter-gatherers live
a precarious, hand-to-mouth existence. Instead, Lee found that the !Kung,
depending more on vegetable foods than meat, actually spent little time collecting food and managed to live long and fruitful lives in their difficult desert home.
The update by Lee and Megan Biesele that appears at the end of the article details
the events that have led the !Kung to settle down permanently to life as small-
scale farmers and cattle raisers.*

The current anthropological view of hunter-gatherer subsistence rests on
two questionable assumptions. First is the notion that these people are primarily dependent on the hunting of game animals, and second is the assumption that their way of life is generally a precarious and arduous struggle for
existence.

Recent data on living hunter-gatherers show a radically different picture. We have learned that in many societies, plant and marine resources are
far more important than are game animals in the diet. More important, it is
becoming clear that, with few conspicuous exceptions, the hunter-gatherer
subsistence base is at least routine and reliable and at best surprisingly abundant. Anthropologists have consistently tended to underestimate the viability
of even those "marginal isolates" of hunting peoples that have been available
to ethnographers.

The purpose of this paper is to analyze the food-getting activities of one
such "marginal" people, the !Kung Bushmen of the Kalahari Desert. Three related
questions are posed: How do the Bushmen make a living? How easy or difficult
is it for them to do this? What kinds of evidence are necessary to measure and
evaluate the precariousness or security of a way of life? And after the relevant
data are presented, two further questions are asked: What makes this security
of life possible? To what extent are the Bushmen typical of hunter-gatherers in
general?

Bushman Subsistence

The !Kung Bushmen of Botswana are an apt case for analysis. They inhabit the
semi-arid northwest region of the Kalahari Desert. With only six to nine inches
of rainfall per year, this is, by any account, a marginal environment for human
habitation. In fact, it is precisely the unattractiveness of their homeland that has
kept the !Kung isolated from extensive contact with their agricultural and pastoral neighbors.

Fieldwork was carried out in the Dobe area, a line of eight permanent water-holes near the South-West Africa border and 125 miles south of the Okavango River. The population of the Dobe area consists of 466 Bushmen, including 379 permanent residents living in independent camps or associated with Bantu cattle posts, as well as 87 seasonal visitors. The Bushmen share the area with some 340 Bantu pastoralists largely of the Herero and Tswana tribes. The ethnographic present refers to the period of fieldwork: October 1963 to January 1965.

The Bushmen living in independent camps lack firearms, livestock, and agriculture. Apart from occasional visits to the Herero for milk, these !Kung are entirely dependent upon hunting and gathering for their subsistence. Politically they are under the nominal authority of the Tswana headman, although they pay no taxes and receive very few government services. European presence amounts to one overnight government patrol every six to eight weeks. Although Dobe-area !Kung have had some contact with outsiders since the 1880s, the majority of them continue to hunt and gather because there is no viable alternative locally available to them.

Each of the fourteen independent camps is associated with one of the permanent waterholes. During the dry season (May–October) the entire population is clustered around these wells. Table 1 shows the numbers at each well at the end of the 1964 dry season. Two wells had no camp residents and one large well supported five camps. The number of camps at each well and the size of each camp changed frequently during the course of the year. The "camp" is an open aggregate of cooperating persons which changes in size and composition from day to day. Therefore, I have avoided the term "band" in describing the !Kung Bushman living groups.

Each waterhole has a hinterland lying within a six-mile radius that is regularly exploited for vegetable and animal foods. These areas are not territories in the zoological sense, since they are not defended against outsiders. Rather, they constitute the resources that lie within a convenient walking distance of a

TABLE 1   Numbers and Distribution of Resident Bushmen and Bantu by Waterhole*

Name of Waterhole	No. of Camps	Population of Camps	Other Bushmen	Total Bushmen	Bantu
Dobe	2	37	—	37	—
!angwa	1	16	23	39	84
Bate	2	30	12	42	21
!ubi	1	19	—	19	65
!gose	3	52	9	61	18
/ai/ai	5	94	13	107	67
!xabe	—	—	8	8	12
Mahopa	—	—	23	23	73
Total	14	248	88	336	340

*Figures do not include 130 Bushmen outside area on the date of census.

waterhole. The camp is a self-sufficient subsistence unit. The members move out each day to hunt and gather, and return in the evening to pool the collected foods in such a way that every person present receives an equitable share. Trade in foodstuffs between camps is minimal; personnel do move freely from camp to camp, however. The net effect is of a population constantly in motion. On the average, an individual spends a third of his time living only with close relatives, a third visiting other camps, and a third entertaining visitors from other camps.

Because of the strong emphasis on sharing, and the frequency of movement, surplus accumulation of storable plant foods and dried meat is kept to a minimum. There is rarely more than two or three days' supply of food on hand in a camp at any time. The result of this lack of surplus is that a constant subsistence effort must be maintained throughout the year. Unlike agriculturalists, who work hard during the planting and harvesting seasons and undergo "seasonal unemployment" for several months, the Bushmen hunter-gatherers collect food every third or fourth day throughout the year.

Vegetable foods comprise from 60 to 80 percent of the total diet by weight, and collecting involves two or three days of work per woman per week. The men also collect plants and small animals, but their major contribution to the diet is the hunting of medium and large game. The men are conscientious but not particularly successful hunters; although men's and women's work input is roughly equivalent in terms of man-day of effort, the women provide two to three times as much food by weight as the men.

Table 2 summarizes the seasonal activity cycle observed among the Dobe-area !Kung in 1964. For the greater part of the year, food is locally abundant and easily collected. It is only during the end of the dry season in September and October, when desirable foods have been eaten out in the immediate vicinity of the waterholes, that the people have to plan longer hikes of 10 to 15 miles and carry their own water to those areas where the mongongo nut is still available. The important point is that food is a constant, but distance required to reach food is a variable; it is short in the summer, fall, and early winter, and reaches its maximum in the spring.

This analysis attempts to provide quantitative measures of subsistence status, including data on the following topics: abundance and variety of resources, diet selectivity, range size and population density, the composition of the work force, the ratio of work to leisure time, and the caloric and protein levels in the diet. The value of quantitative data is that they can be used comparatively and also may be useful in archeological reconstruction. In addition, one can avoid the pitfalls of subjective and qualitative impressions; for example, statements about food "anxiety" have proven to be difficult to generalize across cultures.

Abundance and Variety of Resources

It is impossible to define "abundance" of resources absolutely. However, one index of *relative* abundance is whether or not a population exhausts all the food available from a given area. By this criterion, the habitat of the Dobe-area Bushmen

TABLE 2 The Bushman Annual Round

	Jan.	Feb.	Mar.	April	May	June	July	Aug.	Sept.	Oct.	Nov.	Dec.
Season	*Summer Rains*			*Autumn Dry*		*Winter Dry*				*Spring Dry*		*First Rains*
Availability of water	Temporary summer pools everywhere			Large summer pools		Permanent waterholes only						Summer pools developing
Group moves	Widely dispersed at summer pools			At large summer pools		All population restricted to permanent waterholes						Moving out to summer pools
Men's subsistence activities	1. Hunting with bow, arrows, and dogs (year-round) 2. Running down immatures 3. Some gathering (year-round)					Trapping small game in snares				Running down newborn animals		
Women's subsistence activities	1. Gathering of mongongo nuts (year-round) 2. Fruits, berries, melons					Roots, bulbs, resins				Roots, leafy greens		
Ritual activities	Dancing, trance performances, and ritual curing (year-round)				Boys' initiation*							†
Relative subsistence hardship		Water-food distance minimal				Increasing distance from water to food				Water-food distance minimal		

*Held once every five years; none in 1963–64.
† New Year's: Bushmen join the celebrations of their missionized Bantu neighbors.

92

is abundant in naturally occurring foods. By far the most important food is the mongongo (mangetti) nut (*Ricinodendron rautanenii* Schinz). Although tens of thousands of pounds of these nuts are harvested and eaten each year, thousands more rot on the ground each year for want of picking.

The mongongo nut, because of its abundance and reliability, alone accounts for 50 percent of the vegetable diet by weight. In this respect it resembles a cultivated staple crop such as maize or rice. Nutritionally it is even more remarkable, for it contains five times the calories and ten times the protein per cooked unit of the cereal crops. The average daily per capita consumption of 300 nuts yields about 1,260 calories and 56 grams of protein. This modest portion, weighing only about 7.5 ounces, contains the caloric equivalent of 2.5 pounds of cooked rice and the protein equivalent of 14 ounces of lean beef.

Furthermore, the mongongo nut is drought resistant, and it will still be abundant in the dry years when cultivated crops may fail. The extremely hard outer shell protects the inner kernel from rot and allows the nuts to be harvested for up to twelve months after they have fallen to the ground. A diet based on mongongo nuts is in fact more reliable than one based on cultivated foods, and it is not surprising, therefore, that when a Bushman was asked why he hadn't taken to agriculture, he replied: "Why should we plant, when there are so many mongongo nuts in the world?"

Apart from the mongongo, the Bushmen have available eighty-four other species of edible food plants, including twenty-nine species of fruits, berries, and melons and thirty species of roots and bulbs. The existence of this variety allows for a wide range of alternatives in subsistence strategy. During the summer months the Bushmen have no problem other than to choose among the tastiest and most easily collected foods. Many species, which are quite edible but less attractive, are bypassed, so that gathering never exhausts *all* the available plant foods of an area. During the dry season the diet becomes much more eclectic and the many species of roots, bulbs, and edible resins make an important contribution. It is this broad base that provides an essential margin of safety during the end of the dry season, when the mongongo nut forests are difficult to reach. In addition, it is likely that these rarely utilized species provide important nutritional and mineral trace elements that may be lacking in the more popular foods.

Diet Selectivity

If the Bushmen were living close to the "starvation" level, then one would expect them to exploit every available source of nutrition. That their life is well above this level is indicated by the data in Table 3. Here all the edible plant species are arranged in classes according to the frequency with which they were observed to be eaten. It should be noted that although there are some eighty-five species available, about 90 percent of the vegetable diet by weight is drawn from only twenty-three species. In other words, 75 percent of the listed species provide only 10 percent of the food value.

In their meat-eating habits, the Bushmen show a similar selectivity. Of the 223 local species of animals known and named by the Bushmen, 54 species are

TABLE 3 !Kung Bushman Plant Foods

Food Class	Part Eaten								Total Number of Species in Class	Totals (percentages)	
	Fruit and Nut	Bean and Root	Fruit and Stalk	Root, Bulb	Fruit, Berry, Melon	Resin	Leaves	Seed, Bean		Estimated Contribution by Weight to Vegetable Diet	Estimated Contribution of Each Species
I. Primary Eaten daily throughout year (mongongo nut)	1	—	—	—	—	—	—	—	1	c.50	c.50*
II. Major Eaten daily in season	1	1	1	1	4	—	—	—	8	c.25	c.3†
III. Minor Eaten several times per week in season	—	—	—	7	3	2	2	—	14	c.15	c.1
IV. Supplementary Eaten when classes I–III locally unavailable	—	—	—	9	12	10	1	—	32	c.7	c.0.2
V. Rare Eaten several times per year	—	—	—	9	4	—	—	—	13	c.3	c.0.1‡
VI. Problematic Edible but not observed to be eaten	—	—	—	4	6	4	1	2	17	nil	nil
Total Species	2	1	1	30	29	16	4	2	85	100	—

*1 species constitutes 50 percent of the vegetable diet by weight.
† 23 species constitute 90 percent of the vegetable diet by weight.
‡ 62 species constitute the remaining 10 percent of the diet.

classified as edible, and of these only 17 species were hunted on a regular basis. Only a handful of the dozens of edible species of small mammals, birds, reptiles, and insects that occur locally are regarded as food. Such animals as rodents, snakes, lizards, termites, and grasshoppers, which in the literature are included in the Bushman diet, are despised by the Bushmen of the Dobe area.

Range Size and Population Density

The necessity to travel long distances, the high frequency of moves, and the maintenance of populations at low densities are also features commonly associated with the hunting and gathering way of life. Density estimates for hunters in western North America and Australia have ranged from 3 persons/square mile to as low as 1 person/100 square miles. In 1963–65, the resident and visiting Bushmen were observed to utilize an area of about 1,000 square miles during the course of the annual round for an effective population density of 41 persons/100 square miles. Within this area, however, the amount of ground covered by members of an individual camp was surprisingly small. A day's round-trip of twelve miles serves to define a "core" area six miles in radius surrounding each water point. By fanning out in all directions from their well, the members of a camp can gain access to the food resources of well over 100 square miles of territory within a two-hour hike. Except for a few weeks each year, areas lying beyond this six-mile radius are rarely utilized, even though they are no less rich in plants and game than are the core areas.

Although the Bushmen move their camps frequently (five or six times a year), they do not move them very far. A rainy season camp in the nut forests is rarely more than ten or twelve miles from the home waterhole, and often new campsites are occupied only a few hundred yards away from the previous one. By these criteria, the Bushmen do not lead a free-ranging nomadic way of life. For example, they do not undertake long marches of 30 to 100 miles to get food, since this task can be readily fulfilled within a day's walk of home base. When such long marches do occur they are invariably for visiting, trading, and marriage arrangements, and should not be confused with the normal routine of subsistence.

Demographic Factors

Another indicator of the harshness of a way of life is the age at which people die. Ever since Hobbes characterized life in the state of nature as "nasty, brutish and short," the assumption has been that hunting and gathering is so rigorous that members of such societies are rapidly worn out and meet an early death. Silberbauer, for example, says of the Gwi Bushmen of the central Kalahari that "life expectancy . . . is difficult to calculate, but I do not believe that many live beyond 45." And Coon has said of hunters in general:

> The practice of abandoning the hopelessly ill and aged has been observed in many parts of the world. It is always done by people living in poor environments where

it is necessary to move about frequently to obtain food, where food is scarce, and transportation difficult. . . . Among peoples who are forced to live in this way the oldest generation, the generation of individuals who have passed their physical peak, is reduced in numbers and influence. There is no body of elders to hand on tradition and control the affairs of younger men and women, and no formal system of age grading.

The !Kung Bushmen of the Dobe area flatly contradict this view. In a total population of 466, no fewer than 46 individuals (17 men and 29 women) were determined to be over sixty years of age, a proportion that compares favorably to the percentage of elderly in industrialized populations.

The aged hold a respected position in Bushmen society and are the effective leaders of the camps. Senilicide is extremely rare. Long after their productive years have passed, the old people are fed and cared for by their children and grandchildren. The blind, the senile, and the crippled are respected for the special ritual and technical skills they possess. For instance, the four elders at !gose waterhole were totally or partially blind, but this handicap did not prevent their active participation in decision making and ritual curing.

Another significant feature of the composition of the work force is the late assumption of adult responsibility by the adolescents. Young people are not expected to provide food regularly until they are married. Girls typically marry between the ages of fifteen and twenty, and boys about five years later, so that it is not unusual to find healthy, active teenagers visiting from camp to camp while their older relatives provide food for them.

As a result, the people in the twenty to sixty age group support a surprisingly large percentage of nonproductive young and old people. About 40 percent of the population in camps contributes little to the food supplies. This allocation of work to young and middle-aged adults allows for a relatively carefree childhood and adolescence and a relatively unstrenuous old age.

Leisure and Work

Another important index of ease or difficulty of subsistence is the amount of time devoted to the food quest. Hunting has usually been regarded by social scientists as a way of life in which merely keeping alive is so formidable a task that members of such societies lack the leisure time necessary to "build culture." The !Kung Bushmen would appear to conform to the rule, for as Lorna Marshall says:

> It is vividly apparent that among the !Kung Bushmen, ethos, or "the spirit which actuates manners and customs," is survival. Their time and energies are almost wholly given to this task, for life in their environment requires that they spend their days mainly in procuring food.

It is certainly true that getting food is the most important single activity in Bushman life. However, this statement would apply equally well to small-scale agricultural and pastoral societies too. How much time is *actually* devoted to the food quest is fortunately an empirical question. And an analysis of the work effort of the Dobe Bushmen shows some unexpected results. From July 6 to August 2, 1964, I recorded all the daily activities of the Bushmen living at the Dobe waterhole. Because of the coming and going of visitors, the camp population fluctuated in size day by day, from a low of 23 to a high of 40, with a mean of 31.8 persons. Each day some of the adult members of the camp went out to hunt and/or gather while others stayed home or went visiting. The daily recording of all personnel on hand made it possible to calculate the number of man-days of work as a percentage of total number of man-days of consumption.

Although the Bushmen do not organize their activities on the basis of a seven-day week, I have divided the data this way to make them more intelligible. The workweek was calculated to show how many days out of seven each adult spent in subsistence activities (Table 4, Column 7). Week II has been eliminated from the totals since the investigator contributed food. In week I, the people spent an average of 2.3 days in subsistence activities, in week II, 1.9 days, and in week IV, 3.2 days. In all, the adults of the Dobe camp worked about two and a half days a week. Since the average working day was about six hours long, the fact emerges that !Kung Bushmen of Dobe, despite their harsh environment, devote from twelve to nineteen hours a week to getting food. Even the hardest-working individual in the camp, a man named ≠oma who went out hunting on sixteen of the twenty-eight days, spent a maximum of thirty-two hours a week in the food quest.

TABLE 4   Summary of Dobe Work Diary

Week	(1) Mean Group Size	(2) Adult-Days	(3) Child-Days	(4) Total Man-Days of Consumption	(5) Man-Days of Work	(6) Meat (lbs.)	(7) Average Workweek /Adult	(8) Index of Subsistence Effort
I	25.6	114	65	179	37	104	2.3	.21
(July 6–12)	(23–29)							
II	28.3	125	73	198	22	80	1.2	.11
(July 13–19)	(23–27)							
III	34.3	156	84	240	42	177	1.9	.18
(July 20–26)	(29–40)							
IV	35.6	167	82	249	77	129	3.2	.31
(July 27–Aug. 2)	(32–40)							
4-wk. total	30.9	562	304	866	178	490	2.2	.21
Adjusted total*	31.8	437	231	668	156	410	2.5	.23

*See text

Key: Column 1: Mean group size = $\dfrac{\text{total man-days of consumption}}{7}$.

Column 7: Workweek = the number of workdays per adult per week.

Column 8: Index of subsistence effort = $\dfrac{\text{man-days of work}}{\text{man-days of consumption}}$ (e.g., in Week I, the value of "S" = 21, i.e., 21 days of work/100 days of consumption or 1 workday produces food for 5 consumption days).

Because the Bushmen do not amass a surplus of foods, there are no seasons of exceptionally intensive activities such as planting and harvesting, and
no seasons of unemployment. The level of work observed is an accurate reflection of the effort required to meet the immediate caloric needs of the group. This
work diary covers the midwinter dry season, a period when food is neither at
its most plentiful nor at its scarcest levels, and the diary documents the transition from better to worse conditions (see Table 5). During the fourth week the
gatherers were making overnight trips to camps in the mongongo nut forests
seven to ten miles distant from the waterhole. These longer trips account for the
rise in the level of work, from twelve or thirteen to nineteen hours per week.

If food getting occupies such a small proportion of a Bushman's waking
hours, then how *do* people allocate their time? A woman gathers on one day
enough food to feed her family for three days, and spends the rest of her time
resting in camp, doing embroidery, visiting other camps, or entertaining visitors from other camps. For each day at home, kitchen routines, such as cooking, nut cracking, collecting firewood, and fetching water, occupy one to three
hours of her time. This rhythm of steady work and steady leisure is maintained
throughout the year.

The hunters tend to work more frequently than the women, but their
schedule is uneven. It is not unusual for a man to hunt avidly for a week and
then do nothing at all for two or three weeks. Since hunting is an unpredictable
business and subject to magical control, hunters sometimes experience a run
of bad luck and stop hunting for a month or longer. During these periods, visiting, entertaining, and especially dancing are the primary activities of men.
(Unlike the Hadza, gambling is only a minor leisure activity.)

The trance dance is the focus of Bushman ritual life; over 50 percent of the
men have trained as trance-performers and regularly enter trance during the
course of the all-night dances. At some camps, trance dances occur as frequently
as two or three times a week, and those who have entered trances the night
before rarely go out hunting the following day. . . . In a camp with five or more

**TABLE 5   Caloric and Protein Levels in the !Kung Bushman Diet,
July–August, 1964**

| | Per-Capita Consumption | | | | |
Class of Food	Percentage Contribution to Diet by Weight	Weight in Grams	Protein in Grams	Calories per Person per Day	Percentage Caloric Contribution of Meat and Vegetables
Meat	37	230	34.5	690	33
Mongongo nuts	33	210	56.7	1,260	67
Other vegetable foods	30	190	1.9	190	
Total all sources	100	630	93.1	2,140	100

hunters, there are usually two or three who are actively hunting and several others who are inactive. The net effect is to phase the hunting and non-hunting so that a fairly steady supply of meat is brought into camp.

Caloric Returns

Is the modest work effort of the Bushmen sufficient to provide the calories necessary to maintain the health of the population? Or have the !Kung, in common with some agricultural peoples, adjusted to a permanently substandard nutritional level?

During my fieldwork I did not encounter any cases of kwashiorkor, the most common nutritional disease in the children of African agricultural societies. However, without medical examinations, it is impossible to exclude the possibility that subclinical signs of malnutrition existed.

Another measure of nutritional adequacy is the average consumption of calories and proteins per person per day. The estimate for the Bushmen is based on observations of the weights of foods of known composition that were brought into Dobe camp on each day of the study period. The per-capita figure is obtained by dividing the total weight of foodstuffs by the total number of persons in the camp. These results are set out in detail elsewhere and can only be summarized here. During the study period 410 pounds of meat were brought in by the hunters of the Dobe camp, for a daily share of nine ounces of meat per person. About 700 pounds of vegetables were gathered and consumed during the same period. Table 5 sets out the calories and proteins available per capita in the !Kung Bushman diet from meat, mongongo nuts, and other vegetable sources.

This output of 2,140 calories and 93.1 grams of protein per person per day may be compared with the Recommended Daily Allowances (RDA) for persons of the small size and stature but vigorous activity regime of the !Kung Bushmen. The RDA for Bushmen can be estimated at 1,975 calories and 60 grams of protein per person per day. Thus it is apparent that food output exceeds energy requirements by 165 calories and 33 grams of protein. One can tentatively conclude that even a modest subsistence effort of two or three days' work per week is enough to provide an adequate diet for the !Kung Bushmen.

The Security of Bushman Life

I have attempted to evaluate the subsistence base of one contemporary hunter-gatherer society living in a marginal environment. The !Kung Bushmen have available to them some relatively abundant high-quality foods, and they do not have to walk very far or work very hard to get them. Furthermore, this modest work effort provides sufficient calories to support not only active adults, but also a large number of middle-aged and elderly people. The Bushmen do not have to press their youngsters into the service of the food quest, nor do they have to dispose of the oldsters after they have ceased to be productive.

The evidence presented assumes an added significance because this security of life was observed during the third year of one of the most severe droughts in South Africa's history. Most of the 576,000 people of Botswana are pastoralists and agriculturalists. After the crops had failed three years in succession and over 100,000 head of cattle had died on the range for lack of water, the World Food Program of the United Nations instituted a famine relief program which has grown to include 180,000 people, over 30 percent of the population. This program did not touch the Dobe area in the isolated northwest corner of the country, and the Herero and Tswana women there were able to feed their families only by joining the Bushman women to forage for wild foods. Thus the natural plant resources of the Dobe area were carrying a higher proportion of population than would be the case in years when the Bantu harvested crops. Yet this added pressure on the land did not seem to adversely affect the Bushmen.

In one sense it was unfortunate that the period of my fieldwork happened to coincide with the drought, since I was unable to witness a "typical" annual subsistence cycle. However, in another sense, the coincidence was a lucky one, for the drought put the Bushmen and their subsistence system to the acid test and, in terms of adaptation to scarce resources, they passed with flying colors. One can postulate that their subsistence base would be even more substantial during years of higher rainfall.

What are the crucial factors that make this way of life possible? I suggest that the primary factor is the Bushmen's strong emphasis on vegetable food sources. Although hunting involves a great deal of effort and prestige, plant foods provide from 60 to 80 percent of the annual diet by weight. Meat has come to be regarded as a special treat; when available, it is welcomed as a break from the routine of vegetable foods, but it is never depended upon as a staple. No one ever goes hungry when hunting fails.

The reason for this emphasis is not hard to find. Vegetable foods are abundant, sedentary, and predictable. They grow in the same place year after year, and the gatherer is guaranteed a day's return of food for a day's expenditure of energy. Game animals, by contrast, are scarce, mobile, unpredictable, and difficult to catch. A hunter has no guarantee of success and may in fact go for days or weeks without killing a large mammal. During the study period, there were eleven men in the Dobe camp, of whom four did no hunting at all. The seven active men spent a total of 78 man-days hunting, and this work input yielded eighteen animals killed, or one kill for every four man-days of hunting. The probability of any one hunter making a kill on a given day was 0.23. By contrast, the probability of a woman finding plant food on a given day was 1.00. In other words, hunting and gathering are not equally felicitous subsistence alternatives.

Consider the productivity per man-hour of the two kinds of subsistence activities. One man-hour of hunting produces about 100 edible calories, and of gathering, 240 calories. Gathering is thus seen to be 2.4 times more productive than hunting. In short, hunting is a *high-risk, low-return* subsistence activity, while gathering is a *low-risk, high-return* subsistence activity.

It is not at all contradictory that the hunting complex holds a central place in the Bushmen ethos and that meat is valued more highly than vegetable foods. Analogously, steak is valued more highly than potatoes in the food preferences of our own society. In both situations the meat is more "costly" than the vegetable food. In the Bushman case, the cost of food can be measured in terms of time and energy expended. By this standard, 1,000 calories of meat "costs" ten man-hours, while the "cost" of 1,000 calories of vegetable foods is only four man-hours. Further, it is to be expected that the less predictable, more expensive food source would have a greater accretion of myth and ritual built up around it than would the routine staples of life, which rarely if ever fail.

Conclusions

Three points ought to be stressed. First, life in the state of nature is not necessarily nasty, brutish, and short. The Dobe-area Bushmen live well today on wild plants and meat, in spite of the fact that they are confined to the least productive portion of the range in which Bushman peoples were formerly found. It is likely that an even more substantial subsistence would have been characteristic of these hunters and gatherers in the past, when they had the pick of African habitats to choose from.

Second, the basis of Bushman diet is derived from sources other than meat. This emphasis makes good ecological sense to the !Kung Bushmen and appears to be a common feature among hunters and gatherers in general. Since a 30 to 40 percent input of meat is such a consistent target for modern hunters in a variety of habitats, is it not reasonable to postulate a similar percentage for prehistoric hunters? Certainly the absence of plant remains on archeological sites is by itself not sufficient evidence for the absence of gathering. Recently abandoned Bushman campsites show a similar absence of vegetable remains, although this paper has clearly shown that plant foods comprise over 60 percent of the actual diet.

Finally, one gets the impression that hunting societies have been chosen by ethnologists to illustrate a dominant theme, such as the extreme importance of environment in the molding of certain cultures. Such a theme can best be exemplified by cases in which the technology is simple and/or the environment is harsh. This emphasis on the dramatic may have been pedagogically useful, but unfortunately it has led to the assumption that a precarious hunting subsistence base was characteristic of all cultures in the Pleistocene. This view of both modern and ancient hunters ought to be reconsidered. Specifically I am suggesting a shift in focus away from the dramatic and unusual cases, and toward a consideration of hunting and gathering as a persistent and well-adapted way of life.

Epilogue: The Ju/'hoansi in 1994[1]

In 1963 perhaps three-quarters of the Dobe Ju/'hoansi were living in camps based primarily on hunting and gathering while the rest were attached to Black cattle posts. Back then there had been no trading stores, schools, or clinics, no government feeding programs, boreholes, or airstrips, and no resident civil servants (apart from the tribally-appointed headman, his clerk, and constable). By 1994 all these institutions and facilities were in place and the Dobe people were well into their third decade of rapid social change; they had been transformed in a generation from a society of foragers, some of whom herded and worked for others, to a society of small-holders who eked out a living by herding, farming, and craft production, along with some hunting and gathering.

Ju villages today look like others in Botswana. The beehive-shaped grass huts are gone, replaced by semi-permanent mud-walled houses behind makeshift stockades to keep out cattle. Villages ceased to be circular and tight-knit. Twenty-five people who lived in a space twenty by twenty meters now spread themselves out in a line village several hundred meters long. Instead of looking across the central open space at each other, the houses face the kraal where cattle and goats are kept, inscribing spatially a symbolic shift from reliance on each other to reliance on property in the form of herds.

Hunting and gathering, which provided Dobe Ju with over 85 percent of their subsistence as recently as 1964, now supplies perhaps 30 percent of their food. The rest is made up of milk and meat from domestic stock, store-bought mealie (corn) meal, and vast quantities of heavily-sugared tea whitened with powdered milk. Game meat and foraged foods and occasional produce from gardens makes up the rest of the diet. However, for most of the 1980s government and foreign drought relief provided the bulk of the diet. . . .

In the long run, Dobe-area Ju/'hoansi face serious difficulties. Since 1975, wealthy Tswana have formed borehole syndicates to stake out ranches in remote areas. With 99-year leases, which can be bought and sold, ownership is tantamount to private tenure. By the late 1980s borehole drilling was approaching the Dobe area. If the Dobe Ju do not form borehole syndicates soon, with overseas help, their traditional foraging areas may be permanently cut off from them by commercial ranching.

Review Questions

1. How does Lee assess the day-to-day quality of !Kung life when they lived as foragers? How does this view compare with that held by many anthropologists in the early 1960s?

2. What evidence does Lee give to support his view about the !Kung?

[1]Excerpted from Richard B. Lee and Megan Biesele, "A Local Culture in the Global System: The Ju/'hoansi-!Kung Today," *General Anthropology* 1(1) (Fall 1994): pp. 1, 3–5.

3. According to Lee, !Kung children are not expected to work until after they are married; old people are supported and respected. How does this arrangement differ from behavior in our own society, and what might explain the difference?

4. What was a key to successful subsistence for the !Kung and other hunter-gatherers, according to Lee?

5. In what ways has life changed for the !Kung since 1964? What has caused these changes?

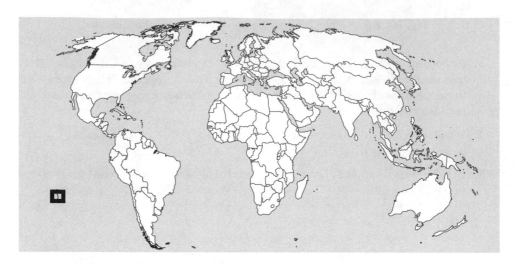

11

Adaptive Failure: Easter's End

Jared Diamond

Customs can often be explained as human responses to material necessity. But people may not always adapt successfully, as Jared Diamond shows in this discussion of the rise and fall of Easter Island civilization. Basing his conclusions on recent archaeological excavations, he notes that in A.D. 400, when the Polynesian ancestors of today's Easter Island population arrived on the island, they found a heavily forested and fertile land. Within a few hundred years, the islanders numbered between 7,000 to 20,000 and lived in a politically complex, prosperous society. By the 1400s, however, the forest was destroyed, making it impossible for people to build ocean-going canoes or continue the manufacture of stone heads, for which the island later became famous. Bird and sea mammal populations, once a major source of food, had also been decimated. Political chaos ensued and islanders turned to cannibalism as a dietary supplement. Diamond concludes that Easter Island civilization declined

From Jared Diamond, "Easter's End," *Discover*, August 1995. Used by permission of Jared Diamond.

because environmental destruction occurred slowly and because social concerns took precedence over conservation. In this sense, the island's fate serves as a warning about humanity's future in a highly stressed world environment.

———

Among the most riveting mysteries of human history are those posed by vanished civilizations. Everyone who has seen the abandoned buildings of the Khmer, the Maya, or the Anasazi is immediately moved to ask the same question: Why did the societies that erected those structures disappear?

Their vanishing touches us as the disappearance of other animals, even the dinosaurs, never can. No matter how exotic those lost civilizations seem, their framers were humans like us. Who is to say we won't succumb to the same fate? Perhaps someday New York's skyscrapers will stand derelict and overgrown with vegetation, like the temples at Angkor Wat and Tikal.

Among all such vanished civilizations, that of the former Polynesian society on Easter Island remains unsurpassed in mystery and isolation. The mystery stems especially from the island's gigantic stone statues and its impoverished landscape, but it is enhanced by our associations with the specific people involved: Polynesians represent for us the ultimate in exotic romance, the background for many a child's, and an adult's, vision of paradise. My own interest in Easter was kindled over 30 years ago when I read Thor Heyerdahl's fabulous accounts of his *Kon-Tiki* voyage.

But my interest has been revived recently by a much more exciting account, one not of heroic voyages but of painstaking research and analysis. My friend David Steadman, a paleontologist, has been working with a number of other researchers who are carrying out the first systematic excavations on Easter intended to identify the animals and plants that once lived there. Their work is contributing to a new interpretation of the island's history that makes it a tale not only of wonder but of warning as well.

Easter Island, with an area of only 64 square miles, is the world's most isolated scrap of habitable land. It lies in the Pacific Ocean more than 2,000 miles west of the nearest continent (South America), 1,400 miles from even the nearest habitable island (Pitcairn). Its subtropical location and latitude— at 27 degrees south, it is approximately as far below the equator as Houston is north of it—help give it a rather mild climate, while its volcanic origins make its soil fertile. In theory, this combination of blessings should have made Easter a miniature paradise, remote from problems that beset the rest of the world.

The island derives its name from its "discovery" by the Dutch explorer Jacob Roggeveen, on Easter (April 5) in 1722. Roggeveen's first impression was not of a paradise but of a wasteland: "We originally, from a further distance, have considered the said Easter Island as sandy; the reason for that is this, that we counted as sand the withered grass, hay, or other scorched and burnt vegetation, because its wasted appearance could give no other impression than of a singular poverty and barrenness."

The island Roggeveen saw was a grassland without a single tree or bush over ten feet high. Modern botanists have identified only 47 species of higher plants native to Easter, most of them grasses, sedges, and ferns. The list includes just two species of small trees and two of woody shrubs. With such flora, the islanders Roggeveen encountered had no source of real firewood to warm themselves during Easter's cool, wet, windy winters. Their native animals included nothing larger than insects, not even a single species of native bat, land bird, land snail, or lizard. For domestic animals, they had only chickens.

European visitors throughout the eighteenth and early nineteenth centuries estimated Easter's human population at about 2,000, a modest number considering the island's fertility. As Captain James Cook recognized during his brief visit in 1774, the islanders were Polynesians (a Tahitian man accompanying Cook was able to converse with them). Yet despite the Polynesians' well-deserved fame as a great seafaring people, the Easter Islanders who came out to Roggeveen's and Cook's ships did so by swimming or paddling canoes that Roggeveen described as "bad and frail." Their craft, he wrote, were "put together with manifold small planks and light inner timbers, which they cleverly stitched together with very fine twisted threads. . . . But as they lack the knowledge and particularly the materials for caulking and making tight the great number of seams of the canoes, these are accordingly very leaky, for which reason they are compelled to spend half the time in bailing." The canoes, only ten feet long, held at most two people, and only three or four canoes were observed on the entire island.

With such flimsy craft, Polynesians could never have colonized Easter from even the nearest island, nor could they have traveled far offshore to fish. The islanders Roggeveen met were totally isolated, unaware that other people existed. Investigators in all the years since his visit have discovered no trace of the islanders' having any outside contacts: not a single Easter Island rock or product has turned up elsewhere, nor has anything been found on the island that could have been brought by anyone other than the original settlers or the Europeans. Yet the people living on Easter claimed memories of visiting the uninhabited Sala y Gomez reef 260 miles away, far beyond the range of the leaky canoes seen by Roggeveen. How did the islanders' ancestors reach that reef from Easter, or reach Easter from anywhere else?

Easter Island's most famous feature is its huge stone statues, more than 200 of which once stood on massive stone platforms lining the coast. At least 700 more, in all stages of completion, were abandoned in quarries or on ancient roads between the quarries and the coast, as if the carvers and moving crews had thrown down their tools and walked off the job. Most of the erected statues were carved in a single quarry and then somehow transported as far as six miles—despite heights as great as 33 feet and weights up to 82 tons. The abandoned statues, meanwhile, were as much as 65 feet tall and weighed up to 270 tons. The stone platforms were equally gigantic: up to 500 feet long and 10 feet high, with facing slabs weighing up to 10 tons.

Roggeveen himself quickly recognized the problem the statues posed: "The stone images at first caused us to be struck with astonishment," he wrote, "because we could not comprehend how it was possible that these people, who are devoid of heavy thick timber for making any machines, as well as strong ropes, nevertheless had been able to erect such images." Roggeveen might have added that the islanders had no wheels, no draft animals, and no source of power except their own muscles. How did they transport the giant statues for miles, even before erecting them? To deepen the mystery, the statues were still standing in 1770, but by 1864 all of them had been pulled down, by the islanders themselves. Why then did they carve them in the first place? And why did they stop?

The statues imply a society very different from the one Roggeveen saw in 1722. Their sheer number and size suggest a population much larger than 2,000 people. What became of everyone? Furthermore, that society must have been highly organized. Easter's resources were scattered across the island: the best stone for the statues was quarried at Rano Raraku near Easter's northeast end; red stone, used for large crowns adorning some of the statues, was quarried at Puna Pau, inland in the southwest; stone carving tools came mostly from Aroi in the northwest. Meanwhile, the best farmland lay in the south and east, and the best fishing grounds on the north and west coasts. Extracting and redistributing all those goods required complex political organization. What happened to that organization, and how could it ever have arisen in such a barren landscape?

Easter Island's mysteries have spawned volumes of speculation for more than two and a half centuries. Many Europeans were incredulous that Polynesians—commonly characterized as "mere savages"—could have created the statues or the beautifully constructed stone platforms. In the 1950s, Heyerdahl argued that Polynesia must have been settled by advanced societies of American Indians, who in turn must have received civilization across the Atlantic from more advanced societies of the Old World. Heyerdahl's raft voyages aimed to prove the feasibility of such prehistoric transoceanic contacts. In the 1960s the Swiss writer Erich von Däniken, an ardent believer in Earth visits by extraterrestrial astronauts, went further, claiming that Easter's statues were the work of intelligent beings who owned ultramodern tools, became stranded on Easter, and were finally rescued.

Heyerdahl and von Däniken both brushed aside overwhelming evidence that the Easter Islanders were typical Polynesians derived from Asia rather than from the Americas and that their culture (including their statues) grew out of Polynesian culture. Their language was Polynesian, as Cook had already concluded. Specifically, they spoke an eastern Polynesian dialect related to Hawaiian and Marquesan, a dialect isolated since about A.D. 400, as estimated from slight differences in vocabulary. Their fishhooks and stone adzes resembled early Marquesan models. Last year DNA extracted from 12 Easter Island skeletons was also shown to be Polynesian. The islanders grew bananas, taro, sweet potatoes, sugarcane, and paper mulberry—typical Polynesian crops, mostly of Southeast Asian origin. Their sole domestic animal, the chicken, was also typically Polynesian and ultimately Asian, as were the rats that arrived as stowaways in the canoes of the first settlers.

What happened to those settlers? The fanciful theories of the past must give way to evidence gathered by hardworking practitioners in three fields: archeology, pollen analysis, and paleontology.

Modern archeological excavations on Easter have continued since Heyerdahl's 1955 expedition. The earliest radiocarbon dates associated with human activities are around A.D. 400 to 700, in reasonable agreement with the approximate settlement date of 400 estimated by linguists. The period of statue construction peaked around 1200 to 1500, with few if any statues erected thereafter. Densities of archeological sites suggest a large population; an estimate of 7,000 people is widely quoted by archeologists, but other estimates range up to 20,000, which does not seem implausible for an island of Easter's area and fertility.

Archeologists have also enlisted surviving islanders in experiments aimed at figuring out how the statues might have been carved and erected. Twenty people, using only stone chisels, could have carved even the largest completed statue within a year. Given enough timber and fiber for making ropes, teams of at most a few hundred people could have loaded the statues onto wooden sleds, dragged them over lubricated wooden tracks or rollers, and used logs as levers to maneuver them into a standing position. Rope could have been made from the fiber of a small native tree, related to the linden, called the hauhau. However, that tree is now extremely scarce on Easter, and hauling one statue would have required hundreds of yards of rope. Did Easter's now barren landscape once support the necessary trees?

That question can be answered by the technique of pollen analysis, which involves boring out a column of sediment from a swamp or pond, with the most recent deposits at the top and relatively more ancient deposits at the bottom. The absolute age of each layer can be dated by radiocarbon methods. Then begins the hard work: examining tens of thousands of pollen grains under a microscope, counting them, and identifying the plant species that produced each one by comparing the grains with modern pollen from known plant species. For Easter Island, the bleary-eyed scientists who performed that task were John Flenley, now at Massey University in New Zealand, and Sarah King of the University of Hull in England.

Flenley and King's heroic efforts were rewarded by the striking new picture that emerged of Easter's prehistoric landscape. For at least 30,000 years before human arrival and during the early years of Polynesian settlement, Easter was not a wasteland at all. Instead, a subtropical forest of trees and woody bushes towered over a ground layer of shrubs, herbs, ferns, and grasses. In the forest grew tree daisies, the rope-yielding hauhau tree, and the toromiro tree, which furnishes a dense, mesquite-like firewood. The most common tree in the forest was a species of palm now absent on Easter but formerly so abundant that the bottom strata of the sediment column were packed with its pollen. The Easter Island palm was closely related to the still-surviving Chilean wine palm, which grows up to 82 feet tall and 6 feet in diameter. The tall, unbranched trunks of the Easter Island palm would have been ideal for transporting and erecting statues and constructing large canoes. The palm would also have been a valuable food source, since its Chilean relative yields edible nuts as well as sap from which Chileans make sugar, syrup, honey, and wine.

What did the first settlers of Easter Island eat when they were not glutting themselves on the local equivalent of maple syrup? Recent excavations by David Steadman, of the New York State Museum at Albany, have yielded a picture of Easter's original animal world as surprising as Flenley and King's picture of its plant world. Steadman's expectations for Easter were conditioned by his experiences elsewhere in Polynesia, where fish are overwhelmingly the main food at archeological sites, typically accounting for more than 90 percent of the bones in ancient Polynesian garbage heaps. Easter, though, is too cool for the coral reefs beloved by fish, and its cliffgirded coastline permits shallow-water fishing in only a few places. Less than a quarter of the bones in its early garbage heaps (from the period 900 to 1300) belonged to fish; instead, nearly one-third of all bones came from porpoises.

Nowhere else in Polynesia do porpoises account for even 1 percent of discarded food bones. But most other Polynesian islands offered animal food in the form of birds and mammals, such as New Zealand's now extinct giant moas and Hawaii's now extinct flightless geese. Most other islanders also had domestic pigs and dogs. On Easter, porpoises would have been the largest animal available—other than humans. The porpoise species identified at Easter, the common dolphin, weighs up to 165 pounds. It generally lives out at sea, so it could not have been hunted by line fishing or spearfishing from shore. Instead, it must have been harpooned far offshore, in big seaworthy canoes built from the extinct palm tree.

In addition to porpoise meat, Steadman found, the early Polynesian settlers were feasting on seabirds. For those birds, Easter's remoteness and lack of predators made it an ideal haven as a breeding site, at least until humans arrived. Among the prodigious numbers of seabirds that bred on Easter were albatross, boobies, frigate birds, fulmars, petrels, prions, shearwaters, storm petrels, terns, and tropic birds. With at least 25 nesting species, Easter was the richest seabird breeding site in Polynesia and probably in the whole Pacific.

Land birds as well went into early Easter Island cooking pots. Steadman identified bones of at least six species, including barn owls, herons, parrots, and rail. Bird stew would have been seasoned with meat from large numbers of rats, which the Polynesian colonists inadvertently brought with them; Easter Island is the sole known Polynesian island where rat bones outnumber fish bones at archeological sites. (In case you're squeamish and consider rats inedible, I still recall recipes for creamed laboratory rat that my British biologist friends used to supplement their diet during their years of wartime food rationing.)

Porpoises, seabirds, land birds, and rats did not complete the list of meat sources formerly available on Easter. A few bones hint at the possibility of breeding seal colonies as well. All these delicacies were cooked in ovens fired by wood from the island's forests.

Such evidence lets us imagine the island onto which Easter's first Polynesian colonists stepped ashore some 1,600 years ago, after a long canoe voyage from eastern Polynesia. They found themselves in a pristine paradise. What then happened to it? The pollen grains and the bones yield a grim answer.

Pollen records show that destruction of Easter's forests was well under way by the year 800, just a few centuries after the start of human settlement. Then charcoal from wood fires came to fill the sediment cores, while pollen of palms and other trees and woody shrubs decreased or disappeared, and pollen of the grasses that replaced the forest became more abundant. Not long after 1400 the palm finally became extinct, not only as a result of being chopped down but also because the now ubiquitous rats prevented its regeneration: of the dozens of preserved palm nuts discovered in caves on Easter, all had been chewed by rats and could no longer germinate. While the hauhau tree did not become extinct in Polynesian times, its numbers declined drastically until there weren't enough left to make ropes from. By the time Heyerdahl visited Easter, only a single, nearly dead toromiro tree remained on the island, and even that lone survivor has now disappeared. (Fortunately, the toromiro still grows in botanical gardens elsewhere.)

The fifteenth century marked the end not only for Easter's palm but for the forest itself. Its doom had been approaching as people cleared land to plant gardens; as they felled trees to build canoes, to transport and erect statues, and to burn; as rats devoured seeds; and probably as the native birds died out that had pollinated the trees' flowers and dispersed their fruit. The overall picture is among the most extreme examples of forest destruction anywhere in the world: the whole forest gone, and most of its tree species extinct.

The destruction of the island's animals was as extreme as that of the forest: without exception, every species of native land bird became extinct. Even shellfish were overexploited, until people had to settle for small sea snails instead of larger cowries. Porpoise bones disappeared abruptly from garbage heaps around 1500; no one could harpoon porpoises anymore, since the trees used for constructing the big seagoing canoes no longer existed. The colonies of more than half of the seabird species breeding on Easter or on its offshore islets were wiped out.

In place of these meat supplies, the Easter Islanders intensified their production of chickens, which had been only an occasional food item. They also turned to the largest remaining meat source available: humans, whose bones became common in late Easter Island garbage heaps. Oral traditions of the islanders are rife with cannibalism; the most inflammatory taunt that could be snarled at an enemy was "The flesh of your mother sticks between my teeth." With no wood available to cook these new goodies, the islanders resorted to sugarcane scraps, grass, and sedges to fuel their fires.

All these strands of evidence can be wound into a coherent narrative of a society's decline and fall. The first Polynesian colonists found themselves on an island with fertile soil, abundant food, bountiful building materials, ample lebensraum, and all the prerequisites for comfortable living. They prospered and multiplied.

After a few centuries, they began erecting stone statues on platforms, like the ones their Polynesian forebears had carved. With passing years, the statues and platforms became larger and larger, and the statues began sporting ten-ton red crowns—probably in an escalating spiral of one-upmanship, as rival clans tried to surpass each other with shows of wealth and power. (In the same way, successive Egyptian pharaohs built ever-larger pyramids. Today Hollywood movie moguls near my home in Los Angeles are displaying their wealth and power by building ever more ostentatious mansions. Tycoon Marvin Davis topped previous moguls with plans for a 50,000-square-foot house, so now Aaron Spelling has topped Davis with a 56,000-square-foot house. All that those buildings lack to make the message explicit are ten-ton red crowns.) On Easter, as in modern America, society was held together by a complex political system to redistribute locally available resources and to integrate the economies of different areas.

Eventually Easter's growing population was cutting the forest more rapidly than the forest was regenerating. The people used the land for gardens and the wood for fuel, canoes, and houses—and, of course, for lugging statues. As forest disappeared, the islanders ran out of timber and rope to transport and erect their statues. Life became more uncomfortable—springs and streams dried up, and wood was no longer available for fires.

People also found it harder to fill their stomachs, as land birds, large sea snails, and many seabirds disappeared. Because timber for building seagoing canoes vanished, fish catches declined and porpoises disappeared from the table. Crop yields also declined, since deforestation allowed the soil to be eroded by rain and wind, dried by the sun, and its nutrients to be leeched from it. Intensified chicken production and cannibalism replaced only part of all those lost foods. Preserved statuettes with sunken cheeks and visible ribs suggest that people were starving.

With the disappearance of food surpluses, Easter Island could no longer feed the chiefs, bureaucrats, and priests who had kept a complex society running. Surviving islanders described to early European visitors how local chaos replaced centralized government and a warrior class took over from the hereditary chiefs. The stone points of spears and daggers, made by the warriors during their heyday in the 1600s and 1700s, still litter the ground of Easter today. By around 1700, the population began to crash toward between one-quarter and one-tenth of its former number. People took to living in caves for protection against their enemies. Around 1770 rival clans started to topple each other's statues, breaking the heads off. By 1864 the last statue had been thrown down and desecrated.

As we try to imagine the decline of Easter's civilization, we ask ourselves, "Why didn't they look around, realize what they were doing, and stop before it was too late? What were they thinking when they cut down the last palm tree?"

I suspect, though, that the disaster happened not with a bang but with a whimper. After all, there are those hundreds of abandoned statues to consider. The forest the islanders depended on for rollers and rope didn't simply disappear one day—it vanished slowly, over decades. Perhaps war interrupted the moving teams; perhaps by the time the carvers had finished their work, the last rope snapped. In the meantime, any islander who tried to warn about the dangers of progressive deforestation would have been overridden by vested interests of carvers, bureaucrats, and chiefs, whose jobs depended on continued deforestation. Our Pacific Northwest loggers are only the latest in a long line of loggers to cry, "Jobs over trees!" The changes in forest cover from year to year would have been hard to detect: yes, this year we cleared those woods over there, but trees are starting to grow back again on this abandoned garden site here. Only older people, recollecting their childhoods decades earlier, could have recognized a difference. Their children could no more have comprehended their parents' tales than my eight-year-old sons today can comprehend my wife's and my tales of what Los Angeles was like 30 years ago.

Gradually trees became fewer, smaller, and less important. By the time the last fruit-bearing adult palm tree was cut, palms had long since ceased to be of economic significance. That left only smaller and smaller palm saplings to clear each year, along with other bushes and treelets. No one would have noticed the felling of the last small palm.

By now the meaning of Easter Island for us should be chillingly obvious. Easter Island is Earth writ small. Today, again, a rising population confronts shrinking resources. We too have no emigration valve, because all human societies are linked by international transport, and we can no more escape into space than the Easter Islanders could flee into the ocean. If we continue to follow our present course, we shall have exhausted the world's major fisheries, tropical rain forests, fossil fuels, and much of our soil by the time my sons reach my current age.

Every day newspapers report details of famished countries—Afghanistan, Liberia, Rwanda, Sierra Leone, Somalia, the former Yugoslavia, Zaire—where soldiers have appropriated the wealth or where central government is yielding to local gangs of thugs. With the risk of nuclear war receding, the threat of our ending with a bang no longer has a chance of galvanizing us to halt our course. Our risk now is of winding down, slowly, in a whimper. Corrective action is blocked by vested interests, by well-intentioned political and business leaders, and by their electorates, all of whom are perfectly correct in not noticing big changes from year to year. Instead, each year there are just somewhat more people, and somewhat fewer resources, on Earth.

It would be easy to close our eyes or to give up in despair. If mere thousands of Easter Islanders with only stone tools and their own muscle power sufficed to destroy their society, how can billions of people with metal tools and machine power fail to do worse? But there is one crucial difference. The Easter Islanders had no books and no histories of other doomed societies. Unlike the Easter Islanders, we have histories of the past—information that can save us. My main hope for my sons' generation is that we may now choose to learn from the fates of societies like Easter's.

Review Questions

1. What was the ecology of Easter Island when Polynesians first arrived on the island about A.D. 400, according to Jared Diamond?

2. What were the main sources of food eaten by Easter Islanders in the early years of island habitation?

3. What changes occurred in the Easter Island environment due to human exploitation? How did these changes affect the life and social organization of the islanders?

4. How does Diamond explain the inability of Easter Islanders to see the effect they were having on their island's habitat?

5. How does the Easter Island case apply to what is happening in the world today?

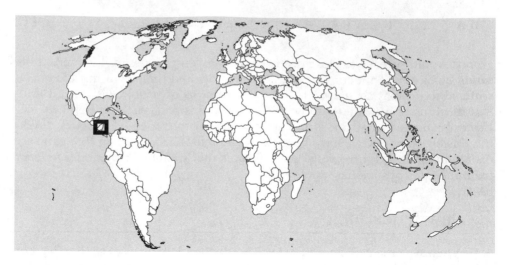

12

Subsistence and Market: When the Turtle Collapses

Bernard Nietschmann

For most of our history, we humans lived in relatively small groups and subsisted on wild foods. Inland, we collected vegetable foods, hunted a variety of animals, and if there were streams and lakes nearby, caught and ate fish. We moved from time to time with the seasons to exploit new territories when food at one location was exhausted. As we domesticated plants and animals, however, our populations grew and dependence on wild foods declined. Today, few of us could easily subsist for any length of time on land-based wild foods: There are too many of us and too few of them.

Shore dwellers, on the other hand, relied much more heavily on the sea for their food. Shellfish, fish, and other sea animals made up a greater

From Bernard Nietschmann, "When the Turtle Collapses, the World Ends," *Natural History*, June/July 1974. Reprinted from *Natural History* June/July 1974; copyright © Natural History Magazine, Inc., 1974.

proportion of their diet. While domestication advanced among inland communities, it was largely only fishing technology rather than the source of seafood that changed for maritime peoples. In essence, even today we still "hunt" sea creatures rather than farm them. (There are, of course, fish and shrimp farms, but the open sea remains the main source of seafood.)

Today there is a growing demand for seafood but a declining supply. Fish stocks, such as cod, have deteriorated to near extinction as the animals are unable to reproduce themselves quickly enough. As sea species disappear, we have mined more ocean ecozones to find those that remain. The result is an ecological disaster in the making, not only for fish but also for the traditional fishing communities that depended on catching them. Without other sources of food and income, the maritime way of life has disappeared in many parts of the world.

In this article, Bernard Nietschmann traces the disturbing effect of the international market for green sea turtles on the Miskito Indians, who once harpooned the large sea reptiles only for food. Trapped in a vicious circle, Indians began to catch the turtles to sell rather than to eat. With no turtle meat to eat came a need for money to buy food. Money came only from catching and selling more turtles. The need for cash also reduced the Indians' ability to perform reciprocal economic obligations. In the end, the new economy began to disappear because of the diminished catch of overexploited turtles, leaving the Miskito without even their original means of subsistence.

In the half-light of dawn, a sailing canoe approaches a shoal where nets have been set the day before. A Miskito turtleman stands in the bow and points to a distant splash that breaks the gray sheen of the Caribbean waters. Even from a hundred yards, he can tell that a green turtle has been caught in one of the nets. His two companions quickly bring the craft alongside the turtle, and as they pull it from the sea, its glistening shell reflects the first rays of the rising sun. As two men work to remove the heavy reptile from the net, the third keeps the canoe headed into the swells and beside the anchored net. After its fins have been pierced and lashed with bark fiber cord, the 250-pound turtle is placed on its back in the bottom of the canoe. The turtlemen are happy. Perhaps their luck will be good today and their other nets will also yield many turtles.

These green turtles, caught by Miskito Indian turtlemen off the eastern coast of Nicaragua, are destined for distant markets. Their butchered bodies will pass through many hands, local and foreign, eventually ending up in tins, bottles, and freezers far away. Their meat, leather, shell, oil, and calipee, a gelatinous substance that is the base for turtle soup, will be used to produce goods consumed in more affluent parts of the world.

The coastal Miskito Indians are very dependent on green turtles. Their culture has long been adapted to utilizing the once vast populations that inhabited the largest sea turtle feeding grounds in the Western Hemisphere. As the most important link between livelihood, social interaction, and environment, green turtles were the pivotal resource around which traditional Miskito Indian society revolved. These large reptiles also provided the major source of protein for Miskito subsistence. Now this priceless and limited resource has become a prized commodity that is being exploited almost entirely for economic reasons.

In the past, turtles fulfilled the nutritional needs as well as the social responsibilities of Miskito society. Today, however, the Miskito depend mainly on the sale of turtles to provide them with the money they need to purchase household goods and other necessities. But turtles are a declining resource; overdependence on them is leading the Miskito into an ecological blind alley. The cultural control mechanisms that once adapted the Miskito to their environment and faunal resources are now circumvented or inoperative, and they are caught up in a system of continued intensification of turtle fishing, which threatens to provide neither cash nor subsistence.

I have been studying this situation for several years, unraveling its historical context and piecing together its past and future effect on Miskito society, economy, and diet, and on the turtle population.

The coastal Miskito Indians are among the world's most adept smallcraft seamen and turtlemen. Their traditional subsistence system provided dependable yields from the judicious scheduling of resource procurement activities. Agriculture, hunting, fishing, and gathering were organized in accordance with seasonal fluctuations in weather and resource availability and provided adequate amounts of food and materials without overexploiting any one species or site. Women cultivated the crops while men hunted and fished. Turtle fishing was the backbone of subsistence, providing meat throughout the year.

Miskito society and economy were interdependent. There was no economic activity without a social context and every social act had a reciprocal economic aspect. To the Miskito, meat, especially turtle meat, was the most esteemed and valuable resource, for it was not only a mainstay of subsistence, it was the item most commonly distributed to relatives and friends. Meat shared in this way satisfied mutual obligations and responsibilities and smoothed out daily and seasonal differences in the acquisition of animal protein. In this way, those too young, old, sick, or otherwise unable to secure meat received their share, and a certain balance in the village was achieved: minimal food requirements were met, meat surplus was disposed of to others, and social responsibilities were satisfied.

Today, the older Miskito recall that when meat was scarce in the village, a few turtlemen would put out to sea in their dugout canoes for a day's harpooning on the turtle feeding grounds. In the afternoon, the men would return, sailing before the northeast trade wind, bringing meat for all. Gathered on the beach, the villagers helped drag the canoes into thatched storage sheds. After the turtles were butchered and the meat distributed, everyone returned home to the cooking fires.

Historical circumstances and a series of boom-bust economic cycles disrupted the Miskito's society and environment. In the seventeenth and eighteenth centuries, intermittent trade with English and French buccaneers—based on the exchange of forest and marine resources for metal tools and utensils, rum, and firearms—prompted the Miskito to extend hunting, fishing, and gathering beyond subsistence needs to exploitative enterprises.

During the nineteenth and early twentieth centuries, foreign-owned companies operating in eastern Nicaragua exported rubber, lumber, and gold, and initiated commercial banana production. As alien economic and ecological influences were intensified, contract wage labor replaced seasonal, short-term economic relationships; company commissaries replaced limited trade goods; and large-scale exploitation of natural resources replaced sporadic, selective extraction. During economic boom periods the relationship between resources, subsistence, and environment was drastically altered for the Miskito. Resources became a commodity with a price tag, market exploitation a livelihood, and foreign wages and goods a necessity.

For more than two hundred years, relations between the coastal Miskito and the English were based on sea turtles. It was from the Miskito that the English learned the art of turtling, which they then organized into intensive commercial exploitation of Caribbean turtle grounds and nesting beaches. Sea turtles were among the first resources involved in trade relations and foreign commerce in the Caribbean. Zoologist Archie Carr, an authority on sea turtles, has remarked that "more than any other dietary factor, the green turtle supported the opening up of the Caribbean." The once abundant turtle populations provided sustenance to ships' crews and to the new settlers and plantation laborers.

The Cayman Islands, settled by the English, became in the seventeenth and eighteenth centuries the center of commercial turtle fishing in the Caribbean. By the early nineteenth century, pressure on the Cayman turtle grounds and nesting beaches to supply meat to Caribbean and European markets became so great that the turtle population was decimated. The Cayman Islanders were forced to shift to other turtle areas off Cuba, the Gulf of Honduras, and the coast of eastern Nicaragua. They made annual expeditions, lasting four to seven weeks, to the Miskito turtle grounds to net green turtles, occasionally purchasing live ones, dried calipee, and the shells of hawksbill turtles (*Eretmochelys imbricata*) from the Miskito Indians. Reported catches of green turtles by the Cayman turtles generally ranged between two thousand and three thousand a year up to the early 1960s, when the Nicaraguan government failed to renew the islanders' fishing privileges.

Intensive resource extraction by foreign companies led to seriously depleted and altered environments. By the 1940s, many of the economic booms had turned to busts. As the resources ran out and operating costs mounted, companies shut down production and moved to other areas in Central America. Thus, the economic mainstays that had helped provide the Miskito with jobs, currency, markets, and foreign goods were gone. The company supply ships and commissaries disappeared, money became scarce, and store-bought items expensive.

In the backwater of the passing golden boom period, the Miskito were left with an ethic of poverty, but they still had the subsistence skills that had maintained their culture for hundreds of years. Their land and water environment was still capable of providing reliable resources for local consumption. As it had been in the past, turtle fishing became a way of life, a provider of life itself. But traditional subsistence culture could no longer integrate Miskito society and environment in a state of equilibrium. Resources were now viewed as having a value and labor a price tag. All that was needed was a market.

Recently, two foreign turtle companies began operations along the east coast of Nicaragua. One was built in Puerto Cabezas in late 1968, and another was completed in Bluefields in 1969. Both companies were capable of processing and shipping large amounts of green turtle meat and byproducts to markets in North America and Europe. Turtles were acquired by purchase from the Miskito. Each week company boats visited coastal Miskito communities and offshore island turtle camps to buy green turtles. The "company" was back, money was again available, and the Miskito were expert in securing the desired commodity. Another economic boom period was at hand. But the significant difference between this boom and previous ones was that the Miskito were now selling a subsistence resource.

As a result, the last large surviving green turtle population in the Caribbean was opened to intensive, almost year-round exploitation. Paradoxically, it would be the Miskito Indians, who once caught only what they needed for food, who would conduct the assault on the remaining turtle population. . . .

Green turtles, *Chelonia mydas*, are large, air-breathing, herbivorous marine reptiles. They congregate in large populations and graze on underwater beds of vegetation in relatively clear, shallow, tropical waters. A mature turtle can weigh two hundred fifty pounds or more and when caught, can live indefinitely in a saltwater enclosure or for a couple of weeks if kept in shade on land. Green turtles have at least six behavioral characteristics that are important in their exploitation: they occur in large numbers in localized areas; they are air breathing, so they have to surface; they are mass social nesters; they have an acute location-finding ability; when mature, they migrate seasonally on an overlapping two- or three-year cycle for mating and nesting; and they exhibit predictable local distributional patterns.

The extensive shallow shelf off eastern Nicaragua is dotted with numerous small coral islands, thousands of reefs, and vast underwater pastures of marine vegetation called "turtle banks." During the day, a large group of turtles may be found feeding at one of the many turtle banks, while adjacent marine pastures may have only a few turtles. They graze on the vegetation, rising periodically to the surface for air and to float for a while before diving again. In the late afternoon, groups of turtles will leave the feeding areas and swim to shoals, some up to four or five miles away, to spend the night. By five the next morning, they gather to depart again for the banks. The turtles' precise, commuter-like behavior between sleeping and feeding areas is well known to the Miskito and helps insure good turtling.

Each coastal turtling village exploits an immense sea area, containing many turtle banks and shoals. For example, the Miskito of Tasbapauni utilize a marine area of approximately six hundred square miles, with twenty major turtle banks and almost forty important shoals.

Having rather predictable patterns of movement and habitat preference, green turtles are commonly caught by the Miskito in three ways: on the turtle banks with harpoons; along the shoal-to-feeding area route with harpoons; and on the shoals using nets, which entangle the turtles when they surface for air.

The Miskito's traditional means of taking turtles was by harpoon—an eight- to ten-foot shaft fitted with a detachable short point tied to a strong line. The simple technology pitted two turtlemen in a small, seagoing canoe against the elusive turtles. Successful turtling with harpoons requires an extensive knowledge of turtle behavior and habits and tremendous skill and experience in handling a small canoe in what can be very rough seas. Turtlemen work in partnerships: a "strikerman" in the bow; the "captain" in the stern. Together, they make a single unit engaged in the delicate and almost silent pursuit of a wary prey, their movements coordinated by experience and rewarded by proficiency. Turtlemen have mental maps of all the banks and shoals in their area, each one named and located through a complex system of celestial navigation, distance reckoning, wind and current direction, and the individual surface-swell motion over each site. Traditionally, not all Miskito were sufficiently expert in seamanship and turtle lore to become respected "strikermen," capable of securing turtles even during hazardous sea conditions. Theirs was a very specialized calling. Harpooning restrained possible over-exploitation since turtles were taken one at a time by two men directly involved in the chase, and there were only a limited number of really proficient "strikermen" in each village.

Those who still use harpoons must leave early to take advantage of the land breeze and to have enough time to reach the distant offshore turtle grounds by first light. Turtlemen who are going for the day, or for several days, will meet on the beach by 2:00 A.M. They drag the canoes on bamboo rollers from beachfront sheds to the water's edge. There, in the swash of spent breakers, food, water, paddles, lines, harpoons, and sails are loaded and secured. Using a long pole, the standing bowman propels the canoe through the foaming surf while the captain in the stern keeps the craft running straight with a six-foot mahogany paddle. Once past the inside break, the men count the dark rolling seas building outside until there is a momentary pause in the sets; then with paddles digging deep, they drive the narrow, twenty-foot canoe over the cresting swells, rising precipitously on each wave face and then plunging down the far side as the sea and sky seesaw into view. Once past the breakers, they rig the sail and, running with the land breeze, point the canoe toward a star in the eastern sky.

A course is set by star fix and by backsight on a prominent coconut palm on the mainland horizon. Course alterations are made to correct for the direction and intensity of winds and currents. After two or three hours of sailing the men reach a distant spot located between a turtle sleeping shoal and feeding bank. There they intercept and follow the turtles as they leave for specific banks.

On the banks the turtlemen paddle quietly, listening for the sound of a "blowing" turtle. When a turtle surfaces for air it emits a hissing sound audible for fifty yards or more on a calm day. Since a turtle will stay near the surface for only a minute or two before diving to feed, the men must approach quickly and silently, maneuvering the canoe directly in front of or behind the turtle. These are its blind spots. Once harpooned, a turtle explodes into a frenzy of action, pulling the canoe along at high speeds in its hopeless, underwater dash for escape until it tires and can be pulled alongside the canoe.

But turtle harpooning is a dying art. The dominant method of turtling today is the use of nets. Since their introduction, the widespread use of turtle nets has drastically altered turtling strategy and productivity. Originally brought to the Miskito by the Cayman Islanders, nets are now extensively distributed on credit by the turtle companies. This simple technological change, along with a market demand for turtles, has resulted in intensified pressure on green turtle populations.

Buoyed by wooden floats and anchored to the bottom by a single line, the fifty-foot-long by fourteen-foot-wide nets hang from the surface like underwater flags, shifting direction with the current. Nets are set in place during midday when the turtlemen can see the dark shoal areas. Two Miskito will set five to thirty nets from one canoe, often completely saturating a small shoal. In the late afternoon, green turtles return to their shoals to spend the night. There they will sleep beside or beneath a coral outcrop, periodically surfacing for air where a canopy of nets awaits them.

Catching turtles with nets requires little skill; anyone with a canoe can now be a turtleman. The Miskito set thousands of nets daily, providing continuous coverage in densely populated nocturnal habitats. Younger Miskito can become turtlemen almost overnight simply by following more experienced men to the shoal areas, thus circumventing the need for years of accumulated skill and knowledge that once were the domain of the "strikermen." All one has to do is learn where to set the nets, retire for the night, remove the entangled turtles the next morning, and reset the nets. The outcome is predictable: more turtlemen, using more effective methods, catch more turtles.

With an assured market for turtles, the Miskito devote more time to catching turtles, traveling farther, and staying at sea longer. Increased dependence on turtles as a source of income and greater time inputs have meant disruption of subsistence agriculture and hunting and fishing. The Miskito no longer produce foodstuffs for themselves; they buy imported foods with money gained from the sale of turtles. Caught between contradictory priorities—their traditional subsistence system and the market economy—the Miskito are opting for cash.

The Miskito are now enveloped in a positive feedback system where change spawns change. Coastal villages rely on turtles for a livelihood. Decline of subsistence provisioning has led to the need to secure food from local shopkeepers on credit to feed the families in the villages and the men during their turtling expeditions. Initial high catches of turtles encouraged more Miskito to participate, and by 1972 the per-person and per-day catch began to decline noticeably.

In late 1972, several months after I had returned to Michigan, I received a letter from an old turtleman, who wrote: "Turtle is getting scarce, Mr. Barney. You said it would happen in five or ten years but it is happening now."

Burdened by an overdependence on an endangered species and with accumulating debts for food and nets, the Miskito are finding it increasingly difficult to break even, much less secure a profit. With few other economic alternatives, the inevitable step is to use more nets and stay out at sea longer.

The turtle companies encourage the Miskito to expand turtling activities by providing them with building materials so that they can construct houses on offshore cays, thereby eliminating the need to return to the mainland during rough weather. On their weekly runs up and down the coast, company boats bring food, turtle gear, and cash for turtles to fishing camps from the Miskito Cays to the Set Net Cays. Frequent visits keep the Miskito from becoming discouraged and returning to their villages with the turtles. On Saturdays, villagers look to sea, watching for returning canoes. A few men will bring turtle for their families; the majority will bring only money. Many return with neither.

Most Miskito prefer to be home on Sunday to visit with friends and for religious reasons. (There are Moravian, Anglican, and Catholic mission churches in many of the villages.) But more and more, turtlemen are staying out for two to four weeks. The church may promise salvation, but only the turtle companies can provide money.

Returning to their villages, turtlemen are confronted with a complex dilemma: how to satisfy both social and economic demands with a limited resource. Traditional Miskito social rules stipulate that turtle meat should be shared among kin, but the new economic system requires that turtles be sold for personal economic gain. Kin expect gifts of meat, and friends expect to be sold meat. Turtlemen are besieged with requests forcing them to decide between who will or will not receive meat. This is contrary to the traditional Miskito ethic, which is based on generosity and mutual concern for the well-being of others. The older Miskito ask why the turtlemen should have to allocate a food that was once abundant and available to all. Turtlemen sell and give to other turtlemen, thereby ensuring reciprocal treatment for themselves, but there simply are not enough turtles to accommodate other economic and social requirements. In order to have enough turtles to sell, fewer are butchered in the villages. This means that less meat is being consumed than before the turtle companies began operations. The Miskito presently sell 70 to 90 percent of the turtles they catch; in the near future they will sell even more and eat less. . . .

Social tension and friction are growing in the villages. Kinship relationships are being strained by what some villagers interpret as preferential and stingy meat distribution. Rather than endure the trauma caused by having to ration a limited item to fellow villagers, many turtlemen prefer to sell all their turtles to the company and return with money, which does not have to be shared. However, if a Miskito sells out to the company, he will probably be unable to acquire meat for himself in the village, regardless of kinship or purchasing power. I overheard an elderly turtleman muttering to himself as he butchered a turtle: "I no going to sell, neither give dem meat. Let dem eat de money."

The situation is bad and getting worse. Individuals too old or sick to provide for themselves often receive little meat or money from relatives. Families without turtlemen are families without money or access to meat. The trend is toward the individualization of nuclear families, operating for their own economic ends. Miskito villages are becoming neighborhoods rather than communities.

The Miskito diet has suffered in quality and quantity. Less protein and fewer diverse vegetables and fruits are consumed. Present dietary staples—rice, white flour, beans, sugar, and coffee—come from the store. In one Miskito village, 65 percent of all food eaten in a year was purchased.

Besides the nutritional significance of what is becoming a largely carbohydrate diet, dependence on purchased foods has also had major economic reverberations. Generated by national and international scarcities, inflationary fallout has hit the Miskito. Most of their purchased foods are imported, much coming from the United States. In the last five years prices for staples have increased 100 to 150 percent. This has had an overwhelming impact on the Miskito, who spend 50 to 75 percent of their income for food. Consequently, their entry into the market by selling a subsistence resource, diverting labor from agriculture, and intensifying exploitation of a vanishing species has resulted in their living off poorer-quality, higher-priced foods.

The Miskito now depend on outside systems to supply them with money and materials that are subject to world market fluctuations. They have lost their autonomy and their adaptive relationship with their environment. Life is no longer socially rewarding, nor is their diet satisfying. The coastal Miskito have become a specialized and highly vulnerable sector of the global market economy.

Loss of turtle markets would be a serious economic blow to the Miskito, who have almost no other means of securing cash for what have now become necessities. Nevertheless, continued exploitation will surely reduce the turtle population to a critical level.

National and international legislation is urgently needed. At the very least, commercial turtle fishing must be curtailed for several years until the *Chelonia* population can rebound and exploitation quotas can be set. While turtle fishing for subsistence should be permitted, exportation of sea turtle products used in the gourmet, cosmetic, or jewelry trade should be banned.

Restrictive environmental legislation, however, is not a popular subject in Nicaragua, a country that has recently been torn by earthquakes, volcanic eruption, and hurricanes. A program for sea turtle conservation submitted to the Nicaraguan government for consideration ended up in a pile of rubble during the earthquake that devastated Managua in December 1972, adding a sad footnote to the Miskito-sea turtle situation. With other problems to face, the government has not yet reviewed what is happening on the distant east coast, separated from the capital by more than two hundred miles of rain forest—and years of neglect.

As it is now, the turtles are going down and, along with them, the Miskito—seemingly a small problem in terms of the scale of ongoing ecological and cultural change in the world. But each localized situation involves species and societies with long histories and, perhaps, short futures. They are weathervanes in the conflicting winds of economic and environmental priorities. As Bob Dylan sang: "You don't need a weatherman to tell which way the wind blows."

Review Questions

1. What does Nietschmann mean by *subsistence economy?*

2. How has the Miskito Indians' exploitation of the green sea turtle affected their economy?

3. What does Nietschmann mean when he says that the Miskito Indian economy is "enveloped in a positive feedback system"?

4. How has the world market affected the Miskito economy?

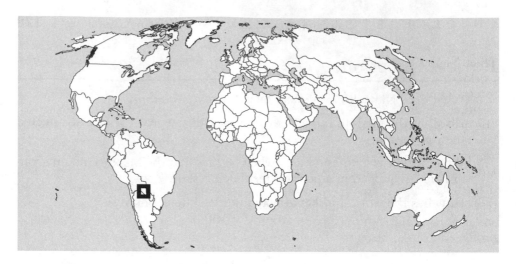

13

Forest Development the Indian Way

Richard K. Reed

To most industrialized peoples, the practice of slash-and-burn agriculture seems wasteful. Horticulturalists use axes and machetes to fell forests, burn the debris, and then plant in the ashes. Within a few short years, the fields are abandoned and the farmer moves on. For people used to thinking of agriculture as intensively planted permanent fields, slash-and-burn agriculture seems destructive. In this article, Richard Reed challenges this simplistic notion. Describing the production practices of the Guaraní Indians living in the tropical forests of Paraguay, and detailing the destruction of their original way of life by the infiltration of colonos (non-Indian colonists), he shows that Indian slash-and-burn agriculture combined with commercial harvesting of natural products offers a more sustainable and economically sound means for all people to prosper in these fragile forests.

From Richard K. Reed, "Forest Development the Indian Way." Used by permission of the author.

When I arrived in Itanaramí that very first time, it felt like I had left the modern world behind. This small Guaraní Indian village was hidden deep in the Paraguayan forests, surrounded by hundreds of miles of wilderness. I took a jeep to the end of a rutted dirt road and followed winding footpaths for two days into the heart of one of South America's great natural areas. Trees shaded the trail I took over the low hills, and clear streams offered cool refreshment in the valleys. Entering the community, the path opened into a small clearing and Veraju's small thatch roof jutted up through the tangle of the family's overgrown garden. His family was busy in the house yard, preparing manioc from the garden and game from the hunt. The rest of the settlement was similarly embedded in the forest, each home set in a small clearing along the narrow footpath. Houses seemed isolated from the world, protected from modernity by the high trees and verdant foliage of this vast forest.

I soon discovered that the isolation was illusory. Their house lots were strewn with machetes from Costa Rica and clothes were sewn from Brazilian polyester cloth. Even the most isolated households bought salt and soap and fish hooks from traders.

Guaraní made their living by gardening and hunting, but they also obtained cash by gathering and selling goods from the forest, especially the leaves of the wild yerba-maté plant (*Ilex Paraguayensis*), which is brewed in a caffeinated infusion throughout southern South America. And the commercial work was not new. A little research showed that the Guaraní had sold the leaf to Brazilian, Argentine, and Bolivian merchants since at least 1590. They had developed a way to mine the forest for its wealth without destroying the resources on which they depend.

The Threatened Forests

But the Guaraní's environment was threatened even then. The world's great tropical regions had become prime targets for a new kind of economic development. Ranchers and farmers, from Brazil to Indonesia, flocked to the jungle frontiers armed with chainsaws and bulldozers. They built roads, clear-cut timber, and denuded the land of foliage, often burning the trees and brush as they went.

The scope of this human invasion staggers the mind. In recent times, development destroys hundreds of square miles of virgin tropical forest each day. In the Amazon alone, an area half the size of Louisiana is cleared every year. We are discovering that not only are the forests finite, but they are rapidly disappearing. At this rate, authorities predict that the forests will be gone by the year 2050!

The future of this development is as finite as the resources it depends on. The march of progress, which seems so powerful and necessary, will soon destroy the very resources it requires. We can either choose to abandon our current development strategies or we will be forced to change.

As a result, the modern world is searching for models of development that promote growth within the world's finite resources. This *sustainable development* differs from conventional strategies in several important respects. First, it recognizes that resources are finite and protects those resources even as we benefit from them. Second, sustainable development emphasizes the relationship between economic, ecological, and social systems, striving to protect the integrity of all three. Third, sustainable development promotes social stability by distributing the benefits and raising the standard of living of all people.

As the modern world searches for technological solutions to its increasingly obvious problems, I discovered that the Guaraní offered a proven model for sustainable tropical forest development. More than simply providing their subsistence, they had developed a *commercial* system that gave them access to the world marketplace without destroying the forests they depended on.

We may ask what accounts for this successful adaptation. What subsistence strategies permit them to live within the ecological limits of the forest? Can such people provide a model for successful tropical forest management? If so, perhaps indigenous peoples will be as important to our future as the oxygen-giving forests they live in. Let's look at the factors that allowed the Guaraní of eastern Paraguay to prosper in the forest and the lessons we may learn from them.

The Guaraní

Before the encroachment of outsiders, the Guaraní Indians were well adapted to their forest environment. Like most horticulturalists, they lived in small, widely scattered communities. Because their population densities were low, and because they practiced a mixture of slash-and-burn agriculture and foraging, they placed a light demand on forest resources. Small size also meant a more personal social organization and an emphasis on cooperation and sharing. Although of greater size and complexity than hunter-gatherer bands, Guaraní villages contained many of the cultural values found in these nomadic societies.

Since that first visit twenty years ago, I have continued to conduct ethnographic fieldwork in the small group of Guaraní villages that include Itanaramí. The residents of these communities are among the last of the Guaraní Indians still living in the forests of southern South America. They are the remnants of an ethnic group that 400 years ago dominated southern Brazil and Paraguay from the Atlantic Ocean to the Andes. The Guaraní have suffered as disease, slavers, and colonists have invaded their forests. Today, only 30,500 Guaraní remain in isolated settlements where the tropical forest survives—and even these are threatened.

The forests of Itanaramí have high canopies that shelter both animal and human populations. When I first arrived in the region, the expanse of trees was broken only by streams and rivers that drain westward to the broad, marshy valley of the Paraná River. Viewed from the ground, the density of the forest growth was matched only by the diversity of plant species.

Itanaramí itself is built along a small stream that gives the settlement its name. To my uninformed eye, it was difficult to recognize the existence of a village at all when I first arrived there. Homesteads—which consisted of a clearing, a thatched hut, and a field—were scattered in the forest, often out of sight of one another. A closer look revealed that pathways through the forest connected houses to each other and to a slightly larger homestead, that of the *tamoi* (literally grandfather), the group's religious leader. As in many small societies, households were tied together by kinship, which wove a tapestry of relations that organized social affairs and linked Itanaramí to other Guaraní communities.

I discovered that Guaraní culture emphasized sharing and cooperation. Sisters often shared work and childcare. Brothers usually hunted together. Food was distributed among members of the extended family, including cousins, aunts, and uncles. Families distributed abundance with compatriots who had less—and expected the same treatment in return. People emphasized the general welfare, not personal wealth.

The *tamoi*, although in no sense a leader with formal authority, commanded considerable respect in the community. He settled disputes, chastised errant juniors, and led the entire community in evening religious ceremonies where all drank *kanguijy* (fermented corn), danced, and chanted to the gods.

The people of Itanaramí not only lived in the forest, they saw themselves as of it. The forest was basic to indigenous cosmology. The people referred to themselves as *ka'aguygua*, or "people of the forest." Villagers often named their children after the numerous forest songbirds, symbolizing their close personal ties to the environment.

Sustainable Production

Guaraní had lived in their present locale for centuries and had dwelled throughout the tropical forests of lowland South America for thousands of years. During all this time, they had exploited flora, fauna, and soils of the forests without doing permanent harm. The secret of their success was their production strategy. The Indians mixed agriculture with gathering, hunting, and fishing in a way that permitted the environment to recover. They even collected forest products for sale to outsiders, again without causing environmental damage.

Guaraní farming was well suited to forest maintenance. Using a form of shifting agriculture called slash-and-burn farming, the Indians permitted the forest to recover from the damage of field clearing. The way Veraju, the tamoi of Itanaramí, and his wife, Kitu, farmed provides a typical example. When the family needed to prepare a new field, it was Veraju who did the heavy work. He cut the trees and undergrowth to make a half-acre clearing near his house. Then he, Kitu, and some of their five children burned the fallen trees and brush, creating an ash that provided a powerful fertilizer for the thin forest soils. When the field was prepared, Kitu used a digging stick fashioned from a sapling to poke small holes in the ground, and planted the staple Guaraní crops, beans and manioc root (from which tapioca is made). Interspersed with the basic staples, they added the slower-growing banana, sugar cane, and orange trees to round out their diet. When the crops matured, it was Kitu and her daughters who harvested them.

The secret to successful slash-and-burn agriculture is field "shifting" or rotation. Crops flourish the first year and are plentiful the next, but the sun and rain soon take their toll on the exposed soil. The thin loam layer, so typical of tropical forests, degenerates rapidly to sand and clay. Grasses, weeds, and insect pests, rare in the deep forest, eventually discover the vulnerable crops. By the third year, the poor soils are thick with weeds and grow only a sparse corn crop and few small manioc roots. Rather than replant a fourth time, Veraju and Kitu would clear a new field nearby where soils are naturally more fertile and the forest can be burned for additional ash fertilizer. Although fallow, their old field was not abandoned. They continued to return periodically for fruit and to root out the remaining manioc.

The surrounding forest quickly reclaims the old field; roots penetrate the opening from the forest edge and animals wander through it dropping seeds in their path. As the forest returns, the decaying matter once again strengthens the depleted soil. After several years the plot will be distinguished only as one of the citrus groves that are scattered throughout the unbroken forest. In this way, the forest produces a sustained yield without degrading the natural ecosystem.

The forest recovers sufficiently fast for the same plot to be cleared and replanted within ten or fifteen years. This "swidden" system results in the cyclic use of a large area of forest, with a part under cultivation and a much larger portion lying fallow in various stages of recomposition.

If farming formed the only subsistence base, the Guaraní would have had to clear much larger gardens. But they also turned to other forest resources— game, fish, and forest products—to meet their needs. Guaraní men often formed small groups to hunt large animals such as deer, tapir, and peccary with guns purchased from outsiders or with the more traditional bows and arrows they make themselves. A successful hunt provides enough meat to share liberally with friends. Men also trapped smaller mammals, such as armadillo and paca (a large rodent). They fashioned snares and deadfall traps from saplings, tree trunks, and cactus fiber twine. These were set near homesteads, along streams, and at the edges of gardens. Traps not only provided meat, but also killed animals that would otherwise eat the crops.

Fish also supplied protein for the Guaraní diet and reduced dependence on agricultural produce. Many rivers and streams flow near Itanaramí on flat bottomland. These watercourses meander in broad loops that may be cut off as the river or stream changes course during a flood. Meanders, called oxbows, make ideal fishing spots. In addition to hook and line, men captured the fish by using a poison extracted from the bark of the *timbo* vine. Floated over the surface of the water, the poison stuns the fish and allows them to be caught by hand.

The forest also supplied a variety of useful products for the Guaraní. They made houses from tree trunks and bamboo stalks; rhododendron vines secured thatched roofs. Villagers collected wild honey and fruit to add sweetness to their diets. If the manioc in the fields were insufficient, wild tubers provided a basic staple. Even several species of insect larva and ants were collected as tasty and nutritious supplements to the daily meal. Finally, the Indians knew about a wide variety of medicinal plants. They processed roots, leaves, flowers, and seeds to release powerful alkaloids, making teas and poultices for the sick and injured.

But the Guaraní were not isolated from commercial goods. Almost five hundred years ago, White traders entered the forests of the Guaraní and gave Indians access to world markets. The Guaraní continued to produce for most of their needs, but items such as machetes, hooks, soap, and salt were more easily bought than manufactured or collected. As they did with farming and hunting, Guaraní turned to the forest to meet such economic needs. They regularly collected two forest products, yerba-maté and leaves from wild orange trees, which have an oil used in flavorings and perfumes, to raise the necessary funds.

It is important to note the special Guaraní knowledge and values associated with subsistence activities. Because they lived in the forest for such a long time, and because they would have nowhere to turn if their own resources disappeared, they relied on a special and complex knowledge of how the forest works and how it can be used.

For example, Guaraní, such as Veraju, distinguished among a variety of "ecozones," each with a unique combination of soil, flora, and fauna. They recognized obvious differences between the high forests on the hills, the deep swamps of river basins, and the grassy savannahs of the high plains. But they made more subtle distinctions within these larger regions. For example, they called the low scrub along rivers *ca'ati*. Flooded each year during the rainy season, this region supported bamboo groves that harbored small animals for trapping and provided material for house construction. The forests immediately above the flood plain look like an extension of the ca'ati, but to the Guaraní they differed in important ways. This ecozone supported varieties of bamboo that were useless in house construction but that attracted larger animals, such as peccary, which they hunted. In all, the Guaraní distinguished among nine resource zones, each with distinctive soils, flora, fauna, and uses. These subtle distinctions among ecozones enabled the Guaraní to use the forest to its best benefit. By shifting their subsistence efforts from one zone to another, just as they shifted their fields from one spot to the next, the Guaraní assured that the forest environment, with its rich variety of life, would always be able to renew itself.

The Impact of Unsustainable Development

In the last few years, intensive commercial development has come to the region in which Itanaramí lies. Paraguay's deforestation rates are among the highest in the world, raising the specter of complete ecological destruction. White *colonos* (settlers), armed with chain saws and earthmovers, attack the trees. They vandalize the land without awareness of the carefully integrated ecozones. As the trees fall, the forest products, such as yerba maté, are destroyed. So are the mammals and fish, the bamboo and the rhododendron vines, the honey and the fruits, and the fallow fields. As these resources disappear, so does the economy of the once self-sufficient Guaraní. Without their traditional mode of subsistence, it has become impossible to maintain their kin-organized society, the influence of the tamoi, and the willingness to share. Indian communities are destroyed by poverty and disease, and the members who remain join the legions of poor laborers who form the lowest class of the national society. In short, the Guaraní lose their ability to survive as an independent ethnic group.

Recent intensive development began near Itanaramí with a road that colonists cut through the jungle to the village. Through this gash in the forest moved logging trucks, bulldozers, farm equipment, and buses. Accompanying the machinery of development were farmers, ranchers, and speculators, hoping to make a quick profit from the verdant land. They descended from their vehicles onto the muddy streets of a newly built frontier town. They cleared land for general stores and bars, which were soon filled with merchandise and warm beer. By day, the air in the town was fouled by truck noise and exhaust fumes; by night it was infused with the glare of electric lights and the noise of blaring tape players.

Soon the settlers began to fell the forest creating fields for cotton, soybeans, and pasture. Survey teams cleared boundaries and drew maps. Lumber gangs camped in the forests, clear-cutting vast tracts of trees. Valuable timber was hauled off to new lumber mills; everything else was piled and burned. Massive bulldozers created expanses of sunlight in the previously unbroken forest. Within months, grass, cotton, and soybeans sprouted in the exposed soils. Where once the land had been home for game, it now provided for cattle. Herds often clogged the roads, competing with trucks hauling cotton to market and busses loaded with new colonists. Settlers fenced in the fields and cut lanes through the remaining forest to mark off portions that would be private property (off-limits to Indians).

The road and fields reached Itanaramí in 1994. A cement bridge was built over the stream and chainsaws, logging trucks, and bulldozers assaulted the forests the Guaraní once used for gardens, farming, and hunting. The footpath that once carried Guaraní to the tamoi's house now carries their timber to market in Brazil. The families are left with barren house lots.

Moreover, by destroying the forest resources surrounding the Guaraní villages of the region, colonos set in motion a process that destroyed the native culture and society. Guaraní communities became islands surrounded by a sea of pastures and farm fields. Although the Indians held onto their gardens, they lost the forest resources needed to sustain their original mode of subsistence, which depended on hunting, fishing, and gathering in the forest as well as farming. These economic changes forced alterations in the Indian community.

First, without the forest to provide game, fish, and other products, the Guaraní became dependent on farming alone for their survival. Without wild foods, they had to plant more corn and beans. Without the forest production of yerba maté leaves to collect for sale, they were also forced to plant cash crops such as cotton and tobacco. These changes forced them to clear gardens that were over twice the size of their previous plots.

While the loss of the forest for hunting and gathering increased their dependence on agriculture, the fences and land titles of the new settlers reduced the land available to the Indians for cultivation. Families soon cleared the last of the remaining high forests that they controlled. Even the once forested stream banks were denuded.

After they had cleared their communities' high forest, Indian farmers were forced to replant fields without allowing sufficient fallow time for soils to rejuvenate. Crops suffered from lack of nutrients and yields declined despite additional effort devoted to clearing and weeding. Commercial crops, poorly suited to the forest soils, did even worse. As production suffered, the Indians cleared and farmed even larger areas. The resulting spiral of poor harvests and enlarged farms outstripped the soil's capacity to produce and the Guaraní's ability to care for the crops. Food in the Indian communities grew scarce. The diet was increasingly restricted to nonnutritious manioc as a dietary staple because it was the only plant that could survive in the exhausted soils.

The Guaraní felt the ecological decline in other ways. The loss of game and poor crop yields exacerbated health problems. Settlers brought new diseases such as colds and flu into the forest. The Guaraní have little inherited resistance to these illnesses and poor nutrition reduced their defenses even further. Disease not only sapped the adults' energy for farming and childcare, it increased death rates at all ages. Tuberculosis, which well-fed Guaraní had rarely contracted, became the major killer in the community.

The environmental destruction took a psychological toll as well. Guaraní began to fall into depression, get drunk on cheap cane liquor, and, all too often, commit suicide. A number of suicides were noted among the Guaraní in Brazil in the 1990s and subsequent research in Paraguay showed that indigenous peoples were killing themselves at almost fifty times the national average. The epidemic hit 15- to 24-year-olds the hardest. These young people saw little future for themselves, their families, and their people.

Deforestation also disrupted social institutions. Without their subsistence base, many Guaraní needed additional cash to buy food and goods. Indian men were forced to seek work as farmhands, planting pastures and picking cotton on land where they once hunted. Women stayed at home to tend children and till the deteriorating soils of the family farms.

The search for wage labor eventually forced whole Guaraní families to move. Many jobs were available on the new farms that had replaced the forest. Entire families left home for hovels they constructed on the land of their employers. From independent farmers and gatherers, they became tenants of *patrones* (landowners). Patrones prohibited the Guaraní farmhands from planting gardens of their own, so the displaced Indians were forced to buy all their food, usually from the patrones themselves. Worse, patrones set their own inflated prices on the food and goods sold to Indians. Dependence on the patrones displaced the mutual interdependence of traditional Guaraní social organization.

As individuals and families left the Guaraní villages in search of work on surrounding farms and ranches, tamoi leaders lost influence. It became impossible to gather disparate relatives and friends for religious ritual. The distances were too great for the elders' nieces and nephews to seek out counsel and medicines. Moreover, the diseases and problems suffered by the Guaraní were increasingly caused by people and powers outside the forest. The tamoi could neither control nor explain the changing world.

Finally, as the forest disappeared, so did its power to symbolize Guaraní entity. No longer did young Indians see themselves as "people of the forest." Increasingly, they called themselves *indios*, the pejorative slur used by their non-Indian neighbors.

Today, many of the Guaraní of eastern Paraguay remain in small but impoverished communities in the midst of a frontier society based on soybean farming and cattle ranching. The households that previously were isolated individual plots are now concentrated in one small area without forest for farming or privacy. The traditional tamoi continue to be the center of the social and religious life of the community, but no longer exert influence over village decisions, which are increasingly dominated by affairs external to the local community.

Development and Ecology

Some people might argue that the Guaraní need to learn from their new neighbors, that they need to change their traditional ways and adopt the economy and culture of the more modern, prosperous society. The problems the Guaraní suffer, they claim, are a result of their traditional economy and culture. Change might be painful for today's Indians, but will provide unequaled opportunity for their descendents.

Unfortunately, this argument ignores the fact that recent development is destroying the resources on which the new farming and ranching depend. The long-run implications of forest clearing are disastrous, not simply for the Guaraní and other Indians, but for settlers and developers as well. The tropical forest ecosystem is extremely fragile. When the vegetable cover is destroyed, the soil quickly disappears. Erosion clogs rivers with silt and the soils left behind are baked to a hardpan on which few plants can survive. Rainwater previously captured by foliage and soil is quickly lost to runoff, drying the winds that feed the regional rain systems. Although first harvests in frontier areas seem bountiful, long-term farming and ranching are unprofitable as the soils, deprived of moisture and the rejuvenating forces of the original forest, are reduced to a "red desert."

Returning to Itanaramí today, one notices that many of the fields first cleared by ranchers in 1996 have already been abandoned. And even worse, leaving the cleared land fallow does not restore it. Once destroyed, the forest plants cannot reclaim the huge expanses of hardpan left by unsustainable development.

Nor have developers been interested in husbanding the land. The colonos who clear the forests are concerned with short-term profit. Entrepreneurs and peasant farmers maximize immediate returns on their labor and investment, unaware of the environmental costs that subsidize their earnings. When the trees and soils of one area are exhausted, the farmers, ranchers, and loggers move farther into the virgin forest in search of new resources. The process creates a wave of development that leaves destruction in its wake. Unlike the Guaraní who have developed sustainable systems, developers do not stay and contend with the environmental destruction caused by their activities.

Indigenous Models for Sustainable Development

Rather than the Guaraní learning to adapt to our models of development, perhaps we need to take a lesson from indigenous peoples. If we hope to survive in the rain forest, we must learn from the people who have not only survived, but prospered commercially in this fragile environment. International agencies and national governments have begun to recognize that our development strategies are doomed to failure. Although deforestation continues unchecked in many regions of the Amazon Basin, forest conservation programs are using the experience of indigenous people to promote sustainable development in the forest.

Such is the case in Paraguay where a program is being implemented to preserve the remaining tropical forests. Groups like the Guaraní of Itanaramí, so recently threatened by encroaching development, are providing a model for newcomers to earn a profit from the natural resources, while protecting the existing environment. The natural forests of some of the Guaraní are the last remaining undisturbed subtropical forest in eastern Paraguay. With the help of Nature Conservancy, an area of 280 square miles has been set aside as a biosphere reserve. Although small, the program is attempting to protect a much larger buffer zone around the reserve by promoting rational land use by colonists. Aided by anthropologists who have made detailed studies of Indian commercial harvesting, planners are integrating the Indians' own models of agro-forestry into new production strategies for colonos. Guaraní techniques of commercial extraction have been of special interest, particularly the harvest of yerba maté, as it will economically outperform destructive farming in the long run. Teams of planners are teaching newcomers to tend and harvest their own tree crops. Far from being backward and inefficient, the mixed horticultural subsistence strategies of indigenous forest groups have turned out to be the most practical way to manage the fragile tropical forest environment.

Review Questions

1. Anthropologists claim that subsistence strategies affect a society's social organization and ideology. Evaluate this assertion in light of reading about the way the Guaraní live in their rain forest environment.

2. Why is horticulture more environmentally sensible than intensive agricultural and pastoral exploitation of the Amazonian rain forest?

3. Guaraní Indians are largely subsistence farmers and foragers. How do they use their forest environment without destroying it?

4. How have *colonos* disrupted the lives of Guaraní villagers? What does this tell us about the relationship between subsistence and social structure?

5. How can the Guaraní use their rain forest habitat to make money, and what does their experience suggest as a way to integrate forest exploitation into a market economy without environmental destruction?

FOUR

ECONOMIC SYSTEMS

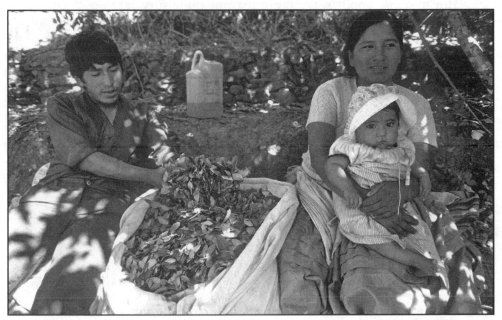

Magnum Photos, Inc.

READINGS IN THIS SECTION

Reciprocity and the Power of Giving   139
Lee Cronk

Global Women in the New Economy   146
Barbara Ehrenreich and Arlie Russell Hochschild

Cocaine and the Economic Deterioration of Bolivia   156
Jack Weatherford

Malawi versus the World Bank   167
Sonia Patten

People everywhere experience wants that can be satisfied only by the acquisition and use of material goods and the services of others. To meet such wants, humans rely on an aspect of their cultural inventory, the **economic system,** which we will define as the provision of goods and services to meet biological and social wants.

The meaning of the term *want* can be confusing. It can refer to what humans *need* for their survival. We must eat, drink, maintain a constant body temperature, defend ourselves, and deal with injury and illness. The economic system meets these needs by providing food, water, clothing, shelter, weapons, medicines, and the cooperative services of others.

But material goods serve more than just our survival needs: they meet our culturally defined *wants* as well. We need clothes to stay warm, but we want garments of a particular style, cut, and fabric to signal our status, rank, or anything else we wish to communicate socially. We need food to sustain life, but we want particular foods prepared in special ways to fill our aesthetic and social desires. Services and goods may also be exchanged to strengthen ties between people or groups. Birthday presents may not always meet physical needs, but they clearly function to strengthen the ties between the parties to the exchange.

Part of the economic system is concerned with **production,** which means rendering material items useful and available for human consumption. Production systems must designate ways to allocate resources. The **allocation of resources** refers to the cultural rules people use to assign rights to the ownership and use of resources. Production systems must also include technologies. Americans usually associate technology with the tools and machines used for manufacturing, rather than with the knowledge for doing it. But many anthropologists link the concept directly to culture. Here we will define **technology** as the cultural knowledge for making and using tools and extracting and refining raw materials.

Production systems also include a **division of labor,** which refers to the rules that govern the assignment of jobs to people. In hunting and gathering societies, labor is most often divided along the lines of gender, and sometimes age. In these societies, almost everyone knows how to produce, use, and collect the necessary material goods. In industrial society, however, jobs are highly specialized, and labor is divided, at least ideally, on the basis of skill and experience. Rarely do we know how to do someone else's job in our complex society.

The **unit of production,** meaning the persons or groups responsible for producing goods, follows a pattern similar to the way labor is divided in various societies. Among hunter-gatherers, there is little specialization; individuals, families, groups of friends, or sometimes bands form the units of production. But in our own complex society, we are surrounded by groups specially organized to manufacture, transport, and sell goods.

Another part of the economic system is **distribution.** There are three basic modes of distribution: market exchange, reciprocal exchange, and redistribution.

We are most conscious of market exchange because it lies at the heart of our capitalist system. **Market exchange** is the transfer of goods and services based on price, supply, and demand. Every time we enter a store and pay for something, we engage in market exchange. The price of an item may change with the supply. For example, a discount store may lower the price of a television set because it has too many of the appliances on hand. Prices may go up, however, if everyone wants the sets when there are few to sell. Money is often used in market systems; it enables people to exchange a large variety of items easily. Barter involves the trading of goods, not money, but it, too, is a form of market exchange because the number of items exchanged may also vary with supply and demand. Market exchange appears in human history when societies become larger and more complex. It is well suited for exchange between the strangers who make up these larger groups.

Although we are not so aware of it, we also engage in reciprocal exchange. **Reciprocal exchange** involves the transfer of goods and services between two people or groups based on role obligations. Birthday and holiday gift giving is a fine example of reciprocity. On these occasions we exchange goods not because we necessarily need or want them, but because we are expected to do so as part of our status and role. Parents should give gifts to their children, for example; children should reciprocate. If we fail in our reciprocal obligations, we signal an unwillingness to continue the relationship. Small, simply organized societies, such as the !Kung described earlier, base their exchange systems on reciprocity. Complex ones like ours, although largely organized around the market or redistribution, still manifest reciprocity between kin and close friends.

Finally, there is **redistribution,** the transfer of goods and services between a central collecting source and a group of individuals. Like reciprocity, redistribution is based on role obligation. Taxes typify this sort of exchange in the United States. We must pay our taxes because we are citizens, not because we are buying something. We receive goods and services back—education, transportation, roads, defense—but not necessarily in proportion to the amount we contribute. Redistribution may be the predominant mode of exchange in socialist societies.

Anthropologists also frequently talk about two kinds of economies. In the past, many of the world's societies had **subsistence economies** organized around the need to meet material necessities and social obligations. Subsistence economies are typically associated with smaller groups. They occur at a local level. Such economies depend most on the non-market-exchange mechanisms: reciprocity and redistribution. Their members are occupational generalists. Most people can do most jobs, although there may be distinctions on the basis of gender and age. The !Kung described by Richard Lee in Parts One and Three of this book had subsistence economies as do most horticulturalists.

Market economies differ from subsistence economies in their size and motive for production. Although reciprocity and redistribution exist in market economies, market exchange drives production and consumption. Market economies are larger (indeed, there is a growing world market economy that includes almost everyone) and are characterized by high economic specialization, as well as impersonality. The American economy is market-driven as are most national systems. If they have not been already, most subsistence economies will, in the near future, be absorbed into national market systems.

The selections in Part Four illustrate several of the concepts discussed above. In the first article, Lee Cronk looks at gift giving, a classic example of reciprocity. He finds that gifts can cement relationships, confer prestige, and obligate subordinates as well as being used to attack enemies. In the second article, Barbara Ehrenreich and Arlie Russell Hochschild discuss a growing labor trend, the movement of women from poor societies to take low-paying jobs in rich ones. Often aided by their countries of origin, women immigrants are expected to send money home and leave their children in the hands of others. In the next article, Jack Weatherford deals with the negative impact of the world market on the social organization and economy of the indigenous peoples of Peru, Bolivia, and Colombia who grow coca and prepare the drug for market. The final selection by Sonia Patten details the effect of free-market World Bank and IMF policies on the agricultural subsistence economy of Malawi. With its people starving because they could not afford the market price of fertilizer, the African country's government decided to subsidize the chemical. The result was a bumper crop and the end of malnutrition.

Key Terms

allocation of resources p. 136	production p. 136
distribution p. 136	reciprocal exchange p. 137
division of labor p. 136	redistribution p. 137
economic system p. 136	subsistence economies p. 137
market economies p. 137	technology p. 136
market exchange p. 137	unit of production p. 136

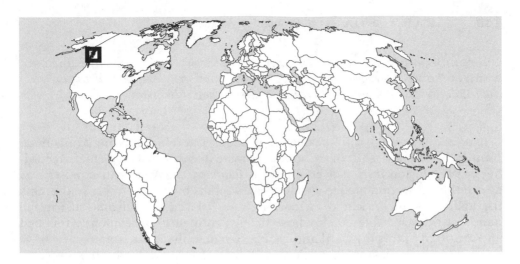

14

Reciprocity and the Power of Giving

Lee Cronk

As we saw in the introduction to Part Four, reciprocity constitutes an important exchange system in every society. At the heart of reciprocal exchange is the idea of giving. In this article, Lee Cronk explores the functions of giving using a variety of examples from societies around the world. Giving may be benevolent. It may be used to strengthen existing relationships or to form new ones. Gifts may also be used aggressively to "fight" people, to "flatten" them with generosity. Givers often gain position and prestige in this way. Gifts may also be used to place others in debt so that one can control them

Reprinted with the permission of the New York Academy of Sciences, 7 World Trade Center, 250 Greenwich St., 40th Floor, New York, NY 10007. www.nyas.org

and require their loyalty. Cronk shows that, in every society, from !Kung hxaro exchange to American foreign aid, there are "strings attached" to giving that affect how people and groups relate to each other.

During a trek through the Rockies in the 1830s, Captain Benjamin Louis E. de Bonneville received a gift of a fine young horse from a Nez Percé chief. According to Washington Irving's account of the incident, the American explorer was aware that "a parting pledge was necessary on his own part, to prove that this friendship was reciprocated." Accordingly, he "placed a handsome rifle in the hands of the venerable chief; whose benevolent heart was evidently touched and gratified by this outward and visible sign of amity."

Even the earliest white settlers in New England understood that presents from natives required reciprocity, and by 1764, "Indian gift" was so common a phrase that the Massachusetts colonial historian Thomas Hutchinson identified it as "a proverbial expression, signifying a present for which an equivalent return is expected." Then, over time, the custom's meaning was lost. Indeed, the phrase now is used derisively, to refer to one who demands the return of a gift. How this cross-cultural misunderstanding occurred is unclear, but the poet Lewis Hyde, in his book *The Gift,* has imagined a scenario that probably approaches the truth.

Say that an Englishman newly arrived in America is welcomed to an Indian lodge with the present of a pipe. Thinking the pipe a wonderful artifact, he takes it home and sets it on his mantelpiece. When he later learns that the Indians expect to have the pipe back, as a gesture of goodwill, he is shocked by what he views as their short-lived generosity. The newcomer did not realize that, to the natives, the point of the gift was not to provide an interesting trinket but to inaugurate a friendly relationship that would be maintained through a series of mutual exchanges. Thus, his failure to reciprocate appeared not only rude and thoughtless but downright hostile. "White man keeping" was as offensive to native Americans as "Indian giving" was to settlers.

In fact, the Indians' tradition of gift giving is much more common than our own. Like our European ancestors, we think that presents ought to be offered freely, without strings attached. But through most of the world, the strings themselves are the main consideration. In some societies, gift giving is a tie between friends, a way of maintaining good relationships, whereas in others it has developed into an elaborate, expensive, and antagonistic ritual designed to humiliate rivals by showering them with wealth and obligating them to give more in return.

In truth, the dichotomy between the two traditions of gift giving is less behavioral than rhetorical: our generosity is not as unconditional as we would like to believe. Like European colonists, most modern Westerners are blind to the purpose of reciprocal gift giving, not only in non-Western societies but also, to some extent, in our own. Public declarations to the contrary, we, too, use gifts to nurture long-term relationships of mutual obligation, as well as to embarrass our rivals and to foster feelings of indebtedness. And this ethic touches all aspects of contemporary life, from the behavior of scientists in research networks to superpower diplomacy. Failing to acknowledge this fact, especially as we give money, machines, and technical advice to peoples around the world, we run the risk of being misinterpreted and, worse, of causing harm.

Much of what we know about the ethics of gift giving comes from the attempts of anthropologists to give things to the people they are studying. Richard Lee, of the University of Toronto, learned a difficult lesson from the !Kung hunter-gatherers, of the Kalahari desert, when, as a token of goodwill, he gave them an ox to slaughter at Christmas. Expecting gratitude, he was shocked when the !Kung complained about having to make do with such a scrawny "bag of bones." Only later did Lee learn, with relief, that the !Kung belittle all gifts. In their eyes, no act is completely generous, or free of calculation; ridiculing gifts is their way of diminishing the expected return and of enforcing humility on those who would use gifts to raise their own status within the group.

Rada Dyson-Hudson, of Cornell University, had a similar experience among the Turkana, a pastoral people of northwestern Kenya. To compensate her informants for their help, Dyson-Hudson gave away pots, maize meal, tobacco, and other items. The Turkana reaction was less than heartwarming. A typical response to a gift of a pot, for example, might be, "Where is the maize meal to go in this pot?" or, "Don't you have a bigger one to give me?" To the Turkana, these are legitimate and expected questions.

The Mukogodo, another group of Kenyan natives, responded in a similar way to gifts Beth Leech and I presented to them during our fieldwork in 1986. Clothing was never nice enough, containers never big enough, tobacco and candies never plentiful enough. Every gift horse was examined carefully, in the mouth and elsewhere. Like the !Kung, the Mukogodo believe that all gifts have an element of calculation, and they were right to think that ours were no exception. We needed their help, and their efforts to diminish our expectations and lessen their obligations to repay were as fair as our attempts to get on their good side.

The idea that gifts carry obligations is instilled early in life. When we gave Mukogodo children candies after visiting their villages, their mothers reminded them of the tie: "Remember these white people? They are the ones who gave you candy." They also reinforced the notion that gifts are meant to circulate, by asking their children to part with their precious candies, already in their mouths. Most of the youngsters reluctantly surrendered their sweets, only to have them immediately returned. A mother might take, at most, a symbolic nibble from her child's candy, just to drive home the lesson.

The way food, utensils, and other goods are received in many societies is only the first stage of the behavior surrounding gift giving. Although repayment is expected, it is crucial that it be deferred. To reciprocate at once indicates a desire to end the relationship, to cut the strings; delayed repayment makes the strings longer and stronger. This is especially clear on the Truk Islands, of Micronesia, where a special word—*niffag*—is used to designate objects moving through the island's exchange network. From the Trukese viewpoint, to return niffag on the same day it is received alters its nature from that of a gift to that of a sale, in which all that matters is material gain.

After deciding the proper time for response, a recipient must consider how to make repayment, and that is dictated largely by the motive behind the gift. Some exchange customs are designed solely to preserve a relationship. The !Kung have a system, called *hxaro*, in which little attention is paid to whether the items exchanged are equivalent. Richard Lee's informant !Xoma explained to him that "Hxaro is when I take a thing of value and give it to you. Later, much later, when you find some good thing, you give it back to me. When I find something good I will give it to you, and so we will pass the years together." When Lee tried to determine the exact exchange values of various items (Is a spear worth three strings of beads, two strings, or one?), !Xoma explained that any return would be all right: "You see, we don't trade with things, we trade with people!"

One of the most elaborate systems of reciprocal gift giving, known as *kula*, exists in a ring of islands off New Guinea. Kula gifts are limited largely to shell necklaces, called *soulava*, and armbands, called *mwali*. A necklace given at one time is answered months or years later with an armband, the necklaces usually circulating clockwise, and the armbands counterclockwise, through the archipelago. Kula shells vary in quality and value, and men gain fame and prestige by having their names associated with noteworthy necklaces or armbands. The shells also gain value from their association with famous and successful kula partners.

Although the act of giving gifts seems intrinsically benevolent, a gift's power to embarrass the recipient and to force repayment has, in some societies, made it attractive as a weapon. Such antagonistic generosity reached its most elaborate expression, during the late nineteenth century, among the Kwakiutl, of British Columbia.

The Kwakiutl were acutely conscious of status, and every tribal division, clan, and individual had a specific rank. Disputes about status were resolved by means of enormous ceremonies (which outsiders usually refer to by the Chinook Indian term *potlatch*), at which rivals competed for the honor and prestige of giving away the greatest amount of property. Although nearly everything of value was fair game—blankets, canoes, food, pots, and, until the mid-nineteenth century, even slaves—the most highly prized items were decorated sheets of beaten copper, shaped like shields and etched with designs in the distinctive style of the Northwest Coast Indians.

As with the kula necklaces and armbands, the value of a copper sheet was determined by its history—by where it had been and who had owned it—and a single sheet could be worth thousands of blankets, a fact often reflected in its name. One was called "Drawing All Property from the House," and another, "About Whose Possession All Are Quarreling." After the Kwakiutl began to acquire trade goods from the Hudson's Bay Company's Fort Rupert post, in 1849, the potlatches underwent a period of extreme inflation, and by the 1920s, when items of exchange included sewing machines and pool tables, tens of thousands of Hudson's Bay blankets might be given away during a single ceremony.

In the 1880s, after the Canadian government began to suppress warfare between tribes, potlatching also became a substitute for battle. As a Kwakiutl man once said to the anthropologist Franz Boas, "The time of fighting is past. . . . We do not fight now with weapons: we fight with property." The usual Kwakiutl word for potlatch was *p!Esa*, meaning to flatten (as when one flattens a rival under a pile of blankets), and the prospect of being given a large gift engendered real fear. Still, the Kwakiutl seemed to prefer the new "war of wealth" to the old "war of blood."

Gift giving has served as a substitute for war in other societies, as well. Among the Siuai, of the Solomon Islands, guests at feasts are referred to as attackers, while hosts are defenders, and invitations to feasts are given on short notice in the manner of "surprise attacks." And like the Kwakiutl of British Columbia, the Mount Hagen tribes of New Guinea use a system of gift giving called *moka* as a way of gaining prestige and shaming rivals. The goal is to become a tribal leader, a "big-man." One moka gift in the 1970s consisted of several hundred pigs, thousands of dollars in cash, some cows and wild birds, a truck, and a motorbike. The donor, quite pleased with himself, said to the recipient, "I have won. I have knocked you down by giving so much."

Although we tend not to recognize it as such, the ethic of reciprocal gift giving manifests itself throughout our own society, as well. We, too, often expect something, even if only gratitude and a sense of indebtedness, in exchange for gifts, and we use gifts to establish friendships and to manipulate our positions in society. As in non-Western societies, gift giving in America sometimes takes a benevolent and helpful form; at other times, the power of gifts to create obligations is used in a hostile way.

The Duke University anthropologist Carol Stack found a robust tradition of benevolent exchange in an Illinois ghetto known as the Flats, where poor blacks engage in a practice called swapping. Among residents of the Flats, wealth comes in spurts; hard times are frequent and unpredictable. Swapping, of clothes, food, furniture, and the like, is a way of guaranteeing security, of making sure that someone will be there to help out when one is in need and that one will get a share of any windfalls that come along.

Such networks of exchange are not limited to the poor, nor do they always involve objects. Just as the exchange of clothes creates a gift community in the Flats, so the swapping of knowledge may create one among scientists. Warren

Hagstrom, a sociologist at the University of Wisconsin, in Madison, has pointed out that papers submitted to scientific journals often are called contributions, and, because no payment is received for them, they truly are gifts. In contrast, articles written for profit—such as this one—often are held in low esteem: scientific status can be achieved only through *giving* gifts of knowledge.

Recognition also can be traded upon, with scientists building up their gift-giving networks by paying careful attention to citations and acknowledgments. Like participants in kula exchange, they try to associate themselves with renowned and prestigious articles, books, and institutions. A desire for recognition, however, cannot be openly acknowledged as a motivation for research, and it is a rare scientist who is able to discuss such desires candidly. Hagstrom was able to find just one mathematician (whom he described as "something of a social isolate") to confirm that "junior mathematicians want recognition from big shots and, consequently, work in areas prized by them."

Hagstrom also points out that the inability of scientists to acknowledge a desire for recognition does not mean that such recognition is not expected by those who offer gifts of knowledge, any more than a kula trader believes it is all right if his trading partner does not answer his gift of a necklace with an armband. While failure to reciprocate in New Guinean society might once have meant warfare, among scientists it may cause factionalism and the creation of rivalries.

Whether in the Flats of Illinois or in the halls of academia, swapping is, for the most part, benign. But manipulative gift giving exists in modern societies, too—particularly in paternalistic government practices. The technique is to offer a present that cannot be repaid, coupled with a claim of beneficence and omniscience. The Johns Hopkins University anthropologist Grace Goodell documented one example in Iran's Khūzestān Province, which, because it contains most of the country's oil fields and is next door to Iraq, is a strategically sensitive area. Goodell focused on the World Bank–funded Dez irrigation project, a showpiece of the shah's ambitious "white revolution" development plan. The scheme involved the irrigation of tens of thousands of acres and the forced relocation of people from their villages to new, model towns. According to Goodell, the purpose behind dismantling local institutions was to enhance central government control of the region. Before development, each Khūzestāni village had been a miniature city-state, managing its own internal affairs and determining its own relations with outsiders. In the new settlements, decisions were made by government bureaucrats, not townsmen, whose autonomy was crushed under the weight of a large and strategically placed gift.

On a global scale, both the benevolent and aggressive dimensions of gift giving are at work in superpower diplomacy. Just as the Kwakiutl were left only with blankets with which to fight after warfare was banned, the United States and the Soviet Union now find, with war out of the question, that they are left only with gifts—called concessions—with which to do battle. Offers of military cutbacks are easy ways to score points in the public arena of international opinion and to shame rivals, and failure either to accept such offers or to respond with even more extreme proposals may be seen as cowardice or as bellicosity. Mikhail Gorbachev is a virtuoso, a master potlatcher, in this new kind of competition, and, predictably, Americans often see his offers of disarmament and openness as gifts with long strings attached. One reason U.S. officials were buoyed last December [1988], when, for the first time since the Second World War, the Soviet Union accepted American assistance, in the aftermath of the Armenian earthquake, is that it seemed to signal a wish for reciprocity rather than dominance—an unspoken understanding of the power of gifts to bind people together.

Japan, faced with a similar desire to expand its influence, also has begun to exploit gift giving in its international relations. In 1989, it will spend more than ten billion dollars on foreign aid, putting it ahead of the United States for the second consecutive year as the world's greatest donor nation. Although this move was publicly welcomed in the United States as the sharing of a burden, fears, too, were expressed that the resultant blow to American prestige might cause a further slip in our international status. Third World leaders also have complained that too much Japanese aid is targeted at countries in which Japan has an economic stake and that too much is restricted to the purchase of Japanese goods—that Japan's generosity has less to do with addressing the problems of underdeveloped countries than with exploiting those problems to its own advantage.

The danger in all of this is that wealthy nations may be competing for the prestige that comes from giving gifts at the expense of Third World nations. With assistance sometimes being given with more regard to the donors' status than to the recipients' welfare, it is no surprise that, in recent years, development aid often has been more effective in creating relationships of dependency, as in the case of Iran's Khūzestān irrigation scheme, than in producing real development. Nor that, given the fine line between donation and domination, offers of help are sometimes met with resistance, apprehension and, in extreme cases, such as the Iranian revolution, even violence.

The Indians understood a gift's ambivalent power to unify, antagonize, or subjugate. We, too, would do well to remember that a present can be a surprisingly potent thing, as dangerous in the hands of the ignorant as it is useful in the hands of the wise.

Review Questions

1. What does Cronk mean by *reciprocity*? What is the social outcome of reciprocal gift giving?

2. According to Cronk, what are some examples of benevolent gift giving?

3. How can giving be used to intimidate other people or groups? Give some examples cited by Cronk and think of some from your own experience.

4. How does Cronk classify gift-giving strategies such as government foreign aid? Can you think of other examples of the use of exchange as a political device?

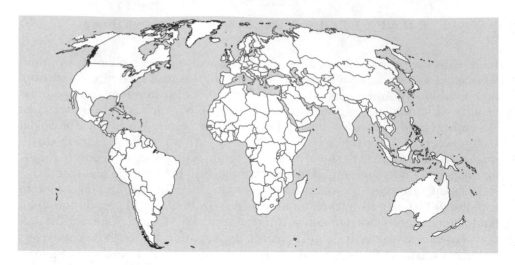

15

Global Women in the New Economy

Barbara Ehrenreich and Arlie Russell Hochschild

Movement is a key feature of today's world economy. Manufacturing jobs move from wealthier nations to poorer ones. An enormous variety of goods and raw materials travels by sea and rail to every part of the world. And more and more, so do people. Most come from poor nations to find work in rich ones. At first most were men; today many are women. In this selection, Barbara Ehrenreich and Arlie Russell Hochschild describe the history of female immigration, the reasons women migrate, the kinds of jobs they take in wealthier nations, the stresses their absence has on their own families, their lives in the families of others when they serve as nannies, and consequences for relative wealth among the world's nations. The authors conclude that women, both rich and poor, seek to better their condition and that migration increases interdependence among nations.

"Whose baby are you?" Josephine Perera, a nanny from Sri Lanka, asks Isadora, her pudgy two-year-old charge in Athens, Greece.

Thoughtful for a moment, the child glances toward the closed door of the next room, in which her mother is working, as if to say, "That's my mother in there."

"No, you're *my* baby," Josephine teases, tickling Isadora lightly. Then, to settle the issue, Isadora answers, "Together!" She has two mommies—her mother and Josephine. And surely a child loved by many adults is richly blessed.

In some ways, Josephine's story—which unfolds in an extraordinary documentary film, *When Mother Comes Home for Christmas*, directed by Nilita Vachani—describes an unparalleled success. Josephine has ventured around the world, achieving a degree of independence her mother could not have imagined, and amply supporting her three children with no help from her ex-husband, their father. Each month she mails a remittance check from Athens to Hatton, Sri Lanka, to pay the children's living expenses and school fees. On her Christmas visit home, she bears gifts of pots, pans, and dishes. While she makes payments on a new bus that Suresh, her oldest son, now drives for a living, she is also saving for a modest dowry for her daughter, Norma. She dreams of buying a new house in which the whole family can live. In the meantime, her work as a nanny enables Isadora's parents to devote themselves to their careers and avocations.

But Josephine's story is also one of wrenching global inequality. While Isadora enjoys the attention of three adults, Josephine's three children in Sri Lanka have been far less lucky. According to Vachani, Josephine's youngest child, Suminda, was two—Isadora's age—when his mother first left home to work in Saudi Arabia. Her middle child, Norma, was nine; her oldest son, Suresh, thirteen. From Saudi Arabia, Josephine found her way first to Kuwait, then to Greece. Except for one two-month trip home, she has lived apart from her children for ten years. She writes them weekly letters, seeking news of relatives, asking about school, and complaining that Norma doesn't write back.

Although Josephine left the children under her sister's supervision, the two youngest have shown signs of real distress. Norma has attempted suicide three times. Suminda, who was twelve when the film was made, boards in a grim, Dickensian orphanage that forbids talk during meals and showers. He visits his aunt on holidays. Although the oldest, Suresh, seems to be on good terms with his mother, Norma is tearful and sullen, and Suminda does poorly in school, picks quarrels, and otherwise seems withdrawn from the world. Still, at the end of the film, we see Josephine once again leave her three children in Sri Lanka to return to Isadora in Athens. For Josephine can either live with her children in desperate poverty or make money by living apart from them. Unlike her affluent First World employers, she cannot both live with her family and support it.

Thanks to the process we loosely call "globalization," women are on the move as never before in history. In images familiar to the West from television commercials for credit cards, cell phones, and airlines, female executives jet about the world, phoning home from luxury hotels and reuniting with eager children in airports. But we hear much less about a far more prodigious flow of female labor and energy: the increasing migration of millions of women from poor countries to rich ones, where they serve as nannies, maids, and sometimes sex workers. In the absence of help from male partners, many women have succeeded in tough "male world" careers only by turning over the care of their children, elderly parents, and homes to women from the Third World. This is the female underside of globalization, whereby millions of Josephines from poor countries in the south migrate to do the "women's work" of the north—work that affluent women are no longer able or willing to do. These migrant workers often leave their own children in the care of grandmothers, sisters, and sisters-in-law. Sometimes a young daughter is drawn out of school to care for her younger siblings.

This pattern of female migration reflects what could be called a worldwide gender revolution. In both rich and poor countries, fewer families can rely solely on a male breadwinner. In the United States, the earning power of most men has declined since 1970, and many women have gone out to "make up the difference." By one recent estimate, women were the sole, primary, or coequal earners in more than half of American families. So the question arises: Who will take care of the children, the sick, the elderly? Who will make dinner and clean house?

While the European or American woman commutes to work an average twenty-eight minutes a day, many nannies from the Philippines, Sri Lanka, and India cross the globe to get to their jobs. Some female migrants from the Third World do find something like "liberation," or at least the chance to become independent breadwinners and to improve their children's material lives. Other, less fortunate migrant women end up in the control of criminal employers—their passports stolen, their mobility blocked, forced to work without pay in brothels or to provide sex along with cleaning and child-care services in affluent homes. But even in more typical cases, where benign employers pay wages on time, Third World migrant women achieve their success only by assuming the cast-off domestic roles of middle- and high-income women in the First World—roles that have been previously rejected, of course, by men. And their "commute" entails a cost we have yet to fully comprehend.

The migration of women from the Third World to do "women's work" in affluent countries has so far received little media attention—for reasons that are easy enough to guess. First, many, though by no means all, of the new female migrant workers are women of color, and therefore subject to the racial "discounting" routinely experienced by, say, Algerians in France, Mexicans in the United States, and Asians in the United Kingdom. Add to racism the private "indoor" nature of so much of the new migrants' work. Unlike factory workers, who congregate in large numbers, or taxi drivers, who are visible on the street, nannies and maids are often hidden away, one or two at a time, behind closed doors in private homes. Because of the illegal nature of their work, most sex workers are even further concealed from public view.

At least in the case of nannies and maids, another factor contributes to the invisibility of migrant women and their work—one that, for their affluent employers, touches closer to home. The Western culture of individualism, which finds extreme expression in the United States, militates against acknowledging help or human interdependency of nearly any kind. Thus, in the time-pressed upper middle class, servants are no longer displayed as status symbols, decked out in white caps and aprons, but often remain in the background, or disappear when company comes. Furthermore, affluent careerwomen increasingly earn their status not through leisure, as they might have a century ago, but by apparently "doing it all"—producing a full-time career, thriving children, a contented spouse, and a well-managed home. In order to preserve this illusion, domestic workers and nannies make the house hotel-room perfect, feed and bathe the children, cook and clean up—and then magically fade from sight.

The lifestyles of the First World are made possible by a global transfer of the services associated with a wife's traditional role—child care, home-making, and sex—from poor countries to rich ones. To generalize and perhaps oversimplify: in an earlier phase of imperialism, northern countries extracted natural resources and agricultural products—rubber, metals, and sugar, for example—from lands they conquered and colonized. Today, while still relying on Third World countries for agricultural and industrial labor, the wealthy countries also seek to extract something harder to measure and quantify, something that can look very much like love. Nannies like Josephine bring the distant families that employ them real maternal affection, no doubt enhanced by the heartbreaking absence of their own children in the poor countries they leave behind. Similarly, women who migrate from country to country to work as maids bring not only their muscle power but an attentiveness to detail and to the human relationships in the household that might otherwise have been invested in their own families. Sex workers offer the simulation of sexual and romantic love, or at least transient sexual companionship. It is as if the wealthy parts of the world are running short on precious emotional and sexual resources and have had to turn to poorer regions for fresh supplies.

There are plenty of historical precedents for this globalization of traditional female services. In the ancient Middle East, the women of populations defeated in war were routinely enslaved and hauled off to serve as household workers and concubines for the victors. Among the Africans brought to North America as slaves in the sixteenth through nineteenth centuries, about a third were women and children, and many of those women were pressed to be concubines, domestic servants, or both. Nineteenth-century Irishwomen—along with many rural Englishwomen—migrated to English towns and cities to work as domestics in the homes of the growing upper middle class. Services thought to be innately feminine—child care, housework, and sex—often win little recognition or pay. But they have always been sufficiently in demand to transport over long distances if necessary. What is new today is the sheer number of female migrants and the very long distances they travel. Immigration statistics show huge numbers of women in motion, typically from poor countries to rich. Although the gross statistics give little clue as to the jobs women eventually take, there are reasons to infer that much of their work is "caring work," performed either in private homes or in institutional settings such as hospitals, hospices, child-care centers, and nursing homes.

The statistics are, in many ways, frustrating. We have information on legal migrants but not on illegal migrants, who, experts tell us, travel in equal if not greater numbers. Furthermore, many Third World countries lack data for past years, which makes it hard to trace trends over time; or they use varying methods of gathering information, which makes it hard to compare one country with another. . . . From 1950 to 1970, for example, men predominated in labor migration to northern Europe from Turkey, Greece, and North Africa. Since then, women have been replacing men. In 1946, women were fewer than 3 percent of the Algerians and Moroccans living in France; by 1990, they were more than 40 percent. Overall, half of the world's 120 million legal and illegal migrants are now believed to be women.

Patterns of international migration vary from region to region, but women migrants from a surprising number of sending countries actually outnumber men, sometimes by a wide margin. For example, in the 1990s, women make up over half of Filipino migrants to all countries and 84 percent of Sri Lankan migrants to the Middle East. Indeed, by 1993 statistics, Sri Lankan women such as Josephine vastly outnumbered Sri Lankan men as migrant workers who'd left for Saudi Arabia, Kuwait, Lebanon, Oman, Bahrain, Jordan, and Qatar, as well as to all countries of the Far East, Africa, and Asia. About half of the migrants leaving Mexico, India, Korea, Malaysia, Cyprus, and Swaziland to work elsewhere are also women. Throughout the 1990s women outnumbered men among migrants to the United States, Canada, Sweden, the United Kingdom, Argentina, and Israel.

Most women, like men, migrate from the south to the north and from poor countries to rich ones. Typically, migrants go to the nearest comparatively rich country, preferably one whose language they speak or whose religion and culture they share. There are also local migratory flows: from northern to southern Thailand, for instance, or from East Germany to West. But of the regional or cross-regional flows, four stand out. One goes from Southeast Asia to the oil-rich Middle and Far East—from Bangladesh, Indonesia, the Philippines, and Sri Lanka to Bahrain, Oman, Kuwait, Saudi Arabia, Hong Kong, Malaysia, and Singapore. Another stream of migration goes from the former Soviet bloc to western Europe—from Russia, Romania, Bulgaria, and Albania to Scandinavia,

Germany, France, Spain, Portugal, and England. A third goes from south to north in the Americas, including the stream from Mexico to the United States, which scholars say is the longest-running labor migration in the world. A fourth stream moves from Africa to various parts of Europe. France receives many female migrants from Morocco, Tunisia, and Algeria. Italy receives female workers from Ethiopia, Eritrea, and Cape Verde.

Female migrants overwhelmingly take up work as maids or domestics. As women have become an ever greater proportion of migrant workers, receiving countries reflect a dramatic influx of foreign-born domestics. In the United States, African-American women, who accounted for 60 percent of domestics in the 1940s, have been largely replaced by Latinas, many of them recent migrants from Mexico and Central America. In England, Asian migrant women have displaced the Irish and Portuguese domestics of the past. In French cities, North African women have replaced rural French girls. In western Germany, Turks and women from the former East Germany have replaced rural native-born women. Foreign females from countries outside the European Union made up only 6 percent of all domestic workers in 1984. By 1987, the percentage had jumped to 52, with most coming from the Philippines, Sri Lanka, Thailand, Argentina, Colombia, Brazil, El Salvador, and Peru.

The governments of some sending countries actively encourage women to migrate in search of domestic jobs, reasoning that migrant women are more likely than their male counterparts to send their hard-earned wages to their families rather than spending the money on themselves. In general, women send home anywhere from half to nearly all of what they earn. These remittances have a significant impact on the lives of children, parents, siblings, and wider networks of kin—as well as on cash-strapped Third World governments. Thus, before Josephine left for Athens, a program sponsored by the Sri Lankan government taught her how to use a microwave oven, a vacuum cleaner, and an electric mixer. As she awaited her flight, a song piped into the airport departure lounge extolled the opportunity to earn money abroad. The songwriter was in the pay of the Sri Lanka Bureau of Foreign Employment, an office devised to encourage women to migrate. The lyrics say:

> *After much hardship, such difficult times*
> *How lucky I am to work in a foreign land.*
> *As the gold gathers so do many greedy flies.*
> *But our good government protects us from them.*
> *After much hardship, such difficult times,*
> *How lucky I am to work in a foreign land.*
> *I promise to return home with treasures for everyone.*

Why this transfer of women's traditional services from poor to rich parts of the world? The reasons are, in a crude way, easy to guess. Women in Western countries have increasingly taken on paid work, and hence need other—paid domestics and caretakers for children and elderly people—to replace them. For their part, women in poor countries have an obvious incentive to migrate: relative and absolute poverty. The "care deficit" that has emerged in the wealthier countries as women enter the workforce *pulls* migrants from the Third World and postcommunist nations; poverty *pushes* them.

In broad outline, this explanation holds true. Throughout western Europe, Taiwan, and Japan, but above all in the United States, England, and Sweden, women's employment has increased dramatically since the 1970s. In the United States, for example, the proportion of women in paid work rose from 15 percent of mothers of children six and under in 1950 to 65 percent today. Women now make up 46 percent of the U.S. labor force. Three-quarters of mothers of children eighteen and under and nearly two-thirds of mothers of children age one and younger now work for pay. Furthermore, according to a recent International Labor Organization study, working Americans averaged longer hours at work in the late 1990s than they did in the 1970s. By some measures, the number of hours spent at work have increased more for women than for men, and especially for women in managerial and professional jobs.

Meanwhile, over the last thirty years, as the rich countries have grown much richer, the poor countries have become—in both absolute and relative terms—poorer. Global inequalities in wages are particularly striking. In Hong Kong, for instance, the wages of a Filipina domestic are about fifteen times the amount she could make as a schoolteacher back in the Philippines. In addition, poor countries turning to the IMF or World Bank for loans are often forced to undertake measures of so-called structural adjustment, with disastrous results for the poor and especially for poor women and children. To qualify for loans, governments are usually required to devalue their currencies, which turns the hard currencies of rich countries into gold and the soft currencies of poor countries into straw. Structural adjustment programs also call for cuts in support for "noncompetitive industries," and for the reduction of public services such as health care and food subsidies for the poor. Citizens of poor countries, women as well as men, thus have a strong incentive to seek work in more fortunate parts of the world.

But it would be a mistake to attribute the globalization of women's work to a simple synergy of needs among women—one group, in the affluent countries, needing help and the other, in poor countries, needing jobs. For one thing, this formulation fails to account for the marked failure of First World governments to meet the needs created by its women's entry into the work-force. The downsized American—and to a lesser degree, western European—welfare state has become a "deadbeat dad." Unlike the rest of the industrialized world, the United States does not offer public child care for working mothers, nor does it ensure paid family and medical leave. Moreover, a series of state tax revolts in the 1980s reduced the number of hours public libraries were open and slashed school-enrichment and after-school programs. Europe did not experience anything comparable. Still, tens of millions of western European women are in the workforce who were not before—and there has been no proportionate expansion in public services.

Secondly, any view of the globalization of domestic work as simply an arrangement among women completely omits the role of men. Numerous studies, including some of our own, have shown that as American women took on paid employment, the men in their families did little to increase their contribution to the work of the home. For example, only one out of every five men among the working couples whom Hochschild interviewed for *The Second Shift* in the 1980s shared the work at home, and later studies suggest that while working mothers are doing somewhat less housework than their counterparts twenty years ago, most men are doing only a little more. With divorce, men frequently abdicate their child-care responsibilities to their ex-wives. In most cultures of the First World outside the United States, powerful traditions even more firmly discourage husbands from doing "women's work." So, strictly speaking, the presence of immigrant nannies does not enable affluent women to enter the workforce; it enables affluent *men* to continue avoiding the second shift.

The men in wealthier countries are also, of course, directly responsible for the demand for immigrant sex workers—as well as for the sexual abuse of many migrant women who work as domestics. Why, we wondered, is there a particular demand for "imported" sexual partners? Part of the answer may lie in the fact that new immigrants often take up the least desirable work, and, thanks to the AIDS epidemic, prostitution has become a job that ever fewer women deliberately choose. But perhaps some of this demand . . . grows out of the erotic lure of the "exotic." Immigrant women may seem desirable sexual partners for the same reason that First World employers believe them to be especially gifted as caregivers: they are thought to embody the traditional feminine qualities of nurturance, docility, and eagerness to please. Some men feel nostalgic for these qualities, which they associate with a bygone way of life. Even as many wage-earning Western women assimilate to the competitive culture of "male" work and ask respect for making it in a man's world, some men seek in the "exotic Orient" or "hot-blooded tropics" a woman from the imagined past.

Of course, not all sex workers migrate voluntarily. An alarming number of women and girls are trafficked by smugglers and sold into bondage. Because trafficking is illegal and secret, the numbers are hard to know with any certainty. Kevin Bales estimates that in Thailand alone, a country of 60 million, half a million to a million women are prostitutes, and one out of every twenty of these is enslaved. . . . Many of these women are daughters whom northern hill-tribe families have sold to brothels in the cities of the south. Believing the promises of jobs and money, some begin the voyage willingly, only to discover days later that the "arrangers" are traffickers who steal their passports, define them as debtors, and enslave them as prostitutes. Other women and girls are kidnapped, or sold by their impoverished families, and then trafficked to brothels. Even worse fates befall women from neighboring Laos and Burma, who flee crushing poverty and repression at home only to fall into the hands of Thai slave traders.

If the factors that pull migrant women workers to affluent countries are not as simple as they at first appear, neither are the factors that push them. Certainly relative poverty plays a major role, but, interestingly, migrant women often do not come from the poorest classes of their societies. In fact, they are typically more affluent and better educated than male migrants. Many female migrants from the Philippines and Mexico, for example, have high school or college diplomas and have held middle-class—albeit low-paid—jobs back home. One study of Mexican migrants suggests that the trend is toward increasingly better-educated female migrants. Thirty years ago, most Mexican-born maids in the United States had been poorly educated maids in Mexico. Now a majority have high school degrees and have held clerical, retail, or professional jobs before leaving for the United States. Such women are likely to be enterprising and adventurous enough to resist the social pressures to stay home and accept their lot in life.

Noneconomic factors—or at least factors that are not immediately and directly economic—also influence a woman's decision to emigrate. By migrating, a woman may escape the expectation that she care for elderly family members, relinquish her paycheck to a husband or father, or defer to an abusive husband. Migration may also be a practical response to a failed marriage and the need to provide for children without male help. In the Philippines, . . . Rhacel Salazar Parrenas tells us, migration is sometimes called a "Philippine divorce." And there are forces at work that may be making the men of poor countries less desirable as husbands. Male unemployment runs high in the countries that supply female domestics to the First World. Unable to make a living, these men often grow demoralized and cease contributing to their families in other ways. Many female migrants tell of unemployed husbands who drink or gamble their remittances away. Notes one study of Sri Lankan women working as maids in the Persian Gulf: "It is not unusual . . . for the women to find upon their return that their Gulf wages by and large have been squandered on alcohol, gambling and other dubious undertakings while they were away."

To an extent then, the globalization of child care and housework brings the ambitious and independent women of the world together: the career-oriented upper-middle-class woman of an affluent nation and the striving woman from a crumbling Third World or postcommunist economy. Only it does not bring them together in the way that second-wave feminists in affluent countries once liked to imagine—as sisters and allies struggling to achieve common goals. Instead, they come together as mistress and maid, employer and employee, across a great divide of privilege and opportunity.

This trend toward global redivision of women's traditional work throws new light on the entire process of globalization. Conventionally, it is the poorer countries that are thought to be dependent on the richer ones—a dependency symbolized by the huge debt they owe to global financial institutions. What we explore in this book, however, is a dependency that works in the other direction, and it is a dependency of a particularly intimate kind. Increasingly often, as affluent and middle-class families in the First World come to depend on migrants from poorer regions to provide child care, homemaking, and sexual services, a global relationship arises that in some ways mirrors the traditional relationship between the sexes. The First World takes on a role like that of the old-fashioned male in the family—pampered, entitled, unable to cook, clean, or find his socks. Poor countries take on a role like that of the traditional woman within the family—patient, nurturing, and self-denying. A division of labor feminists critiqued when it was "local" has now, metaphorically speaking, gone global.

To press this metaphor a bit further, the resulting relationship is by no means a "marriage," in the sense of being openly acknowledged. In fact, it is striking how invisible the globalization of women's work remains, how little it is noted or discussed in the First World. Trend spotters have had almost nothing to say about the fact that increasing numbers of affluent First World children and elderly persons are tended by immigrant care workers or live in homes cleaned by immigrant maids. Even the political groups we might expect to be concerned about this trend—antiglobalization and feminist activists—often seem to have noticed only the most extravagant abuses, such as trafficking and female enslavement. So if a metaphorically gendered relationship has developed between rich and poor countries, it is less like a marriage and more like a secret affair.

But it is a "secret affair" conducted in plain view of the children. Little Isadora and the other children of the First World raised by "two mommies" may be learning more than their ABC's from a loving surrogate parent. In their own living rooms, they are learning a vast and tragic global politics. Children see. But they also learn how to disregard what they see. They learn how adults make the visible invisible. That is their "early childhood education." . . .

The globalization of women's traditional role poses important challenges to anyone concerned about gender and economic inequity. How can we improve the lives and opportunities of migrant women engaged in legal occupations such as nannies and maids? How can we prevent trafficking and enslavement? More basically, can we find a way to counterbalance the systematic transfer of caring work from poor countries to rich, and the inevitable trauma of the children left behind? . . .

Review Questions

1. What kind of work do most female immigrants do when they move from poorer to richer countries?

2. What are the advantages of working in another country for women immigrants?

3. What are the negative aspects of the work in which female immigrants engage?

4. What are the four main "flows" of immigrants from poorer to richer countries?

5. What do the female immigrants and the women in wealthier societies have in common economically?

6. The authors argue that immigration has actually made rich countries dependent on poor countries. On what do they base their assertion?

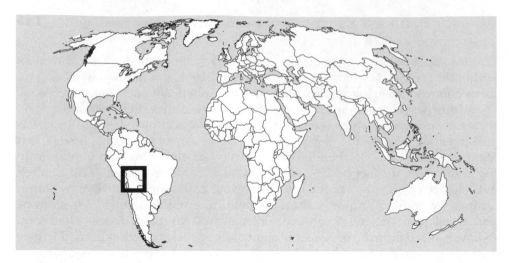

16

Cocaine and the Economic Deterioration of Bolivia

Jack Weatherford

The demands of the world market have eroded local subsistence economies for centuries. Lands once farmed by individual families to meet their own needs now grow sugarcane, cotton, grain, or vegetables for market. Deprived of their access to land, householders must work as day laborers or migrate to cities to find jobs. Villages are denuded of the men, who have gone elsewhere for work, leaving women to farm and manage the family. The rhythm and structure of daily village life are altered dramatically. In

This article was written especially for *Conformity and Conflict,* Copyright © 1986 by Jack Weatherford. Reprinted by permission.

this article, Jack Weatherford describes the impact of a new world market for cocaine on the structure and lives of rural Bolivians. Fed by an insatiable demand in Europe and the United States, the Bolivian cocaine trade has drawn males from the countryside, disrupted communications, destroyed families, unbalanced the local diet, and upset traditional social organization.

"They say you Americans can do anything. So, why can't you make your own cocaine and let our children come home from the coca plantations in the Chapare?" The Indian woman asked the question with confused resignation. In the silence that followed, I could hear only the rats scurrying around in the thatched roof. We continued shelling corn in the dark. The large house around us had once been home to an extended clan but was now nearly empty.

There was no answer to give her. Yet it was becoming increasingly obvious that the traditional Andean system of production and distribution built over thousands of years was now crumbling. Accompanying the destruction of the economic system was a marked distortion of the social and cultural patterns of the Quechua Indians. Since early in Inca history, the village of Pocona where I was working had been a trading village connecting the highlands, which produced potatoes, with the lowlands, which produced coca, a mildly narcotic plant used by the Incas. Over the past decade, however, new market demands from Europe and the United States have warped this system. Now the commodity is cocaine rather than the coca leaves, and the trade route bypasses the village of Pocona.

Bolivian subsistence patterns range from hunting and gathering in the jungle to intensive farming in the highlands, and since Inca times many parts of the country have depended heavily on mining. In the 1980s all of these patterns have been disrupted by the Western fad for one particular drug. Adoption of cocaine as the "drug of choice" by the urban elite of Europe and America has opened up new jungle lands and brought new Indian groups into Western economic systems. At the same time, the cocaine trade has cut off many communities such as Pocona from their traditional role in the national economy. Denied participation in the legal economy, they have been driven back into a world of barter and renewed isolation.

The vagaries of Western consumerism produce extensive and profound effects on Third World countries. It makes little difference whether the demand is for legitimate products such as coffee, tungsten, rubber, and furs marketed through legal corporations, or for illegal commodities such as opium, marijuana, cocaine, and heroin handled through criminal corporations. The same economic principles that govern the open, legal market also govern the clandestine, illegal markets, and the effects of both are frequently brutal.

Before coming to this Bolivian village, I assumed that if Americans and Europeans wanted to waste their money on cocaine, it was probably good that some of the poor countries such as Bolivia profit from it. In Cochabamba, the city in the heart of the cocaine-producing area, I had seen the benefits of this trade among the *narco chic* who lived in a new suburb of houses styled to look like Swiss chalets, Spanish haciendas, and English country homes. All these homes were surrounded by large wrought-iron fences, walls with broken glass set in the tops, and with large dogs that barked loudly and frequently. Such homes cost up to a hundred thousand dollars, an astronomical sum for Bolivia. I had also seen the narco elite of Cochabamba wearing gold chains and the latest Miami fashions and driving Nissans, Audis, Ford Broncos, an occasional BMW, or even a Mercedes through the muddy streets of the city. Some of their children attended the expensive English-speaking school; much of Cochabamba's meager nightlife catered to the elite. But as affluent as they may be in Bolivia, this elite would probably not earn as much as working-class families in such cities as Detroit, Frankfurt, or Tokyo.

Traveling outside of Cochabamba for six hours on the back of a truck, fording the same river three times, and following a rugged path for the last twenty-five kilometers, I reached Pocona and saw a different face of the cocaine trade. Located in a valley a mile and a half above sea level, Pocona is much too high to grow the coca bush. Coca grows best below six thousand feet, in the lush area called the Chapare where the eastern Andes meet the western edge of the Amazon basin and rain forest.

Like the woman with whom I was shelling corn, most of the people of Pocona are older, and community life is dominated by women together with their children who are still too young to leave. This particular woman had already lost both of her sons to the Chapare. She did not know it at the time, but within a few months, she was to lose her husband to the same work as well. With so few men, the women are left alone to plant, work, and harvest the fields of potatoes, corn, and fava beans, but with most of the work force missing, the productivity of Pocona has declined substantially.

In what was once a moderately fertile valley, hunger is now a part of life. The daily diet consists almost exclusively of bread, potato soup, boiled potatoes, corn, and tea. The majority of their daily calories comes from the potatoes and from the sugar that they put in their tea. They have virtually no meat or dairy products and very few fresh vegetables. These products are now sent to the Chapare to feed the workers in the coca fields, and the people of Pocona cannot compete against them. The crops that the people of Pocona produce are now difficult to sell because truck drivers find it much more profitable to take goods in and out of the Chapare rather than face the long and unprofitable trip to reach such remote villages as Pocona.

Despite all the hardships caused by so many people being away from the village, one might assume that more cash should be flowing into Pocona from the Chapare, where young men easily earn three dollars a day—three times the average daily wage of porters or laborers in Cochabamba. But this assumption was contradicted by the evidence of Pocona. As one widowed Indian mother of four explained, the first time her sixteen-year-old son came home, he brought bags of food, presents, and money for her and the younger children. She was very glad that he was working in the Chapare. On the second visit home he brought only a plastic bag of white powder for himself, and instead of bringing food, he took away as much as he could carry on the two-day trip back into the Chapare.

The third time, he told his mother that he could not find enough work in the Chapare. As a way to earn more money he made his mother bake as much bread as she could, and he took Mariana, his ten-year-old sister, with him to sell the bread to the workers in the Chapare. According to the mother, he beat the little girl and abused her repeatedly. Moreover, the money she made disappeared. On one of Mariana's trips home to get more bread, the mother had no more wheat or corn flour to supply her son. So, she sent Mariana away to Cochabamba to work as a maid. The enraged son found where Mariana was working and went to the home to demand that she be returned to him. When the family refused, he tried but failed to have her wages paid to him rather than to his mother. Mariana was separated from her family and community, but at least she was not going to be one more of the prostitutes in the Chapare, and for her mother that was more important.

The standard of living in Pocona was never very high, but with the advent of the cocaine boom in Bolivia, the standard has declined. Ten years ago, Pocona's gasoline-powered generator furnished the homes with a few hours of electric light each night. The electricity also allowed a few families to purchase radios, and occasionally someone brought in a movie projector to show a film in a large adobe building on the main square. For the past two years, the people of Pocona have not been able to buy gasoline for their generator. This has left the village not only without electricity but without entertainment and radio or film contact with the outside world. A few boys have bought portable radios with their earnings from the Chapare, but their families were unable to replace the batteries. Nights in Pocona are now both dark and silent.

In recent years the national economy of Bolivia has been virtually destroyed, and peasants in communities such as Pocona are reverting to barter as the only means of exchange. The value of the peso may rise or fall by as much as 30 percent in a day; the peasants cannot take a chance on trading their crops for money that may be worth nothing in a week. Cocaine alone has not been responsible for the destruction of the Bolivian economy, but it has been a major contributor. It is not mere coincidence that the world's largest producer of coca is also the country with the world's worst inflation.

During part of 1986, inflation in Bolivia varied at a rate between 2,000 and 13,000 percent, if calculated on a yearly basis. Prices in the cities changed by the hour, and on some days the dollar would rise at the rate of more than 1 percent per hour. A piece of bread cost 150,000 pesos, and an American dollar bought between two and three million pesos on the black market. Large items such as airplane tickets were calculated in the billions of pesos, and on one occasion I helped a man carry a large box of money to pay for such a ticket. It took two professional counters half an hour to count the bills. Workers were paid in stacks of bills that were often half a meter high. Because Bolivia is too undeveloped to print its money, the importation of its own bills printed in West Germany and Brazil was one of the leading imports in the mid-1980s.

Ironically, by no longer being able to participate fully in the money economy, the villagers of Pocona who have chewed coca leaves for centuries now find it difficult to afford the leaves. The narcotics industry pays such a high price that the people of Pocona can afford only the rejected trash from the cocaine industry. Whether chewed or made into a tea, the coca produces a mild lift somewhat like a cup of coffee but without the jagged comedown that follows a coffee high. Coca also reduces hunger, thirst, headaches, stomach pains, and the type of altitude sickness known as *sorroche*.

Were this all, coca use might be viewed as merely a bad habit somewhat like drinking coffee, smoking cigarettes, or overindulging in chocolates, but unlike these practices coca actually has a number of marked health benefits. The coca leaf is very high in calcium. In a population with widespread lactose intolerance and in a country without a national system of milk distribution, this calcium source is very important. The calcium also severely reduces cavities in a population with virtually no dental services outside the city. Coca also contains large amounts of vitamins A, C, and D, which are often lacking in the starchy diets of the mountain peasants.

Without coca, and with an excess of corn that they cannot get to market, the people of Pocona now make more *chicha*, a form of home-fermented corn beer that tastes somewhat like the silage that American dairymen feed their cows. It is ironic that as an affluent generation of Americans are decreasing their consumption of alcohol in favor of drugs such as cocaine, the people of Pocona are drinking more alcohol to replace their traditional coca. *Chicha*, like most beers, is more nutritious than other kinds of distilled spirits but lacks the health benefits of the coca leaves. It also produces intoxication, something that no amount of coca leaves can do. Coca chewing is such a slow process and produces such a mild effect that a user would have to chew a bushel of leaves to equal the impact of one mixed drink or one snort of cocaine.

In many ways, the problems and complaints of Pocona echo those of any Third World country with a cash crop, particularly those caught in the boom-and-bust cycle characteristic of capitalist systems. Whether it is the sisal boom of the Yucatán, the banana boom of Central America, the rubber boom of Brazil, or the cocaine boom in Bolivia, the same pattern develops. Rural villages are depleted of their work forces. Family and traditional cultural patterns disintegrate. And the people are no longer able to afford certain local products that suddenly become valued in the West. This is what happened to Pocona.

Frequently, the part of a country that produces the boom crop benefits greatly, while other areas suffer greatly. If this were true in Bolivia, benefits accruing in the coca-producing area of the Chapare would outweigh the adjustment problems of such villages as Pocona. As it turns out, however, the Chapare has been even more adversely affected.

Most of the young men who go to the Chapare do not actually work in the coca fields. The coca bush originated in this area and does not require extensive care. One hectare can easily produce eight hundred kilograms of coca leaves in a year, but not much labor is needed to pick them. After harvesting, the leaves are dried in the sun for three to four days. Most of these tasks can easily be done by the farmer and his family. Wherever one goes in the Chapare one sees coca leaves spread out on large drying cloths. Old people or young children walk up and down these cloths, turning the drying leaves with their whisk brooms.

The need for labor, especially the labor of strong young men, comes in the first stage of cocaine production, in the reduction of large piles of leaves into a small quantity of *pasta,* or coca paste from which the active ingredient, cocaine, can then be refined. Three hundred to five hundred kilograms of leaves must be used to make one kilogram of pure cocaine. The leaves are made into *pasta* by soaking them in vats of kerosene and by applying salt, acetone, and sulfuric acid. To make the chemical reaction occur, someone must trample on the leaves for several days—a process very much like tromping on grapes to make wine, only longer. Because the corrosive mixture dissolves shoes or boots, the young men walk barefooted. These men are called *pisacocas* and usually work in the cool of the night, pounding the green slime with their feet. Each night the chemicals eat away more skin and very quickly open ulcers erupt. Some young men in the Chapare now have feet that are so diseased that they are incapable of standing, much less walking. So, instead, they use their hands to mix the *pasta,* but their hands are eaten away even faster than their feet. Thousands and possibly tens of thousands of young Bolivian men now look like lepers with permanently disfigured hands and feet. It is unlikely that any could return to Pocona and make a decent farmer.

Because this work is painful, the *pisacocas* smoke addictive cigarettes coated with *pasta.* This alleviates their pain and allows them to continue walking the coca throughout the night. The *pasta* is contaminated with chemical residues, and smoking it warps their minds as quickly as the acids eat their hands and feet. Like Mariana's brother, the users become irrational, easily angered, and frequently violent.

Once the boys are no longer able to mix coca because of their mental or their physical condition, they usually become unemployed. If their wounds heal, they may be able to work as loaders or haulers, carrying the cocaine or transporting the controlled chemicals used to process it. By and large, however, women and very small children, called *hormigas* (ants), are better at this work. Some of the young men then return home to their villages; others wander to Cochabamba, where they might live on the streets or try to earn money buying and selling dollars on the black market.

The cocaine manufacturers not only supply their workers with food and drugs, they keep them sexually supplied with young girls who serve as prostitutes as well. Bolivian health officials estimate that nearly half of the people living in the Chapare today have venereal disease. As the boys and girls working there return to their villages, they take these diseases with them. Increasing numbers of children born to infected mothers now have bodies covered in syphilitic sores. In 1985, a worse disease hit with the first case of AIDS. Soon after the victim died, a second victim was diagnosed.

In an effort to control its own drug problem, the United States is putting pressure on Bolivia to eradicate coca production in the Andean countries. The army invaded the Chapare during January of 1986, but after nearly three weeks of being surrounded by the workers in the narcotics industry and cut off from their supply bases, the army surrendered. In a nation the size of Texas and California combined, but with a population approximately the size of the city of Chicago, it is difficult for the government to control its own territory. Neither the Incas nor the Spanish conquistadores were ever able to conquer and administer the jungles of Bolivia, where there are still nomadic bands of Indians who have retreated deep into the jungle to escape Western encroachment. The army of the poorest government in South America is no better able to control this country than its predecessors. The government runs the cities, but the countryside and the jungles operate under their own laws.

One of the most significant effects of the coca trade and of the campaigns to eradicate it has come on the most remote Indians of the jungle area. As the campaign against drugs has pushed production into more inaccessible places and as the world demand has promoted greater cultivation of coca, the coca growers are moving into previously unexplored areas. A coca plantation has been opened along the Chimore river less than an hour's walk from one of the few surviving bands of Yuqui Indians. The Yuquis, famous for their eight-foot-long bows and their six-foot arrows, are now hovering on the brink of extinction. In the past year, the three bands of a few hundred Yuquis have lost eleven members in skirmishes with outsiders. In turn, they killed several outsiders this year and even shot the missionary who is their main champion against outside invaders.

According to the reports of missionaries, other Indian bands have been enlisted as workers in cocaine production and trafficking, making virtual slaves out of them. A Bolivian medical doctor explained to me that the Indians are fed the cocaine in their food as a way of keeping them working and preventing their escape. Through cocaine, the drug traffickers may be able to conquer and control these last remnants of the great Indian nations of the Americas. If so, they will accomplish what many have failed to do in the five-hundred-year campaign of Europeans to conquer the free Indians.

The fate of the Indians driven out of their homelands is shown in the case of Juan, a thirteen-year-old Indian boy from the Chimore river where the Yuquis live. I found him one night in a soup kitchen for street children operated in the corner of a potato warehouse by the Maryknoll priests. Juan wore a bright orange undershirt that proclaimed in bold letters Fairfax District Public Schools. I sat with him at the table coated in potato dust while he ate his soup with his fellow street children, some of whom were as young as four years old.

He told me what he could remember of his life on the Chimore; he did not know to which tribe he was born or what language he had spoken with his mother. It was difficult for Juan to talk about his Indian past in a country where it is a grave insult to be called an Indian. Rather than talk about the Chimore or the Chapare, he wanted to ask me questions because I was the first American he had ever met. Was I stronger than everyone else, because he had heard that Americans were the strongest people in the world? Did we really have wolves and bears in North America, and was I afraid of them? Had I been to the Chapare? Did I use cocaine?

In between his questions, I found out that Juan had come to Cochabamba several years ago with his mother. The two had fled the Chapare, but he did not know why. Once in the city they lived on the streets for a few years until his mother died, and he had been living alone ever since. He had become a *polilla* (moth), as they call such street boys. To earn money he washed cars and sold cigarettes laced with *pasta*. When he tired of talking about himself and asking about the animals of North America, he and his two friends made plans to go out to one of the nearby *pasta* villages the next day.

Both the Chapare (which supplied the land for growing coca) and highland villages such as Pocona (which supplied the labor) were suffering from the cocaine boom. Where, then, is the profit? The only other sites in Bolivia are the newly developed manufacturing towns where cocaine is refined. Whereas in the past most of this refining took place in Colombia, both the manufacturers and the traffickers find it easier and cheaper to have the work done in Bolivia, closer to the source of coca leaves and closer to much cheaper sources of labor. The strength of the Colombian government and its closeness to the United States also make the drug trafficking more difficult there than in Bolivia, with its weak, unstable government in La Paz.

Toco is one of the villages that has turned into a processing point for cocaine. Located at about the same altitude as Pocona but only a half-day by truck from the Chapare, Toco cannot grow coca, but the village is close enough to the source to become a major producer of the *pasta*. Traffickers bring in the large shipments of coca leaves and work them in backyard "kitchens." Not only does Toco still have its young men at home and still have food and electricity, but it has work for a few hundred young men from other villages.

Unlike Pocona, for which there are only a few trucks each week, trucks flow in and out of Toco every day. Emblazoned with names such as Rambo, El Padrino (The Godfather), and Charles Bronson rather than the traditional truck names of San José, Virgen de Copacabana, or Flor de Urkupina, these are the newest and finest trucks found in Bolivia. Going in with a Bolivian physician and another anthropologist from the United States, I easily got a ride, along with a dozen Indians, on a truck which was hauling old car batteries splattered with what appeared to be vomit.

A few kilometers outside of Toco we were stopped by a large crowd of Indian peasants. Several dozen women sat around on the ground and in the road spinning yarn and knitting. Most of the women had babies tied to their shoulders in the brightly colored *awayu* cloth, which the women use to carry everything from potatoes to lambs. Men stood around with farm tools, which they now used to block the roads. The men brandished their machetes and rakes at us, accusing us all of being smugglers and *pisacocas*. Like the Indians on the truck with us, the three of us stood silent and expressionless in the melee.

The hostile peasants were staging an ad hoc strike against the coca trade. They had just had their own fields of potatoes washed away in a flash flood. Now without food and without money to replant, they were demanding that someone help them or they would disrupt all traffic to and from Toco. Shouting at us, several of them climbed on board the truck. Moving among the nervous passengers, they checked for a shipment of coca leaves, kerosene, acid, or anything else that might be a part of the coca trade. Having found nothing, they reluctantly let us pass with stern warnings not to return with cocaine or *pasta*. A few weeks after our encounter with the strikers, their strike ended and most of the men went off to look for work in the Chapare and in Toco; without a crop, the cocaine traffic was their only hope of food for the year.

On our arrival in Toco we found out that the batteries loaded with us in the back of the truck had been hollowed out and filled with acid to be used in making *pasta*. *Chicha* vomit had been smeared around to discourage anyone from checking them. After removal of the acid, the same batteries were then filled with plastic bags of cocaine to be smuggled out of Toco and into the town of Cliza and on to Cochabamba and the outside world.

Toco is an expanding village with new cement-block buildings going up on the edge of town and a variety of large plumbing pipes, tanks, and drains being installed. It also has a large number of motorcycles and cars. By Bolivian standards it is a rich village, but it is still poorer than the average village in Mexico or Brazil. Soon after our arrival in Toco, we were followed by a handful of men wanting to sell us *pasta*, and within a few minutes the few had grown to nearly fifty young men anxious to assist us. Most of them were on foot, but some of them circled us in motorcycles, and many of them were armed with guns and machetes. They became suspicious and then openly hostile when we convinced them that we did not want to buy *pasta*. To escape them we took refuge in the home of an Indian family and waited for the mob to disperse.

When we tried to leave the village a few hours later, we were trapped by a truckload of young men who did not release us until they had checked with everyone we had met with in the village. They wondered why we were there if not to buy *pasta*. We were rescued by the doctor who accompanied us; she happened to be the niece of a popular Quechua writer. Evoking the memory of her uncle who had done so much for the Quechua people, she convinced the villagers of Toco that we were Bolivian doctors who worked with her in Cochabamba, and that we were not foreigners coming to buy *pasta* or to spy on them. An old veteran who claimed that he had served in the Chaco War with her uncle vouched for us, but in return for having saved us he then wanted us to buy *pasta* from him.

The wealth generated by the coca trade from Bolivia is easy to see. It is in the European cars cruising the streets of Cochabamba and Santa Cruz, and in the nice houses in the suburbs. It is in the motorcycles and jeeps in Toco, Cliza, and Trinidad. The poverty is difficult to see because it is in the remote villages like Pocona, among the impoverished miners in the village of Porco, and intertwined in the lives of peasants throughout the highland districts of Potosí and Oruro. But it is in communities such as Pocona that 70 percent of the population of Bolivia lives. For every modern home built with cocaine money in Cochabamba, a tin mine lies abandoned in Potosí that lost many of its miners when the world price for tin fell and they had to go to the Chapare for food. For every new car in Santa Cruz or every new motorcycle in Toco, a whole village is going hungry in the mountains.

The money for coca does not go to the Bolivians. It goes to the criminal organizations that smuggle the drugs out of the country and into the United States and Europe. A gram of pure cocaine on the streets of Cochabamba costs five dollars; the same gram on the streets of New York, Paris, or Berlin costs over a hundred dollars. The price increase occurs outside Bolivia.

The financial differential is evident in the case of the American housewife and mother sentenced to the Cochabamba prison after being caught with six and a half kilograms of cocaine at the airport. Like all the other women in the prison, she now earns money washing laundry by hand at a cold-water tap in the middle of the prison yard. She receives the equivalent of twenty cents for each pair of pants she washes, dries, and irons. In Bolivian prisons, the prisoner has to furnish his or her own food, clothes, medical attention, and even furniture.

She was paid five thousand dollars to smuggle the cocaine out of Bolivia to the Caribbean. Presumably someone else was then to be paid even more to smuggle it into the United States or Europe. The money that the American housewife received to smuggle the cocaine out of the country would pay the salary of eighty *pisacocas* for a month. It would also pay the monthly wages of two hundred fifty Bolivian schoolteachers, who earn the equivalent of twenty U.S. dollars per month in pay. Even though her price seemed high by Bolivian standards, it is a small part of the final money generated by the drugs. When cut and sold on the streets of the United States, her shipment of cocaine would probably bring in five to seven million dollars. Of that amount, however, only about five hundred dollars goes to the Bolivian farmer.

The peasant in the Chapare growing the coca earns three times as much for a field of coca as he would for a field of papayas. But he is only the first in a long line of people and transactions that brings the final product of cocaine to the streets of the West. At the end of the line, cocaine sells for four to five times its weight in gold.

The United States government made all aid programs and loans to Bolivia dependent on the country's efforts to destroy coca. This produces programs in which Bolivian troops go into the most accessible areas and uproot a few fields of aging or diseased coca plants. Visiting drug-enforcement agents from the United States together with American congressmen applaud, make their reports on the escalating war against drugs, and then retire to a city hotel where they drink hot cups of coca tea and cocktails.

These programs hurt primarily the poor farmer who tries to make a slightly better living by growing coca rather than papayas. The raids on the fields and cocaine factories usually lead to the imprisonment of ulcerated *pisococas* and women and children *hormigas* from villages throughout Bolivia. Local authorities present the burned fields and full prisons to Washington visitors as proof that the Bolivian government has taken a hard stance against drug trafficking.

International crime figures with bank accounts in New York and Zurich get the money. Bolivia ends up with hunger in its villages, young men with their hands and feet permanently maimed, higher rates of venereal disease, chronic food shortages, less kerosene, higher school dropout rates, increased drug addiction, and a worthless peso.

Review Questions

1. List and describe the major effects of the cocaine trade on rural Bolivian life.

2. Why have the production of coca and the manufacture of cocaine created a health hazard in Bolivia?

3. Why has the cocaine trade benefited the Bolivian economy so little?

4. How has the cocaine trade disrupted village social organization in Bolivia?

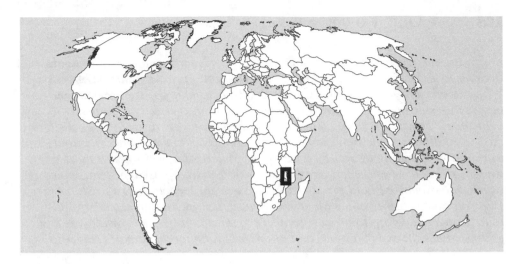

17

Malawi Versus the World Bank

Sonia Patten

Market economics rules in most industrialized countries, especially since the decline of communism. In market systems, goods are produced for sale, prices affect demand and vice-versa, and demand drives production. Underlying the system is the profit motive to get the greatest gain for the least cost. The market not only applies to manufacturing and providing services in industrialized societies but also governs agriculture although most governments interfere with it to some extent in that economic sphere. It is no wonder that most economists from industrialized nations believe that the free market system is the key to development in nonindustrialized societies, and this has led institutions such as the World Bank and the International Monetary Fund (IMF) to drop social and agricultural support programs in favor of market-based development as a requirement of receiving loans.

There is a problem, however, at least initially, with the market-based approach to development especially as it applies to agriculture. In many nonindustrialized societies, a majority of the people farm small plots of land in order to feed their families and meet social obligations to kin and neighbors. When floods, draught, exhausted soils, and other factors reduce yields and people face starvation, only government aid, not market-based programs, can help them. That is the point Sonia Patten makes in this article as she discusses conditions in the small south African country of Malawi. She notes that international lending agencies required the Malawian government to cease underwriting the cost of fertilizer in favor of a market-based system. As a result, the exhausted land produced less maize and people began to starve. Eventually, the government of Malawi overruled their international lenders and reinstituted a program to provide fertilizer to farm families. The result was a grain surplus, the end of famine, and improved health for the nation's citizens.

This article is about the impact a group of economic organizations called the "Washington Consensus" has on rural families living in the small southern African nation of Malawi. The "Washington Consensus," which is located in Washington, D.C., as the name implies, and its associated economists and policymakers created a situation in Malawi that forced rural farmers there to trade a day's labor for a day's food, dismantle their homes to sell timbers and roofing for cash so they could purchase food, beg for food, or go hungry. One can challenge statements about the causal relationships between macro-level and micro-level socioeconomic decisions and events, but in this instance the connections seem clear. A review of "Washington Consensus" policy and the information provided by women in ten rural Malawi households over a period of eighteen months helps us understand just how individuals and families struggle to survive when macro-level economic policies have an adverse impact on them.

The "Washington Consensus" refers to a set of economic prescriptions derived from policies of the International Monetary Fund (IMF) and the World Bank (both headquartered in Washington, D.C.) and endorsed by the U.S. Treasury Department. The goal for these policies and prescriptions is to bring about basic economic reform in poor nations, rapidly moving their economies in the direction of capitalism and incorporation into the global marketplace. When a government applies for a loan from these international lending agencies, it must agree to abide by a structural adjustment program (SAP) based on these economic policies and prescriptions. Thus, the conditions for securing a loan include the following: (1) cuts in spending for health, education, and all forms of social welfare; (2) privatization of all state-owned enterprises; (3) opening the economy to foreign competition and direct foreign investment; (4) allowing the market to determine interest rates; (5) managing currency exchange rates to keep them stable. Additionally, governments are to broaden the tax base in order to collect more revenue, deregulate labor markets, and stop using public monies to subsidize commodities, thus increasing the cost to consumers. It is this last point, the withdrawal of subsidies, that I will focus on. The commodity in question is commercial fertilizer, an absolutely essential agricultural input for even the smallest subsistence farmer.

Malawi is one of the poorest nations in the world. It has a population of about thirteen million people, 95 percent engaged in rain-fed agriculture, mostly on smallholdings of about one to four acres. It takes about two-thirds of an acre per person to have a reasonable chance of producing sufficient food to meet subsistence needs for a family. The nation has more or less reached the limit of its possible area of cultivation, and is suffering from the problems that accompany deforestation as people have cut trees to clear land for firewood for cooking and brick-making. There is no longer a fallow period for cropland—farmers plant all of their land every year.

The staple crop is white maize (corn); it is consumed at every meal. Over 90 percent of cultivable land in Malawi is planted to maize. It is hard on the soil, rapidly leaching it of nutrients, especially nitrogen. Presently, if commercial fertilizer high in nitrogen is not applied during the growing season, the amount of maize harvested is greatly diminished. Households are unable to meet their subsistence needs and have no surplus to put on the market. The "season of hunger," that period of time between family consumption of the last store of maize from the previous harvest (any time between early September and late December) and the beginning of the next harvest (in late March or April) grows longer, and families have to find a way to cope.

Fertilizer subsidies have a long history in Malawi. They began in 1952 while the country was still a British colony. The objectives of the subsidy were to ensure distribution of a vital agricultural input at a low cost to even the most geographically remote smallholder farmer, thus increasing output of maize, the priority crop, and to maintain soil fertility. The subsidies continued after independence and into the 1970s. In 1981 the country experienced a balance of payments problem and turned to the World Bank and IMF for assistance in the form of loans. Thus, Malawi has been indebted to and under the influence of these international lending agencies longer than any other African nation, and the involvement continues up to the present. As early as 1984, the World Bank and IMF began attributing problems in the economy to government subsidy policies, particularly with regard to commercial fertilizer. By 1985 the government began progressive reduction of the fertilizer subsidy. By the 1990s, there was complete deregulation and liberalization of the fertilizer and seed markets in Malawi, under the tutelage of the international lending institutions. The process was finalized in 1994/95 with complete removal of all types of subsidies and price controls on all agricultural inputs and products. At the same time there was 40 percent depreciation in the value of the currency and inflation soared from 20 percent to 53 percent.

This was an absolute crisis for small farmers. Harvests fell and malnutrition rose. By the month of June, most rural families were reduced to eating two meals a day. Over a third of rural families were running out of stored maize by September and 80 percent by September. More than 25 percent of under-five children were underweight and more than half were stunted by long-term malnutrition. The country was struggling with the heavy burden of HIV/AIDS, and life expectancy had fallen to 37 years. World Bank economists had begun to get a sense that all was not well, all was not going according to plan, and perhaps a social safety net was needed to "catch" those who were most vulnerable. A number of fertilizer programs were begun to try and meet the needs of smallholders and allow them to have a greater likelihood of producing sufficient food to feed their families.

Government programs like the Starter Pak Initiative and Targeted Input Programme were created to distribute free or subsidized fertilizer. The results were mixed at best.

Big farmers were not eligible for these programs, which relied on the distribution of vouchers to smallholders through village headmen. A voucher could then be exchanged for a 50 kg bag of fertilizer free or at a subsidized price, depending on the program. But headmen sometimes sold the vouchers rather than distribute them. And big farmers would have vendors with coupons buy bags of fertilizer at the subsidized price, then pay the vendors a fee for this service, and re-sell the bags for a handsome profit. The supply of subsidized fertilizer was quickly depleted, long before most small farmers had secured any. Another social safety net program put rural men and women to work building roads, and at the end of several days of work, they were paid with a 50 kg bag of fertilizer. It took so much work to earn a bag that many people refused to participate, saying it seemed like a kind of slavery.

How did individual households cope with these dire circumstances? This is what I learned from ten women in one village where few families could afford a sufficient amount of fertilizer. Some of the families were able to secure one bag, allowing them one application on their maize crop; it takes three applications during a growing season for optimal results. Most of the families used no fertilizer at all. In 2005, all but one family consumed all of their stored food by September, and some as early as August. Normally August is the time of year when weddings take place, when ancestors are honored. These events require contributions of food from each household, but in 2005 the village headman decreed that no household should make these contributions because everyone was suffering from insufficient food.

The first strategy that families turned to in the hunger crisis was to skip meals. When there is sufficient food, people eat *nsima* (maize porridge) three times a day—breakfast, lunch and supper. When there is a food shortage, breakfast is no longer prepared. As the situation continued to deteriorate, women began to mix maize flour, the regular ingredient for *nsima*, with maize bran, which is usually used for animal feed. The next step was to use cassava rather than maize for the noon meal. Cassava is nutrient poor, and most people in the Central Region don't like it. By this time men and women were actively seeking work that they could exchange for food—a day's work in a rich farmer's fields in exchange for enough maize flour to prepare a meal. If such work could not be found, people began to sell off their assets in order to buy maize, which was in short supply and thus very expensive. They sold animals, bricks, sheets of corrugated metal roofing, timbers that had supported their houses—whatever they had that could be sold for money or exchanged for maize. The absolute last resort was to sell land or exchange land for maize. And I was told that some older women who had no family in the vicinity were so desperately hungry that they went door to door begging for something to eat.

It is during this season of hunger that the land must be prepared and the next crop planted and cultivated. When hunger is great, maize will be harvested and cooked while it is still green and other foodstuffs like pumpkins will be cooked when they are small. People can't wait for them to mature—they might starve in the interim.

So how it is that World Bank and IMF economists would mandate a policy that causes so much human suffering? The current president of Malawi, Bingu wa Mutharika, must have asked the same question. He is an economist trained at a prominent U.S. university, and is well aware that Western nations heavily subsidize their farmers. After the disastrous 2005 harvest that required emergency food aid for five million Malawians, he reinstated and deepened fertilizer subsidies over the protests of the U.S. The result? The 2007 maize harvest was so big that Malawi is exporting hundreds of thousands of tons to neighboring countries. The national granaries are full. Acute hunger in children has fallen so sharply that the UN-donated powdered milk stockpiled for treating hungry children has been sent on to other African nations still in need. In sum, it appears that the policies generated by the Washington Consensus may need to be reconfigured when it comes to public investment in African agriculture, especially agriculture practiced by subsistence farmers who are unable to produce enough grain for sale to pay for the fertilizer that will ensure a surplus.

Review Questions

1. What is the "Washington Consensus"?

2. What are the five points of the Washington Consensus' Structural Adjustment Program (SAP)? What is the economic theory behind them?

3. What is the history of farm support in Malawi and how did taking loans from the World Bank and IMF change that history?

4. Why is chemical fertilizer so important to farming in Malawi?

5. When it followed SAP guidelines, the government of Malawi ceased to provide fertilizer for its farmers. How did that impact the country's people and agricultural output?

6. What happened when the government of Malawi recently again began to provide fertilizer for its farmers? What does that say about World Bank and IMF policy?

FIVE

KINSHIP
AND FAMILY

Getty Images, Inc.

READINGS IN THIS SECTION

Mother's Love: Death without Weeping   176
Nancy Scheper-Hughes

Family and Kinship in Village India   186
David W. McCurdy

Polyandry: When Brothers Take a Wife   195
Melvyn C. Goldstein

Uterine Families and the Women's Community   203
Margery Wolf

Social life is essential to human existence. We remain in the company of other people from the day we are born to the time of our death. People teach us to speak. They show us how to relate to our surroundings. They give us the help and the support we need to achieve personal security and mental well-being. Alone, we are relatively frail, defenseless primates; in groups we are astonishingly adaptive and powerful. Yet despite these advantages, well-organized human societies are difficult to achieve. Some species manage to produce social organization genetically. But people are not like bees or ants. We lack the genetically coded directions for behavior that make these insects successful social animals. Although we seem to inherit a general need for social approval, we also harbor individual interests and ambitions that can block or destroy close social ties. To overcome these divisive tendencies, human groups organize around several principles designed to foster cooperation and group loyalty. Kinship is among the strongest of these.

We may define **kinship** as the complex system of culturally defined social relationships based on marriage (the principle of **affinity**) and birth (the principle of **consanguinity**). The study of kinship involves consideration of such principles as descent, kinship status and roles, family and other kinship groups, marriage, and residence. In fact, kinship has been such an important organizing factor in many of the societies studied by anthropologists that it is one of the most elaborate areas of the discipline. What are some of the important concepts?

First is descent. **Descent** is based on the notion of a common heritage. It is a cultural rule tying together people on the basis of reputed common ancestry. Descent functions to guide inheritance, group loyalty, and, above all, the formation of families and extended kinship groups.

There are three main rules of descent. One is **patrilineal descent,** which links relatives through males only. In patrilineal systems, females are part of their father's line, but their children descend from the husbands. **Matrilineal descent** links relatives through females only. Males belong to their mother's line; the children of males descend from the wives. **Bilateral descent** links a person to kin through both males and females simultaneously. Americans are said to have bilateral descent, whereas most of the people in India, Japan, and China are patrilineal. Such groups as the Apache and Trobriand Islanders are matrilineal.

Descent often defines groups called, not surprisingly, **descent groups.** One of these is the **lineage,** a localized group that is based on unilineal (patrilineal or matrilineal) descent and that usually has some corporate powers. In the Marshall Islands, for example, the matriline holds rights to land, which, in turn, it allots to its members. Lineages in India sometimes hold rights to land but are a more important arena for other kinds of decisions such as marriage. Lineage mates must be consulted about the advisability, timing, and arrangements for weddings.

Clans are composed of lineages. Clan members believe they are all descended from a common ancestor, but because clans are larger, members cannot trace their genealogical relationships to everyone in the group. In some societies, clans may be linked together in even larger groups called **phratries.** Because phratries are usually large, the feeling of common descent they offer is weaker.

Ramages, or cognatic kin groups, are based on bilateral descent. They often resemble lineages in size and function but provide more recruiting flexibility. An individual can choose membership from among several ramages where he or she has relatives.

Another important kinship group is the family. This unit is more difficult to define than we may think, because people have found so many different ways to organize "familylike" groups. Here we will follow anthropologist George P. Murdock's approach and define the **family** as a kin group consisting of at least one married couple sharing the same residence with their children and performing sexual, reproductive, economic, and educational functions. A **nuclear family** consists of a single married couple and their children. An **extended family** consists of two or more married couples and their children. Extended families have a quality all their own and are often found in societies where family performance and honor are paramount to the reputation of individual family members. Extended families are most commonly based on patrilineal descent. Women marry into such families and must establish themselves among the line members and other women who live there.

Marriage, the socially approved union of two people, is a second major principle of kinship. The regulation of marriage takes elaborate forms from one society to the next. Marriage may be **exogamous,** meaning marriage outside any particular named group, or **endogamous,** indicating the opposite. Bhil tribals of India, for example, are clan and village exogamous (they should marry outside these groups), but tribal endogamous (they should marry other Bhils).

Marriage may also be **monogamous,** where it is preferred that only one woman should be married to one man at a time, or **polygamous,** meaning that one person may be married to more than one person simultaneously. There are two kinds of polygamy, **polygyny,** the marriage of one man with more than one woman simultaneously, and **polyandry,** the marriage of one woman with more than one man.

Many anthropologists view marriage as a system of alliances between families and descent lines. Viewed in these terms, rules such as endogamy and exogamy can be explained as devices to link or internally strengthen various kinship groups. The **incest taboo,** a legal rule that prohibits sexual intercourse or marriage between particular classes of kin, is often explained as a way to extend alliances between kin groups.

Finally, the regulation of marriage falls to the parents and close relatives of eligible young people in many societies. These elders concern themselves with more than wedding preparations; they must also see to it that young people marry appropriately, which means they consider the reputation of prospective spouses and their families' economic strength and social rank.

The selections in Part Five illustrate several aspects of kinship systems. In the first article, Nancy Scheper-Hughes looks at the relationship that poor Brazilian mothers have with their infants. Because babies die so often, mothers must delay forming attachments to them until their children show that they can survive. The second article, by David McCurdy, looks at the way kinship organizes life for the inhabitants of a Rajasthani Bhil village. Arranging a marriage requires use and consideration of clans, lineages, families, and weddings. Despite its origin in peasant society, the Indian kinship system is proving useful as people try to cope with a modernizing society. The third article, by Melvyn Goldstein, describes a rare form of marriage—polyandry—and shows why, despite other choices, Tibetan brothers often choose to share a single wife among them. Finally, Margery Wolf looks at the structure of the Taiwanese extended family from the point of view of the women who constitute it. It is only by establishing her own uterine family that a woman can gain power within the patrilineal group.

Key Terms

affinity   p. 173
bilateral descent   p. 173
clan   p. 174
consanguinity   p. 173
descent   p. 173
descent groups   p. 173
endogamy p. 174
exogamy p. 174
extended family   p. 174
family   p. 174
incest taboo   p. 174
kinship   p. 173

lineage   p. 173
marriage   p. 174
matrilineal descent   p. 173
monogamy   p. 174
nuclear family   p. 174
patrilineal descent   p. 173
phratry   p. 174
polyandry   p. 174
polygamy   p. 174
polygyny   p. 174
ramage   p. 174

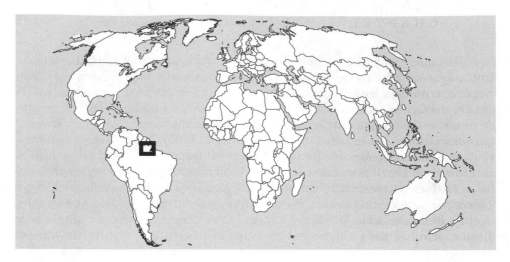

18

Mother's Love: Death without Weeping

Nancy Scheper-Hughes

Kinship systems are based on marriage and birth. Both, anthropologists assume, create ties that can link kin into close, cooperative, enduring structures. What happens to such ties, however, in the face of severe hardship imposed by grinding poverty and urban migration? Can we continue to assume, for example, that there will be a close bond between mother and child? This is the question pursued by Nancy Scheper-Hughes in the following article about the mother–infant relationship among poor women in a Brazilian shantytown. The author became interested in the question following a "baby die-off" in the town of Bom Jesus in 1965. She noticed that mothers seemed to take these events casually. After twenty-five years of research in the Alto do Cruzeiro shantytown there, she has come to see such indifference as a cultural response to high rates of infant death due to poverty and malnutrition. Mothers, and surrounding social institutions such as the Catholic church, expect babies to die easily. Mothers concentrate their support

From "Death Without Weeping," *Natural History,* October 1989. Copyright © 1989 by Nancy Scheper-Hughes, with an update in 2009. Reprinted by permission of the publisher.

on babies who are "fighters" and let themselves grow attached to their children only when they are reasonably sure that the offspring will survive. The article also provides an excellent illustration of what happens to kinship systems in the face of poverty and social dislocation. Such conditions may easily result in the formation of woman-headed families and in a lack of the extended kinship networks so often found in more stable, rural societies.

In a current epilogue to this article, Scheper-Hughes notes that political changes in Brazil since the 1980s have led to improved health for mothers and babies. Mothers have fewer babies and no longer give up on offspring who in the past would have seemed destined to die. Unfortunately, the rise of drugs and gangs along with vigilante death squads have become a major threat to survival and social life in Bom Jesus.

I have seen death without weeping

The destiny of the Northeast is death

Cattle they kill

To the people they do something worse

> *—Anonymous Brazilian singer (1965)*

"Why do the church bells ring so often?" I asked Nailza de Arruda soon after I moved into a corner of her tiny mud-walled hut near the top of the shantytown called the Alto do Cruzeiro (Crucifix Hill). I was then a Peace Corps volunteer and a community development/health worker. It was the dry and blazing hot summer of 1965, the months following the military coup in Brazil, and save for the rusty, clanging bells of N.S. das Dores Church, an eerie quiet had settled over the market town that I call Bom Jesus da Mata. Beneath the quiet, however, there was chaos and panic. "It's nothing," replied Nailza, "just another little angel gone to heaven."

Nailza had sent more than her share of little angels to heaven, and sometimes at night I could hear her engaged in a muffled but passionate discourse with one of them, two-year-old Joana. Joana's photograph, taken as she lay propped up in her tiny cardboard coffin, her eyes open, hung on a wall next to one of Nailza and Ze Antonio taken on the day they eloped.

Nailza could barely remember the other infants and babies who came and went in close succession. Most had died unnamed and were hastily baptized in their coffins. Few lived more than a month or two. Only Joana, properly baptized in church at the close of her first year and placed under the protection of a powerful saint, Joan of Arc, had been expected to live. And Nailza had dangerously allowed herself to love the little girl.

In addressing the dead child, Nailza's voice would range from tearful imploring to angry recrimination: "Why did you leave me? Was your patron saint so greedy that she could not allow me one child on this earth?" Ze Antonio advised me to ignore Nailza's odd behavior, which he understood as a kind of madness that, like the birth and death of children, came and went. Indeed, the premature birth of a stillborn son some months later "cured" Nailza of her "inappropriate" grief, and the day came when she removed Joana's photo and carefully packed it away.

More than fifteen years elapsed before I returned to the Alto do Cruzeiro, and it was anthropology that provided the vehicle of my return. Since 1982 I have returned several times in order to pursue a problem that first attracted my attention in the 1960s. My involvement with the people of the Alto do Cruzeiro now spans a quarter of a century and three generations of parenting in a community where mothers and daughters are often simultaneously pregnant.

The Alto do Cruzeiro is one of three shantytowns surrounding the large market town of Bom Jesus in the sugar plantation zone of Pernambuco in Northeast Brazil, one of the many zones of neglect that have emerged in the shadow of the now tarnished economic miracle of Brazil. For the women and children of the Alto do Cruzeiro the only miracle is that some of them have managed to stay alive at all.

The Northeast is a region of vast proportions (approximately twice the size of Texas) and of equally vast social and developmental problems. The nine states that make up the region are the poorest in the country and are representative of the Third World within a dynamic and rapidly industrializing nation. Despite waves of migrations from the interior to the teeming shantytowns of coastal cities, the majority still live in rural areas on farms and ranches, sugar plantations and mills.

Life expectancy in the Northeast is only forty years, largely because of the appallingly high rate of infant and child mortality. Approximately one million children in Brazil under the age of five die each year. The children of the Northeast, especially those born in shantytowns on the periphery of urban life, are at a very high risk of death. In these areas, children are born without the traditional protection of breast-feeding, subsistence gardens, stable marriages, and multiple adult caretakers that exists in the interior. In the hillside shantytowns that spring up around cities or, in this case, interior market towns, marriages are brittle, single parenting is the norm, and women are frequently forced into the shadow economy of domestic work in the homes of the rich or into unprotected and oftentimes "scab" wage labor on the surrounding sugar plantations, where they clear land for planting and weed for a pittance, sometimes less than a dollar a day. The women of the Alto may not bring their babies with them into the homes of the wealthy, where the often-sick infants are considered sources of contamination, and they cannot carry the little ones to the riverbanks where they wash clothes because the river is heavily infested with schistosomes and other deadly parasites. Nor can they carry their young children to the plantations, which are often several miles away. At wages of a dollar a day, the women of the Alto cannot hire baby sitters. Older children who are not in school will sometimes serve as somewhat indifferent caretakers. But any child not in school is also expected to find wage work. In most cases, babies are simply left at home alone, the door securely fastened. And so many also die alone and unattended.

Bom Jesus da Mata, centrally located in the plantation zone of Pernambuco, is within commuting distance of several sugar plantations and mills. Consequently, Bom Jesus has been a magnet for rural workers forced off their small subsistence plots by large landowners wanting to use every available piece of land for sugar cultivation. Initially, the rural migrants to Bom Jesus were squatters who were given tacit approval by the mayor to put up temporary straw huts on each of the three hills overlooking the town. The Alto do Cruzeiro is the oldest, the largest, and the poorest of the shantytowns. Over the past three decades many of the original migrants have become permanent residents, and the primitive and temporary straw huts have been replaced by small homes (usually of two rooms) made of wattle and daub, sometimes covered with plaster. The more affluent residents use bricks and tiles. In most Alto homes, dangerous kerosene lamps have been replaced by light bulbs. The once tattered rural garb, often fashioned from used sugar sacking, has likewise been replaced by store-bought clothes, often castoffs from a wealthy *patrão* (boss). The trappings are modern, but the hunger, sickness, and death that they conceal are traditional, deeply rooted in a history of feudalism, exploitation, and institutionalized dependency.

My research agenda never wavered. The questions I addressed first crystallized during a veritable "die-off" of Alto babies during a severe drought in 1965. The food and water shortages and the political and economic chaos occasioned by the military coup were reflected in the handwritten entries of births and deaths in the dusty, yellowed pages of the ledger books kept at the public registry office in Bom Jesus. More than 350 babies died in the Alto during 1965 alone—this from a shantytown population of little more than 5,000. But that wasn't what surprised me. There were reasons enough for the deaths in the miserable conditions of shantytown life. What puzzled me was the seeming indifference of Alto women to the death of their infants, and their willingness to attribute to their own tiny offspring an aversion to life that made their death seem wholly natural, indeed all but anticipated.

Although I found that it was possible, and hardly difficult, to rescue infants and toddlers from death by diarrhea and dehydration with a simple sugar, salt, and water solution (even bottled Coca-Cola worked fine), it was more difficult to enlist a mother herself in the rescue of a child she perceived as ill-fated for life or better off dead, or to convince her to take back into her threatened and besieged home a baby she had already come to think of as an angel rather than as a son or daughter.

I learned that the high expectancy of death, and the ability to face child death with stoicism and equanimity, produced patterns of nurturing that differentiated between those infants thought of as thrivers and survivors and those thought of as born already "wanting to die." The survivors were nurtured, while stigmatized, doomed infants were left to die, as mothers say, *a mingua*, "of neglect." Mothers stepped back and allowed nature to take its course. This pattern, which I call mortal selective neglect, is called passive infanticide by anthropologist Marvin Harris. The Alto situation, although culturally specific in the form that it takes, is not unique to Third World shantytown communities and may have its correlates in our own impoverished urban communities in some cases of "failure to thrive" infants.

I use as an example the story of Zezinho, the thirteen-month-old toddler of one of my neighbors, Lourdes. I became involved with Zezinho when I was called in to help Lourdes in the delivery of another child, this one a fair and robust little tyke with a lusty cry. I noted that while Lourdes showed great interest in the newborn, she totally ignored Zezinho who, wasted and severely malnourished, was curled up in a fetal position on a piece of urine- and feces-soaked cardboard placed under his mother's hammock. Eyes open and vacant, mouth slack, the little boy seemed doomed.

When I carried Zezinho up to the community day-care center at the top of the hill, the Alto women who took turns caring for one another's children (in order to free themselves for part-time work in the cane fields or washing clothes) laughed at my efforts to save Ze, agreeing with Lourdes that here was a baby without a ghost of a chance. Leave him alone, they cautioned. It makes no sense to fight with death. But I did do battle with Ze, and after several weeks of force-feeding (malnourished babies lose their interest in food), Ze began to succumb to my ministrations. He acquired some flesh across his taut chest bones, learned to sit up, and even tried to smile. When he seemed well enough, I returned him to Lourdes in her miserable scrap-material lean-to, but not without guilt about what I had done. I wondered whether returning Ze was at all fair to Lourdes and to his little brother. But I was busy and washed my hands of the matter. And Lourdes did seem more interested in Ze now that he was looking more human.

When I returned in 1982, there was Lourdes among the women who formed my sample of Alto mothers—still struggling to put together some semblance of life for a now grown Ze and her five other surviving children. Much was made of my reunion with Ze in 1982, and everyone enjoyed retelling the story of Ze's rescue and of how his mother had given him up for dead. Ze would laugh the loudest when told how I had had to force-feed him like a fiesta turkey. There was no hint of guilt on the part of Lourdes and no resentment on the part of Ze. In fact, when questioned in private as to who was the best friend he ever had in life, Ze took a long drag on his cigarette and answered without a trace of irony, "Why my mother, of course!" "But of course," I replied.

Part of learning how to mother in the Alto do Cruzeiro is learning when to let go of a child who shows that it "wants" to die or that it has no "knack" or no "taste" for life. Another part is learning when it is safe to let oneself love a child. Frequent child death remains a powerful shaper of maternal thinking and practice. In the absence of firm expectation that a child will survive, mother love as we conceptualize it (whether in popular terms or in the psychobiological notion of maternal bonding) is attenuated and delayed with consequences for infant survival. In an environment already precarious to young life, the emotional detachment of mothers toward some of their babies contributes even further to the spiral of high mortality–high fertility in a kind of macabre lock-step dance of death.

The average woman of the Alto experiences 9.5 pregnancies, 3.5 child deaths, and 1.5 stillbirths. Seventy percent of all child deaths in the Alto occur in the first six months of life, and 82 percent by the end of the first year. Of all deaths in the community each year, about 45 percent are of children under the age of five.

Women of the Alto distinguish between child deaths understood as natural (caused by diarrhea and communicable diseases) and those resulting from sorcery, the evil eye, or other magical or supernatural afflictions. They also recognize a large category of infant deaths seen as fated and inevitable. These hopeless cases are classified by mothers under the folk terminology "child sickness" or "child attack." Women say that there are at least fourteen different types of hopeless child sickness, but most can be subsumed under two categories—chronic and acute. The chronic cases refer to infants who are born small and wasted. They are deathly pale, mothers say, as well as weak and passive. They demonstrate no vital force, no liveliness. They do not suck vigorously; they hardly cry. Such babies can be this way at birth or they can be born sound but soon show no resistance, no "fight" against the common crises of infancy: diarrhea, respiratory infections, tropical fevers.

The acute cases are those doomed infants who die suddenly and violently. They are taken by stealth overnight, often following convulsions that bring on head banging, shaking, grimacing, and shrieking. Women say it is horrible to look at such a baby. If the infant begins to foam at the mouth or gnash its teeth or go rigid with its eyes turned back inside its head, there is absolutely no hope. The infant is "put aside"—left alone—often on the floor in a back room, and allowed to die. These symptoms (which accompany high fevers, dehydration, third-stage malnutrition, and encephalitis) are equated by Alto women with madness, epilepsy, and worst of all, rabies, which is greatly feared and highly stigmatized.

Most of the infants presented to me as suffering from chronic child sickness were tiny, wasted famine victims, while those labeled as victims of acute child attack seemed to be infants suffering from the deliriums of high fever or the convulsions that can accompany electrolyte imbalance in dehydrated babies.

Local midwives and traditional healers, praying women, as they are called, advise Alto women on when to allow a baby to die. One midwife explained: "If I can see that a baby was born unfortuitously, I tell the mother that she need not wash the infant or give it a cleansing tea. I tell her just to dust the infant with baby powder and wait for it to die." Allowing nature to take its course is not seen as sinful by these often very devout Catholic women. Rather, it is understood as cooperating with God's plan.

Often I have been asked how consciously women of the Alto behave in this regard. I would have to say that consciousness is always shifting between allowed and disallowed levels of awareness. For example, I was awakened early one morning in 1987 by two neighborhood children who had been sent to fetch me to a hastily organized wake for a two-month-old infant whose mother I had unsuccessfully urged to breast-feed. The infant was being sustained on sugar water, which the mother referred to as *soro* (serum), using a medical term for the infant's starvation regime in light of his chronic diarrhea. I had cautioned the mother that an infant could not live on *soro* forever.

The two girls urged me to console the young mother by telling her that it was "too bad" that her infant was so weak that Jesus had to take him. They were coaching me in proper Alto etiquette. I agreed, of course, but asked, "And what do *you* think?" Xoxa, the eleven-year-old, looked down at her dusty flip-flops and blurted out, "Oh, Dona Nanci, that baby never got enough to eat, but you must never say that!" And so the death of hungry babies remains one of the best kept secrets of life in Bom Jesus da Mata.

Most victims are waked quickly and with a minimum of ceremony. No tears are shed, and the neighborhood children form a tiny procession, carrying the baby to the town graveyard where it will join a multitude of others. Although a few fresh flowers may be scattered over the tiny grave, no stone or wooden cross will mark the place, and the same spot will be reused within a few months' time. The mother will never visit the grave, which soon becomes an anonymous one.

What, then, can be said of these women? What emotions, what sentiments motivate them? How are they able to do what, in fact, must be done? What does mother love mean in this inhospitable context? Are grief, mourning, and melancholia present, although deeply repressed? If so, where shall we look for them? And if not, how are we to understand the moral visions and moral sensibilities that guide their actions?

I have been criticized more than once for presenting an unflattering portrait of poor Brazilian women, women who are, after all, themselves the victims of severe social and institutional neglect. I have described these women as allowing some of their children to die, as if this were an unnatural and inhuman act rather than, as I would assert, the way any one of us might act, reasonably and rationally, under similarly desperate conditions. Perhaps I have not emphasized enough the real pathogens in this environment of high risk: poverty, deprivation, sexism, chronic hunger, and economic exploitation. If mother love is, as many psychologists and some feminists believe, a seemingly natural and universal maternal script, what does it mean to women for whom scarcity, loss, sickness, and deprivation have made that love frantic and robbed them of their grief, seeming to turn their hearts to stone?

Throughout much of human history—as in a great deal of the impoverished Third World today—women have had to give birth and to nurture children under ecological conditions and social arrangements hostile to child survival, as well as to their own well-being. Under circumstances of high childhood mortality, patterns of selective neglect and passive infanticide may be seen as active survival strategies.

They also seem to be fairly common practices historically and across cultures. In societies characterized by high childhood mortality and by a correspondingly high (replacement) fertility, cultural practices of infant and child care tend to be organized primarily around survival goals. But what this means is a pragmatic recognition that not all of one's children can be expected to live. The nervousness about child survival in areas of northeast Brazil, northern India, or Bangladesh, where a 30 percent or 40 percent mortality rate in the first years of life is common, can lead to forms of delayed attachment and a casual or benign neglect that serves to weed out the worst bets so as to enhance the life chances of healthier siblings, including those yet to be born. Practices similar to those that I am describing have been recorded for parts of Africa, India, and Central America.

Life in the Alto do Cruzeiro resembles nothing so much as a battlefield or an emergency room in an overcrowded inner-city public hospital. Consequently, morality is guided by a kind of "lifeboat ethics," the morality of triage. The seemingly studied indifference toward the suffering of some of their infants, conveyed in such sayings as "little critters have no feelings," is understandable in light of these women's obligation to carry on with their reproductive and nurturing lives.

In their slowness to anthropomorphize and personalize their infants, everything is mobilized so as to prevent maternal overattachment and, therefore, grief at death. The bereaved mother is told not to cry, that her tears will dampen the wings of her little angel so that she cannot fly up to her heavenly home. Grief at the death of an angel is not only inappropriate, it is a symptom of madness and of a profound lack of faith.

Infant death becomes routine in an environment in which death is anticipated and bets are hedged. While the routinization of death in the context of shantytown life is not hard to understand, and quite possible to empathize with, its routinization in the formal institutions of public life in Bom Jesus is not as easy to accept uncritically. Here the social production of indifference takes on a different, even a malevolent, cast.

In a society where triplicates of every form are required for the most banal events (registering a car, for example), the registration of infant and child death is informal, incomplete, and rapid. It requires no documentation, takes less than five minutes, and demands no witnesses other than office clerks. No questions are asked concerning the circumstances of the death, and the cause of death is left blank, unquestioned and unexamined. A neighbor, grandmother, older sibling, or common-law husband may register the death. Since most infants die at home, there is no question of a medical record.

From the registry office, the parent proceeds to the town hall, where the mayor will give him or her a voucher for a free baby coffin. The full-time municipal coffinmaker cannot tell you exactly how many baby coffins are dispatched each week. It varies, he says, with the seasons. There are more needed during the drought months and during the big festivals of Carnaval and Christmas and São Joao's Day because people are too busy, he supposes, to take their babies to the clinic. Record keeping is sloppy.

Similarly, there is a failure on the part of city-employed doctors working at two free clinics to recognize the malnutrition of babies who are weighed, measured, and immunized without comment and as if they were not, in fact, anemic, stunted, fussy, and irritated starvation babies. At best the mothers are told to pick up free vitamins or a health "tonic" at the municipal chambers. At worst, clinic personnel will give tranquilizers and sleeping pills to quiet the hungry cries of "sick-to-death" Alto babies.

The church, too, contributes to the routinization of, and indifference toward, child death. Traditionally, the local Catholic church taught patience and resignation to domestic tragedies that were said to reveal the imponderable workings of God's will. If an infant died suddenly, it was because a particular saint had claimed the child. The infant would be an angel in the service of his or her heavenly patron. It would be wrong, a sign of a lack of faith, to weep for a child with such good fortune. The infant funeral was, in the past, an event celebrated with joy. Today, however, under the new regime of "liberation theology," the bells of N.S. das Dores parish church no longer peal for the death of Alto babies, and no priest accompanies the procession of angels to the cemetery where their bodies are disposed of casually and without ceremony. Children bury children in Bom Jesus da Mata. In this most Catholic of communities, the coffin is handed to the disabled and irritable municipal gravedigger, who often chides the children for one reason or another. It may be that the coffin is larger than expected and the gravedigger can find no appropriate space. The children do not wait for the gravedigger to complete his task. No prayers are recited and no sign of the cross made as the tiny coffin goes into its shallow grave.

When I asked the local priest, Padre Marcos, about the lack of church ceremony surrounding infant and childhood death today in Bom Jesus, he replied: "In the old days, child death was richly celebrated. But those were the baroque customs of a conservative church that wallowed in death and misery. The new church is a church of hope and joy. We no longer celebrate the death of child angels. We try to tell mothers that Jesus doesn't want all the dead babies they send him." Similarly, the new church has changed its baptismal customs, now often refusing to baptize dying babies brought to the back door of a church or rectory. The mothers are scolded by the church attendants and told to go home and take care of their sick babies. Baptism, they are told, is for the living; it is not to be confused with the sacrament of extreme unction, which is the anointing of the dying. And so it appears to the women of the Alto that even the church has turned away from them, denying the traditional comfort of folk Catholicism.

The contemporary Catholic church is caught in the clutches of a double bind. The new theology of liberation imagines a kingdom of God on earth based on justice and equality, a world without hunger, sickness, or childhood mortality. At the same time, the church has not changed its official position on sexuality and reproduction, including its sanctions against birth control, abortion, and sterilization. The padre of Bom Jesus da Mata recognizes this contradiction intuitively, although he shies away from discussions on the topic, saying that he prefers to leave questions of family planning to the discretion and the "good consciences" of his impoverished parishioners. But this, of course, sidesteps the extent to which those good consciences have been shaped by traditional church teachings in Bom Jesus, especially by his recent predecessors. Hence, we can begin to see that the seeming indifference of Alto mothers toward the death of some of their infants is but a pale reflection of the official indifference of church and state to the plight of poor women and children.

Nonetheless, the women of Bom Jesus are survivors. One woman, Biu, told me her life history, returning again and again to the themes of child death, her first husband's suicide, abandonment by her father and later by her second husband, and all the other losses and disappointments she had suffered in her long forty-five years. She concluded with great force, reflecting on the days of Carnaval '88 that were fast approaching:

> No, Dona Nanci, I won't cry, and I won't waste my life thinking about it from morning to night. . . . Can I argue with God for the state that I'm in? No! And so I'll dance and I'll jump and I'll play Carnaval! And yes, I'll laugh and people will wonder at a *pobre* like me who can have such a good time.

And no one did blame Biu for dancing in the streets during the four days of Carnaval—not even on Ash Wednesday, the day following Carnaval '88 when we all assembled hurriedly to assist in the burial of Mercea, Biu's beloved *casula*, her last-born daughter who had died at home of pneumonia during the festivities. The rest of the family barely had time to change out of their costumes. Severino, the child's uncle and godfather, sprinkled holy water over the little angel while he prayed: "Mercea, I don't know whether you were called, taken, or thrown out of this world. But look down at us from your heavenly home with tenderness, with pity, and with mercy." So be it.

Brief Epilogue

Many students write after reading this article asking me whether the situation has changed in the Alto do Cruzeiro. Is life better or worse for mothers and newborn babies? One of the advantages of long-term ethnographic research is seeing history in the making. I began my engagements with the people of the Alto in 1964 at the start of twenty years of military rule, a ruthless regime that produced deep impoverishment among those living in urban *favelas* and in rural areas. The scarcities and insecurities of that era contributed to the death of infants and small babies. By the time I completed my study of mother love and child death in the early 1990s Brazil was well on its way to democratization which ushered in many important changes, most notably a free, public, national health care system (SUS) which guaranteed poor women adequate pre- and post-natal care.

The decade of the 1990s witnessed what population experts call the demographic or epidemiologic transition. As both births and infant deaths declined, mothers began to treat their infants as potentially capable of survival and the old stance of maternal "watchful waiting" accompanied by "letting go" of infants thought of as having no "taste" or "talent" for life, was replaced by a maternal ethos of "holding on" and "holding dear" each infant. Today, young women of the Alto can expect to give birth to three or fewer babies and to see all of them live to adolescence. Many factors produced this reproductive transition: the 'modernization' of Catholic beliefs about infant death; the under-the-counter availability of Cytotec, a risky "morning after" pill; the implementation under the national health care system (Serviço Único de Saúde) of local 'health agents' who went door to door in poor communities, identifying and rescuing vulnerable infants, toddlers and old people. The primary cause of the decline in infant mortality on the Alto do Cruzeiro, however, was the "simple" installation of water pipes reaching virtually all the homes in the shantytown with sufficient, clean water. Water = life! It is painful to consider how "culture," "belief," and even "maternal sentiments" follow basic changes in the material conditions—and therefore the possibilities—of everyday life.

Motherhood is not only a social and a cultural construction, but a constellation of embodied practices responding to the requirements and limitations of the political and economic conditions that determine the resilience or vulnerability of infants and their mothers. Today, new problems have beset the people of the Alto do Cruzeiro. Since the publication of "Death without Weeping" drugs and gangs have made their ugly mark on the community and death squads have sprung up to impose a kind of vigilante justice. These anti-social features of life in "Bom Jesus" take some of the pleasure away, as one sees the young men of the Alto who survived that dangerous first year of life, felled by bullets and knife wounds at the hands of gang leaders, *bandidos*, and local police in almost equal measure.

Review Questions

1. What did Scheper-Hughes notice about mothers' reactions during the baby die-off of 1965 in Bom Jesus, Brazil?

2. How do poor Brazilian mothers react to their infants' illnesses and death? How do other institutions, such as the church, clinic, and civil authorities respond? Give examples.

3. How does Scheper-Hughes explain the apparent indifference of mothers to the death of their infants?

4. What does the indifference of mothers to the deaths of their children say about basic human nature, especially the mother–child bond?

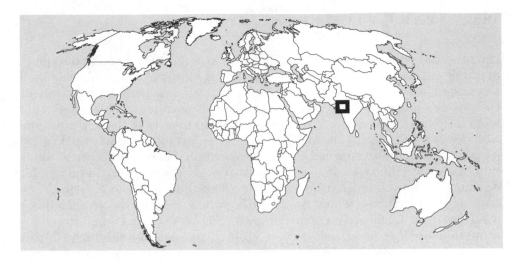

19

Family and Kinship in Village India

David W. McCurdy

Anyone who reads older ethnographic accounts of different cultures will inevitably run across terms such as clan, lineage, avunculocal, levirate, extended family, polyandry, cross-cousin, *and* Crow *terminology. All these terms and many more were created by anthropologists to describe categories, groups, social arrangements, and roles associated with the complex kinship systems that characterized so many of the groups they studied. The importance of kinship for one of these societies, that found in an Indian village, is the topic of this article by David McCurdy. He argues that kinship forms the core social groups and associations in rural India in a system well adapted to family-centered land-holding and small-scale farming. He concludes by pointing out that Indians have used their close family ties to adapt to life in the emerging cash-labor-oriented modernizing world.*

On a hot afternoon in May, 1962, I sat talking with three Bhil men in the village of Ratakote, located in southern Rajasthan, India.[1] We spoke about the results of recent national elections, their worry over a cattle disease that was afflicting the village herds, and predictions about when the monsoon rains would start. But our longest discussion concerned kin—the terms used to refer to them, the responsibilities they had toward one another, and the importance of marrying them off properly. It was toward the end of this conversation that one of the men, Kanji, said, "Now sāb (Bhili for sāhīb), you are finally asking about a good thing. This is what we want you to tell people about us when you go back to America."

As I thought about it later, I was struck by how different this social outlook was from mine. I doubt that I or any of my friends in the United States would say something like this. Americans do have kin. We have parents, although our parents may not always live together, and we often know other relatives, some of whom are likely to play important parts in our lives. We grow up in families and we often create new ones if we have children. But we also live in a social network of other people whom we meet at work or encounter in various "outside" social settings, and these people can be of equal or even greater importance to us than kin. Our social worlds include such non-kin structures as companies and other work organizations, schools, neighborhoods, churches and other religious groups, and voluntary associations, including recreational groups and social clubs. We are not likely to worry much about our obligations to relatives with the notable exceptions of our children and grandchildren (middle-class American parents are notoriously child-centered), and more grudgingly, our aging parents. We are not supposed to "live off" relatives or lean too heavily on them.

Not so in Ratakote. Ratakote's society, like many agrarian villages around the world, is kinship-centered. Villagers anchor themselves in their families. They spend great energy on creating and maintaining their kinship system. This actually is not so surprising. Elaborate kinship systems work well in agrarian societies where families tend to be corporate units and where peoples' social horizons are often limited to the distance they can walk in a day. For the same reasons, families in the United States were also stronger in the past when more of them owned farms and neighborhood businesses.

What may come as a surprise, however, is how resilient and strong Indian kinship systems such as Ratakote's have been in the face of recent economic changes, especially the growth of wage labor. Let us look more closely at the Bhil kinship system, especially at arranged marriage, to illustrate these ideas.

Arranging a Marriage

If there is anything that my American students have trouble understanding about India, it is arranged marriage. They can not imagine sitting passively by while

---

[1]Ratakote is a Bhil tribal village located 21 miles southwest of Udaipur, Rajasthan, in the Aravalli hills. I did ethnographic research in the village from 1961 to 1963, and again in 1985, 1991, and 1994 for shorter periods of time.

their parents advertise their charms and evaluate emerging nuptial candidates. The thought of living—to say nothing of having sex with—a total stranger seems out of the question to them. In our country, personal independence takes precedence over loyalty to family.

Not so in India. There, arranged marriage is the norm, and most young people, as well as their elders, accept and support the custom. (They often find it sexually exciting, too.) There are many reasons why this is so, but one stands out for discussion here. Marriage constructs alliances between families, lineages, and clans. The resulting kinship network is a pivotal structure in Indian society. It confers social strength and security. People's personal reputations depend on the quality and number of their allied kin. There is little question in their minds about who should arrange marriages. The decision is too important to leave up to inexperienced and impressionable young people.

As an aside I should note that young Indians play a greater part in the process than they used to. Middle-class boys often visit the families of prospective brides, where they manage to briefly "interview" them. They also tap into their kinship network to find out personal information about prospects. Young women also seek out information about prospective grooms. Bhils are no exception. They often conspire to meet those to whom they have been betrothed, usually at a fair or other public event where their contact is likely to go unnoticed. If they don't like each other, they will begin to pressure their parents to back out of the arrangement.

The importance of arranging a marriage was brought home to me several times during fieldwork in Ratakote, but one instance stands out most clearly. When I arrived in the swvillage for a short stay in 1985, Kanji had just concluded marriage arrangements for his daughter, Rupani.[2] What he told me about the process underscored the important role kinship plays in the life of the village.

Kanji started by saying that he and his wife first discussed Rupani's marriage the previous year when the girl first menstruated. She seemed too young for such a union then so they had waited nine months before committing to the marriage process. Even then, Rupani was still only 15 years old. Kanji explained that everyone preferred early marriage for their children because young people were likely to become sexually active as they grew older and might fall in love and elope, preempting the arrangement process altogether. Now they figured that the time had come, and they began a series of steps to find a suitable spouse that would eventually involve most of their kin.

The first step was to consult the members of Kanji's *lineage*. Lineage is an anthropological term, not one used by Bhils. But Bhils share membership in local groups of relatives that meet the anthropological definition. Lineages (in this case patrilineages) include closely related men who are all descended from a known ancestor. Kanji's lineage consists of his two married brothers, three married sons of his deceased father's brother (his father is also dead), and his own married son when the latter is home. All are the descendants of his grandfather who had migrated to Ratakote many years earlier. He had talked with all

---

[2]Kanji and Rupani are not real people. Their experiences are a composite of several life histories.

of them informally about the possibility of his daughter's marriage before this. Now he called them together for formal approval.

The approval of lineage mates is necessary because they are essential to the marriage process. Each one of them will help spread the word to other villages that Rupani is available for marriage. They will loan money to Kanji for wedding expenses, and when it comes time for the wedding ceremony, they will provide much of the labor needed to prepare food and arrange required activities. Each family belonging to the lineage will host a special meal for the bride (the groom is similarly entertained in his village) during the wedding period, and one or two will help her make offerings to their lineal ancestors. The groom will also experience this ritual.

The lineage also has functions not directly related to marriage. It has the right to redistribute the land of deceased childless, male members, and it provides its members with political support. It sees to memorial feasts for deceased members. Its members may cooperatively plow and sow fields together and combine their animals for herding.

With lineage approval in hand, Kanji announced Rupani's eligibility in other villages. (Bhils are village exogamous, meaning they prefer to marry spouses from other communities.) Kanji and his lineage mates went about this by paying visits to feminal relatives in other villages. These are kin of the women, now living in Ratakote, who have married into his family. They also include the daughters of his family line who have married and gone to live in other villages, along with their husbands and husbands' kin.

Once the word has been spread, news of prospective candidates begins to filter in. It may arrive with feminal kin from other villages when they visit Ratakote. Or it may come from neighbors who are acting as go-betweens in Ratakote for kin who live in other villages and who seek partners for their children. Either way, a process of evaluation starts. Does the family of the suggested boy or girl have a good reputation? Are they hospitable to their in-laws? Do they meet their obligations to others? What is the reputation of the boy or girl they are offering in marriage? Is he or she tall or short, light or dark, robust or frail, cheerful or complaining, hardworking or lazy? What about their level of education? Does the family have sufficient land and animals? Have they treated other sons- and daughters-in-law well?

The most fundamental question to ask, however, is whether the prospective spouse is from the right clan. In anthropology, the term *clan* refers to an aggregate of people who all believe they are descended from a common ancestor. In Ratakote this group is called an *arak*. Araks are named and the names are used as surnames when Bhils identify themselves. Kanji comes from the pargi arak and is thus known as Kanji Pargi. There is Lalu Bodar, Naraji Katara, Dita Hiravat, Nathu Airi—all men named for one of the 36 araks found in Ratakote. Women also belong to their father's clan, but unlike many American women who adopt their husband's surname at marriage, they keep their arak name all their lives.

Araks are based on a rule of patrilineal descent. This means that their members trace ancestry through males only. (Matrilineal descent traces the line through females only, and bilateral descent, which is found in U.S. society, includes both sexes.) Patrilineal descent not only defines arak membership, it governs inheritance. (Sons inherit equally from their fathers in Ratakote; daughters do not inherit despite a national law giving them that right.) It says that the children of divorced parents stay with the father's family. It bolsters the authority of men over their wives and children. It supports the rule of patrilocality. It even defines the village view of conception. Men plant the "seeds" that grow into children; women provide the fields in which the seeds germinate and grow.

The arak symbolizes patrilineal descent. It is not an organized group, although the members of an arak worship the same mother goddess no matter where they live. Instead it is an identity, an indicator that tells people who their lineal blood relatives are. There are pargis in hundreds of other Bhil villages. Most are strangers to Kanji but if he meets pargis elsewhere, he knows they share a common blood heritage with him.

It is this sense of common heritage that affects marriage. Bhils, like most Indians, believe that clan (arak) mates are close relatives even though they may be strangers. Marriage with them is forbidden. To make sure incest is impossible, it is also forbidden to marry anyone from your mother's arak or your father's mother's arak, to say nothing of anyone else you know you are related to.

This point was driven home to me on another occasion when a neighbor of Kanji's, Kamalaji Kharadi, who was sitting smoking with several other men, asked me which arak I belonged to. Instead of letting it go at "McCurdy," I said that I didn't have an arak. I explained that Americans didn't have a kinship group similar to this, and that was why I had to ask questions about kinship.

My listeners didn't believe me. After all, I must have a father and you get your arak automatically from him. It is a matter of birth and all people are born. They looked at each other as if to say, "We wonder why he won't tell us what his arak is?", then tried again to get me to answer. My second denial led them to ask, "OK, then what is your wife's arak?" (If you can't get at it one way, then try another.) I answered that she didn't have an arak either. This caused a mild sensation. "Then how do you know if you have not married your own relative?", they asked, secretly, I think, delighted by the scandalous prospect.

The third step that occurred during the arrangement of Rupani's marriage came after the family had settled on a prospective groom. This step is the betrothal, and it took place when the groom's father and some of his lineage mates and neighbors paid a formal visit to Kanji's house. When they arrive, Kanji must offer his guests a formal meal, usually slaughtering a goat and distilling some liquor for the occasion. The bride, her face covered by her sari, will be brought out for a brief viewing, as well. But most of the time will be spent making arrangements—when will the actual wedding take place?; who will check the couple's horoscopes for fit?; how much will the bride price (also called bride wealth by many anthropologists) be?

Bride price (*dapa*) deserves special comment. It is usually a standard sum of money (about 700 rupees in 1985), although it may also include silver ornaments or other valuables. The dapa is given by the groom's father and his line to the parents of the bride. Bhils view this exchange as a compensation for the loss of the bride's services to her family. It also pays for a shift in her loyalty.

The exchange points up an important strain on families in patrilineal societies, the transfer of a woman from her natal family and line to those of her husband. This transfer includes not only her person, but her loyalty, labor, and children. Although she always will belong to her father's arak, she is now part of her husband's family, not his.

This problem is especially troublesome in India because of the close ties formed there by a girl and her parents. Parents know their daughter will leave when she marries, and they know that in her husband's house and village, she will be at a disadvantage. She will be alone, and out of respect for his parents her husband may not favor her wishes, at least in public. Because of this, they tend to give her extra freedom and support. In addition, they recognize the strain she will be under when she first goes to live with her new husband and his family. To ease her transition, they permit her to visit her parents frequently for a year or two. They also may try to marry her into a village where other women from Ratakote have married, so that she has some kin or at least supporters.

After her marriage, a woman's parents and especially her brothers find it hard not to care about her welfare. Their potential interest presents a built-in structural conflict that could strain relations between the two families if nothing were done about it.

A solution to this problem is to make the marriage into an exchange, and bride price is one result. Bride price also helps to dramatize the change in loyalty and obligation accompanying the bride's entrance into her new family.

Bhils have also devised a number of wedding rituals to dramatize the bride's shift in family membership. The bride must cry to symbolize that she is leaving her home. The groom ritually storms the bride's house at the beginning of the final ceremony. He does so like a conquering hero, drawing his sword to strike a ceremonial arch placed over the entrance while simultaneously stepping on a small fire (he wears a slipper to protect his foot), ritually violating the household's sacred hearth. At the end of the wedding, the groom, with some friends, engages in a mock battle with the bride's brothers and other young men, and symbolically abducts her. The meaning of this ritual is a dramatic equivalent of a father "giving away the bride" at American weddings.

One additional way of managing possible tension between in-laws is the application of respect behavior. The parents of the bride must always treat those of the groom and their relatives with respect. They must not joke in their presence, and they must use respectful language and defer to the groom's parents in normal conversation. In keeping with the strong patrilineal system, a groom may not accept important gifts from his wife's family except on ritual occasions, such as weddings, when exchange is expected. A groom may help support his own father, but he should not do so with his in-laws. That is up to their sons.

Bride price exchange also sets in motion a life-long process of mutual hospitality between the two families. Once the marriage has taken place, the families will become part of each other's feminal kin. They will exchange gifts on some ritual occasions, open their houses to each other, and, of course, help one another make future marriages.

The Future of Indian Kinship

On our last trip to India in 1994, my wife and I learned that Rupani had delivered three children since her wedding. Kanji had visited them a few months before we arrived, and he said that Rupani was happy and that he had wonderful grandchildren. But he also mentioned that her husband now spent most of his time in the nearby city of Udaipur working in construction there. He sent money home, but his absence left Rupani to run the house and raise the children by herself, although she did so with the assistance of his parents and lineage mates.

Rupani's case is not unusual. Every morning 70 or 80 men board one of the 20 or so busses that travel the road, now paved, that runs through Ratakote to the city. There they wait to be recruited by contractors for day labor at a low wage. If they are successful, gain special skills, or make good connections, they may get more permanent, better-paying jobs and live for weeks at a time in the city.

The reason they have to take this kind of work is simple. Ratakote has more than doubled in population since 1962. (The village had a population of 1,184 in 1963. By 1994 an estimate put the number at about 2,600.) There is not enough land for everyone to farm nor can the land produce enough to feed the growing population, even in abundant years. Work in the city is the answer, especially for householders whose land is not irrigated like Kanji's.

Cash labor has a potential to break down the kinship system that Bhils value so highly. It frees men and women from economic dependence on the family (since they make their own money working for someone else). It takes up time, too, making it difficult for them to attend the leisurely eleven-day weddings of relatives or meet other obligations to kin that require their presence. With cash labor, one's reputation is likely to hinge less on family than on work. For some, work means moving the family altogether. Devaji Katara, one of Kanji's neighbors, has a son who has moved with his wife and children to the Central Indian city of Indore. He has a good factory job there, and the move has kept them together. By doing so, however, he and they are largely removed from the kinship loop.

Despite these structural changes, kinship in Ratakote and for India as a whole remains exceptionally strong. Even though they may live farther away, Bhil sons and daughters still visit their families regularly. They send money home, and they try to attend weddings. They talk about their kin, too, and surprisingly, they continue the long process of arranging marriage for their children.

Perhaps one reason for kinship's vitality is the use to which kinship is put by many Indians. The people of Ratakote and other Indians have never given up teaching their children to respect their elders and subordinate their interests to those of the family. Family loyalty is still a paramount value. They use this loyalty to help each other economically. Family members hire each other in business. They take one another in during hard times. They offer hospitality to each other. Unlike Americans who feel guilty about accepting one-sided help from relatives, Indians look to the future. Giving aid now may pay off with a job or a favor later. Even if it doesn't, it is the proper thing to do.

Instead of breaking up the kinship network, work that takes men and families away from the village has simply stretched it out. An Indian student I know has found relatives in every American city he has visited. He knows of kin in Europe and southeast Asia too. Anywhere he goes he is likely to have relatives to stay with and to help him. When he settles down he will be expected to return the favor. Another Indian acquaintance, who went to graduate school in the United States and who continues to work here, has sent his father thousands of dollars to help with the building of a house. This act, which would surprise many Americans, seems perfectly normal to him.

Kanji is not disturbed by the economic changes that are overtaking the quiet agricultural pace of Ratakote. I last left him standing in front of his house with a grandson in his arms. His son, who had left the village in 1982 to be a "wiper" on a truck, returned to run the farm. He will be able to meet the family's obligation to lineage and feminal kin. For Kanji, traditional rules of inheritance have pulled a son and, for the moment at least, a grandson, back into the bosom of the family where they belong.

Review Questions

1. What are the main ways that kinship organizes Bhil society in Ratakote, according to McCurdy?

2. What is meant by the terms *clan, lineage, family, patrilineal descent, patrilocal residence, alliance,* and *feminal kin group?* Give examples of each.

3. Why do Bhil parents feel that marriage is too important a matter to be left up to their children?

4. What attributes do Bhil parents look for in a prospective bride or groom? How do young people try to influence the marriage partner their parents choose for them?

5. Although the U.S. kinship system seems limited by comparison to India's, many argue that it is more important than most of us think. Can you think of ways this might be true?

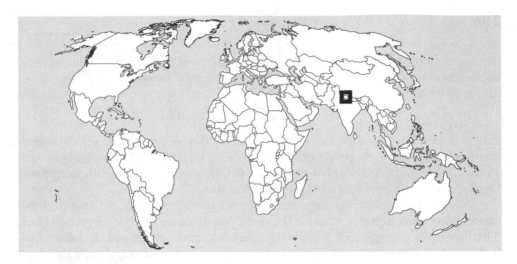

20

Polyandry: When Brothers Take a Wife

Melvyn C. Goldstein

Many of the world's societies permit polygamy, the marriage of an individual to more than one spouse. The most common form of polygamy is polygyny, an arrangement in which a man marries more than one wife. Polygyny may exist for many reasons, not the least of which is its relationship to the substantial economic contributions of women. But there is a second kind of polygamy called polyandry, organized around the marriage of a woman to more than one husband, and its causes may seem less clear. In this article, Melvyn Goldstein describes the fraternal polyandry practiced by Tibetans living in Northern Nepal and seeks to explain why, despite having a choice of marriage forms including monogamy and polygyny, men and women often choose this rare form of marriage. He argues that, by marrying a single wife,

From Melvyn C. Goldstein, "When a Brother Takes a Wife," *Natural History,* March 1987. Reprinted from *Natural History* March 1987; copyright © Natural History Magazine, Inc., 1987.

a group of brothers can more easily preserve their family resources, whereas monogamous or polygynous marriage usually costs a man his inheritance and requires him to make a fresh start.

———————————

Eager to reach home. Dorje drives his yaks hard over the seventeen-thousand-foot mountain pass, stopping only once to rest. He and his two older brothers, Pema and Sonam, are jointly marrying a woman from the next village in a few weeks, and he has to help with the preparations.

Dorje, Pema, and Sonam are Tibetans living in Limi, a two-hundred-square-mile area in the northwest corner of Nepal, across the border from Tibet. The form of marriage they are about to enter—fraternal polyandry in anthropological parlance—is one of the world's rarest forms of marriage but is not uncommon in Tibetan society, where it has been practiced from time immemorial. For many Tibetan social strata, it traditionally represented the ideal form of marriage and family.

The mechanics of fraternal polyandry are simple. Two, three, four, or more brothers jointly take a wife, who leaves her home to come and live with them. Traditionally, marriage was arranged by parents, with children, particularly females, having little or no say. This is changing somewhat nowadays, but it is still unusual for children to marry without their parents' consent. Marriage ceremonies vary by income and region and range from all the brothers sitting together as grooms to only the eldest one formally doing so. The age of the brothers plays an important role in determining this: very young brothers almost never participate in actual marriage ceremonies, although they typically join the marriage when they reach their midteens.

The eldest brother is normally dominant in terms of authority, that is, in managing the household, but all the brothers share the work and participate as sexual partners. Tibetan males and females do not find the sexual aspect of sharing a spouse the least bit unusual, repulsive, or scandalous, and the norm is for the wife to treat all the brothers the same.

Offspring are treated similarly. There is no attempt to link children biologically to particular brothers, and a brother shows no favoritism toward his child even if he knows he is the real father because, for example, his other brothers were away at the time the wife became pregnant. The children, in turn, consider all of the brothers as their fathers and treat them equally, even if they also know who is their real father. In some regions children use the term "father" for the eldest brother and "father's brother" for the others, while in other areas they call all the brothers by one term, modifying this by the use of "elder" and "younger."

Unlike our own society, where monogamy is the only form of marriage permitted, Tibetan society allows a variety of marriage types, including monogamy, fraternal polyandry, and polygyny. Fraternal polyandry and monogamy are the most common forms of marriage, while polygyny typically occurs in cases where the first wife is barren. The widespread practice of fraternal polyandry, therefore, is not the outcome of a law requiring brothers to marry jointly. There is choice, and in fact, divorce traditionally was relatively simple in Tibetan society. If a brother in a polyandrous marriage became dissatisfied and wanted to separate, he simply left the main house and set up his own household. In such cases, all the children stayed in the main household with the remaining brother(s), even if the departing brother was known to be the real father of one or more of the children.

The Tibetans' own explanation for choosing fraternal polyandry is materialistic. For example, when I asked Dorje why he decided to marry with his two brothers rather than take his own wife, he thought for a moment, then said it prevented the division of his family's farm (and animals) and thus facilitated all of them achieving a higher standard of living. And when I later asked Dorje's bride whether it wasn't difficult for her to cope with three brothers as husbands, she laughed and echoed the rationale of avoiding fragmentation of the family and land, adding that she expected to be better off economically, since she would have three husbands working for her and her children.

Exotic as it may seem to Westerners, Tibetan fraternal polyandry is thus in many ways analogous to the way primogeniture functioned in nineteenth-century England. Primogeniture dictated that the eldest son inherited the family estate, while younger sons had to leave home and seek their own employment—for example, in the military or the clergy. Primogeniture maintained family estates intact over generations by permitting only one heir per generation. Fraternal polyandry also accomplishes this but does so by keeping all the brothers together with just one wife so that there is only one *set* of heirs per generation.

While Tibetans believe that in this way fraternal polyandry reduces the risk of family fission, monogamous marriages among brothers need not necessarily precipitate the division of the family estate: brothers could continue to live together, and the family land could continue to be worked jointly. When I asked Tibetans about this, however, they invariably responded that such joint families are unstable because each wife is primarily oriented to her own children and interested in their success and well-being over that of the children of the other wives. For example, if the youngest brother's wife had three sons while the eldest brother's wife had only one daughter, the wife of the youngest brother might begin to demand more resources for her children since, as males, they represent the future of the family. Thus the children from different wives in the same generation are competing sets of heirs, and this makes such families inherently unstable. Tibetans perceive that conflict will spread from the wives to their husbands and consider this likely to cause family fission. Consequently, it is almost never done.

Although Tibetans see an economic advantage to fraternal polyandry, they do not value the sharing of a wife as an end in itself. On the contrary, they articulate a number of problems inherent in the practice. For example, because authority is customarily exercised by the eldest brother, his younger male siblings have to subordinate themselves with little hope of changing their status within the family. When these younger brothers are aggressive and individualistic, tensions and difficulties often occur despite there being only one set of heirs.

In addition, tension and conflict may arise in polyandrous families because of sexual favoritism. The bride normally sleeps with the eldest brother, and the two have the responsibility to see to it that the other males have opportunities for sexual access. Since the Tibetan subsistence economy requires males to travel a lot, the temporary absence of one or more brothers facilitates this, but there are also other rotation practices. The cultural ideal unambiguously calls for the wife to show equal affection and sexuality to each of the brothers (and vice versa), but deviations from this ideal occur, especially when there is a sizable difference in age between the partners in the marriage.

Dorje's family represents just such a potential situation. He is fifteen years old and his two older brothers are twenty-five and twenty-two years old. The new bride is twenty-three years old, eight years Dorje's senior. Sometimes such a bride finds the youngest husband immature and adolescent and does not treat him with equal affection; alternatively, she may find his youth attractive and lavish special attention on him. Apart from that consideration, when a younger male like Dorje grows up, he may consider his wife "ancient" and prefer the company of a woman his own age or younger. Consequently, although men and women do not find the idea of sharing a bride or a bridegroom repulsive, individual likes and dislikes can cause familial discord.

Two reasons have commonly been offered for the perpetuation of fraternal polyandry in Tibet: that Tibetans practice female infanticide and therefore have to marry polyandrously, owing to a shortage of females; and that Tibet, lying at extremely high altitudes, is so barren and bleak that Tibetans would starve without resort to this mechanism. A Jesuit who lived in Tibet during the eighteenth century articulated this second view: "One reason for this most odious custom is the sterility of the soil, and the small amount of land that can be cultivated owing to the lack of water. The crops may suffice if the brothers all live together, but if they form separate families they would be reduced to beggary."

Both explanations are wrong, however. Not only has there never been institutionalized female infanticide in Tibet, but Tibetan society gives females considerable rights, including inheriting the family estate in the absence of brothers. In such cases, the woman takes a bridegroom who comes to live in her family and adopts her family's name and identity. Moreover, there is no demographic evidence of a shortage of females. In Limi, for example, there were (in 1974) sixty females and fifty-three males in the fifteen- to thirty-five-year age category, and many adult females were unmarried.

The second reason is incorrect because the climate in Tibet is extremely harsh, and ecological factors do play a major role in perpetuating polyandry, but polyandry is not a means of preventing starvation. It is characteristic, not of the poorest segments of the society, but rather of the peasant landowning families.

In the old society, the landless poor could not realistically aspire to prosperity, but they did not fear starvation. There was a persistent labor shortage throughout Tibet, and very poor families with little or no land and few animals could subsist through agricultural labor, tenant farming, craft occupations such as carpentry, or by working as servants. Although the per-person family income could increase somewhat if brothers married polyandrously and pooled their wages, in the absence of inheritable land, the advantage of fraternal polyandry was not generally sufficient to prevent them from setting up their own households. A more skilled or energetic younger brother could do as well or better alone, since he would completely control his income and would not have to share it with his siblings. Consequently, while there was and is some polyandry among the poor, it is much less frequent and more prone to result in divorce and family fission.

An alternative reason for the persistence of fraternal polyandry is that it reduces population growth (and thereby reduces the pressure on resources) by relegating some females to lifetime spinsterhood (see Figure 1). Fraternal polyandrous marriages in Limi (in 1974) averaged 2.35 men per woman, and not surprisingly, 31 percent of the females of child-bearing age (twenty to forty-nine) were unmarried. These spinsters either continued to live at home, set up their own households, or worked as servants for other families. They could also become Buddhist nuns. Being unmarried is not synonymous with exclusion from the reproductive pool. Discreet extramarital relationships are tolerated, and actually half of the adult unmarried women in Limi had one or more children. They raised these children as single mothers, working for wages or weaving cloth and blankets for sale. As a group, however, the unmarried women had far fewer offspring than the married women, averaging only 0.7 children per woman, compared with 3.3 for married women, whether polyandrous, monogamous, or polygynous. When polyandry helps regulate population, this function of polyandry is not consciously perceived by Tibetans and is not the reason they consistently choose it.

If neither a shortage of females nor the fear of starvation perpetuates fraternal polyandry, what motivates brothers, particularly younger brothers, to opt for this system of marriage? From the perspective of the younger brother in a landholding family, the main incentive is the attainment or maintenance of the good life. With polyandry, he can expect a more secure and higher standard of living, with access not only to his family's land and animals but also to its inherited collection of clothes, jewelry, rugs, saddles, and horses. In addition, he will experience less work pressure and much greater security because all responsibility does not fall on one "father." For Tibetan brothers, the question is whether to trade off the greater personal freedom inherent in monogamy for the real or potential economic security, affluence, and social prestige associated with life in a larger, labor-rich polyandrous family.

A brother thinking of separating from his polyandrous marriage and taking his own wife would face various disadvantages. Although in the majority of Tibetan regions all brothers theoretically have rights to their family's estate, in reality Tibetans are reluctant to divide their land into small fragments. Generally, a

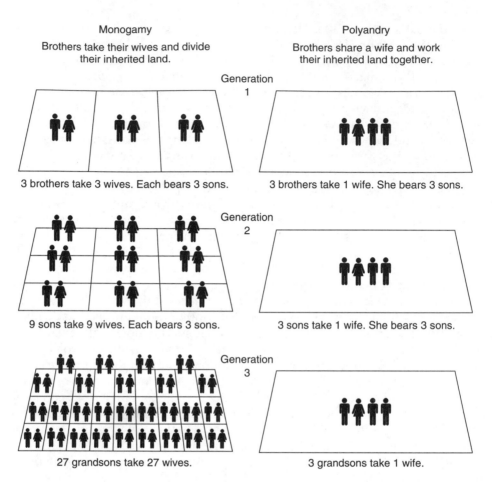

Monogamy

Brothers take their wives and divide
their inherited land.

Polyandry

Brothers share a wife and work
their inherited land together.

Generation
1

3 brothers take 3 wives. Each bears 3 sons.

3 brothers take 1 wife. She bears 3 sons.

Generation
2

9 sons take 9 wives. Each bears 3 sons.

3 sons take 1 wife. She bears 3 sons.

Generation
3

27 grandsons take 27 wives.

3 grandsons take 1 wife.

FIGURE 1   Family Planning in Tibet
An economic rationale for fraternal polyandry is outlined in the diagram above, which
emphasizes only the male offspring in each generation. If every wife is assumed
to bear three sons, a family splitting up into monogamous households would rapidly
multiply and fragment the family land. In this case, a rule of inheritance, such as
primogeniture, could retain the family land intact, but only at the cost of creating
many landless male offspring. In contrast, the family practicing fraternal
polyandry maintains a steady ratio of persons to land.

younger brother who insists on leaving the family will receive only a small plot of
land, if that. Because of its power and wealth, the rest of the family usually can
block any attempt of the younger brother to increase his share of land through lit-
igation. Moreover, a younger brother may not even get a house and cannot expect
to receive much above the minimum in terms of movable possessions, such as
furniture, pots, and pans. Thus a brother contemplating going it on his own must
plan on achieving economic security and the good life not through inheritance
but through his own work.

The obvious solution for younger brothers—creating new fields from virgin land—is generally not a feasible option. Most Tibetan populations live at high altitudes (above 12,000 feet), where arable land is extremely scarce. For example, in Dorje's village, agriculture ranges only from about 12,900 feet, the lowest point in the area, to 13,300 feet. Above that altitude, early frost and snow destroy the staple barley crop. Furthermore, because of the low rainfall caused by the Himalayan rain shadow, many areas in Tibet and northern Nepal that are within the appropriate altitude range for agriculture have no reliable sources of irrigation. In the end, although there is plenty of unused land in such areas, most of it is either too high or too arid.

Even where unused land capable of being farmed exists, clearing the land and building the substantial terraces necessary for irrigation constitute a great undertaking. Each plot has to be completely dug out to a depth of two to two and a half feet so that the large rocks and boulders can be removed. At best, a man might be able to bring a few new fields under cultivation in the first years after separating from his brothers, but he could not expect to acquire substantial amounts of arable land this way.

In addition, because of the limited farmland, the Tibetan subsistence economy characteristically includes a strong emphasis on animal husbandry. Tibetan farmers regularly maintain cattle, yaks, goats, and sheep, grazing them in the areas too high for agriculture. These herds produce wool, milk, cheese, butter, meat, and skins. To obtain these resources, however, shepherds must accompany the animals on a daily basis. When first setting up a monogamous household, a younger brother like Dorje would find it difficult to both farm and manage animals.

In traditional Tibetan society, there was an even more critical factor that operated to perpetuate fraternal polyandry—a form of hereditary servitude somewhat analogous to serfdom in Europe. Peasants were tied to large estates held by aristocrats, monasteries, and the Lhasa government. They were allowed the use of some farmland to produce their own subsistence but were required to provide taxes in kind and corvée (free labor) to their lords. The corvée was a substantial hardship, since a peasant household was in many cases required to furnish the lord with one laborer daily for most of the year and more on specific occasions such as the harvest. This enforced labor, along with the lack of new land and the ecological pressure to pursue both agriculture and animal husbandry, made polyandrous families particularly beneficial. The polyandrous family allowed an internal division of adult labor, maximizing economic advantage. For example, while the wife worked the family fields, one brother could perform the lord's corvée, another could look after the animals, and a third could engage in trade.

Although social scientists often discount other people's explanations of why they do things, in the case of Tibetan fraternal polyandry, such explanations are very close to the truth. The custom, however, is very sensitive to changes in its political and economic milieu and, not surprisingly, is in decline in most Tibetan areas. Made less important by the elimination of the traditional serf-based economy, it is disparaged by the dominant non-Tibetan leaders of India, China, and Nepal.

New opportunities for economic and social mobility in these countries, such as the tourist trade and government employment, are also eroding the rationale for polyandry, and so it may vanish within the next generation.

Review Questions

1. What is fraternal polyandry, and how does this form of marriage manage potential conflict over sex, children, and inheritance?

2. Why do many Tibetans choose polyandry over monogamous or polygynous marriage?

3. According to Tibetans, what are some of the disadvantages of polyandry?

4. What is wrong with the theory that Tibetan polyandry is caused either by a shortage of women due to infanticide or is a way to prevent famine by limiting population and land pressure?

5. Why might Tibetan polyandry disappear under modern conditions?

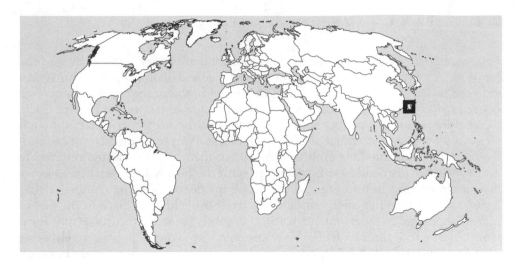

21

Uterine Families and the Women's Community

Margery Wolf

The size and organization of extended families vary from one society to the next, but extended families often share some important attributes. They are most often based on a rule of patrilineal descent. For men, the patrilineal family extends in an unbroken line of ancestors and descendants. Membership is permanent; loyalty assured. For women, the patrilineal family is temporary. Born into one family and married into another, women discover that their happiness and interests depend on bearing children to create their own uterine family. This and the importance of a local women's group are the subjects of this article by Margery Wolf in her discussion of Taiwanese family life.

Few women in China experience the continuity that is typical of the lives of the menfolk. A woman can and, if she is ever to have any economic security, must provide the links in the male chain of descent, but she will never appear in anyone's genealogy as that all-important name connecting the past to the future. If she dies before she is married, her tablet will not appear on her father's altar; although she was a temporary member of his household, she was not a member of his family. A man is born into his family and remains a member of it throughout his life and even after his death. He is identified with the family from birth, and every action concerning him, up to and including his death, is in the context of that group. Whatever other uncertainties may trouble his life, his place in the line of ancestors provides a permanent setting. There is no such secure setting for a woman. She will abruptly leave the household into which she is born, either as an infant or as an adult bride, and enter another whose members treat her with suspicion or even hostility.

A man defines his family as a large group that includes the dead, and not-yet-born, and the living members of his household. But how does a woman define her family? This is not a question that China specialists often consider, but from their treatment of the family in general, it would seem that a woman's family is identical with that of the senior male in the household in which she lives. Although I have never asked, I imagine a Taiwanese man would define a woman's family in very much those same terms. Women, I think, would give quite a different answer. They do not have an unchanging place, assigned at birth, in any group, and their view of the family reflects this.

When she is a child, a woman's family is defined for her by her mother and to some extent by her grandmother. No matter how fond of his daughter the father may be, she is only a temporary member of his household and useless to his family—he cannot even marry her to one of his sons as he could an adopted daughter. Her irrelevance to her father's family in turn affects the daughter's attitude toward it. It is of no particular interest to her, and the need to maintain its continuity has little meaning for her beyond the fact that this continuity matters a great deal to some of the people she loves. As a child she probably accepts to some degree her grandmother's orientation toward the family: the household, that is, those people who live together and eat together, including perhaps one or more of her father's married brothers and their children. But the group that has the most meaning for her and with which she will have the most lasting ties is the smaller, more cohesive unit centering on her mother, that is, the uterine family—her mother and her mother's children. Father is important to the group, just as grandmother is important to some of the children, but he is not quite a member of it, and for some uterine families he may even be "the enemy." As the girl grows up and her grandmother dies and a brother or two marries, she discovers that her mother's definition of the family is becoming less exclusive and may even include such outsiders as her brother's new wife. Without knowing precisely when it happened, she finds that her brother's interests and goals have shifted in a direction she cannot follow. Her mother does not push her aside, but when the mother speaks of the future, she speaks in terms of her son's future. Although the mother sees her uterine family as adding new members and another generation, her daughter sees it as dissolving, leaving her with strong particular relationships, but with no group to which she has permanent loyalties and obligations.

When a young woman marries, her formal ties with the household of her father are severed. In one of the rituals of the wedding ceremony the bride's father or brothers symbolically inform her by means of spilt water that she, like the water, may never return, and when her wedding sedan chair passes over the threshold of her father's house, the doors are slammed shut behind her. If she is ill-treated by her husband's family, her father's family may intervene, but unless her parents are willing to bring her home and support her for the rest of her life (and most parents are not), there is little they can do beyond shaming the other family. This is usually enough.

As long as her mother is alive, the daughter will continue her contacts with her father's household by as many visits as her new situation allows. If she lives nearby she may visit every few days, and no matter where she lives she must at least be allowed to return at New Year. After her mother dies her visits may become perfunctory, but her relations with at least one member of her uterine family, the group that centered on her mother, remain strong. Her brother plays an important ritual role throughout her life. She may gradually lose contact with her sisters as she and they become more involved with their own children, but her relations with her brother continue. When her sons marry, he is the guest of honor at the wedding feasts, and when her daughters marry he must give a small banquet in their honor. If her sons wish to divide their father's estate, it is their mother's brother who is called on to supervise. And when she dies, the coffin cannot be closed until her brother determines to his own satisfaction that she died a natural death and that her husband's family did everything possible to prevent it.

With the ritual slam of her father's door on her wedding day, a young woman finds herself quite literally without a family. She enters the household of her husband—a man who in an earlier time, say fifty years ago, she would never have met and who even today, in modern rural Taiwan, she is unlikely to know very well. She is an outsider, and for Chinese an outsider is always an object of deep suspicion. Her husband and her father-in-law do not see her as a member of their family. But they do see her as essential to it; they have gone to great expense to bring her into their household for the purpose of bearing a new generation for their family. Her mother-in-law, who was mainly responsible for negotiating the terms of her entry, may harbor some resentment over the hard bargaining, but she is nonetheless eager to see another generation added to *her* uterine family. A mother-in-law often has the same kind of ambivalence toward her daughter-in-law as she has toward her husband—the younger woman seems a member of her family at times and merely a member of the household at others. The new bride may find that her husband's sister is hostile or at best condescending, both attitudes reflecting the daughter's distress at an outsider who seems to be making her way right into the heart of the family.

Chinese children are taught by proverb, by example, and by experience that the family is the source of their security, and relatives the only people who can be depended on. Ostracism from the family is one of the harshest sanctions that can be imposed on erring youth. One of the reasons mainlanders as individuals are considered so untrustworthy on Taiwan is the fact that they are not subject to the controls of (and therefore have no fear of ostracism from) their families. If a timid new bride is considered an object of suspicion and potentially dangerous because she is a stranger, think how uneasy her own first few months must be surrounded by strangers. Her irrelevance to her father's family may result in her having little reverence for descent lines, but she has warm memories of the security of the family her mother created. If she is ever to return to this certainty and sense of belonging, a woman must create her own uterine family by bearing children, a goal that happily corresponds to the goals of the family into which she has married. She may gradually create a tolerable niche for herself in the household of her mother-in-law, but her family will not be formed until she herself forms it of her own children and grandchildren. In most cases, by the time she adds grandchildren, the uterine family and the household will almost completely overlap, and there will be another daughter-in-law struggling with loneliness and beginning a new uterine family.

The ambiguity of a man's position in relation to the uterine families accounts for much of the hostility between mother-in-law and daughter-in-law. There is no question in the mind of the older woman but that her son is her family. The daughter-in-law might be content with this situation once her sons are old enough to represent her interests in the household and in areas strictly under men's control, but until then, she is dependent on her husband. If she were to be completely absorbed into her mother-in-law's family—a rare occurrence unless she is a *simpua*—there would be little or no conflict; but under most circumstances she must rely on her husband, her mother-in-law's son, as her spokesman, and here is where the trouble begins. Since it is usually events within the household that she wishes to affect, and the household more or less overlaps with her mother-in-law's uterine family, even a minor foray by the younger woman suggests to the older one an all-out attack on everything she has worked so hard to build in the years of her own loneliness and insecurity. The birth of grandchildren further complicates their relations, for the one sees them as new members for her family and the other as desperately needed recruits to her own small circle of security.

In summary, my thesis contends . . . that because we have heretofore focused on men when examining the Chinese family—a reasonable approach to a patrilineal system—we have missed not only some of the system's subtleties but also its near-fatal weaknesses. With a male focus we see the Chinese family as a line of descent, bulging to encompass all the members of a man's household and spreading out through his descendants. With a female focus, however, we see the Chinese family not as a continuous line stretching between the vague horizons of past and future, but as a contemporary group that comes into existence out of one woman's need and is held together insofar as she has the strength to do so, or, for that matter, the need to do so. After her death the uterine family survives only in the mind of her son and is symbolized by the special attention he gives her earthly remains and her ancestral tablet. The rites themselves are demanded by the ideology of the patriliny, but the meaning they hold for most sons is formed in the uterine family. The uterine family has no ideology, no formal structure, and no public existence. It is built out of sentiments and loyalties that die with its members, but it is no less real for all that. The descent lines of men are born and nourished in the uterine families of women, and it is here that a male ideology that excludes women makes its accommodations with reality.

Women in rural Taiwan do not live their lives in the walled courtyards of their husband's households. If they did, they might be as powerless as their stereotype. It is in their relations in the outside world (and for women in rural Taiwan that world consists almost entirely of the village) that women develop sufficient backing to maintain some independence under their powerful mothers-in-law and even occasionally to bring the men's world to terms. A successful venture into the men's world is no small feat when one recalls that the men of a village were born there and are often related to one another, whereas the women are unlikely to have either the ties of childhood or the ties of kinship to unite them. All the same, the needs, shared interests, and common problems of women are reflected in every village in a loosely knit society that can when needed be called on to exercise considerable influence.

Women carry on as many of their activities as possible outside the house. They wash clothes on the riverbank, clean and pare vegetables at a communal pump, mend under a tree that is a known meetingplace, and stop to rest on a bench or group of stones with other women. There is a continual moving back and forth between kitchens, and conversations are carried on from open doorways through the long, hot afternoons of summer. The shy young girl who enters the village as a bride is examined as frankly and suspiciously by the women as an animal that is up for sale. If she is deferential to her elders, does not criticize or compare her new world unfavorably with the one she has left, the older residents will gradually accept her presence on the edge of their conversations and stop changing the topic to general subjects when she brings the family laundry to scrub on the rocks near them. As the young bride meets other girls in her position, she makes allies for the future, but she must also develop relationships with the older women. She learns to use considerable discretion in making and receiving confidences, for a girl who gossips freely about the affairs of her husband's household may find herself labeled a troublemaker. On the other hand, a girl who is too reticent may find herself always on the outside of the group, or worse yet, accused of snobbery. I described in *The House of Lim* the plight of Lim Chui-ieng, who had little village backing in her troubles with her husband and his family as the result of her arrogance toward the women's community. In Peihotien the young wife of the storekeeper's son suffered a similar lack of support. Warned by her husband's parents not to be too "easy" with the other villagers lest they try to buy things on credit, she obeyed to the point of being considered unfriendly by the women of the village. When she began to have serious troubles with her husband and eventually his family, there was no one in the village she could turn to for solace, advice, and, most important, peacemaking.

Once a young bride has established herself as a member of the women's community, she has also established for herself a certain amount of protection. If the members of her husband's family step beyond the limits of propriety in their treatment of her—such as refusing to allow her to return to her natal home for her brother's wedding or beating her without serious justification—she can complain to a woman friend, preferably older, while they are washing vegetables at the communal pump. The story will quickly spread to the other women, and one of them will take it on herself to check the facts with another member of the girl's household. For a few days the matter will be thoroughly discussed whenever a few women gather. In a young wife's first few years in the community, she can expect to have her mother-in-law's side of any disagreement given fuller weight than her own—her mother-in-law has, after all, been a part of the community a lot longer. However, the discussion itself will serve to curb many offenses. Even if the older woman knows that public opinion is falling to her side, she will still be somewhat more judicious about refusing her daughter-in-law's next request. Still, the daughter-in-law who hopes to make use of the village forum to depose her mother-in-law or at least gain herself special privilege will discover just how important the prerogatives of age and length of residence are. Although the women can serve as a powerful protective force for their defenseless younger members, they are also a very conservative force in the village.

Taiwanese women can and do make use of their collective power to lose face for their menfolk in order to influence decisions that are ostensibly not theirs to make. Although young women may have little or no influence over their husbands and would not dare express an unsolicited opinion (and perhaps not even a solicited one) to their fathers-in-law, older women who have raised their sons properly retain considerable influence over their sons' actions, even in activities exclusive to men. Further, older women who have displayed years of good judgment are regularly consulted by their husbands about major as well as minor economic and social projects. But even men who think themselves free to ignore the opinions of their women are never free of their own concept, face. It is much easier to lose face than to have face. We once asked a male friend in Peihotien just what "having face" amounted to. He replied, "When no one is talking about a family, you can say it has face." This is precisely where women wield their power. When a man behaves in a way that they consider wrong, they talk about him—not only among themselves, but to their sons and husbands. No one "tells him how to mind his own business," but it becomes abundantly clear that he is losing face and by continuing in this manner may bring shame to the family of his ancestors and descendants. Few men will risk that.

The rules that a Taiwanese man must learn and obey to be a successful member of his society are well developed, clear, and relatively easy to stay within. A Taiwanese woman must also learn the rules, but if she is to be a successful woman, she must learn not to stay within them, but to *appear* to stay within them; to manipulate them, but not to appear to be manipulating them; to teach them to her children, but not to depend on her children for her protection. A truly successful Taiwanese woman is a rugged individualist who has learned to depend largely on herself while appearing to lean on her father, her husband, and her son. The contrast between the terrified young bride and the loud, confident, often lewd old woman who has outlived her mother-in-law and her husband reflects the tests met and passed by not strictly following the rules and by making purposeful use of those who must. The Chinese male's conception of women as "narrow-hearted" and socially inept may well be his vague recognition of this facet of women's power and technique.

The women's subculture in rural Taiwan is, I believe, below the level of consciousness. Mothers do not tell their about-to-be-married daughters how to establish themselves in village society so that they may have some protection from an oppressive family situation, nor do they warn them to gather their children into an exclusive circle under their own control. But girls grow up in village society and see their mothers and sisters-in-law settling their differences to keep them from a public airing or presenting them for the women's community to judge. Their mothers have created around them the meaningful unit in their father's households, and when they are desperately lonely and unhappy in the households of their husbands, what they long for is what they have lost. . . . [Some] areas in the subculture of women . . . mesh perfectly into the main culture of the society. The two cultures are not symbiotic because they are not sufficiently independent of one another, but neither do they share identical goals or necessarily use the same means to reach the goals they do share. Outside the village the women's subculture seems not to exist. The uterine family also has no public existence, and appears almost as a response to the traditional family organized in terms of a male ideology.

Review Questions

1. According to Wolf, what is a uterine family, and what relatives are likely to be members?

2. Why is the uterine family important to Chinese women who live in their husband's patrilineal extended families?

3. What is the relationship between a woman's uterine family and her power within her husband's family?

4. Why might the existence of the uterine family contribute to the division of extended families into smaller constituent parts?

5. How do you think a Chinese woman's desire to have a uterine family affects attempts to limit the Chinese population?

SIX

IDENTITY, ROLES, AND GROUPS

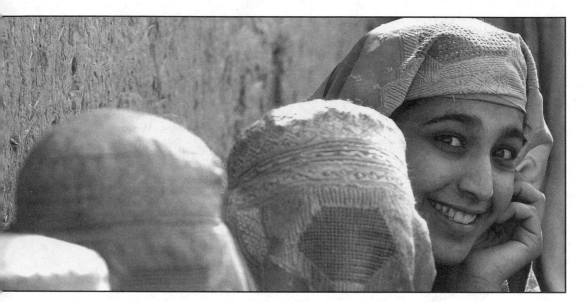

Emmanuel Dunand/Getty Images, Inc.—Agence France Presse

READINGS IN THIS SECTION

Heading Home: Women, Work, and Identity in America   215
Dianna Shandy and Karine Moe

Poverty at Work: Office Employment and the Crack Alternative   227
Philippe Bourgois

Symbolizing Roles: Behind the Veil   240
Elizabeth W. Fernea and Robert A. Fernea

Mixed Blood   248
Jeffrey M. Fish

For most of us, social interaction is unconscious and automatic. We associate with other people from the time we are born. Of course we experience moments when we feel socially awkward and out of place, but generally we learn to act toward others with confidence. Yet our unconscious ease masks an enormously complex process. When we enter a social situation, how do we know what to do? What should we say? How are we supposed to act? Are we dressed appropriately? Are we talking to the right person? Without knowing it, we have learned a complex set of cultural categories for social interaction that enables us to estimate the social situation, identify the people in it, act appropriately, and recognize larger groups of people.

Status and roles are basic to social intercourse. **Status** refers to the categories of different kinds of people who interact. The old saying, "You can't tell the players without a program," goes for our daily associations as well. Instead of a program, however, we identify the actors by a range of signs, from the way they dress to the claims they make about themselves. Most statuses are named, so we may be heard to say things like, "That's President Gavin," or "She's a lawyer," when we explain social situations to others. This identification of actors is a prerequisite for appropriate social interaction.

Roles are the rules for action associated with particular statuses. We use them to interpret and generate social behavior. For example, a professor plays a role in the classroom. Although often not conscious of this role, the professor will stand, use the blackboard, look at notes, and speak with a slightly more formal air than usual. The professor does not wear blue jeans and a T-shirt, chew gum, sit cross-legged on the podium, or sing. These actions might be appropriate for this person when assuming the identity of "friend" at a party, but they are out of place in the classroom.

People also always relate to each other in **social situations,** the settings in which social interaction takes place. Social situations consist of a combination of times, places, objects, and events. For example, if we see a stranger carrying a television set across campus at four o'clock in the afternoon, we will probably ignore the activity. Most likely someone is simply moving. But if we see the same person carrying the set at four in the morning, we may suspect a theft. Only the time has changed, but it is a significant marker of the social situation. Similarly, we expect classrooms to be associated with lectures, and stethoscopes to be part of medical exams. Such places and objects mark the social situations of which they are part.

People also belong to groups. **Social groups** are organized collections of individuals. They are often named—the Republican Party, American Motorcyclist Association, General Motors—although some, such as friends who meet for drinks after work on Fridays, may be anonymous and less formal. Social groups have several attributes. The people who belong to them normally recognize their common membership and share the goals of the group. The group should share an "inside" culture and its members should interact with each other. Groups are also organized internally in some way. Tasks are often divided among members. Finally, groups usually link to one another. For example, when a couple marries, their union connects the families of the bride and groom. There are some collections of people that we might think of as groups that do not fit this definition. "Middle-class" people, for example, are an aggregate, not a social group, because they are not an interacting organized collective. No one says, "I am meeting tonight with my middle-class men's association."

As societies around the world grow larger, it becomes more difficult to identify groups. People may do most of their socializing in **social networks,** the individuals with whom they regularly interact. Networks are not groups; they are defined only in relation to a particular individual. Nonetheless they are important because they may involve a substantial part of an individual's social interaction. A "social messiness" also afflicts interaction worldwide. People freely travel and enter new social situations where culture is not fully shared. Individuals can interact in dozens of different social situations each day.

Groups form around several principles. Every society has kinship groups, the topic of the previous section of this book. Ethnic groups organize around a shared cultural background. Some groups, such as the American Association of Retired Persons, are based on age. Others, like the National Organization for Women, are based on gender. The Macalester/Groveland Community Association is a territorial group. Many groups, such as the Gold Wing Road Riders Association (a national motorcycle group), Ford Motor Company (an economic group), and Mothers Against Drunk Driving (an interest group) organize around common goals and interests. Many groups are built around several of these design principles at once.

Finally groups can also be organized around social hierarchy. Some degree of **inequality** is part of most human interaction. One spouse may dominate another; a child may receive more attention than his or her siblings; the boss's friends may be promoted faster than other employees. But inequality becomes most noticeable when it systematically affects whole classes of people. In its most obvious form, inequality emerges as **social stratification,** which is characterized by regularly experienced unequal access to valued economic resources and prestige.

Anthropologists recognize at least two kinds of social stratification: class and caste. **Class** stratification restricts individuals' access to valued resources and prestige within a partially flexible system. Although it is often a difficult process, individuals may change rank in a class system if they manage to acquire the necessary prerequisites.

Many sociologists and anthropologists believe that there is an American class system and use terms such as *lower class, working class, middle class,* and *upper class* to designate the unequal positions within it. Americans born into poverty lack access to goods and prestige in this system but can change class standing if they acquire wealth and symbols of higher standing on a continuing basis. Upward mobility is difficult to achieve, however, and few people at the bottom of the system manage to change rank significantly. Indeed, many social scientists feel there is now a permanent underclass in the United States.

Caste defines a second kind of social stratification, one based on permanent membership. People are born into castes and cannot change membership, no matter what they do. In India, for example, caste is a pervasive feature of social organization. South Asians are born into castes and remain members for life; intercaste marriage is forbidden. In the past, castes formed the building blocks of rural Indian society. They were governed by strict rules of deference and served to allocate access to jobs, land, wealth, and power. Cash labor and new industrial jobs have eroded the economic aspect of the system today, but caste persists as a form of rank throughout most of the Indian subcontinent.

Several anthropologists and sociologists have argued that American racial groups are the equivalent of Indian castes. Black and white Americans keep their racial identity for life; nothing can change one's race. Racial identity clearly affects chances for the acquisition of prestige and economic success.

Caste identity, whether Indian or American, tends to preserve and create cultural difference. There is noticeable cultural variation among members of castes in most Indian villages, just as cultural variation occurs among black and white people in the United States.

Using the idea of social stratification, anthropologists have constructed a rough classification of societies into three types: egalitarian, rank, and stratified. **Egalitarian societies** lack formal social stratification. They may display inequality in personal relations based on age, gender, or personal ability, but no category of persons within the same sex or age group has special privilege. Hunter-gatherer societies are most likely to be egalitarian.

Rank societies contain unequal access to prestige, but not to valued economic resources. In such societies there may be chiefs or other persons with authority and prestige, and they may gain access to rank by birth, but their positions give them no substantial economic advantage. Horticultural societies, including some chiefdomships, fit this category.

Stratified societies organize around formal modes of social stratification, as their name suggests. Members of stratified societies are likely to form classes or castes, and inequality affects access to both prestige and economic resources. Most complex societies, including agrarian and industrialized states, fit into this type.

Inequality may also be based on other human attributes, such as age and gender. In many societies, including our own, age and gender affect access to prestige, power, and resources. It is common for men to publicly outrank women along these dimensions, particularly in societies threatened by war or other adversity that requires male intervention.

The articles in this part explore the nature of status, role, and inequality. The first, by Dianna Shandy and Karine Moe, looks at a recent trend, the tendency for young, professionally trained women to leave high-paying jobs once only open to men, to be at home with their children. Stressed by the need to compete full-time at work yet drawn by the needs and pleasure of being with their children, the move seems a sensible solution if a husband's salary is sufficient or other money is available. Returning to work later when the children are grown is an option but may require a change of career. The second article, by Philippe Bourgois, deals with the plight of poorly educated Puerto Rican men living in New York City. Once able to work at steady, adequately paid, manufacturing jobs, they now can find only minimum wage work in New York's service economy because manufacturers have left the city. The lack of income and respect they find there makes selling crack more appealing. The article by Elizabeth and Robert Fernea describes the importance of the veil as a symbol defining the role and rank of women in the Middle East. Viewed by many Western women as a sign of female degradation, more Middle Eastern women have begun to wear the veil to symbolize their Muslim identity. Finally, the fourth article, by Jeffrey Fish, looks at the way Americans define race. Seen by most Americans as a biologically determined subspecies of human beings, but actually a culturally defined taxonomy based on the classification of one's parents, race in the United States is entirely different from racial categories in Brazil.

Key Terms

caste   p. 213

class   p. 212

egalitarian societies   p. 213

inequality   p. 212

rank societies   p. 213

role   p. 211

social groups   p. 211

social networks   p. 212

social situation   p. 211

social stratification   p. 212

status   p. 211

stratified societies   p. 213

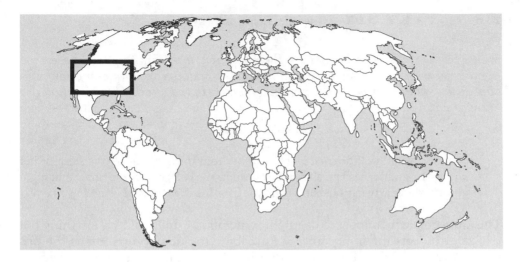

22

Heading Home: Women, Work, and Identity in America

Dianna Shandy and Karine Moe

Young, successfully employed college-educated women face a dilemma when they decide to have children. Can they continue to work full-time with the same intensity that up to then has brought them occupational success, or will they have to cut back? What will adjustments required by motherhood and family do to their occupational identity and ability to compete on an equal basis with men? In this article, Dianna Shandy and Karine Moe discuss these and other questions concerning women's work and place in the home once they have children. Basing their comments on extensive interviews and focus groups as well as labor statistics, they argue that younger professional women, pushed by the stress of trying to do everything and

Original article from Dianna J. Shandy and Karine S. Moe, "Heading for Home: Women, Work, and Identity in America." Used by permission of the authors.

pulled by the pleasure of being with their children, are beginning to choose home over work once they have a family. Despite doing so, they can often continue to hold their past occupational identity in the minds of those who know them.

Jennifer, a tall, well-dressed woman in her mid-thirties, fingers the stem of her wine glass and braces herself for the question she will get a dozen times that night at a cocktail party her husband is holding for his clients: *"And what do you do?"*

This question, which most of us might write off as "small talk," is anything but trivial. It reflects the importance we attribute to one's occupation as the primary source of our public social identity. So normally when we answer the what-do-you-do question, we identity ourselves by our occupation. We might say things such as, "I am a college professor at Metro State," or "I'm a wealth management consultant over at Grant and Smith Securities."

Although most North Americans don't like to admit there is a class system (we prefer to believe we accept people for "who they are"), we actually, and often without thinking, rank each other on the basis of our occupational identity. For example, Jennifer's husband is president of an advertising company with both local and regional accounts. The clients at his cocktail party tend to be presidents, vice presidents, or division managers who work for the companies his firm promotes. They represent a more affluent class of people than, say, firefighters, fast-food restaurant managers, or administrative assistants although some of these jobs, such as firefighting, confer prestige.

Occupational identity conveys more than just one's class, however. It implies relative status between individuals. When men and women work at the same jobs, their work signifies that they are approximately equal. This assertion not only gains credence from observations of contemporary U.S. society, but from anthropological fieldwork and cross-cultural comparison. Take a well-known study by Ernestine Friedl, for example.[1] She points out that decades of ethnographic research in a variety of the world's societies have caused many anthropologists to conclude that males inherit a predisposition to dominate females everywhere. Friedl argues against this position by citing evidence about gender relations in four contrasting hunting and gathering societies. She asserts that control of publicly (beyond the family) shared resources, especially animal protein, determines the degree to which females are equal to males. First, she notes that among the Washo Indians (a foraging group that lived in the Sierra Nevada Mountains of southern California) both men and women foraged for edible plants and both caught rabbits and other small animals as a source of protein. The result was relative gender equality. Men and women were not segregated in daily activities. Both sexes could take lovers, dissolve marriages, and make decisions for the group. The Hadza of

---

[1]Ernestine Friedl, "Society and Sex Roles," *Human Nature*, April 1978.

Tanzania, she points out, also display relative gender equality largely because men and women forage separately and work to meet their own individual needs for food.

On the other hand, the Tiwi living on islands off the North coast of Australia show a more typical hunter/gatherer pattern. The men hunt and the women gather, and the male control of meat (protein), which is shared publicly by the whole group, results in domination over women. Men hunt and control the public distribution of meat; women gather only for family needs.

Finally, in the fourth case represented by the Inuit of the Arctic, males provide virtually all the food by hunting seals, walruses, whales, and fish. As a result, Inuit women are "used, abused, and traded," as Friedl puts it. Friedl also notes that gender inequality continues in many agriculturally based societies where men control most of the food that is publicly exchanged. Anthropologists Jane Collier and Michelle Rosaldo have also argued that while women's roles as gatherers contributed significantly to the food supply, these contributions were symbolically less important than the men's hunting activities.[2]

Friedl's argument appears to inform what is happening to U.S. women. Women have increasingly gained power and equality as they hold jobs once reserved for men. This has long been a goal for women in our society, and women in America now wield governmental and corporate power at levels never before seen in the history of this country. Women now have unprecedented access to education, jobs, and income.

And that's not all. A large part of the growth in the post-World War II U.S. economy can be attributed to the dramatic increase in the labor force participation by women, especially those who are married. And this participation extends to management and leadership positions and the ownership of one-third of all U.S. businesses that employ a quarter of the workforce.

Going hand in hand with this surge in women's contributions to economic productivity is the fact that women are at least as well educated as men. Women make up a full 58% of the nation's college students and are, overall, the majority in graduate and professional schools. They are hired in equal numbers by the country's most prestigious law firms. The majority of veterinarians and accountants are women. Women physicians will soon dominate certain sub-specialties within medicine.

In addition, while the number of women in the labor force has increased over the last few decades, fewer males have sought work. Labor economists note that if current trends continue, by 2020 only 70% of men will participate in the U.S. labor force, and by 2050, their participation will decline to 66%.

To be sure, there continues to be a wage gap between males and females for the labor force as a whole. However, when you look at specific niches within the population a different picture emerges. Without children, men and women

[2]Jane F. Collier and Michelle Z. Rosaldo, "Politics and Gender in Simple Societies," in Sherry B. Ortner and Harriet S. Whitehead (eds.), *On Sexual Meanings: The Cultural Construction of Gender and Sexuality* (Cambridge: Cambridge University Press, 1981).

pursue their careers neck in neck in terms of pay when they work similar jobs for similar hours. In fact, the gender wage gap for childless people between the ages of 27 and 33 is practically zero. Does this all mean that gender bias is absent in the world of work in America today? No. However, while gender discrimination at work continues, women have seen substantial gains in job equality over the past three or four decades.

Returning Home

And this brings us back to Jennifer's unease about the what-do-you-do question. Despite the statistics presented above, she, like an increasing number of young, married women with children, decided to give up her career for life as an at-home mother. She did so despite the fact that her personal history fit the trend toward job equality and the growing public influence of women. She graduated from a prestigious eastern college with honors and gained her degree as an attorney at a "top 10" law school. She obtained a high-paying job in a firm specializing in mergers and acquisitions where she was in line to become a partner. Then something happened that changed her promising career: she had one, then two children. Now, as an at-home mom, she grapples with the issue of identity in settings like business cocktail parties where occupational achievement outranks motherhood as an acceptable identity.

Jennifer's decision to leave her career is not unique. A study of well-educated women that we have been conducting reveals that a growing number of young, professional women are leaving work to become "at-home moms." As we have discovered, this attorney turned at-home mother is emblematic of a growing number of American women today. In fact, the full-time labor force participation of married women with professional degrees and children under 18 fell from nearly two-thirds to just over a half between 1998 and 2005. From a labor market perspective, this is a significant and remarkable shift, with dramatic ramifications for economic growth. Having gained a foothold in formerly male-dominated positions, it becomes paradoxical that many highly educated, accomplished women are leaving their careers, often as a consequence of becoming mothers. This article is about why we think this is happening and at least partly, how women are managing to do this without losing status.

Who Drops Out

To better understand this conundrum, we (an anthropologist and a labor economist) joined forces to look at national trends and learn more through interviews and focus groups about what kinds of women leave work. We discovered from national labor force participation data that a surprising number of college-educated, especially professional, women were opting out of the labor force. From here we designed interviews and focus groups with women who were making or had made the decision to leave their jobs in order to stay home with their children, as well as those who were continuing to juggle home and office.

The first thing we discovered was that age counts. We learned that women in their twenties and thirties seemed to approach childbirth, child rearing, and employment differently than their mothers and grandmothers. This older generation, the so-called Baby Boomers (women in their late forties to early sixties) were the first large wave of women to compete for prominent positions in the labor force. They entered work with high expectations and demonstrated ability, and like today's younger women, soon found that work conflicted with marriage and the need to raise children. Overall their response has been to try to manage both work and family by attempting to adjust to both, although with varying degrees of success. Nonetheless, these women were pioneering in their ability to anticipate and overcome obstacles and thereby created occupational opportunities for their daughters.

The second thing we discovered was that daughters of Baby Boomers (women in their early thirties to mid-forties and usually labeled Gen Xers or Millennials) benefited from the pioneering work of their mother's generation; however, they were the most likely to report having been "blindsided" by the realities of juggling career and children. Angie, a mother of two children in her mid-thirties with an MBA typifies this group. When she considered her own expectations for combining work with motherhood she said: "I thought women could do it all but just that my [own] mother did not do it well."

The third thing we discovered was that Millennials, married and well-educated women with young children, seemed to be far more pragmatic than older women about the conflict between work and family. Accordingly, they were also the most creative in the strategies they had devised to manage this conflict. They were still gunning for top spots educationally, but they reported being more mindful about how they would negotiate career and family. We found that women in their twenties and early thirties were more likely than older women to have reduced their responsibilities at work for family reasons. For some this meant selecting a career that was more flexible and amenable to the demands of child rearing. Others were planning to have careers and children sequentially. Still others intended to have children first and move into a career at some undefined future point when their children were older. But as we have noted above, many, faced with the need and desire to raise children, have left work behind, at least for the time being.

Finally, we should note that men rarely drop out of work to become at-home dads. Among married couples, when one parent leaves the labor force, 97 times out of 100 it is the woman who does so. The phenomenon of at-home dads is a growing trend, but when you look at the bigger picture of labor force participation, the number of men who do this is quite small. In this case couples bend to traditional gender roles—mom quits her job and dad presses even harder in his.

Before we go any further, we should note that by virtue of our focus on college-educated women for both our surveys and our interviews, we are *de facto* conducting a study of elite women. We realize that the notion of having a so-called "choice" not to work is available only to a narrow slice of American women, while many others need two incomes to keep their household afloat. In this respect our study does not tell the story of all women.

However, we argue that it is important to focus on college-educated and therefore relatively elite women because their experiences shape the lives of all American women. These women represent the potential leaders, the voices for change. If we don't have a critical mass of women executives, how can we expect the culture of companies to change? How can we expect laws to keep pace with women's lives if they aren't represented in Washington? Therefore, while at first glance middle- and upper-middle-class mothers are targeted most directly by our analysis, we believe the implications of our argument affect all women in America.

Why Do Women "Opt Out"?

So why do women "opt out" now when they have unprecedented access to education, jobs, and income, and potentially suffer the loss of their occupational identity? One suggested answer focuses solely on generation. It says that members of the younger generation, both men and women, are more likely to exit the work force than their elders. Although we don't deny the importance of generation, we feel gender has to be part of the explanation too. In our research, we have grappled with the intersection of gender and generation to understand the outflow of professional women from the labor force. And we agree that younger women approach issues of work and family differently than older women. However, it is important to acknowledge that while gender and generation vie with one another for explanatory power, gender is crucial to what is happening here. Indeed, we believe that gender is more important than generation as a way to understand current intersections of gender, work, and identity in America today.

So if it is not just a generational difference, what are the gender-related factors that bear on women's decision to return home?

What "Pushes" Women to Go Home?

There are several things that "push" women to leave the workforce. Let's look at a few of them.

The 100-Hour Couple

One of the most intriguing explanations for why women leave the workforce is the phenomenon of the 100-hour couple. Let's consider Valerie's situation. Valerie was an English and Political Science double major in college. A child of a single mother who single-handedly supported and raised five children, Valerie attended a state university and worked her way through school. She went on to attend law school and to work as a real estate attorney. She married her husband, also an attorney, who worked in banking. By the time they had their second child, their careers were at a zenith, with Valerie and her husband each working an average of 75-hours a week. To meet their work obligations, they had a full-time and a part-time nanny. When they discovered they needed yet a third nanny to help out because of work obligations that increasingly spilled over into evenings and weekends, they decided to re-evaluate their situation. They concluded that one of them had to reduce hours at work or quit his or her job altogether. They recognized that they could live on either Valerie's or her husband's salary alone, although her husband's income was significantly larger than hers. Therefore, for financial as well as for other less tangible reasons that could not be tallied on a spreadsheet, Valerie decided to leave her job and to stay home with their children. Valerie described her decision in the following way:

> If we were financially able, one of us needed to quit our jobs. What was the point of having kids if we weren't spending time with them? Strangers were raising my children—65 hours per week of child care. Deciding to quit my job and stay home with my children was the right thing to do.

Valerie's case illustrates some key points. As women's educational qualifications rise, so too have their occupational aspirations and their chance for marriage with economically successful men. It's not surprising that well-educated women gravitate toward high-powered, high-paying jobs and marry elite men who have done the same. Whereas previous generations saw a surplus of professional men relative to women, the educational gap has closed. Instead of the CEO marrying his secretary or the doctor marrying his nurse, the CEO is marrying the CFO and the doctor is marrying the doctor. With this larger pool of well-educated, well-employed women, we have transitioned to high-powered couples resulting in a rapid and significant increase in the percent of high earning couples that together work over 100 hours per week.

In Valerie's case, she and her husband surpassed 150-hour workweeks, but when we look across a larger sample of families, 100 hours is a threshold for couples who make a decision for one, and as pointed out it is usually the woman, to alter their work situation.

The Second Shift

Another factor pushing women out of the workforce is what sociologist Arlie Hochschild calls the second shift. Here she gives life to the old adage, "A man may work from sun to sun, but a woman's work is never done." The second shift refers to the work women do to maintain and sustain the household in addition to their paid employment. The second shift is commonly seen as a significant stressor for women across socioeconomic groups. It is well documented that women shoulder a disproportionate percentage of housework. For example, one study reports that women do an average of 27 hours of housework a week, compared to 16 hours a week for men. Important here is that while women have made significant gains in the workplace itself, the sexual division of labor at home endures. A recent trend to hire household help is opening possibilities to redefine this aspect of women's lives, but even when families hire people to watch their children or clean their homes, women tend to take on the burden of managing the work that is done in the home and caring for the children.

Although it might strike many as a significant luxury to be able to afford to pay someone to clean their homes and watch their children, in our interviews we found that hiring and supervising staff to care for the home and the children placed additional stress on women and was cited by them as part of the decision to quit their jobs. Women also mentioned moral and ethical concerns. Is it "right and fair," to hire women who often have to leave their own children behind to work these jobs? Then, too, was it advisable to hire nannies with lower educational levels to care for their children, and how does one manage the inevitabilities of sick children and/or sick child care providers?

The women we interviewed did not just describe trying to balance the needs of their children and their jobs, but also the reality of their responsibility to manage their homes. For many the solution was to stay home full-time.

The Glass Ceiling

Women mentioned a third factor that caused them to consider resigning their jobs. They talked about encountering a "glass ceiling" at work, one that is a form of discrimination that limits a woman's advancement. They felt they were being blocked from moving upward in the institution because of some tacit or unwritten set of norms about women, especially married women with children. The women we interviewed were frustrated by seeing their counterparts without children (or with a spouse at home caring for their children and managing the household) advance more swiftly in their careers then they did. It seemed unfair since these co-workers did not have to take parental leave to care for children and were more available to work longer hours. One woman lamented that her peers who had not taken time off for children were now vice presidents sitting in corner offices.

One way to look at this is that women quit their jobs not because of their families but because the pressures and inflexibility of their work situations actually leave them no way to maintain both. This is why many women we spoke with take issue with the term "opting out." Work conditions permitting, some of the women we interviewed would have preferred to "opt in," albeit on terms that better allowed them to both keep their jobs and raise their children.

When we raised the possibility during a focus group of reducing their hours at the job while still remaining employed, one advertising executive summarized the opinion of many of her counterparts when she said, "Part time is just a joke." Another woman with an MBA said, "My boss was reluctant to let me go part time at all. When I cut my hours my boss said he'd pay me less per hour. After three months of fighting and going several levels above him [in the company], I was able to keep my same hourly wage."

We should point out that when viewed cross-culturally, different countries manage the intersection of parenting and labor force participation in other ways. The United States, when compared to other industrialized countries, rarely accommodates the need for parents to have and care for children. One woman we interviewed who ironically worked for a children's museum took 12 weeks of unpaid leave when her first child was born. The only thing the museum guaranteed was that she would get her job back when she returned from leave. In its Feburary 1, 2007 issue, *USA Today* reported that the United States and Australia are the only industrialized countries that fail to provide paid leave for new mothers, although there are exceptions in some U.S. states. Australian mothers have it better, however, with one year of job-protected leave. The U.S. Family and Medical Leave Act provides for 12 weeks of job-protected leave, but it only covers those who work for larger companies. Out of 168 nations in a Harvard University study, 163 had some form of paid maternity leave, putting the United States at the end of the list in company with Lesotho, Papua New Guinea, and Swaziland.[3]

Factors That "Pull" Women Home

Beyond understanding some of the reasons women are "pushed" out of the work force, it is also important to understand what "pulls" them there.

Being with Their Children

One of the reasons women gave us for why they liked being "at-home" revolved around being with their children. Take for example the case of Carol. Carol loves being home with her three kids—all in school now—and is thankful that she is able to do this. She loves spending time with the kids, talking to them, being the one they turn to with their questions. And, she likes the freedom and flexibility. Last summer she drove across the country with her children to visit her mom for a month. Having the latitude to make this trip was especially meaningful to her when her mother died the following winter after a long battle with cancer.

Sara introduces a long list of activities her children participate in by saying that Ryan and Aidan "get a lot of mommy time." She notes that she is able to do this because she has "a flexible enough schedule. I can just cart them

---

[3]"The Work, Family, and Equality Index: How Does the United States Measure Up?" by Jody, Heymann, Alison Earle, and Jeffrey Hayes, published by The Project on Global Working Families, Boston, MA and Montreal, Quebec. The information is on their website: http://www.mcgill.ca/files/ihsp/WFFIFinal2007.pdf.

wherever they need to go." She goes on to describe visits to grandparents in New Mexico and Florida. "When we go we stay for a week. So, before I quit working at General Mills I would max out my vacation." Having control over their time tended to be a central concern for many of these women.

Lower Stress

Many women seek to pursue a less hectic life. One woman's husband credits her with running "a great back office" such that the family spends their weekends together playing and not running errands. Most were tired of the "juggle and struggle" they encountered when they were still working. They had had to negotiate with their spouses over when, where, who, and how to cover child care. Another woman pointed out that staying at home "made my husband's life easier" and that "he enjoys his children more because he is not worrying about the day-to-day." And women freely point out that this arrangement also allows them to get their needs met by allowing them "time for themselves."

Sense of Responsibility

Women also discussed the moral importance and timing of their decision to head home. One attorney noted, "Conventional wisdom says we need to be there because we have infants. In hindsight, it's absolutely flipped. Now that the kids are getting older, it's more important for me to be there." Another bond trader noted that it was easier to hire someone to care for her children when they were "cute naughty" as toddlers, but now that they were not so cute as misbehaving adolescents she felt the need to be more in charge of her kids' care.

Nostalgia

We also found that many women are pulled home by a longing to reproduce what for them was a pleasant upbringing. Some had at-home mothers who were there for them with amenities such as milk and cookies after school. On the other hand, some felt the need to redress the rejection they felt as latchkey kids when mothers were not there for them.

Group Support

Finally, it seems to be increasingly easier for young women to leave work as other like-minded women make the same choice. In one veterinarian turned at-home mom's words, "I run with a pack of smart women." The result is the formation of social networks of women with their children providing a sense of support, occasions for conversation about domestic matters, and opportunities for their children to play together. Although it's not fun to be an ex-veterinarian who stays home by herself with her kids, it is easier to do so when all your friends are doing it too.

Financial Costs

What happens when women give up their paychecks? As one woman aptly noted, "The paycheck gives you a tangible sense of value." Other women we interviewed described how their husband's work time, as the sole income earner, expands as his home effort decreases. Still other women lament the loss of what they called the "fuck you money," or the financial independence their own earnings afforded them and that potentially allowed them to leave their marriage if they ever felt they needed to. Still others argue that their power did not change because their husbands appreciated their efforts at home. The threat that they might return to work and thus destroy the comfortable support system they provided moderates\d the increased power that a husband might otherwise enjoy. But it is clear that by leaving work and a paycheck, divorce or the death of a husband will likely have a greater impact on their lives.

Returning to Work

A lot has been written about the difficulty of re-entering the workforce after significant absences. One problem is the limited shelf life of a professional degree. For example, a physician who does not practice for ten years would have to overcome significant hurdles to get back into clinical work. On the other hand, opportunities to work in the medical sector of the economy may still be available.

However, the chance for them to return to their original occupations did not seem to matter to some of our respondents. Many of the women we interviewed said they would prefer to change professions if they returned to work in the future. Some thought of starting their own businesses. Others described transitioning to a care-giving profession. Many of the bond traders, financial managers, and attorneys we interviewed indicated that when, and if, they returned to work they had their eyes on jobs such as elementary school teacher, social worker for the elderly, or advocate for patients in hospitals.

Maintaining Status

So how can Jennifer and many other young at-home mothers manage to maintain the prestige and power that accompanied the up-scale jobs they once trained for and held? A traditional way that was more common in the past was to associate themselves with their husband's status. If she did so, Jennifer might have answered the what-do-you-do question by simply saying, "Oh, I am Paul's wife." But this kind of answer diminishes her past academic and occupational achievements. So she is more likely to mention what she used to do by saying "I am an attorney" or "I was an attorney with Brand and Cockrin but I am home with the kids for a while."

Finally, if they remain outside the workplace for long, women may choose to maintain a sense of occupational worth by serving in "quasi-professional" settings such as membership on the boards of civic associations, positions with nonprofit organizations, and aides at their children's schools.

Finally, it is difficult at this point for us to predict what these young professionals, now turned full-time mothers, will do in the future as their children grow up and they are once again free to work. The move home may only be one phase in a life of shifting pressures, opportunities, and associated identities.

Review Questions

1. What is the relationship between occupation, class, and social identity in the U.S.?

2. Shandy and Moe described Ernestine Friedl's work on the degree to which males dominate females. What is Friedl's main argument and what evidence does she use to support it?

3. At what age are women likely to move from work to home, according to Shandy and Moe?

4. What factors push women to "head home" instead of continuing to work?

5. What factors pull women to do so?

6. How do women who have left work to raise their children at home deal with the apparent loss of gender equality that comes with their domestic identity over their occupational one?

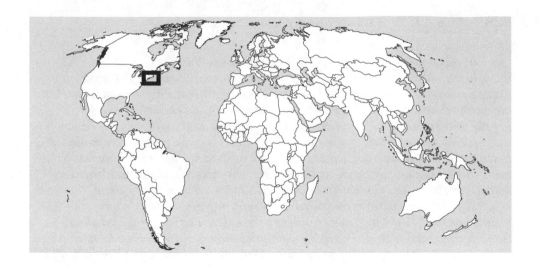

23

Poverty at Work: Office Employment and the Crack Alternative

Philippe Bourgois

There was a time in the United States when people with little education and money could find work in manufacturing plants or other settings requiring manual labor. Many of the skills they needed could be learned on the job and they could make a modest but decent living and support a family. And despite their working class identity, their jobs gave them dignity and a place in society. But in today's America, manufacturing jobs have often disappeared leaving thousands of poorly educated people without equivalent work.

227

In this article, Philippe Bourgois illustrates how this problem has affected unskilled and largely uneducated Puerto Rican men and women in New York City's Spanish Harlem. Manufacturing jobs once provided dignified and stable employment for Puerto Rican men and women. As factories closed during the 1960s, '70s, and '80s, the unemployed could find work only in service industries such as security corporations, law firms, and insurance companies. Because they were uneducated and culturally different, they could hold only minimum wage jobs in such worlds, as they are usually controlled by educated, largely Anglo people who openly look down on them. In the end, they could achieve higher status and often higher income in their own ethnic community by dealing drugs. The result has been a destructive spiral into addiction, murder, and prison. Bourgois concludes the article with an addendum noting that high employment in the late 1990s provided more work opportunities for Puerto Ricans in the formal economy and that crack dealing has largely given way to the less visible sale of marijuana and heroin.

For a total of approximately three and a half years during the late 1980s and early 1990s, I lived with my wife and young son in an irregularly heated, rat-filled tenement in East Harlem, New York. This two-hundred-square-block neighborhood—better known locally as *El Barrio* or Spanish Harlem—is visibly impoverished yet it is located in the heart of New York, the richest city in the Western Hemisphere. It is literally a stone's throw from multimillion-dollar condominiums. Although one in three families survived on some form of public assistance in 1990, the majority of El Barrio's 110,600 Puerto Rican and African-American residents fall into the ranks of the working poor.[1] They eke out an uneasy subsistence in entry-level service and manufacturing jobs in one of the most expensive cities in the world.

The public sector (e.g., the police, social welfare agencies, the Sanitation Department) has broken down in El Barrio and does not function effectively. This has caused the legally employed residents of the neighborhood to lose control of their streets and public spaces to the drug economy. My tenement's block was not atypical and within a few hundred yards' radius I could obtain heroin, crack, powder cocaine, hypodermic needles, methadone, Valium, angel dust, marijuana, mescaline, bootleg alcohol, and tobacco. Within two hundred feet of my stoop there were three competing crack houses selling vials at two, three, and five dollars. Several doctors operated "pill mills" on the blocks around me, writing prescriptions for opiates and barbiturates upon demand. In the projects within view of my living-room window, the Housing Authority police

[1]According to the 1990 Census, in East Harlem 48.3 percent of males and 35.2 percent of females over sixteen were officially reported as employed—compared to a citywide average of 64.3 percent for men and 49 percent for women. Another 10.4 percent of the men and 5.7 percent of the women in East Harlem were actively looking for legal work. . . . In El Barrio as a whole, 60 percent of all households reported legally earned incomes. Twenty-six percent received Public Assistance, 6.3 percent received Supplemental Security Income, and 5 percent received Medicaid benefits.

arrested a fifty-five-year-old mother and her twenty-two-year-old daughter while they were "bagging" twenty-two pounds of cocaine into ten-dollar quarter-gram "Jumbo" vials of adulterated product worth over a million dollars on the streets. The police found twenty-five thousand dollars in cash in small-denomination bills in this same apartment.[2] In other words, there are millions of dollars' worth of business going on directly in front of the youths growing up in East Harlem tenements and housing projects. Why should these young men and women take the subway downtown to work minimum-wage jobs—or even double minimum-wage jobs—in downtown offices when they can usually earn more, at least in the short run, by selling drugs on the street corner in front of their apartment or schoolyard?

This dynamic underground economy is predicated on violence and substance abuse. It has spawned what I call a "street culture" of resistance and self-destruction. The central concern of my study is the relationship of street culture to the worlds of work accessible to street dealers—that is, the legal and illegal labor markets that employ them and give meaning to their lives. I hope to show the local-level implications of the global-level restructuring of the U.S. economy away from factory production and toward services. In the process, I have recorded the words and experiences of some unrepentant victims who are part of a network of some twenty-five street-level crack dealers operating on and around my block. To summarize, I am arguing that the transformation from manufacturing to service employment—especially in the professional office work setting—is much more culturally disruptive than the already revealing statistics on reductions in income, employment, unionization, and worker's benefits would indicate. Low-level service sector employment engenders a humiliating ideological—or cultural—confrontation between a powerful corps of white office executives and their assistants versus a younger generation of poorly educated, alienated, "colored" workers. It also often takes the form of a sharply polarized confrontation over gender roles.

Shattered Working-Class Dreams

All the crack dealers and addicts whom I have interviewed had worked at one or more legal jobs in their early youth. In fact, most entered the labor market at a younger age than the typical American. Before they were twelve years old they were bagging groceries at the supermarket for tips, stocking beers off-the-books in local *bodegas,* or shining shoes. For example, Primo, the night manager at a video game arcade that sells five-dollar vials of crack on the block where I lived, pursued a traditional working-class dream in his early adolescence. With the

---

[2]Both of these police actions were reported in the local print and television media, but I am withholding the cities to protect the anonymity of my street address.

support of his extended kin who were all immersed in a working-class "common sense," he dropped out of junior high school to work in a local garment factory:

> I was like fourteen or fifteen playing hooky and pressing dresses and whatever they were making on the steamer. They was cheap, cheap clothes.
>
> My mother's sister was working there first and then her son, my cousin Willie—the one who's in jail now—was the one they hired first, because his mother agreed: "If you don't want to go to school, you gotta work."
>
> So I started hanging out with him. I wasn't planning on working in the factory. I was supposed to be in school; but it just sort of happened.

Ironically, young Primo actually became the agent who physically moved the factory out of the inner city. In the process, he became merely one more of the 445,900 manufacturing workers in New York City who lost their jobs as factory employment dropped 50 percent from 1963 to 1983 . . . .

Almost all the crack dealers had similar tales of former factory jobs. For poor adolescents, the decision to drop out of school and become a marginal factory worker is attractive. It provides the employed youth with access to the childhood "necessities"—sneakers, basketballs, store-bought snacks—that sixteen-year-olds who stay in school cannot afford. In the descriptions of their first forays into legal factory-based employment, one hears clearly the extent to which they, and their families, subscribed to mainstream working-class ideologies about the dignity of engaging in "hard work" rather than education.

Had these enterprising, early-adolescent workers from El Barrio not been confined to the weakest sector of manufacturing in a period of rapid job loss, their teenage working-class dreams might have stabilized. Instead, upon reaching their mid-twenties, they discovered themselves to be unemployable high school dropouts. This painful realization of social marginalization expresses itself across a generational divide. The parents and grandparents of the dealers continue to maintain working-class values of honesty and hard work which conflict violently with the reality of their children's immersion in street culture. They are constantly accused of slothfulness by their mothers and even by friends who have managed to maintain legal jobs. They do not have a regional perspective on the dearth of adequate entry-level jobs available to "functional illiterates" in New York, and they begin to suspect that they might indeed be *vago bons* [lazy bums] who do not *want* to work hard and cannot help themselves. Confused, they take refuge in an alternative search for career, meaning, and ecstasy in substance abuse.

Formerly, when most entry-level jobs were found in factories, the contradiction between an oppositional street culture and traditional working-class, masculine, shop-floor culture was less pronounced—especially when the work site was protected by a union. Factories are inevitably rife with confrontational hierarchies. Nevertheless, on the shop-floor, surrounded by older union workers, high school dropouts who are well versed in the latest and toughest street culture styles function effectively. In the factory, being tough and violently macho has high cultural value; a certain degree of opposition to the foreman and the "bossman" is expected and is considered appropriate.

In contrast, this same oppositional street-identity is nonfunctional in the professional office worker service sector that has burgeoned in New York's high-finance-driven economy. It does not allow for the humble, obedient, social inter-action—often across gender lines—that professional office workers routinely impose on their subordinates. A qualitative change has occurred, therefore, in the tenor of social interaction in office-based employment. Workers in a mail room or behind a photocopy machine cannot publicly maintain their cultural autonomy. Most concretely, they have no union; more subtly, there are few fel-low workers surrounding them to insulate them and to provide them with a culturally based sense of class solidarity.[3] Instead they are besieged by super-visors and bosses from an alien, hostile, and obviously dominant culture who ridicule street culture. Workers like Primo appear inarticulate to their profes-sional supervisors when they try to imitate the language of power in the work-place and instead stumble pathetically over the enunciation of unfamiliar words. They cannot decipher the hastily scribbled instructions—rife with mysterious abbreviations—that are left for them by harried office managers. The "com-mon sense" of white-collar work is foreign to them; they do not, for example, understand the logic for filing triplicate copies of memos or for post-dating invoices. When they attempt to improvise or show initiative they fail miserably and instead appear inefficient, or even hostile, for failing to follow "clearly spec-ified" instructions.

Their "social skills" are even more inadequate than their limited profes-sional capacities. They do not know how to look at their fellow co-service work-ers, let alone their supervisors, without intimidating them. They cannot walk down the hallway to the water fountain without unconsciously swaying their shoulders aggressively as if patrolling their home turf. Gender barriers are an even more culturally charged realm. They are repeatedly reprimanded for harassing female co-workers.

The cultural clash between white "yuppie" power and inner-city "scram-bling jive" in the service sector is much more than a superficial question of style. It is about access to power. Service workers who are incapable of obey-ing the rules of interpersonal interaction dictated by professional office culture will never be upwardly mobile. Their supervisors will think they are dumb or have a "bad attitude." Once again, a gender dynamic exacerbates the confusion and sense of insult experienced by young, male inner-city employees because most supervisors in the lowest reaches of the service sector are women. Street culture does not allow males to be subordinate across gender lines.

---

[3]Significantly, there are subsectors of the service industry that are relatively unionized—such as hos-pital and custodial work—where there is a limited autonomous space for street culture and working-class resistance.

"Gettin' Dissed"

On the street, the trauma of experiencing a threat to one's personal dignity has been frozen linguistically in the commonly used phrase "to diss," which is short for "to disrespect." Significantly, one generation ago ethnographers working in rural Puerto Rico specifically noted the importance of the traditional Puerto Rican concept of *respeto* in mediating labor relations:

> The good owner "respects" (*respeta*) the laborer. . . . It is probably to the interest of the landowner to make concessions to his best workers, to deal with them on a respect basis, and to enmesh them in a network of mutual obligations.[4]

Puerto Rican street-dealers do not find respect in the entry-level service sector jobs that have increased two-fold in New York's economy since the 1950s. On the contrary, they "get dissed" in the new jobs that are available to them. Primo, for example, remembers the humiliation of his former work experiences as an "office boy," and he speaks of them in a race- and gender-charged idiom:

> I had a prejudiced boss. She was a fucking "ho'," Gloria. She was white. Her name was Christian. No, not Christian, Kirschman. I don't know if she was Jewish or not. When she was talking to people she would say, "He's illiterate."
>
> So what I did one day was, I just looked up the word, "illiterate," in the dictionary and I saw that she's saying to her associates that I'm stupid or something!
>
> Well, I am illiterate anyway.

The most profound dimension of Primo's humiliation was being obliged to look up in the dictionary the word used to insult him. In contrast, in the underground economy, he is sheltered from this kind of threat:

> Rocky [the crack house franchise owner] he would never disrespect me that way. He wouldn't tell me that because he's illiterate too. Plus I've got more education than him. I got a GED. . . .

Primo excels in the street's underground economy. His very persona inspires fear and respect. In contrast, in order to succeed in his former office job, Primo would have had to self-consciously alter his street identity and mimic the professional cultural style that office managers require of their subordinates and colleagues. Primo refused to accept his boss's insults and he was unable to imitate her interactional styles. He was doomed, consequently, to a marginal position behind a photocopy machine or at the mail meter. Behavior considered appropriate in street culture is considered dysfunctional in

---

[4]Eric Wolf, "San Jose: Subcultures of a 'Traditional' Coffee Municipality," in Julian Stewart (ed.), *The People of Puerto Rico* (Chicago: University of Chicago Press, 1956), p. 235.

office settings. In other words, job requirements in the service sector are largely cultural style and this conjugates powerfully with racism.

> I wouldn't have mind that she said I was illiterate. What bothered me was that when she called on the telephone, she wouldn't want me to answer even if my supervisor who was the receptionist was not there. [Note how Primo is so low in the office hierarchy that his immediate supervisor is a receptionist.]
>
> When she hears my voice it sounds like she's going to get a heart attack. She'd go, "Why are you answering the phones?"
>
> That bitch just didn't like my Puerto Rican accent.

Primo's manner of resisting this insult to his cultural dignity exacerbated his marginal position in the labor hierarchy:

> And then, when I did pick up the phone, I used to just sound *Porta'rrrican* on purpose.

In contrast to the old factory sweatshop positions, these just-above-minimum-wage office jobs require intense interpersonal contact with the middle and upper-middle classes. Close contact across class lines and the absence of a working class autonomous space for eight hours a day in the office can be a claustrophobic experience for an otherwise ambitious, energetic, young, inner-city worker.

Caesar, who worked for Primo as lookout and bodyguard at the crack house, interpreted this requirement to obey white, middle-class norms as an affront to his dignity that specifically challenged his definition of masculinity:

> I had a few jobs like that [referring to Primo's "telephone diss"] where you gotta take a lot of shit from bitches and be a wimp.
>
> I didn't like it but I kept on working, because "Fuck it!" you don't want to fuck up the relationship. So you just be a punk [shrugging his shoulders dejectedly].

One alternative for surviving at a workplace that does not tolerate a street-based cultural identity is to become bicultural: to play politely by "the white woman's" rules downtown only to come home and revert to street culture within the safety of one's tenement or housing project at night. Tens of thousands of East Harlem residents manage this tightrope, but it often engenders accusations of betrayal and internalized racism on the part of neighbors and childhood friends who do not have—or do not want—these bicultural skills.

This is the case, for example, of Ray, a rival crack dealer whose tough street demeanor conflates with his black skin to "disqualify" him from legal office work. He quit a "nickel-and-dime messenger job downtown" in order to sell crack full time in his project stairway shortly after a white woman fled from him shrieking down the hallway of a high-rise office building. Ray and the terrified woman had ridden the elevator together, and, coincidentally, Ray had stepped off on the same floor as her to make a delivery. Worse yet, Ray had been trying to act like a "debonair male" and suspected the contradiction between his inadequate appearance and his chivalric intentions was responsible for the woman's terror:

> You know how you let a woman go off the elevator first? Well that's what I did to her but I may have looked a little shabby on the ends. Sometime my hair not combed. You know. So I could look a little sloppy to her maybe when I let her off first.

What Ray did not quite admit until I probed further is that he too had been intimidated by the lone white woman. He had been so disoriented by her taboo, unsupervised proximity that he had forgotten to press the elevator button when he originally stepped on after her:

> She went in the elevator first but then she just waits there to see what floor I press. She's playing like she don't know what floor she wants to go to because she wants to wait for me to press my floor. And I'm standing there and I forgot to press the button. I'm thinking about something else—I don't know what was the matter with me. And she's thinking like, "He's not pressing the button; I guess he's following me!"

As a crack dealer, Ray no longer has to confront this kind of confusing humiliation. Instead, he can righteously condemn his "successful" neighbors who work downtown for being ashamed of who they were born to be:

> When you see someone go downtown and get a good job, if they be Puerto Rican, you see them fix up their hair and put some contact lens in their eyes. Then they fit in. And they do it! I seen it.
>
> They turn-overs. They people who want to be white. Man, if you call them in Spanish, it wind up a problem.
>
> When they get nice jobs like that, all of a sudden, you know, they start talking proper.

Self-Destructive Resistance

During the 1980s, the real value of the minimum wage for legally employed workers declined by one-third. At the same time, social services were cut. The federal government, for example, decreased the proportion of its contribution to New York City's budget by over 50 percent. . . . The breakdown of the inner city's public sector is no longer an economic threat to the expansion of New York's economy because the native-born labor force it shelters is increasingly irrelevant.

New immigrants arrive every day, and they are fully prepared to work hard for low wages under unsavory conditions. Like the parents and grandparents of Primo and Caesar, many of New York's newest immigrants are from isolated rural communities or squalid shanty towns where meat is eaten only once a week and there is no running water or electricity. Half a century ago Primo's mother fled precisely the same living conditions these new immigrants are only just struggling to escape. Her reminiscences about childhood in her natal village reveal the time warp of improved material conditions, cultural dislocation, and crushed working-class dreams that is propelling her second-generation son into a destructive street culture:

> I loved that life in Puerto Rico, because it was a healthy, healthy, healthy life.
>
> We always ate because my father always had work, and in those days the custom was to have a garden in your patio to grow food and everything that you ate.
>
> We only ate meat on Sundays because everything was cultivated on the same little parcel of land. We didn't have a refrigerator, so we ate *bacalao* [salted codfish], which can stay outside and a meat that they call *carne de vieja* [shredded beef], and sardines from a can. But thanks to God, we never felt hunger. My mother made a lot of cornflour.
>
> Some people have done better by coming here, but many people haven't. Even people from my barrio, who came trying to find a better life [*buen ambiente*] just found disaster. Married couples right from my neighborhood came only to have the husband run off with another woman.
>
> In those days in Puerto Rico, when we were in poverty, life was better. Everyone will tell you life was healthier and you could trust people. Now you can't trust anybody.
>
> What I like best was that we kept all our traditions . . . our feasts. In my village, everyone was either an Uncle or an Aunt. And when you walked by someone older, you had to ask for their blessing. It was respect. There was a lot of respect in those days [original quote in Spanish].

The Jewish and Italian-American white workers that Primo's mother replaced a generation ago when she came to New York City in hope of building a better future for her children were largely absorbed into an expanding economy that allowed them to be upwardly mobile. New York's economy always suffered periodic fluctuations, such as during the Great Depression, but those difficult periods were always temporary. The overall trend was one of economic growth. Primo's generation has not been so lucky. The contemporary economy does not particularly need them, and ethnic discrimination and cultural barriers overwhelm them whenever they attempt to work legally and seek service-sector jobs. Worse yet, an extraordinarily dynamic underground drug economy beckons them.

Rather than bemoaning the structural adjustment which is destroying their capacity to survive on legal wages, streetbound Puerto Rican youths celebrate their "decision" to bank on the underground economy and to cultivate their street identities. Caesar and Primo repeatedly assert their pride in their street careers. For example, one Saturday night after they finished their midnight shift at the crack house, I accompanied them on their way to purchase *"El Sapo Verde"*

[The Green Toad], a twenty-dollar bag of powder cocaine sold by a new company three blocks away. While waiting for Primo and Caesar to be "served" by the coke seller a few yards away, I engaged three undocumented Mexican men drinking beer on a neighboring stoop in a conversation about finding work in New York. One of the new immigrants was already earning five hundred dollars a week fixing deep-fat-fry machines. He had a straightforward racist explanation for why Caesar—who was standing next to me—was "unemployed":

> OK, OK, I'll explain it to you in one word: Because the Puerto Ricans are brutes! [Pointing at Caesar] Brutes! Do you understand?
>
> Puerto Ricans like to make easy money. They like to leech off of other people. But not us Mexicans! No way! We like to work for our money. We don't steal. We came here to work and that's all [original quote in Spanish].

Instead of physically assaulting the employed immigrant for insulting him, Caesar embraced the racist tirade, ironically turning it into the basis for a new, generational-based, "American-born," urban cultural pride. In fact, in his response, he ridicules what he interprets to be the hillbilly naiveté of the Mexicans who still believe in the "American Dream." He spoke slowly in street-English as if to mark sarcastically the contrast between his "savvy" Nuyorican (New York-born Puerto Rican) identity versus the limited English proficiency of his detractor:

> That's right, m'a man! We is real vermin lunatics that sell drugs. We don't want no part of society. "Fight the Power!"[5]
>
> What do we wanna be working for? We rather live off the system. Gain weight, lay women.
>
> When we was younger, we used to break our asses too [gesturing towards the Mexican men who were straining to understand his English]. I had all kinds of stupid jobs too . . . advertising agencies . . . computers.
>
> But not no more! Now we're in a rebellious stage. We rather evade taxes, make quick money, and just survive. But we're not satisfied with that either. Ha!

Conclusion: Ethnography and Oppression

The underground economy and the social relations thriving off of it are best understood as modes of resistance to subordination in the service sector of the new U.S. economy. This resistance, however, results in individual self destruction and wider community devastation through substance abuse and violence. This complex and contradictory dynamic whereby resistance leads to self-destruction in the inner city is difficult to convey to readers in a clear and

---

[5]"Fight the Power" is a rap song composed in 1990 by the African-American group, Public Enemy.

responsible manner. Mainstream society's "common sense" understanding of social stratification around ethnicity and class assumes the existence of racial hierarchies and blames individual victims for their failures. This makes it difficult to present ethnographic data from inner-city streets without falling prey to a "pornography of violence" or a racist voyeurism.

The public is not persuaded by a structural economic understanding of Caesar and Primo's "self-destruction." Even the victims themselves psychologize their unsatisfactory lives. Similarly, politicians and, more broadly, public policy ignore the fundamental structural economic facts of marginalization in America. Instead the first priority of federal and local social "welfare" agencies is to change the psychological—or at best the "cultural"—orientations of misguided individuals . . . U.S. politicians furiously debate family values while multinational corporations establish global free-trade zones and unionized factory employment in the U.S. continues to disappear as overseas sweatshops multiply. Social science researchers, meanwhile, have remained silent for the most part. They politely ignore the urgent social problems engulfing the urban United States. The few marginal academic publications that do address issues of poverty and racism are easily ignored by the media and mainstream society. . . .

Epilogue

In the six years since this article was first published, four major dynamics have altered the tenor of daily life on the streets of East Harlem and have deeply affected the lives of the crack dealers and their families depicted in these pages: (1) the U.S. economy entered the most prolonged period of sustained growth in its recorded history, (2) the size of the Mexican immigrant population in New York City and especially in East Harlem increased dramatically, (3) the War on Drugs escalated into a quasi-official public policy of criminalizing and incarcerating the poor and the socially marginal, and (4) drug fashion trends among inner-city youth rendered marijuana even more popular and crack and heroin even less popular among Latinos and African Americans.

Crack, cocaine, and heroin are still all sold on the block where I lived, but they are sold less visibly by a smaller number of people. It is still easy to purchase narcotics throughout East Harlem, but much of the drug dealing has moved indoors, out of sight, dealers no longer shouting out the brand names of their drugs. Most importantly, heroin and crack continue to be spurned by Latino and African-American youth who have seen the ravages those drugs committed on the older generations in their community. Nevertheless, in the U.S. inner city there remains an aging hardcore cohort of addicts. In most large cities crack is most visibly ensconced in predominantly African-American neighborhoods on the poorest blocks, often surrounding large public housing projects. In New York City, Puerto Rican households also continue to be at the epicenter of this ongoing, but now more self-contained, stationary cyclone of crack consumption.

In contrast to crack, heroin consumption has increased. Throughout most of the United States, heroin is cheaper and purer than in the early 1990s, belying any claims that the War on Drugs is winnable. Heroin's new appeal, however, is primarily among younger whites outside the ghetto for whom crack was never a drug of choice. It is not a drug of choice among Latino and African-American youth.

To summarize, both heroin and crack continue to be part of a multi-billion-dollar business that ravages inner-city families with special virulence. The younger generations of East Harlem residents, however, are more involved as sellers rather than consumers. Those Latino and African-American youth who do use crack or heroin generally try to hide the fact from their friends.

More important than changing drug-consumption fashions or the posturing of politicians over drug war campaigns has been the dramatic long-term improvement in the U.S. economy resulting in record low rates of unemployment. Somewhat to my surprise, some of the crack dealers and their families have benefited from this sustained economic growth. Slightly less than half have been allowed to enter the lower echelons of the legal labor market. For example, during the summer of 2000: one dealer was a unionized doorman, another was a home health care attendant, another was a plumber's assistant, three others were construction workers for small-time unlicensed contractors, and one was a cashier in a discount tourist souvenir store. Three or four of the dealers were still selling drugs, but most of them tended to be selling marijuana instead of crack or heroin. Three other dealers were in prison with long-term sentences and ironically were probably employed at well below minimum wage in the United States' burgeoning prison-based manufacturing sector. In short, the dramatic improvement in the U.S. economy has forced employers and unions to integrate more formally marginalized Puerto Ricans and African Americans into the labor market than was the case in the late 1980s and early 1990s when the research for this [article] was conducted. Nevertheless, even at the height of the growth in the U.S. economy in the year 2000, a large sector of street youth found themselves excluded. These marginals have become almost completely superfluous to the legal economy; they remain enmeshed in a still-lucrative drug economy, a burgeoning prison system, and a quagmire of chronic substance abuse. From a long-term political and economic perspective, the future does not bode well for inner-city poor of New York. In the year 2000, the United States had the largest disparity between rich and poor of any industrialized nation in the world—and this gap was not decreasing.

Review Questions

1. What kinds of jobs in the formal economy could Puerto Ricans living in East Harlem hold forty years ago? How did these jobs enable the men to preserve respect as it was defined in their culture?

2. What kinds of jobs are currently available to Puerto Rican men in New York's service economy? How do these jobs challenge the men's self-respect?

3. What structural changes in New York's formal economy have changed over the past forty years? How have these changes affected the lives of young men living in Spanish Harlem?

4. Why do Puerto Rican men take pride in their street identities?

5. Why does Bourgois claim that the Puerto Rican men's resistance to work in the legal economy leads to "self-destruction" and "wider community devastation"?

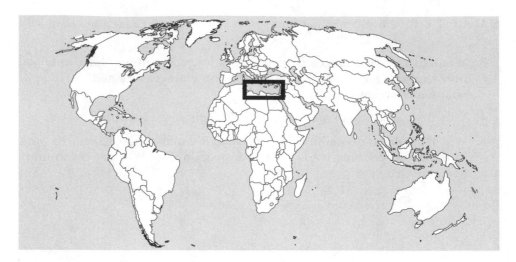

24

Symbolizing Roles: Behind the Veil

Elizabeth W. Fernea and Robert A. Fernea

Most societies have some things that serve as key symbols. The flag of the United States, for example, stands not only for the nation, but for a variety of important values that guide American behavior and perception. In this article, Elizabeth Fernea and Robert Fernea trace the meaning of another key symbol: the veil worn by women in the Middle East. Instead of reference to a national group, the veil codes many of the values surrounding the role of women. Often viewed by Westerners as a symbol of female restriction and inequality, for the women who wear it the veil signals honor, personal protection, the sanctity and privacy of the family, wealth and high status, and city life.

Blue jeans have come to mean America all over the world; three-piece wool suits signal businessmen; and in the 1980s pink or green hair said "punk." What do we notice, however, in societies other than our own? Ishi, the last of a "lost" tribe of North American Indians who stumbled into twentieth-century California in 1911, is reported to have said that the truly interesting objects in the white culture were pockets and matches. Rifa'ah Tahtawi, one of the first young Egyptians to be sent to Europe to study in 1826, wrote an account of French society in which he noted that Parisians used many unusual objects of dress, among them something called a belt. Women wore belts, he said, apparently to keep their bosoms erect, and to show off the slimness of their waists and the fullness of their hips. Europeans are still fascinated by the Stetson hats worn by American cowboys; an elderly Dutch woman of our acquaintance recently carried six enormous Stetsons back to the Hague as presents for the male members of her family.

Like languages (Inca, French) or food (tacos, hamburgers), clothing has special meaning for people who wear it that strangers may not understand. But some objects become charged with meaning to other cultures. The veil is one article of clothing used in Middle Eastern societies that stirs strong emotions in the West. "The feminine veil has become a symbol: that of the slavery of one portion of humanity," wrote French ethnologist Germaine Tillion in 1966. A hundred years earlier, Sir Richard Burton, British traveler, explorer, and translator of the *Arabian Nights,* recorded a different view. "Europeans inveigh against this article [the face veil] . . . for its hideousness and jealous concealment of charms made to be admired," he wrote in 1855. "It is, on the contrary, the most coquettish article of women's attire . . . it conceals coarse skins, fleshy noses, wide mouths and vanishing chins, whilst it sets off to best advantage what in these lands is most lustrous and liquid—the eye. Who has not remarked this at a masquerade ball?"

In the present generation, the veil has become a focus of attention for Western writers, both popular and academic, who take a measure of Burton's irony and Tillion's anger to equate modernization of the Middle East with the discarding of the veil and to look at its return in Iran and in a number of Arab countries as a sure sign of retrogression. "Iran's 16 million women have come a long way since their floor-length cotton veil officially was abolished in 1935," an article noted in the 1970s, just before the Shah was toppled. Today [1986], with Ayatollah Khomeini in power, those 16 million Iranian women have put their veils back on again, as if to say that the long way they have come is not in the direction of the West.

The thousands of words written about the appearance and disappearance of the veil and of *purdah* (the seclusion of women) do little to help us understand the Middle East or the cultures that grew out of the same Judeo-Christian roots as our own. The veil and the all-enveloping garments that inevitably accompany it (the *milayah* in Egypt, the *abbayah* in Iraq, the *chadoor* in Iran, the *yashmak* in Turkey, the *burga'* in Afghanistan, and the *djellabah* and the *haik* in North Africa) are only the outward manifestations of cultural practices and meanings that are rooted deep in the history of Mediterranean and Southwest Asian society and are now finding expression once again. Today, with the resurgence of Islam, the veil has become a statement of difference between the Middle East and the Western world, a boundary no easier to cross now than it was during the Crusades or during the nineteenth century, when Western colonial powers ruled the area.

In English, the word *veil* has many definitions, and some of them are religious, just as in the Middle East. In addition to a face cover, the term also means "a piece of material worn over the head and shoulders, a part of a nun's head dress." The Arabic word for veiling and secluding comes from the root word *hajaba*, meaning "barrier." A *hijab* is an amulet worn to keep away the evil eye; it also means a diaphragm used to prevent conception. The gatekeeper or doorkeeper who guards the entrance to a government minister's office is a *hijab*, and in a casual conversation a person might say, "I want to be more informal with my friend so-and-so, but she always puts a *hijab* [barrier] between us."

In Islam, the Koranic verse that sanctions a barrier between men and women is called the Sura of the *hijab* (curtain): "Prophet, enjoin your wives, your daughters and the wives of true believers to draw their garments close round them. That is more proper, so that they may be recognized and not molested. Allah is forgiving and merciful." Notice, however, that veils of the first true believers did not conceal but rather announced the religious status of the women who wore them, drawing attention to the fact that they were Muslims and therefore to be treated with respect. The special Islamic dress worn by increasing numbers of modern Muslim women has much the same effect; it also says, "Treat me with respect."

Certainly some form of seclusion and of veiling was practiced before the time of Muhammad, at least among the urban elites and ruling families, but it was his followers, the first converts to Islam, who used veiling to signal religious faith. According to historic traditions, the *hijab* was established after the wives of the Prophet Muhammad were insulted by people coming to the mosque in search of the Prophet. Muhammad's wives, they said, had been mistaken for slaves. The custom of the *hijab* was thus established, and in the words of historian Nabia Abbott, "Muhammad's women found themselves, on the one hand, deprived of personal liberty, and on the other hand, raised to a position of honor and dignity." It is true, nonetheless, that the forms and uses of veiling and seclusion have varied greatly in practice over the last thousand years since the time of the Prophet, and millions of Muslim women have never been veiled at all. It is a luxury poorer families cannot afford, since any form of arduous activity, such as working in the fields, makes its use impossible. Thus it is likely that the use of the veil was envied by those who could not afford it, for it signaled a style of life that was generally admired. Burton, commenting on the Muslims portrayed in the *Arabian Nights,* says, "The women, who delight in restrictions which tend to their honour, accepted it willingly and still affect it, they do not desire a liberty or rather a license which they have learned to regard as inconsistent with their time-honored notions of feminine decorum and delicacy. They would think very meanly of a husband who permitted them to be exposed, like hetairae, to the public gaze."

The veil bears many messages about its wearers and their society, and many men and women in Middle Eastern communities today would quickly denounce nineteenth-century Orientalists like Sir Richard Burton and deny its importance. Nouha al Hejelan, wife of the Saudi Arabian ambassador to London, told Sally Quinn of *The Washington Post,* "If I wanted to take it all off [the *abbayah* and veil], I would have long ago. It wouldn't mean as much to me as it does to you." Basima Bezirgan, a contemporary Iraqi feminist, says, "Compared to the real issues that are involved between men and women in the Middle East today, the veil itself is unimportant." A Moroccan linguist, who buys her clothes in Paris, laughs when asked about the veil. "My mother wears a *djellabah* and a veil. I have never worn them. But so what? I still cannot get divorced as easily as a man, and I am still a member of my family group and responsible to them for everything I do. What is the veil? A piece of cloth." However, early Middle Eastern feminists felt differently. Huda Sharawi, an early Egyptian activist who formed the first Women's Union, removed her veil in public in 1923, a dramatic gesture to demonstrate her dislike of society's attitude toward women and her defiance of the system.

"The seclusion of women has many purposes," states Egyptian anthropologist Nadia Abu Zahra. "It expresses men's status, power, wealth, and manliness. It also helps preserve men's image of virility and masculinity, but men do not admit this; on the contrary they claim that one of the purposes of the veil is to guard women's honor." The veil and *purdah* are symbols of restriction, in men's behavior as well as women's. A respectable woman wearing conservative Islamic dress today on a public street is signaling, "Hands off! Don't touch me or you'll be sorry." Cowboy Jim Sayre of Deadwood, South Dakota, says, "If you deform a cowboy's hat, he'll likely deform you." A man who approaches a veiled woman is asking for similar trouble; not only the woman but also her family is shamed, and serious problems may result. "It is clear," says Egyptian anthropologist Ahmed Abou Zeid, "that honor and shame which are usually attributed to a certain individual or a certain kinship group have in fact a bearing on the total social structure, since most acts involving honor or shame are likely to affect the existing social equilibrium."

Veiling and seclusion almost always can be related to the maintenance of social status. The extreme example of the way the rich could use this practice was found among the wealthy sultans of pre-revolutionary Turkey. Stories of their women, kept in harems and guarded by eunuchs, formed the basis for much of the Western folklore concerning the nature of male-female relationships in Middle Eastern society. The forbidden nature of seclusion inflamed the Western imagination, but the Westerners who created erotic fantasies in films and novels would not have been able to enter the sultans' palaces any more than they could have penetrated their harems! It was eroticism plus opulence and luxury, the signs of wealth, that captured the imagination of the Westerners—and still does, as witnessed by the popularity of "Dallas" and "Dynasty."

The meaning associated with veiling or a lack of veiling changes according to locality. Most village women in the Egyptian delta have not veiled, nor have the Berber women of North Africa, but no one criticizes them for this. "In the village, no one veils, because everyone is considered a member of the same large family," explained Aisha Bint Muhammad, a working-class wife of Marrakesh. "But in the city, veiling is *sunnah,* required by our religion." Veiling has generally been found in towns and cities, among all classes, where families feel that it is necessary to distinguish themselves from strangers. Some women who must work without the veil in factories and hotels may put such garments on when they go out on holidays or even walk on the streets after work.

Veiling and *purdah* not only indicate status and wealth; they also have some religious sanction and protect women from the world outside the home. *Purdah* delineates private space and distinguishes between the public and private sectors of society, as does the traditional architecture of the area. Older Middle Eastern houses do not have picture windows facing on the street, nor do they have walks leading invitingly to front doors. Family life is hidden away from strangers; behind blank walls may lie courtyards and gardens, refuges from the heat, cold, and bustle of the outside world, the world of nonkin that is not to be trusted. Outsiders are pointedly excluded.

Even within the household, among her close relatives, a traditional Muslim woman may veil before those kinsmen whom she could legally marry. If her maternal or paternal cousins, her brothers-in-law, or her sons-in-law come to call, she covers her head, or perhaps her whole face. To do otherwise, to neglect such acts of respect and modesty, would be considered shameless.

The veil does more than protect its wearers from known and unknown intruders; it can also conceal identity. Behind the anonymity of the veil, women can go about a city unrecognized and uncriticized. Nadia Abu Zahra reports anecdotes of men donning women's veils in order to visit their lovers undetected; women may do the same. The veil is such an effective disguise that Nouri Al-Sa'id, the late prime minister of Iraq, attempted to escape death from revolutionary forces in 1958 by wearing the *abbayah* and veil of a woman; only his shoes gave him away. When houses of prostitution were closed in Baghdad in the early 1950s, the prostitutes donned the same clothing to cruise the streets. Flashing open their outer garments was an advertisement to potential customers.

Political dissidents in many countries have used the veil for their own ends. The women who marched, veiled, through Cairo during the Nationalist demonstrations against the British after World War I were counting on the strength of Western respect for the veil to protect them against British gunfire. At first they were right. Algerian women also used the protection of the veil to carry bombs through French army checkpoints during the Algerian revolution. But when the French discovered the ruse, Algerian women discarded the veil and dressed like Europeans to move about freely.

The multiple meanings and uses of *purdah* and the veil do not fully explain how such practices came to be so deeply embedded in Mediterranean society. However, their origins lie in the asymmetrical relationship between men and women and the resulting attitudes about men's and women's roles. Women, according to Fatma Mernissi, a Moroccan sociologist, are seen by men in Islamic societies as in need of protection because they are unable to control their sexuality and hence are a danger to the social order. In other words, they need to be restrained and controlled so that men do not give way to the impassioned desire they inspire, and society can thus function in an orderly way.

The notion that women present a danger to the social order is scarcely limited to Muslim society. Anthropologist Julian Pitt-Rivers has pointed out that the supervision and seclusion of women was also found in Christian Europe, even though veiling was not usually practiced there. "The idea that women not subjected to male authority are a danger is a fundamental one in the writings of the moralists from the Archpriest of Talavera to Padre Haro, and it is echoed in the modern Andalusian *pueblo*. It is bound up with the fear of ungoverned female sexuality which had been an integral element of European folklore ever since prudent Odysseus lashed himself to the mast to escape the sirens."

Pitt-Rivers is writing about northern Mediterranean communities, which, like those of the Middle Eastern societies, have been greatly concerned with family honor and shame rather than with individual guilt. The honor of the Middle Eastern extended family, its ancestors and its descendants, is the highest social value. The misdeeds of the grandparents are indeed visited on their grandchildren, but so also grandparents may be disgraced by grandchildren. Men and women always remain members of their natal families. Marriage is a legal contract, but a fragile one that is often broken; the ties between brother and sister, mother and child, father and child are lifelong and enduring. The larger natal family is the group to which the individual man or woman belongs and to which the individual owes responsibility in exchange for the social and economic security that the family group provides. It is the group that is socially honored—or dishonored—by the behavior of the individual.

Both male honor and female honor are involved in the honor of the family, but each is expressed differently. The honor of a man, *sharaf*, is a public matter, involving bravery, hospitality, and piety. It may be lost, but it may also be regained. The honor of a woman, *'ard*, is a private matter involving only one thing, her sexual chastity. Once believed to be lost, it cannot be regained. If the loss of female honor remains only privately known, a rebuke may be all that takes place. But if the loss of female honor becomes public knowledge, the other members of the family may feel bound to cleanse the family name. In extreme cases, the cleansing may require the death of the offending female member. Although such killings are now criminal offenses in the Middle East, suspended sentences are often given, and the newspapers in Cairo and Baghdad frequently carry sad stories of runaway sisters "gone bad" in the city, and the revenge taken upon them in the name of family honor by their brothers or cousins.

This emphasis on female chastity, many say, originated in the patrilineal society's concern with the paternity of the child and the inheritance that follows the male line. How could the husband know that the child in his wife's womb was his son? He could not know unless his wife was a virgin at marriage. Marriages were arranged by parents, and keeping daughters secluded from men was the best way of seeing that a girl remained a virgin until her wedding night.

Middle Eastern women also look upon seclusion as practical protection. In the Iraqi village where we lived from 1956 to 1958, one of us (Elizabeth) wore the *abbayah* and found that it provided a great deal of protection from prying eyes, dust, heat, and flies. Parisian women visiting Istanbul in the sixteenth century were so impressed by the ability of the all-enveloping garment to keep dresses clean of mud and manure and to keep women from being attacked by importuning men that they tried to introduce it into French fashion. Many women have told us that they felt self-conscious, vulnerable, and even naked when they first walked on a public street without the veil and *abbayah*—as if they were making a display of themselves.

The veil, as it has returned in the last decade in a movement away from wearing Western dress, has been called a form of "portable seclusion," allowing women to maintain a modest appearance that indicates respectability and religious piety in the midst of modern Middle Eastern urban life. This new style of dress always includes long skirts, long sleeves, and a head covering (scarf or turban). Some outfits are belted, some are loose, and some include face veils and shapeless robes, as well as gloves so that no skin whatsoever is exposed to the public eye. However, these clothes are seldom black, like the older garments. The women wearing such clothes in Egypt may work in shops or offices or go to college; they are members of the growing middle class.

This new fashion has been described by some scholars as an attempt by men to reassert their Muslim identity and to reestablish their position as heads of families, even though both spouses often must work outside the home. According to this analysis, the presence of the veil is a sign that the males of the household are in control of their women and are more able to assume the responsibilities disturbed or usurped by foreign colonial powers, responsibilities which continue to be threatened by Western politics and materialism. Other scholars argue that it is not men who are choosing the garb today but women themselves, using modest dress as a way of communicating to the rest of the world that though they may work outside their homes, they are nonetheless pious Muslims and respectable women.

The veil is the outward sign of a complex reality. Observers are often deceived by the absence of that sign and fail to see that in Middle Eastern societies (and in many parts of Europe) where the garb no longer exists, basic attitudes are unchanged. Women who have taken off the veil continue to play the old roles within the family, and their chastity remains crucial. A woman's behavior is still the key to the honor and the reputation of her family, no matter what she wears.

In Middle Eastern societies, feminine and masculine continue to be strong poles of identification. This is in marked contrast to Western society, where for more than a generation greater equality between men and women has been reflected in the blurring of distinctions between male and female clothing. Western feminists continue to state that biology is not the basis of behavior and therefore should not be the basis for understanding men's and women's roles. But almost all Middle Eastern reformers, whether upper or middle class, intellectuals or clerics, argue from the assumption of a fundamental, God-given difference, social and psychological as well as physical, between men and women. There are important disagreements among these reformers today about what should be done, however.

Those Muslim reformers still strongly influenced by Western models call for equal access to divorce, child custody, and inheritance; equal opportunities for education and employment; abolition of female circumcision and "crimes of honor"; an end to polygamy; and a law regulating the age of marriage. But of growing importance are reformers of social practice who call for a return to the example set by the Prophet Muhammad and his early followers; they wish to begin by eliminating what they feel to be the licentious practices introduced by Western influence, such as sexual laxity and the consumption of alcohol. To them, change in the laws affecting women should be in strict accord with their view of Islamic law, and women should begin by expressing their modesty and piety by wearing the new forms of veiling in public life. Seclusion may be impossible in modern urban societies, but conservative dress, the new form of veiling, is an option for women that sets the faithful Muslim apart from the corrupt world of the nonbeliever as it was believed to do in the time of the Prophet.

A female English film director, after several months in Morocco, said in an interview, "This business about the veil is nonsense. We all have our veils, between ourselves and other people. The question is what the veils are used for, and by whom." Today the use of the veil continues to trigger Western reaction, for as Islamic dress, it is not only a statement about the honor of the family or the boundary between family and stranger. Just as the changes in the nun's dress in the United States tell us something about the woman who wears it and the society of which she is a part, the various forms of veiling today communicate attitudes and beliefs about politics and religious morality as well as the roles of men and women in the Middle East.

Review Questions

1. What is the meaning to Westerners of the veil worn by Middle Eastern women? How does this view reflect Western values?

2. List the symbolic meanings of the veil to Middle Eastern women. How do these meanings relate to the Muslim concept of *purdah* and to other important Middle Eastern values?

3. There has been a resurgence of the veil in several Middle Eastern societies over the past few years. How can you explain this change?

4. Using this article as a model, analyze the meaning of some American articles of clothing. How do these relate to core values in the United States?

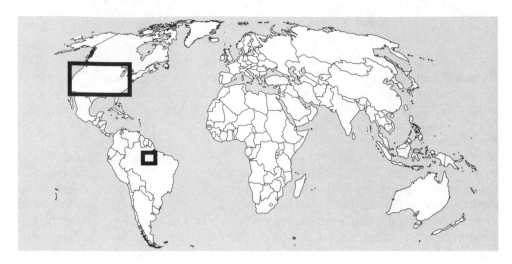

25

Mixed Blood

Jeffrey M. Fish

Many Americans believe that people can be divided into races. For them, races are biologically defined groups. Anthropologists, on the other hand, have long argued that U.S. racial groups are American cultural constructions; they represent the way Americans classify people rather than a genetically determined reality. In this article, Jeffrey Fish demonstrates the cultural basis of race by comparing how races are defined in the United States and Brazil. In America, a person's race is determined not by how he or she looks, but by his or her heritage. A person will be classified as black, for example, if one of his or her parents is classified that way no matter what the person looks like. In Brazil, on the other hand, people are classified into a series of tipos *on the basis of how they look. The same couple may have children classified into three or four different* tipos *based on a number of physical markers such as skin color and nose shape. As a result, Fish's daughter, who has brown skin and whose mother is black, can change her race from black in the United States to* moreno *(brunette), a category just behind* branca *(blond) in Brazil, by simply taking a plane there.*

Last year my daughter, who had been living in Rio de Janeiro, and her Brazilian boyfriend paid a visit to my cross-cultural psychology class. They had agreed to be interviewed about Brazilian culture. At one point in the interview I asked her, "Are you black?" She said, "Yes." I then asked him the question, and he said "No."

"How can that be?" I asked. "He's darker than she is."

Psychologists have begun talking about race again. They think that it may be useful in explaining the biological bases of behavior. For example, following publication of *The Bell Curve*, there has been renewed debate about whether black–white group differences in scores on IQ tests reflect racial differences in intelligence. (Because this article is about race, it will mainly use racial terms, like black and white, rather than cultural terms, like African-American and European-American.)

The problem with debates like the one over race and IQ is that psychologists on both sides of the controversy make a totally unwarranted assumption: that there is a biological entity called "race." If there were such an entity, then it would at least be possible that differences in behavior between "races" might be biologically based.

Before considering the controversy, however, it is reasonable to step back and ask ourselves "What is race?" If, as happens to be the case, race is not a biologically meaningful concept, then looking for biologically based racial differences in behavior is simply a waste of time.

The question "What is race?" can be divided into two more limited ones. The answers to both questions have long been known by anthropologists, but seem not to have reached other social or behavioral scientists, let alone the public at large. And both answers differ strikingly from what we Americans think of as race.

The first question is "How can we understand the variation in physical appearance among human beings?" It is interesting to discover that Americans (including researchers, who should know better) view only a part of the variation as "racial," while other equally evident variability is not so viewed.

The second question is "How can we understand the kinds of racial classifications applied to differences in physical appearance among human beings?" Surprisingly, different cultures label these physical differences in different ways. Far from describing biological entities, American racial categories are merely one of numerous, very culture-specific schemes for reducing uncertainty about how people should respond to other people. The fact that Americans believe that Asians, blacks, Hispanics, and whites constitute biological entities called races is a matter of cultural interest rather than scientific substance. It tells us something about American culture—but nothing at all about the human species.

The short answer to the question "What is race?" is: There is no such thing. Race is a myth. And our racial classification scheme is loaded with pure fantasy.

Let's start with human physical variation. Human beings are a species, which means that people from anywhere on the planet can mate with others from anywhere else and produce fertile offspring. (Horses and donkeys are two different species because, even though they can mate with each other, their off-spring—mules—are sterile.)

Our species evolved in Africa from earlier forms and eventually spread out around the planet. Over time, human populations that were geographically separated from one another came to differ in physical appearance. They came by these differences through three major pathways: mutation, natural selection, and genetic drift. Since genetic mutations occur randomly, different mutations occur and accumulate over time in geographically separated populations. Also, as we have known since Darwin, different geographical environments select for different physical traits that confer a survival advantage. But the largest proportion of variability among populations may well result from purely random factors; this random change in the frequencies of already existing genes is known as genetic drift.

If an earthquake or disease kills off a large segment of a population, those who survive to reproduce are likely to differ from the original population in many ways. Similarly, if a group divides and a subgroup moves away, the two groups will, by chance, differ in the frequency of various genes. Even the mere fact of physical separation will, over time, lead two equivalent populations to differ in the frequency of genes. These randomly acquired population differences will accumulate over successive generations along with any others due to mutation or natural selection.

A number of differences in physical appearance among populations around the globe appear to have adaptive value. For example, people in the tropics of Africa and South America came to have dark skins, presumably, through natural selection, as protection against the sun. In cold areas, like northern Europe or northern North America, which are dark for long periods of time, and where people covered their bodies for warmth, people came to have light skins—light skins make maximum use of sunlight to produce vitamin D.

The indigenous peoples of the New World arrived about 15,000 years ago, during the last ice age, following game across the Bering Strait. (The sea level was low enough to create a land bridge because so much water was in the form of ice.) Thus, the dark-skinned Indians of the South American tropics are descended from light-skinned ancestors, similar in appearance to the Eskimo. In other words, even though skin color is the most salient feature thought by Americans to be an indicator of race—and race is assumed to have great time depth—it is subject to relatively rapid evolutionary change.

Meanwhile, the extra ("epicanthic") fold of eyelid skin, which Americans also view as racial, and which evolved in Asian populations to protect the eye against the cold, continues to exist among South American native peoples because its presence (unlike a light skin) offers no reproductive disadvantage. Hence, skin color and eyelid form, which Americans think of as traits of different races, occur together or separately in different populations.

Like skin color, there are other physical differences that also appear to have evolved through natural selection—but which Americans do not think of as racial. Take, for example, body shape. Some populations in very cold climates, like the Eskimo, developed rounded bodies. This is because the more spherical an object is, the less surface area it has to radiate heat. In contrast, some populations in very hot climates, like the Masai, developed lanky bodies. Like the tubular pipes of an old-fashioned radiator, the high ratio of surface area to volume allows people to radiate a lot of heat.

In terms of American's way of thinking about race, lanky people and rounded people are simply two kinds of whites or blacks. But it is equally reasonable to view light-skinned people and dark-skinned people as two kinds of "lankys" or "roundeds." In other words, our categories for racial classification of people arbitrarily include certain dimensions (light versus dark skin) and exclude others (rounded versus elongated bodies).

There is no biological basis for classifying race according to skin color instead of body form—or according to any other variable, for that matter. All that exists is variability in what people look like—and the arbitrary and culturally specific ways different societies classify that variability. There is nothing left over that can be called race. This is why race is a myth.

Skin color and body form do not vary together: Not all dark-skinned people are lanky; similarly, light-skinned people may be lanky or rounded. The same can be said of the facial features Americans think of as racial—eye color, nose width (actually, the ratio of width to length), lip thickness ("evertedness"), hair form, and hair color. They do not vary together either. If they did, then a "totally white" person would have very light skin color, straight blond hair, blue eyes, a narrow nose, and thin lips; a "totally black" person would have very dark skin color, black tight curly hair, dark brown eyes, a broad nose, and thick lips; those in between would have—to a correlated degree—wavy light brown hair, light brown eyes, and intermediate nose and lip forms.

While people of mixed European and African ancestry who look like this do exist, they are the exception rather than the rule. Anyone who wants to can make up a chart of facial features (choose a location with a diverse population, say, the New York City subway) and verify that there are people with all possible admixtures of facial features. One might see someone with tight curly blond hair, light skin, blue eyes, broad nose, and thick lips—whose features are half "black" and half "white." That is, each of the person's facial features occupies one end or the other of a supposedly racial continuum, with no intermediary forms (like wavy light brown hair). Such people are living proof that supposedly racial features do not vary together.

Since the human species has spent most of its existence in Africa, different populations in Africa have been separated from each other longer than East Asians or Northern Europeans have been separated from each other or from Africans. As a result, there is remarkable physical variation among the peoples of Africa, which goes unrecognized by Americans who view them all as belonging to the same race.

In contrast to the very tall Masai, the diminutive stature of the very short Pygmies may have evolved as an advantage in moving rapidly through tangled forest vegetation. The Bushmen of the Kalahari desert have very large ("steatopygous") buttocks, presumably to store body fat in one place for times of food scarcity, while leaving the rest of the body uninsulated to radiate heat. They also have "peppercorn" hair. Hair in separated tufts, like tight curly hair, leaves space to radiate the heat that rises through the body to the scalp; straight hair lies flat and holds in body heat, like a cap. By viewing Africans as constituting a single race, Americans ignore their greater physical variability, while assigning racial significance to lesser differences between them.

Although it is true that most inhabitants of northern Europe, east Asia, and central Africa look like Americans' conceptions of one or another of the three purported races, most inhabitants of south Asia, southwest Asia, north Africa, and the Pacific islands do not. Thus, the 19th century view of the human species as comprised of Caucasoid, Mongoloid, and Negroid races, still held by many Americans, is based on a partial and unrepresentative view of human variability. In other words, what is now known about human physical variation does not correspond to what Americans think of as race.

In contrast to the question of the actual physical variation among human beings, there is the question of how people classify that variation. Scientists classify things in scientific taxonomies—chemists' periodic table of the elements, biologists' classification of life forms into kingdoms, phyla, and so forth.

In every culture, people also classify things along culture-specific dimensions of meaning. For example, paper clips and staples are understood by Americans as paper fasteners, and nails are not, even though, in terms of their physical properties, all three consist of differently shaped pieces of metal wire. The physical variation in pieces of metal wire can be seen as analogous to human physical variation; and the categories of cultural meaning, like paper fasteners versus wood fasteners, can be seen as analogous to races. Anthropologists refer to these kinds of classifications as folk taxonomies.

Consider the avocado—is it a fruit or a vegetable? Americans insist it is a vegetable. We eat it in salads with oil and vinegar. Brazilians, on the other hand, would say it is a fruit. They eat it for dessert with lemon juice and sugar.

How can we explain this difference in classification?

The avocado is an edible plant, and the American and Brazilian folk taxonomies, while containing cognate terms, classify some edible plants differently. The avocado does not change. It is the same biological entity, but its folk classification changes, depending on who's doing the classifying.

Human beings are also biological entities. Just as we can ask if an avocado is a fruit or a vegetable, we can ask if a person is white or black. And when we ask race questions, the answers we get come from folk taxonomies, not scientific ones. Terms like "white" or "black" applied to people—or "vegetable" or "fruit" applied to avocados—do not give us biological information about people or avocados. Rather, they exemplify how cultural groups (Brazilians or Americans) classify people and avocados.

Americans believe in "blood," a folk term for the quality presumed to be carried by members of so-called races. And the way offspring—regardless of their physical appearance—always inherit the less prestigious racial category of mixed parentage is called "hypo-descent" by anthropologists. A sentence thoroughly intelligible to most Americans might be,"Since Mary's father is white and her mother is black, Mary is black because she has black 'blood.'" American researchers who think they are studying racial differences in behavior would, like other Americans, classify Mary as black—although she has just as much white "blood."

According to hypo-descent, the various purported racial categories are arranged in a hierarchy along a single dimension, from the most prestigious ("white"), through intermediary forms ("Asian"), to the least prestigious ("black"). And when a couple come from two different categories, all their children (the "descent" in "hypo-descent") are classified as belonging to the less prestigious category (thus, the "hypo"). Hence, all the offspring of one "white" parent and one "black" parent—regardless of the children's physical appearance—are called "black" in the United States.

The American folk concept of "blood" does not behave like genes. Genes are units which cannot be subdivided. When several genes jointly determine a trait, chance decides which ones come from each parent. For example, if eight genes determine a trait, a child gets four from each parent. If a mother and a father each have the hypothetical genes BBBBWWWW, then a child could be born with any combination of B and W genes, from BBBBBBBB to WWWWWWWW. In contrast, the folk concept "blood" behaves like a uniform and continuous entity. It can be divided in two indefinitely—for example, quadroons and octoroons are said to be people who have one-quarter and one-eighth black "blood," respectively. Oddly, because of hypo-descent, Americans consider people with one-eighth black "blood" to be black rather than white, despite their having seven-eighths white "blood."

Hypo-descent, or "blood," is not informative about the physical appearance of people. For example, when two parents called black in the United States have a number of children, the children are likely to vary in physical appearance. In the case of skin color, they might vary from lighter than the lighter parent to darker than the darker parent. However, they would all receive the same racial classification—black—regardless of their skin color.

All that hypo-descent tells you is that, when someone is classified as something other than white (e.g., Asian), at least one of his or her parents is classified in the same way, and that neither parent has a less prestigious classification (e.g., black). That is, hypo-descent is informative about ancestry—specifically, parental classification—rather than physical appearance.

There are many strange consequences of our folk taxonomy. For example, someone who inherited no genes that produce "African"-appearing physical features would still be considered black if he or she has a parent classified as black. The category "passing for white" includes many such people. Americans have the curious belief that people who look white but have a parent classified as black are "really" black in some biological sense, and are being deceptive if they present themselves as white. Such examples make it clear that race is a social rather than a physical classification.

From infancy, human beings learn to recognize very subtle differences in the faces of those around them. Black babies see a wider variety of black faces than white faces, and white babies see a wider variety of white faces than black faces. Because they are exposed only to a limited range of human variation, adult members of each "race" come to see their own group as containing much wider variation than others. Thus, because of this perceptual learning, blacks see greater physical variation among themselves than among whites, while whites see the opposite. In this case, however, there is a clear answer to the question of which group contains greater physical variability. Blacks are correct.

Why is this the case?

Take a moment. Think of yourself as an amateur anthropologist and try to step out of American culture, however briefly.

It is often difficult to get white people to accept what at first appears to contradict the evidence they can see clearly with their own eyes—but which is really the result of a history of perceptual learning. However, the reason that blacks view themselves as more varied is not that their vision is more accurate. Rather, it is that blacks too have a long—but different—history of perceptual learning from that of whites (and also that they have been observers of a larger range of human variation).

The fact of greater physical variation among blacks than whites in America goes back to the principle of hypo-descent, which classifies all people with one black parent and one white parent as black. If they were all considered white, then there would be more physical variation among whites. Someone with one-eighth white "blood" and seven-eighths black "blood" would be considered white; anyone with any white ancestry would be considered white. In other words, what appears to be a difference in biological variability is really a difference in cultural classification.

Perhaps the clearest way to understand that the American folk taxonomy of race is merely one of many—arbitrary and unscientific like all the others—is to contrast it with a very different one, that of Brazil. The Portuguese word that in the Brazilian folk taxonomy corresponds to the American "race" is *"tipo."* *Tipo*, a cognate of the English word "type," is a descriptive term that serves as a kind of shorthand for a series of physical features. Because people's physical features vary separately from one another, there are an awful lot of tipos in Brazil.

Since tipos are descriptive terms, they vary regionally in Brazil—in part reflecting regional differences in the development of colloquial Portuguese, but in part because the physical variation they describe is different in different regions. The Brazilian situation is so complex I will limit my delineation of tipos to some of the main ones used in the city of Salvador, Bahia, to describe people whose physical appearance is understood to be made up of African and European features. (I will use the female terms throughout; in nearly all cases the male term simply changes the last letter from *a* to *o*.)

Proceeding along a dimension from the "whitest" to the "blackest" tipos, a *loura* is whiter-than-white, with straight blond hair, blue or green eyes, light skin color, narrow nose, and thin lips. Brazilians who come to the United States think that a *loura* means a "blond" and are surprised to find that the American term refers to hair color only. A *branca* has light skin color, eyes of any color, hair of any color or form except tight curly, a nose that is not broad, and lips that are not thick. *Branca* translates as "white," though Brazilians of this tipo who come to the United States—especially those from elite families—are often dismayed to find that they are not considered white here, and, even worse, are viewed as Hispanic despite the fact that they speak Portuguese.

A *morena* has brown or black hair that is wavy or curly but not tight curly, tan skin, a nose that is not narrow, and lips that are not thin. Brazilians who come to the United States think that a *morena* is a "brunette," and are surprised to find that brunettes are considered white but *morenas* are not. Americans have difficulty classifying *morenas*, many of whom are of Latin American origin: Are they black or Hispanic? (One might also observe that *morenas* have trouble with Americans, for not just accepting their appearance as a given, but asking instead "Where do you come from?" "What language did you speak at home?" "What was your maiden name?" or even, more crudely, "What *are* you?")

A *mulata* looks like a *morena*, except with tight curly hair and a slightly darker range of hair colors and skin colors. A *preta* looks like a *mulata*, except with dark brown skin, broad nose, and thick lips. To Americans, *mulatas* and *pretas* are both black, and if forced to distinguish between them would refer to them as light-skinned blacks and dark-skinned blacks, respectively.

If Brazilians were forced to divide the range of tipos, from *loura* to *preta*, into "kinds of whites" and "kinds of blacks" (a distinction they do not ordinarily make), they would draw the line between *morenas* and *mulatas;* whereas Americans, if offered only visual information, would draw the line between *brancas* and *morenas*.

The proliferation of tipos, and the difference in the white–black dividing line, do not, however, exhaust the differences between Brazilian and American folk taxonomies. There are tipos in the Afro-European domain that are considered to be neither black nor white—an idea that is difficult for Americans visiting Brazil to comprehend. A person with tight curly blond (or red) hair, light skin, blue (or green) eyes, broad nose, and thick lips, is a *sarará*. The opposite features—straight black hair, dark skin, brown eyes, narrow nose, and thin lips—are those of a *cabo verde*. *Sarará* and *cabo verde* are both tipos that are considered by Brazilians in Salvador, Bahia, to be neither black nor white.

When I interviewed my American daughter and her Brazilian boyfriend, she said she was black because her mother is black (even though I am white).

That is, from her American perspective, she has "black blood"—though she is a *morena* in Brazil. Her boyfriend said that he was not black because, viewing himself in terms of Brazilian tipos, he is a *mulato* (not a *preto*).

There are many differences between the Brazilian and American folk taxonomies of race. The American system tells you about how people's parents are classified but not what they look like. The Brazilian system tells you what they look like but not about their parents. When two parents of intermediate appearance have many children in the United States, the children are all of one race; in Brazil they are of many tipos.

Americans believe that race is an immutable biological given, but people (like my daughter and her boyfriend) can change their race by getting on a plane and going from the United States to Brazil—just as, if they take an avocado with them, it changes from a vegetable into a fruit. In both cases, what changes is not the physical appearance of the person or avocado, but the way they are classified.

I have focused on the Brazilian system to make clear how profoundly folk taxonomies of race vary from one place to another. But the Brazilian system is just one of many. Haiti's folk taxonomy, for example, includes elements of both ancestry and physical appearance, and even includes the amazing term (for foreigners of African appearance) *un blanc noir*—literally, "a black white." In the classic study *Patterns of Race in the Americas,* anthropologist Marvin Harris gives a good introduction to the ways in which the conquests by differing European powers of differing New World peoples and ecologies combined with differing patterns of slavery to produce a variety of folk taxonomies. Folk taxonomies of race can be found in many—though by no means all—cultures in other parts of the world as well.

The American concept of race does not correspond to the ways in which human physical appearance varies. Further, the American view of race ("hypo-descent") is just one among many folk taxonomies, [none] of which correspond to the facts of human physical variation. This is why race is a myth and why races as conceived by Americans (and others) do not exist. It is also why differences in behavior between "races" cannot be explained by biological differences between them.

When examining the origins of IQ scores (or other behavior), psychologists sometimes use the term "heritability"—a statistical concept that is not based on observations of genes or chromosomes. It is important to understand that questions about heritability of IQ have nothing to do with racial differences in IQ. "Heritability" refers only to the relative ranking of individuals *within* a population, under given environmental conditions, and not to differences *between* populations. Thus, among the population of American whites, it may be that those with high IQs tend to have higher-IQ children than do those with low IQs. Similarly, among American blacks, it may be that those with high IQs also tend to have higher-IQ children.

In both cases, it is possible that the link between the IQs of parents and children may exist for reasons that are not entirely environmental. This heritability of IQ *within* the two populations, even if it exists, would in no way contradict the average social advantages of American whites as a group compared to the average social disadvantages of American blacks as a group. Such differences in social environments can easily account for any differences in the average test scores *between* the two groups. Thus, the heritability of IQ *within* each group is irrelevant to understanding differences *between* the groups.

Beyond this, though, studies of differences in behavior between "populations" of whites and blacks, which seek to find biological causes rather than only social ones, make a serious logical error. They assume that blacks and whites are populations in some biological sense, as sub-units of the human species. (Most likely, the researchers make this assumption because they are American and approach race in terms of the American folk taxonomy.)

In fact, though, the groups are sorted by a purely social rule for statistical purposes. This can easily be demonstrated by asking researchers how they know that the white subjects are really white and the black subjects are really black. There is no biological answer to this question, because race as a biological category does not exist. All that researchers can say is, "The tester classified them based on their physical appearance," or "Their school records listed their race," or otherwise give a social rather than biological answer.

So when American researchers study racial differences in behavior, in search of biological rather than social causes for differences between socially defined groups, they are wasting their time. Computers are wonderful machines, but we have learned about "garbage in/garbage out." Applying complex computations to bad data yields worthless results. In the same way, the most elegant experimental designs and statistical analyses, applied flawlessly to biologically meaningless racial categories, can only produce a very expensive waste of time.

As immigrants of varied physical appearance come to the United States from countries with racial folk taxonomies different from our own, they are often perplexed and dismayed to find that the ways they classify themselves and others are irrelevant to the American reality. Brazilians, Haitians, and others may find themselves labeled by strange, apparently inappropriate, even pejorative terms, and grouped together with people who are different from and unreceptive to them. This can cause psychological complications (a Brazilian immigrant—who views himself as white—being treated by an American therapist who assumes that he is not).

Immigration has increased, especially from geographical regions whose people do not resemble American images of blacks, whites, or Asians. Intermarriage is also increasing, as the stigma associated with it diminishes. These two trends are augmenting the physical diversity among those who marry each other—and, as a result, among their children. The American folk taxonomy of race (purportedly comprised of stable biological entities) is beginning to change to accommodate this new reality. After all, what race is someone whose four grandparents are black, white, Asian, and Hispanic?

Currently, the most rapidly growing census category is "Other," as increasing numbers of people fail to fit available options. Changes in the census categories every 10 years reflect the government's attempts to grapple with the changing self-identifications of Americans—even as statisticians try to maintain the same categories over time in order to make demographic comparisons. Perhaps they will invent one or more "multiracial" categories, to accommodate the wide range of people whose existence defies current classification. Perhaps they will drop the term "race" altogether. Already some institutions are including an option to "check as many as apply," when asking individuals to classify themselves on a list of racial and ethnic terms.

Thinking in terms of physical appearance and folk taxonomies helps to clarify the emotionally charged but confused topics of race. Understanding that different cultures have different folk taxonomies suggests that we respond to the question "What race is that person?" not by "Black" or "White," but by "Where?" and "When?"

Review Questions

1. What is Jeffrey Fish's main point about the way Americans define race?

2. What is the difference between the way race is defined in the United States and in Brazil? List the Brazilian folk taxonomy of *tipos* and how to translate *tipos* into U.S. racial categories.

3. What evidence challenges the view that races are biologically defined types? What evidence would have to exist to prove that the human species is genetically divided into races?

4. Why does Fish feel it is important to understand that race as Americans define it does not represent a biological reality?

SEVEN

LAW AND POLITICS

Oleg Nikishin/Getty Images

READINGS IN THIS SECTION

Cross-Cultural Law: The Case of the Gypsy Offender   263
Anne Sutherland

Life without Chiefs   272
Marvin Harris

The Founding Indian Fathers   281
Jack Weatherford

The Kindness of Strangers: The United States and Iraq   291
Robin Fox

Ideally, culture provides the blueprint for a smoothly oiled social machine whose parts work together under all circumstances. But human society is not like a rigidly constructed machine. It is made of individuals who have their own special needs and desires. Personal interest, competition for scarce resources, and simple accident can cause nonconformity and disputes, resulting in serious disorganization.

One way we manage social disruption is through the socialization of children. As we acquire our culture, we learn the appropriate ways to look at experience, to define our existence, and to feel about life. Each system of cultural knowledge contains implicit values of what is desirable, and we come to share these values with other people. Slowly, with the acquisition of culture, most people find they *want* to do what they *must* do; the requirements of an orderly social life become personal goals.

Enculturation, however, is rarely enough. Disputes among individuals regularly occur in all societies, and how such disagreements are handled defines what anthropologists mean by the legal system. Some disputes are **infralegal;** they never reach a point where they are settled by individuals with special authority. Neighbors, for example, would engage in an infralegal dispute if they argued over who should pay for the damage caused by water that runs off one's land into the other's basement. So long as they don't take the matter to court or resort to violence, the dispute will remain infralegal. This dispute may become **extralegal,** however, if it occurs outside the law and escalates into violence. Had the neighbors come to blows over the waterlogged basement, the dispute would have become extralegal. Feuds and wars are the best examples of this kind of dispute.

Legal disputes, on the other hand, involve socially approved mechanisms for their settlement. **Law** is the cultural knowledge that people use to settle disputes by means of agents who have the recognized authority to do so. Thus if the argument between neighbors cited previously ended up in court before a judge or referee, it would have become legal.

Although Americans often think of courts as synonymous with the legal system, societies have evolved a variety of structures for settling disputes. For example, some disputes may be settled by **self-redress,** meaning that wronged individuals are given the right to settle matters themselves. **Contests** requiring physical or mental combat between disputants may also be used to settle disputes. A trusted third party, or **go-between,** may be asked to negotiate with each side until a settlement is achieved. In some societies, supernatural power or beings may be used. In parts of India, for example, disputants are asked to take an oath in the name of a powerful deity or (at least in the past) to submit to a supernaturally controlled, painful, or physically dangerous test called an **ordeal.** Disputes may also be taken to a **moot,** an informal community meeting where conflict may be aired. At the moot, talk continues until a settlement is reached. Finally, disputes are often taken to **courts,** which are formally organized and include officials with authority to make and enforce decisions.

Political systems are closely related to legal ones and often involve some of the same offices and actors. The **political system** contains the process for making and carrying out public policy according to cultural categories and rules; **policy** refers to guidelines for action. The **public** are the people affected by the policy. Every society must make decisions that affect all or most of its members. The Mbuti Pygmies of the Ituri Forest described by anthropologist Colin Turnbull, for example, occasionally decide to conduct a communal hunt. Hunters set their nets together and wait for the appearance of forest game. Men, women, and children must work together as beaters to drive the animals toward the nets. When the Mbuti decide to hold a hunt, they make a political decision.

The political process requires that people make and abide by a particular policy, often in the face of competing plans. To do so a policy must have **support,** which is anything that contributes to its adoption and enforcement. Anthropologists recognize two main kinds of support: legitimacy and coercion. **Legitimacy** refers to people's positive evaluation of public officials and public policy. A college faculty, for example, may decide to institute the quarter system because a majority feel that quarters rather than semesters represent the "right length" for courses. Theirs is a positive evaluation of the policy. Some faculty members will oppose the change but will abide by the decision because they value the authority of faculty governance. For them the decision, although unfortunate, is legitimate.

Coercion, on the other hand, is support derived from the threat or use of force or the promise of short-term gain. Had the faculty members adopted the quarter system because they had been threatened with termination by the administration, they would have acted under coercion.

There are also other important aspects of the political process. Some members of a society may be given **authority,** the right to make and enforce public policy. In our country, elected officials are given authority to make certain decisions and exercise particular powers. However, formal political offices with authority do not occur in every society. Most hunting and gathering societies lack such positions, as do many horticulturalists. **Leadership,** which is the ability to influence others to act, must be exercised informally in these societies.

In the first article, Anne Sutherland describes what happens when the substantive laws of two culturally different groups collide in court. A young Gypsy man is convicted of using another family member's social security number although he had no intention of defrauding anyone. The second selection, by Marvin Harris, traces the development of political leadership. He argues that small groups characterized by reciprocal exchange have no recognizable political officers and that many horticultural societies with redistributive economic exchange may develop "big men" who lead by example but still have no formal authority. Jack Weatherford writes about the impact that American Indian political systems had on the formation of the United States. Informed largely by kingships and councils of nobles, early colonists encountered a confederation

of states called the League of the Iroquois, which served as a model for the federation that colonialists eventually built into the U.S. constitution. In the last
article, Robin Fox, argues that people rarely feel comfortable about accepting
gifts from strangers. Despite such discomfort, colonial governments and today,
the United States, display a missionary zeal to give "civilization" and, in America's case, democracy, to other people. Applied to Iraq, at least, the gift seems
doomed to failure. The British cobbled the country together out of a variety of
peoples after World War I, and its people direct their loyalty not to a state, but
to family, clan, tribe, and sect.

Key Terms

authority   p. 261
coercion   p. 261
contest   p. 260
court   p. 260
extralegal dispute   p. 260
go-between   p. 260
infralegal dispute   p. 260
law   p. 260
leadership   p. 261

legitimacy   p. 261
moot   p. 260
ordeal   p. 260
policy   p. 261
political system   p. 261
public   p. 261
self-redress   p. 260
support   p. 261

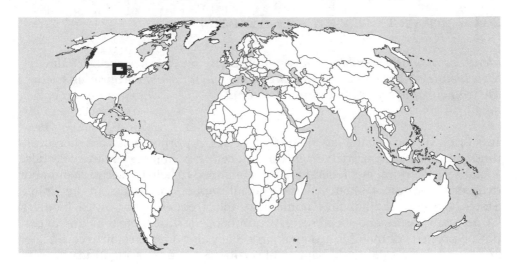

26

Cross-Cultural Law: The Case of the Gypsy Offender

Anne Sutherland

Every society recognizes a list of legal statutes, which anthropologists call substantive law, that define right from wrong. In the United States, for example, it is against the law for an individual to marry more than one person at a time. But what is proper in one country may be a crime in another. Unlike the United States, for example, in Iran it is legal for a person to be married simultaneously to more than one person. So what happens when members of one society live within and under the legal jurisdiction of another? This is the question explored by Anne Sutherland in this article on the legal plight of a young Gypsy man who is arrested for using the Social Security number of a relative on a car loan application. Despite the claim that using different identities of family members is a common Gypsy practice designed to hide their identities, and that he had no intention to defraud anyone by doing so, the young man receives a six-month jail term.

It is often the case that a law made for one set of purposes has another, unintended impact on a particular group. A recent law making the use of a false social security number a federal felony is intended to help prosecution of major drug crime syndicates, but it has a special impact on Gypsies in the United States. Gypsies, traditionally a nomadic people, frequently borrow each others' "American" names and social security numbers, viewing them as a kind of corporate property of their kin group or *vitsa*. They also often lack birth certificates and must obtain midwife or baptismal certificates to use for identification purposes when they try to obtain credit, enter school, or apply for welfare.

In this article, I shall examine the case of a nineteen-year-old Gypsy man who was convicted under the new social security law and served six months in jail. Arguments for the defense in the case followed three lines of reasoning: 1) that this law unfairly singled out Gypsies for punishment; 2) that there was no intent to commit a crime; and 3) that in using the social security numbers of relatives, Gypsies were following a time-honored tradition to remain anonymous and separate from non-Gypsy society.

Facts of the Case

In the fall of 1991 in St. Paul, Minnesota, a nineteen-year-old Gypsy man was convicted of the crime of using his five-year-old nephew's social security number to obtain credit to purchase a car. When the purchase was questioned by the car dealership, he returned the car and was arrested on a felony charge of using a false social security number. After he was arrested, police searched the apartment where he was staying. They found lists of names, addresses and social security numbers, leading them to suspect an organized crime ring.

In *The United States of America v. S.N.,*[1] it was "alleged that the defendant, S.N., while in the process of obtaining a new Ford Mustang from a car dealership, used a social security number that was not his own with intent to deceive." Under the statute 42 U.S.C. 408 (g)(2), a person who, with intent to deceive, falsely represents his or her number to obtain something of value or for any other purpose, is a felon.

In Mr. S.N.'s case there is no specific allegation that he intended to deprive another person permanently of property because the focus of the charging

---

[1]*United States v. Sonny Nicholas,* U.S. District Court, State of Minnesota, CR 4-91-137 (1991). Quotes from Philip Leavenworth, memorandum in support of a motion to declare 42 U.S.C.408(g)(2) unconstitutional.

statute is false representation of numbers. The underlying purpose which motivates a person to falsely represent his or her number may be an essentially innocent purpose, but the statute, at least as it has been interpreted, does not appear to impose a burden of proof as to wrongful purpose.

The statute punishes the means (false number) which a person may employ to achieve any number of ends and it punishes those means as a felony. The lawyer for the defense argued that the statute's failure to address the nature of the purpose to which false credentials are used is a serious flaw in the law and may punish those who would use the number for petty misconduct as felons. He also argued that there is a potential for discriminatory impact on Gypsies who use false credentials to conceal themselves from mainstream society. A Gypsy household may obtain a telephone by providing a false social security number and even if they pay the telephone bill without fail for years, they are felons under this law. S.N. not only made the payments for his car, but he returned it when the number was questioned. He is still a felon under this law.

The defense lawyer argued that the law is objectionable for two reasons. First, the law's disproportionate impact on the Gypsies is objectionable under the equal protection guaranteed in the Fifth Amendment of the U.S. Constitution. He argued that the law denies Gypsies equal protection of the law by irrationally and disproportionately punishing at the felony level certain traditional Gypsy actions which cause no positive injury to anyone. As evidence he used material from my book, *Gypsies: The Hidden Americans*, for testimony that Gypsies routinely use false social security numbers to acquire credit but do pay their bills and are available for repossession in case of default of payment. They get phone service, buy houses and cars and other household items on credit and have a record of payment that is probably better than the general population (*United States v. S.N., 1991*). They do this primarily to remain unknown by mainstream society rather than to cause loss or injury to any person.

Second, as the defense lawyer pointed out, there is a Supreme Court decision that requires the government to prove felonious intent when it seeks to punish a person for wrongful acquisition of another's property. S.N. maintained that he used a false social security number because of a Gypsy tradition to remain anonymous and because his own number had been used by other Gypsies. The government argued that there was a "ring" of Gypsies in the area where S.N. was living. At S.N.'s residence a number of false credentials and social security numbers were found which had been used to obtain cars illegally. Some of these cars are still missing. In other words, there was evidence that false identity had been used recently in the area to steal. In this case, however, S.N. had not stolen anything and was not being accused of stealing, but only of using a false social security number.

Because of the evidence of a ring of car thieves in the area, the prosecution hoped to use the threat of prosecution against S.N., the only Gypsy they had been able to arrest, to plea bargain for information regarding the other people involved in the alleged ring. These other people had disappeared immediately as soon as S.N. was arrested.

One of the problems in the case was that both the prosecution and even the defense had difficulty obtaining complete and accurate information on S.N. For example, they had difficulty determining his "real" name, a moot point for the Gypsies since they have a practice of using many "American" names although they only have one "Gypsy" name (*nav romano*). The Gypsy name of o *Spiro le Stevanosko* (or Spiro the son of Stevan) uses the noun declension characteristic of the Sanskrit-rooted Rom language and is not immediately translatable into English since it does not employ a surname. Spiro's identity can be pinned down by finding out what *vitsa* (a cognatic descent group) he belongs to so that he will not be confused with any other Spiro le Stevanoskos. The Spiro of our example is a *Kashtare* which is part of a larger "nation" of Gypsies or *natsia* called *Kalderasha* (coppersmith). For his "American" names he may take any of a number used by his relatives such as Spiro Costello, John Costello, John Marks, John Miller, Spiro John or Spiro Miller. His nickname is Rattlesnake Pete.

The Anthropologist as Cultural Broker

S.N.'s defense attorney contacted me after finding that he was less confused about S.N. after reading my book about Gypsies. He sought my help in determining whether S.N. was a Gypsy, what his name was, and any other cultural information (such as the use of social security numbers by Gypsies) that would help him with his case.

Consequently, one cold autumn day I drove to the federal holding prison, one and a half hours from the city, and met S.N. He was a thin young man, perpetually fearful of pollution from contact with non-Gypsies and suffering from the effects of several months of what for him was solitary confinement since he had not seen any of his people since being incarcerated. The telephone was his only link with people to whom he could relate, people from his own culture who spoke his language. His main contact was with a non-Gypsy woman who lived with one of his relatives. She was his link with the world he had known and the only "American" household he had been in before prison. Since my primary task was to determine if he was a Gypsy, first I talked to him about his relatives in Los Angeles and his *vitsa* (Yowane) and tried to establish what section of the *vitsa* I personally knew. This exchange of information about *vitsa* and Gypsies of mutual acquaintance is a normal one between Gypsies. The purpose was to establish a link between us.

Then I asked him about why he was in Minnesota. He talked about a seasonal expedition he and his brothers and cousins make to Minnesota to buy and sell cars and fix fenders before winter sets in. He claimed not to know where his brothers and cousins had gone or how he got into his present predicament.

For S.N., the most immediately effective action I could take was to see that he got the food he needed to stay "clean" in jail. When I met him he had lost fifteen pounds and was suffering demonstrable distress and nervousness. He was upset at being cut off from his culture and people for the first time in his life. In addition, he was distressed at being incarcerated and fearful for his safety. More importantly, he was worried he would become defiled or *marime*. A major concern of his was that if he ate food prepared by non-Gypsies who did not follow rules of cleanliness considered essential in the Gypsy culture, he would become *marime*, a condition of ritual impurity that would result in his being shunned by his relatives and other Gypsies. To protect himself, he avoided eating prison food in the hopes that when he was released from prison he would be able to return to his family without a period of physical exile, also called *marime* (or "rejected" as the Gypsies translate it into English). I arranged for his lawyer to provide him with money to buy food from the concession because it is packaged and untouched by non-Gypsies and therefore considered clean by Gypsy standards. He bought milk in cartons, candy bars and soft drinks and other packaged foods that, though they may lack in nutrition, at least were not defiling and kept him from starvation.

A further complicating factor for S.N. was that he spoke English as a second language. He had only a rudimentary ability to read, thus straining his grasp of his defense. And his only contact with relatives was by telephone since neither he nor they could write with any ease. Even though his limited English made it difficult for him to follow his own trial, the court did not provide a translator.

The Trial

The trial was held in Federal Court and centered around the constitutionality of a law that unfairly targets a particular ethnic group and the question of intent to commit a crime. My testimony was intended to establish that Gypsies may use false identification for a number of cultural reasons which may have no connection to any intent to commit a crime. For a traditionally nomadic group with pariah status in the wider society and a pattern of secretiveness and autonomy, concealing identity is a long-established pattern.

This pattern is widespread in all Gypsy groups in Eastern Europe, Western Europe, Russia, Latin America and the United States. It is a mechanism they have developed over centuries to protect themselves from a wider society that has persecuted them or driven them away. The recent case of the German government paying large sums to Romania to take back Gypsy refugees is only the latest in a historically established tradition of discrimination against Gypsies. The persecution of Gypsies in the Holocaust, in medieval Europe and in the early part of the 20th century in the United States has been well documented. Current events in Eastern Europe have shown a resurgence of extreme prejudice against Gypsies. Interviews in recent *New York Times* articles have pointed to a hatred of Gypsies so deep that there is talk of extermination.[2] Because of the history of violence against them, Gypsies have developed elaborate mechanisms of secrecy and have hidden their identity in order to survive. It will not be easy to get them to change this pattern that has stood them in good stead for so many centuries.

The purpose of my testimony was to establish that S.N. *was* a Gypsy and that Gypsies often use false identification without intent to defraud. They do so because as members of a *vitsa*, or cognatic descent group, identification is corporate in nature. Members of the group have corporate access to property owned by other members of the group. That property includes forms of identification.

An additional problem in the S.N. case was the question of identification from photographs. Here we encountered the age-old problem that members of one culture and race have trouble identifying individuals from another culture and race. In simple terms, to many non-Gypsies, all Gypsies look alike. Part of the case involved clearing up erroneous identification of S.N. in photos provided by the prosecution.

I was also asked to testify on my own personal experience with discrimination against Gypsies by the Minneapolis Police Department. One instance of discrimination I related to the court occurred during a talk I gave to some twenty police officers to help them understand Gypsy culture. When I had spoken about the strong sense of family and community among the Gypsies and how much they value their children, a police officer suggested that since the main problem law enforcement officers have is how to detain the Gypsies long enough to prosecute them, removing Gypsy children from their homes on any pretext would be an effective way to keep the parents in town.

Prejudice against Gypsies often goes unrecognized even by culturally and racially sensitive people. The assistant district attorney prosecuting S.N. offered me an article that he used to understand the Gypsies, entitled "Gypsies, the People and their Criminal Propensity,"[3] which quotes extensively from my work, including the fact that Gypsies have several names and that the same or similar non-Gypsy names are used over and over. The article concentrates on "criminal" behavior and never mentions the possibility that there are Gypsies who may not engage in criminal activities. In one section, quotations from my book on the ways Gypsies deal with the welfare bureaucracy were placed under the title, "Welfare Fraud," although by far most of the practices I described were legal. These concluding words in Part II are representative of the tone of the article:

> Officers should not be misled into thinking these people are not organized. They are indeed organized and operate under established rules of behavior, including those that govern marriage, living quarters, child rearing, the division of money and participation in criminal acts.

[2]See *New York Times*, November 17 and 28, 1993, for recent accounts of extreme prejudice against Gypsies.

[3]Terry Getsay, *Kansas State FOP Journal*, Parts I, II, and III (1982): 18–30.

The implication of such statements is inflammatory. Gypsies have a culture, history, language and social structure, but that fact is distorted to imply that their social organization is partly for the purpose of facilitating criminal behavior. Their culture is viewed as a criminal culture. Gypsies have been fighting this view for hundreds of years. It is the view that they still combat in their relations with law enforcement and the criminal justice system. It is the view that was promoted by the prosecution in this case.

In spite of the best efforts of S.N.'s attorney and my testimony that use of a false social security number did not necessarily indicate intent to commit a crime, he was convicted of illegally using a social security number and served about six months in jail.

Conclusions: Anthropology and Cultural Differences in the Courtroom

Anthropologists are often called in as expert witnesses in cases involving cultural difference. Most Native American legal cases, such as the *Mashpee* case reported by James Clifford,[4] center around Indian status, treaties and land rights. In St. Paul, a number of Hmong legal cases highlighted the conflict between traditional marriage (specifically, the age at which children may marry) and the legal status of minors in American law. With the Gypsies, there is yet another set of cultural issues in their contact with American law.

First is the question of the cultural conflict between a historically nomadic group and the state bureaucracy of settled people. Identification—a serious legal issue in a bureaucratic society composed of people with fixed abodes and a written language—has virtually no meaning for the nomadic Gypsies who consider descent and extended family ties the defining factor for identification.

Second is the conflict between Gypsy religious rules regarding ritual pollution and prison regulations. The Gypsies avoid situations, such as a job or jail, that require them to be in prolonged contact with non-Gypsies. Jail presents special problems because the Gypsies can become *marime*, that is, defiled by unclean food and living conditions. The psychological trauma that results from isolation from their community is compounded if they then emerge from jail and have to undergo a further isolation from relatives because of becoming *marime* in jail.

Finally, this case illustrates a cultural clash between the Rom Gypsy value on corporate kinship and the American value on individual rights. The rights and status of an individual Rom Gypsy is directly linked to his or her membership in the *vitsa*. Furthermore, the status of all members of the *vitsa* is affected by the behavior of each individual *vitsa* member. Since they are so

---

[4]"Identity in Mashpee," in *The Predicament of Culture* (Cambridge: Harvard University Press, 1988), pp. 277–346.

intricately linked, reciprocity between *vitsi* members is expected. Members of a *vitsa* and family share economic resources, stay in each other's homes, help each other in work and preparation of rituals, loan each other cars, information, identification, and money. They also share the shame of immoral or incorrect behavior by one member and the stigma (*marime*) attached to going to jail. For the Gypsies, the American ideal of each individual having only one name, one social security number, or a reputation based entirely on their own behavior is contrary to their experience and culture.

The analysis of an event such as a trial, especially an event that brings to the fore cultural difference, can be instructive for both cultures. In this article I have tried to present fundamental differences in the practices of American culture and U.S. law and the practices of Roma law and Gypsy culture. Understanding difference does not necessarily resolve conflict, but it can lead to a more humanitarian application of the law to different cultures. The United States, a country based on immigration and diversity, is in no position to ignore the cultural foundations of different ethnic groups, nor are different cultures in the United States exempt from a law because it is contrary to custom. However, the more aware the legal system is of cultural histories and custom, the greater its capacity for justice.

S.N. chose to pursue his case through the U.S. legal system. He made this choice partly because of the influence and advice of a brother who was married to an American lawyer. The rest of his family strongly opposed this decision, preferring to do it the way they always have, by fleeing or lying to avoid contact with the legal system. While he was in jail, the Gypsies in his community held a *Kris* (formal meeting) to explain his decision to work through the American courts rather than the traditional Gypsy way and to raise money for his defense. The outcome of that trial was that on his release S.N., as well as his brother and brother's wife, who was his lawyer, were "rejected" (*marime*) and totally ostracized by his family. At the same time, the conditions of his probation stipulated that S.N. could not associate with his family, and he was released early into the custody of his brother and his brother's wife. Ironically, in the end, both U.S. and Roma law were in agreement on the consequences of his "crime" but for opposite reasons. The American legal system viewed S.N.'s family as "criminal associates"; his family, on the other hand, viewed S.N. and his brother as *marime* for rejecting Gypsy culture. Nevertheless, the strength of Gypsy culture has always been its ability to keep its closely knit ties, and today S.N. and his brother are back in the bosom of the family.

As the world changes into the next millennium, more people than ever before in human history are on the move as migrants, immigrants, guest workers, refugees and even as tourists. At this time in history, many people are living in places that do not share their cultural and legal traditions. Studies of society and legal systems must search for ways to deal with this cultural encounter. Gypsies have probably the longest recorded history of continuous movement and adaptation to other societies and cultures. Their treatment is a barometer of justice and civilization.

Review Questions

1. What aspect of the "crime" committed by a young Gypsy man is due to cross-cultural difference, according to Sutherland?

2. How did the police interpret the lists of social security numbers and other evidence found in the young man's apartment? How did their interpretation of this evidence differ from the Gypsy's?

3. How does this case illustrate the role cultural anthropologists can play in everyday American life?

4. Can you think of other cases where immigrants or culturally different people run afoul of American substantive law?

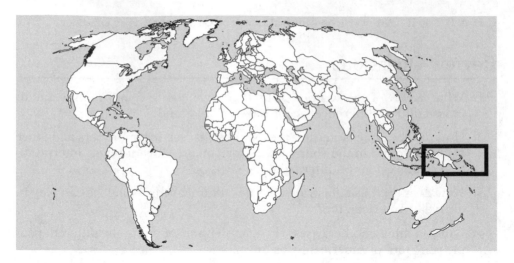

27

Life without Chiefs

Marvin Harris

It may come as a surprise to most Americans, but there were, and in a few cases still are, societies in the world that lack formal political structure. Instead of presidents, mayors, senators, and directors of homeland security, there are headmen, big men, and chiefs who lead by their ability to persuade and impress without the authority to make *people act. In this article, Marvin Harris traces the evolution of political leadership, associating* headmen *with small hunting and gathering societies marked by reciprocal exchange, and* big men *with slightly larger horticultural societies that employ redistributive exchange. Chiefs also occupied the center of redistribution systems but their societies were larger and chiefs could inherit their positions. He concludes that human biological inheritance was shaped by a hunter-gatherer existence; there is nothing inherited about the political formalism and social inequality that characterize large state societies.*

Can humans exist without some people ruling and others being ruled? To look at the modern world, you wouldn't think so. Democratic states may have done away with emperors and kings, but they have hardly dispensed with gross inequalities in wealth, rank, and power.

However, humanity hasn't always lived this way. For about 98 percent of our existence as a species (and for four million years before then), our ancestors lived in small, largely nomadic hunting-and-gathering bands containing about 30 to 50 people apiece. It was in this social context that human nature evolved. It has been only about ten thousand years since people began to settle down into villages, some of which eventually grew into cities. And it has been only in the last two thousand years that the majority of people in the world have not lived in hunting-and-gathering societies. This brief period of time is not nearly sufficient for noticeable evolution to have taken place. Thus, the few remaining foraging societies are the closest analogues we have to the "natural" state of humanity.

To judge from surviving examples of hunting-and-gathering bands and villages, our kind got along quite well for the greater part of prehistory without so much as a paramount chief. In fact, for tens of thousands of years, life went on without kings, queens, prime ministers, presidents, parliaments, congresses, cabinets, governors, and mayors—not to mention the police officers, sheriffs, marshals, generals, lawyers, bailiffs, judges, district attorneys, court clerks, patrol cars, paddy wagons, jails, and penitentiaries that help keep them in power. How in the world did our ancestors ever manage to leave home without them?

Small populations provide part of the answer. With 50 people per band or 150 per village, everybody knew everybody else intimately. People gave with the expectation of taking and took with the expectation of giving. Because chance played a great role in the capture of animals, collection of wild foodstuffs, and success of rudimentary forms of agriculture, the individuals who had the luck of the catch on one day needed a handout on the next. So the best way for them to provide for their inevitable rainy day was to be generous. As expressed by anthropologist Richard Gould, "The greater the amount of risk, the greater the extent of sharing." Reciprocity is a small society's bank.

In reciprocal exchange, people do not specify how much or exactly what they expect to get back or when they expect to get it. That would besmirch the quality of that transaction and make it similar to mere barter or to buying and selling. The distinction lingers on in societies dominated by other forms of exchange, even capitalist ones. For we do carry out a give-and-take among close kin and friends that is informal, uncalculating, and imbued with a spirit of generosity. Teenagers do not pay cash for their meals at home or for the use of the family car, wives do not bill their husbands for cooking a meal, and friends give each other birthday gifts and Christmas presents. But much of this is marred by the expectation that our generosity will be acknowledged with expression of thanks.

Where reciprocity really prevails in daily life, etiquette requires that generosity be taken for granted. As Robert Dentan discovered during his fieldwork among the Semai of Central Malaysia, no one ever says "thank you" for the meat received from another hunter. Having struggled all day to lug the carcass of a pig home through the jungle heat, the hunter allows his prize to be cut up into exactly equal portions, which he then gives away to the entire group. Dentan explains that to express gratitude for the portion received indicates that you are the kind of ungenerous person who calculates how much you give and take: "In this context, saying 'thank you' is very rude, for it suggests, first, that one has calculated the amount of a gift and, second, that one did not expect the donor to be so generous." To call attention to one's generosity is to indicate that others are in debt to you and that you expect them to repay you. It is repugnant to egalitarian peoples even to suggest that they have been treated generously.

Canadian anthropologist Richard Lee tells how, through a revealing incident, he learned about this aspect of reciprocity. To please the !Kung, the "bushmen" of the Kalahari desert, he decided to buy a large ox and have it slaughtered as a present. After days of searching Bantu agricultural villages for the largest and fattest ox in the region, he acquired what appeared to be a perfect specimen. But his friends took him aside and assured him that he had been duped into buying an absolutely worthless animal. "Of course, we will eat it," they said, "but it won't fill us up—we will eat and go home to bed with stomachs rumbling." Yet, when Lee's ox was slaughtered, it turned out to be covered with a thick layer of fat. Later, his friends explained why they had said his gift was valueless, even though they knew better than he what lay under the animal's skin.

"Yes, when a young man kills much meat he comes to think of himself as a chief or a big man, and he thinks of the rest of us as his servants or inferiors. We can't accept this. We refuse one who boasts, for someday his pride will make him kill somebody. So we always speak of his meat as worthless. This way we cool his heart and make him gentle."

Lee watched small groups of men and women returning home every evening with the animals and wild fruits and plants that they had killed or collected. They shared everything equally, even with campmates who had stayed behind and spent the day sleeping or taking care of their tools and weapons.

"Not only do families pool that day's production, but the entire camp— residents and visitors alike—shares equally in the total quantity of food available," Lee observed. "The evening meal of any one family is made up of portions of food from each of the other families resident. There is a constant flow of nuts, berries, roots, and melons from one family fire-place to another, until each person has received an equitable portion. The following morning a different combination of foragers moves out of camp, and when they return late in the day, the distribution of foodstuffs is repeated."

In small, prestate societies, it was in everybody's best interest to maintain each other's freedom of access to the natural habitat. Suppose a !Kung with a lust for power were to get up and tell his campmates, "From now on, all this land and everything on it belongs to me. I'll let you use it but only with my permission and on the condition that I get first choice of anything you capture, collect, or grow." His campmates, thinking that he had certainly gone crazy, would pack up their few belongings, take a long walk, make a new camp, and resume their usual life of egalitarian reciprocity. The man who would be king would be left by himself to exercise a useless sovereignty.

The Headman: Leadership, Not Power

To the extent that political leadership exists at all among band-and-village societies, it is exercised by individuals called headmen. These headmen, however, lack the power to compel others to obey their orders. How can a leader be powerless and still lead?

The political power of genuine rulers depends on their ability to expel or exterminate disobedient individuals and groups. When a headman gives a command, however, he has no certain physical means of punishing those who disobey. So, if he wants to stay in "office," he gives few commands. Among the Eskimo, for instance, a group will follow an outstanding hunter and defer to his opinion with respect to choice of hunting spots. But in all other matters, the leader's opinion carries no more weight than any other man's. Similarly, among the !Kung, each band has its recognized leaders, most of whom are males. These men speak out more than others and are listened to with a bit more deference. But they have no formal authority and can only persuade, never command. When Lee asked the !Kung whether they had headmen—meaning powerful chiefs—they told him, "Of course we have headmen! In fact, we are all headmen. Each one of us is headman over himself."

Headmanship can be a frustrating and irksome job. Among Indian groups such as the Mehinacu of Brazil's Zingu National Park, headmen behave something like zealous scoutmasters on overnight cookouts. The first one up in the morning, the headman tries to rouse his companions by standing in the middle of the village plaza and shouting to them. If something needs to be done, it is the headman who starts doing it, and it is the headman who works harder than anyone else. He sets an example not only for hard work but also for generosity: After a fishing or hunting expedition, he gives away more of his catch than anyone else does. In trading with other groups, he must be careful not to keep the best items for himself.

In the evening, the headman stands in the center of the plaza and exhorts his people to be good. He calls upon them to control their sexual appetites, work hard in their gardens, and take frequent baths in the river. He tells them not to sleep during the day or bear grudges against each other.

Coping with Freeloaders

During the reign of reciprocal exchange and egalitarian headmen, no individual, family, or group smaller than the band or village itself could control access to natural resources. Rivers, lakes, beaches, oceans, plants and animals, the soil and subsoil were all communal property.

Among the !Kung, a core of people born in a particular territory say that they "own" the water holes and hunting rights, but this has no effect on the people who happen to be visiting and living with them at any given time. Since !Kung from neighboring bands are related through marriage, they often visit each other for months at a time and have free use of whatever resources they need without having to ask permission. Though people from distant bands must make a request to use another band's territory, the "owners" seldom refuse them.

The absence of private possession in land and other vital resources means that a form of communism probably existed among prehistoric hunting and collecting bands and small villages. Perhaps I should emphasize that this did not rule out the existence of private property. People in simple band-and-village societies own personal effects such as weapons, clothing, containers, ornaments, and tools. But why should anyone want to steal such objects? People who have a bush camp and move about a lot have no use for extra possessions. And since the group is small enough that everybody knows everybody else, stolen items cannot be used anonymously. If you want something, better to ask for it openly, since by the rules of reciprocity such requests cannot be denied.

I don't want to create the impression that life within egalitarian band-and-village societies unfolded entirely without disputes over possessions. As in every social group, nonconformists and malcontents tried to use the system for their own advantage. Inevitably there were freeloaders, individuals who consistently took more than they gave and lay back in their hammocks while others did the work. Despite the absence of a criminal justice system, such behavior eventually was punished. A widespread belief among band-and-village peoples attributes death and misfortune to the malevolent conspiracy of sorcerers. The task of identifying these evildoers falls to a group's shamans, who remain responsive to public opinion during their divinatory trances. Well-liked individuals who enjoy strong support from their families need not fear the shaman. But quarrelsome, stingy people who do not give as well as take had better watch out.

From Headman to Big Man

Reciprocity was not the only form of exchange practiced by egalitarian band-and-village peoples. Our kind long ago found other ways to give and take. Among them the form of exchange known as redistribution played a crucial role in creating distinctions of rank during the evolution of chiefdoms and states.

Redistribution occurs when people turn over food and other valuables to a prestigious figure such as a headman, to be pooled, divided into separate portions, and given out again. The primordial form of redistribution was probably keyed to seasonal hunts and harvests, when more food than usual became available.

True to their calling, headmen-redistributors not only work harder than their followers but also give more generously and reserve smaller and less desirable portions for themselves than for anyone else. Initially, therefore, redistribution strictly reinforced the political and economic equality associated with reciprocal exchange. The redistributors were compensated purely with admiration and in proportion to their success in giving bigger feasts, in personally contributing more than anybody else, and in asking little or nothing for their effort, all of which initially seemed an innocent extension of the basic principle of reciprocity.

But how little our ancestors understood what they were getting themselves into! For if it is a good thing to have a headman give feasts, why not have several headmen give feasts? Or, better yet, why not let success in organizing and giving feasts be the measure of one's legitimacy as a headman? Soon, where conditions permit, there are several would-be headmen vying with each other to hold the most lavish feasts and redistribute the most food and other valuables. In this fashion there evolved the nemesis that Richard Lee's !Kung informants had warned about: the youth who wants to be a "big man."

A classic anthropological study of big men was carried out by Douglas Oliver among the Siuai, a village people who live on the South Pacific island of Bougainville, in the Solomon Islands. In the Siuai language, big men were known as *mumis*. Every Siuai boy's highest ambition was to become a *mumi*. He began by getting married, working hard, and restricting his own consumption of meats and coconuts. His wife and parents, impressed with the seriousness of his intentions, vowed to help him prepare for his first feast. Soon his circle of supporters widened and he began to construct a clubhouse in which his male followers could lounge about and guests could be entertained and fed. He gave a feast at the consecration of the clubhouse; if this was a success, the circle of people willing to work for him grew larger still, and he began to hear himself spoken of as a mumi. Larger and larger feasts meant that the mumi's demands on his supporters became more irksome. Although they grumbled about how hard they had to work, they remained loyal as long as their mumi continued to maintain and increase his renown as a "great provider."

Finally the time came for the new mumi to challenge the older ones. He did this at a *muminai* feast, where both sides kept a tally of all the pigs, coconut pies, and sago-almond puddings given away by the host mumi and his followers to the guest mumi and his followers. If the guests could not reciprocate with a feast as lavish as that of the challengers, their mumi suffered a great social humiliation, and his fall from mumihood was immediate.

At the end of a successful feast, the greatest of mumis still faced a lifetime of personal toil and dependence on the moods and inclinations of his followers. Mumihood did not confer the power to coerce others into doing one's bidding, nor did it elevate one's standard of living above anyone else's. In fact, because giving things away was the essence of mumihood, great mumis consumed less meat and other delicacies than ordinary men. Among the Kaoka, another Solomon Islands group, there is the saying, "The giver of the feast takes the bones and the stale cakes; the meat and the fat go to the others." At one great feast attended by 1,100 people, the host mumi, whose name was Soni, gave away thirty-two pigs and a large quantity of sago-almond puddings. Soni himself and some of his closest followers went hungry. "We shall eat Soni's renown," they said.

From Big Man to Chief

The slide (or ascent?) toward social stratification gained momentum wherever extra food produced by the inspired diligence of redistributors could be stored while awaiting muminai feasts, potlatches, and other occasions of redistribution. The more concentrated and abundant the harvest and the less perishable the crop, the greater its potential for endowing the big man with power. Though others would possess some stored-up foods of their own, the redistributor's stores would be the largest. In times of scarcity, people would come to him, expecting to be fed; in return, he could call upon those who had special skills to make cloth, pots, canoes, or a fine house for his own use. Eventually, the redistributor no longer needed to work in the fields to gain and surpass bigman status. Management of the harvest surpluses, a portion of which continued to be given to him for use in communal feasts and other communal projects (such as trading expeditions and warfare), was sufficient to validate his status. And, increasingly, people viewed this status as an office, a sacred trust, passed on from one generation to the next according to the rules of hereditary succession. His dominion was no longer a small, autonomous village but a large political community. The big man had become a chief.

Returning to the South Pacific and the Trobriand Islands, one can catch a glimpse of how these pieces of encroaching stratification fell into place. The Trobrianders had hereditary chiefs who held sway over more than a dozen villages containing several thousand people. Only chiefs could wear certain shell ornaments as the insignia of high rank, and it was forbidden for commoners to stand or sit in a position that put a chief's head at a lower elevation. British anthropologist Bronislaw Malinowski tells of seeing all the people present in the village of Bwoytalu drop from their verandas "as if blown down by a hurricane" at the sound of a drawn-out cry warning that an important chief was approaching.

Yams were the Trobrianders' staff of life; the chiefs validated their status by storing and redistributing copious quantities of them acquired through donations from their brothers-in-law at harvest time. Similar "gifts" were received by husbands who were commoners, but chiefs were polygymous and, having as many as a dozen wives, received many more yams than anyone else. Chiefs placed their yam supply on display racks specifically built for this purpose next to their houses. Commoners did the same, but a chief's yam racks towered over all the others.

This same pattern recurs, with minor variations, on several continents. Striking parallels were seen, for example, twelve thousand miles away from the Trobrianders, among chiefdoms that flourished throughout the southeastern region of the United States—specifically among the Cherokee, former inhabitants of Tennessee, as described by the eighteenth-century naturalist William Bartram.

At the center of the principal Cherokee settlements stood a large circular house where a council of chiefs discussed issues involving their villages and where redistributive feasts were held. The council of chiefs had a paramount who was the principal figure in the Cherokee redistributive network. At the harvest time a large crib, identified as the "chief's granary," was erected in each field. "To this," explained Bartram, "each family carries and deposits a certain quantity according to his ability or inclination, or none at all if he so chooses." The chief's granaries functioned as a public treasury in case of crop failure, a source of food for strangers or travelers, and as military store. Although every citizen enjoyed free access to the store, commoners had to acknowledge that it really belonged to the supreme chief, who had "an exclusive right and ability . . . to distribute comfort and blessings to the necessitous."

Supported by voluntary donations, chiefs could now enjoy lifestyles that set them increasingly apart from their followers. They could build bigger and finer houses for themselves, eat and dress more sumptuously, and enjoy the sexual favors and personal services of several wives. Despite these harbingers, people in chiefdoms voluntarily invested unprecedented amounts of labor on behalf of communal projects. They dug moats, threw up defensive earthen embankments, and erected great log palisades around their villages. They heaped up small mountains of rubble and soil to form platforms and mounds on top of which they built temples and big houses for their chief. Working in teams and using nothing but levers and rollers, they moved rocks weighing fifty tons or more and set them in precise lines and perfect circles, forming sacred precincts for communal rituals marking the change of seasons.

If this seems remarkable, remember that donated labor created the megalithic alignments of Stonehenge and Carnac, put up the great statues on Easter Island, shaped the huge stone heads of the Olmec in Vera Cruz, dotted Polynesia with ritual precincts set on great stone platforms, and filled the Ohio, Tennessee, and Mississippi valleys with hundreds of large mounds. Not until it was too late did people realize that their beautiful chiefs were about to keep the meat and fat for themselves while giving nothing but bones and stale cakes to their followers.

In the End

As we know, chiefdoms would eventually evolve into states, states into empires. From peaceful origins, humans created and mounted a wild beast that ate continents. Now that beast has taken us to the brink of global annihilation.

Will nature's experiment with mind and culture end in nuclear war? No one knows the answer. But I believe it is essential that we understand our past before we can create the best possible future. Once we are clear about the roots of human nature, for example, we can refute, once and for all, the notion that it is a biological imperative for our kind to form hierarchical groups. An observer viewing human life shortly after cultural takeoff would easily have concluded that our species was destined to be irredeemably egalitarian except for distinctions of sex and age. That someday the world would be divided into aristocrats and commoners, masters and slaves, billionaires and homeless beggars would have seemed wholly contrary to human nature as evidenced in the affairs of every human society then on Earth.

Of course, we can no more reverse the course of thousands of years of cultural evolution than our egalitarian ancestors could have designed and built the space shuttle. Yet, in striving for the preservation of mind and culture on Earth, it is vital that we recognize the significance of cultural takeoff and the great difference between biological and cultural evolution. We must rid ourselves of the notion that we are an innately aggressive species for whom war is inevitable. We must reject as unscientific claims that there are superior and inferior races and that the hierarchical divisions within and between societies are the consequences of natural selection rather than of a long process of cultural evolution. We must struggle to gain control over cultural selection through objective studies of the human condition and the recurrent process of history. Not only a more just society, but our very survival as a species may depend on it.

Review Questions

1. What is the difference among headmen, big men, and chiefs according to Harris?

2. What does Harris see as the connection between forms of leadership and modes of economic exchange? How does this connection work?

3. Harris makes a distinction between biological evolution and cultural evolution. What is the distinction and how does he apply it to types of leadership?

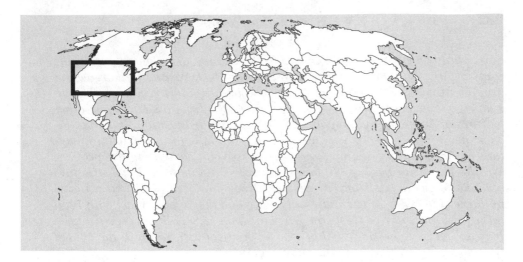

28

The Founding Indian Fathers

Jack Weatherford

As we saw in the last article, the members of small societies could make political decisions without the presence of complex, hierarchical political organization. But as societies have grown both in population and territory, the complexity of political institutions has grown with them. Chieftainships gave way to kingdoms and then states. The regulation of trade; the distribution of goods, services, and wealth; and relations between states including warfare demanded the formation of more complex political systems. Political hierarchies evolved, usually led by hereditary, often divine, rulers supported by ruling elites and a large number of bureaucrats. Although rulers could often depend on their birthright and supernatural power to claim political legitimacy, coercion was also an important tool for the maintenance of power. Large-scale societies, it seemed, could not institutionalize the democratic processes that characterized small societies. Yet the colonists who founded the United States did manage to do so.

Many Americans believe that U.S. democracy stems directly from the ideas of Athenian philosophers. In this article, Jack Weatherford argues for another, unrecognized, political model also used by our founding fathers to shape governmental structure, the League of the Iroquois and some other features of American Indian political process and organization. Indian influence, he argues, found its way into colonial thinking through such individuals as Benjamin Franklin, who had extensive contact with native peoples. Weatherford describes how Indian, especially Iroquoian, political structure served as a model that helped to produce a democratic federal structure incorporating states with substantial local power, and that later, contact with Indians as colonists moved west continued to shape U.S. political organization. It is no accident, he claims, that a basic political institution in the United States is called by the Algonquin name, caucus.

Every day of the school year, troops of children march across the lawn of the United States Capitol perched atop the District of Columbia's highest elevation. The building dominates the Washington skyline, a model of classical symmetry and precision. Two giant wings of precisely equal proportion reach out from a Roman dome that surveys the city of Washington. If reduced to a ruin, the forest of Greek columns decorating the building would appear to be as much at home in Rome or Naples as in Athens or Corinth. The building revels in its Old World heritage.

Indian schoolchildren walking through the halls of Congress would rarely see a hint that the building sits in America overlooking the Potomac River and not along the shores of the Mediterranean Sea. The building copies European, primarily classical, styles, and its halls proudly display pictures, friezes, and busts of famous political thinkers from Hammurabi and Solomon to Rousseau and Voltaire. In the hallways stand statues of American politicians posing in Greek tunics and Roman togas as though they were Roman senators or Athenian orators. Greek busts of the vice-presidents of the United States line the halls of the Senate, lending them the aura of a classical cemetery.

The children pass under doorways that bear weighty engravings and quotations from European documents such as the Magna Carta interspersed with quotes from the United States Declaration of Independence or Constitution. The building and its appointments proudly proclaim their part in the great march of European progress and civilization. They portray the blessed dove of democracy hatching in Athens and then taking wing for a torturous flight of two millennia, pausing only momentarily over Republican Rome, the field of Runnymede, and the desk of Voltaire before finally alighting to rest permanently and securely in the virgin land of America.

A child standing squarely in the middle of the Capitol beneath the great dome sees a painted band circling the upper wall representing the history of America. In that work, the Indians appear as just one more dangerous obstacle, like the wild animals, the Appalachian Mountains, the Mississippi River, and the western deserts, that blocked the progress of European civilization and technology in the white man's march across America. The most peaceful picture with an Indian theme in the rotunda shows the baptism of Pocahontas, daughter of the Indian leader Powhatan. Surrounded by Europeans and dressed in English clothes, she symbolically renounces the savage life of the Indians for the civilization of the British.

The lesson in this august setting presents itself forcefully on every visitor. The United States government derives from European precedents, and the Americans gave civilization to the Indians. Nothing in the Capitol hints that contemporary Americans owe the slightest debt to the Indians for teaching us about democratic institutions.

Despite these civic myths surrounding the creation of American government, America's settlers from Europe knew little of democracy. The English came from a nation ruled by monarchs who claimed that God conferred their right to rule and even allowed them to wage wars of extinction against the Irish. Colonists also fled to America from France, which was wandering aimlessly through history under the extravagances of a succession of kings named Louis, most of whom pursued debauched and extravagant reigns that oppressed, exploited, and at times even starved their subjects.

Despite the ideal government sketched by Plato in *The Republic*, and the different constitutions analyzed by Aristotle in his *Politics*, the Old World offered America few democratic models for government. Democratic government had no fortress in the Old World. Despite the democratic rhetoric that came into fashion in eighteenth-century Europe, no such systems existed there at that time. The monarchy and the aristocracy of England were engaged in a protracted struggle that would eventually lead to the supremacy of Parliament (and a closely limited electoral franchise until the reforms of the nineteenth century). France had not yet begun its experiments with participatory democracy. The Founding Fathers of the United States judiciously assembled bits and pieces of many different systems to invent a completely new one. In fashioning the new system, they even borrowed some distinctive elements from the American Indians.

The Founding Fathers faced a major problem when it came time to invent the United States. They represented, under the Articles of Confederation, thirteen separate and sovereign states. How could one country be made from all thirteen without each one yielding its own power?

Reportedly, the first person to propose a union of all the colonies and to propose a federal model for it was the Iroquois chief Canassatego, speaking at an Indian-British assembly in Pennsylvania in July 1744. He complained that the Indians found it difficult to deal with so many different colonial administrations, each with its own policy. It would make life easier for everyone involved if the colonists could have a union which allowed them to speak with one voice. He not only proposed that the colonies unify themselves, but told them how they might do it. He suggested that they do as his people had done and form a union like the League of the Iroquois.

Hiawatha and Deganwidah founded the League of the Iroquois sometime between A.D. 1000 and 1450 under a constitution they called the *Kaianerekowa* or Great Law of Peace. When the Europeans arrived in America, the league constituted the most extensive and important political unit north of the Aztec civilization. From earliest contact the Iroquois intrigued the Europeans, and they were the subject of many amazed reports. Benjamin Franklin, however, seems to have been the first to take their system as a potentially important model by which the settlers might be able to fashion a new government.

Benjamin Franklin first became acquainted with the operation of Indian political organization in his capacity as official printer for the colony of Pennsylvania. His job included publication of the records and speeches of the various Indian assemblies and treaty negotiations, but following his instinctive curiosity, he broadened this into a study of Indian culture and institutions. Because of his expertise and interest in Indian matters, the colonial government of Pennsylvania offered him his first diplomatic assignment as their Indian commissioner. He held this post during the 1750s and became intimately familiar with the intricacies of Indian political culture and in particular with the League of the Iroquois. After this taste of Indian diplomacy, Franklin became a lifelong champion of the Indian political structure and advocated its use by the Americans. During this time he also refined his political techniques of persuasion, compromise, and slow consensus building that proved so important to his later negotiations as the ambassador to France and as a delegate to the Constitutional Convention.

Echoing the original proposal of Canassatego, Franklin advocated that the new American government incorporate many of the same features as the government of the Iroquois. Speaking to the Albany Congress in 1754, Franklin called on the delegates of the various English colonies to unite and emulate the Iroquois League, a call that was not heeded until the Constitution was written three decades later. Even though the Founding Fathers finally adopted some of the essential features of the Iroquois League, they never followed it in quite the detail advocated by Franklin.

The Iroquois League united five principal Indian nations—the Mohawk, Onondaga, Seneca, Oneida, and Cayuga. Each of these nations had a council composed of delegates called sachems who were elected by the tribes of that nation. The Seneca Nation elected eight sachems to its council, the Mohawk and Oneida nations each had councils of nine sachems, the Cayuga Nation had a council of ten, and the Onondaga Nation had a council of fourteen. Each of these nations governed its own territory, and its own council met to decide the issues of public policy for each one. But these councils exercised jurisdiction over the internal concerns of that one nation only; in this regard they exercised powers somewhat like the individual governments of the colonies.

In addition to the individual councils of each separate nation, the sachems formed a grand Council of the League in which all fifty sachems of the six nations sat together to discuss issues of common concern. The sachems represented their individual nations, but at the same time they represented the whole League of the Iroquois, thereby making the decisions of the council the law for all five nations. In this council each sachem had equal authority and privileges, with his power dependent on his oratorical power to persuade. The council met in the autumn of at least one year in five in a longhouse in the Onondaga Nation; if needed they could be called into session at other times as well. Their power extended to all matters of common concern among the member nations. In the words of Lewis Henry Morgan, America's first modern anthropologist, the council "declared war and made peace, sent and received embassies, entered into treaties of alliance, regulated the affairs of subjugated nations, received new members into the League, extended its protection over feeble tribes, in a word, took all needful measures to promote their prosperity, and enlarge their dominion."[1]

Through this government the nations of the Iroquois controlled territory from New England to the Mississippi River, and they built a league that endured for centuries. Unlike European governments, the league blended the sovereignty of several nations into one government. This model of several sovereign units united into one government presented precisely the solution to the problem confronting the writers of the United States Constitution. Today we call this a "federal" system in which each state retains power over internal affairs and the national government regulates affairs common to all. Henry Steele Commager later wrote of this crucial time that even "if Americans did not actually invent federalism, they were able to take out an historical patent on it."[2] The Indians invented it even though the United States patented it.

Another student of the Iroquois political organization was Charles Thomson, the perpetual secretary of the Continental Congress. He spent so much energy studying the Indians and their way of life that the Delaware Nation adopted him as a full member. Following Thomas Jefferson's request, Thomson wrote at length on Indian social and political institutions for inclusion in an appendix to Jefferson's *Notes on the State of Virginia*. According to his description of Indian political tradition, each Indian town built a council house for making local decisions and for electing delegates to the tribal council. The tribal council in turn elected delegates to the national council. Even though Thomson wrote this several years before the Constitutional Convention, this description reads like a blueprint for the United States Constitution, especially when we remember that the Constitution allowed the state legislatures (rather than the general populace) to elect senators. Thomson stresses that the sachems or political leaders do not acquire their positions by heredity but by election, and he adds that because outsiders can be naturalized into the Indian nation, even they can be elected to such offices.

The Americans followed the model of the Iroquois League not only in broad outline but also in many of the specific provisions of their *Kaianerekowa*. According to the *Kaianerekowa*, the sachems were not chiefs, a position frequently associated with leadership in war. As a lawmaker, the sachem could never go to war in his official capacity as a sachem. "If disposed to take the warpath, he laid aside his civil office, for the time being, and became a common warrior."[3] This

[1]Lewis Henry Morgan, *League of the Iroquois* (Rochester: Sage, 1851), pp. 66–67.

[2]Henry Steele Commager. *The Empire of Reason: How Europe Imagined and America Realized the Enlightenment* (Garden City, NY: Anchor), p. 207.

[3]Morgan, p. 72.

followed the tradition in many Indian tribes that relied upon separate leaders for peace and for war. The colonists followed this model too in eventually separating civilian authorities from military ones. Members of Congress, judges, and other officials could not also act as military leaders without giving up their elected office; similarly, military leaders could not be elected to political office without first resigning their military position. This contrasted with British traditions; church and military leaders frequently served as members of the House of Lords and frequently played major political roles in the House of Commons as well. Similarly, this inability to separate the civil government and the military has doomed many of the imitators of American democracy, particularly in Africa and Latin America.

If the conduct of any sachem appeared improper to the populace or if he lost the confidence of his electorate, the women of his clan impeached him and expelled him by official action, whereupon the women then choose a new sachem. This concept of impeachment ran counter to European tradition, in which the monarch ruled until death, even if he became insane or incapacitated, as in the case of George III. The Americans followed the Iroquois precedent of always providing for ways to remove leaders when necessary, but the Founding Fathers saw no reason to follow the example of the Iroquois in granting women the right to vote or any other major role in the political structure.

One of the most important characteristics of the Iroquois League permitted it to expand as needed; the council could vote to admit new members. This proved to be an important feature of the system after the Tuscarora Indians of North Carolina faced attack in 1712 by the army of Colonel John Barnwell and again in 1713 by the army of Colonel James Moore. Having thoroughly defeated the Tuscaroras, the Carolina colonists demanded reparations from the Indians to pay the colonists' expenses incurred in the war. Because the Indians had no money to pay, the colonists seized four hundred of them and sold them into slavery at the rate of ten pounds sterling apiece. The surviving Tuscaroras fled North Carolina to seek refuge among the Iroquois. In 1714 the Tuscaroras applied for formal membership in the league, and the Iroquois admitted them in 1722 as the Sixth Nation. Similarly the league later incorporated other decimated groups such as the Erie, but the league did not allow for an entity such as a colony, which had played such an important part in European governments since the times of the ancient Greeks.

In a radical break with Old World tradition, the emerging government of the United States emulated this Iroquois tradition of admitting new states as members rather than keeping them as colonies. The west became a series of territories and then states, but the United States treated each new territory as a future partner rather than as a colony. The new government codified this Indian practice into American law through the Congressional Resolution of 1780, the Land Ordinances of 1784 and 1785, and the Northwest Ordinance, together with similar provisions written directly into the Constitution. No direct proof links these laws with the Iroquois, but it seems likely to be more than mere coincidence that both the Iroquois and the United States governments enacted such similar procedures.

Although the Iroquois recognized no supreme leader in their system analogous to the president of the United States, the framers of the Constitution deliberately or inadvertently imitated the Great Council in establishing the electoral college system to select a president. Each state legislature selected a group of electors equal in number to that state's combined total of senators and representatives. Like the sachems, each elector then had one vote in the electoral college.

In the two centuries since the Constitution went into effect, some aspects of the system have changed. The voters rather than the state legislatures now elect both the electoral college and the senators through popular vote, but the system preserves the general features of the League of the Iroquois.

Upon election to the council, the new sachem "lost" his name and thenceforth other sachems called him by the title of his office. In much the same way, proceedings of the United States Senate do not permit the use of names such as "Senator Kennedy" or "Rudy Boschwitz." Instead the senators must be addressed by their office title as "the Senior Senator from Massachusetts" or "the Junior Senator from Minnesota." Other titles such as "Majority Leader," "Mr. Chairman," or "Mr. President" may be used, but all personal names remain strictly taboo.

Another imitation of the Iroquois came in the simple practice of allowing only one person to speak at a time in political meetings. This contrasts with the British tradition of noisy interruptions of one another as the members of Parliament shout out agreement or disagreement with the speaker. Europeans were accustomed to shouting down any speaker who displeased them; in some cases they might even stone him or inflict worse damage.

The Iroquois permitted no interruptions or shouting. They even imposed a short period of silence at the end of each oration in case the speaker had forgotten some point or wished to elaborate or change something he had said. Even though the American Congress and legislatures did not adopt the practice of silence at the end, they did allow speakers "to revise and extend" the written record after speaking.

The purpose of debate in Indian councils was to persuade and educate, not to confront. Unlike European parliaments, where opposing factions battle out an issue in the public arena, the council of the Indians sought to reach an agreement through compromise. This important difference in nuance led Bruce Burton to observe in his study of American law that "American democracy owes its distinctive character of debate and compromise to the principles and structures of American Indian civil government."[4] Still today, this difference separates the operation of the United States Congress and the state legislatures from their European counterparts. American legislative bodies are composed primarily of individuals forming shifting factions from one issue to another, whereas the legislative bodies of Europe operate through opposing political parties that control the votes of individual representatives.

---

[4]Bruce A. Burton, "Iroquois Confederate Law and the Origins of the U.S. Constitution," *Northeast Indian Quarterly*, Fall 1986, p. 4.

In keeping with Iroquois tradition, Franklin proposed that since the sachems did not own land or receive any financial compensation for their work, the officials of the United States should not be paid. They should perform their work as a sacred trust freely given to the communal welfare. Even though the Founding Fathers did not incorporate this, they did work to prevent property qualifications for holding office and for exercising the right to vote. They also tended to limit salaries paid to officeholders to a minimum to cover basic expenses of life rather than making public office a sinecure or a route to wealth. . . .

From Hollywood films and adventure novels Americans often conclude that strong chiefs usually commanded the Indian tribes. More often, however, as in the case of the Iroquois, a council ruled, and any person called the "head" of the tribe usually occupied a largely honorary position of respect rather than power. Chiefs mostly played ceremonial and religious roles rather than political or economic ones. Unlike the words "caucus" and "powwow," which are Indian-derived and indicative of Indian political traditions, the word "chief" is an English word of French origin that British officials tried to force onto Indian tribes in order that they might have someone with whom to trade and sign treaties.

In Massachusetts the British tried to make one leader into *King* Philip. The British imputed monarchy to the Indian system when no such institution existed. Thus while the English settlers learned from the Indians how to speak and act in group councils, they simultaneously pushed the Indians toward a monarchical and thus less democratic system. . . .

In almost every North American tribe, clan, or nation for which we have detailed political information, the supreme authority rested in a group rather than in an individual. It took many generations of close interaction between colonists and Indians before the principles of group decision-making replaced the European traditions of relying on a single supreme authority. The importance of these Indian councils and groups shows clearly in the English lack of words to explain such a process.

One of the most important political institutions borrowed from the Indians was the caucus. Even though the word appears to be proper Latin and some law students with a semester of Latin occasionally decline the plural as *cauci*, the word comes from the Algonquian languages. The caucus permits informal discussion of an issue without necessitating a yea or nay vote on any particular question. This agreed with the traditional Indian way of talking through an issue or of making a powwow; it made political decisions less divisive and combative. The caucus became a mainstay of American democracy both in the Congress and in political and community groups all over the country. The caucus evolved into such an important aspect of American politics that the political parties adopted it to nominate their presidential candidates. In time this evolved into the political convention, which still functions as an important part of contemporary American politics but is largely absent from European politics. . . .

Even after the founding of the United States, the Indians continued to play a significant role in the evolution of democracy because of their sustained interactions with Americans on the frontier. The frontiersmen constantly reinvented democracy and channeled it into the eastern establishment of the United States.

Time and again the people of the frontier rebelled against the entrenched and conservative values of an ever more staid coastal elite. As the frontier gradually moved westward, the settlements on the edge sent such rebels as Henry Clay, Andrew Jackson, David Crockett, and Abraham Lincoln back to reinvest the spirit of democracy into the political institutions of the east. Some of these men, such as Sam Houston, lived for long periods with Indians. Houston spent so much time with the Cherokee that they adopted him into their nation about 1829. The influence of the Cherokees stayed with him throughout his tenure as president of Texas from 1836 to 1838 and again from 1841 to 1844. Throughout his life he maintained close working relations with a variety of Indian nations and a strong commitment to liberty.

Even Alexis de Tocqueville, who denigrated the achievements of the Indians, noticed that the settlers on the frontier "mix the ideas and customs of savage life with the civilization of their fathers." In general he found this reprehensible, for it made their "passions more intense" and "their religious morality less authoritative,"[5] but these traits certainly may be interpreted by others as among the virtues of a democratic people.

Most democratic and egalitarian reforms of the past two hundred years in America originated on the frontier and not in the settled cities of the east. The frontier states dropped property and religious requirements for voters. They extended the franchise to women, and in 1916 Montana elected Jeannette Rankin as the first woman in Congress four years before the Nineteenth Amendment to the Constitution gave women the right to vote. The western states started the public election of senators in place of selection by the legislature. They also pioneered the use of primary elections and electoral recalls of unpopular officers. Even today they have more elective offices, such as judges; such offices in the east are usually filled by appointment by the governor or the legislature. This strong bias toward the electoral process and equal votes for all has been reinforced repeatedly by the people who have had the closest and the longest connections with the Indians on the frontier. . . .

Washington, D.C., has never recognized the role of the Indians in the writing of the United States Constitution or in the creation of political institutions that seem so uniquely American. But an inadvertent memorial does exist. An older woman from Israel pointed this out to me one spring day as I cut across the lawn of the United States Capitol, where I then worked for Senator John Glenn. She stopped me, and in a husky voice asked me who was the Indian woman atop the Capitol dome. Suddenly looking at it through her eyes, I too saw the figure as an Indian even though I knew that it was not.

When the United States government embarked on an expansion of the Capitol in the middle of the nineteenth century, the architects proposed to cap

[5]Alexis de Tocqueville, *Democracy in America 2*, vols, in Phillips Bradley (ed.) (New York: Random House, 1945), p. 334.

the dome with a symbol of freedom. They chose for this a nineteen-foot bronze statue of a Roman woman who would stand on the pinnacle of the Capitol. Sculptor Thomas Crawford crowned the woman with a Phrygian cap, which in Roman history had been the sign of the freed slave. At that time Jefferson Davis, the future president of the Confederate States of America, still served as the secretary of war for the United States, and he objected strongly to what he interpreted as an antisouthern and antislavery symbol. He compelled Crawford to cap her with something less antagonistic to southern politicians. Crawford designed a helmet covered with a crown of feathers, but in putting this headdress on the figure, her whole appearance changed. Now instead of looking like a classical Greek or Roman, she looked like an Indian.

She still stands today on the pseudoclassical Capitol overlooking the city of Washington. The Washington Monument rises to the same height, but no other building has been allowed to rise higher than she. Even though no one intended her to be an Indian, she now reigns as the nearest thing to a monument that Washington ever built to honor the Indians who contributed to the building of a federal union based on democracy.

Review Questions

1. Weatherford argues that American Indian political structure served as a model for the U.S Constitution. What evidence does he cite to support his assertion?

2. As Weatherford described, what were the main structural features of the League of the Iroquois?

3. What organizational features characteristic of the Iriquoi are reflected in the U.S. Constitution devised by the founding fathers?

4. What life experiences enabled some colonial leaders as opposed to others to bring information about Indian political structure to those who framed the U.S. Constitution?

5. How did the western movement of American settlers affect the development of democracy in the United States? Why?

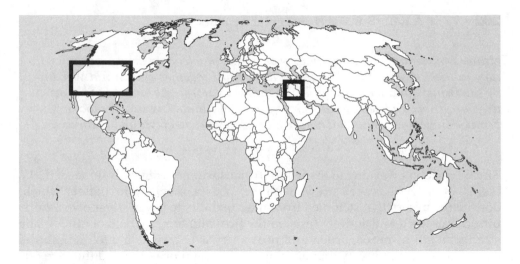

29

The Kindness
of Strangers: The U.S.
and Iraq

Robin Fox

We typically view the era of Western colonialism and more recently some aspects of U.S. foreign policy as systems of exploitation. Colonials, we claim, were there to extract raw materials and tap cheap labor; today the U.S. also wants raw materials, especially oil, as it enters the affairs of other countries. Although there is ample evidence to support this view, we should recognize another motive for Western intervention in other countries: the gift of civilization and for Americans, our view of freedom and democracy. In this selection, Robin Fox stresses this last point. He notes that like Protestant missionaries, we believe that the "love of freedom" and "democracy" are part of human nature. All we need to do is give it to people, and they will naturally see the light. When people don't accept the gift, we treat them as if we are stern parents "helping" them to do what is best for them. Our invasion

Reprinted with kind permission from Springer Science and Business Media: *Society,* "The Kindness of Strangers." September/October 2007, Robin Fox.

of Iraq was certainly about oil, but it was just as much about bringing democracy to the "Iraqi people." But Iraq was cobbled together after World War I by the British, and its people direct their loyalty not to the state but to family, clan, tribe, and sect. Rather than a part of human nature, democracy, Fox concludes, defies human nature and takes work to create and maintain.

Since Laocoön's warning to his fellow Trojans went so tragically unheeded, the course of history has been strewn with the corpses of ungrateful nations which, despite the misery that stemmed from their inability to govern their own affairs, bitterly resented and actively resisted the firm and forceful help of others. The stranger's gift of peace, order, and prosperity is less welcome to us than the death, chaos, and poverty that are our own doing. For in the end they are our own, and that is what matters to us. Like truculent adolescents, we do not want to be told how to do things or have them done for us; we want to make our own, even fatal, mistakes. We will take what we can use from what is offered, but we want, at last, to do it ourselves: to manage our own lives, however badly. The main thing about the stranger, after all, is that he is strange. He is not like us; he will never understand us. Our greatest fear, perhaps because the possibility is often so seductive, is that we will become like him and lose our selves. The stranger's gift never comes without strings, and we do not want to be tied.

We of the post-Enlightenment Anglophone West are among the most earnest of the givers. We are not, like our medieval Catholic ancestors, really proponents of the Crusade and the holy war against the heathen. We are at heart Protestant missionaries. We want to bring the good news and the benefits of civilization to the benighted of the earth. And if they don't want it, then like Protestant parents, and entirely for their own good of course, we must sternly make them accept it. Certainly, we hoped to make profits and attain political power in the process, but these were small prices the benighted had to pay for the incomparable gifts we had to offer. Critics of colonialism miss the point if all they see is the profits and the power. Our civilizing mission was, and still is, as dear to us as the jihad is to Muslims. Even when it is not Protestantism per se that we are offering, it is the children of the Protestant Ethic that we know as democracy, liberty, equality, and the free market. Our learned men tell us we are the foreordained bearers of a truth so fundamental that with its triumph history will come to an end, there being nothing left for mankind to achieve. If this is so, how can the benighted so stubbornly, and even violently, refuse our gift of a free leg up onto the stage of world history?

There is no question that we went into Iraq to defend our oil interests: that, at least, was the rational part. But the holy warriors of the White House saw a far greater opportunity. They could plant the banner of liberal democracy in the heartland of Arab totalitarianism, and thus change the world for the better. To do this was to collaborate with the inevitable progress of mankind—a sure winner of a policy. We would simply give the inevitable progress a friendly shove in the right direction. The "Iraqi People" (much invoked) would greet us as liberators and gratefully accept our gift of free elections. How could they possibly prefer the savagery of Saddam and the hegemony of the brutes of Baath? Once rid of these monsters, the "Iraqi People"—like people everywhere, as "lovers of freedom"— would set up a representative democracy modeled on our own. Ballot boxes and purple finger paint would be provided, political parties would be free to form, the press would be unrestricted. This model democracy would stand as a rebuke and an example to the monstrous regimes in the Middle East, which would gradually succumb to the same happy fate. What is more, it would be an Arab democracy, thus saving the Arabs from the embarrassment of Israel being the only democratic state in the region. Since democracies are inherently peaceful, the more of them in the region the better, and the better for our "national security." And above all, as the guarantors of this liberal democratic paradise, we would have a continuing benign influence in the area, which would, incidentally, protect our oil interests.

For the missionaries this was a chance too good to be missed. Saddam's regime was ripe for the plucking. There was no way its army could stand up to the superior Western forces, and once the army was disbanded, the criminals tried, and "de-Baathification" completed, the grateful freed "People of Iraq" would take it from there. They would need help and firm guidance from the missionaries, of course. They would make mistakes, and there would be all the baggage of dictatorship to unpack. But it had been done in Japan and Germany with startling success (both totally misleading examples, as it happens), why not in Iraq? To suggest otherwise, said George W. Bush, was to suggest that the "Iraqi People" were inherently incapable of "freedom and democracy." That was to be condescending and colonialist. Everyone everywhere wanted these benefits, and only wicked regimes prevented them from realizing these universal human goals, toward which, we must not forget, mankind was inevitably evolving anyway.

I am not caricaturing this position. Those who would see the ideology as a cynical cover for the arms industry, Halliburton, and Big Oil are missing what is truly at issue here, and what is much more frightening. The colonial powers always look out for their economic and strategic interests; it would be foolish of them not to. But they have also always believed the "civilizing mission" to be just as important. This was justified partly by religion—bringing Christianity to the heathen—but was also seen as an end in itself: the production of an industrial, peaceful, democratic (sometimes socialist) world.

As societies evolved from military to industrial institutions, so would peace and democracy spread around the globe. Free-trade advocates repeat it today: the more we are dependent on each other through trade, the less likely will we be to fight each other. Trade requires the rule of law, the rule of law promotes democracy, and democracies don't fight each other—we know the logic. This is the fundamental belief of the missionaries. We have a precious gift that we can give the nations of the world, and whether they want it or not, we are going to give it to them. If they think they don't want it, then they must be re-educated, with force if necessary, to realize that they do. History is going to end in universal liberal democracy, so they might as well learn to co-operate with the inevitable.

The problem for liberal and radical critics of Bushism in the West is that they really believe this too. It is no longer fashionable to think that some form of communism or socialism will be the inevitable end product, but some kind of democratic open society is seen as the only alternative for the decolonized peoples of the world. It is hard to find any fervent postcolonialist who will agree that, having thrown off the imperial yoke, the ex-colonial peoples should be free to choose dictatorship, theocracy, tribalism, nepotism, clitoridectomy, or the rule of warlords. Respect for "indigenous cultures" goes only so far. The left-liberals assume as fervently as the Bushites that people everywhere aspire to a state of liberal democratic polity where human rights and the rights of women will be assured and tolerance and religious freedom will be institutionalized. It is to their constant embarrassment that this does not happen, and fifty years later the excuse that the failure lies in the pernicious aftereffects of colonialism is wearing thin; they do not really believe it themselves. (They have substituted neocolonialism, neoliberalism, globalization, transnational corporations.) But the alternative is hard to bear for the progressive mentality that assumes we can indeed write our own script and exclude all those factors of "human nature" that seem so stubbornly to resist our enlightened blandishments.

Against this naive optimism of the missionaries of whatever stripe, we can set an opposing view that is historical and what we might call naturalistic. It sees that the institutions we so prize are not the *product of* a freedom-loving human nature but the result of many centuries of effort to *overcome* human nature. However desirable they may be, they are not natural to us. We maintain them with constant vigilance and the support of hard-won economic, political, legal, and social structures. These have taken literally thousands of years to put in place. In England universal suffrage had to wait until 1928, when women under thirty were finally included. In the United States it was only after the Voting Rights Act of 1965 that we can be said to have achieved true democracy. Far from being a fact of human nature, the voluntary ceding of power after elections, the basic feature of liberal democracy, actually flies in the face of nature. It is self-evidently absurd. Our political opponents are always disreputable and their accession to power will be the ruin of the country. Listen to the rhetoric of campaigns: allowing the opponents to take over amounts to almost criminal malfeasance. Yet that is what we do after a mere counting of heads—cede control to the villains and incompetents.

The cynic will say that we allow this to happen only because we know there is no real difference between political parties in these systems, and so we join in a conspiracy of the willing to take our turns. Even so, this willingness that we take for granted is an amazing, unusual, and fragile thing. Our Western democracies still struggle with nepotism and corruption whose energetic persistence should tell us something. How could we believe then that we could walk into a country like Iraq and do in a few months, or even a few years, or even several decades, what millennia had failed to evolve spontaneously? Because the "Iraqi People," like everyone else, "loved freedom"?

For a start, there are no "Iraqi People." The phrase is pure rhetoric. Iraq as a "nation" (like the "nation" of Kuwait) was devised by the compasses and protractors of Gertrude Bell when the British and French divided up the Middle East after World War I. We know well enough the ethnic-religious division into Kurd, Sunni, and Shiite. But what is not understood is that Iraq, like the other countries of the region, still stands at a level of social evolution where the family, clan, tribe, and sect command major allegiance, and the idea of the individual autonomous voter, necessary and commonplace in our own systems, is totally foreign, and would not make sense to the "average Ahmed."

I received a call in 2003 from a *New York Times* reporter, John Tierney, who was baffled by what he discovered in his Baghdad hotel. Each week there was a lavish wedding in the dining room and ball-room. It looked very Western until he discovered that the bride and groom were inevitably cousins, and, more than that, they were most often paternal parallel first cousins, as the jargon has it; they were the children of two brothers, and if they were not that close, then the bride was usually from the same paternal clan as the groom. Occasionally, a woman from the mother's paternal clan was married, as in the case of Saddam Hussein. When questioned about this, the young people told the reporter, "Of course we marry a cousin. What would you have us do, marry a stranger? We cannot trust strangers." Such a system of close-cousin marriage, the commonest form of preferred marriage in Arab society, literally keeps the marriage in the family. These groups are inward-looking and suspicious of strangers. It is the "Mafia solution" to life: never go against the family. Trust is only possible, ultimately, between close relatives, and preferably those of the paternal clan. The idea of voluntarily doing anything for strangers has to be worked at. It is another of those things we in Western democracies do every day without thought. It is "human nature" for us. We give large sums of our money to complete strangers to distribute to other strangers for purposes often unknown to us. This is taxation. It is everywhere hated, but absolutely necessary to run a complex society. We trust strangers to do things absolutely essential to our lives and welfare. We take it for granted they will do them: they are doing their jobs. But this is as foreign to much of the world as our odd acceptance of the relinquishment of power. And to that same world it borders on the immoral as well as the insane. In those places where the state cannot be trusted with the welfare of individuals, they turn to the older and wiser certainty of kinship.

When there was no electricity in Baghdad, the reason was that as soon as copper cable was laid, the Iraqis came out in the night and stole it. Copper brought a good price. When the troops expostulated with those caught and tried to make them see that their theft was against the "Iraqi People," the indignant thieves demanded to know who these "Iraqi People" were who stood between them and the feeding of their starving families. They were responsible not for some mythical Iraqi People but for their kin: their cousins who were their spouses. The few ambulances in Baghdad cannot function properly to get the injured from bombings to the hospitals. The armed clansmen of the injured commandeer the ambulances and turn out the unrelated wounded. Firefights often break out between armed groups competing for the ambulances. Remember the graphic scene in *Lawrence of Arabia* when the tribal chief Auda, played by Anthony Quinn, is told he should join in the attack on the Turks in Aqaba for the sake of "the

Arabs." "What tribe is that?" he asks. He recites the tribes he knows, but demands to know what tribe is "the Arabs" that he should sacrifice for them. "The English" he understands as a tribe he can ally with against his enemies, including the Turks if it suits him. Thus some of the sheikhs in Anbar ally with the Americans against Al Qaeda and its allies if it suits them. But their and Auda's sole concern is with their tribal advantage. This was Auda's highest moral imperative. And Auda loved freedom above all other things.

If this tribal "mentality" is closer to the default system of human nature than is our cherished individualistic democracy, then we ignore its appeal at our peril. The marriage of close cousins may appear to us backward, unhygienic, or immoral, but it is the pattern that has dominated the world until fairly recently. If we could get into God's memory, we would find that the majority of marriages throughout history have been with close cousins. In the West we had to move from tribalism, through empire, feudalism, mercantile capitalism, and the Industrial Revolution to reach our present state of fragile democracy (shrugging off communism and fascism along the way). We were helped in the shedding of dominant kinship groups by the relative individualism of the Angles and Saxons with their emphasis on the independent nuclear family, and then by Christian monogamy and the banning of cousin marriages by the Church. And we had to do it by our own efforts, to pull ourselves up by the social bootstraps, to make it stick. We have seen in Germany, in Italy, and in Spain how fragile this really is. Russia never did make it. France is always problematic. Latin America and the Balkans continue to be a mess. But in making this move we had to change the entire communalistic, ritualistic, kinship-dominated society that is natural to us. We had to transform "nepotism" and "corruption" from tribal virtues into criminal offenses, and we have to keep at it all the time. I live in New Jersey and I stare into the pit.

The future is hypothetical. The old formula "no bourgeoisie, no democracy" still holds. What independent professional class there was in Iraq, with its need for the rule of law to guarantee contracts, was destroyed by Saddam. It is something we cannot re-create with any amount of aid or surges, nor can we force it upon the "Iraqi People." The price of failure, says Bush, is too high. But failure was written all over this enterprise from the start. The goals set, beyond the toppling of Saddam, were impossible, and the real mystery is why our leaders ever thought they could be achieved. The administration may, by increased force and bribery (the "Iraqi People" understand both very well), patch up some kind of "order" for a while. But it cannot create the whole civil infrastructure and the sea change of values that underpin a functioning liberal democracy. To do that you have to turn tribesmen into citizens.

These White House children of the Protestant Ethic should understand how hard won is the open society we live in, how much it is the work of centuries of struggle and suffering, how fragile it is, and how *we had to do it for ourselves*. Our fundamentalist Islamic opponents have on their side the atavistic attractions of the closed society, and we should take them at least as seriously as they take us. Before we try to make them over in our image, we should remember how unnervingly recent was our own makeover, and act with becoming humility and caution. A helping hand here and there may not be amiss, but we should never be surprised at the rejection of the stranger's gift.

Review Questions

1. According to Fox, how do people usually act when strangers try to give them things?

2. What mission has characterized Western colonial intervention in other people's countries?

3. Americans believe that people everywhere long for something. What is it, and how does this belief relate to our actions toward Iraq?

4. Why is the phrase "Iraqi people" wrong, according to Fox?

5. Where do most people in Iraq place their loyalty, and how does this affect how they see the U.S. presence in their country?

6. Why is it important to know who Iraqis marry, and what does this tell us about political structures in Iraq?

7. How has democracy emerged in the world, and what does that say about human nature and prospects for U.S. success in Iraq?

EIGHT

RELIGION, MAGIC, AND WORLDVIEW

John Petrovic/AP Wide World Photos

READINGS IN THIS SECTION

Taraka's Ghost   303
Stanley A. Freed and Ruth S. Freed

Baseball Magic   310
George Gmelch

Run for the Wall: An American Pilgrimage   320
Jill Dubisch

Body Ritual among the Nacirema   334
Horace Miner

People seem most content when they are confident about themselves and the order of things around them. Uncertainty breeds debilitating anxiety; insecurity saps people's sense of purpose and their willingness to participate in social activity. Most of the time cultural institutions serve as a lens through which to view and interpret the world and respond realistically to its demands. But from time to time the unexpected or contradictory intervenes to shake people's assurance. A farmer may wonder about his skill when a properly planted and tended crop fails to grow. A wife may feel bewildered when the man she has treated with tenderness and justice for many years runs off with another woman. Death, natural disaster, and countless other forms of adversity strike without warning, eating away at the foundations of confidence. At these crucial points in life, many people use religion to help account for the vagaries of their experience.

Religion is the cultural knowledge of the supernatural that people use to cope with the ultimate problems of human existence.[1] In this definition, the term **supernatural** refers to a realm beyond normal experience. Belief in gods, spirits, ghosts, and magical power often defines the supernatural, but the matter is complicated by cultural variation and the lack of a clear distinction in many societies between the natural and the supernatural world. **Ultimate problems,** on the other hand, emerge from universal features of human life and include life's meaning, death, evil, and transcendent values. People everywhere wonder why they are alive, why they must die, and why evil strikes some individuals and not others. In every society, people's personal desires and goals may conflict with the values of the larger group. Religion often provides a set of **transcendent values** that override differences and unify the group.

An aspect of religion that is more difficult to comprehend is its link to emotion. Ultimate problems "are more appropriately seen as deep-seated emotional needs," not as conscious, rational constructs, according to sociologist Milton Yinger.[2] Anthropologists may describe and analyze religious ritual and belief but find it harder to get at religion's deeper meanings and personal feelings.

Anthropologists have identified two kinds of supernatural power: personified and impersonal. **Personified supernatural force** resides in supernatural beings, in the deities, ghosts, ancestors, and other beings found in the divine world. For the Bhils of India, a *bhut*, or ghost, has the power to cause skin lesions and wasting diseases. *Bhagwan*, the equivalent of the Christian deity, controls the universe. Both possess and use personified supernatural force.

Impersonal supernatural force is a more difficult concept to grasp. Often called **mana,** the term used in Polynesian and Melanesian belief, it represents a kind of free-floating force lodged in many things and places. The concept is akin to the Western term *luck* and works like an electrical charge that can be introduced into things or discharged from them. Melanesians, for example, might attribute the spectacular growth of yams to some rocks lying in the fields.

[1]This definition draws on the work of Milton Yinger, *Religion, Society, and the Individual: An Introduction to the Sociology of Religion* (New York: Macmillan, 1957).

[2]Yinger, p. 9.

The rocks possess mana, which is increasing fertility. If yams fail to grow in subsequent years, they may feel that the stones have lost their power.

Supernatural force, both personified and impersonal, may be used by people in many societies. **Magic** refers to the strategies people use to control supernatural power. Magicians have clear ends in mind when they perform magic, and use a set of well-defined procedures to control and manipulate supernatural forces. For example, a Trobriand Island religious specialist will ensure a sunny day for a political event by repeating powerful sayings thought to affect the weather.

Sorcery uses magic to cause harm. For example, some Bhil *bhopas*, who regularly use magic for positive purposes, may also be hired to work revenge. They will recite powerful *mantras* (ritual sayings) over effigies to cause harm to their victims.

Witchcraft is closely related to sorcery because both use supernatural force to cause evil. But many anthropologists use the term to designate envious individuals who are born with or acquire evil power and who knowingly or unknowingly project it to hurt others. The Azande of Africa believe that most unfortunate events are due to witchcraft, and most Azande witches claim they were unaware of their power and apologize for its use.

Most religions possess ways to influence supernatural power or, if spirits are nearby, to communicate with them directly. For example, people may say **prayers** to petition supernatural beings. They may also give gifts in the form of **sacrifices** and offerings. Direct communication takes different forms. **Spirit possession** occurs when a supernatural being enters and controls the behavior of a human being. With the spirit in possession, others may talk directly with someone from the divine world. **Divination** is a second way to communicate with the supernatural. It usually requires material objects or animals to provide answers to human-directed questions. The Bhils of India, for example, predict the abundance of summer rainfall by watching where a small bird specially caught for the purpose lands when it is released. If it settles on something green, rainfall will be plentiful; if it rests on something brown, the year will be dry.

Almost all religions involve people with special knowledge who either control supernatural power outright or facilitate others in their attempt to influence it. **Shamans** are religious specialists who directly control supernatural power. They may have personal relationships with spiritual beings or know powerful secret medicines and sayings. They are usually associated with curing. **Priests** are religious specialists who mediate between people and supernatural beings. They don't control divine power; instead, they lead congregations in ceremonies and help others petition the gods.

Worldview refers to a system of concepts and often unstated assumptions about life. It usually contains a **cosmology** about the way things are and a **mythology** about how things have come to be. Worldview presents answers to the ultimate questions: life, death, evil, and conflicting values.

Finally, anthropologists also study and report on the formation of new religions, especially those that occur as a result of deprivation and stress. These

revitalization movements, as Anthony F. C. Wallace called them in 1956, are "deliberate, organized, conscious efforts by members of a society to construct a more satisfying culture."[3] Revitalization movements are usually related to rapid change that renders a traditional way of life ineffective. For example, when one cultural group becomes dominated by another, rapid change and loss of authority may make its original meaning system seem thin, ineffective, and contradictory. The resulting state of deprivation often causes members to rebuild their culture along what they consider to be more satisfying lines.

Wallace argued that revitalization movements go through five stages:

1. *A Steady State.* This is a normal state of society in which people, through their culture, are able to manage the chronic stresses of daily life.

2. *Period of Increased Individual Stress.* Individuals in a society experience new stress caused by such events as culture contact, defeat in war, political domination, or climatic change.

3. *Period of Cultural Distortion.* Stress levels continue to rise as normal stress-reducing techniques fail to work. Social organization begins to break down, causing additional stress, and various cultural elements become distorted and disjointed.

4. *Period of Revitalization.* This period is marked by its own stages. First, a prophet or leader comes forward with a new vision of the culture that requires change. Called a *mazeway reformulation,* this vision is intended to produce a more integrated, satisfying, and adaptive culture. This is followed by the *communication* of the revitalization plan and, if it proves attractive, the plan's *organization* for wider dissemination, its *adoption* by many people, its *cultural transformation* of the society, and its *routinization* in daily life.

5. *A New Steady State.* If no additional stresses occur, the society should attain a new steady state at the end of the process.

Although not all revitalization movements are religious—the Marxist doctrine and communist revolution in Russia exemplify a political revitalization movement—most of the world's major religions probably started as revitalization movements and many smaller sects and movements fit the revitalization pattern today.

The first article, by Stanley Freed and Ruth Freed, describes how Sita, a low-caste Indian woman, is chronically possessed by the ghost of a friend who committed suicide. Stressed by the prospect of sexual relations with a new and strange husband, lack of support in her conjugal household, and the deaths of many friends and family members, ghost possession, argue the Freeds, reduces Sita's anxiety and gives her needed family support. The second article, by George Gmelch, is the latest revision of his earlier classic piece on the use of magic by

[3]Anthony F. C. Wallace, "Revitalization Movements: Some Theoretical Considerations for Their Comparative Study," *American Anthropologist* 58, no. 2 (1956): 264–281.

American baseball players. He looks in detail at the rituals, taboos, and fetishes employed by the athletes. In the third article, Jill Dubisch illustrates the meaning and impact of ritual and pilgrimage. Using the "Run For the Wall," a motorcycle pilgrimage that involves travel from Los Angeles to the Vietnam Memorial in Washington, D.C., as an example, she shows how this difficult motorcycle ride evokes strong emotions and personal transformation among its participants. The fourth article is Horace Miner's classic article describing the body ritual of a North American group, the Nacerima. The Nacerima's concern for the health and beauty of their bodies has led them to establish an elaborate ritual system including the building of holy fonts in their houses and the presence of a variety of ritual specialists.

Key Terms

cosmology   p. 300

divination   p. 300

magic   p. 300

mana   p. 299

mythology   p. 300

personified supernatural
   force   p. 299

prayer   p. 300

priest   p. 300

religion   p. 299

revitalization movement   p. 301

sacrifice   p. 300

shaman   p. 300

sorcery   p. 300

spirit possession   p. 300

supernatural   p. 299

transcendent values   p. 299

ultimate problems   p. 299

witchcraft   p. 300

worldview   p. 300

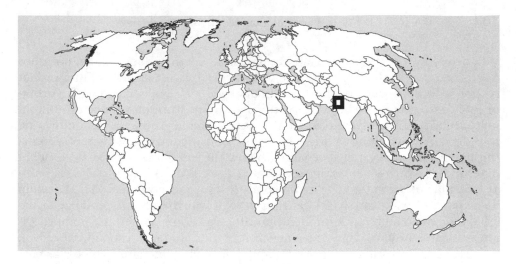

30

Taraka's Ghost

Stanley A. Freed and Ruth S. Freed

Most people meet life's challenges by using an array of normal, and often effective, cultural responses. U.S. traffic is dangerous, for example, but we use driving skills we have learned to survive with confidence on the road. But some circumstances fall beyond our everyday abilities. We exercise and eat properly, but still may unexpectedly become ill. We work diligently and skill-fully at our jobs, yet fail to be promoted. Many anthropologists see a relationship between religion and the anxieties that are caused by stressful and seemingly unmanageable aspects of life. In this article, Stanley Freed and Ruth Freed describe such an association. They report that a low-caste girl, Sita, is possessed by Taraka, the ghost of a childhood friend who committed suicide. Sita is stressed by the need to have sex with a new husband, the lack of support that meets a bride in her husband's household, and the deaths of three friends and several brothers and sisters. Ghost possession reduces her anxiety and gains her the support of her natal and conjugal families.

From Stanley A. Freed and Ruth S. Freed, "Taraka's Ghost," *Natural History,* October 1999, pp. 84–91.
Reprinted from *Natural History,* October 1999, copyright © Natural History Magazine, Inc., 1999.

When we saw our first ghost possession in a North Indian village, on a hot September day in the late 1950s, we were struck by the villagers' matter-of-fact response to what seemed an extraordinary event. We were seated with a group of low-caste villagers who were softly chatting in front of a mud hut. Sita, a newly married fifteen-year-old girl, was sitting on the ground, and, conforming to the proper behavior of a bride, she was inconspicuous and silent. Still wearing her bridal finery, her face veiled below the eyes, she worked her sewing machine, of which she was proud.

A man of her caste, who had recently lost his job, commented that sewing on a machine was man's work (at that time, it was mainly the province of the village tailor). The remark implied that Sita was doing something inappropriate, an insinuation to which, as a new bride, she could not respond. Moreover, the criticism struck at Sita's pride and joy, her sewing machine, which was part of her dowry. To her it was a talisman, protecting her and providing her with higher status than other brides of her caste, for she was the first to possess one.

Sita's mother-in-law, who had witnessed earlier ghost possessions of the girl, realized that the criticism had distressed Sita, and anticipating that Sita would again be possessed, the older woman abruptly began to discuss the ghost attacks that plagued the teenager. We couldn't imagine why the conversation had taken such a turn until Sita began to shiver, a symptom preceding possession. Despite the heat, she complained of feeling cold, so some women covered her with quilts. She moaned, breathed with difficulty, and then collapsed in a semi-conscious state.

The spectators accepted that a ghost had possessed her and tried a variety of standard curing techniques. These ranged from engaging the ghost in conversation, identifying it, and trying to satisfy its wishes or demands so that it would leave voluntarily, to attempting to drive it away with verbal abuse and, if necessary, physically painful or unpleasant measures (applied to the victim but aimed at the ghost). First, the women propped Sita up in a sitting position and wafted smoke from some smoldering cow dung under her nose. She jerked violently, so they had to restrain her. Then they shouted at the ghost: "Who are you? Are you going?" The ghost, speaking through Sita, promised to leave, and the women released the girl. But they were not deluded. They suspected that the ghost would not leave permanently and that a cure would be difficult. "Ghosts don't keep their promises," they confided to us.

Sita again fell unconscious, a sign that the ghost had returned. To revive her, the women dropped stinging hookah water in her eyes and pulled her braids. Sita returned to semiconsciousness and emitted a high-pitched wail, which announced the ghost's presence and readiness to talk. There followed a conversation between the ghost (speaking through Sita) and Sita's in-laws and a few other women, in the course of which the ghost identified herself as Sita's cousin Taraka, who had committed suicide by drowning in a well. Taraka's ghost declared that she would not leave Sita. The spectators again attempted to drive out the ghost, but Sita finally relapsed into unconsciousness.

For a fortnight thereafter, Sita experienced a series of possessions, so her father-in-law called various exorcists. They used generally similar techniques, calling on their familiars—supernatural beings who served them—to assist with the cure. Among these familiars were Hanuman, the monkey god; Kalkaji, goddess of the cremation grounds, with whom ghosts are closely linked; Jahar or Guga Pir, a Hindu-Muslim saint, who cut off his maternal cousins' heads in battle and later buried himself alive; and the ghost of a conjurer from Dacca. Each curer began a session by calling on his familiars, thus reassuring Sita and her relatives as to his curing powers.

When Sita's possessions persisted, her father was notified. He brought two exorcists to collaborate in an all-night session to drive off the ghost. They first induced possession in Sita by the power of suggestion and by the hypnotic effects of chanting mantras (hymns) believed to have supernatural power and using a fire to focus her concentration. Then they tried to exorcise Taraka's ghost by verbal abuse, hitting Sita, squeezing rock salt between her fingers (which was painful), pulling her braids, and throwing bits of her hair into the fire. During the session, Sita alternated between seeing a ghost, falling into a semiconscious state while a ghost spoke through her, unconsciousness, and intermittent returns to consciousness. Sita was not cured, however, and soon thereafter left for an extended visit with her parents, who lived in another village.

During the rest of our stay in India, we came to learn more about the villagers' beliefs in ghosts and the particular circumstances that led to Sita's afflictions. In rural North India, almost all Hindus believe that the soul goes through a cycle of rebirths. Following a person's death, it becomes a ghost, lingering for thirteen days in the village cremation grounds. Villagers who adhere to the doctrines of the Arya Samaj, a reform sect of Hinduism, believe in only one God, Bhagwan, and expect his judgment after cremation. The majority of villagers, who follow a more traditional version of Hinduism with multiple supernatural beings, believe that the soul travels to the Land of the Dead, ruled by Yama, Lord of the Dead. There Yama and his scribe review the soul's past actions before deciding on its future.

The important element in what happens to the soul at death is its karma, the sum of its good and bad actions from all its past lives. After being judged, the soul may be reborn or, if the sum of its actions is unusually good, released from the cycle of rebirths to join with many other souls and the Universal Absolute, a neuter deity known also as the Ultimate Reality, the joining of all souls in one.

Many Hindus believe in an additional possibility: a soul may become a ghost that lingers, possibly for decades, haunting the places where it lived and died. These are the souls of people who die tortured, from disease, accident, suicide, or murder; who violate village norms of behavior; who die before the years allotted to them by Yama; or who never attain the satisfactions of adult life. The ghosts of persons who are murdered or commit suicide are the most malevolent and tarry longest.

Ghosts are feared because they are believed to attack the living to seize their souls. Many villagers, but not all, believe that being seized by a ghost can cause illness or death. Ghost possession is the most vivid form of attack, in which a ghost enters and speaks through its victim, who has fallen into semiconsciousness. After recovering, the victim does not remember what took place.

Because people in a state of possession may attempt to commit suicide by drowning in a well or by jumping in front of a train, they are usually watched by relatives and neighbors.

There is often a relationship between a ghost and its victim. For example, we learned that Taraka was not only a cousin but also a very close friend of Sita's. Sita had lived with Taraka's family for six months. Engaged to a man of another village, Taraka had an illicit affair with a boy of her own village. Because she became pregnant, the loss of her premarital chastity could not be long concealed.

The virtue of daughters is crucial to family honor in North India, and a daughter's sexual misbehavior, if it becomes generally known, may force a father to get rid of her by inducing suicide or even by murder. Taraka's parents learned of her pregnancy and quickly arranged her wedding to her fiancé. They handed over only a small dowry, in case Taraka's in-laws, realizing she was pregnant, returned her.

When Taraka went to her husband's family to begin her marital life, her husband's parents immediately discovered that she was pregnant. Renouncing all rights to her, they returned her to her father. Despite Taraka's pleas, her father was unforgiving and told her to commit suicide. Shortly thereafter, when Taraka, Sita, and some other girls were playing, Taraka decided to leave the group and asked Sita to accompany her. Sita refused. Taraka ran from the group, went to a nearby well, jumped in, and drowned. Sita blamed herself for the suicide.

Taraka was one of Sita's three close childhood friends, all of whom she lost during the three years before her own marriage. Prior to Taraka's indiscretions and suicide, a schoolmate had been murdered by her father. She was raped by a schoolteacher, and even though the girl was the victim and the identity of the assailant was known, her father was furious and blamed her. He flew into a rage, raped and murdered her, and threw her into a well (villagers regard such crimes as family business and rarely interfere). Another of Sita's schoolmates died of typhoid and malaria, shortly after beginning sexual relations with her husband.

The episode of the untrustworthy schoolteacher worried Sita's mother, who took her daughter out of school. The abrupt end of her education was a shock to Sita, who wanted to be a schoolteacher herself. Instead, Sita and her mother went to visit her mother's brother in her mother's natal village. This was when Sita's life became entwined with Taraka's, for Taraka was this man's daughter.

In Sita's mind, the deaths of her friends were linked with mating, marriage, childbirth, and disappointed dreams of further education. This link was reinforced by other painful memories. As her parents' first-born child, Sita had lived through the deaths of four infant brothers and five infant sisters, who had died because they could not digest their mother's milk. Mother, daughter, and other villagers believed that a ghost had taken these infants' souls. (Two brothers born subsequently had survived.) With the memory of the deaths of her friends and infant siblings, the fifteen-year-old Sita went to her husband to consummate her marriage, on her second visit to her in-laws.

On the first night, Sita told her sister-in-law that she was afraid to sleep with her husband and implored her to stay with her instead. The sister-in-law did so, but when Sita awoke in the night, she found her husband sleeping beside her. They did not have sexual relations that night. The following day, Sita went to the well for water and either jumped or accidentally slipped and fell in. Fortunately, two men who were nearby threw her a rope and pulled her out. As a result of this incident, the young couple did not have sexual relations that night either, and the next day Sita returned to her parents' home.

The marriage was finally consummated on Sita's next visit to her husband, some months later. During the fourth night of sexual relations, however, Sita was possessed by Taraka's ghost, who said that Sita's husband was her husband. The statement indicated that Taraka's ghost had been with Sita at the time of Sita's wedding, which meant that both women were married to Sita's husband.

At best, a North Indian rural woman must make an extraordinary social and psychological adjustment when she marries. At an early age, she moves from her natal family, where she is loved, cherished, and indulged, to her marital family, where she is chaperoned and required to restrict her movements. She leaves her natal village to settle in the unfamiliar surroundings of her husband's village. She must adjust to her husband and his often large family, especially his parents, sisters, and brothers' wives. And in this rural society, where marriages are arranged by parents, the bride may not have even seen her husband before the wedding day (although nowadays at least some families arrange for the young couple to meet at the time of the engagement).

A married woman and her kin are regarded as social inferiors to her husband's kin. A new bride is expected to shoulder harder and more onerous household chores and farm work than the daughters in her husband's family (they too, when they marry and go to live with their husbands, will go through a similar experience). A new bride also is generally uninformed about the relation between menarche and childbirth and is apprehensive about beginning sexual relations with her husband. The social and psychological vulnerability of a bride makes her a prime candidate for attacks by ghosts. In Sita's case, with three friends who had all died before their allotted time and without issue, the ghosts were waiting in the wings. All three possessed Sita at one time or another, but Taraka's ghost was her main tormentor.

The transition from beloved and only surviving daughter to daughter-in-law was particularly stressful for Sita. Moreover, having been raised in a one caste village, she had faced little caste discrimination, but her husband's village was multicaste, and her caste was near the bottom of the hierarchy. Her fear of mating and bearing infants whose souls might be seized by ghosts was a source of stress, as were various physical ailments. These cultural, psychological, and physical stresses were preconditions for her possessions. Research by neuroscientists during the past two decades may shed light on the underlying physiological mechanism of ghost possession. Under the stress of mental or physical pain, the body produces morphinelike substances called endorphins, which relieve the pain and may trigger mental states called alternate, altered, or dissociative. Ghost possession is one such dissociative mental state.

Stress is not confined to brides or women in North India nor is ghost possession. On a return visit to the village in 1978, we recorded the cases of three young men who were troubled by ghosts. Although some of the details of the cases were different, they all involved the stresses of modern life, especially school examinations and job hunting. Education and employment are signs of economic responsibility that a girl's parents often require before entrusting their daughter to a young husband. For example, one of the young men, a 22-year-old member of the Potter caste, was desperate for a job because his wife's parents would not let their daughter come to live with him unless he found one.

The young man was possessed, according to his mother and sister, by the ghost of his mother's first husband's first wife. The belief that the ghost of a first wife will haunt her husband's next wife and children was a strong motif in village culture. In this case, the husband had subsequently passed away too, and his next wife had remarried and the children were of this marriage; but the principle was similar. Known as the Lady, this ghost had possessed the young man's older brother twenty years before under similar circumstances and was now intermittently possessing the younger man.

The young man was treated by two village exorcists. One was a high-caste Brahman. The other was the man whose remark had disturbed Sita twenty years before: unemployed at the time and subsequently saddened by the deaths of many of his infants and by his wife's long illness, he believed that the great god Shiva visited his home. Following this experience, he became an exorcist.

During our 1978 stay, we also interviewed Sita, who recounted her medical history. Now a poised, intelligent, 35-year-old woman, she recalled her early possessions, which had lasted three years until the birth of her first child. Then the possessions had become fits, which she described as follows:

> They start from the head. I feel giddy and drowsy. Then I can't see anything and everything goes dark. My legs, hands, and veins stiffen, then a pain goes to my stomach. I don't know what happens, but I have a pain in my heart, my eyes shut, and my tongue comes out. I shriek so loud that the whole village, even the Brahmans, know that I am having a fit. I have a weak heart. Whenever there is a fight in the family or elsewhere, or if I see a dead body, I have fits.

In 1978 Sita's fits were still taking place. Well acquainted with modern medicine—she went to modern hospitals for what she recognized as biological problems—she nonetheless blamed her twenty years of possessions and fits on Taraka's ghost. According to Sita, Taraka's ghost had possessed Taraka's mother, and she herself had then been infected through contact with Taraka's mother. She continued to consult indigenous curers, mainly exorcists, who drove off the ghost or gave her amulets to control it.

In the intervening years, Sita told us, her mother had given birth to three more infants who had died. The older of Sita's surviving brothers had died at age fourteen, and her grieving mother had died soon after. Sita's remaining brother became a schoolteacher with Sita's assistance, and she accompanied him and his wife on their honeymoon.

Sita's father was still alive, retired from military service. As a small child, Sita had idolized him—a soldier who traveled to other countries but came home every year for two months. The relationship persisted through the years. When she visited him every summer, free from the stress and anxiety of life in her marital family, she never had fits.

Sita detailed her pregnancies, illnesses, and operations in the years since we first met her. Pregnant nine times, she had six children born alive (one of whom died at age three), two miscarriages, and one induced abortion, prior to being sterilized in 1972. Sita's family had a history of an inability to digest milk, and her first child, a daughter, did not take Sita's milk. Sita's father arranged for Sita and her daughter to be hospitalized while the infant was fed glucose. Because of her father's influence, Sita thereafter went to hospitals for physical problems that she considered serious. She had an operation for kidney stones. She suffered from menstrual complaints and side effects from being sterilized. A constant worrier, she was badly disturbed when one of her brothers-in-law was diagnosed as having tuberculosis, for she feared that she might have it.

Nevertheless, with regard to her appearance, the maintenance of her household, and care of her children, she managed very well and, except for her fits, was in control of her life. The treatment for ghost possession and fits by exorcists and the various amulets they gave her for protection from Taraka's ghost relieved her anxiety and helped to reduce stress. They also brought her other advantages, especially support from her natal and marital families, a reduction in her workload, and permission to visit her retired father every summer. When we last saw her, Sita was the leader of the women of her family, confidently planning the education and future of her children.

Review Questions

1. What aspects of her life make Sita a prime candidate for ghost possession in Indian society?

2. What happens to the souls of dead people according to Hindu village belief? What accounts for the presence of ghosts?

3. How did ghost possession help Sita adjust to her life as a married woman?

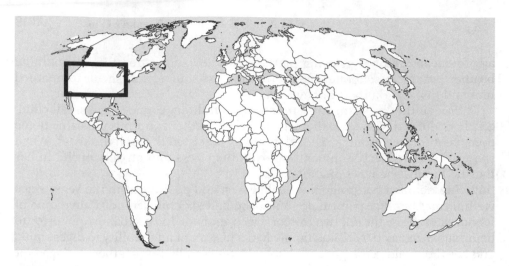

31

Baseball Magic

George Gmelch

Americans pride themselves on their scientific approach to life and problem solving. But as George Gmelch demonstrates in this updated article, U.S. baseball players, much like people in many parts of the world, also turn to supernatural forces to ensure success. Following the pioneering analysis of Trobriand magic by Bronislaw Malinowski, Gmelch shows that, like Tro-briand Islanders, baseball players use magic, including ritual, taboos, and fetishes, to manage the anxiety generated by unpredictable events that challenge human control.

On each pitching day for the first three months of a winning season, Dennis Grossini, a pitcher on a Detroit Tiger farm team, arose from bed at exactly 10:00 A.M. At 1:00 P.M. he went to the nearest restaurant for two glasses of iced tea and a tuna fish sandwich. When he got to the ballpark at 3:00 P.M., he put on the sweatshirt and jock he wore during his last winning game; one hour before the game he chewed a wad of Beech-Nut chewing tobacco. After each pitch during the game he touched the letters on his uniform and straightened his cap after each ball. Before the start of each inning he replaced the pitcher's rosin bag next to the spot where it was the inning before. And after every inning in which he gave up a run, he washed his hands.

When I asked which part of his ritual was most important, he said, "You can't really tell what's most important so it all becomes important. I'd be afraid to change anything. As long as I'm winning, I do everything the same."

Trobriand Islanders, according to anthropologist Bronislaw Malinowski, felt the same way about their fishing magic. Trobrianders fished in two different settings: in the *inner lagoon* where fish were plentiful and there was little danger, and on the *open sea* where fishing was dangerous and yields varied widely. Malinowski found that magic was not used in lagoon fishing, where men could rely solely on their knowledge and skill. But when fishing on the open sea, Trobrianders used a great deal of magical ritual to ensure safety and increase their catch.

Baseball, America's national pastime, is an arena in which players behave remarkably like Malinowski's Trobriand fishermen. To professional ballplayers, baseball is more than just a game, it is an occupation. Since their livelihoods depend on how well they perform, many use magic in an attempt to control the chance that is built into baseball. There are three essential activities of the game—pitching, hitting, and fielding. In the first two, chance can play a surprisingly important role. The pitcher is the player least able to control the outcome of his efforts. He may feel great and have good stuff warming up in the bullpen and then get in the game and get clobbered. He may make a bad pitch and see the batter miss it for a strike or see it hit hard but right into the hands of a fielder for an out. Conversely, his best pitch may be blooped for a base hit. He may limit the opposing team to just a few hits yet lose the game, and he may give up many hits and win. And the good and bad luck don't always average out over the course of a season. For instance, this past season (2007) Matt Cain gave up fewer runs per game than his teammate Noah Lowry but only won seven games while losing sixteen while Lowry won fourteen games and only lost eight. Both pitched for the same team—the San Francisco Giants—which meant they had the same fielders behind them. By chance, when Cain pitched the Giants scored few runs while his teammate Lowry enjoyed considerable run support. Regardless of how well a pitcher performs, the outcome of the game also depends upon the proficiency of his teammates, the ineptitude of the opposition, and luck.

Hitting, which many observers call the single most difficult task in the world of sports, is also full of uncertainty. Unless it's a home run, no matter how hard the batter hits the ball, fate determines whether it will go into a waiting glove or find a gap between the fielders. The uncertainty is compounded by the low success rate of hitting: the average hitter gets only one hit in every four trips to the plate, while the very best hitters average only one hit in every three trips. Fielding, which we will return to later, is the one part of baseball where chance does not play much of a role.

How do the risk and uncertainty in pitching and hitting affect players? How do they try to control the outcomes of their performance? These are questions that I first became interested in many years ago both as a ballplayer and as an anthropology student. I had devoted much of my youth to baseball, and played professionally as a first baseman in the Detroit Tiger organization in the 1960s. It was shortly after the end of one baseball season that I took an anthropology course called "Magic, Religion, and Witchcraft." As I listened to my professor describe the magical rituals of the Trobriand Islanders, it occurred to me that what these so-called "primitive" people did wasn't all that different from what my teammates and I did for luck and confidence at the ballpark.

Routines and Rituals

The most common way players attempt to reduce chance and their feelings of uncertainty is to develop a *routine*—a course of action that is regularly followed. Talking about the routines of ballplayers, Pittsburgh Pirates coach Rich Donnelly said:

> They're like trained animals. They come out here [ballpark] and everything has to be the same, they don't like anything that knocks them off their routine. Just look at the dugout and you'll see every guy sitting in the same spot every night. It's amazing, everybody in the same spot. And don't you dare take someone's seat. If a guy comes up from the minors and sits here, they'll say, "Hey, Jim sits here, find another seat." You watch the pitcher warm up and he'll do the same thing every time. . . . You got a routine and you adhere to it and you don't want anybody knocking you off it.

Routines are comforting; they bring order into a world in which players have little control. The varied elements in routines can produce the tangible benefit of helping the player concentrate. All ballplayers know that it is difficult to think and hit at the same time, and that following a routine can keep them from thinking too much. But often what players do goes beyond mere routine. These actions become what anthropologists define as *ritual*—prescribed behaviors in which there is no empirical connection between the means (e.g., tapping home plate three times) and the desired end (e.g., getting a base hit). Because there is no real connection between the two, rituals are not rational. Sometimes they are quite irrational. Similar to rituals are the nonrational beliefs that form the basis of taboos and fetishes, which players also use to bring luck to their side. But first let's take a close look at rituals.

Baseball rituals are infinitely varied. Most are personal, and are performed by individuals rather than by a team or group. Most are done in a private and unemotional manner, in much the same way players apply pine tar and rosin to their bats to improve the grip. A ballplayer may ritualize any activity that he considers important or somehow linked to good performance. Recall the variety of things that Dennis Grossini does, from specific times for waking and eating to foods and dress. Many pitchers listen to the same song on their I-pods on the day they are scheduled to start. Pitcher Al Holland always played with two dollar bills in his back pocket. The Oriole's Glenn Davis used to chew the same gum every day during hitting streaks, saving it under his cap. Astros infielder Julio Gotay always played with a cheese sandwich in his back pocket (he had a big appetite, so there might also have been a measure of practicality here). Red Sox Wade Boggs ate chicken before every game during his career, and that was just one of many elements in his pre- and postgame routine, which also included leaving his house for the ballpark at precisely the same time each day (1:47 for a night game), running wind sprints at 7:17 for a 7:35 start, and drawing a chai—the Hebrew symbol for life—upon entering the batter's box.

Many hitters go through a series of preparatory rituals before stepping into the batter's box. These include tugging on their caps, touching their uniform letters or medallions, crossing themselves, and swinging, tapping, or bouncing the bat on the plate a prescribed number of times. Consider the Dodger's Nomar Garciaparra. After each pitch he steps out of the batters box, kicks the dirt with each toe, adjusts his right batting glove, adjusts his left batting glove, and touches his helmet before getting back into the box. He insists that it is a routine, not superstition. "I'm just doing it to get everything tight. I like everything tight, that's all it is, really." Mike Hargrove, former Cleveland Indian first baseman, had so many time-consuming elements in his batting ritual that he was nicknamed "the human rain delay." Both players believe their batting rituals helped them regain their concentration after each pitch. But others wondered if the two had become prisoners of their elaborate superstitions.

Players who have too many or particularly bizarre rituals risk being labeled as flakes, and not just by teammates but also by fans and the media as well. For example, ex-Mets pitcher Turk Wendell's eccentric rituals, which include chewing black licorice while pitching, only to spit it out, brush his teeth and reload the candy between innings, and wearing a necklace of teeth from animals he has killed, made him a cover story subject in the *New York Times Sunday Magazine*.

Baseball fans observe a lot of this ritual behavior, such as pitchers smoothing the dirt on the mound before each new batter and position players tagging a base when leaving and returning to the dugout between innings, never realizing its importance to the player. The one ritual many fans do recognize, largely because it's a favorite of TV cameramen, is the "rally cap"—players in the dugout folding their caps and wearing them bill up in hopes of sparking a rally.

Rituals grow out of exceptionally good performances. When a player does well, he seldom attributes his success to skill alone; he knows that his skills don't change much from day to day. So, then, what was different about today which can explain his three hits? He makes a correlation. That is, he attributes his success, in part, to an object, a food he ate, not having shaved, a new shirt he bought that day, or just about any behavior out of the ordinary. By repeating those behaviors, the player seeks to gain control over his performance, to bring more good luck. Outfielder John White explained how one of his rituals started:

> I was jogging out to centerfield after the national anthem when I picked up a scrap of paper. I got some good hits that night and I guess I decided that the paper had something to do with it. The next night I picked up a gum wrapper and had another good night at the plate . . . I've been picking up paper every night since.

When outfielder Ron Wright played for the Calgary Cannons he shaved his arms once a week. It all began two years before when after an injury he shaved his arm so it could be taped, and then hit three homers. Now he not only has one of the smoothest swings in the minor leagues, but two of the smoothest forearms. Wade Boggs' routine of eating chicken before every game began when he was a rookie in 1982 and noticed a correlation between multiple-hit games and poultry plates (his wife has 40 chicken recipes). One of Montreal Expo farmhand Mike Saccocio's rituals also concerned food: "I got three hits one night after eating at Long John Silver's. After that when we'd pull into town, my first question would be, "Do you have a Long John Silver's?" Unlike Boggs, Saccocio abandoned his ritual and looked for a new one when he stopped hitting well.

During one game New York Yankee manager Joe Torre stood on the dugout steps instead of sitting on the bench when his team was batting. The Yankees scored a few runs, so he decided to keep on doing it. As the Yankees won nine games in a row, Torre kept standing. Torre explained, "I have a little routine going now. . . . As long as we score, I'll be doing the same thing."

When in a slump, most players make a deliberate effort to change their routines and rituals in an attempt to shake off their bad luck. One player tried taking different routes to the ballpark, another tried sitting in a different place in the dugout, another shaved his head, and several reported changing what they ate before the game. I had one manager who would rattle the bat bin when the team was not hitting well, as if the bats were in a stupor and could be aroused by a good shaking. Some of my teammates rubbed their hands along the handles of the bats protruding from the bat bin in hopes of picking up some luck from the bats of others. Diamondbacks left fielder Luis Gonzalez sometimes places his bats in the room where Baseball Chapel—a Sunday church service—is about to get underway. Gonzalez hopes his bats will get some benefit, though he doesn't usually attend the service himself.

Taboo

Taboos (the word comes from a Polynesian term meaning prohibition) are the opposite of rituals. These are things you shouldn't do. Breaking a taboo, players believe, leads to undesirable consequences or bad luck. Most players observe at least a few taboos, such as never stepping on the chalk foul lines. A few, like Nomar Garciaparra, leap over the entire base path. One teammate of mine would never watch a movie on a game day, despite our playing virtually every day from April to September. Another teammate refused to read anything before a game because he believed it weakened his batting eye.

Many taboos take place off the field, out of public view. On the day a pitcher is scheduled to start, he is likely to avoid activities he believes will sap his strength and detract from his effectiveness. On the day they are to start, some pitchers avoid shaving, eating certain foods and even having sex (this nostrum is probably based on an eighteenth century belief about preserving vital body fluids, but experts now agree there is no ill effect and there may actually be a small benefit).

Taboos usually grow out of exceptionally poor performances, which players attribute to a particular behavior. During my first season of pro ball I ate pancakes before a game in which I struck out three times. A few weeks later I had another terrible game, again after eating pancakes. The result was a pancake taboo: I never again ate pancakes during the season. (Conversely, Orioles pitcher Jim Palmer, after some success, insisted on eating pancakes before each of his starts).

While most taboos are idiosyncratic, there are a few that all ballplayers hold and that do not develop out of individual experience or misfortune. These form part of the culture of baseball, and are sometimes learned as early as Little League. Mentioning a no-hitter while one is in progress is a well-known example. The origins of such shared beliefs are lost in time, though some scholars have proposed theories. For example, the taboo against stepping on the chalk foul lines when running onto or off the field between innings, suggests National Baseball Hall of Fame research director Tim Wiles, may be rooted in the children's superstition, "step on a crack, break your mother's back."

Fetishes

Fetishes are charms, material objects believed to embody supernatural power that can aid or protect the owner. Good-luck charms are standard equipment for some ballplayers. These include a wide assortment of objects from coins, chains, and crucifixes to a favorite baseball hat. The fetishized object may be a new possession or something a player found that coincided with the start of a streak and which he holds responsible for his good fortune. While playing in the Pacific Coast League, Alan Foster forgot his baseball shoes on a road trip and borrowed a pair from a teammate. That night he pitched a no-hitter, which he attributed to the shoes. Afterwards he bought them from his teammate and they became a fetish. Expo farmhand Mark LaRosa's rock has a different origin and use:

> I found it on the field in Elmira after I had gotten bombed. It's unusual, perfectly round, and it caught my attention. I keep it to remind me of how important it is to concentrate. When I am going well I look at the rock and remember to keep my focus. The rock reminds me of what can happen when I lose my concentration.

For one season Marge Schott, former owner of the Cincinnati Reds, insisted that her field manager rub her St. Bernard "Schotzie" for good luck before each game. When the Reds were on the road, Schott would sometimes send a bag of the dog's hair to the field manager's hotel room. Religious medallions, which many Latino players wear around their necks and sometimes touch before going to the plate or mound, are also fetishes, though tied to their Roman Catholicism. Also relating to their religion, some players make the sign of the cross or bless themselves before every at bat (a few like Pudge Rodriguez do so before every pitch), and a few point or blow a kiss to the heavens after hitting a home run.

Some players regard certain uniform numbers as lucky. When Ricky Henderson came to the Blue Jays in 1993, he paid teammate Turner Ward $25,000 for the right to wear number 24. Don Sutton got off cheaper. When he joined the Dodgers he convinced teammate Bruce Boche to give up number 20 in exchange for a new set of golf clubs. Oddly enough, there is no consensus about the effect of wearing number 13. Some players shun it, while a few request it. When Jason Giambi arrived with the Oakland A's his favorite number 7 was already taken, so he settled for 16 (the two numbers add up to 7). When he signed with the Yankees, number 7 (Mickey Mantle's old number) was retired and 16 was taken, so he settled for 25 (again, the numbers add up to 7).

Number preferences emerge in different ways. A young player may request the number of a former star, sometimes hoping that it will bring him the same success. Or he may request a number he associates with good luck. Colorado Rockies' Larry Walker's fixation with the number 3 has become well known to baseball fans. Besides wearing 33, he takes three practice swings before stepping into the box, he showers from the third nozzle, sets his alarm for three minutes past the hour and he was wed on November 3 at 3:33 p.m.[1] Fans in ballparks all across America rise from their seats for the seventh-inning stretch before the home club comes to bat because the number 7 is lucky, although the specific origin of this tradition has been lost.

Clothing, both the choice and the order in which it is put on, combine elements of both ritual and fetish. Some players put on the parts of their uniform in a particular order. Expos farmhand Jim Austin always puts on his left sleeve, left pants leg, and left shoe before the right. Most players, however, single out one or two lucky articles or quirks of dress for ritual elaboration. After hitting two home runs in a game, for example, ex-Giant infielder Jim Davenport discovered that he had missed a buttonhole while dressing for the game. For the remainder of his career he left the same button undone. Phillies' Len Dykstra would discard his batting gloves if he failed to get a hit in a single at-bat. In a hitless game, he might go through four pair of gloves. For outfielder Brian Hunter the focus is shoes: "I have a pair of high tops and a pair of low tops. Whichever shoes don't get a hit that game, I switch to the other pair." At the time of our interview, he was struggling at the plate and switching shoes almost every day. For Birmingham Baron pitcher Bo Kennedy the arrangement of the different pairs of baseball shoes in his locker is critical:

> I tell the clubbies [clubhouse boys] when you hang stuff in my locker don't touch my shoes. If you bump them move them back. I want the Ponys in front, the turfs to the right, and I want them nice and neat with each pair touching each other. . . . Everyone on the team knows not to mess with my shoes when I pitch.

[1]Lee Allen, "The Superstitions of Baseball Players," *New York Folklore Quarterly* 20, no. 20 (1964): 98–109.

During hitting or winning streaks players may wear the same clothes day after day. Once I changed sweatshirts midway through the game for seven consecutive nights to keep a hitting streak going. Clothing rituals, however, can become impractical. Catcher Matt Allen was wearing a long sleeve turtleneck shirt on a cool evening in the New York-Penn League when he had a three-hit game. "I kept wearing the shirt and had a good week," he explained. "Then the weather got hot as hell, 85 degrees and muggy, but I would not take that shirt off. I wore it for another ten days—catching—and people thought I was crazy." Perhaps taking a ritual to the extreme, Leo Durocher, managing the Brooklyn Dodgers to a pennant in 1941, spent three and a half weeks in the same gray slacks, blue coat, and knitted blue tie. Losing streaks often produce the opposite effect, such as the Oakland A's players who went out and bought new street clothes after losing fourteen in a row.

Former Oakland A's manager Art Howe often wouldn't wash his socks after the A's were victorious; and he would also write the line up card with the same pen, and tape the pregame radio show in the same place on the field. In the words of one veteran, "It all comes down to the philosophy of not messing with success—or deliberately messing with failure."

Baseball's superstitions, like most everything else, change over time. Many of the rituals and beliefs of early baseball are no longer observed. In the 1920s–30s sportswriters reported that a player who tripped en route to the field would often retrace his steps and carefully walk over the stumbling block for "insurance." A century ago players spent time on and off the field intently looking for items that would bring them luck. To find a hairpin on the street, for example, assured a batter of hitting safely in that day's game. A few managers were known to strategically place a hairpin on the ground where a slumping player would be sure to find it. Today few women wear hairpins—a good reason the belief has died out. In the same era, Philadelphia Athletics manager Connie Mack hoped to ward off bad luck by employing a hunchback as a mascot. Hall of Famer Ty Cobb took on a young black boy as a good luck charm, even taking him on the road during the 1908 season. It was not uncommon then for players to rub the head of a black child for good luck.

To catch sight of a white horse or a wagonload of barrels were also good omens. In 1904 the manager of the New York Giants, John McGraw, hired a driver with a team of white horses to drive past the Polo Grounds around the time his players were arriving at the ballpark. He knew that if his players saw white horses, they would have more confidence and that could only help them during the game. Belief in the power of white horses survived in a few backwaters until the 1960s. A gray-haired manager of a team I played for in Drummondville, Quebec, would drive around the countryside before important games and during the playoffs looking for a white horse. When he was successful, he would announce it to everyone in the clubhouse.

One belief that appears to have died out recently is a taboo about crossed bats. Several of my Latino teammates in the 1960s took it seriously. I can still recall one Dominican player becoming agitated when another player tossed a bat from the batting cage and it landed on top of his bat. He believed that the top bat might steal hits from the lower one. In his view, bats contained a finite number of hits. It was once commonly believed that when the hits in a bat were used up no amount of good hitting would produce any more. Hall of Famer Honus Wagner believed each bat contained only 100 hits. Regardless of the quality of the bat, he would discard it after its 100th hit. This belief would have little relevance today, in the era of light bats with thin handles—so thin that the typical modern bat is lucky to survive a dozen hits without being broken. Other superstitions about bats do survive, however. Position players on the Class A Asheville Tourists would not let pitchers touch or swing their bats, not even to warm up. Poor-hitting players, as most pitchers are, were said to pollute or weaken the bats.

Although the elements in many rituals have changed over time, the reliance of players on them has not. Moreover, that reliance seems fairly impervious to advances in education. Way back in the 1890s, in an article I found in the archives of the National Baseball Hall of Fame, one observer predicted that the current influx of better educated players into the game and the "gradual weeding out of bummers and thugs" would raise the intellectual standard of the game and reduce baseball's rampant superstitions. It didn't. I first researched baseball magic in the late 1960s; when I returned 30 years later to study the culture of baseball, I expected to find less superstition. After all, I reasoned, unlike in my playing days most of today's players have had some college. I did find that today's players are less willing to admit to having superstitions, but when I asked instead about their "routines" they described rituals and fetishes little different from my teammates in the 60s.

Uncertainty and Magic

The best evidence that players turn to rituals, taboos, and fetishes to control chance and uncertainty is found in their uneven application. They are associated mainly with pitching and hitting—the activities with the highest degree of chance—and not fielding. I met only one player who had any ritual in connection with fielding, and he was an error-prone shortstop. Unlike hitting and pitching, a fielder has almost complete control over the outcome of his performance. Once a ball has been hit in his direction, no one can intervene and ruin his chances of catching it for an out (except in the unlikely event of two fielders colliding). Compared with the pitcher or the hitter, the fielder has little to worry about. He knows that in better than 9.7 times out of 10 he will execute his task flawlessly. With odds like that there is little need for ritual.

Clearly, the rituals of American ballplayers are not unlike those of the Trobriand Islanders studied by Malinowski many years ago.[2] In professional baseball, fielding is the equivalent of the inner lagoon while hitting and pitching are like the open sea.

[2]Bronislaw Malinowski, *Magic, Science and Religion and Other Essays* (Glencoe, IL: Free Press, 1948).

While Malinowski helps us understand how ballplayers respond to chance and uncertainty, behavioral psychologist B. F. Skinner sheds light on why personal rituals get established in the first place.[3] With a few grains of seed Skinner could get pigeons to do anything he wanted. He merely waited for the desired behavior (e.g., pecking) and then rewarded it with some food. Skinner then decided to see what would happen if pigeons were rewarded with food pellets regularly, every fifteen seconds, regardless of what they did. He found that the birds associate the arrival of the food with a particular action, such as tucking their head under a wing or walking in clockwise circles. About ten seconds after the arrival of the last pellet, a bird would begin doing whatever it associated with getting the food and keep doing it until the next pellet arrived. In short, the pigeons behaved as if their actions made the food appear. They learned to associate particular behaviors with the reward of being given seed.

Ballplayers also associate a reward—successful performance—with prior behavior. If a player touches his crucifix and then gets a hit, he may decide the gesture was responsible for his good fortune and touch his crucifix the next time he comes to the plate. Unlike pigeons, however, most ballplayers are quicker to change their rituals once they no longer seem to work. Skinner found that once a pigeon associated one of its actions with the arrival of food or water, only sporadic rewards were necessary to keep the ritual going. One pigeon, believing that hopping from side to side brought pellets into its feeding cup, hopped ten thousand times without a pellet before finally giving up. But, then, Wade Boggs ate chicken before every game, through slumps and good times, for seventeen years.

Obviously the rituals and superstitions of baseball do not make a pitch travel faster or a batted ball find the gaps between the fielders, nor do the Trobriand rituals calm the seas or bring fish. What both do, however, is give their practitioners a sense of control, and with that, added confidence. And we all know how important that is. If you really believe eating chicken or hopping over the foul lines will make you a better hitter, it probably will.

Review Questions

1. According to Gmelch, what is magic, and why do people practice it?

2. What parts of baseball are most likely to lead to magical practice? Why?

3. What is meant by the terms *ritual*, *taboo*, and *fetish*? Illustrate these concepts using examples from this article.

4. How are Malinowski's and Skinner's theories of magic alike and different? What is each designed to explain?

5. Can you think of other areas of U.S. life where magic is practiced? Do the same theories used in this article account for these examples, too?

---

[3]B.F. Skinner, *Behavior of Organisms: An Experimental Analysis* (New York: Appleton Century, 1938).

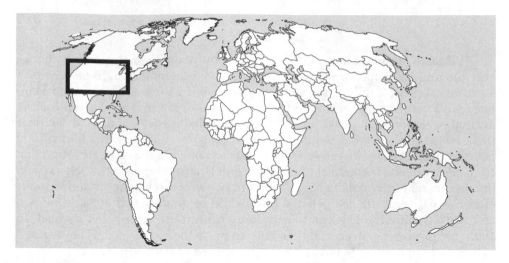

32

Run for the Wall: An American Pilgrimage

Jill Dubisch

Pilgrimages involve ritually structured travel that physically removes people from their everyday lives as they journey to places that evoke important, often life-changing, emotions. As a ritual, pilgrimages are structured around repetitive acts that symbolize past events, places, stories, and meanings. They involve a ritual of separation, a liminal period, and a final reincorporation into normal life for those who embark on them. We often associate pilgrimages with religion, but they may also occur in more secular contexts with much the same effect. This is the case for a pilgrimage called the Run for the Wall, described by Jill Dubisch in this article. The "run" is a pilgrimage undertaken by motorcyclists who travel for ten days each spring from Los Angeles to Washington, D.C., to commemorate soldiers lost during the Vietnam War. Started years ago by Vietnam veterans, it has grown to include other riders over the years as well. After they leave Los Angeles, riders cross the United States, stopping in towns along the way and occasionally participating in commemorations dedicated to the memory of veterans. Additional riders may join the run along the way, while others may drop out. Those who make it to Washington visit "the wall," their name for the Vietnam War Memorial bearing the names of all those who died in the war. Finally, they participate in "rolling thunder," a parade of thousands of motorcyclists ending at the U.S. Capitol, as a way to honor and "remember" soldiers who were captured, missing, and killed in the Vietnam War. Dubisch describes the ritual nature of the pilgrimage and details its emotional effect and transformative power for motorcyclists who participate.

They roared off the I-40 exit west of Flagstaff, Arizona, a motley crew of leather-clad, long-haired bikers on their Harleys. *Here they are,* we thought, as my partner Ray and I scrambled to pull our Honda Gold Wing motorcycle in behind them. Excitement washed over us, mingled with a large dose of anxiety. Could we really become part of this rough-looking crowd, we wondered, these wild looking riders with their black leather jackets, chains, headscarves, long hair, and beards? After all, these were *real* bikers—not the sort of riders we were used to from our mostly middle-aged Honda Gold Wing motorcycle club. And yet this was the group with whom we planned to spend the next ten days, accompanying them on a cross-country journey from Flagstaff to the Vietnam Veterans Memorial in Washington, D.C., an annual pilgrimage known as the Run for the Wall.

As we parked nervously at the end of the line of bikes on the shoulder of the road, waiting for our police escort for the parade into downtown Flagstaff, little did we know what awaited us in the days ahead. For on this journey across America, both we and the mostly Vietnam veterans with whom we rode would develop emotional bonds that extended well beyond the Run, and we would experience a transformation that would change our lives. Such a trans-formation was not to be won easily, however, for the journey, a gruelling ten-day motorcycle ride, was fraught not only with all the dangers of the road that any motorcycle journey entails, but also with the emotional dangers involved in reawakening memories of a difficult period in our history—the era of the Vietnam War and the political protest and social disruption that were the con-sequences of that war. What's more, in the course of this journey, our very view of the country in which we lived would change, as we were fed and lodged and greeted with smiles, tears, and ceremonies—and occasionally with hostility or fear—in small communities all across America. The couple that finally returned home three weeks later on their motorcycle were not the same people who left Flagstaff that day in early May of 1996. The ride turned out to be a pilgrimage, a ritual passage that personally transformed both us and those with whom we road.

But who were these people who streamed off the highway and into our lives that day? Why did they term their journey a pilgrimage and why were they making such a pilgrimage so many years after the Vietnam War had ended? And why did they make this journey on motorcycles? Why would those who are not veterans choose to accompany them? And why would communities along the journey's route turn out to feed and celebrate the veterans and to wish them "welcome home"? In order to answer these questions, it is necessary to address not only the issue of the still-unhealed "wounds" of the Vietnam War and to examine the nature of pilgrimage, but also more generally to consider the nature of ritual and its role in American life.

The Run for the Wall: An American Ritual

The Run for the Wall begins every year in mid-May as several hundred motorcycle riders gather at a motel in southern California in preparation for their journey across the United States from California to Washington, D.C. Although many of the riders might be mistaken for outlaw bikers, with their beards, headscarves, boots, and black leather jackets, in fact, most are Vietnam veterans, and the journey they are about to undertake is no mere outing or biker joy ride. Rather, they are at the beginning of a serious, and often emotional and painful endeavor, a journey with a mission, a pilgrimage, whose final destination is the most powerful of American secular shrines, the Vietnam Veterans Memorial—the Wall.

The Run first took place in 1989, when a group of Vietnam veterans decided to ride their motorcycles across the country to the recently inaugurated Vietnam Veterans Memorial. Their intention was, as one of those original riders explained to me, "to say goodbye" to their fallen comrades whose names were on the Wall, and they saw the journey as a one-time event. However, the enthusiastic welcome the group received in the communities where they stopped in the course of their ride, and the ceremonies and hospitality with which they were greeted, as one rider told me, made them realize "we had to do it again." And so the Run for the Wall has taken place every year, and grown every year, so much that recently it has added a more southern route to the original Midwestern route with which the Run began.

During this ten-day journey across the United States, the riders travel several hundred miles a day on their motorcycles. Some go "all the way" to D.C., while others travel shorter distances with the group, replaced by others who join along the route, so that at times the group may have from 200 to 300 riders, forming a line stretching several miles down the highway. During the journey, the riders are greeted with ceremonies performed by local organizations such as veterans' groups and local motorcycle organizations. They visit VFW and American legion halls, Vietnam memorials, local parks and community halls. They are honored and fed and put up for the night at local camping grounds. Few of them pay for a single meal along the way, and camping is always free.

But many of these veterans are making another journey as well—a journey into the past and their own painful memories, to a time of personal danger and fear and grief, and of national dissention and conflict that split a generation— to that painful period of American history, the Vietnam War, a war that (as the

2004 presidential campaign showed) remains controversial to this day. And when the group arrives at its final destination, the Vietnam Veterans Memorial, an arrival always timed for the Friday of Memorial Day weekend, the memories become intensely painful, as the riders confront the names of dead comrades—and the non-veterans the names of dead relatives and friends—and relive once more all the traumatic memories of the war.

And yet the aim of this journey is not simply to confront the past, or to evoke its pain. Rather, the participants describe the aims of their pilgrimage as twofold: as a means of healing the individual wounds of the war and as a ride on behalf of all veterans, but especially those "left behind," the prisoners of war (POWs) and those missing in action (MIAs). Nor are these causes the concern of veterans alone. On this ritual journey, veterans are accompanied by family, friends, and other supporters, and also, since that day in 1996 when we first joined the Run, by two social scientists.

The Anthropology of Pilgrimage

When I joined the Run for the Wall it was not the first time I had been involved with a pilgrimage, however. For a number of years I had done anthropological fieldwork at the shrine of the Madonna of the Annunciation on the Greek island of Tinos, one of that country's most famous pilgrimage sites and the destination of thousands of Orthodox Christian pilgrims every year.[1] Although my work on Tinos was deeply involving and often emotional, I was an outsider, not a Greek Orthodox Christian, and from a different culture, and I did not myself participate in pilgrimage. Thus when I joined the Run for the Wall, it was the first time I had really been a pilgrim myself, and had taken part in a journey with a personal, as well as professional, significance.

"Pilgrimage" is a word that usually conjures up visions of sacred journeys connected with the great world religions—the Muslim pilgrimage to Mecca, Catholic pilgrimage to Lourdes or Santiago, or perhaps a journey of Hindus to the sacred waters of the Ganges in India. But pilgrimage is by no means limited to such religious traditions, and in fact it can take a variety of forms. Pilgrimage can range from large-scale journeys such as those that devout Muslims make to Mecca, to small individual journeys such as the Irish make to a healing well, or Americans to a family reunion. It can be mandated and structured by religious traditions or religious authorities, or undertaken as a purely individual quest. It can be motivated by spiritual needs or by the desire for solutions to such pragmatic physical problems as illness or the inability to bear a child. It is, in short, a highly flexible, variable, and multi-faceted ritual activity.

This notion of a journey, whether it is actual physical travel or metaphoric, is part of what gives pilgrimages their common structure and their widespread appeal. The journey is a powerful symbol and is connected with the idea that

---

[1]See Jill Dubisch, *In a Different Place* (Princeton, NJ: Princeton University Press, 1995).

one needs to go to a "different place"—to the wilderness, to a sacred locale, to the site of powerful events and away from the place of one's ordinary life—in order to achieve transformation, to touch the sacred, or to receive important messages from the other world. Thus while pilgrimage is a journey, it is not just any kind of journey. It is not taken out of pleasure or simple practical necessity (though it may also include these elements). Rather it is a journey with a purpose, a mission, a ritual act that carries the pilgrim to a place with special meaning or power. Nor need such journeys be strictly religious in nature. The Run for the Wall and journeys to Elvis Presley's home at Graceland or to Ground Zero at the World Trade Center in New York City, for example, do not fit within established religious traditions, yet they are seen by many of their participants as pilgrimages.

Pilgrimage destinations themselves draw people for a variety of reasons. Certain places are special, often by virtue of things that have happened there, whether a human event, such as the Battle of Gettysburg, or the appearance or act of a divine being, such as an apparition of the Virgin Mary at Lourdes in France. In other cases, the origins of the pilgrimage site may be lost in time, and the site simply known for its miraculous powers, as is the case with the healing wells of Ireland. And some pilgrimage sites attract people through the physical powers of place, as with mountains in Chinese pilgrimage, or the red rock "vortexes" of Sedona, Arizona. But journeys are also metaphorical. The idea of life as a moral and spiritual journey is deeply ingrained in the Christian religion. (And it is no coincidence that in the 1960s a psychedelic experience, in which one journeyed in mind but not in body, was termed a "trip"!)

The Anthropology of Ritual

I have spoken of pilgrimage as a "ritual," but what, exactly, are rituals, and why are they important? And what sort of ritual is pilgrimage?

Robbie Davis-Floyd, in her book *Birth as an American Rite of Passage*, defines ritual as "a patterned, repetitive, and symbolic enactment of a cultural belief or value."[2] According to Davis-Floyd, the primary purpose of ritual is "transformation," and for this reason rituals are often performed to mark important occasions, times, or transitions. From the perspective of those performing the rituals, there are a variety of purposes in carrying out ritual activities: to maintain order in the world, to connect with gods or ancestors, to protect, to express group or individual identity, or because the rituals are mandated by the religious system of the society. Rituals can bring about changes, as when rites of passage such as baptism or marriage transform individuals by moving them from one social status or stage of life to another. Rituals also mark off ordinary life from times when special activities are permitted or required. The carnival

[2]Robbie Davis-Floyd, *Birth as an American Rite of Passage* (Berkeley, CA: University of California Press, 1992), p. 8.

period preceding Lent in Catholic cultures both allows creativity and license absent in ordinary life and at the same time signals the beginning of the period of abstinence to follow, a period that itself parallels and dramatizes the sufferings of Christ before the crucifixion and resurrection. Similarly, a pilgrimage is an activity and time set apart, and pilgrimage may take place at times of special significance, such as holy days or national days of commemoration. Thus the Run for the Wall is timed so that its arrival at the Vietnam Veterans Memorial takes place on Memorial Day weekend, a period of remembering the war dead and of patriotic activities.

This brings up another important feature of rituals. As the famous scholar of religion, Mircea Eliade pointed out, rituals often reenact the important myths of society, showing us why they are the way they are. Thus Christian Easter rituals enact the crucifixion and resurrection, while the Jewish Passover meal, the Seder, recounts the Jews' flight from Egypt. Nor need such rituals be religious in nature. The Fourth of July in the United States, for example, commemorates the signing of the Declaration of Independence and serves as an occasion to proclaim American values of freedom, patriotism, and community. Rituals may also seek to rewrite or reshape the past. In the Run for the Wall, as I will show, veterans seek, among other things, to transform the meaning of being a Vietnam veteran from shame to pride, and to give veterans a chance for the homecoming reception most never had when they returned from Vietnam. ("Welcome home, brother" is the ritual greeting extended to these veterans by other veterans on the Run and by those who greet them along the way.)

Symbolism plays an important role in rituals. Victor Turner, an anthropologist who devoted much of his work to the study of ritual, saw symbols as having two poles: the ideological and the sensory. On the one hand, rituals engage our senses of sound, touch, sight, taste and smell (the sensory pole). On the other hand, they also convey important messages about social values (the ideological pole). Although contemporary anthropologists would see these two dimensions as intertwined, with each embedded in the other (rather than as opposite poles), they would agree that it is the combination of the ideological and the sensory that makes rituals so powerful and moving, for they engage more than just our intellects. For this reason, people sometimes find themselves moved by the rituals of other groups or cultures, even when they themselves do not share the values of those performing the ritual.

Although rituals are often perceived as being "traditional," passed on in the same form from generation to generation, the fact is that rituals are an ongoing human activity and must be re-created every time they are performed. Hence rituals are subject to both intentional and unintentional change. Moreover, new rituals are created regularly, and old ones modified. The Run for the Wall has now become a yearly "tradition," the ritual activities carried out in the course of its journey modified and added to every year by both the participants and by those who host them along the way.

It is clear that rituals are a rich source of data for the anthropologist and important windows on the culture in which they occur. For this reason, I like

Renato Rosaldo's description of rituals as "busy intersections," places where "a number of distinct social processes interact."[3] It is just such a "busy intersection" that we find in the annual motorcycle pilgrimage known as the Run for the Wall.

Pilgrimage as Ritual

One reason that the journey—as both symbol and as an actual activity—is so powerful is that it has the potential to create what anthropologists call a "liminal" state. Liminality is an important feature of those rituals we call "rites of passage," in which individuals or groups move from one stage or condition to another. Victor Turner and his wife, Edith Turner, saw pilgrimage as one type of rite of passage. When one is on a pilgrimage, the liminal period is marked by the physical separation created by the journey itself. Ordinary duties are left behind, and time and space take on different meanings. This may induce an altered state of consciousness that renders the pilgrim more receptive to both the messages of the journey and the healing or other transformations that pilgrimage can effect. Thus once the pilgrimage is over, the pilgrim often has experienced an inner transformation, such as healing of physical or psychological ills, atonement for sin, or spiritual renewal. Transformation of social status or identity may also take place. Vietnam veterans who participate in the Run for the Wall may return home with newly created identities *as* veterans (an identity they may have previously played down or denied), and they may also find that they have finally begun to heal the long-buried wounds of Vietnam.

To see how these various features of pilgrimage and ritual are represented on the Run for the Wall, let us look at some of the events that take place in the course of this ten-day journey. But before that, it is necessary to address two important elements of American culture that come together to define this pilgrimage: the Vietnam War and motorcycle riding.

The Vietnam War

The Run for the Wall's focus on the POW/MIA issue carries the message that the Vietnam War in some sense is not really over (a message also made clear in the 2004 presidential campaign and the frequent comparisons of the Iraq war to Vietnam). Despite the fact that the Vietnam war officially ended thirty years ago, unresolved conflicts over the meaning of the war, and the fact that it is a war that the United States did not "win," have made the memories of the war difficult and contentious, not only for veterans but for Americans generally. In addition, many veterans are still struggling to come to terms with their own roles in the war, as their faith in themselves—and in the values of their culture—was shaken by the experience. When these veterans returned home, their belief that they

[3]*Culture and Truth* (New York: Beacon, 1989), p. 17.

would be honored for having fought and risked their lives in defense of their country by those they thought they were defending was undermined by the indifference, and sometimes outright hostility, with which a number of homecoming veterans were received.

Because of such a reception, many veterans were reluctant to speak of their experiences in Vietnam or to connect or identify themselves with other veterans. They saw their postcombat symptoms as signs of their own craziness, and not the consequences of a shared experience. Although veterans who ended up in therapy groups in veterans' hospitals had some opportunity to talk about their experiences, many, if not most, Vietnam veterans bore their emotional burdens alone.

Many of these returning veterans thus sought to put Vietnam behind them and to "get on with their lives." It was only later that some of them, at least, began to feel the delayed traumatic effects of their wartime experience and found their carefully constructed postwar lives crumbling. It is from the need to address both the long-term and delayed consequences of the war, both for themselves and others, that many of the participants came to be involved in the Run for the Wall.

But why motorcycles?

Motorcycles in American Culture

Motorcycles have long held an attraction for veterans, from the returning veterans of World War II (some of whom formed the first Hell's Angels club) to current veterans of the Iraq war. For many of those who ride them, motorcycles symbolize important American values of freedom, self-reliance, patriotism, and individualism. Assertion of these values, and particularly patriotism, is evident among at least some groups of bikers—and certainly on the Run for the Wall—in the form of American flags, eagles, and other similar emblems decorating the motorcycles, the jackets, and the tee shirts of the bikers.

Many bikers also see themselves as a breed apart, "rebels" against the norms and restrictions of conventional society (even if only for the weekends they can "escape" on their motorcycles). The sense of marginality that some veterans felt on their return to civilian life, and the difficulty they may experience in adapting to that life, thus fit with the marginality of at least some segments of motorcycle culture, especially that of the "outlaw" bikers and similar groups. Motorcycle riding can also have important therapeutic effects, providing a space in which veterans feel that they can "clear their heads" and find some peace from the memories and emotional traumas that continue to haunt them.

There is a sense of solidarity and "brotherhood" that exists among bikers that is also important in the Run for the Wall. This sense of brotherhood echoes the camaraderie of warriors in combat; indeed, participating in the Run for the Wall is for some like going into battle again—this time for the POW/MIA cause and for the healing of fellow veterans. This is echoed in the military formation of the riders, rolling two by two in a long column down the highway, and in the element of danger present in any motorcycle ride, as well as in the roar of the motorcycles themselves.

By riding motorcycles, the participants in the Run for the Wall also set themselves apart from those making a cross-country journey by ordinary means. The parade of motorcycles (at points numbering several hundred bikes) riding side by side in formation down the highway presents an impressive sight, which is part of the strategy employed by the Run in its political agenda—calling attention to the POW/MIA issue. At the same time, riding motorcycles represents a more conventional element of pilgrimage—the role that hardship and suffering often play in the pilgrim's journey. Such suffering emphasizes the importance of the journey and leads to a feeling of accomplishment among those who have succeeded in reaching their destination. This sense of accomplishment is reflected in the honoring of those who have gone "all the way," that is, made the entire journey from California to Washington, D.C. The physical sensations of motorcycle riding—the noise, the motion, the riding in formation with several hundred other motorcycles, the hazards of the road—also combine to create a psychological receptivity to the ritual messages imparted along the journey's route.

But what are these messages, and how are they imparted in the course of the Run's many rituals? In order to answer this question, let us look at several of the ritual stops made during the Run for the Wall's long cross-country journey.

The Navajo Reservation and the Brotherhood of Warriors

Since its inception, the Run for the Wall, while maintaining the same basic itinerary (from California to Washington in ten days, arriving the Friday of Memorial Day weekend), has also regularly altered, added, and sometimes eliminated the various stops and ceremonies that punctuate the journey. In 1998, a new stop was added to the Run for the Wall, as the organizers of the Run responded to an invitation from the Navajo Reservation to ride to the still in progress Navajo Vietnam Veterans Memorial at Window Rock on the Run's third day out.

That particular year, the Run had endured snow on its way through the mountains of Northern Arizona and temperatures hovering around forty degrees Fahrenheit as we crossed the high desert along Interstate 40 toward Gallup (with a wind chill close to zero for those riding on motorcycles). As we turned off the interstate toward the Navajo Nation administrative center of Window Rock, we were met by a contingent of Navajo police who escorted us along the narrow two-lane road that led through the reservation. All along the route, groups of Navajo stood next to cars and pick-up trucks, waving and applauding as we rode by. As we pulled into the parking lot beneath the dramatic red rock formation that gives the town of Window Rock its name, we saw crowds of Navajo gathered around the lot and on the rocks above. We rolled to a stop and the crowd burst into enthusiastic applause. In response, the bikers gunned their engines in a collective roar. From the podium at one end of the parking lot, a Navajo leader said, "Look around you, white men—you're surrounded by Indians. We'll take your bikes. You can have our horses." His comment acknowledged both the differences that separated the Navajo from the mostly Anglo group of bikers and the shared military history that connected them. In the ceremonies that followed, Navajo leaders gave the Run a Navajo Nation flag to carry to the Wall, a Navajo folk singer performed a song he wrote in memory of a brother who died in Vietnam, Navajo children took our pictures while balancing precariously on the rocks above, and there was a demonstration by the last living World War II "code talkers" (Navajo who had participated in a secret military operation that used the Navajo language as a code). Then, as the desert light dimmed around the mystical formation of Window Rock, Navajo and non-Navajo warriors saluted while a bugler played "Taps."

At Window Rock what might be seen as an opposition (Anglo/Native American) is transformed into a common culture of the brotherhood of warriors. The horse and the motorcycle are both warrior's symbols, a dead warrior is memorialized (reminding all those present of the common sacrifices made by Navajo and non-Navajo), Navajo are connected to the riders and to the riders' destination—the Vietnam Memorial—through the presentation of the flag that the riders will carry to D.C., tying the Navajo not only to the pilgrims but also to the powerful symbols of the nation's capital and thus to the nation itself. The cold, grueling ride that preceded these ceremonies for the Run for the Wall participants placed us all in an altered and receptive state that made this ceremony at Window Rock one of the most emotionally powerful events of our pilgrimage.

The Power of Places: Evoking the Memory and Emotion of the Past at Angel Fire, New Mexico

On its fourth day out, the Run stops at the Vietnam Memorial at Angel Fire, New Mexico, high in the mountains near Taos. Although to most people it is best known as a ski area, to those who have participated in the Run for the Wall it will always be one of the most beautiful and powerful places associated with their pilgrimage. Here, high on a knoll and surrounded by a wind-swept alpine valley and snow-topped mountain peaks, stands a beautiful chapel, shaped like a white wing rising against the New Mexico sky. Next to the chapel is a memorial and museum of the Vietnam War, with photographs and exhibits. In the chapel itself, photographs of New Mexican men who died in Vietnam, looking terribly young in their military uniforms, stretches across the wall above a tier of seats descending to the lower part of the chapel and the simple cross that is the building's only ornament. There are often flowers or other offerings at the base of the cross, and on each tier of seats sits a box of tissues, mute testimony to the powerful emotions this stark and simple memorial evokes.

The memorial and chapel were built by Dr. Victor Westphal who lost his son in Vietnam, and who is now himself buried on the memorial's grounds. (Until 2004, Dr. Westphal was there to greet the Run every year, the latter years in a wheelchair.) The first year we were on the Run, there was a service held in the chapel for a veteran who had died the year before and who had been one of the original organizers of the Run. His wife spoke eloquently of what the Run's support had meant to her in her own mourning. Her words had particular resonance with this group of Vietnam veterans, many of whom still grieve for the loss of comrades in a war that was over decades ago. Then a young woman with an incredibly pure voice sang "Amazing Grace." There was not one of those wild tough bikers who had so intimidated us at the beginning of our journey who was not at that point in tears.

Many veterans have spoken to us about the significance of Angel Fire in their own spiritual and psychic journey toward healing. For those who felt they had gotten past the traumas of Vietnam and moved on with their lives, for those who had come on the Run thinking they were "just going for a ride" with fellow biker vets, Angel Fire awakened memories and reopened wounds that had never completely healed. At this point, many began to realize they had much left from the past that they had not confronted, that had continued to affect their lives and the lives of those around them. For these individuals, Angel Fire was not simply a stop on their pilgrimage; rather, it was the beginning of their *real* pilgrimage.

Part of the power of Angel Fire lies in its setting—the remoteness, the beauty, the steep, winding and somewhat hazardous mountain roads that must be traversed to get there. This creates a receptivity to the emotions of the past that are evoked by the memorial. Nor is it only those on the Run who journey here for pilgrimage. Ceremonies are held here on other days as well: on Veterans' Day and on Father's Day, in honor of the men killed in Vietnam whose children never had a chance to know them. And in between such events, more solitary pilgrimages are made by those drawn by the power of the site.

Limon, Colorado: Remembering the Missing and the Dead

Limon, Colorado is the Run's stop on its fifth night. It is a long day, riding from Cimarron, New Mexico, the previous night's stop, making several ceremonial stops along the way (including, one year, at the Colorado Vietnam memorial in Pueblo), ending up at this small town in eastern Colorado on the edge of the Great Plains. After checking into motels or the local KOA campground (where camping, as everywhere on the Run's journey, is free), many riders mount up again for the half hour ride east to the town of Hugo, where they will be served a wonderful feast prepared by the local women. Afterwards, everyone regroups at the KOA for the evening's ceremony, conducted by members of Task Force Omega, a group of families of POWs and MIAs. Here every year, as dusk falls, the names of the Colorado Missing in Action are read in a candlelight ritual that varies from year to year. On the 1999 Run, a "V" of candelabra was set up in a space near the tents, and we formed into couples, each couple assigned a month and given a list of names of those who had gone missing in Vietnam in that month. As each month was called, the woman read the names on her list. As each name was read in the gathering darkness, the man called out, "Still on patrol, sir!" Afterwards we all joined hands in a "healing circle."

The Run for the Wall's journey is punctuated with rituals such as these, rituals created by Run for the Wall participants and by the individuals and groups that host them along the way. Most of these rituals, in one way or another, commemorate the missing and the dead of the Vietnam War. In the ritual at Limon, it is specifically the missing who are memorialized, providing a ritual for those who have been left in limbo—both the missing themselves and those they have left behind, who have had no space provided for mourning those they have lost. The audience participation in the ritual joins all of us with those who are missing, and with those who mourn. The light of candles, the growing darkness, the open spaces of the looming plains ahead and the mountains behind us create a powerful ritual atmosphere, as do the voices of the dead responding to the calling of their names. They are still here, they remind us, still connected, and we should not forget. ("Missing but not forgotten," we responded in unison another year, as the names of the missing were read at this same ceremony.)

At the Wall: Confronting the Sacred Space

The Vietnam Veterans Memorial, with its two black granite wings engraved with the names of the over 58,000 American soldiers who died in Vietnam, is a particularly powerful symbol in that it memorializes both the individual and the collective dead. For many veterans, it is the Wall, and not individual grave sites, where the spirits of their dead comrades reside. And for many veterans, it is such an emotional and powerful place that they can scarcely bear to think about it, let alone visit. On my first journey with the Run, one veteran, also riding with the group for the first time, told me how terrified he was as we drew closer to our destination. He did manage to complete the journey, but, like many others, he was overcome with grief once he reached the memorial. For many, it is only because they have the support of the other pilgrims on this journey that they are able to make this pilgrimage and to confront its destination at the end.

There are no collective rituals at the Wall. Each of the pilgrims from the Run carries out his (or her) own symbolic acts, whether that be leaving important objects (wreaths, military objects, photographs, letters, and flowers), making rubbings of names, praying, or simply sitting in sorrow and contemplating the many names carved on the black granite surface. Although individual in their expression of grief and remembrance, these are rituals that would be recognized by pilgrims everywhere. Indeed, it is such activities—both the acts themselves and the many physical markers they leave behind—that often mark powerful and popular pilgrimage sites.

For many who are involved with the Run, the Wall has almost mystical powers. People speak of "Wall magic," the force that draws people to the Wall and to each other for healing. To touch a name on the Wall, I was told, is to call forth the soul of the person who died. And some veterans who keep vigil at the Wall the night after the Run arrives (the "Night Patrol") report hearing a cacophony of voices coming from the black granite surface, as if all the dead were trying to speak to them at once. Thus the Wall serves as a place of connection between worlds, between the living and the dead, as well as a place for remembering and for healing.

The Return

There are no special rituals marking the homeward journey of the Run for the Wall participants. Riders return home singly or with groups of friends, make a quick and direct journey or stop to visit friends and family, as they wish. But they return as different people, for the Run for the Wall, like many pilgrimages, is, among other things, a rite of passage and a ritual of transformation. Some have found at least a measure of peace and healing through their journey, through the support of other veterans and of those who host them along the way, and through their confrontation with the Wall and all that it represents. Others have "come out of the woods," out of the shame and guilt and sense of isolation that being a veteran has entailed, and have begun to acknowledge, and even to be proud of, their status as veterans. All have been given an opportunity—and space and support—to mourn the dead for whom the veteran's grief is often still intense and surprisingly fresh. And in a sense, many have been given the opportunity to ritually reenact the Vietnam War by riding for a cause (the POW/MIA issue) with fellow veterans, on an intense, difficult, and sometimes dangerous mission, arriving—this time in triumph—in the nation's capitol. Here, instead of the indifference and even hostility that met them when they returned from Vietnam, they are greeted with warmth and enthusiasm. Thus through ritual, they, in some sense, at least, "rewrite" their own history, as well as that of the war, and become heroes, at last, in what is for many "the parade they never had."

Conclusion: The Journey That Has No End

Pilgrimage, an ancient ritual, continues to flourish today in a range of forms. To understand its continuing popularity, we must also look to the many reasons why people undertake such ritual journeys. One of the answers to this may lie in the creative potential of pilgrimage itself, for, as the Run for the Wall illustrates, it is a ritual readily adapted to a variety of situations and to a range of human needs. Indeed, pilgrimage may be a perfect ritual for a contemporary global world, as it both lends itself to our individual purposes and desires and connects us to the larger world.

Like most rituals, the Run for the Wall, also offers itself to many meanings and interpretations. That two individuals who opposed the Vietnam War, and who find some of the kinds of patriotic sentiments celebrated on the Run distasteful, can nonetheless find their participation in the Run for the Wall one of the most moving and powerful experiences of their lives, is testimony to this. It became clearer to me through my own participation the ways in which a pilgrimage, like other rituals, can be many, even contradictory, things at once: a political movement and a personal journey of healing, a celebration of the warrior and a memorial to the tragedy of war, an experience of liminality by the marginal and a mode of integration and the overcoming of marginality, a journey away and a coming home.

As I write this article, the United States is once again engaged in foreign wars, in Iraq and in Afghanistan, and these wars are increasingly reflected in the Run for the Wall and its rituals. (Even prior to these wars, the Run had already attracted some Gulf War veterans, and had begun to broaden its mission to include the veterans, and the missing and the dead, of all American wars.) In 2003, Lori Piestewa, the first Native American woman to die in combat, was memorialized at Run for the Wall ceremonies in Gallup, New Mexico. In the 2004 Run, we were joined by both returning Iraq veterans and those about to be deployed, and prayers were offered daily for the safety of all those serving. Remembering their own treatment when they returned from war, several veterans reminded participants to be sure that today's returning veterans were better received and cared for. As the Vietnam veterans on the Run can testify, the wounds of war are deep and long lasting. For these reasons, then, the Run for the Wall is a ritual journey whose end is nowhere in sight.

Review Questions

1. What does Dubisch mean by the term *ritual?* What are the basic parts of rituals?

2. What is a pilgrimage, according to Dubisch? What are the common features of a pilgrimage?

3. What kind of people started the Run for the Wall? Why? What effect does Dubisch say the run has on its participants?

4. Dubisch argues that the Run for the Wall has a strong emotional and transformative impact on those who participate. What appears to generate such intense feelings?

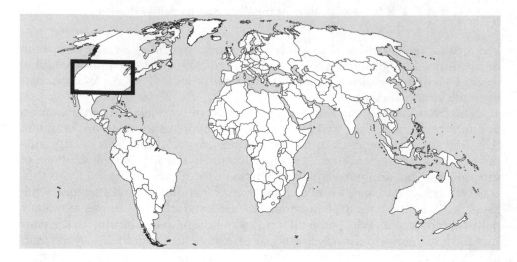

33

Body Ritual among the Nacirema

Horace Miner

Ritual involving repeated symbolic acts can be about many things—the growth of crops, the response to death, movement from one social identity to another, community solidarity, and much more. It can also be about one's body, including how to care for it, how to make it socially acceptable, and how to make it impressive to others. This classic article written in 1958 by Horace Miner describes the extensive body ritual of a North American group, the Nacirema, whose houses contain special shrines in which body ritual takes place. From the article, it is clear that the society's elaborate variety of body rituals reveals important Nacirema cultural values.

From Horace Miller, "Body Ritual among the Nacirema," *The American Anthropologist*, vol. 58, June 1956. Used by permission of Blackwell Publishing.

The anthropologist has become so familiar with the diversity of ways in which different peoples behave in similar situations that he is not apt to be surprised by even the most exotic customs. In fact, if all of the logically possible combinations of behavior have not been found somewhere in the world, he is apt to suspect that they must be present in some yet undescribed tribe. This point has, in fact, been expressed with respect to clan organization by Murdock. In this light, the magical beliefs and practices of the Nacirema present such unusual aspects that it seems desirable to describe them as an example of the extremes to which human behavior can go.

Professor Linton first brought the ritual of the Nacirema to the attention of anthropologists twenty years ago, but the culture of this people is still very poorly understood. They are a North American group living in the territory between the Canadian Cree, the Yaqui and Tarahumare of Mexico, and the Carib and Arawak of the Antilles. Little is known of their origin, although tradition states that they came from the east. . . .

Nacirema culture is characterized by a highly developed market economy which has evolved in a rich natural habitat. While much of the people's time is devoted to economic pursuits, a large part of the fruits of these labors and a considerable portion of the day are spent in ritual activity. The focus of this activity is the human body, the appearance and health of which loom as a dominant concern in the ethos of the people. While such a concern is certainly not unusual, its ceremonial aspects and associated philosophy are unique.

The fundamental belief underlying the whole system appears to be that the human body is ugly and that its natural tendency is to debility and disease. Incarcerated in such a body, man's only hope is to avert these characteristics through the use of the powerful influences of ritual and ceremony. Every household has one or more shrines devoted to this purpose. The more powerful individuals in the society have several shrines in their houses and, in fact, the opulence of a house is often referred to in terms of the number of such ritual centers it possesses. Most houses are of wattle and daub construction, but the shrine rooms of the more weathly are walled with stone. Poorer families imitate the rich by applying pottery plaques to their shrine walls.

While each family has at least one such shrine, the rituals associated with it are not family ceremonies but are private and secret. The rites are normally only discussed with children, and then only during the period when they are being initiated into these mysteries. I was able, however, to establish sufficient rapport with the natives to examine these shrines and to have the rituals described to me.

The focal point of the shrine is a box or chest which is built into the wall. In this chest are kept the many charms and magical potions without which no native believes he could live. These preparations are secured from a variety of specialized practitioners. The most powerful of these are the medicine men, whose assistance must be rewarded with substantial gifts. However, the medicine men do not provide the curative potions for their clients, but decide what the ingredients should be and then write them down in an ancient and secret language. This writing is understood only by the medicine men and by the herbalists who, for another gift, provide the required charm.

The charm is not disposed of after it has served its purpose, but is placed in the charm–box of the household shrine. As these magical materials are specific for certain ills, and the real or imagined maladies of the people are many, the charm–box is usually full to overflowing. The magical packets are so numerous that people forget what their purposes were and fear to use them again. While the natives are very vague on this point, we can only assume that the idea in retaining all the old magical materials is that their presence in the charm–box, before which the body rituals are conducted, will in some way protect the worshipper.

Beneath the charm–box is a small font. Each day every member of the family, in succession, enters the shrine room, bows his head before the charm–box, mingles different sorts of holy water in the font, and proceeds with a brief rite of ablution. The holy waters are secured from the Water Temple of the community, where the priests conduct elaborate ceremonies to make the liquid ritually pure.

In the hierarchy of magical practitioners, and below the medicine men in prestige, are specialists whose designation is best translated "holy–mouth–men." The Nacirema have an almost pathological horror of and fascination with the mouth, the condition of which is believed to have a supernatural influence on all social relationships. Were it not for the rituals of the mouth, they believe that their teeth would fall out, their gums bleed, their jaws shrink, their friends desert them, and their lovers reject them. They also believe that a strong relationship exists between oral and moral characteristics. For example, there is a ritual ablution of the mouth for children which is supposed to improve their moral fiber.

The daily body ritual performed by everyone includes a mouth–rite. Despite the fact that these people are so punctilious about care of the mouth, this rite involves a practice which strikes the uninitiated stranger as revolting. It was reported to me that the ritual consists of inserting a small bundle of hog hairs into the mouth, along with certain magical powders, and then moving the bundle in a highly formalized series of gestures.

In addition to the private mouth–rite, the people seek out a holy–mouth–man once or twice a year. These practitioners have an impressive set of paraphernalia, consisting of a variety of augers, awls, probes, and prods. The use of these objects in the exorcism of the evils of the mouth involves almost unbelievable ritual torture of the client. The holy–mouth–man opens the client's mouth and, using the above mentioned tools, enlarges any holes which decay may have created in the teeth. Magical materials are put into these holes. If there are no naturally occurring holes in the teeth, large sections of one or more teeth are gouged out so that the supernatural substance can be applied. In the client's view, the purpose of these ministrations is to arrest decay and to draw friends. The extremely sacred and traditional character of the rite is evident in the fact that the natives return to the holy–mouth–men year after year, despite the fact that their teeth continue to decay.

It is to be hoped that, when a thorough study of the Nacirema is made, there will be careful inquiry into the personality structure of these people. One has but to watch the gleam in the eye of a holy–mouth–man, as he jabs an awl into an exposed nerve, to suspect that a certain amount of sadism is involved. If this can be established, a very interesting pattern emerges, for most of the population shows definite masochistic tendencies. It was to these that Professor Linton referred in discussing a distinctive part of the daily body ritual which is performed only by men. This part of the rite involves scraping and lacerating the surface of the face with a sharp instrument. Special women's rites are performed only four times during each lunar month, but what they lack in frequency is made up in barbarity. As part of this ceremony, women bake their heads in small ovens for about an hour. The theoretically interesting point is that what seems to be a preponderantly masochistic people have developed sadistic specialists.

The medicine men have an imposing temple, or *latipso*, in every community of any size. The more elaborate ceremonies required to treat very sick patients can only be performed at this temple. These ceremonies involve not only the thaumaturge but a permanent group of vestal maidens who move sedately about the temple chambers in distinctive costume and headdress.

The *latipso* ceremonies are so harsh that it is phenomenal that a fair proportion of the really sick natives who enter the temple ever recover. Small children whose indoctrination is still incomplete have been known to resist attempts to take them to the temple because "that is where you go to die." Despite this fact, sick adults are not only willing but eager to undergo the protracted ritual purification, if they can afford to do so. No matter how ill the supplicant or how grave the emergency, the guardians of many temples will not admit a client if he cannot give a rich gift to the custodian. Even after one has gained admission and survived the ceremonies, the guardians will not permit the neophyte to leave until he makes still another gift.

The supplicant entering the temple is first stripped of all his or her clothes. In everyday life the Nacirema avoids exposure of his body and its natural functions. Bathing and excretory acts are performed only in the secrecy of the household shrine, where they are ritualized as part of the body–rites. Psychological shock results from the fact that body secrecy is suddenly lost upon entry into the *latipso*. A man, whose own wife has never seen him in an excretory act, suddenly finds himself naked and assisted by a vestal maiden while he performs his natural functions into a sacred vessel. This sort of ceremonial treatment is necessitated by the fact that the excreta are used by a diviner to ascertain the course and nature of the client's sickness. Female clients, on the other hand, find their naked bodies are subjected to the scrutiny, manipulation and prodding of the medicine men.

Few supplicants in the temple are well enough to do anything but lie on their hard beds. The daily ceremonies, like the rites of the holy–mouth–men, involve discomfort and torture. With ritual precision, the vestals awaken their miserable charges each dawn and roll them about on their beds of pain while performing ablutions, in the formal movements of which the maidens are highly trained. At other times they insert magic wands in the supplicant's mouth or force him to eat substances which are supposed to be healing. From time to time the medicine men come to their clients and jab magically treated needles into their flesh. The fact that these temple ceremonies may not cure, and may even kill the neophyte, in no way decreases the people's faith in the medicine men.

There remains one other kind of practitioner, known as a "listener." This witchdoctor has the power to exorcise the devils that lodge in the heads of people who have been bewitched. The Nacirema believe that parents bewitch their own children. Mothers are particularly suspected of putting a curse on children while teaching them the secret body rituals. The counter-magic of the witchdoctor is unusual in its lack of ritual. The patient simply tells the "listener" all his troubles and fears, beginning with the earliest difficulties he can remember. The memory displayed by the Nacirema in these exorcism sessions is truly remarkable. It is not uncommon for the patient to bemoan the rejection he felt upon being weaned as a babe, and a few individuals even see their troubles going back to the traumatic effects of their own birth.

In conclusion, mention must be made of certain practices which have their base in native esthetics but which depend upon the pervasive aversion to the natural body and its functions. There are ritual fasts to make fat people thin and ceremonial feasts to make thin people fat. Still other rites are used to make women's breasts larger if they are small, and smaller if they are large. General dissatisfaction with breast shape is symbolized in the fact that the ideal form is virtually outside the range of human variation. A few women afflicted with almost inhuman hyper-mammary development are so idolized that they make a handsome living by simply going from village to village and permitting the natives to stare at them for a fee.

Reference has already been made to the fact that excretory functions are ritualized, routinized, and relegated to secrecy. Natural reproductive functions are similarly distorted. Intercourse is taboo as a topic and scheduled as an act. Efforts are made to avoid pregnancy by the use of magical materials or by limiting intercourse to certain phases of the moon. Conception is actually very infrequent. When pregnant, women dress so as to hide their condition. Parturition takes place in secret, without friends or relatives to assist, and the majority of women do not nurse their infants.

Our review of the ritual life of the Nacirema has certainly shown them to be a magic–ridden people. It is hard to understand how they have managed to exist so long under the burdens which they have imposed upon themselves. But even such exotic customs as these take on real meaning when they are viewed with the insight provided by Malinowski when he wrote:

"Looking from far and above, from our high places of safety in the developed civilization, it is easy to see all the crudity and irrelevance of magic. But without its power and guidance early man could not have mastered his practical difficulties as he has done, nor could man have advanced to the higher stages of civilization."

Review Questions

1. Where are the Nacirema located?

2. Describe the main body rituals that occur in Nacireman household shrines.

3. What kinds of ritual specialists does Miner describe for the Nacirema in this article? What do they function to do for people?

4. What is the *latipso,* and for what is it used?

5. What do you think the psychological functions of Nacireman body ritual are, and how do these fit with Malinowski's theory about the functions of religion and magic described in the earlier article on baseball magic?

NINE

GLOBALIZATION

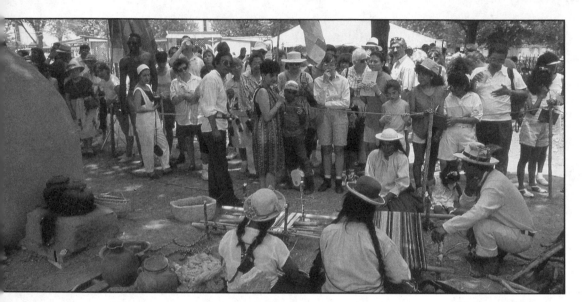

Paul Conklin/PhotoEdit Inc.

READINGS IN THIS SECTION

The Road to Refugee Resettlement   344
Dianna Shandy

Why Tourism Matters   354
Sharon Bohn Gmelch

Japanese Hip-Hop and the Globalization of Popular Culture   365
Ian Condry

Several times a week, a small island freighter leaves Granada's Saint George's harbor loaded with fuel drums, crates of processed food, boxes containing manufactured goods, and an occasional motor scooter or car. When its hold is filled, 60 or 70 passengers, many of them women, troop across the gang plank and settle down among the freight or take a seat in a small cabin set aside for them on the upper aft deck. They are bound for their small island home, Carriacou, located about 35 miles by sea to the north. Most are returning from overseas work in New York, Britain, or mainland Europe, where they worked for a few years as maids and cleaners or at other service jobs. Carrying gifts of CD players, clothing, shoes, and other items manufactured outside their island, they will be greeted warmly by their relatives, whom they have alerted by phone or e-mail about the time of their arrival. Most returnees have already wired home money they saved from their off-island work and are beginning to think about using it to build a house or buy items that will make their lives easier and more secure.

The people returning to Carriacou illustrate a major trend that is sweeping the world: globalization. **Globalization** consists of powerful forces that reshape local conditions on an ever-intensifying scale.[1] Although places such as Carriacou may seem peripheral to globalization, the impact of international money, tourists, transportation, goods, and the movement of the island's peoples to other parts of the world have all affected the way people live there. And their experience is repeated in many other parts of the world.

Globalization may occur on several levels. In the most general and formal sense, we can talk about it as a world system. The **world system** is often defined in market terms and links nations and people together economically. More accurately, it is **transnational;** it consists of companies and patterns of exchange that transcend national borders and may evade control by individual governments. An international company may have a headquarters located in Bermuda; manufacturing facilities in Atlanta, Mexico, and Shanghai; customer service representatives in Mumbai; and investors from thirty or forty different countries. Japanese cars and motorcycles sold in the United States reflect the transnational world system. So do the tuna caught by American trawlers in the Atlantic and shipped overnight to Japan to make sushi.

The world system affects local conditions by providing goods, stimulating production, and introducing ideas. As a result, local people can easily find themselves both motivated by and at the mercy of world markets. For example, the government of India, through its state and district development offices, encouraged tribals living in Southern Rajasthan to dedicate some of their cropland to sericulture (silk worm production). Local farmers borrowed money to

---

[1]This definition is taken from Emily Schultz and Robert Lavenda, *Cultural Anthropology: A Perspective on the Human Condition,* 6th ed. (New York: Oxford University Press, 2005), p. 363.

build "cocoon houses," and to underwrite the cost of fertilizing mulberry bushes for the silk worms to eat. The World Bank advanced money for a small cocoon processing factory. The program was a success—farmers doubled their money each year; women earned wages in the processing plant—until, that is, the Chinese government arbitrarily lowered the price of the silk its farmers produced by half. Unable to compete, the Indian program failed, disrupting the lives of people who embraced it. Stories like this should not come as a surprise to American workers who have lost jobs to "outsourcing," and to factory workers in other countries who are now employed to take their place.

The international movement of people also illustrates globalization. **Refugees,** people who immigrate to other parts of the world because it is too dangerous for them to stay in their homeland, have moved to many countries. **Guest workers** (people granted permission to work in a country other than their own) are found in many parts of the world. Legal immigrants (and illegal immigrants) diversify populations in many nations. The result is that some societies are becoming **multicultural;** people with different cultural backgrounds live side by side. Just as companies can be transnational, so can immigrants, workers, and refugees. People who originate from the same cultural areas often communicate with one another, calling or e-mailing home, wiring money to each other, and forming a visiting network. Tourism is the world's largest industry and regularly brings people with different backgrounds into contact.

Finally, globalization is marked by cultural diffusion. **Cultural diffusion,** or cultural borrowing, represents the movement of cultural ideas and artifacts from one society to another. Coca Cola has diffused from the United States to many parts of the world; sushi has diffused from Japan to the United States and Europe. So have musical styles, forms of dress, words, and a variety of other cultural items.

In almost every case, societies that borrow aspects of another group's culture adapt them to their own ways of life. Borrowed items usually undergo **cultural hybridization;** they are a mixture of the borrowed and the local. A hamburger in China will probably not taste exactly like one cooked on the backyard grill of an American family. Curry in the United States tastes different from the "real thing" prepared in India. (Note that as the local size of immigrant populations rise, more genuine, meaning closer to its ethnic origins, food becomes available to the original residents as well.)

The articles in Part Nine illustrate several of these points. The first, by Dianna Shandy, is an updated version of an article included in the previous edition. It describes the ordeal faced by Nuer refugees as they attempt to gain admittance and establish a life in the United States. Fleeing the civil war that has wracked their home in southern Sudan, Nuer refugees must develop the skill and determination to pass through a series of bureaucratic hurdles to reach and adjust to life in the United States. Personal initiative, education, using U.S. Nongovernmental organizations (NGOs), and the sharing of information about what works are keys to their success. The second article, by Sharon Bohn Gmelch, stresses the importance of tourism as a global phenomenon. It is the world's largest business and is not only economically important but also a major agent of culture change. In the third article, Ian Condry describes a form of pop culture, hip-hop, that has spread from the United States to Japan. Reviewing more general globalization theory, he shows how hip-hop has been hybridized in the Japanese context and how anthropologists, with their emphasis on local settings, can show what globalization means to people as they conduct their daily lives.

Key Terms

cultural diffusion   p. 342
cultural hybridization   p. 342
globalization   p. 341
guest workers   p. 342

multicultural   p. 342
refugees   p. 342
transnational   p. 341
world system   p. 341

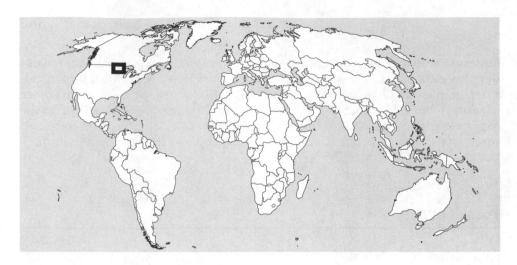

34

The Road to Refugee Resettlement

Dianna Shandy

In the early days of the discipline, anthropologists usually studied non-Western groups that they assumed were bounded and clearly definable. Such groups were named (often by outsiders) and were thought to have territories and a common language and culture. Although anthropologists recognized that many of the groups they studied had outside connections—that they freely borrowed culture, intermarried, and migrated—most still felt it was reasonable to talk about groups as if they were bounded units. However, the picture is changing, as this updated article by Dianna Shandy clearly shows. Today people are on the move. Some are migrants looking for economic opportunity; others are refugees. Here Shandy, using the case of the Nuer from southern Sudan, shows how refugees fleeing a perpetual civil war manage to gain relocation in the United States and how they have sought to adapt to the demands of life among Americans. A key to the process is the role played by the United Nations and social service agencies and the Nuer's own determination to better (in their terms) themselves.

―――――――――

A Nuer youth, Thok Ding (not his real name) lies prone alongside two other boys on the dusty, clay ground on the outskirts of a village in southern Sudan. A man crouches over him with a razor blade. Beginning with the right side, the man makes six parallel cuts from each side of the youth's forehead to the center to create scars called *gaar*. This ritual scarification, which has been outlawed in Nuer areas since the 1980s, still marks entry into manhood for many Nuer young men.

A few years later in Minneapolis, Minnesota, Thok sits in pained concentration in front of a computer screen in a driver's license examination office. Still weak in English, he struggles to recall the multiple choice response sequence he memorized to pass the exam, in this stressful, but less painful, American rite of passage into adulthood.

When I began ethnographic work among Nuer refugees living in Minnesota, Iowa, and several other regions of the United States in 1997, I immediately was struck by the incongruity of their lives. The Nuer are a famous people in anthropology. They were the subject of three books by the well-known late British social anthropologist, Sir Edward E. Evans-Pritchard, who described their pastoralist mode of subsistence, complex segmented kinship system, and religion. Evans-Pritchard conducted research among the Nuer in the 1930s. He described the Nuer as a tall, independent, confident people whose existence revolved around the needs of their cattle, especially the requirement to move the animals from high to low ground and back again each year. During the dry season from September to April, the cattle were herded to lower ground where there was still water and grass. During the rainy season, the lowlands became a swampy lagoon and the herds had to be moved to the highlands where rain had restored the range. This transhumant lifestyle and the need to guard cattle against raiders from nearby tribes had shaped Nuer society. (The Nuer were also the subject of a well-known ethnographic film, "The Nuer," made by Robert Gardner and released in 1970, which showed them to be much as Evans-Pritchard had described them.)

So when I first met Nuer people in Minnesota in the mid-1990s, these Northeast African pastoralists seemed out of place. Tall (most men are well over six feet in height) and still displaying the (for men) prominent forehead scars received at their initiations, the Nuer had come to live in one of the coldest parts of the United States. Why had they left their ancestral home? What did their status as refugees mean and how did they get it? How had they managed to come to the United States? Why had they been located, as it turns out, in more than 30 different U.S. states? How would a people raised as cattle herders adapt to American urban settings? Would they remain in the United States on a temporary or permanent basis? How would they maintain a relationship with the families they left behind? And finally in a broader sense, what does all this tell us about the interconnectedness of a globalizing world and about anthropology's role in it?

Becoming a Refugee

Until recently, most Americans called the people who settled here, *immigrants*. No distinctions were made based on the reasons people came here or the circumstances they had left behind. In general, their arrival was encouraged and welcome because the country was spacious and their skills and labor were needed.

Today, things are different. There are immigrants and *refugees*. In the past, refugees were a kind of immigrant. They were people who came here to escape from intolerable conditions in their homelands, such as pogroms, the threat of military conscription, civil wars, and famine. The fact that they were escaping from something, however, did not affect whether or not they could enter the United States. Most people, especially those from Europe, were welcome.

Over the last fifty years, however, refugees have come to occupy a formal status, both in the eyes of the United Nations and U.S. immigration officials. They are not just *internally displaced persons* or *(IDPs)*, those who have left their homes but who are still in their own country. Officially, meaning how the United Nations and national governments define them, a refugee group is one that shares a "well founded fear of persecution" based on any of five factors such as race, religion, nationality, membership in a particular social group, or political opinion, and who has left their home country. How the UN or national governments apply this definition when they seek to certify individuals as refugees varies. But the number of people that claim to fit this description and who seek asylum skyrocketed at the end of the cold war in 1989 to an estimated 14 million in 2008.

Bureaucracies control who can be classified as a refugee. In 1950 the United Nations established a formal agency to help with the refugee "problem" headed by the United Nations High Commissioner for Refugees (UNHCR). The agency recognizes three options, or what it calls "durable solutions," to address the situation of refugees around the world: voluntary repatriation to the country of origin, integration into a country of asylum, or rarely, third country resettlement, meaning a move from one country of asylum to one that offers possibilities for a more permanent home. Initially housed in refugee camps, displaced people can apply for official refugee status with the hope of resettlement in another country, or that conditions will stabilize in their own country, allowing them to return home.

Many countries have agreed to take in a limited number of refugees as a way of settling them more permanently, and the United States is one of them. To do this the U.S. sets a limit on the number of refugees it will accept each year and uses a bureaucratic process to screen prospective refugees it might be willing to take in. Over the past decade, the U.S. has resettled an average of 57,895 refugees here each year, with a sharp dip in numbers in the wake of September 11, 2001. The process is complicated by the fact that the criteria for admission can change, different government officials interpret the criteria dissimilarly, and resettlement policy can shift from one year to the next. It is also complicated by cross-cultural misunderstanding. The U.S. bureaucracy works differently from the way governments operate in the refugee's country of origin. Languages are a major barrier. Categories of meaning are not shared. The screening process is intended to determine "real" refugees, or those who cannot be protected by their home governments, and "economic" migrants who leave their home voluntarily to seek a better life. In practice the distinction is often difficult to establish.

The Nuer living in Minnesota and other regions of the United States have managed to come through this process successfully. They have made it to camps that process refugees, discovered how to enter the bureaucratic process designed to certify them as refugees, learned how to tell a sufficiently convincing refugee story to gain certification and found a way to get on the list to be resettled in the U.S.

Thok Ding's life illustrates this process. Thok was born in southern Sudan and lived in a small village. As in most Nuer households, Thok lived with his mother, father, siblings, and his father's extended family. Thok had family members who lived in town and attended school, but there was no school in his village. His first memory is of going to the forest to take care of his calves when he was seven or eight. He would leave home in the early morning with other boys his age, taking food with him to eat while he was grazing the cattle and protecting the calves from wild animals. Girls, on the other hand, would stay closer to home and were charged with milking the cows.

When he was in his early teens, he, along with other boys who were the same age, underwent the ritual scarification *gaar* ceremony ushering him into manhood. After undergoing this painful ritual, Thok said that now that he was a man, he could be "free." "You can do whatever you like. You can have a woman. You can have a home by yourself. You can live away from your parents."

Shortly after his initiation, the civil war that wracked the southern Sudan caught up with him. Fueled by events that extend back much further in time, civil war engulfed Sudan for much of the period since it gained independence from joint English-Egyptian colonial rule in 1956, with just a brief interlude of peace from the early 1970s until 1983. In 2005, a peace agreement was signed between southern rebels and the Khartoum government ending what is known as the North-South war in Sudan. This conflict in the Sudan frequently is attributed to social distinctions based on geography (north-south), ethnicity (Arab-African), and religion (Muslim-Christian). But, as the more recent and ongoing Darfur crisis has illustrated, these are fluid categories. From a southern perspective, northern Muslim Arabs entered their land in the 1800s looking for ivory and slaves. Northerners were favored under colonial rule, which gave them more power and increased tension with people, such as the Nuer, living in the south. From 1983–2005, it was the Khartoum government, located in the north, that was engaged in war with southerners who were seeking self-government. As of this writing, it remains unclear whether the peace agreement will endure and, if so, for how long.

Nuer society has suffered cataclysmic shifts in the decades since Evans-Pritchard conducted his fieldwork, a fact well documented by anthropologist Sharon Hutchinson in her book entitled *Nuer Dilemmas* published in

1996. For example, instead of merely regulating Nuer seasonal cattle drives, the change of seasons in the southern Sudan also dictates the rhythm of the civil war. The dry season makes it possible to move heavy artillery across the clay plains; during the wet season the same plains are impassable. The war and the displacement of Nuer and other southern Sudanese it has caused are the major cause of migration.

In the late 1980s, government troops attacked Thok's village, killing many people including his father. Although many of the survivors elected to stay and to keep herding cattle, with his father dead Thok felt it was wisest to leave Sudan after this tragedy. He traveled on foot for three days with his mother and siblings and their cattle to an Ethiopian refugee camp called Itang.

One feature of camp life was the presence of a Christian mission school, which provided Thok with his first taste of formal education, something that would prove useful later as he sought refugee status. He advanced quickly in school, skipping several grades. Seventh grade stands out for him as the real beginning of his education, however, because he passed a national exam. As a result, he was transferred to Gambela, another Ethiopian camp, to attend school, leaving his mother and siblings behind. Food scarcity made life in Gambela very difficult. Thok recalls that students were given only a small amount of corn each month. They would grind the grain into flour, cook the mixture with water, and eat it plain without a stew.

His education at Gambela progressed nicely, but was ended when war now broke out in Ethiopia. Threatened by the dangers it posed, Thok rejoined his mother and siblings. Together they returned to Sudan where the U.N. had established a temporary camp to care for the Sudanese refugees who were streaming back across the border from Ethiopia. Thok weighed his options and decided to return to Ethiopia on his own. He went to the capital of Ethiopia, Addis Ababa, where he encountered some friends from school who shared information on how to get to refugee camps in Kenya.

He traveled to Kenya by bus, negotiating his way past border and police checkpoints along the way. He was arrested once by Kenyan police and had to spend the night in jail before they turned him over to the U.N. authorities that ran the nearby refugee camp. Once in the camp, he filled out a form that documented his background, and requested that he be considered for resettlement in another country. Since Thok had no relatives who had been resettled in other countries, he applied for resettlement anywhere that would accept refugees from the Sudan. These included Australia, Canada, and Sweden as well as the United States, the country that finally admitted him.

Two years elapsed from the time Thok arrived in the camp until he was sent to the United States. Life in the Kenyan camp was much more difficult than the one he had stayed at in Ethiopia. There was nothing to do, no river, no place to keep cattle, and no garden plots. Thok did, however, meet some friends he had made earlier in school, and together they cooked food and found ways to pass the long days in the camp. He and his friends also listened to the stories other Nuer told of their encounters with the refugee officials who interviewed people requesting resettlement. In a tragic commentary on how devastation can seem "normal," they learned that the biggest mistake people made was to invent dramatic stories to make themselves eligible for resettlement. For example, one Nuer man said, "People feel they need a reason, so they tell the person interviewing them that they killed someone and if they return to Sudan they will be put in jail. But the story didn't work because the interviewer thought the refugee must be a violent man." The Nuer men who worked as interpreters in the camps believed there was a better approach. "We told the community, we need to tell them the reality. Don't say you killed someone, just say you were caught in the crossfire." They had learned that the refugee officials were looking for certain kinds of experiences to determine who fit the criteria for refugee resettlement.

In addition to recounting a plausible story that indicates why they would be persecuted if they returned home, refugees must also pass a medical screening, and they must also sign a promissory note to repay the cost of their airfare to the United States once they have settled and found work. Thok passed through this process successfully, and with a ticket provided for him by the International Organization for Migration, flew to the United States. He was met at the airport by a representative from Lutheran Social Services, one of many U.S. voluntary agencies responsible for resettling refugees.

Adapting to America

Some immigrants to the United States rely on family or friends to help them find a home, job, and place in America. But many refugees depend on voluntary agencies or "volags" to help with settlement. These agencies are under contract to the U.S. government and receive a stipend for each refugee that they place. Volags help refugees with such necessities as finding a find a place to live, getting a job, learning to ride the bus, and buying food. They also help them complete paperwork documenting the existence of family members who were left behind, since there may be a chance to bring them over later. Volags emphasize how important it is for refugees to find a job and become self-sufficient. Volags provide refugees with a small initial cash stipend to help them get established. But the money doesn't last long and refugees are encouraged to start working as soon as possible, often within the first week or two after arrival. An agency helped place Thok in Minnesota, find him an apartment, and assisted with a job search.

There were about 30 refugees from Sudan and Somalia on Thok's flight from Nairobi, Kenya, to New York's JFK International Airport. When Thok boarded the plane, he knew no one. By the time he arrived in New York many hours later, he felt like the eight Sudanese men he had traveled with were his new best friends. In a wrenching sort of dispersal, the eight men were all directed by airline staff to different gates at the airport to await the next leg of their journey to far-flung destinations, like San Diego, California; Nashville, Tennessee; Dallas, Texas; and Minneapolis, Minnesota.

A representative from Lutheran Social Services and a volunteer from a local church greeted Thok when he arrived on his own in Minneapolis. His few possessions fit in a small bag that he carried with him on the plane. The man from Lutheran Social Services gave him shampoo and a toothbrush and took him to Burger King. Thok found the food very strange and difficult to eat. Thok stayed the first night in the volunteer's home—a widower in his mid-sixties who regularly helped out Lutheran Social Services in this way. Thok spoke some English, but he relied mostly on gestures to communicate with his host. The next day the volunteer took Thok to Lutheran Social Services to complete paperwork.

When they finished with the paperwork, the case manager who had met Thok at the airport took him to what was to be his apartment. Thok found the place to be very dirty, particularly the carpeting that had not been cleaned after the last tenants departed. There was a strong smell of cigarette smoke, cockroaches in the kitchen, and a very leaky faucet in the bathroom. Despite these problems, Thok would have his own place that would be affordable when he got a job. Later, the man Thok had stayed with the previous night brought over some furniture that had been donated by church members.

Over the coming week, Thok met with his case manager to discuss getting a job. Where refugees work and the kinds of jobs that they can get depend somewhat on the level of education and training they received prior to arrival in the United States. Upon arrival, most Nuer have little formal education and can, unfortunately, only find jobs that most people born in the U.S. do not want such as unskilled factory worker, security guard, parking lot attendant, fast food server, and nursing home assistant. Or, if they do have a degree when they arrive, like many immigrants, they are "underemployed," or work in jobs below their level of credentials. Many of the Nuer who have settled in the upper Midwest have found work in meat packing plants. Thok first got a job filling beverage trays for airplanes at the airport after he arrived in the United States. His back and arms ached from the lifting he was required to do, and he did not like his boss.

Several weeks later, Thok spotted another Nuer man while he was shopping at Target. Thok did not know him personally, but after they started talking he discovered that he knew the village where the man was from in the Sudan. It was good to see someone from "home," and Thok invited him back to his apartment to cook a meal and eat together. This man had moved to Minnesota from Iowa and was able to tell Thok the names and even the phone numbers of some Nuer who were living in Des Moines. Thok knew some of these people from the refugee camps in Ethiopia, and the next day he bought a phone card to get in touch. Thok could hardly believe his ears when he heard his friend John Wal answer the phone. After a conversation that lasted until the phone card expired, Thok decided to board a bus and leave Minnesota to move to Iowa. John had talked about the sizable Nuer community living in Des Moines and the well-paying jobs offered by a meat packing company. Thok called his case manager and left a message saying that he was going. He packed his personal items, left the furniture in the apartment, and boarded a Greyhound bus.

In Des Moines, Thok moved in with John and another Nuer man. Thok worked in a packing plant for a while, but found it very difficult. At first his job was to kill pigs as they entered the processing line. He found it so hard to sleep at night after doing this over and over again all day that he asked to be transferred to some other part of the line. He still found the work exceedingly hard. One motivation to find a job quickly is to make it possible to bring over his family members to join him, but Thok has not managed to do this yet.

In addition to his mother and siblings, Thok would also like to bring over a wife. There are roughly three Nuer men for every Nuer woman in the United States, and most of the women are already married or engaged to be married. Thok and other Nuer men struggle with what they perceive as "the unreasonable levels of freedom" afforded to women in U.S. society. One way to marry a wife with more "traditional" Nuer values, or so men think, is to let their family facilitate a marriage in the Sudan or in Ethiopia and try to bring the wife over as a spouse or a refugee.

Staying in Touch

Refugee groups are deliberately "scattered" geographically across the United States when they are resettled. Policymakers believe that dispersal increases individuals' ability to adapt successfully to their new environment and that it decreases any disruptive impact on the host community that receives the refugees. However, even though refugees are "placed" in particular locales in the United States, they seldom stay put. Hmong, originally from the highlands of South East Asia, and now residents of Saint Paul, Minnesota, are a case in point. They, like the Nuer, are well known for moving frequently after arrival in the United States. Nuer, who moved regularly as part of their lives in southern Sudan, continue a kind of nomadism in the U.S. Nuer move frequently—from apartment to apartment, from city to city, and from state to state. As a result of having been resettled in more than thirty different states in America, Nuer have many residency options to consider and have a tendency to move where they have relatives, friends, or jobs.

Staying in contact is very important to many Nuer refugees. They are adept at devising strategies for remaining in contact with other Nuer dispersed across the United States and those whom they left behind in Africa. The process of incorporation into the United States as a refugee is also about maintaining ties to Africa. One aspect of Nuer life that sets them apart from the experiences of previous waves of immigrants to the United States is the means by which they keep in contact with those who remain at home in the Sudan, in refugee camps in neighboring African states, and around the world.

Immigrants have always retained some ties with the homes they left. But, in a twenty-first century context the possibilities for frequent, affordable, and rapid contact are greatly expanded. Anthropologists refer to these crosscutting social ties that span the borders of nation-states as *transnationalism*. For instance, Thok, who wants to marry, could phone his brother in Gambela, Ethiopia, to arrange the event. He can use Western Union to send money to his brother to buy cows to give to the prospective bride's father. In Nuer eyes, the groom does not even need to be present for the marriage to be legitimate, but this is not true in the eyes of immigration authorities. Even though the groom can do his part to sponsor the marriage from the United States, he still must travel to Ethiopia for the marriage to be recognized officially for immigration purposes. The bride can apply as a refugee herself but increases her chances of resettlement by also applying as a spouse joining her husband.

Sudan ranks third, after Palestine and Afghanistan, in a list of countries that has produced the most refugees. Those in the diaspora maintain close ties with friends and family in the Sudan, in other African countries, and around the world. Therefore, a focus on the lives of Sudanese refugees in Africa is an important part of understanding Nuer refugees' lives in the United States. These transnational linkages influence Nuer peoples' decisions in the United States.

Conclusion

Refugees are a special category of immigrant to the United States. Often seen as victims of tragic circumstances, refugees are also amazingly adept at finding ways to survive these same circumstances. Refugees' lives depend on an international and national bureaucracy, and those who pass through the process represent a very small percentage of people who are displaced. Starting a life in a vastly different cultural environment than the one they were raised in presents a number of hardships. Refugees cope with these challenges by trying to maintain their original ethnic group identity. Transnational communication is one way to do this. So is moving to find people they know from their homelands.

Anthropologists, such as Evans-Pritchard, used to journey to faraway places to study distant "others." Nowadays it is often the objects of study that make the journey to the land of the anthropologists. Refugees such as the Nuer are among the latest newcomers to urban and suburban areas in the United States, and anthropologists can play a role in the adaptation process of Nuer in America. For example, some anthropologists work for voluntary agencies where what they learn about refugees through their ability to conduct ethnographic research helps to ease refugee adjustment to unfamiliar surroundings. Other anthropologists work at the federal and state levels to advise about the efficacy of the social programs designed to meet the needs of recently arrived populations and suggest changes if they are needed. Sometimes these roles take the form of advocacy.

But through it all, anthropologists still do fieldwork in much the same way. They learn the language of refugee populations, ask open-ended questions in interviews, conduct participant observation at such events as weddings, funerals, graduation ceremonies, and political meetings, and try to understand life from their informants' perspective.

Although he now knows an anthropologist, Thok Ding goes about his new life in America with the same independent determination that got him here in the first place. He will continue to move his residence if he thinks it will help him, increase his level of education, find better paying jobs, and eventually if all works out, marry a woman from the Sudan, bring his whole family to the United States and in the end, become a new American.

Review Questions

1. According to Shandy, what is the formal United Nations definition of a refugee?

2. What steps do displaced persons have to take to achieve resettlement as refugees?

3. How have Nuer refugees reorganized their lives to live successfully in the United States?

4. How have migrants to the United States changed the way anthropologists define groups they study and the focus of their research?

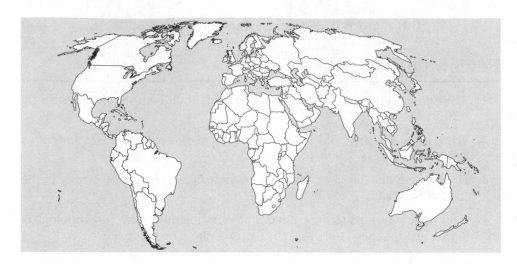

35

Why Tourism Matters

Sharon Bohn Gmelch

On a hot humid morning in 2001, sixty people transferred from an excursion yacht to a small flotilla of outboard-motor powered dugout canoes. After a two-hour trip from the ocean bay where the yacht was anchored to a river and one of its side tributaries, they arrived near a small village. Young boys and girls greeted them at the riverbank and took them by the hand up a forest path to a village of open-faced houses built on stilts. Once there, they were greeted by bare-breasted women who showed them baskets and other craft items for sale and offered to paint their arms and faces in traditional fashion.

The tourists were part of an Elder Hostel tour to Panama. They were on a one-day ecotour to visit the Embera in the Panamanian province of Darien. Before the trip, an anthropologist who had lived and worked with the Embera gave the tourists a careful orientation. Armed with this knowledge, their trip to the village not only taught them something about cultural diversity but also brought money and change to the Embera community. It was, however, also the beginning of a change in the way the Embera villagers lived, thought about themselves, and viewed the world outside their community.

The Embera trip is only one small example of a worldwide phenomenon, the meteoric rise of tourism in today's world. For many, despite its prevalence, tourism is viewed as a trivial matter. It is simply a form of recreation, a time for people to vacation or view exotic peoples like customers at a sideshow. For anthropology, however, tourism is a major global force. As Sharon Gmelch points out in this article, tourism is the world's largest business; it brings cross-cultural difference to tourist and natives alike. It has major economic, ecological, and cultural consequences. For anthropologists, she argues, the study of tourism is imperative.

Why would anyone study tourism? What's there to study? People lie on the beach, they swim, they drink rum punch, they eat. . . . Who cares?

Well, locals care—especially those who rake the beaches, clean the pools, serve the drinks, and prepare the food. So do governments, environmentalists, and multinationals. Tourism is the world's largest industry, employing one out of every twelve workers. That's more people than work to produce the food we eat. In 2006 there were 840 million international tourist arrivals. By 2020 it is estimated that there will be 1.6 billion generating 2,000 billion USD. That's a lot of people traveling around the world, crossing national borders, and interacting with other cultures. It also represents a lot of jet fuel and carbon emissions, which is just one reason environmentalists are concerned, and a lot of foreign exchange, which is why so many governments view tourism as an instrument of economic development. And in this era of globalization, what activity could be more global? Tourism is clearly more than its frivolous stereotype.

When anthropologists study tourism they look at many things: what tourists seek (e.g., adventure, authenticity, relaxation), how they decide where to go, how destinations market themselves, the tourist experience, interaction between locals and tourists, culture change, the lives of tourism workers, the economic benefits and costs of tourism, its impact on the environment, the similarities and differences between tourism and other forms of travel, tourist art. . . . The possibilities are almost as broad as anthropology itself. I first became interested in tourism as a research topic when I was living on the Caribbean island of Barbados in the early 1980s and couldn't help observing the impact tourists had. The population of Barbados is 90 percent Afro-Caribbean and most tourists were white Europeans or North Americans, so they automatically stood out. They also stood out because of their dress and behavior. To them, Barbados represented a fantasy isle; its resorts promoted this feeling with names like "Discovery Bay" and "Treasure Island." Souvenir shops sold T-shirts with images of spiff-smoking Rastas and the words "No worries." Their vacation represented a time-out from their normal lives; as tourists they occupied a liminal status that allowed them to do things they never would have considered at home like standing in line for groceries wearing a bikini.

My anthropology students got upset whenever they were identified as tourists and quickly tried to correct that misapprehension. After all, they were living there in the homes of village families and studying the culture, not just having fun. They were appalled at some tourist behavior and their general ignorance of the island and its people. The white Barbadian minority also went to lengths to separate itself from tourists. A few sported T-shirts proclaiming, "I live here." Although anthropologists like Valene Smith and Dennison Nash had studied tourism, at the time the subject still was not quite a "legitimate" research topic—the frivolous stereotype again. Tourism seemed light weight, like sport, not serious like the economy or inequality—although it is clearly related to both. So it was some years before I actively began to study it.

A Brief History

The impulse to travel for more than necessity (e.g., for subsistence or trade) is very old, but it has not always been possible. At one time, travel outside of a person's home locale was considered dangerous—the terrain, the absence of reliable maps, bandits, anything could happen. Religious pilgrims were some of the earliest "tourists." Most traveled by foot to holy sites like Mecca and Jerusalem to fulfill a lifetime goal and perhaps, to secure a better afterlife. For the medieval pilgrims in Chaucer's *The Canterbury Tales,* the trip to martyr St. Thomas Becket's shrine combined a spiritual quest with pleasure and adventure. Along the way, they enjoyed new sights and experiences and each other's sometimes ribald companionship.

Travel has long been associated with education. The Roman statesman Seneca recognized as early as the first century that "Travel and change of place impart new vigor to the mind." In the seventeenth and eighteenth centuries young English and American elites, usually men, polished their education by taking the "Grand Tour," in the company of a tutor, to the great sites of European architecture, art, history, and culture. Today, international exchange programs, which combine structured learning with touristic travel, are an important part of college curricula.

People have also traveled for health. Destinations boasting hot springs, pure mountain air, or warm water and salubrious sea breezes promised both mental and physical recuperation. In 1751 George Washington took his half-brother Lawrence to Barbados hoping he would recover from his tuberculosis there (he died on the voyage home). Spa resorts sprang up throughout Europe in the eighteenth century and remain popular there and elsewhere today. Medical tourism is one of the newer trends with people traveling to exotic locales to receive more economical treatment but also pampered care and the opportunity to recover in an interesting place. Brazil is currently popular for cosmetic surgery; India for heart surgery.

Tourism for the average person only became possible with advances in transportation. Thomas Cook, a Baptist minister and temperance worker, used Britain's new railway system in 1841 to transport factory workers from Leicester to Loughborough, just 19 miles away, for a temperance rally. He soon organized excursions throughout England, and later went on to develop elaborate journeys via railway and steamship to the Continent, Egypt, and the Holy Land, combining people's fascination with the novelty of new modes of travel and their emerging curiosity about new places. He issued tickets at favorable rates, hired local guides, and even handled their lodging and currency changes. The travel agency he built still bears his name.

The transportation industry itself has played a key role in promoting tourism: American railways encouraged people to travel to the Southwest, steamships lured early visitors to Alaska with images of glaciers, totem poles, and Native people. In the 1970s travel for the masses literally took off with the growth in jet travel (particularly the Boeing 747 jumbo jet) and the introduction of charter flights and all-inclusive holidays.

The reasons people travel and how they decide where to go are complex. Cost and safety are important considerations for most. After that, much depends on how well a destination has been marketed through web sites, brochures, advertisements, and feature articles. Destinations are advertised like any other "product" through pictures and words which create appealing images and fantasies—idyllic beaches, majestic vistas, glamorous resorts, remote and exotic cultures. Individual tourists also have their own pre-established ideas about certain places. The iconic tourism sites in the early twentieth century were the Taj Mahal, the pyramids of Giza, Victoria Falls in Zimbabwe, Old Faithful Geyser in Yellowstone. Today they include Peru's Machu Pichu and even the wineries of Napa Valley. Other sites become desirable based on word-of-mouth recommendations or the mental associations created by books and films. Since 1989, American baseball enthusiasts have traveled to a cornfield in Iowa to see the "field of dreams" made famous by the movie of the same name. Japanese tourists travel to Prince Edward Island to visit the fictional home of Anne Shirley, the beloved Canadian heroine of Lucy Maude Montgomery's 1908 novel *Anne of Green Gables* (and a more recent television miniseries). Anne's spunk and determination have made her a popular character in Japan ever since 1954 when the book was translated and introduced into the junior high curriculum. Tourists from all over the world visit Anne Frank's house in Amsterdam, the World War II–related site made vividly real in her published diary. Status considerations can also determine where tourists go: some destinations have more *cachet* than others based on their distance, expense, challenge, perceived exclusivity, associations with "high culture" or celebrities, and a host of other factors.

Some people travel to satisfy a desire for change or simply to find a place to relax. Others seek to fulfill their fantasies by visiting and experiencing exotic places. They travel to marvel at the Great Wall of China or the Grand Canyon, to experience the rush of sighting wildlife in Kenya or rafting the Colorado, to enjoy good wine and food in France, to absorb the spirituality of Varanasi or Tibet, to luxuriate on a tropical island or at a European spa, to physically challenge themselves by walking the Inca Way, to see the Maasai or the Mona Lisa.

A Unique Form of Globalization

Unlike most forms of globalization, tourism often brings consumers (i.e., the tourists) and producers (e.g., local service providers, ethnic Others) into direct contact with one another. When abroad, the food we eat or the art we buy is often purchased straight from the people who made it. When we buy bananas at a supermarket at home or jeans from our local Gap, we seldom think about who produced them or the conditions under which they were made. Increasingly, however, the things we buy at home are made by the people we visit aboard—by workers in Vietnam, China, Indonesia, or Mexico. As tourists, we experience their local economics, observe their standard of living, and often develop some empathy and interest in their lives.

Globalization is usually viewed as a homogenizing force; countries' increasing economic and political ties and the accelerating flow of information, goods, and people worldwide is seen as diminishing cultural differences. The tourism industry, however, has an interest in preserving the local. Government tourism boards, travel services, resorts, and the like, aggressively promote aspects of local heritage, culture, cuisine, and place in order to emphasize a destination's uniqueness and to distinguish it from other possible places tourists could visit. Consequently, despite the uniformity imposed by the spread of international standards in accommodation, hygiene, food, and travel and hospitality services, tourism does not necessarily destroy cultural differences. Folk dances and festivals, historical events, "traditional" dress-styles, indigenous arts and crafts, vernacular architecture, local markets and foods are just some of the cultural differences it promotes.

Tourism's Many Impacts

Tourism affects not only the people who travel, but also the people and places they visit. Exactly what happens and the scale of the impact depends on many factors, including the number of tourists who come, whether they visit during a single season or arrive the year round, the size and population of the country being visited, how developed the local economy and infrastructure are, and who controls the industry and profits from it—multinationals, local elites, and/or the average resident.

When large numbers of tourists visit a place, especially if they visit the year round, residents often feel overwhelmed. In Barbados, three times the total population of the island visit it as tourists each year. Yet because most people arrive on cruise ships and don't stay long or else come primarily to enjoy the beach, some parts of the small island remain relatively untouched. In a small town like Sitka, Alaska, with a population of less than 8,000 (and only 14 miles of road) the arrival of a cruise ship can have a dramatic impact. On cruise ship days—ships are posted in the newspaper—most locals avoid the downtown as the tourists take over, clogging the sidewalks and stores and wandering absent-mindedly into traffic to take photographs. Tourists can be especially intrusive when they visit places primarily to see "native" people and their ceremonies, to take photographs, and to shop for indigenous arts and crafts. The Pueblo Indians in the American southwest control the impact of tourists who come to their reservations by making some areas of their villages off-limits, by keeping the performance of many ceremonies secret, and by being evasive or uncommunicative when questioned. Similar strategies are used in other parts of the world.

When local people become objects of the "tourist gaze"—when they are watched and photographed even while doing the most mundane things—their lives may be altered. The Eskimo hunters of Kotzebue, Alaska, stopped butchering their seals on the beach and moved their activities indoors in order to escape being watched and photographed. The "love market" at SaPa in Vietnam's northern highlands is another example. Historically it was a Red Dao tradition to seek marriage partners while trading and socializing at the market. Courting couples would serenade one another with mouth harps and personalized songs that revealed their attraction for the other person and touted their own domestic abilities and work ethic. Today, the market has all but lost this function since couples felt too much on display and now meet elsewhere in order to avoid tourists. Recently, SaPa organized a new festival to attract more visitors. Called the "Festival of the Clouds," it joins tourists with ethnic minority people to play traditional games, drink local wine, and eat *thang co* (a horse meat hotpot).

In many places, residents post signs explaining local customs and laying out rules for visitors—remove shoes in a temple, do not photograph or touch religious icons, do not give candy to local children, do not kiss in public, ask permission to photograph local people, do not look at a woman's face, do not touch a person's head, dress modestly. In Barbados, one shopkeeper posted the following: "We value your business and we know that you're cool, but please leave exposed tummies around the pool."

To attract tourists, destinations need to differentiate themselves from other places. Some do so by commodifying local rituals and celebrations and marketing them as tourist "spectacles." When this happens, their meaning and value for local people can be lost. When the Chambri of Papua New Guinea opened their initiation ceremony to visiting tourists, they unwittingly turned it into a "performance." The presence of a tourist audience combined with the small changes that were made in order not to frighten the tourists removed the ceremony's mystery and impact on the initiates. The Alarde ceremony in Spain—a large-scale, elaborately costumed re-enactment of the Basque town of Hondarribia's victory over the French in the seventeenth century—declined after Spain's Ministry of Tourism and Information included it in its national advertising in the 1970s. As more tourists arrived, the municipal government decided the ceremony should be performed twice so that more visitors could watch it, thus re-defining it as a public spectacle for tourists rather than a local expression of Basque pride. As a result, participation dropped dramatically. More recently, however, the festival has acquired new local significance as part of the struggle for regional political rights in Spain.

The Hawaiian hula is another example of an indigenous custom that has been thoroughly commodified for tourism. It was once a sacred temple dance that celebrated the procreative powers of the Hawaiian chiefly class; today it is performed for tourists in entirely secular contexts—the airport, hotel lobbies, and theme parks. Yet to most tourists it represents "authentic" Hawaiian culture—an age-old tradition that is real and unmediated. Terms like "authentic" and "traditional" are frequently used to describe aspects of local culture marketed to tourists. Most travelers like to think that what they are seeing is "real"—an historical and internally generated part of local culture. Yet new dances, songs, and festivals are created all the time to provide visitors with entertaining "cultural" or "folkloric" events to watch. Some of these creations like Barbados's Crop Over festival (celebrating the end of the sugarcane harvest) have become part of local culture. It was developed in 1974 by the country's tourism board to promote tourism during the slack summer season but now has been embraced by residents and Barbadians living abroad who return home to visit at this time of year. Dances created specifically for tourism in Bali have now been incorporated into Balinese culture; the "frog dance" created for tourists in the 1970s is now performed at Balinese weddings.

Some researchers talk about the "demonstration effects" of tourism and the changes these produce. When foreign tourists arrive in less developed countries they bring with them an affluence that can create a sense of relative deprivation and unrealistic desires in local people of modest means for the lifestyle and possessions tourists have. (Of course, television, films, the Internet, and other outside influences also contribute to this.) Raising the expectations of people who do not yet have the resource base or opportunities to acquire what comparatively wealthy visitors have, can result in some locals searching for ways to get rich quick—activities like street crime, hustling, gambling, and drug dealing. Tourists also provide the opportunity and sometimes the market (e.g., in the case of drugs) for such activities.

Prostitution is found in virtually every tourist location. Some young women (and men) move to tourist areas intentionally in hopes of finding a foreign lover or marriage partner or to become prostitutes. Others are lured from rural villages under false pretenses—to become performers, dancers, bar hostesses, factory workers—by middlemen and then get trapped into prostitution. Specialized tour operators in Western countries, Japan, and the Middle East offer package sex tours that market the sexual allure of exotic Others and guarantee their availability. Local governments are not entirely innocent here; some like Thailand have in the past actively marketed their population's physical beauty and availability to tourists. Some cities like Bangkok have become bywords for the sex trade and have developed commercial sex sectors. In the Caribbean, male "beach bums" or gigolos patrol the beaches looking for tourist women to hook up with. Child prostitution is a growing problem in many tourist destinations. The Bangkok-based organization, End Child Prostitution in Asian Tourism (ECPAT), estimates that a million children are involved. According to the World Tourism Organization (WTO), a study of 100 school children in Kalutara, Sri Lanka, found that 86 had their first sexual experience at ages 12 or 13, the majority with a foreign tourist. Recent legislation in the United States, Germany, Britain, and Sweden, has made it a crime to travel abroad for the purpose of having sex with a minor; prosecutions have been brought against some tourists.

On a positive note, tourism usually creates new markets for local arts. Hotels hire local performers—musicians, dancers, singers, theater troops—to entertain their guests and local art to decorate their rooms and lobbies. Tourists often buy local art and crafts as mementos and souvenirs of their trip. Although many people bemoan the emergence of what they consider to be degraded and quasi-mass produced "airport" or "tourist art," the sale of these items creates opportunities for local people of modest means to earn money. It also demonstrates their ability to read the market, that is, to judge what tourists like (e.g., wooden statues of colonial figures in Africa, baskets with novelty shapes in Alaska) and to provide it. Having a more diverse clientele, especially in a small-scale society, also creates room for artistic experimentation.

This brings us to tourism's considerable economic impact. As mentioned at the beginning, tourism is estimated to generate 2,000 billion dollars worldwide by 2020. Unfortunately, much of this money never reaches destination countries. One study in Thailand estimated that 70 percent of all the money spent by tourists left the country via foreign-owned tour operators, airlines, and hotels, and through the use of imported drinks and food—a phenomenon called "leakage." Caribbean countries as a whole lose between 70 and 90 cents of every dollar that tourists spend to holiday. All-inclusive resorts that offer tourists a pre-paid package of airfare, accommodation, entertainment, meals, and other services, put little money into the local economy. Tourists have no reason to leave the resort to eat in a local restaurant, hire a local guide, or shop in local stores when they have already paid for everything.

Cruise ships, which are in essence floating all-inclusives, likewise contribute little to the countries they visit. When ship passengers disembark at a port, many have already purchased their tours through the cruise line, and the car rentals, taxi services, helicopters, and tour-operator booths they first encounter are often controlled either by transnational chains, local elites, or expatriates. These same groups also own many of the larger retail stores tourists are funneled into. Some cruise ship lines lease or own their own Caribbean islands, a practice which further reduces the time and money tourists spend at destination ports. In an attempt to offset this, more destinations now charge cruise lines a passenger head tax.

To encourage tourism, less developed nations usually have to spend large sums of money upgrading their infrastructure—building international airports, excavating deep-water harbors, laying miles of paved road, building new electricity generating plants, increasing the capacity of their water supply and service, and so forth. Major construction projects are often financed with loans from the International Monetary Fund (IMF) or World Bank and must be paid back through local taxes and reduced spending in the public sector. This may siphon money from schools and libraries, hospitals, and the like that directly benefit local inhabitants. Moreover, when services like water or electricity are in short supply, priority is given to maintaining the comfort of tourists (to help guarantee their future business) rather than locals.

Although tourism clearly creates new jobs especially during the construction phase, the downside is that most of the jobs it creates (e.g., hotel maids, waiters, gardeners, bartenders) are seasonal, low paying, and provide little in the way of benefits, long-term security, or opportunities for advancement.

Despite these limitations, many tourism workers are grateful for the jobs they have and like the work they do. Some local people are able to become independent entrepreneurs by opening small guest houses or shops, becoming tour guides, or making crafts to sell. It is the local elites, however, who benefit the most since they are the ones who have the capital, connections, and know-how to take real advantage of emerging opportunities.

When large-scale tourism projects are undertaken—building international airports, deep-water harbors, resorts, and golf courses or establishing game parks and nature preserves—large swathes of agricultural or grazing land and fishing grounds can be removed from use, physically displacing local people and eliminating their subsistence base in the process. About 70 percent of the national parks and game reserves in East Africa are on former Masai grazing land. In the 1990s, hundreds of Filipinos were resettled to make room for the huge Samal Island Tourism estate adjacent to Mindanao. The Philippine government projected the creation of hundreds of replacement jobs, but the job training programs promised to displaced locals were minimal and the construction of the huge complex was repeatedly delayed and scaled back. This left most relocated residents without jobs, without access to their old agricultural land and fishing grounds, and with few of the new services promised them. Too often, tourism's positive and negative impacts are grossly asymmetrical.

Because tourists often seek beautiful places or unique landscapes to visit that are ecologically fragile, local environments are easily degraded. Image the impact that 300,000 hiking boot-clad tourists have on the paths and stone buildings of Machu Pichu each year compared to the 500 or so Incas who once lived there. Japanese geologists have reported land slippage at Machu Pichu of .4 inches a month.

Coral reefs are damaged by tourism; local residents sometimes harvest coral to sell or make into jewelry and tourists who dive and cruise ships that anchor on coral can kill the fragile cephalopods. A single anchor dropped from a cruise ship over a coral reef for just one day can destroy an area half the size of a football field.

The building of hotels, yacht and cruise ship harbors, and other tourism infrastructure in the Caribbean and parts of Central America has destroyed wetlands and mangroves. Wetlands typically provide a habitat and nursery for birds, fish, and crustaceans. They also protect shorelines from hurricanes. Their destruction leads to environmental degradation.

Tourists use a lot of water, usually many times more than do native residents. Think of all the water used each day by guests taking showers, by hotels to launder sheets and towels, and by resorts to replenish swimming pools and fountains and to maintain lush landscaping and golf courses. A single golf course in a tropical country like Thailand can use as much water in a year as 60,000 rural villagers. In places where fresh water comes from wells, over-pumping can cause salt to intrude into the groundwater. The heavy water usage required by tourism also produces a lot of wastewater, and even treated wastewater contains a large amount of phosphates and nitrates. When released into the sea, the discharge stresses living corals, killing them over time. As coral dies the reef too breaks down. Without a reef barrier to absorb wave energy, there is nothing to prevent beach erosion.

Tourists account for at least 60 percent of air travel and, therefore, of the fuel and ozone depleting emissions that jets emit. Tourism also accounts for many other unexpected environmental impacts such as noise and visual pollution. As a result of the noise caused by helicopter tours over the Grand Canyon, stillness—one of the things visitors expect to find in a natural area of such scale—can be found in only one-third of the Grand Canyon. In Yellowstone National Park in the winter of 2000, so many visitors used snow mobiles that researchers found that engine noise was heard 90 percent of the time at eight popular tourist sites including Old Faithful geyser.

Visual pollution occurs when tourist developments are built without any architectural sensitivity to the surrounding landscape or local building styles or when their sheer size overwhelms the landscape or they are prominently situated on mountainsides or shoreline.

Slowly people have become more aware of tourism's environmental impact. Ecotourism is one attempt to address the problem and is currently the fastest growing type of tourism. It involves travel to places of untouched natural beauty where a serious effort has been made to minimize tourism's environmental impact and to promote sustainable development. Ecotourism developments are typically small-scale and their building methods and architecture are low impact and convey a sense of place (e.g., by using local materials and styles). Here tourists are given the opportunity to experience and learn about special ecosystems, like Costa Rica's and Belize's tropical rainforests and coral reefs, and enjoy low-impact environmental adventures (e.g., forest floor and canopy walks, river rafting, snorkeling and scuba diving). Ecotourism also promotes conservation ethics and is committed to improving the local environment and the lives of local people. Yet it only appeals to some tourists and can only cater to small numbers. There is also the phenomenon of "eco-light." Since tourism is a poorly regulated industry, it is easy for destinations to claim to be "green" when they are not.

"Responsible tourism" is a newer notion that asks all of us to examine how often and why we travel as well as the kind of tourism we engage in. It encourages us to do our homework—to learn something in advance about the people and cultures of the places we plan to visit and of the tour operators we plan to travel with.

The next time you travel, enjoy yourself but think like an anthropologist would about the bigger picture and try to minimize the negative impacts of what you do. Be a good global citizen and care. Tourism does matter.

Notes

Many of the ideas expressed in this article can be found in *Tourists and Tourism,* Sharon Gmelch (ed.) (Long Grove, IL: Waveland Press, 2004).

Review Questions

1. What kinds of things do anthropologists study when they investigate tourism, according to Gmelch?

2. What were some of the reasons people traveled to other places in the past before the mid-twentieth century?

3. What is unique about tourism in comparison to other forms of globalization such as international trade and the rise of multinational companies?

4. How do local peoples protect themselves against the "tourist gaze"?

5. Assess the economic impact of tourism on native peoples and the companies that organize such travel.

6. List the impacts that tourism has on such entities as local cultures, local governments, and the environment.

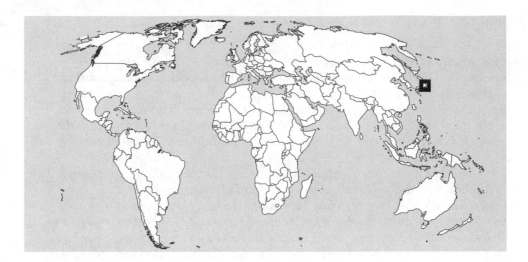

36

Japanese Hip-Hop and the Globalization of Popular Culture

Ian Condry

By now, anyone who travels the world knows that something is afoot. Hilton, Sheraton, Radisson, and other national chain look-alike hotels grace down-town districts in most major international cities. African cab drivers deliver embarking airline passengers to historic "American" districts in our nation's capital. Tourists eat in a Chinese restaurant located in Cusco, high in the Andes. Faxes and e-mails flash around the world in seconds. Clothing and hairstyles look similar from one country to the next. But does this global "sameness" related to population movement, transnational companies, and cross-cultural borrowing mean that a single world culture is emerging? In some ways, perhaps, yes, but in many ways borrowed culture is hybridized

365

by a process of localization. *When new cultural forms arrive, they are often understood and modified by local cultural perspectives. And often their appearance stimulates the creation of new cultural forms. Anthropologists have a long tradition of investigating beliefs, social organization, and events at the local level, so the process of hybridization and cultural creation "on the ground" is where they can make the greatest contribution to an understanding of globalization.*

This is a point made by Ian Condry in this selection. Using the example of hip-hop, originally a North American contribution to pop culture, he shows how this entertainment form has been adapted to the club scene in metropolitan Tokyo. Sporting typical—in most cases American-like—clothing and hairstyles, crowds of Japanese young people jam all-night clubs to hear hip-hop performers do their stuff. But they continue to do this in a Japanese fashion, using the musical form as a way to express their presence as young individuals in traditionally group-oriented, age-ranked Japanese society.

Introduction

Japanese hip-hop, which began in the 1980s and continues to develop today, is an intriguing case study for exploring the globalization of popular culture. Hip-hop is but one example among many of the transnational cultural styles pushed by entertainment and fashion industries, pulled by youth eager for the latest happening thing, and circulated by a wide range of media outlets eager to draw readers and to sell advertising. In Tokyo, a particular combination of local performance sites, artists, and fans points to ways that urban areas are crucibles of new, hybrid cultural forms. Hip-hop was born in the late 1970s in New York City as a form of street art: rapping on sidewalk stoops, outdoor block parties with enormous sound systems, graffiti on public trains, and breakdancing in public parks. In its voyage to Japan, the street ethic of hip-hop remains, but it is performed most intensely in all-night clubs peppered around Tokyo. This paper examines these nightclubs as an urban setting that helps us grasp the cultural dynamics of Japanese hip-hop. In particular, the interaction between artist-entrepreneurs and fans in live shows demonstrates how "global" popular culture is still subject to important processes of localization.

Anthropologists have a special role in analyzing such transnational forms because of their commitment to extended fieldwork in local settings. Ethnography aims to capture the cultural practices and social organization of a people. This offers a useful way of seeing how popular culture is interwoven with everyday life. Yet there is a tension between ethnography and globalization, because in many ways they seem antithetical to each other. While ethnography attempts to evoke the distinctive texture of local experience, globalization is often seen as erasing local differences. An important analytical challenge for today's media-saturated world is finding a way to understand how local culture interacts with such global media flows.

On one hand, it seems as if locales far removed from each other are becoming increasingly the same. It is more than a little eerie to fly from New York to Tokyo and see teenagers in both places wearing the same kinds of fashion characteristic of rap fans: baggy pants with boxers on display, floppy hats or baseball caps, and immaculate space-age Nike sneakers. In Tokyo stores for youth, rap music is the background sound of choice. Graffiti styled after the New York City aerosol artists dons numerous walls, and breakdancers can be found in public parks practicing in the afternoon or late at night. In all-night dance clubs throughout Tokyo, Japanese rappers and DJs take to the stage and declare that they have some "extremely bad shit" (*geki yaba shitto*)—meaning "good music"—to share with the audience. For many urban youth, hip-hop is the defining style of their era. In 1970s Japan, the paradigm of high school cool was long hair and a blistering solo on lead guitar. Today, trendsetters are more likely to sport "dread" hair and show off their scratch techniques with two turntables and a mixer. In the last few years, rap music has become one of the best-selling genres of music in the United States and around the world as diverse youth are adapting the style to their own messages and contexts.

But at the same time, there are reasons to think that such surface appearances of sameness disguise differences at some deeper level. Clearly, cultural setting and social organization have an impact on how movies and television shows are viewed. Yet if we are to understand the shape of cultural forms in a world that is increasingly connected by global media and commodity flows, we must situate Japanese rappers in the context of contemporary Japan. When thinking about how hip-hop is appropriated, we must consider, for example, that most Japanese rappers and fans speak only Japanese. Many of them live at home with their parents, and they all went through the Japanese education system. Moreover, even if the origin of their beloved music genre is overseas, they are caught up in social relations that are ultimately quite local, animated primarily by face-to-face interactions and telephone calls. So while these youth see themselves as "hip-hoppers" and "B-Boys" and "B Girls," and associate themselves with what they call a "global hip-hop culture," they also live in a day-to-day world that is distinctly Japanese.

For those interested in studying the power of popular culture, there is also a more practical question of research methods. How does a lone researcher go about studying something as broad and unwieldy as the globalization of mass culture? One of the tenets of anthropological fieldwork is that you cannot understand a people without being there, but in the case of a music genre, where is "there"? In the fall of 1995, I began a year and a half of fieldwork in Tokyo, and the number of potential sites was daunting. There were places where the music was produced: record companies, recording studios, home studios, and even on commuter trains with handheld synthesizers. There were places where the music was promoted: music magazines, fashion magazines, TV and radio shows, night-clubs, and record stores. There was the interaction between musicians and fans at live shows, or in mediated form on cassettes, CDs, and 12-inch LPs. To make matters worse, rap music is part of the larger category of "hip-hop." Hip-hop encompasses not only rap, but also breakdance, DJ, graffiti, and fashion. The challenge was to understand the current fascination among Japanese youth with hip-hop music and style, while also considering the role of money-making organizations. How does one situate the experiential pleasures within the broader structures of profit that produce mass culture?

As I began interviewing rappers, magazine writers, and record company people, I found a recurring theme that provided a partial answer. Everyone agreed that you cannot understand Japanese rap music without going regularly to the clubs. Clubs were called the "actual site" *(genba)* of the Japanese rap scene.[1] It was there that rappers performed, DJs learned which songs elicit excitement in the crowd, and breakdancers practiced and competed for attention. In what follows, I would like to suggest that an effective tool for understanding the globalization of popular culture is to consider places like Japanese hip-hop nightclubs in terms of what might be called "genba globalism." By using participant–observation methods to explore key sites that are a kind of media crossroads, we can observe how globalized images and sounds are performed, consumed, and then transformed in an ongoing process. I use the Japanese term "genba" to emphasize that the processing of such global forms happens through the local language and in places where local hip-hop culture is produced. In Japanese hip-hop, these clubs are important not only as places where fans can see live shows and hear the latest releases from American and Japanese groups, but also as places for networking among artists, writers, and record company people. In this essay, I would like to point out some of the advantages of considering key sites as places to understand the cross-cutting effects of globalization. To get a sense of what clubs are about, let's visit one.

Going to Harlem
on the Yamanote Line

A visit to Tokyo's Harlem is the best place to begin a discussion of Japanese hip-hop. Opened in the summer of 1997, Harlem is one of many all night dance clubs, but as the largest club solely devoted to hip-hop and R&B, it has become the flagship for the Japanese scene (at least, at the time of this writing in February 2001). Nestled in the love hotel area of the Shibuya section of Tokyo, Harlem is representative of the otherworldliness of clubs as well as their location within the rhythms and spaces of mainstream Japan.

If we were visiting the club, we would most likely meet at Shibuya train station around midnight because the main action seldom gets started before 1 A.M. Most all-night revelers commute by train, a practice that links Tokyo residents

---

[1]The word *"genba"* is made up of the characters "to appear" and "place," and it is used to describe a place where something actually happens, like the scene of an accident or of a crime, or a construction site. In the hip-hop world the term is used to contrast the intense energy of the club scene with the more sterile and suspect marketplace.

in a highly punctual dance. The night is divided between the last train (all lines stop by 1 A.M. at the latest) and the first train of the morning (between 4:30 and 5 A.M.). The intervening period is when clubs (*kurabu*) are most active.[2] Shortly after midnight, Shibuya station is the scene for the changing of the guard: those heading home, running to make their connections for the last train, and those like us heading out, dressed up, and walking leisurely because we will be spending all night on the town. The magazine stands are closing. Homeless men are spread out on cardboard boxes on the steps leading down to the subways. The police observe the masses moving past each other in the station square towards their respective worlds. Three billboard-size TVs looming overhead, normally spouting pop music videos and snowboard ads during the day, are now dark and silent. The throngs of teenagers, many in their school uniforms, that mob Shibuya during afternoons and all weekend have been replaced by a more balanced mix of college students, "salarymen" and "career women," and of course more than a few B-Boys and B-Girls—the hip-hop enthusiasts in baggy pants and headphones. The sidewalks are splashed with light from vending machines—cigarettes, soda, CDs, beer (off for the night), and "valentine call" phone cards. A few drunken men are being carried by friends or lie in their suits unconscious on the sidewalk.

To get to Harlem, we walk uphill along Dôgenzaka Avenue toward a corner with a large neon sign advertising a capsule hotel, where businessmen who have missed their last train can sleep in coffin-like rooms. We pass disposable lamppost signs and phone booth stickers advertising various sex services. An elderly man in the back of a parked van is cooking and selling *takoyaki* (octopus dumplings) to those with the late-night munchies. The karaoke box establishments advertise cheaper rates at this hour. Turning right at a Chinese restaurant, we move along a narrow street packed with love hotels, which advertise different prices for "rest" or "stay." In contrast to the garish yellow sign advertising the live music hall, On-Air East, about fifty meters ahead, a nondescript door with a spiffy, long-haired bouncer out front is all that signals us that Harlem is inside. It seems there are always a couple of clubbers out front talking on their tiny cell phones. Up the stairs, past a table filled with flyers advertising upcoming hip-hop events, we pay our ¥3000 each (around $25, which may seem expensive, but is only about half again as much as a movie ticket). We move into the circulating and sweaty mass inside.

Traveling to a club instills a sense of moving against the mainstream in time and space. Others are going home to bed as the clubber heads out. When the clubber returns home in the morning, reeking of smoke and alcohol, the train cars hold early-bird workers as well. So the movement to and from the club, often from the distant suburbs, gives clubbers a sense of themselves as separate, flaunting

---

[2]Hip-hop is not the only style for club music. Techno, House, Reggae, Jungle/Drum 'n' Bass, and so on, are some of the other popular club music styles. Live music tends to be performed earlier in the evening, usually starting around 7 P.M., and finishing in time for the audience to catch an evening train home. In contrast to "clubs," "discos" must by law close by 1 A.M.

their leisure, their costumes, and their consumer habits. During the course of my year-and-a-half of fieldwork, between the fall of 1995 and the spring of 1997, I went to over a hundred club events around Tokyo and I began to see that clubs help one understand not only the pleasures of rap in Japan, but also the social organization of the scene and the different styles that have emerged. This becomes clear as you spend time inside the clubs.

Inside the Club

Inside the club, the air is warm and thick, humid with the breath and sweat of dancing bodies. Bone-thudding bass lines thump out of enormous speakers. There is the scratch-scratch of a DJ doing his turntable tricks, and the hum of friends talking, yelling really, over the sound of the music. The lighting is subdued, much of it coming from a mirrored ball slowly rotating on the ceiling. The fraternity house smell of stale beer is mostly covered up by the choking cigarette haze, but it is best not to look too closely at what is making the floor alternately slippery and sticky. The darkness, low ceiling, black walls, and smoky murk create a space both intimate and claustrophobic. Almost everyone heads for the bar as soon as they come in. An important aspect of clubbing is the physical experience of the music and crowded setting.

Harlem is a larger space than most of the Tokyo clubs, and can hold upwards of one thousand people on a crowded weekend night. On the wall behind the DJ stage, abstract videos, *anime* clips, or edited Kung Fu movies present a background of violence and mayhem, albeit with an Asian flavor. Strobe lights, steam, and moving spotlights give a strong sense of the space, and compound the crowded, frenetic feeling imposed by the loud music. The drunken revelry gives clubs an atmosphere of excitement that culminates with the live show and the following freestyle session. But an important part of clubbing is also the lull before and after the show, when one circulates among the crowd, flirting, networking, gossiping, or simply checking out the scene. Clubs are a space where the diffuse network of hip-hop fans comes together in an elusive effort to have fun. To the extent that a "community" emerges in the hip-hop scene, it revolves around specific club events and the rap groups that draw the crowd.

Much of the time is spent milling around, talking, drinking, and dancing. The live show often produces a welcome rise in the excitement level of the clubbers. Some events feature several live acts, often followed by a freestyle session. The rap show will usually begin between 1:00 and 1:30 A.M. Formats vary depending on the club and the event. "B-Boy Night" at R-Hall (organized by Crazy-A) was held one Sunday a month and would start with a long breakdancing show, with many groups each doing a five-minute routine. Then a series of rap groups would come on, each doing two or three songs. At other shows, like FG Night, sometimes a series of groups would perform, while on other nights only one group would do a show followed by a more open-ended freestyle. Nevertheless, there were many similarities, and a characteristic live show would proceed as follows. Two rappers take the stage (or step up into the DJ booth), as the DJ prepares the music. For people enamored of live bands, the live show of a rap concert may strike one as a bit lifeless. The music is either pre-recorded on a digital audio tape (DAT) or taken from the breakbeats section of an album.[3] The flourish of a lead guitar, bass, or drum solo is replaced in the hip-hop show by the manic scratching of a record by a DJ who deftly slides a record back and forth across the slip mat laid on the turntable and works the mixer to produce the rhythmic flurries of sampled sound.

The rappers begin with a song introducing themselves as a group. Every group seems to have its own introductory song of self-promotion:

rainutsutaa ga rainut shi ni yatte kita *doko ni kita? Shibuya!*	Rhymester has come to rhyme where are we? Shibuya!
hai faa za dopesuto da *oretachi kyo cho gesuto da*	we are By Phar the Dopest we are tonight's super guests
makka na me o shita fuktuô *ore tojo*	The red-eyed owl [You the Rock] I've arrived on stage

These songs tend to be brief, only a couple of minutes long. Between the first and second song, the rappers ask the audience how they feel. A common catch-phrase was "How do you feel/My crazy brothers."[4] The group will introduce by name the rappers and DJ, and also make sure everyone remembers the name of the group. The rappers will comment about how noisy the crowd is. Crowds are more often criticized for not being worked up enough rather than praised for their excitement.

The second song tends to be the one the group is most famous for. On stage, each rapper holds a cordless microphone right up to his mouth, and a rapper might steady the mic by holding his index finger under his nose. The other arm is gesticulating, palm out in a waving motion at the audience. A bobbing motion in the head and shoulders can be more or less pronounced.

Between the second and third song, the group will usually demand some call-and-response from the audience, almost always as follows:

Call	Response	Call	Response
ie yo ho	*ho*	Say, ho	ho
ie yo ho ho	*ho ho*	Say, ho ho	ho ho
ie yo ho ho ho	*ho ho ho*	Say ho ho ho	ho ho ho
sawage!	[screams]	Make noise!	[screams]

---

[3]The term "breakbeats" refers to the section of a song where only the drums, or drums and bass, play. It is the break between the singing and the melodies of the other instruments, hence "break-beats." This section can be looped by a DJ using two turntables and a mixer with cross-fader, and produces a backing track suitable for rapping.

[4]In Japanese, *chôoshi wa dô dai/ikarera kyôdai*. The masculinity of Japanese rap is here indexed by the calling out to "brothers" and also by the use of the masculine slang *dai* instead of *da*.

The third and usually final song tends to be a new song, often introduced in English as "brand new shit," a revolting image for English-speakers perhaps, but apparently heard by the audience as a cooler way of saying "new song" than the Japanese *shinkyoku*. If the song is about to be released as a record or CD, this information is also announced before the song's performance. If there are other rap groups in the audience, this is also the time for "shout outs" (praise for fellow hip-hoppers) as in "Shakkazombie in da house" or "Props to King Giddra" and once even, "Ian Condry in da house." After the third song, there is seldom talk besides a brief goodbye in English: "Peace" or "We out." Encores are rare, but freestyle sessions, discussed below, are ubiquitous. After the show, rappers retreat backstage or to the bar area, but never linger around the stage after performing. The year 1996 was also a time of a "freestyle boom," when most shows were closed with an open-ended passing of the microphone. Anyone could step on stage and try his or her hand at rapping for a few minutes. This has been an important way for younger performers to get the attention of more established acts. There is a back-and-forth aspect of performance in the clubs that shows how styles are developed, honed, and reworked in a context where the audience is knowledgeable, discriminating, and at times participates in the show itself.

It is important to understand that over the years, this kind of feedback loop has helped determine the shape of current Japanese rap styles. One of my main sites was a weekly Thursday night event that featured another collection of rap groups called Kitchens. Hip-hop collectives such as Kitchens, Little Bird Nation, Funky Grammar Unit, and Rock Steady Crew Japan are called "families" (*famirii*, in Japanese). The different groups often met at clubs or parties, at times getting acquainted after particularly noteworthy freestyle sessions. Over time some would become friends, as well as artistic collaborators, who performed together live or in the studio for each others' albums. Such families define the social organization of the "scene." What is interesting is how they also characterize different aesthetic takes on what Japanese hip-hop should be. Kitchens, for example, aim to combine a pop music sensibility with their love for rap music, and, like many such "party rap" groups, they appeal to a largely female audience. The Funky Grammar Unit aims for a more underground sound that is nonetheless accessible, and they tend to have a more even mix of men and women in the audience. Other families like Urbarian Gym (UBG) are less concerned with being accessible to audiences than with conveying a confrontational, hard-core stance. The lion's share of their audiences are young males, though as UBG's leader, Zeebra, breaks into the pop spotlight, their audiences are becoming more diverse.

The lull that precedes and follows the onstage performance is a key time for networking to build these families. In all, the live show is at most an hour long, at times closer to twenty minutes, and yet there is nowhere for the clubbers to go until the trains start running again around 5 A.M. It is not unusual for music magazine writers to do interviews during club events, and record company representatives often come to shows as well, not only as talent scouts but also to discuss upcoming projects. I found that 3:00 to 4 A.M. was the most productive time for fieldwork because by then the clubbers had mostly exhausted their supply of stories and gossip to tell friends, and were then open to finding out what this strange foreigner jotting things in his notebook was doing in their midst.

Japanese cultural practices do not disappear just because everyone is wearing their hip-hop outfits and listening to the latest rap tunes. To give one example, at the first Kitchens event after the New Year, I was surprised to see all the clubbers who knew each other going around and saying the traditional New Year's greeting in very formal Japanese: "Congratulations on the dawn of the New Year. I humbly request your benevolence this year as well." There was no irony, no joking atmosphere in these statements. This is a good example of the way that globalization may appear to overshadow Japanese culture, but one needs to spend time in clubs with the people to see how surface appearances can be deceiving.

In many ways, then, it is not surprising that rappers, DJs, breakdancers, record company people, and magazine editors all agree you cannot understand the music unless you go to the clubs. There is an intensity of experience in hearing the music at loud volume, surrounded by a crush of dancing people, while drinking alcohol and staying out all night, that gives the music an immediacy and power it lacks when heard, say, on headphones in the quiet of one's room. Indeed, it is difficult to convey in words the feeling of communal excitement during a particularly good show, when one gets wrapped up in a surge of energy that is palpable yet intangible. It is this emotional experience that in many ways counteracts any fears that it is all "merely imitation," which is the most common criticism of the music.

At the same time, going to a club involves a strange mix of the extraordinary and the routine. On one hand, you visit a place with bizarre interior design, listen to music at exceedingly high volume, stay out all night and, often, get drunk. It is a sharp contrast to an ordinary day of school or work. We must also recognize, however, that while a club may strive to be a fantastic microcosm, it is still embedded in Japan's political-economic structures, characteristic social relations, and the contemporary range of cultural forms. It is not by chance that clubs tend to attract people of specific class, age, sexuality, and to some extent locale. Moreover, if you go regularly to clubs, after a while it becomes just another routine. It is largely predictable what kind of pleasures can be expected, and also the generally unpleasant consequences for work or school after a night without sleep.[5] Clubbing offers freedom and constraints. This tension is the key to understanding how clubs socialize the club-goers by structuring pleasure in characteristic ways.

[5]Youthful Japanese clubbers use the mixed English-Japanese construction "all *suru*" (do all) to mean "stay out all night in a club." For example, the following exchange occurred between two members of the female group Now. Here, the sense of routine outweighs the excitement. A: *konban mo ooru suru ka na?* (Are we staying out all night again?) B: *Tabun.* (Probably) A: *Yabai.* (That sucks.)

I have only suggested some of the ways that clubs offer insight into the ways that global hip-hop becomes transformed into a local form of Japanese hip-hop, but we can see how an idea of "genba globalism" can help us understand the process of localization. Globalism is refracted and transformed in important ways through the actual site of urban hip-hop clubs. Japanese rappers perform for local audiences in the Japanese language and use Japanese subjects to build their base of fans. In contrast to club events with techno or house music, hip-hop events emphasize lyrics in the shows and the freestyle sessions. There is a wide range of topics addressed in Japanese hip-hop, but they all speak in some way to the local audience. Dassen 3 uses joking lyrics ridiculing school and television. Scha Dara Parr is also playful, emphasizing things like their love of video games and the kind of verbal repartee characteristic of close buddies. When Zeebra acts out his hard-core stance, he tells of drug use in California, expensive dates with girlfriends, and abstract lyrics about hip-hop as a revolutionary war. Rhymester's lyrics are often set in a club or just after a show, for example, describing an imagined, fleeting love affair with a girl on a passing train. Some songs refer to cultural motifs going back centuries, such as a song performed by Rima and Umedy about a double-suicide pact between lovers, remade as a contemporary R&B and hip-hop jam.

Understanding Globalization in Local Terms

Rap music in Japan offers an interesting case study of the way popular culture is becoming increasingly global in scope, while at the same time becoming domesticated to fit with local ideas and desires. At the dawn of the twenty-first century, entertainment industries are reaching wider markets and larger audiences. The film *Titanic*, for example, grossed over $1.5 billion, the largest amount ever for a film, and two-thirds of this income came from overseas. In music, there are global pop stars too, like Britney Spears and Celine Dion. In rap music, the Fugees could be considered global stars. Their 1996 album "The Score" sold over 17 million copies worldwide. More recently, Lauryn Hill's 1998 solo album revealed that the transnational market for hip-hop is still growing, and most major rap stars do promotional tours in Japan. An important feature of pop culture commodities is that they tend to be expensive to produce initially, but then relatively cheap to reproduce and distribute. Compact disks are one of the most striking examples. Although studio time is expensive (between $25,000 for a practically homemade album to upwards of $250,000 for state-of-the-art productions), the CDs themselves cost about eighty cents to produce, including the packaging. Obviously, the more one can sell, the higher the return, and this helps explain the eagerness of entertainment businesses to develop new markets around the world.

Less clear are the kinds of effects such globalized pop culture forms might have. The fluidity of culture in the contemporary world raises new questions about how we are linked together, what we share and what divides us. The spread of popular culture seems in some ways linked with a spread in values, but we must be cautious in our assessment of how and to what extent this transfer takes place. It is safe to say that the conventional understanding of globalization is that it is producing a homogenization of cultural forms. From this perspective, we are witnessing the McDonaldization and the Coca-Cola colonization of the periphery by powerful economic centers of the world system. The term "cultural imperialism" captures this idea, that political and economic power is being used "to exalt and spread the values and habits of a foreign culture at the expense of the native culture."[6] In some ways, anthropology as a discipline emerged at a time when there was a similar concern that the forces of modernity (especially missionaries and colonial officials) were wiping out "traditional cultures," and thus one role for ethnographers was to salvage, at least in the form of written documents, the cultures of so-called "primitive peoples." Many people view globalization, and particularly the spread of American pop culture, as a similar kind of invasion, but the idea that watching a Disney movie automatically instills certain values must be examined and not simply assumed. In some ways the goals of anthropology—combatting simplistic and potentially dangerous forms of ethnocentrism—remain as important today as when the discipline was born.

The example of Japanese hip-hop gives us a chance to examine some recent theorizing on globalization. The sociologist Malcolm Waters offers a useful overview of globalization, which he defines as follows:

> A social process in which the constraints of geography on social and cultural arrangements recede, and in which people become increasingly aware that they are receding.[7]

A key aspect of this definition is not only that the world is increasingly becoming one place, but that people are becoming increasingly aware of that. This awareness may lead to a heightened sense of risk, such as global warming or the "love bug" virus, or to a rosy view of increased opportunities, for example, to get the most recent hip-hop news in real time or to download the latest music instantly via the Internet.

It is important to recognize, however, that globalization involves much more than Hollywood movies and pop music. Waters does a good job of analyzing three aspects of globalization, namely, economic, political, and cultural. He contends that globalization processes go back five hundred years, and that the relative importance of economic, political, and cultural exchanges has varied over that time.[8] From the sixteenth to nineteenth centuries, economics was key. In particular, the

---

[6]John Tomlinson, *Cultural Imperialism: A Critical Introduction* (London: Printer Publishers, 1991), p. 3.

[7]Malcolm Waters, *Globalization* (London: Routledge, 1995, p. 3).

[8]Waters, pp. 157–164.

growth of the capitalist world system was the driving force in linking diverse regions. During the nineteenth and twentieth centuries, politics moved to the fore. Nation-states produced a system of international relations that characterized global linkages with multinational corporations and integrated national traditions. Now, at the dawn of the twenty-first century, cultural forms are leading global changes in both politics and economics. Waters argues that a "global idealization" is producing politics based on worldwide values (e.g., human rights, the environment, anti-sweatshop movement) and economic exchanges centered on lifestyle consumerism. The key point is that while economics and then politics were the driving forces in globalization of previous centuries, it is cultural flows that are increasingly important today. If he is right, and I would argue he is, this points to the importance of studying the kinds of ideals that are spread around the globe.

What ideals are spread by hip-hop in Japan? Clubbing certainly promotes an attitude that stresses leisure, fashion, and consumer knowledge of music over other kinds of status in work and school. Although it is important to recognize that the effects of lyrics are somewhat complicated, it is worth considering, to some extent, the messages carried by the music. Although rappers deal with a wide variety of subjects, one theme appears again and again, namely, that youth need to speak out for themselves. As rapper MC Shiro of Rhymester puts it, "If I were to say what *hip-hop* is, it would be a 'culture of the first person singular.' In hip-hop, . . . rappers are always yelling, 'I'm this.'" Such a message may seem rather innocuous compared to some of the hard-edged lyrics one is likely to hear in the United States, but it is also a reflection of the kind of lives these Japanese youth are leading. In Japan, the education system tends to emphasize rote memorization and to track students according to exams. Sharply age-graded hierarchies are the norm, and may be especially irksome in a situation where the youth are likely to live with their parents until they get married. Moreover, the dominant ideology that harmony of the group should come before individual expression ("the nail that sticks up gets hammered down") makes for a social context in which the hip-hop idea that one should be speaking for oneself is, in some limited sense, revolutionary. At the very least, it shows how global pop culture forms are leading not to some simple homogenization, but rather adding to a complex mix that in many ways can only be studied ethnographically through extended research in local sites.

Another important theorist of globalization is Arjun Appadurai, who proposes that we consider contemporary cultural flows in terms of movement in five categories: people or ethnicity, ideology, finance, technology, and media. He adds the suffix "-scape" to each to highlight that the deterritorialization of cultural forms is accompanied by new landscapes of cultural exchange, thus we have "ethnoscapes, ideoscapes, financescapes, technoscapes, and mediascapes" (others have added "sacriscapes" to describe the spread of religion, and one might add "leisurescapes" for the spread of popular culture). The key point about these landscapes is that they are "non-isomorphic," that is, they don't map evenly onto each other. Appadurai notes, for example, that the "Japanese are notoriously hospitable to ideas and are stereotyped as inclined to export (all) and import (some) goods, but they are notoriously closed to immigration."[9] Migration and electronic mass media are the main driving forces to Appadurai's theorization. One of the problems with Appadurai's theory, however, is that the notion of "-scapes" draws us away from considering how flows of technology, media, finance, and people are connected. An alternative is to consider key sites, *genba* if you will, of various sorts depending on one's interests as a way to see how new, hybrid forms of culture are produced. "Genba globalism" aims to show how artists, fans, producers, and media people are actively consuming and creating these new forms.

One thing that anthropologists offer to the advancement of human knowledge is a clear sense of the ways people interact in specific places. At one time, anthropologists would choose a village or island to map in elaborate detail. Now in a media-filled world, we face different analytical challenges, but the techniques of fieldwork—learning the language, participating in daily life, observing rituals, and so on—can still be used. One of Appadurai's conclusions is that exchanges along these different "-scapes" are leading not only to a deterritorialization of cultural forms, but also to an increased importance of the "work of the imagination."[10] In other words, as identities can be picked up from a variety of media sources, the construction of "who we are" arises increasingly from how we imagine ourselves, rather than from where we live. Life in urban areas seems to make this aspect of identity—as imagination and as performance—all the more salient. What I hope I have drawn attention to is the way the hip-hop nightclubs give us a chance to bring some of this work of the imagination down to the level of daily life.

Conclusion: Global Pop and Cultural Change

In the end, the globalization of popular culture needs to be understood as two related yet opposing trends of greater massification and deeper compartmentalization. On one hand, the recording industry is reaching larger and larger markets, both within Japan and around the world, as mega-hits continue to set sales records. On the other hand, there is an equally profound if less visible process by which niche scenes are becoming deeper and more widely connected than before, and in the process, new forms of heterogeneity are born. Although I have only been able to touch on a few of its aspects here, Japanese rap music is a revealing case study of the social location, cultural role, and capitalist logic of such micro-mass cultures. It is important to recognize, however, that these micro-mass cultures also have the potential to move into the mainstream.

[9]Arjun Appadurai, *Modernity at large: Cultural dimensions of globalization* (Minneapolis: University of Minnesota Press, 1996), p. 37.

[10]Appadurai, p. 3.

The distinction between "scene" and "market" highlights what is at stake when we try to analyze the cultural and capitalist transformations associated with globalization. Information-based and service industries are growing rapidly, promising to reorganize the bounds of culture and commodities, yet we need close readings of how such emerging economies influence everyday lives. Although B-Boys and B-Girls go to great lengths to distinguish the "cultural" from the "commercial" in their favored genre, it is rather the linkage of the two in the circuits of popular culture that offers the deepest insight. In the end, the winds of global capitalism that carried the seeds of rap music to Japan can only be grasped historically with a close attention to social spaces, media forms, and the rhythms of everyday life.

Walking to a hip-hop club in Tokyo, one is confronted with a tremendous range of consumer options, and it is this heightened sense of "you are what you buy" that has in many ways become the defining feature of identity in advanced capitalist nations, at least among those people with the money to consume their preferred lifestyle. At the same time, it is important to be sensitive to the ways that, outward appearances notwithstanding, the consumers of things like hip-hop are embedded in a quite different range of social relations and cultural meanings. It makes a difference that B-Boys and B-Girls, listening to American hip-hop records, still feel it is important to go around to their friends and associates with the traditional New Year's greeting of deference and obligation. This is an example of the ways social relations within the Japanese rap scene continue to carry the weight of uniquely Japanese practices and understandings.

It is likely, too, that "global pop" will become more heterogeneous as the entertainment industries in other countries develop. There are reasons to think that, in music at least, the domination of American popular music as the leading "global" style seems likely to be a temporary situation. In the immediate postwar period in Japan, Western music initially dominated sales. But sales of Japanese music steadily grew and in 1967 outpaced Western sales. Today, three-fourths of Japan's music market is Japanese music to one-fourth Western. Moreover, although American music currently constitutes about half of global sales, this is down from 80 percent a decade ago. It is quite possible that as local record companies mature in other countries, they will, as in Japan, come to dominate local sales. Certainly, multinational record companies are moving in this direction of developing local talent and relying less on Western pop stars. Moreover, although Japan is a ravenous importer of American popular culture, it has some notable exports as well. Some are more familiar than others, but they include the Mighty Morphin' Power Rangers, karaoke, "Japanimation," *manga* (Japanese comic books), mechanical pets, Nintendo or the Sony PlayStation video games, and of course, Pokémon.

Just as it would seem strange to Americans if someone claimed Pokémon is making U.S. kids "more Japanese," it is dangerous to assume that mass culture goods by themselves threaten to overwhelm other cultures. The anthropologist Daniel Miller has been a proponent for taking a closer look at the ways such goods are woven into everyday lives. He argues that mass commodities are better analyzed in terms of an "unprecedented diversity created by the differential consumption of what had once been thought to be global and homogenizing institutions."[11] Miller's emphasis on the active and creative aspects of consumption is characteristic of a broad trend within the social sciences to view global commodities in terms of their local appropriations, and to represent local consumers with a greater degree of agency than found in other works that emphasize "cultural imperialism." It is this perspective that seems to me the best characterization of what is going on in Japan.

It is easy to see how the "sameness" aspect of globalization is promoted. Music magazines, TV video shows, and record stores promote similar artists whether in Japan or the United States. A new album by Nas is met with a flurry of publicity in the Japanese and English-language hip-hop magazines available in Tokyo. This relates in part to the structure of record companies and their marketing practices. In this sense, the widening and increasingly globalized market for popular culture does appear to be leading to greater homogenization. But it is primarily a process of homogenizing what is available, regardless of where you are. I would argue that the global marketing blitz of megahit productions like the film *Titanic* and the music of Celine Dion and Lauryn Hill reflect a homogenization of *what* is available, but not *how* it is interpreted. Although it is more difficult to see, in part because it is hidden beneath similar clothes, hairstyles, and consumption habits, different interpretations are generated in different social contexts. By attending to "actual sites" of cultural production and consumption, we can more clearly gauge the ways local contexts alter the meanings of globalization. "Keeping it real" for hip-hoppers in Japan means paying attention to local realities.

Review Questions

1. Describe the Tokyo hip-hop scene as it is presented by Condry. Based on your own knowledge of the North American scene, what seems to be different about Japanese hip-hop?

2. Condry notes that an author, Malcolm Waters, identifies three basic kinds of globalization that have occupied three time periods. What are those kinds of globalization and when was each most important?

3. What are "-scapes" as they have been presented in the writings of anthropologist Arjun Appadurai? How do they apply to the Japanese hip-hop scene?

4. What is the major contribution anthropologists can make to the study of globalization according to Condry? How does this article illustrate that contribution?

5. What is cultural imperialism? Can Japanese culture be "imperialistic"?

---

[11]Daniel Miller, "Introduction: Anthropology, modernity and consumption," in Daniel Miller (ed.), *Worlds Apart: Modernity through the Prism of the Local* (London: Routledge, 1995), p. 3.

TEN

CULTURE CHANGE AND APPLIED ANTHROPOLOGY

READINGS IN THIS SECTION

The Kayapo Resistance   385
Terence Turner

Medical Anthropology: Improving Nutrition in Malawi   403
Sonia Patten

Using Anthropology   415
David W. McCurdy

Career Advice for Anthropology Undergraduates   428
John T. Omohundro

Nowhere in the world do human affairs remain precisely constant from year to year. New ways of doing things mark the history of even the most stable groups. Change occurs when an Australian aboriginal dreams about a new myth and teaches it to the members of his band; when a loader in a restaurant kitchen invents a way to stack plates more quickly in the dishwasher; or when a New Guinea Big Man cites the traditional beliefs about ghosts to justify the existence of a new political office devised by a colonial government. Wherever people interpret their natural and social worlds in a new way, cultural change has occurred. Broad or narrow, leisurely or rapid, such change is part of life in every society.

Culture change can originate from two sources: innovation and borrowing. **Innovation** is the invention of qualitatively new forms. It involves the recombination of what people already know into something different. For example, Canadian Joseph-Armand Bombardier became an innovator when he mated tracks, designed to propel earth-moving equipment, to a small bus that originally ran on tires, producing the first snowmobile in the 1950s. Later, the Skolt Lapps of Finland joined him as innovators when they adapted his now smaller, more refined snowmobile for herding reindeer in 1961. The Lapp innovation was not the vehicle itself. That was borrowed. What was new was the use of the vehicle in herding, something usually done by men on skis.

Innovations are more likely to occur and to be adopted during stressful times when traditional culture no longer works well. Bombardier, for example, began work on his snowmobile after he was unable to reach medical help in time to save the life of his critically ill son during a Canadian winter storm. Frustrated by the slowness of his horse and sleigh, he set out to create a faster vehicle.

The other basis of culture change is **borrowing.** Borrowing—or **diffusion,** as it is sometimes called—refers to the adoption of something new from another group. Tobacco, for example, was first domesticated and grown in the New World but quickly diffused to Europe and Asia after 1492. Such items as the umbrella, pajamas, Arabic numerals, and perhaps even the technology to make steel came to Europe from India. Ideologies and religions may diffuse from one society to another.

An extreme diffusionist view has been used to explain most human achievements. For example, author Erich von Däniken argues that features of ancient New World civilizations were brought by space invaders. Englishman G. Elliot Smith claimed that Mayan and Aztec culture diffused from Egypt. Thor Heyerdahl sailed a reed boat, the *Ra II,* from Africa to South America to prove that an Egyptian cultural origin was possible for New World civilization.

Whether something is an innovation or borrowed, it must pass through a process of **social acceptance** before it can become part of a culture. Indeed many, if not most, novel ideas and things remain unattractive and relegated to obscurity. To achieve social acceptance, an innovation must become known to the members of a society, must be accepted as valid, and must fit into a system of cultural knowledge revised to accept it.

Several principles facilitate social acceptance. If a change wins the support of a person in authority, it may gain the approval of others. Timing is also important. It would have made little sense for a Lapp to attempt the introduction of snowmobiles when there was no snow or when the men who do the reindeer herding were scattered over their vast grazing territory. Other factors also affect social acceptance. Changes have a greater chance of acceptance if they meet a felt need, if they appeal to people's prestige (in societies where prestige is important), and if they provide some continuity with traditional customs.

Change may take place under a variety of conditions, from the apparently dull day-to-day routine of a stable society to the frantic climate of a revolution. One situation that has occupied many anthropologists interested in change is **cultural contact,** particularly situations of contact where one society politically dominates another. World history is replete with examples of such domination, which vary in outcome from annihilation—in the case of the Tasmanians and hundreds of tribes in North and South America, Africa, Asia, and even ancient Europe—to the political rule that indentured countless millions of people to colonial powers.

The process of change caused by these conditions is called **acculturation.** Acculturation results from cultural contact. Acculturative change may affect dominant societies as well as subordinate ones. After their ascendance in India, for example, the British came to wear *khaki* clothes, live in *bungalows,* and trek through *jungles*—all Indian concepts.

But those who are subordinated experience the most far-reaching changes in their way of life. From politically independent, self-sufficient people, they usually become subordinate and dependent. Sweeping changes in social structure and values may occur, along with a resulting social disorganization.

Although the age of colonial empires is largely over, the destruction of tribal culture continues at a rapid pace today. As we saw in Reed's article in Part Three of this book, hundreds of thousands of Amazonian Indians have already perished in the last few years because of intrusive frontier and development programs. Following almost exactly the pattern of past colonial exploitation, modern governments bent on "progress" displace and often kill off indigenous tribal populations. The frequent failure of development, coupled with its damaging impact on native peoples, has caused many anthropologists to reassess their role. As a result, more and more anthropologists have become part of native resistance to outside intrusion.

A less dramatic, but in many ways no less important, agent of change is the world economy. No longer can most people live in self-sufficient isolation. Their future is inevitably tied in with an overall system of market exchange. Take the Marshall Islanders described by anthropologist Michael Rynkiewich, for example. Although they cultivate to meet their own subsistence needs, they also raise coconuts for sale on the world market. Receipts from the coconut crop go to pay for outboard motors and gasoline, cooking utensils, and a variety of other goods they don't manufacture themselves but have come to depend on. Several major American food companies have now eliminated coconut oil from their products because of its high level of saturated fat. This loss has created lower demand for copra (dried coconut meat), from which the oil is pressed. Reduced demand, in turn, may cause substantial losses to the Marshall Islanders. A people who once could subsist independently have now become prisoners of the world economic system.

Anthropologists may themselves become agents of change, applying their work to practical problems. **Applied anthropology,** as opposed to academic anthropology, includes any use of anthropological knowledge to influence social interaction, to maintain or change social institutions, or to direct the course of cultural change. There are four basic uses of anthropology contained within the applied field: adjustment anthropology, administrative anthropology, action anthropology, and advocate anthropology.

Adjustment anthropology uses anthropological knowledge to make social interaction more predictable among people who operate with different cultural codes. For example, take the anthropologists who consult with companies and government agencies about intercultural communication. It is often their job to train Americans to interpret the cultural rules that govern interaction in another society. For a businessperson who will work in Latin America, the anthropologist may point out the appropriate culturally defined speaking distances, ways to sit, definitions of time, topics of conversation, times for business talk, and so on. All of these activities would be classified as adjustment anthropology.

Administrative anthropology uses anthropological knowledge for planned change by those who are external to the local cultural group. It is the use of anthropological knowledge by a person with the power to make decisions. If an anthropologist provides knowledge to a mayor about the culture of constituents, he or she is engaged in administrative anthropology. So would advisers to chief administrators of U.S. trust territories such as once existed in places like the Marshall Islands.

Action anthropology uses anthropological knowledge for planned change by the local cultural group. The anthropologist acts as a catalyst, providing information but avoiding decision making, which remains in the hands of the people affected by the decisions.

Advocate anthropology uses anthropological knowledge by the anthropologist to increase the power of self-determination of a particular cultural group. Instead of focusing on the process of innovation, the anthropologist centers attention on discovering the sources of power and how a group can gain access to them. James Spradley took such action when he studied tramps in 1968. He discovered that police and courts systematically deprived tramps of their power to control their lives and of the rights accorded normal citizens. By releasing his findings to the Seattle newspapers, he helped tramps gain additional power and weakened the control of Seattle authorities.

Whether they are doing administrative, advocate, adjustment, or action anthropology, anthropologists take, at least in part, a qualitative approach. They do ethnography, discover the cultural knowledge of their informants, and apply this information in the ways discussed previously. In contrast to the quantitative data so often prized by other social scientists, they use the insider's viewpoint to discover problems, to advise, and to generate policy.

The articles in this part illustrate several aspects of cultural change and applied anthropology. The first, by Terence Turner, relates the case of how one people, the Kayapo of the Brazilian Amazon, have successfully resisted external threats to their existence as a people. By uniting Indians, environmental groups, and legislators, and using the international media, they have managed to protect and expand their forest area and advance the international environmental cause. The second updated selection, by medical anthropologist Sonia Patten, describes her experience as an applied anthropologist. Working with USAID funding, she and a team of specialists designed a program using milk goats to improve children's nutrition in Malawi. The third article, by David McCurdy, discusses the modern uses of anthropology. From studies of General Motors workers, to program assessment for people with AIDS, to participation in government health projects, to international counseling, professional anthropologists put their discipline to work. In this article, McCurdy looks at one way in which the ethnographic perspective can be put to work in a business setting. Finally, in the last article, John Omohundro tackles a question often asked by students: "What do you do with an anthropology major?" Basing his answer on years of work with his institution's career development office, he argues that anthropology teaches a number of skills that are useful in the world of work. The trick, he notes, is for students to translate these skills into résumé language that employers can understand.

Key Terms

acculturation   p. 382
action anthropology   p. 383
adjustment anthropology   p. 383
administrative anthropology   p. 383
advocate anthropology   p. 383
applied anthropology   p. 383

borrowing   p. 381
cultural contact   p. 382
diffusion   p. 381
innovation   p. 381
social acceptance   p. 381

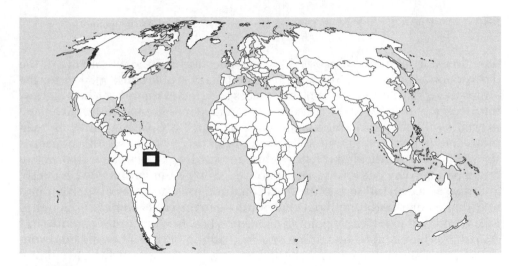

37

The Kayapo Resistance

Terence Turner

Until about 200 years ago, vast areas of the world were inhabited by native, mostly hunter-gatherer or horticultural, peoples. Few native groups have survived the ravages of colonial and economic expansion, though, and those who are left seem destined to become victims of "progress." In this article, however, Terence Turner argues that "Fourth World" peoples—in this case the Kayapo of the Brazilian Amazon—have acted to conserve their own political autonomy while simultaneously aiding the world conservation movement. Apparently doomed to extinction by the relentless encroachment of Brazilian settlers, loggers, miners, and dam builders, the Kayapo have managed to mobilize not only themselves, but other Indians, environmentalists, legislators, and the world press in a united effort to defend the forest and their right to live in it.

Turner, Terence. The Role of Indigenous Peoples in the Environmental Crisis: The Example of the Kayapo of the Brazilian Amazon. *Perspectives in Biology and Medicine* 36:3 (1993), 526–545. © The Johns Hopkins University Press. Reprinted with permission of The Johns Hopkins University Press.

As increasing numbers of people have become aware of the imminence of the destruction of the world's tropical forests and the probable consequences for the atmosphere and climate of the planet, voices have increasingly been heard drawing attention to the need for concern for human populations of forest dwellers, as well as the floral and faunal components of the ecosystem. This has been motivated in part by humanitarian concerns, in part by more specific concerns for indigenous political and legal rights, in part by an awareness that native forest peoples may possess valuable knowledge of their environments, and also, at times, by a realization that the traditional adaptive activities of such peoples may make important functional contributions to the ecosystems in which they live. Whatever their specific point of departure, however, advocates of native forest peoples have tended to assume that recognition of the rights and contributions of the native inhabitants of the forests, as well as their physical and cultural survival, would depend, like the salvation of the forests themselves, upon them. That native forest peoples themselves, many of whom number among the most primitive and remote human societies on earth, should come to play an important role as allies and even leaders in the world struggle to save the forests is a prospect so apparently remote as to seem only a little less improbable than Martians arriving to lend a hand. Yet this is precisely what has been happening in the last few years, nowhere with more impressive scope and success than in the case of the Kayapo Indians of the Brazilian Amazon.

The Kayapo: Ethnographic and Historical Background

The Kayapo are a nation of Ge-speaking Indians who inhabit the middle and lower reaches of the valley of the Xingu River, one of the major southern tributaries of the Amazon. Their total population is currently around 2,500, divided among 14 mutually independent communities. The largest of these communities, Gorotire, has about 800 inhabitants, but several others are little more than hamlets. Kayapo country is a mixture of forest and savannah land, with rather more forest than open country around most of the villages. The total area covered by Kayapo communities and their associated land-use patterns is about the size of Scotland.

The massive destruction of the Amazonian environment represented by the cutting and burning of the forest, the cutting of roads, and the soil erosion and river pollution caused by mining and the building of giant hydroelectric dams, have had a shattering impact on the environment and way of life of many forest Indians of the Amazon. Even groups whose lands have not yet been reached by these activities, or are just beginning to be affected by them, now live in the permanent shadow of the threat. To understand the meaning of this threat for indigenous peoples like the Kayapo, one must stand in a Kayapo village under the dense clouds of smoke that now darken the sky over Kayapo country at the end of every dry season, as Brazilian squatters and ranchers burn off vast stretches of previously forested land to the east and south, rapidly approaching the traditional borders of Kayapo territory along a 700-mile front. It is to feel one's world burning, with the ring of fire drawing even tighter.

For members of modern industrial societies, one of the most difficult points to grasp about the relation of native tropical forest peoples to their environment, as articulated through their modes of subsistence production, is that the relationship is not felt or conceived to comprise a separate, "economic" sphere in our sense. Rather, it forms an integral part of the total social process of producing human beings and social life. The threatened annihilation of such a society's environmental base of subsistence is therefore not felt merely as an "economic" threat, nor one that can be located and confined in an external, "environmental" sphere. It is a threat to the continuity and meaning of social life. Understanding this point is essential, not only to appreciate the traumatic effects of wholesale ecological devastation on traditional societies of subsistence producers like the Kayapo, but also to understand the nature of their political response and resistance to such threats.

The Relation of the Kayapo to the Environment through Subsistence Production

For the Kayapo, like most other contemporary Amazonian native peoples, traditional patterns of subsistence adaptation are still the basic way of life. The Kayapo produce their means of subsistence by a combination of slash-and-burn horticulture, hunting, fishing, and foraging. According to the division of labor by gender and generation, men engage in all productive pursuits incompatible with the care of young children, while women perform those which can be carried out while caring for children. This means that men hunt, fish, do the heavy and dangerous work of clearing gardens, and gather certain wild forest products that grow at great distances, requiring overnight journeys. Women do the planting, weeding, and harvesting of gardens; cut firewood; cook the food; build traditional shelters (now done almost exclusively in trekking camps); forage for such wild products as can be found within a day's round-trip walk from the village or camp; and care for children. Girls begin to help their mothers with household and garden chores while still children, but boys do little productive labor until they are inducted into the men's house, a bachelors' dormitory and men's club which stands apart from the family houses in the middle of the round village plaza.

Kayapo gardens must be cleared from fresh forestland and produce for about three years for most crops. The Kayapo raise an impressive variety of garden produce: manioc (both the bitter and sweet varieties), maize, bananas, yams, sweet potatoes, fava beans, squash, *cissus* (a leafy creeper that is a unique domesticate of their own), tobacco, *urucu* (used to make red body paint), and cotton (used to make string, but not woven). In recent years, many Kayapo have added Brazilian-introduced crops such as papaya, rice, various species of beans, pineapples, watermelon, avocado, and mango. Most families maintain about three gardens in production at any one time and clear a new one every year. After a garden is abandoned, it requires about 25 years for reforestation to render it ready for reuse. A sizable village therefore needs an extensive area of forestland for the rotation of its garden plots.

The Kayapo supplement their horticultural diet with large quantities of fish and game. Included among the latter are wild pig, tapir, deer, monkey, tortoise, armadillo, and various species of birds and rodents. Gathered wild produce is also seasonally important, and includes *babassu* coconuts (used for body and hair oil), *piki, tucum,* and brazil nuts, honey, palmito, *acai, bacaba,* and a variety of less important fruits. Hunting or fishing for the men, and gardening for the women, are more or less daily activities while the community is settled in its base village.

For considerable periods of the year, however, the Kayapo abandon their base villages and go off on collective seminomadic treks through the surrounding forest and savannah. These may last from one to three months, and may take one of several forms. Individual age-sets (most frequently, the male bachelors' set) may be sent out to gather seasonally ripening nuts or fruits; the whole village may go together; the individual senior men's societies may trek as separate groups, each with its associated women, children, and bachelor dependents; or only part of the village may go on trek to gather food for a ceremonial feast, while the rest remain behind in the village. A community may go on two or three such treks per year, so that at least some of the village may spend as much as half the year on trek. Large areas may thus be covered by all the treks undertaken by the members of a single village in a given year. In spite of the low population density of Kayapo country, therefore, most of the area is actually used by the mobile trekking groups which continually sally forth from the widely scattered base villages.

The regular alternation between trekking and base village occupation thus appears to be an integral aspect of Kayapo social organization. Why this should be so is not immediately apparent. Trekking by large collective groups is a relatively inefficient way to exploit the wild floral and faunal resources of an area. Only the adult men of the camp do any hunting. The bachelors and younger boys are typically occupied either with clearing the trail to the next day's campsite and the campsite itself, or bringing up horticultural produce from the village gardens, while the women occupy themselves with pitching or breaking camp, cutting firewood, preparing food, and tending children. The camp is moved every one or two days, but usually only for a distance of one or two kilometers, about a 15-minute walk. More game could doubtless be captured by small groups of men working alone, free to move more rapidly over greater distances. Hunting and fishing are routinely done in this way while the community is residing in the base village, and it is certainly no less productive than the hunting done on trek. Trekking by whole communities or large groups, in other words, cannot be accounted for as the most efficient available method of acquiring needed protein or other foodstuffs.

A similar question arises over the frequency with which Kayapo bands moved their village sites in the days before peaceful relations were established with the Brazilians. There is in fact no ecological reason why Kayapo villages as large as two thousand would ever need to move as a group from their permanent village sites to remain supplied with the foods they require. Notwithstanding this fact, Kayapo villages before pacification tended to move as often as every two, or more usually five to ten years. A given community would have as many as a dozen village sites, and occupy most of them over a twenty-year period. This frequency of movement, again, cannot be accounted for simply as a result of material necessity. In common with trekking, it seems part of a dynamic inherent in Kayapo social organization.

The Social Meaning of Subsistence Production

The high mobility of Kayapo society, and the large amount of territory it requires in consequence, thus cannot be understood, as some have attempted to do, as the result of nutritional deficiencies in the soil or lack of protein or other nutrients in the faunal or floral environment. They are, rather, the corollaries and effects of the organization of Kayapo society, with its central tension between female-centered and male-centered forms of social grouping. These forms themselves, however, are articulated in terms of their complementary roles in production, although this is production understood in the Kayapo sense of the social production of human beings and social relations, which includes but is not reducible to, material subsistence. This notion of social production calls for a more extended exegesis as it is essential to an understanding of the Kayapo relationship to their natural environment and their society per se.

Kayapo patterns of environmental adaptation and subsistence production are intricately interwoven with their ways of producing human individuals. This process of human production includes what we call "socializing" children, but continues through the life cycle and the final rites of death. This individual process, in turn, is treated by the Kayapo as an integral part of the process of reproducing collective social units like extended-family households, age-sets, and ceremonial organizations, and thus of society as a whole. As I have already indicated, the division of labor in the production of material subsistence is defined in relation to the division of labor in the production of social persons and relations, with women specializing in the socialization of children. It must be clearly understood that this is not simply a natural result but a culturally imposed social pattern. Women who do not happen to be raising young children nevertheless do not go hunting and fishing. At a higher level of organization, the nuclear family forms the social unit of cooperation in the production and consumption of material subsistence, but as a social unit it owes its form primarily to its role in producing new social persons, not its functions in expediting subsistence activities. Subsistence production thus finds its place as an integral part of the global process of social production, which also includes the socialization of children, the recruitment and reconstitution of families and collective groups, and the celebration of the great communal ceremonies. In these two-to-four month long symbolic dramas, all of these levels of activity are performed in an orchestrated pattern that asserts their essential interdependence as parts of a single whole.

The Kayapo attitude toward the nonhuman natural environment must be understood as a part of this same global pattern. The Kayapo do not oppose "nature" to human society as mutually exclusive, externally related domains; nor can they be said to possess a single, uniform concept of "nature" in our sense. They recognize that the forest and savannah beyond their village clearings are products of forces that are independent of humans and not under social control. They further recognize that they depend upon these natural forces and products for their own social existence, and that social persons are in fact largely "natural" beings, whose physical bodies, senses, and libidinal energies are as extra-social in origin as any forest tree or wild animal. Disease, death, shamanic trance, insanity, and periods of transition in [life]-crisis ritual are seen as moments when the continuity between the internal natural core of human social actors and the external natural environment of the forest and animal world asserts itself, short-circuiting and blacking out the interposed, insulating social veneer. At such times, the social person reverts to a "natural" state, here conceived as one of entropic dissolution of social form. At other times, as in the rituals of initiation at puberty or the everyday bringing in of game, gathered nuts, or garden produce from the forest, displacing or penetrating the boundary between nature and society has the opposite result: an infusion of energy which, directed into social channels, enables society to exist and renew itself. Human beings and society itself, in sum, are seen as partly "natural" entities, dependent on continual infusions of energy from their natural surroundings. The reproduction of human society, the reproduction of socialized human beings, and the reproduction of the natural forest and savannah environment are thus interconnected parts of a single great process.

Society and its members, in sum, are essentially seen as appropriating and channeling natural energy, and are thus dependent on the ability of the natural world (meaning the forest, animals, birds, rivers, and fish) to reproduce itself and continue as a great reservoir and source of the energy society must continually draw upon to live. The destruction of the forest, the killing or driving away of its animals, or the pollution of the rivers and killing of their fish, therefore, are not seen by the Kayapo simply as an attack on "the natural environment" in our sense, but as a direct assault upon them as a society and as individuals.

This view, it should immediately be added, is fully compatible with the destruction of trees and animals on a considerable scale for appropriation by the Kayapo of the energy stored in their flesh, fruits, or the soil on which they stand. The Kayapo operate with a rough rule of thumb derived from millennia of experience, a sense of the ability of the local environment to accommodate a certain level of destruction, inflicted by their traditional modes and levels of subsistence activity, and still regenerate itself. They have no mystical sense of reverence or respect for individual trees or animals and feel no hesitation about chopping them down or taking them as game whenever their interests demand. What concerns the Kayapo is nature in the aggregate, or more specifically, the survival and reproduction of a sufficient slice of the natural environment to support their traditional way of life. It was only when they realized that this aggregate capacity for regeneration was threatened by the vast scale of the destruction now being inflicted on the area that the Kayapo became aroused over the fate of the forest environment as such. Similarly, ecological concerns for tropical rain forests became transformed into urgent political issues in the developed world only when peoples of the developed countries realized the probable consequences of this destruction from the rest of the world's climate and population. Kayapo and First World modes of "ecological" consciousness and concern converged, in short, when, starting from very different premises, the members of both societies realized that the survival of their societies was at stake. The dramatic results of this convergence are the subject of the rest of this paper.

The Kayapo Resistance and the Environmentalist Movement

The Kayapo area of Southern Para state is a representative microcosm of the destructive processes at work in the Amazon as a whole. Beginning in the late 1960s, the Kayapo have been confronted with virtually every major form of environmental destruction and land depredation found elsewhere in the region.

The Kayapo Face the End of Their World

Since the 1960s there has been constant pressure from small squatters and large ranchers attempting to infiltrate Kayapo areas and clear small farms by burning off patches of forest. Land speculators have attempted to build illegal airstrips and to survey and sell off large chunks of Kayapo land to which they did not even hold legal title. In 1971, the Brazilian government built a major road of the Trans-Amazonica highway system through Kayapo country, secretly altering the route so as to amputate the Kayapo area of the Xingu National Park, which it then attempted to sell off to private owners, mostly speculators, would-be ranchers, and farmers. The road brought heavy truck and bus traffic carrying settlers and supplies to the new settlements farther west, bringing with them the perils of infectious disease and the potential for conflict with the Indians. Timber companies interested in the large stands of virgin mahogany within the boundaries of the remaining officially delimited Kayapo reserve, the Kayapo Indigenous Area, sought and obtained logging concessions for large tracts from Kayapo leaders in exchange for sizable money payments and the construction of modern housing and other facilities in Kayapo villages. Most of the money went into communal accounts in banks in neighboring frontier towns. These accounts were either explicitly or tacitly controlled by chiefs or the few literate Kayapo able to keep the accounts. Some of these individuals began to draw heavily on these "communal" funds for personal use, giving rise to tension and resentment by the rest of their communities. Rivalries between competing companies and their respective Kayapo sponsors almost led to war between two Kayapo villages in 1986.

The discovery of gold at the huge mine of Serra Pelada near the eastern border of the Kayapo Indigenous Area led to intense prospecting and exploratory gold-mining activity within the eastern borders of the Kayapo Indigenous Area. This culminated in 1983 with the opening of two large illegal gold mines only ten kilometers from Gorotire village. Three thousand Brazilian miners swarmed onto Kayapo land, and neither the Brazilian Indian Service (FUNAI) nor any other arm of the Brazilian government seemed willing or able to do anything to stop it. Tons of mercury from the mining operations began to pollute the Rio Fresco, the main fishery of several Kayapo communities. Then, in 1986, an even more ominous form of pollution threatened, when radioactive waste from a cancer treatment facility in the city of Goiania caused two dozen fatalities, and the federal government attempted to dump the material on the western border of Kayapo country.

As if all this were not enough, the Kayapo began to hear rumors that the Brazilian government was planning to build a series of hydroelectric dams along the Xingu and its tributaries, which would result in the flooding of large areas of Kayapo land and end the value of most of the river system as a fishery. The scheme was to be funded by loans from the World Bank. Repeated attempts to learn the truth about the government's plans were met with stonewalling and denials that any such plan existed. The rumors persisted, however, and construction sites began to be cleared at certain points along the river. The Kayapo were outraged by the government's disregard for their political and legal rights to be consulted about a project which would so heavily affect their lands and livelihood. They were equally concerned about the ecological effects. While Kayapo leaders strove unsuccessfully to penetrate the government's cover-up about the dam project, however, they were confronted by an even more direct threat to their legal and political rights, as Indians, to challenge governmental or private Brazilian infringements of their land rights, resources, or communal interests. At the convention called to draw up the new Brazilian constitution, a measure was introduced calling for the redefinition of any Indian who demonstrated the capacity to bring a legal action in a Brazilian court as an "acculturated" person who could no longer be considered an Indian, and therefore could no longer represent or bring an action on behalf of an Indian community in court. This "catch-22" provision would have destroyed the possibility of any legal or political resistance by native peoples against abuses of their rights, persons, lands, or environments within the terms of the Brazilian legal and political process.

This daunting array of threats to the Kayapo environment, communal lands and resource base, political and civil rights is a representative sample of the human face of the environmental crisis in the Amazon. The Kayapo confronted this apparently overwhelming onslaught beginning in the early 1970s as a still largely monolingual people of Ge-speakers scattered over a vast area in 14 mutually autonomous and politically uncoordinated settlements. In most of the villages, some of the men (but almost no women) spoke Portuguese, and a handful had learned to read, write, and do simple arithmetic. A few leaders had obtained some experience of Brazilian administrative and political ways through working in the Indian Service or as members of Brazilian expeditions to contact other tribes. They had a few contacts with the outside world through anthropologists and indigenous advocacy groups, and the Brazilian Indian Service (FUNAI) offered some support, although it could not be counted upon to represent the Indians' interests against the more threatening forms of economic development mounted by government or powerful private interests. Aside from this slender array of assets, the Kayapo had no political resources with which to defend themselves and their forest beyond their own largely intact tribal institutions and culture. These, however, were to serve them well in the trials that lay ahead.

The Kayapo Resistance

This is what they did. The two western communities whose land had been severed by the road began an unrelenting campaign of armed attacks on all Brazilian intruders who attempted to open ranches or settle in the separated area. After 15 years and perhaps 50 Brazilian dead, with no Kayapo casualties, no Brazilian settler remained in the entire area. The leaders of the two Kayapo groups meanwhile carried out a campaign of diplomacy, making repeated trips to Brasília to pressure the government to return the stolen land and thus end the violent standoff in the area. The government capitulated in 1985, returning the area to the Kayapo and ceding an additional area immediately to the north of the old area (this became the Capoto Indigenous Area). The two communities of the region joined again into a single large village and have resolutely banned all Brazilian mining, timber, and agricultural interests and settlers from their reclaimed areas.

Also in 1985, the two illegally opened gold mines were assaulted and captured by 200 Kayapo, armed with a mixture of firearms and traditional weapons. The larger mine was accessible only by air, so the Kayapo seized and blockaded the landing strip, confronting the Brazilian government with a choice: either cede title and administrative authority over the mines to the Kayapo, together with a significant percentage of the proceeds (10% was the amount initially demanded), and legally demarcate the boundaries of the Kayapo Indigenous Area (thus making the government unambiguously responsible for the defense of the area against any further such incursions), or the Kayapo would allow no more planes to land or take off, either to supply or evacuate the three thousand miners at the site. After a tense ten-day standoff, the government gave in to the Kayapo demands.

The leaders of Gorotire, the nearest and largest Kayapo village, used the first income from the mine to purchase a light plane and hire a Brazilian pilot. They put the plane to use to patrol their borders from the air to spot intruders and would-be squatters. If any were seen, patrols were dispatched to expel or eliminate the invaders. Within a year, invasions effectively ceased. They have also used the plane to fly to other Kayapo villages and to Brazilian cities to purchase goods and bring people out for medical assistance. In the nearest town of Redencao, and the state capital of Belem, they have bought houses for the use of Kayapo travelers and shoppers, and in the former they have established a tribal office to deal with their bank accounts and official relations with the local office of FUNAI.

All timber concessions on Kayapo land were suspended by the Indian Service (FUNAI) at the end of 1987, at the urging of the most influential Kayapo leaders, Payakan and Ropni. Some concessions, however, were surreptitiously continued by a few other leaders who have lined their own pockets with the fees paid by the companies. Still other communities and leaders not previously involved with lumbering companies are under great pressure from the companies to grant new concessions. Meanwhile, resistance to any new concessions continues to be strong, and one community (A'Ukre) has declared its part of the Kayapo Indigenous Area an "extractive reserve" closed to all ecologically destructive forms of timber and mineral exploitation. This remains a conflicted issue, with the ultimate outcome in doubt. Meanwhile, a substantial area of the Kayapo Indigenous Area has been clear-cut. The fate of the captured gold mines has also proved a divisive issue. Not only have the Kayapo not closed them down, as they originally said they would do within two years of taking them over, but some Kayapo have opened a couple of small new mines on their own land. Other Kayapo vigorously oppose this and have strictly prohibited all mining activity, whether by Brazilians or Kayapo, from their areas of the reserve. Meanwhile, five Gorotire Kayapo have become wealthy enough from the gold and timber revenues to buy private houses for themselves in Redencao, where they live for much of the time, keeping Brazilian servants and, in two cases, acquiring large ranches outside the reserve. This phenomenon has been paralleled by the chief of the village of Kikretum, who owns an airplane, houses, and a hotel in the neighboring town of Tucuma. The rise of this embryonic "new class" has already given rise to significant tensions within Kayapo society and is a factor in the unresolved conflicts over the future form of accommodation between Kayapo society and the Brazilian economy.

Most of the other threats posed by the enveloping national society proved less divisive, and the Kayapo were able to mount concerted, well-organized responses to them without internal dissension or conflict. When the government's plan to dump the radioactive waste on traditional Kayapo land was announced, the Kayapo sent a hundred men to Brasília to demonstrate against the plan. Suitably painted and feathered, they staged a sit-in in the president's palace. Nothing like this had happened in Brazil in the twenty years since the coup d'etat that established the military regime that was then in the process of relinquishing power. The initial incredulity and indignation of the authorities, however, gave way to acquiescence to the Kayapo's demands, and the dumping plan was abandoned. Pressing their advantage, the Kayapo next sent a deputation of some 50 chiefs and leading citizens to the Constitutional Convention to lobby for the defeat of the "catch-22" acculturation clause and other provisions injurious to Indian interests. Presenting themselves as always, in traditional paint and feathers and carrying traditional weapons, they patiently attended the weeks of debates on the sections bearing on indigenous peoples' rights, gave press conferences, and lobbied the deputies. When the acculturation clause was defeated, and surprisingly strong safeguards of indigenous rights, lands, and resources were adopted by the Convention, the Kayapo received much of the credit in the Brazilian press.

In 1988, two Kayapo leaders were invited to the United States to partici-pate in a conference on tropical forest ecology. From there, they traveled to Washington, met with members of Congress, and spoke with World Bank offi-cials about the effects of the proposed Xingu dam scheme on the peoples and environment of the area. They were able to obtain copies of the entire dam proj-ect, the very existence of which the Brazilian government had continued to deny, from the Bank. Shortly after the Kayapos' visit, the World Bank announced that it was deferring action on the Brazilian loan request. Enraged, elements of the Brazilian national security and political establishment had criminal charges brought against them and their American interpreter under a law prohibiting participation in political activity in Brazil by foreigners. The charges were ridicu-lous in strictly legal terms; since the actions in question had taken place in the United States, the American had been acting in his own country, and the Kayapo were not in any case foreigners. The transparent attempt at legal terrorism boomeranged, as nongovernment organizations (NGOs), anthropologists, and the congressmen whom the Kayapo had met on their tour organized an inter-national outcry.

When one of the Kayapo leaders came to Belem, the capital of the state of Para, where the charges had been brought, to be arraigned, the Kayapo orga-nized a massive protest demonstration. More than five hundred Kayapo men and women danced through the streets and massed in the square before the Palace of Justice to support their kinsman and denounce Brazilian political repression. The defiance turned to ridicule when the judge refused to allow the Kayapo leader to enter the courthouse for arraignment until he changed his paint and feathers for "civilized" (Brazilian) clothes. The Kayapo refused and told the judge he would have to come to the Kayapo village of Gorotire if he wanted another chance to arraign him on the charges. Meanwhile, Kayapo ora-tors unrolled the map of the Xingu dam scheme obtained from the World Bank in Washington on an easel erected in the square and explained the entire secret project in Kayapo and Portuguese for the benefit of the many Brazilian onlook-ers, who included reporters and TV crews. The government never again dared to try to arraign the Kayapo leader, and eventually dropped all the charges.

With the World Bank still actively considering the Brazilian government's request for a loan to enable the building of the Xingu dams, the proposed multi-dam hydroelectric scheme in the Xingu River valley now appeared to the Kayapo as the greatest threat, not only to their environment, but to their political and legal control over their lands and resources. Since the government still refused to disclose its plans to build the dams, the Kayapo resolved to force it to reveal its intentions and to receive, before an audience of national and world news media, their criticisms of the human and environmental effects of the dams, as well as of its deceit in attempting to conceal and deny its plans. To accomplish this, they decided to convene in great congress of Amazonian peoples at the site of the first of the dams the government hoped to build: Altamira, near the mouth of the Xingu. To the meeting would be invited representatives of the Brazilian government's representatives of the World Bank; representatives of the national and world news media; nongovernmental organizations active in the environmentalist, human rights, and indigenous peoples' support fields; delegates from as many indigenous nations of Amazonia as possible; and as many Kayapo as could be transported and accommodated. At the meeting, the government representatives would be asked to present their plans, to give an account of their probable effects on the environment and the human inhabitants of the region (Brazilian as well as native), and to explain why they had tried for so long to keep their plans secret from those who would be most affected by them.

The Kayapo leaders who envisioned this project saw that its success would depend on international public opinion, press attention, and financial support. Only the attendance of a large number of media and NGO representatives, they felt, would compel the Brazilian government to send its representatives to face certain humiliation at such a meeting. The leader chiefly responsible for the plan, Payakan, therefore embarked on a tour of seven European and North American countries (sponsored and coordinated by Friends of the Earth, the World Wildlife Federation, and the Kayapo Support Group of Chicago) in November, 1988, to publicize the Altamira gathering and appeal for support. At a more general level, Payakan also sought to bring the crisis of the Amazon forest and its native peoples to wider public attention, and to lobby government and international development bank officials against supporting economic development projects (such as the Xingu dam scheme) that would irreversibly damage the environment and require the expropriation or destruction of native lands.

Payakan, at the same time, also sought to bring about greater mutual trust, cooperation, and unity of purpose among the various kinds of nongovernmental organizations and sectors of public opinion involved in supporting the Indians and the environmental struggle. These included human rights, indigenous peoples' advocacy, anthropological, and environmentalist organizations. Among the latter were some groups specifically devoted to defending tropical rain forests, others concerned with saving endangered animal species, and still others dedicated to conservation and environmental quality in a more general sense. Payakan, in his dealings with these groups or their representatives, had quickly realized that they tended to work in isolation from one another, often mistrusted one another's politics, or viewed one another's work as irrelevant to their own concerns. With other Kayapo leaders, Payakan saw this situation as not only damaging the effectiveness of the work of these organizations, but as out of touch with the real interconnections of the issues with which the groups were attempting to deal. For both reasons, they felt, the support of the NGOs was less effective than it might otherwise be. Payakan therefore devoted much effort on his tour to appealing to these groups to join forces and recognize that they were really all involved in a single great struggle. As he put it in a speech at the University of Chicago:

> The forest is one big thing; it has people, animals, and plants. There is no point
> saving the animals if the forest is burned down; there is no point saving the forest

if the people and animals who live in it are killed or driven away. The groups trying to save the races of animals cannot win if the people trying to save the forest lose; the people trying to save the Indians cannot win if either of the others lose; the Indians cannot win without the support of these groups; but the groups cannot win either without the support of the Indians, who know the forest and the animals and can tell what is happening to them. No one of us is strong enough to win alone; together, we can be strong enough to win.

Payakan's message was widely heard. His tour became a concrete example of the intergroup cooperation he preached. For many indigenous advocacy organizations, environmentalist groups, human rights groups, Latin Americanist social scientists and anthropologists, helping to organize Payakan's tour and attending his speeches was their first practical experience of cooperating and coming together around a common set of interests and commitments. This experience has been continually repeated since then in a series of cooperative efforts to support the Altamira meeting, aid new organizational initiatives by the Kayapo and other forest peoples in Brazil, and help with subsequent tours by Payakan and other Kayapo leaders. It is generally recognized by activists of the various support organizations concerned that the Kayapo campaign has become an important catalyst of increased contact and cooperation among them at the national and international level, and that this cooperation has brought increased efficacy in lobbying, fund-raising, and public opinion outreach efforts.

Payakan's tour successfully achieved all its goals. Enough money was raised to defray all the costs of the Altamira gathering (which eventually approached $100,000) without drawing upon any of the funds derived from timber or gold concessions, which Payakan and most of his closest Kayapo supporters opposed. Much publicity and media attention was generated, guaranteeing a strong international media presence at the Altamira gathering itself. The support base of the Kayapo campaign among European and American nongovernmental organizations, public opinion, and politicians was greatly strengthened. The stage was now set for one of the most remarkable events in the history of Amazonia, the environmentalist movement, and modern popular protest politics.

From February 19–24, 1989, 600 Amazonian Indians and a roughly equal number of Brazilian and international journalists, photographers, TV crews, documentary filmmakers, Brazilian and foreign politicians, and representatives of various nongovernmental support organizations converged on the small river town of Altamira. Among the Indians were some 500 Kayapo and 100 members of 40 other indigenous nations, whom the Kayapo had invited to join them in confronting the Brazilian government, and to make their own views on the issues of dams and the destruction of the forest known to the government representatives, the news media, and one another. Five days of meetings, speeches, press conferences, and ritual performances by Kayapo and other indigenous groups were programmed and carried out without a major hitch. The event represented an impressive feat of organization and political coordination. It required the transportation, lodging, and feeding of hundreds of indigenous participants, which involved constructing a large encampment with traditional Kayapo shelters outside the town and daily busing of its inhabitants to the meeting hall in the center. Much of the credit for the event belongs to the Brazilian indigenous peoples' support organization, The Ecumenical Center for Documentation and Information (CEDI), which effectively cooperated with Payakan and the rest of the indigenous leadership in handling many of the logistical tasks essential to the success of the meeting.

Some elements of the regional Brazilian populace, especially those linked with landowning and commercial interests who stood to gain from the construction of the dams, were hostile to the Indians and (even more) their Brazilian and foreign environmentalist supporters. There were fears that violent incidents might occur and spread out of control. That this did not happen can be attributed in part to the foresight and discipline of the Kayapo, who carefully sited their encampment far outside of town and refrained from street demonstrations within the city limits, but also in large measure to the presence of so many foreign and domestic media personnel and observers.

The event took on the aspect of an international media circus. The Pope sent a telegram of support. The rock star Sting flew in for a day and gave a press conference at the Kayapo encampment, denouncing the destruction of the forest and promoting his own project for the creation of a new Kayapo reserve. No doubt because this project depended on the goodwill of the Brazilian government, Sting avoided directly committing himself in support of the Kayapo campaign against the dams. Since this was the whole purpose of the Altamira meeting, his Kayapo hosts roundly criticized him for using their platform for his own project and then skipping off. A British member of Parliament, a Belgian member of the European Parliament, and a half-dozen Brazilian deputies of the National Congress, however, mounted the platform and gave unreserved support. A final communique was issued, on behalf of all native peoples of Amazonia, condemning the dam project. By the time the conference closed with a dance from the Kayapo New Corn ceremony (joined in by assorted Indians of other tribes, European and Brazilian activists and media personnel, momentarily giving it the air of a 1960s hippie love-in), the Altamira gathering had become an international media success of such proportions as to generate serious political pressure against any international funding of the dam scheme, or indeed any attempt to go on with the plan by the Brazilian government. Within two weeks after the end of the meeting, the World Bank announced that it would not grant the Brazilian loan earmarked for the dam project, and the Brazilian National Congress had announced plans for a formal investigation and debate on the whole plan.

The Kayapo have not rested on their laurels since Altamira. One major line of effort was the drive to get a large area of the west bank of the Xingu demarcated as a third major Kayapo reserve, linking the two largest existing reserves (the Capoto and Kayapo Indigenous Areas) in a continuous area the size of Britain. In this effort, the Kayapo were supported by Sting and his recently founded Rainforest Foundation, which raised close to two million dollars to support the project. President Sarney of Brazil made several public statements vaguely in favor of the plan, but in January 1990, when Sting came to Brazil with the money from the Rainforest Foundation to present to the government to start the demarcation of the reserve, Sarney noncommitally passed the buck by merely extending the official period for administrative decision on the proposal into the new administration of President-elect Collor without taking action. Collor finally proclaimed the new reserve in 1991; the actual demarcation of the boundary was finished in September 1992. The demarcation of the new reserve bears witness to the political pressure the Kayapo, and the Rainforest Foundation with its international and Brazilian support, were able to bring to bear. Meanwhile, Payakan established a Kayapo Foundation (the "Fundacao Mebengokre") to administer and raise money for the support of a series of programs, including the establishment of an "extractive reserve" within the Kayapo Indigenous Area. This is an area off-limits to all lumbering and mining operations, devoted exclusively to environmentally sustainable forms of forest exploitation such as the gathering of Brazil nuts and other wild forest products.

The Kayapo also made some attempt to follow up on the links of solidarity with other indigenous Amazonian peoples forged at Altamira. In November 1989, several Kayapo leaders and a Kayapo video-cameraman flew (in a Kayapo plane) to Boa Vista in the northern frontier state of Rondonia to investigate an incident in which Yanomamo villagers had been attacked and driven from their land by Brazilian gold miners. The Kayapo denounced the government policies leading to the incident and declared their support for the survivors. The government had banned the area to all non-Indians after the occurrence, attempting to cover up the affair and keep it out of the press. The government was clearly thinking only of local Yanomamo Indians, but the Kayapo, seizing upon the loophole opened up by the wording of the ban and capitalizing on their undeniable identity as "Indians," were able to penetrate the official smokescreen with their fact-finding and support mission.

Wider Implications: The Kayapo Achievement in World Perspective

The Environmentalist Movement

At the level of international environmentalist politics, the Kayapo are now an established presence. In 1990 alone, Kayapo spokesmen have traveled to various European countries, Canada, the U.S.A., and Japan. They were accorded audiences by heads of state (Mitterand of France), cabinet ministers responsible for loans, aid and financial dealings with Brazil, and members of parliaments and national assemblies (Canada, France, Belgium, England, and the U.S.A.). They have also met with indigenous groups and leaders in North America, notably the Cree of Northern Quebec in 1991 and 1992. All of this notoriety and attention has generated for them a measure of immunity from the cruder forms of abuse and exploitation that have so often been the lot of indigenous peoples in Amazonia and elsewhere.

A mere ten years ago, however, they themselves were the targets of many such abuses, as recounted above. They have succeeded, against fantastic odds, in turning the tables on their would-be exploiters and seizing the political advantage, drawing upon the support of international and urban Brazilian public opinion. The strength of this support owes much to the worldwide wave of concern for the fate of the tropical forests, but the Kayapo would not have been able to capitalize so effectively on the general climate of environmental concern without their shrewd grasp of the possibilities of contemporary news and informational media and their effective presentation of themselves and their cause through them. Other factors in the Kayapo successes have been the effective support of numerous nongovernmental organizations and the impressive capacity of the Kayapo themselves for mass organization and militant but disciplined confrontational tactics, as exemplified by their bold but nonviolent demonstrations in Brasília, Belem, and Altamira.

The success of the Kayapo in furthering their own cause, at the same time, has had an important effect upon the politics of the developed world, and in particular, of the environmentalist movement. The support of environmentalist groups and public opinion has been essential to the Kayapo victories, but it is equally true that the Kayapo have won important victories for the environmentalist movement, and partly as a result have exercised an important influence upon its thinking, strategies, and organizational tactics. Perhaps most importantly, in a few short years they have revolutionized the consciousness of many activists and ordinary persons concerned with the fate of the world's tropical forests, teaching them that indigenous forest-dwelling peoples are not just a passive part of the problem, but an active part of the solution. By their own example, they have demonstrated that native forest peoples, no matter how apparently primitive, remote, or numerically insignificant, can become potent combatants and allies in the struggle to avert ecological disaster. In addition, they have helped bring about working relations of mutual trust and collaboration between members of a number of important organizations, scientific specialists, and politicians, who had previously never considered working together, and in many cases mistrusted one another's politics and policies.

Before the advent of the Kayapo on the international stage, many environmentalists had realized that there could be no solution to the problem of saving the forests that did not include the human inhabitants of the forests. Many who had arrived at this relatively enlightened opinion, however, continued to think of aboriginal forest peoples, and even forest-dwelling members of national societies like the Brazilian rubber-tappers, as historical basket cases, with all the capacity for political action in their own behalf of endangered animal species like the black cayman or the Amazonian giant otter. It has been a humbling, disconcerting, but delightful surprise to many of these same good people suddenly to discover that some of these supposedly hapless victims of progress have assumed a leading role in the struggle environmentalists had thought (perhaps a tad condescendingly) *they* were leading, and that these same native peoples have even succeeded in bringing to the effort a degree of unity and effectiveness that had previously eluded its familiar leadership.

The Rise of Ecological Resistance
in the Fourth World

The Kayapo are not a unique case. Their story, in fact, conforms in its essential features to an emerging pattern of ethnic self-assertiveness and ecological militancy on the part of native forest peoples in the Amazon and other parts of the world. It is not new for native peoples (to refer, by this term, to the tribal societies and ethnic minorities comprising the "Fourth World") to attempt to resist the wholesale appropriation of their lands and resources by the peoples and governments of modern states. What is new is the combination of political, economic, environmental, and ideological pressures with revolutionary new media technologies that has enabled native peoples to take their case directly to the peoples and governments of the world, and to find a receptive hearing because of the convergence of their cause with the new levels of popular concern over the environment.

One major manifestation of this worldwide pattern is the organization, over the past twenty years, of many federations of native peoples, for the most part consisting of groups speaking the same or related languages. Over 50 such groups now exist in the Amazon alone. They typically unite around a program of defense of native land and resources, respect for civil and political rights, and the assertion of traditional values and cultural identity. These groups are increasingly in touch with one another, and in some areas intergroup coordinating organizations, such as the recently organized Coordinating Group of the Amazon Basin, COICA, have begun to appear.

The rise of these organizations and the political consciousness they express has been catalyzed by many factors. Among them are the extension of modern transportation and communications networks to many previously inaccessible areas inhabited by tribal peoples; improved medical technology and assistance; greater availability of manufactured tools and goods; the extension of effective national government administrative control over the contiguous national populations; the increase in the strength and effectiveness of nonindigenous, nongovernmental advocacy and support organizations; the increased interest and ability of national and international media to publicize abuse of native lands, rights and peoples; the increase in international economic and political interdependence, which has made many governments more sensitive to the repercussions of bad publicity over indigenous issues; and last but not least, the influence of a steady trickle of anthropological researchers, who have helped both to catalyze native groups' awareness of the value of their traditional cultures in the eyes of the outside world and to inform them of the existence of potential sources of support in that world for their struggles to resist economic, political, and cultural oppression.

These factors have converged in recent years with growing concern in world public opinion for human rights and environmental issues, which have favored the causes of native groups struggling to defend their traditional lands and resource bases. None of these external factors, however, would have been sufficient by themselves to generate the cultural and social resources, or the political organization and will to act, that have been shown by so many native peoples. This is the part of the story that remains least well known to the world at large. It is important that it become known, as an antidote to the hopelessness induced by apocalyptic but often inaccurate news stories of "genocide" and widespread romantic clichés like the inevitable disappearance of primitive peoples in the path of progress. (The two often have more in common than meets the eye.) These myths have had the harmful effect of discouraging support for the struggles of many native peoples with a fighting chance to win. As the Kayapo case shows, such support can make an enormous difference.

That is the rosy side of a picture which is in the main far from rosy. For every indigenous people who have found the courage, leadership, and ability to respond constructively to the threat of despoliation of their ecological bases or the theft of their lands, others have been or are being decimated, dispossessed, or destroyed. In spite of some shining cases of successful resistance to threats to the ambient life-world, other battles have been, or are being, lost. The sheer volume of environmental destruction, and the variety of its forms and causes, make the struggle appear almost hopeless. Nowhere, however, has this been more true than in the Kayapo area of the Amazon. What the Kayapo have managed to do shows that even the most apparently hopeless odds can be faced and overcome.

Review Questions

1. How do the Kayapo Indians of Brazil subsist in their Amazon forest environment?

2. What forces threaten the livelihood and social existence of the Kayapo as a cultural group?

3. How have the Kayapo reacted to defend their forest environment and their existence as a cultural group?

4. Turner argues that the Kayapo have tried to unite and enlist the aid of several kinds of local and world groups in their fight to preserve their forest and lands. What are these groups? Use the case of the encampment at Altamira to illustrate how they could work together.

5. How have the Kayapo affected the world environmentalist movement?

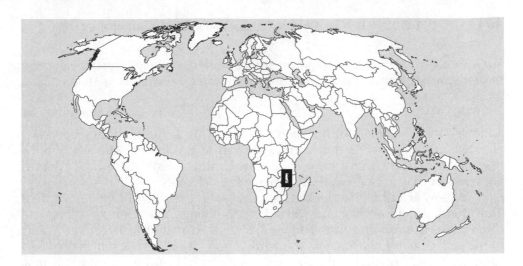

38

Medical Anthropology: Improving Nutrition in Malawi

Sonia Patten

Applied anthropologists work in many settings. They may conduct government program evaluations, work on forest conservation projects, market or advertise products, staff rural development programs, establish foreign offices for nongovernmental organizations or corporations, or advise hospital staff, among other things. In this article, Sonia Patten describes her role as an applied medical anthropologist on a project aimed at the improvement of infant and child nutrition in the African nation of Malawi. As a medical anthropologist, her job was to collect cultural baseline data that would help to shape the program and make it appropriate to village conditions in Malawi.

Malawi—Welcome to the Warm Heart of Africa. This is the sign that greets travelers when they arrive in this southeastern African republic. The warm, open response to visitors that I have enjoyed each time I have traveled to Malawi contrasts starkly to the poverty that plagues its citizens.

Malawi is a small landlocked nation in southeast Africa that lies south of Tanzania, east of Zambia, and west of Mozambique. The country is long and thin with its axis running north and south along the Great African Rift Valley. Part of the valley holds Lake Malawi, the third largest lake in Africa, which accounts for more than 20 percent of the country's total area of 119,100 square kilometers. Malawi is one of the ten poorest countries in the world. Its economy is based predominately on agriculture, which accounts for half the gross domestic product and virtually all the exports. Cotton, tobacco, and sugar are most likely to be sold to other countries. However, despite exports, food security for both households and the nation is a chronic problem, with annual "hungry seasons" a fact of life and the specter of famine never far from people's minds. Maize, or white corn, is the staple food for the nation, and it is rare when the nation's rain-fed agriculture produces enough of it to adequately feed the population. The Malawi government faces the enormous challenges of strengthening the economy, improving educational and health facilities, and dealing with the serious environmental issues of deforestation and erosion. The country depends heavily on the International Monetary Fund, World Bank, and bilateral and multilateral donor assistance. It was a small project funded by the U.S. Agency for International Development (USAID) that brought me as a medical anthropologist to Malawi several times during the 1990s.

Medical anthropology is difficult to define because it covers such a wide scope of research and practical programming. In the broadest sense, it can be defined as the study of human health in a variety of cultural and environmental contexts. Over the past three decades, medical anthropology has become a distinct and important area within anthropology. Presently it has three major areas of emphasis. One is the study of cultural differences in health beliefs and systems of healing such as alternative therapies, shamanism, and folk concepts of disease. A second consists of biomedical studies of human adaptations to disease, including nutrition, genetics, and demography. The third is applied medical anthropology, which focuses on the application of anthropology to health-related problems and possible solutions.

Medical anthropologists often carry out research as members of interdisciplinary teams, where their main contribution is to discover a people's cultural conceptions of health, illness, and the more general cultural context within which ideas about health are situated. It was as an applied medical anthropologist that I came to be a member of such an interdisciplinary team that would work in Malawi.

In the early 1990s, I was on the faculty at one of three universities that had joined together to apply for a USAID grant under a program called University Development Linkages Program (UDLP). Two of the universities were American and one was the agricultural college that forms part of the University of Malawi system. A major goal of the UDLP was to strengthen developing nation colleges and universities by giving them access to U.S. faculties and other American university resources. The program also sought to increase the involvement of U.S. faculty members with faculty in developing nations so that students at U.S. institutions would benefit from an internationalizing of the curriculum.

In this case, scientists from participating universities were asked to devise and implement a project that would benefit all collaborating institutions of higher education. Many teams of UDLP scientists that applied for grants designed projects intended to strengthen curricula at developing nation institutions. Our team, however, opted to design and implement a project addressing a major problem, child undernourishment in Malawi. We recognized that three out of five children in the country were undernourished. Worse, the mortality rate for children under five was 24 percent or nearly one in four. The problem was caused by the fact that children received insufficient protein and calories, which left them vulnerable to a host of infectious diseases, potential mental impairment, serious deficiency diseases such as kwashiorkor and marasmus, and premature death. This is the story of the people from two central Malawi villages and three universities as we worked to craft a program to reduce child undernourishment and increase child survival on a sustainable basis.

Faculty members who were participating in this effort represented a number of disciplines: anthropology, human nutrition, cooperative extension, animal science, veterinary medicine, and crop science. Several of the participating faculty members from Malawi had grown up in small villages, still had extended family in those villages, and were familiar with economic and cultural factors contributing to child undernourishment there. From them and from field research we learned that mothers breastfeed their babies for two to three years, which assured that the children received sufficient protein and calories during these early years. However, that changed when the children were fully weaned. The indigenous weaning food is a gruel of water and maize flour, and babies receive small amounts of it beginning at about four months of age. When mothers wean their toddlers, it is this gruel that the children eat day after day. It is a nutritionally inadequate weaning food and children soon begin to show its effects—swollen bellies, stunted growth, and increased susceptibility to malaria, measles, and other infectious diseases. The weaning food is made from the same crop, maize, that constitutes the staple food for adults, a boiled maize flour dish called *nsima*. The problem of a nutritionally inadequate weaning food is not unique to Malawi—it plagues many developing nations. In these countries there is often a high-carbohydrate food such as corn or rice that makes up as much as 90 percent of children's daily intake. If people survive into adulthood, their bodies have made an adaptation to this low-protein diet. But young children do not thrive.

As our project searched for ideas about how to create a plan for addressing child nutrition, we decided to focus on a simple approach that would use indigenous resources and be manageable at the local level. This was the introduction of a protein and calorie-rich additive, goat milk, to the local weaning food. Although goats are plentiful in Malawi villages, they are meat goats, not dairy goats. They are like walking bank accounts, to be sold when a family needs money to pay school fees for the children, health care, and rites of passage such as weddings and funerals. It would be a bold step to secure approval from male village political leaders and elders for the introduction of milk-producing goats to provide milk for young children. Dairy goats would be put directly into the hands of women, not men. Would it work? Would women be willing to learn new animal management and food handling techniques? Would they have time to carry out the additional labor that would be required? Would the goat milk be given to the children who needed it? Would husbands or brothers take the valuable animals away from the women? Would the goats and the children flourish? As time went on, we learned the answers to all these questions and more. And the village women contributed very valuable insights and suggestions that made the project a model that has been adopted elsewhere in Malawi.

The Program

Our work began with a series of planning meetings. Our goal was to create a program that would enable women to raise and keep dairy goats on a sustainable and manageable basis, and use the milk that was produced to supplement their children's diets and increase food security for their families. The plan we generated would have three parts: (1) generation of a database on the milk production and biological characteristics of goats; (2) development and implementation of demonstrations and outreach programs for distributing milk goats to rural women and teaching them how to care for the animals; and (3) formation and implementation of outreach programs for rural women so they could learn how to safely handle goat milk and use it as a regular part of the diet, especially for their children who were under five years of age. At our planning meetings we had to figure out what we were actually going to do, and in what sequence.

The animal scientists on the team knew that milk goats introduced into local villages would have to be hardy or they would die. They wanted to try out some breeding experiments using local goats and imported breeds of dairy goats to see just what kind of a crossbred doe would result in the best combination of high milk production and ability to adapt to life in the village. So they worked out a breeding scheme using local Malawi goats and imported Saanen dairy goats from South Africa, Damascus goats from Cyprus, and Anglo-Nubian goats from the U.S. The breeding experiments were carried out at the farm that the Malawi members of our team used for teaching and research.

This kind of research can't be done in a hurry. Arranging for the importation of animals is a complex process because one has to find a supplier, arrange for payment, arrange for shipment (very few airlines are willing to transport large animals internationally), work out how to feed and water the animals while they are in transit, secure permits from the Malawi Ministry of Agriculture, and quarantine the animals for a period of weeks when they arrive in country. Only then can the breeding research begin.

To our dismay, none of the imported Anglo-Nubian goats survived for very long in Malawi. And several of the Damascus goats also died. The Saanens, however, proved to be the hardier—not surprising, since they originated from relatively close by South Africa where environmental conditions were similar to those in Malawi. And when bred with local Malawi goats, the resulting cross-breeds turned out to provide substantial weekly milk yields that would be enough for the goats' kids as well as for the young children of rural families. So the team decided to import more Saanens and continue the crossbreeding program. Crossbred does would be distributed to village women and most of the crossbred bucks would be sold to support the project. As the program developed, team members discovered that some local does produced relatively high average milk yields; this finding became important as the project unfolded.

My work as the team anthropologist involved the human side of the project. With the help of team nutritionists and the extension expert, I designed a survey to collect baseline cultural information in the villages where the milk goats would be distributed. It was important to document such things as women's daily activities, the meaning and use of goats, relationships between men and women, and ways children were fed in the target villages before the milk goats were introduced. Later we would look for changes we hoped would occur after the new goats arrived and for unexpected problems.

To proceed with the social research, we selected three villages, all relatively close to the college campus in a rural setting about 25 km from the capital city of Lilongwe. To proceed, however, it was necessary to obtain permission from the people in each community. To do so we held meetings with the village headmen, men and women elders, mothers of young children who would be affected by our project, and anyone else from the village who was interested in learning about the program.

In the Central Region of Malawi where we were working, most people belong to the Chewa ethnic group. The Chewa have a matrilineal descent system and practice matrilocal residence. Thus, Chewa men and women inherit clan and lineage membership from their mothers. It is this membership that gives people the right to farm plots of land surrounding their villages. When women marry, most continue to live in the village of their birth with a group of related females—mother, maternal grandmother, mother's sisters and their children, sisters and their children, and eventually, adult daughters and their young children. When young men marry, most move to the villages of their brides. The village political leader is usually, but not always, a man. He cannot be the son of the prior headman because a son is not part of his father's matriline. Instead, he is likely to be the son of the prior headman's sister—a maternal nephew. This system creates a situation where almost all of the women and the powerful men in a village are maternal kin to one another.

To introduce the project, we had to recognize the matrilineal nature of village social organization and the need for people's approval. We met with groups of interested women and men and the headmen in two villages. We explained what we were proposing to do. We said we wanted to find out how the young children in the village were doing in terms of growth and health. Then we intended to make milk goats available to women who had children under five years old because we felt the children would benefit from goat milk in their diet. We noted that it would not cost the women any money. (Most rural women lack the means to purchase even local goats, because they cost from $30 to $50. Dairy goats would be much more expensive.) We said that women who received milk goats would be asked to return the first healthy kid, whether male or female, to the college farm and that this would constitute payment for the animal. We told them that women who took the goats would be asked to attend demonstrations to help them learn how to care for the animals, handle the milk, and feed the milk to their children. We also said that someone from the project would come to the village each week to weigh and measure the participants' children to see if goat milk in their diet was having an effect on weight and height of their youngsters.

Village women were uniformly positive about the project—they wanted to participate. But men, including the headmen, were more skeptical. They worried about the impact on social relations of such valuable animals going to women—it didn't seem appropriate—couldn't the goats be given to the men of the village? The goats were not to be sold or slaughtered, we said. They would be there for the benefit of the children, and their care would involve extra work for the women. Everyone knew that children were suffering because of malnourishment—sometimes a child would become so seriously malnourished that relatives had to take it to the district hospital for nutritional rehabilitation. This meant a three-week hospital stay with a family member right there to feed and care for the child. The cost to the family was considerable. And the death of a child was a great sorrow. So eventually the men agreed that the project should go forward. The headmen agreed that the goats should belong to the women and said they would resolve any disputes over ownership in favor of the women.

When we were ready to talk with people in a third village about the project, we learned something that quickly dissuaded us from continuing there. It seemed that there was animal theft going on in the area, and the prime suspects were a family living in the third village! Until the local system of justice had solved these crimes and dealt with the perpetrators, we could not take the risk of working in that village. Animal theft became a problem in the other two villages as well. The rural economy in Malawi has weakened in recent years because of droughts, floods, soil depletion, deforestation, erosion, low prices for commodities, and high rates of inflation. The annual hungry season, the period of time between when people consume the last of the food they have stored to the time when the next crops are harvested, used to begin in December and end in March. Now the hungry season often begins in September. People must reduce the amount of food they eat at a time when they have to carry out the heaviest agricultural labor, preparing fields and planting them when the annual rains begin. Both men and women do this work and nearly all agricultural labor is done by hand. In the depth of the hungry season, people may turn to eating maize bran, the portion of the maize kernel that they normally feed to their animals, in order to have something in their bellies to assuage the hunger pangs. Under conditions such as these, it is no surprise that theft of animals is on the rise in the countryside.

Women in the two villages who received milk goats responded vigorously to the threat of theft once a few animals had been stolen. They began to take their milk goats with them as they went to work in the fields, tethering them nearby rather than letting them range free. They built pens against the sides of their mud or brick houses, to provide shade and security. At night they brought the animals into their houses so the whole family could guard them.

Our research team hired two young women who were both native speakers of the local language, Chichewa, and who had grown up in villages. We asked them to administer the baseline survey in the two villages and to continue working on the project. They would help to distribute animals to village women and later pay weekly visits to the recipients to weigh and measure their young children. One of these young women remained with the project throughout, and is dedicated to working with the villagers. She has been a key to the success of our work.

The baseline survey of households with children under five years of age revealed some interesting and useful information. Women headed 30 percent of the households; there was no adult male regularly living with them. Almost 75 percent of the women were nonliterate. A total of 35.4 percent of the children were underweight for their age and 57.7 percent were stunted (short for age). These figures are close to the national averages for a preharvest season, (i.e., the hungry season). A surprising finding was that children in female-headed households were less likely to be undernourished or stunted. We can only speculate about why this was the case. Perhaps it has to do with groups of related women sharing resources in the interest of their children's well being.

We gave women who participated in the baseline survey the opportunity to volunteer to receive a milk goat, with the understanding that they would attend demonstrations that taught ways to manage the animals and keep them healthy, how to milk goats, how to keep the milk from spoiling, and how to add it to their children's food. We also pointed out that they would have to return first-born kids to project personnel so the does could eventually be distributed to other women, but that all kids born after that would be theirs to keep. The female goats would increase their flock of milk-producers, and the males could be sold to give the women much-needed cash. All women who received milk goats would also be provided with a bucket for milking, a pan for cooking, and a measuring cup to help them track milk production.

The program proved popular. Very quickly the project had more participants than it could accommodate, and we had to create a waiting list. We gave priority to those women who had children under five that were most seriously undernourished. Other women on the waiting list agreed to this. We also provided animals to some grandmothers who were raising young grandchildren orphaned when their parents died of AIDS. Care for AIDS orphans has become a major problem in Malawi, and is reflected at the village level. It is common to see women, already struggling to care for immediate family members, stressed to the maximum as they undertake to feed and house children left behind by relatives who have succumbed to the disease.

Team members designed and began to present demonstrations for village women on goat management, goat health, milking, safe milk handling, and incorporation of milk in their children's food. Recipes using local ingredients and goat milk were developed and tested in the home economics kitchens at the college, and taste-tested by the women participants and their children at the village-based demonstrations. The recipes that passed the taste test were routinely used by the women; those that didn't were rejected.

When the women received their animals, all of the does were either pregnant or already had young kids. This is when project field assistants began their weekly visits to the villages. During each visit, the participating women gathered in a central area of the village with their children. Each woman would have her child or children weighed in a sling scale that was suspended from a tree branch. Once a month, team members measured the upper arm circumference and height of the children. The fact of high child mortality was brought home to me in a very graphic way during this process when some women initially objected to having their children's height measured because they thought it was too much like measuring the children for coffins. A few women persisted in their objection. In these cases, our field assistants could only estimate observable changes in height. The field assistants also asked women about the general health of their children during the previous week, the milk production of their goats, and the health of their goats. If a goat was ill, the field assistant arranged for a veterinary assistant or the team member who was a veterinarian to travel to the village and examine the animal. If there was a significant health problem with a child, the field assistant notified faculty team members who would then take the information to the nearest clinic where they could arrange transport of the woman and child to a hospital if that was called for. Almost all the women who received animals were committed to caring for them and using the milk for their children. Ninety-eight percent of the recipients returned the first kid to the project. This is an astonishingly high rate of return and it implies that rural women would be very good risks for other kinds of so-called "payback schemes" that make local efforts to improve economic security sustainable.

We were gratified to see that those children who began to receive even small amounts of goat milk as an ingredient in their daily diets showed steady weight and height gains even when they were sick. In time, however, we began to see children hit growth plateaus or even lose ground temporarily. We learned from village women themselves why this was happening. Women who made up village committees approached the project team with a proposal for a solution. They told us that their milk goats had to have at least two kids before they could get a second high-yield doe, and this meant that there were periods of time when no milk was available for their children. The women asked if we could teach them how to grow soybeans. They were all familiar with soybean flour as a food for undernourished children because this is what they received when they took their malnourished children to maternal and child health clinics for treatment. Their plan was to grow soybeans and grind them into flour to feed their children when no goat milk was available.

Our project team went back to the drawing board and figured out how to incorporate this new effort. The team purchased soybean seed and distributed 5 kg of it to each woman in the two villages. The village headmen approved of this effort and in some instances designated land for use by those women who needed it. Malawi team members developed and presented demonstrations on how to grow and process soybeans. The women agreed to pay back the 5 kg of seed after their first harvest, again a way to perpetuate the program over time and make it sustainable, and all did so. Women have now completed three or four successful growing seasons with soybeans, and many are growing and storing enough beans to see them through the periods of time when their does produce no milk. They also save enough seed for the next planting season.

It also became clear after a short period of time that we would have to change the goat crossbreeding program. The college farm could not breed enough hardy milk goats to keep up with the demand. The animal scientists on our team looked for local Malawi goats that were the highest milk producers and these, when pregnant or with a kid, were distributed to women on the waiting list. Simultaneously, plans were made to build buck stations in each of the villages and to provide each station with a Saanen or crossbred buck to breed with local goats. Village headmen oversaw the building efforts and other men and women helped to feed and water the buck. When a doe comes into heat, the owner can bring it to the station to be inseminated. In this way the Saanen genes for high milk production spread more rapidly into the village flocks. The villagers know that their bucks must be exchanged for others about every three years in order to avoid inbreeding.

I returned to Malawi for a short visit in the summer of 2004 and found that many positive features of the project were still in place. In discussions with groups of women who had received dairy goats, I learned that two-thirds of them still had their original project animals. The remaining third had lost their original animals to disease or injury, but not before the goats had delivered offspring that survived. Only one woman had sold her animal before it had given her viable kids; this is tantamount to a farmer selling or eating her seed! But the woman's situation was quite difficult. Her husband was seriously ill and could not assist with farm work, and as a consequence she had been unable to raise sufficient maize to provide for household subsistence. She was desperate for cash in order to purchase food, and it was out of this desperation that she sold her milk goat.

Several women had a sufficient number of animals that they were able to meet the nutritional needs of their young children and sell surplus goats,

primarily to NGOs planning to launch similar efforts to address child malnutrition. For the most part, money earned in this way was used to buy commercial fertilizer in order to increase the maize harvest. Cooking oil, salt, and
clothing were other items commonly purchased with these earnings. The loss
of animals to theft had decreased due to the introduction of a community
policing effort. Professional police have trained villagers to take turns
patrolling the village and its surrounding area at night in order to discourage
thieves, and it seemed to be working. But another danger had presented itself.
Because the 2004 harvest was not a good one due to erratic rains, people were
anxious about their food reserves, most knowing that they would run out long
before the next harvest. One result of this is that domesticated dogs (every
household has a watchdog) are not fed adequate amounts of cooked maize
bran or leftover cooked maize flour. They are hungry, and they have begun running across the fields in packs, attacking kids and young goats belonging to
people from villages other than their own. Some people have lost valuable
kids in this way and were considering tethering kids while the does free range.
Normally tethering occurs only during the rainy season after planting has
taken place. There is the possibility that marauding dogs will be shot, but this
raises the likelihood of inter-village conflict.

   Of the four village buck stations erected as part of the project, three were
in good repair and the bucks well cared for. The fourth was somewhat rundown
and needed refurbishing. And it was clear that the buck needed better care.
After some discussion and investigation, it became apparent that the headman
had declared the buck was his personal property and only his relatives could use
its services—anyone else would have to pay him a fee if they wished to bring
their animals to the buck. Not surprisingly, people did not take well to this
proclamation. They more or less boycotted the buck station, which meant that
most of the care of the animal fell to the elderly headman and his wife. The station was repaired, the animal was provided with nutritional supplements, the
household was provided with a new bucket for the dedicated purpose of bringing water to the buck, and the headman was informed that the buck would die
or be returned to the college if it did not receive better care. In the end, it became
clear that a miscommunication had occurred between the headman and project personnel, leading the headman to conclude that he was now free to charge
for use of the buck station. By the time I left Malawi, the misunderstanding
had apparently been cleared up. College personnel will continue to check on the
well being of this valuable animal—it would be a great loss to the village if it
were to die or be removed.

   During group and individual discussions with women, everyone acknowledged the value of goat milk as a component of their children's diets. I was told
that, since the milk had become available in the villages, no child had become
so seriously malnourished that he or she had to be taken to the hospital for
nutritional rehabilitation. This was a real change from an earlier point in time,
and a hallmark of success for all of our efforts, researchers and villagers, to
promote the health of children.

Conclusion

Our project team designed and tested a locally sustainable approach to alleviate infant and child malnourishment in rural Malawi. Data on changes in the participating children's weights, heights, and upper arm circumferences show that relatively small amounts of goat milk included in the regular diet make a substantial difference in promoting normal growth in children. Results from a rapid appraisal survey that I helped to design indicate that the project is highly valued by rural women. This is confirmed by key village women and by the fact that more women than project resources would permit sought to join the program. Presently some Malawi nongovernmental organizations (NGOs) have introduced similar efforts in other parts of the country. Several district hospitals that provide rehabilitation for severely malnourished children have established flocks of milk goats on their grounds and use the milk as an important part of the rehabilitation treatment. The agricultural college plans to offer training to Malawians and people from other southern African nations who are interested in replicating the program. And the project villages will be demonstration sites for trainees who want to see how the project works "on the ground."

It was important to have an anthropologist on the project team. As the team anthropologist, I participated in every phase of the project, including management duties at times when it was necessary to keep our efforts on schedule. I was responsible for providing an ethnographic account of local culture and using this information to help shape how we could present the program to villagers. I was not trained to manage goat breeding or conduct some of the health measurements, but I could point out how I thought villagers would respond to our plans and to suggest how best to make them full participants in project planning and implementation. It is easy for people from any society to believe that those who are from elsewhere still see the world in the same way they do. Since cultures differ (Americans, for example, find it difficult to understand the ramifications of a matrilineal descent system) anthropologists can translate information about such differences in ways that are useful to other members of interdisciplinary teams. Thus, we can shape programs to fit local conditions and help with cross-cultural communication. That is what I think happened in Malawi.

In July of 2006 I once again traveled to Malawi. A principal motive for this trip was to explore possibilities for securing boreholes and pumps for the villages that had participated in the milk goat project. I had the opportunity to meet with ten women, all project participants, in one of the villages. On this occasion the update that I received was not encouraging. The national and local economies had grown steadily more difficult for Malawians and especially for those who are rural smallholders. Agricultural inputs such as fertilizer and seed had soared in price and many farmers were simply not able to purchase a sufficient amount of fertilizer to assure a harvest sufficient for meeting the subsistence needs of the family. People began to sell off valuable assets in order to secure cash for the purchase of maize. For nine of the ten women with whom I spoke, these assets were their milk goats. The one woman who managed to keep her animals was in the fortunate position of having a husband who was employed, albeit at a relatively low wage, at a government facility. His small but steady income protected the family from having to sell assets such as animals in order to afford staple food. The women who had sold their milk goats were hopeful that, in a year of good harvest, they would be able to purchase a milk doe.

When I expressed my concern and disappointment about these developments to a Malawian who was a key member of the project team, he suggested that I should think about this in another way—if women had not had these valuable animals to sell for a good price in order to see their families through this difficult time, they might have been forced to resort to such dire acts as dismantling their houses to sell the timbers and sheets of metal roofing. This is one of the last resorts of rural dwellers when faced with chronic hunger and the need for cash to purchase food. So the women were buffered from such a drastic move. And they were convinced of the value of milk goats for the physical health of their young children and their own economic well being. They are resilient and resourceful women, and they viewed the setback as only temporary.

Review Questions

1. What are the social and environmental conditions that lead to child malnutrition in Malawi, according to Patten?

2. What programs did the project team come up with to improve child nutrition in Malawi, and what steps did they take to implement it?

3. How is anthropology useful for programs such as the one described by Patten in this article?

4. In what ways did team members involve local people in the design and implementation of the program?

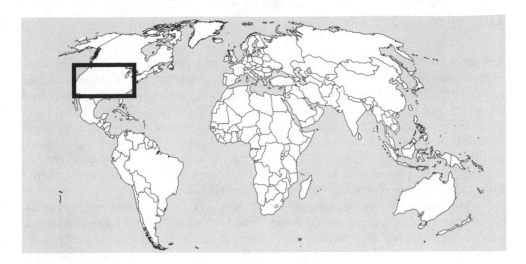

39

Using Anthropology

David W. McCurdy

Some disciplines, such as economics, have an obvious relationship to the nonacademic world. Economic theory, although generated as part of basic research, may often prove useful for understanding the "real" economy. Anthropology, on the other hand, does not seem so applicable. In this article, David McCurdy discusses some of the professional applications of anthropology and argues that there is a basic anthropological perspective that can help anyone cope with the everyday world. He uses the case of a company manager to illustrate this point, asserting that ethnographic "qualitative" research is an important tool for use in the nonacademic world.

In 1990 a student whom I had not seen for fifteen years stopped by my office. He had returned for his college reunion and thought it would be interesting to catch up on news about his (and my) major department, anthropology. The conversation, however, soon shifted from college events to his own life. Following graduation and a stint in the Peace Corps, he noted, he had begun to study for his license as a ship's engineer. He had attended the Maritime Academy and worked for years on freighters. He was finally granted his license, he continued, and currently held the engineer's position on a container ship that made regular trips between Seattle and Alaska. He soon would be promoted to chief engineer and be at the top of his profession.

As he talked, he made an observation about anthropology that may seem surprising. His background in the discipline, he said, had helped him significantly in his work. He found it useful as he went about his daily tasks, maintaining his ship's complex engines and machinery, his relationships with the crew, and his contacts with land-based management.

And his is not an unusual case. Over the years, several anthropology graduates have made the same observation. One, for example, is a community organizer who feels that the cross-cultural perspective he learned in anthropology helps him mediate disputes and facilitate decision making in a multiethnic neighborhood. Another, who works as an advertising account executive, claims that anthropology helps her discover what products mean to customers. This, in turn, permits her to design more effective ad campaigns. A third says she finds anthropology an invaluable tool as she arranges interviews and writes copy. She is a producer for a metropolitan television news program. I have heard the same opinion expressed by many others, including the executive editor of a magazine for home weavers, the founder of a fencing school, a housewife, a physician, several lawyers, the kitchen manager for a catering firm, and a high school teacher.

The idea that anthropology can be useful is also supported by the experience of many new Ph.D.s. A recent survey has shown, for the first time, that more new doctorates in anthropology find employment in professional settings than in college teaching or scholarly research, and the list of nonacademic work settings revealed by the survey is remarkably broad. There is a biological anthropologist, for example, who conducts research on nutrition for a company that manufactures infant formula. A cultural anthropologist works for a major car manufacturer, researching such questions as how employees adapt to working overseas, and how they relate to conditions on domestic production lines. Others formulate government policy; plan patient care in hospitals; design overseas development projects; run famine relief programs; consult on tropical forest management; and advise on product development, advertising campaigns, and marketing strategy for corporations.

This new-found application of cultural anthropology comes as a surprise to many Americans. Unlike political science, for example, which has a name that logically connects it with practical political and legal professions, there is nothing in the term *anthropology* that tells most Americans how it might be useful.

The research subject of anthropology also makes it more difficult to comprehend. Political scientists investigate political processes, structures, and motivations. Economists look at the production and exchange of goods and services. Psychologists study differences and similarities among individuals. The research of cultural anthropologists, on the other hand, is more difficult to characterize. Instead of a focus on particular human institutions, such as politics, law, and economics, anthropologists are interested in cross-cultural differences and similarities among the world's many groups.

This interest produces a broad view of human behavior that gives anthropology its special cross-cultural flavor. It also produces a unique research strategy, called *ethnography*, that tends to be qualitative rather than quantitative. Whereas other social sciences moved toward *quantitative methods* of research designed to test theory by using survey questionnaires and structured, repetitive observations, most anthropologists conduct *qualitative research* designed to elicit the cultural knowledge of the people they seek to understand. To do this, anthropologists often live and work with their subjects, called *informants* within the discipline. The result is a highly detailed ethnographic description of the categories and rules people consult when they behave, and the meanings that things and actions have for them.

It is this ethnographic approach, or cultural perspective, that I think makes anthropology useful in such a broad range of everyday settings. I particularly find important the special anthropological understanding of the culture concept, ethnographic field methods, and social analysis. To illustrate these assertions, let us take a single case in detail, that of a manager working for a large corporation who consciously used the ethnographic approach to solve a persistent company problem.

The Problem

The manager, whom we will name Susan Stanton, works for a large multinational corporation called UTC (not the company's real name). UTC is divided into a number of parts, including divisions, subdivisions, departments, and other units designed to facilitate its highly varied business enterprises. The company is well-diversified, engaging in research, manufacturing, and customer services. In addition to serving a wide cross-section of public and private customers, it also works on a variety of government contracts for both military and nonmilitary agencies.

One of its divisions is educational. UTC has established a large number of customer outlets in cities throughout the United States, forming what it calls its "customer outlet network." They are staffed by educational personnel who are trained to offer a variety of special courses and enrichment programs. These courses and programs are marketed mainly to other businesses or to individuals who desire special training or practical information. For example, a small company might have UTC provide its employees with computer training, including instruction on hardware, programming, computer languages, and computer program applications. Another company might ask for instruction on effective management or accounting procedures. The outlets' courses for individuals include such topics as how to get a job, writing a résumé, or enlarging your own business.

To organize and manage its customer outlet network, UTC has created a special division. The division office is located at the corporate headquarters and is responsible for developing new courses, improving old ones, training customer outlet personnel, and marketing customer outlet courses, or "products" as they are called inside the company. The division also has departments that develop, produce, and distribute the special learning materials used in customer outlet courses. These include books, pamphlets, video and audio tapes and cassettes, slides, overlays, and films. These materials are stored in a warehouse and are shipped, as they are ordered, to customer outlets around the country.

It is with this division that Susan Stanton first worked as a manager. She had started her career with the company in a small section of the division that designed various program materials. She had worked her way into management, holding a series of increasingly important positions. She was then asked to take over the management of a part of the division that had the manufacture, storage, and shipment of learning materials as one of its responsibilities.

But there was a catch. She was given this new management position with instructions to solve a persistent, although vaguely defined, problem. "Improve the service," they had told her, and "get control of the warehouse inventory." In this case, "service" meant the process of filling orders sent in by customer outlets for various materials stored in the warehouse. The admonition to improve the service seemed to indicate that service was poor, but all she was told about the situation was that customer outlet personnel complained about the service; she did not know exactly why or what "poor" meant.

In addition, inventory was "out of control." Later she was to discover the extent of the difficulty.

> We had a problem with inventory. The computer would say we had two hundred of some kind of book in stock, yet it was back ordered because there was nothing on the shelf. We were supposed to have the book but physically there was nothing there. I'm going, "Uh, we have a small problem. The computer never lies, like your bank statement, so why don't we have the books?"

If inventory was difficult to manage, so were the warehouse employees. They were described by another manager as "a bunch of knuckle draggers. All they care about is getting their money. They are lazy and don't last long at the job." Strangely, the company did not view the actions of the warehouse workers as a major problem. Only later did Susan Stanton tie in poor morale in the warehouse with the other problems she had been given to solve.

Management by Defense

Although Stanton would take the ethnographic approach to management problems, that was not what many other managers did. They took a defensive stance, a position opposite to the discovery procedures of ethnography. Their major concern—like that of many people in positions of leadership and responsibility—was to protect their authority and their ability to manage and to get things done. Indeed, Stanton also shared this need. But their solution to maintaining their position was different from hers. For them, claiming ignorance and asking questions—the hallmark of the ethnographic approach—is a sign of weakness. Instead of discovering what is going on when they take on a new management assignment, they often impose new work rules and procedures. Employees learn to fear the arrival of new managers because their appearance usually means a host of new, unrealistic demands. They respond by hiding what they actually do, withholding information that would be useful to the manager. Usually, everyone's performance suffers.

Poor performance leads to elaborate excuses as managers attempt to blame the troubles on others. Stanton described this tendency.

> When I came into the new job, this other manager said, "Guess what? You have got a warehouse. You are now the proud owner of a forklift and a bunch of knuckle draggers." And I thought, management's perception of those people is very low. They are treating them as dispensable, that you can't do anything with them. They say the workers don't have any career motives. They don't care if they do a good job. You have to force them to do anything. You can't motivate them. It's only a warehouse, other managers were saying. You can't really do that much about the problems there so why don't you just sort of try to keep it under control.

Other managers diminished the importance of the problem itself. It was not "poor service" that was the trouble. The warehouse was doing the best it could with what it had. It was just that the customers—the staff at the customer outlets—were complainers. As Susan Stanton noted:

> The people providing the service thought that outlet staff were complainers. They said, "Staff complain about everything. But it can't be that way. We have checked it all out and it isn't that bad."

Making excuses and blaming others lead to low morale and a depressed self-image. Problems essentially are pushed aside in favor of a "let's just get by" philosophy.

Ethnographic Management

By contrast, managers take the offensive when they use ethnographic techniques. That is what Stanton did when she assumed her new managerial assignment over the learning materials manufacturing and distribution system. To understand what the ethnographic approach means, however, we must first look briefly at what anthropologists do when they conduct ethnographic field research. Our discussion necessarily involves a look at the concepts of culture and microculture as well as ethnography. For as we will shortly point out, companies have cultures of their own, a point that has recently received national attention; but more important for the problem we are describing here, companies are normally divided into subgroups, each with its own microculture. It is these cultures and microcultures that anthropologically trained managers can study ethnographically, just as fieldworkers might investigate the culture of a

!Kung band living in the Kalahari Desert of West Africa or the Gypsies living in San Francisco.

Ethnography refers to the process of discovering and describing culture, so it is important to discuss this general and often elusive concept. There are numerous definitions of culture, each stressing particular sets of attributes. The definition we employ here is especially appropriate for ethnographic field-work. We may define culture as the acquired knowledge that people use to generate behavior and interpret experience. In growing up, one learns a system of cultural knowledge appropriate to the group. For example, an American child learns to chew with a closed mouth because that is the cultural rule. The child's parents interpret open-mouthed chewing as an infraction and tell the child to chew "properly." A person uses such cultural knowledge throughout life to guide actions and to give meaning to surroundings.

Because culture is learned, and because people can easily generate new cultural knowledge as they adapt to other people and things, human behavior and perceptions can vary dramatically from one group to another. In parts of India, for example, children learn to chew "properly" with their mouths open. Their cultural worlds are quite different from the ones found in the United States.

Cultures are associated with groups of people. Traditionally, anthropologists associated culture with relatively distinctive ethnic groups. *Culture* referred to the whole life-way of a society, and particular cultures could be named. Anthropologists talked of German culture, Ibo culture, and Bhil culture. Culture was everything that was distinctive about the group.

Culture is still applied in this manner today, but with the advent of complex societies and a growing interest among anthropologists in understanding them, the culture concept has also been used in a more limited way. Complex societies such as our own are composed of thousands of groups. Members of these groups usually share the national culture, including a language and a huge inventory of knowledge for doing things, but the groups themselves have specific cultures of their own. For example, if you were to walk into the regional office of a stock brokerage firm, you would hear the people there talking an apparently foreign language. You might stand in the "bull pen," listen to brokers make "cold calls," "sell short," "negotiate a waffle," or get ready to go to a "dog and pony show." The fact that an event such as this feels strange when you first encounter them is strong evidence to support the notion that you don't yet know the culture that organizes them. We call such specialized groups *microcultures*.

We are surrounded by microcultures, participating in a few, encountering many others. Our family has a microculture. So may our neighborhood, our college, and even our dormitory floor. The waitress who serves us lunch at the corner restaurant shares a culture with her co-workers. So do bank tellers at our local savings and loan. Kin, occupational groups, and recreational associations each tend to display special microcultures. Such cultures can be, and now often are, studied by anthropologists interested in understanding life in complex American society.

The concept of microculture is essential to Susan Stanton as she begins to attack management problems at UTC because she assumes that conflict between different microcultural groups is most likely at the bottom of the difficulty. One microculture she could focus on is UTC company culture. She knows, for example, that there are a variety of rules and expectations—written and unwritten—for how things should be done at the company. She must dress in her "corporates," for example, consisting of a neutral-colored suit, stockings, and conservative shoes. UTC also espouses values about the way employees should be treated, how people are supposed to feel about company products, and a variety of other things that set that particular organization apart from other businesses.

But the specific problems that afflicted the departments under Stanton's jurisdiction had little to do with UTC's corporate culture. They seemed rather to be the result of misunderstanding and misconnection between two units, the warehouse and the customer outlets. Each had its own microculture. Each could be investigated to discover any information that might lead to a solution of the problems she had been given.

Such investigation would depend on the extent of Stanton's ethnographic training. As an undergraduate in college, she had learned how to conduct ethnographic interviews, observe behavior, and analyze and interpret data. She was not a professional anthropologist, but she felt she was a good enough ethnographer to discover some relevant aspects of microcultures at UTC.

Ethnography is the process of discovering and describing a culture. For example, an anthropologist who travels to India to conduct a study of village culture will use ethnographic techniques. The anthropologist will move into a community, occupy a house, watch people's daily routines, attend rituals, and spend hours interviewing informants. The goal is to discover a detailed picture of what is going on by seeing village culture through the eyes of informants. The anthropologist wants the insider's perspective. Villagers become teachers, patiently explaining different aspects of their culture, praising the anthropologist for acting correctly and appearing to understand, laughing when the anthropologist makes mistakes or seems confused. When the anthropologist knows what to do and can explain in local terms what is going on or what is likely to happen, real progress has been made. The clearest evidence of such progress is when informants say, "You are almost human now," or "You are beginning to talk just like us."

The greatest enemy of good ethnography is the preconceived notion. Anthropologists do not conduct ethnographic research by telling informants what they are like based on earlier views of them. They teach the anthropologist how to see their world: the anthropologist does not tell them what their world should really be like. All too often in business, a new manager will take over a department and begin to impose changes on its personnel to fit a preconceived perception of them. The fact that the manager's efforts are likely to fail makes sense in light of this ignorance. The manager doesn't know the microculture. Nor has he or she asked employees about it.

But can a corporate manager really do ethnography? After all, managers have positions of authority to maintain, as we noted earlier. It is all right for professional anthropologists to enter the field and act ignorant; they don't have a position to maintain and they don't have to continue to live with their informants. The key to the problem appears to be the "grace period." Most managers are given one by their employees when they are new on the job. A new manager cannot be expected to know everything. It is permissible to ask basic questions. The grace period may last only a month or two, but it is usually long enough to find out valuable information.

This is the opportunity that Susan Stanton saw as she assumed direction of the warehouse distribution system. As she described it:

> I could use the first month, actually the first six weeks, to find out what was going on, to act dumb and find out what people actually did and why. I talked to end customers. I talked to salespeople, people who were trying to sell things to help customer outlets with their needs. I talked to coordinators at headquarters staff who were trying to help all these customer outlets do their jobs and listened to what kinds of complaints they had heard. I talked to the customer outlet people and the guys in the warehouse. I had this six-week grace period where I could go in and say, "I don't know anything about this. If you were in my position, what would you do, or what would make the biggest difference, and why would it make a difference?" You want to find out what the world they are operating in is like. What do they value? And people were excited because I was asking and listening and, by God, intending to do something about it instead of just disappearing again.

As we shall see shortly, Stanton's approach to the problem worked. But it also resulted in an unexpected bonus. Her ethnographic approach symbolized unexpected interest and concern to her employees. That, combined with realistic management, gave her a position of respect and authority. Their feelings for her were expressed by one warehouse worker when he said:

> When she [Susan] was going to be transferred to another job, we gave her a party. We took her to this country-and-western place and we all got to dance with the boss. We told her that she was the first manager who ever tried to understand what it was like to work in the warehouse. We thought she would come in like the other managers and make a lot of changes that didn't make sense. But she didn't. She made it work better for us.

Problems and Causes

An immediate benefit of her ethnographic inquiry was a much clearer view of what poor service meant to customer outlet personnel. Stanton discovered that learning materials, such as books and cassettes, took too long to arrive after they were ordered. Worse, material did not arrive in the correct quantities. Sometimes there would be too many items, but more often there were too few, a particularly galling discrepancy since customer outlets were charged for what they ordered, not what they received. Books also arrived in poor condition, their covers ripped or scratched, edges frayed, and ends gouged and dented. This, too, bothered customer outlet staff because they were often visited by potential customers who were not impressed by the poor condition of their supplies. Shortages and scruffy books did nothing to retain regular customers either.

The causes of these problems and the difficulties with warehouse inventory also emerged from ethnographic inquiry. Stanton discovered, for example, that most customer outlets operated in large cities, where often they were housed in tall buildings. Materials shipped to their office address often ended up sitting in ground-level lobbies, because few of the buildings had receiving docks or facilities. Books and other items also arrived in large boxes, weighing up to a hundred pounds. Outlet staff, most of whom were women, had to go down to the lobby, open those boxes that were too heavy for them to carry, and haul armloads of supplies up the elevator to the office. Not only was this time-consuming, but customer outlet staff felt it was beneath their dignity to do such work. They were educated specialists, after all.

The poor condition of the books was also readily explained. By packing items loosely in such large boxes, warehouse workers ensured trouble in transit. Books rattled around with ease, smashing into each other and the side of the box. The result was torn covers and frayed edges. Clearly no one had designed the packing and shipping process with customer outlet staff in mind.

The process, of course, originated in the central warehouse, and here as well, ethnographic data yielded interesting information about the causes of the problem. Stanton learned, for example, how materials were stored in loose stacks on the warehouse shelves. When orders arrived at the warehouse, usually through the mail, they were placed in a pile and filled in turn (although there were times when special preference was given to some customer outlets). A warehouse employee filled an order by first checking it against the stock recorded by the computer, then going to the appropriate shelves and picking the items by hand. Items were packed in the large boxes and addressed to customer outlets. With the order complete, the employee was supposed to enter the number of items picked and shipped in the computer so that inventory would be up to date.

But, Stanton discovered, workers in the warehouse were under pressure to work quickly. They often fell behind because materials the computer said were in stock were not there, and because picking by hand took so long. Their solution to the problem of speed resulted in a procedure that even further confused company records.

> Most of the people in the warehouse didn't try to count well. People were looking at the books on the shelves and were going, "Eh, that looks like the right number. You want ten? Gee, that looks like about ten." Most of the time the numbers they shipped were wrong.

The causes of inaccurate amounts in shipping were thus revealed. Later, Stanton discovered that books also disappeared in customer outlet building lobbies. While staff members carried some of the materials upstairs, people passing by the open boxes helped themselves.

Other problems with inventory also became clear. UTC employees, who sometimes walked through the warehouse, would often pick up interesting materials from the loosely stacked shelves. More important, rushed workers often neglected to update records in the computer.

The Shrink-Wrap Solution

The detailed discovery of the nature and causes of service and inventory problems suggested a relatively painless solution to Stanton. If she had taken a defensive management position and failed to learn the insider's point of view, she might have resorted to more usual remedies that were impractical and unworkable. Worker retraining is a common answer to corporate difficulties, but it is difficult to accomplish and often fails. Pay incentives, punishments, and motivation enhancements such as prizes and quotas are also frequently tried. But they tend not to work because they don't address fundamental causes.

Shrink-wrapping books and other materials did. Shrink-wrapping is a packaging method in which clear plastic sheeting is placed around items to be packaged, then through a rapid heating and cooling process, shrunk into a tight covering. The plastic molds itself like a tight skin around the things it contains, preventing any internal movement or external contamination. Stanton described her decision.

> I decided to have the books shrink-wrapped. For a few cents more, before the books ever arrived in the warehouse, I had them shrink-wrapped in quantities of five and ten. I made it part of the contract with the people who produced the books for us.

On the first day that shrink-wrapped books arrived at the warehouse, Stanton discovered that they were immediately unwrapped by workers who thought a new impediment had been placed in their way. But the positive effect of shrink-wrapping soon became apparent. For example, most customer outlets ordered books in units of fives and tens. Warehouse personnel could now easily count out orders in fives and tens, instead of having to count each book or estimate numbers in piles. Suddenly, orders filled at the warehouse contained the correct number of items.

Employees were also able to work more quickly, since they no longer had to count each book. Orders were filled faster, the customer outlet staff was pleased, and warehouse employees no longer felt the pressure of time so intensely. Shrink-wrapped materials also traveled more securely. Books, protected by their plastic covering, arrived in good condition, again delighting the personnel at customer outlets.

Stanton also changed the way materials were shipped, based on what she had learned from talking to employees. She limited the maximum size of shipments to twenty-five pounds by using smaller boxes. She also had packages marked "inside delivery" so that deliverymen would carry the materials directly to the customer outlet offices. If they failed to do so, boxes were light enough to carry upstairs. No longer would items be lost in skyscraper lobbies.

Inventory control became more effective. Because they could package and ship materials more quickly, the workers in the warehouse had enough time to enter the size and nature of shipments in the computer. Other UTC employees no longer walked off with books from the warehouse, because the shrink-wrapped bundles were larger and more conspicuous, and because taking five or ten books is more like stealing than "borrowing" one.

Finally, the improved service dramatically changed morale in the division. Customer outlet staff members, with their new and improved service, felt that finally someone had cared about them. They were more positive and they let people at corporate headquarters know about their feelings. "What's happening down there?" they asked. "The guys in the warehouse must be taking vitamins."

Morale soared in the warehouse. For the first time, other people liked the service workers there provided. Turnover decreased as pride in their work rose. They began to care more about the job, working faster with greater care. Managers who had previously given up on the "knuckle draggers" now asked openly about what had got into them.

Stanton believes the ethnographic approach is the key. She has managers who work for her read anthropology, especially books on ethnography, and she insists that they "find out what is going on."

Conclusion

Anthropology is, before all, an academic discipline with a strong emphasis on scholarship and basic research. But, as we have also seen, anthropology is a discipline that contains several intellectual tools—the concept of culture, the ethnographic approach to fieldwork, a cross-cultural perspective, a holistic view of human behavior—that make it useful in a broad range of nonacademic settings. In particular, it is the ability to do qualitative research that makes anthropologists successful in the professional world.

A few years ago an anthropologist consultant was asked by a utility company to answer a puzzling question: Why were its suburban customers, whose questionnaire responses indicated an attempt at conservation, failing to reduce their consumption of natural gas? To answer the question, the anthropologist conducted ethnographic interviews with members of several families, listening as they told him about how warm they liked their houses and how they set the heat throughout the day. He also received permission to install several video cameras aimed at thermostats in private houses. When the results were in, the answer to the question was deceptively simple: Fathers fill out questionnaires and turn down thermostats; wives, children, and cleaning workers, all of whom, in this case, spent time in the houses when fathers were absent, turn them up. Conservation, the anthropologist concluded, would have to involve family decisions, not just admonitions to save gas.

Over the past two or three years, anthropology's usefulness in the world of work has been discovered by the United States press. For example, *U.S. News and World Report* carried a story in 1998 entitled "Into the Wild Unknown of Workplace Culture: Anthropologists Revitalize Their Discipline," which traced changing trends in academic anthropology and highlighted the growth of the discipline's penetration of the business world.[1] Included in the article were examples of useful ethnography, such as the discovery by one anthropologist consultant that rank-and-file union members were upset with shop stewards because the latter spent more time recruiting new members than responding to grievances. In another instance, the article reported on the work of anthropologist Ken Erickson. Hired to find out why immigrant meatpackers had launched a wildcat strike, he was able to show that the workers struck because they felt their supervisors treated them as unskilled laborers, not because there was a language problem, as proposed by management. The workers had developed elaborate strategies to work quickly, effectively, and safely that were ignored or unknown to their supervisors.

In 1999, *USA Today* carried a story that further emphasized anthropology's usefulness. Entitled "Hot Asset in Corporate: Anthropology Degrees," the article began with, "Don't throw away the MBA degree yet. But as companies go global and crave leaders for a diverse workforce, a new hot degree is emerging for aspiring executives: anthropology."[2] The piece carried numerous examples—the hiring of anthropologist Steve Barnett as a vice president at Citicorp following his discovery of the early warning signs that identify people who do not pay credit card bills; the case of Hallmark, which sent anthropologists into immigrant homes to discover how holidays and birthdays are celebrated so that the company could design appropriate cards for such occasions; the example of a marketing consultant firm that sent anthropologists into bathrooms to watch how women shave their legs, and in the process, to discover what women want in a razor.

The article also listed executives who stressed how important their anthropology degree has been for their business successes. Motorola corporate lawyer Robert Faulkner says that the anthropology degree he received before going to law school has become increasingly valuable in his management job. Warned by his father that most problems are people problems, Michael Koss, CEO of the Koss headphone company, is another example. He received his anthropology degree from Beloit College. Katherine Burr, CEO of The Hanseatic Group, has an MA in anthropology and was quoted as saying, "My competitive edge came completely out of anthropology. The world is so unknown, changes so rapidly. Preconceptions can kill you." The article concluded with the observations of Ken Erickson of the Center for Ethnographic Research. "It takes trained observation. Observation is what anthropologists are trained to do."

[1]Brendan I. Koerner, "Into the Wild Unknown of Workplace Culture: Anthropologists Revitalize Their Discipline," *U.S. News & World Report,* August 10, 1998, p. 56.

[2]Del Jones, "Hot Asset in Corporate: Anthropology Degrees," *USA Today,* February 18, 1999, section B, p. 1.

In short, cultural anthropology has entered the world of business over the past twenty years. I argue that the key to its special utility and value in the commercial world is the ethnographic approach. Anthropologists have this ethnographic field experience and a sense of how social systems work and how people use their cultural knowledge. They have the special background, originally developed to discover and describe the cultural knowledge and behavior of unknown societies, needed to, in the words of Susan Stanton, "find out what is going on."

Review Questions

1. What kinds of jobs do professional anthropologists do?

2. What is special about anthropology that makes fundamental knowledge of it valuable to some jobs?

3. What is meant by *qualitative research?* Why is such research valuable to business and government?

4. What difficulties did the company manager described in this article face? What solutions did she invent to deal with them? How did her knowledge of anthropology help her with this problem?

5. Why is ethnography useful in everyday life? Can you think of situations in which you could use ethnographic research?

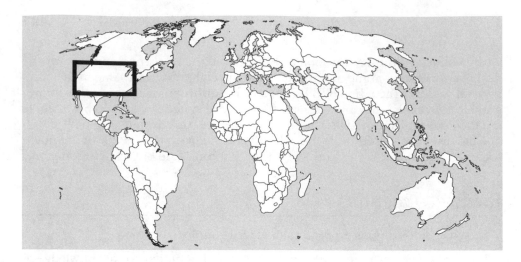

40

Career Advice for Anthropology Undergraduates

John T. Omohundro

In the previous article we learned that anthropologists regularly use their skills in the world of work and that employers are beginning to recognize the value of employees who are trained in anthropology. But the fact remains that many Americans do not fully understand what anthropology is and have little idea what students who major in anthropology can do for them. Worse, students themselves may not consciously recognize the work skills that anthropology has taught them or how to translate these skills into a language prospective employers can understand. John Omohundro tackles this

From John T. Omohundro, *Careers in Anthropology,* pp. 1–4 (New York: McGraw-Hill). Used by permission of the publisher.

problem of recognition and translation in this selection. Using a concept he calls "transcultural presentation," he lists some of the skills that anthropology teaches students and shows how these skills can be translated by graduating students into résumé language for employers.

The following scene happens at least once a semester. A distraught student pokes her (or his) head through my office door.

"Scuse me. . . . Are you busy? I need to ask you something."

"No, Grebbleberry, come in, sit down. What's bothering you?"

"Well, I really like anthropology. In fact, I want to drop my major in [deleted] and declare anthropology. But I told my parents and they were freaked out. My mother cried and my father threatened to cut me off. And my friends think I've lost it completely. Now they have me scared. I'm afraid I won't be able to get a job. What am I going to do?"

This student has all the symptoms of anthro shock. I'm tempted to smile in recognition of the syndrome but to Grebbleberry there is nothing amusing here. I have two answers: the difficult answer and the easy answer. The difficult answer, which I would like to give, is a problem because students are not prepared to believe me. The difficult answer is:

"For most careers, it doesn't matter much what you major in, as long as you like the subject and are good at it. The point of a major in a liberal arts education is to give practice at studying something in depth. One's major is not the same thing as job training. The careers that follow from most undergraduate majors are not and cannot be specified, even if the world doesn't change— but it does, frequently. There is no direct, obvious, and inevitable connection between college disciplines and the occupational titles people carry."

Although many years of teaching and advising convince me that the difficult answer I've just described is true, I don't respond with that answer anymore. First, I have to treat the "anthro shock"—the fear gripping the student that, ". . . mocked and alone, I'm going to starve." So, instead I reply with the easy answer:

"Take courage. There are many things you can do for a living that use your anthropological knowledge and skills. I can help you discover them and prepare for them."

Only then does the student's color begin to return; the anthro shock is in remission. Later, perhaps, after we've begun a career development program, I might introduce the difficult answer. But Grebbleberry still won't believe me, because my answer goes against most of what pundits, peers, parents, and even some professors have told her. This article presents some of the evidence that I have gathered for the claims made in the "easy" answer, to assist advisors to respond quickly and effectively to anthro shock.

Becoming a Career Advisor

Good advice is sorely needed and in short supply. Too many of the students I have supervised appeared flustered and ill-prepared when people ask them naive but usually sincere questions about what anthropology is, what it is good for, and what the student is going to "do with it." My advisees usually answered these questions apologetically or parried them with self-deprecating humor. Bill Gates can get away with being apologetic and self-deprecating; my students need to present themselves more positively. Furthermore, many students and parents acquire their understanding of anthropology through students rather than professors, so it behooves us to raise the quality of the understanding that our major students impart. In turn, by improving their self-presentation our students will become more confident, more ambitious, and ultimately more successful in finding good work.

My career advising grew out of efforts to be a good teacher of the liberal arts, one who helps students move on to self-actualization in the world after college. The advising also grew out of my research in adaptive problem-solving by residents of small coastal communities in Newfoundland. Using the adaptive problem-solving approach, I ask, how do students find out about the world of work and how do they find their place in it? Twenty years ago, I began to develop career workshops within my department, then expanded them into workshops at anthropology conferences, and lately assembled those materials into a workbook, *Careers in Anthropology* (1998).[1] I use the book as a supplementary text in courses, as a workbook in careers workshops, and as an advising guide to students who declare anthropology as a major. This article is drawn from that book.

Because my experience with careers has been limited to academic ones, I collaborate with my college's career planning counselor. Lacking important parts of the whole picture, we are insufficient individually to advise anthropology majors. I have learned about résumés, interviews, and employer expectations, while my career planning colleagues have learned about the usefulness of anthropological perspectives and methods. Even if students consult both of us separately, they tend to perceive us as talking past one another, so they sometimes become frustrated and drop out of the process. But when the career planner and I work together, we see the value in each other's knowledge and how to blend it with concepts from our own fields. The career planners, for example, are delighted to learn that anthropology includes training in participant observation, object reconstruction and cataloging, and cognitive mapping, among other activities. They in turn have taught me what employers call those activities and how to highlight them on student résumés to increase what linguistic anthropologists call "indexicality," or talking on the same wavelength.

---

[1]John T. Omohundro, *Careers in Anthropology* (Mountain View, CA: Mayfield Publishing Company, 1998).

While working with the career planners, and counseling and tracking my advisees, I discovered that undergraduate anthropology alumni not only find meaningful work in which they use their anthropology, but they can use their anthropology to get hired to do that work. To demonstrate this idea I drafted and field tested exercises in which anthropological research techniques, such as ethnosemantics, life history, demography, participant observation, social network analysis, key informant interviews, and survey data analysis, are applied to the tasks of selecting and pursuing interesting work. I also realized that when they are advising for careers, professors can use anthropological perspectives and data-collection techniques to better understand what students and employers know and need. Let us look briefly at what that might be.

Career Planning in Cross-Cultural Perspective

Except for a handful of publications distributed by the American Anthropological Association, few anthropologists have addressed the subject of career planning for undergraduate majors. One exception, James Spradley's "Career Education from a Cultural Perspective,"[2] shaped my conception of the problem. Spradley observes that in most cultures, such as the Amish in northern New York, the Inuit in central Canada, or the Masai in Kenya, children live close to the world of adult work. As they approach their own adulthood, youths understand clearly what adult work is and what they must do to take it up. There aren't many choices, but there isn't much anxiety either. The transition is smooth and supported by ritual, such as coming-of-age ceremonies.

The modern West, Spradley continues, is quite different. Career options are unclear to the beginner. A gulf yawns between their lives and what adults do. What kinds of careers are there over that gulf? What do people do in those positions? How do I decide which position is for me? How do I cross this gulf and get into the picture? The small-scale, nonindustrial cultures allowed twenty years of enculturation to adult careers. By comparison, Spradley observes, the postindustrial world expects youths to make a more complex transition from sixteen years of schooling to adult work in a matter of months or as little as a single weekend. And our culture has no ritual to ease the change.

It takes each student a while to assemble some kind of bridge across that gulf between college life and adult life. The average length of time in the U.S. between graduating with a B.A. and getting hired is six months to one year. That delay isn't usually because there aren't any jobs for liberal arts students. The delay is largely a cultural problem: new graduates simply don't know what to do next. A career counselor at Dartmouth College puts the problem like this: "Although liberal arts majors are qualified for dozens of jobs, they have no idea

[2]James P. Spradley, "Career Education from a Cultural Perspective," in Larry McClure and Carolyn Buan (eds.), *Essays in Career Education* (Portland, OR: Northwest Regional Educational Laboratory, 1973), pp. 3–16.

how to market themselves successfully."[3] They eventually figure it out and get back in the picture. Two years after graduation, two-thirds are employed full time (many of the others are in further study). Three-quarters of the employed are in positions related to their field of study.

My counseling efforts have aimed to enculturate students to the career life while they are still in college, thus abbreviating that liminal state after the baccalaureate degree. Of course, that's a tactical calculation. Looking back on sixteen years of formal education and looking ahead to a worklife of forty or more years, many of my advisees want to enter a liminal state for awhile. Nevertheless, other students are eager to move on. Those who made the effort during their college years to select a starting career, identify some employers, and prepare themselves for that career were rewarded by finding interesting work more quickly than those who waited until after they graduated. Students will have to make some time for this work in a busy college life. As my career planning colleague says, "Looking for a job is itself a job."

If students take up this job of career planning, their anthropology teachers can be valuable motivators and informants. However, not all professors say much about careers to their advisees or their classes. I know this is so because for years I have advised students from other colleges who sought me out at conferences, or when they were home visiting their parents, because they were suffering from anthro shock untreated by their own professors.

Why are some professors avoiding giving career advice? Some feel that after years in the ivory tower they don't understand the work world that their students want to enter. Times have changed, they say, since they were looking for a position. It is widely repeated in the college community that after graduation many students will enter careers that don't exist yet. Also, it is widely repeated that most people change careers (not just employers, but lines of work) several times in their working life. My career planning colleagues have amassed evidence to support these popular conceptions. So, "how can we know what to advise students today?" some of my colleagues wonder. Other professors define career advice, just as they do elementary writing instruction, as a task someone else should do.

A third reason that some professors avoid counseling for careers is that they don't approve of the idea of college as a place to credential people for jobs. In their view, student "vocationalism," or seeing college as a route to a good career, shifts the professor's role from liberator of young minds to gatekeeper of yuppiedom. Professors who teach critical approaches to culture want to inculcate resistance and a desire to change, not a desire to join, the system.

Anthropologist Michael Moffatt, in an insightful ethnography of residence halls and student culture, caused me to re-think student concern about jobs.[4] Moffatt suggests that professors who disdain student "vocationalism" are being hypocritical. After all, professors got their job by going to college, so why shouldn't the

[3]Burton Nadler, *Liberal Arts Power: What It Is and How to Sell It on Your Resume,* 2nd ed. (Princeton, NJ: Peterson's, 1989).

[4]Michael Moffat, *Coming of Age in New Jersey* (Brunswick, NJ: Rutgers University Press, 1986).

students want the same? Students expect that what they call their "job" will place them in the American middle classes, where their occupation will be a key element in their identity. They expect that job to offer them challenge, growth, rewards, security, and a chance to make the world a better place—all of which are goals deserving support from anthropology professors.

Translating the Skills

What does the student need to find that job and thus meet those goals? Career advice is partly a matter of teaching students to imagine themselves in a new way (the ethnographic "other's" way) and to construct a few basic models of what it's like in the working world.

Imagining themselves in a new way involves learning what employers (one of those ethnographic "others") really want (or think they want) and then reviewing one's education and experience for evidence of having acquired those desirable qualities. Seen in an anthropological light, this process may be called "trans-cultural self-presentation" and is similar to what the ethnographer initiates when entering the field and attempting to build rapport. Here are some data to assist that process.

Anthro shock contains the fear that one will acquire no marketable skills. "Marketable skills" implies there are other kinds as well. In fact, there are few skills that a liberal arts student acquires that aren't marketable. But there are temporary enthusiasms influencing which skills are considered desirable this year and what vocabulary is used to describe those skills. Anthropology students are well equipped to examine language, identify trends, and adapt to them by translating their own skills and knowledge into language appropriate for the setting.

Table 1 describes some skills that anthropology majors have an opportunity to develop at my college and, I am sure, at many other undergraduate institutions supporting a major. These are phrased in language immediately recognizable by the anthropology student and teacher.

Table 2 identifies twelve abilities often acquired through the undergraduate anthropology major. Fewer students and teachers will recognize their major as rephrased in this table, but employers will take notice. I advise my students to select anthropology and other courses intentionally to increase their competence in the abilities listed in Table 1 and then, when presenting themselves to potential graduate schools or employers, to highlight those abilities in the terms used in Table 2. Summer jobs, internships, volunteer work, as well as college classes may provide practice in the desirable activities (read "marketable skills").

Advanced majors in our senior seminar practice this transcultural self-presentation with exercises in composing résumé language. I begin by examining a résumé as a cultural text, an element in the process of seeking and offering jobs. We consider when and how their intended readers approach résumés. I argue that the résumé, in little more than a page, is intended to provoke interest in the writer as a person who can do (or learn to do) what the

TABLE 1   Some Transferable Skills in the Anthropology Major

—Interacting with people of diverse cultures, making allowance for difference in customs and beliefs
—Providing insight into social problems by supplying information about how problems—such as aging, conflict, or bereavement—are dealt with in other cultures
—Interviewing people to obtain information about their attitudes, knowledge, and behavior
—Using statistics and computers to analyze data
—Adapting approaches used in public relations, marketing, or politics to different population groups
—Appraising; classifying; and cataloging rare, old, or valuable objects
—Repairing, reconstructing, and preserving cultural artifacts by selecting chemical treatment, temperature, humidity, and storage methods
—Drawing maps and constructing scale models
—Photographing sites, objects, people, and events
—Interpreting or translating
—Using scientific equipment and measuring devices
—Analyzing craft techniques
—Cooperating in an ethnographic or archaeological research team
—Making policy based on social science research data, problem-solving methods, and professional ethical standards
—Designing research projects and applying for grants
—Producing a research paper in appropriate format and style
—Orally presenting research results
—Applying a variety of ethnographic data collection techniques: ethnosemantics, proxemics, life histories, ethnohistory, folklore, event analysis, genealogies, etc.
—Producing and editing a scholarly journal
—Leading a pre-professional organization such as a student anthropology society or honors society
—Developing public relations for a museum, field project, or conference
—Designing, building, installing, and acting as docent for museum exhibits
—Coaching, instructing, tutoring, and team-teaching with peers
—Studying a second language

Source: Adapted from John T. Omohundro, *Careers in Anthropology* (Mountain View, CA: Mayfield, 1998).

reader wants. In one column students list in their own language the experiences, both in their major and in their lives, that they think might have value. In a second column they conduct the "first-order" extraction of what skills and abilities were expected or practiced in those activities. In the third column they rephrase these skills and abilities in résumé language. Usually an anxiety-generating activity, composing résumés this way seems to generate more self-confidence.

What Careers Do Anthropology B.A.'s Pursue?

Students can be brought out of anthro shock by infusions of empirical data. Surveys have been conducted to assess what work anthropology students are prepared for and what fields alumni actually entered. In *Anthropology and Jobs,* H. Russell Bernard and Willis Sibley identified thirteen fields that the

TABLE 2   Résumé Language for Anthropological Abilities

Social agility—In an unfamiliar social or career-related setting, you learn to size up quickly the "rules of the game." You can become accepted more quickly than you could without anthropology.

Observation—As you must often learn about a culture from within it, you learn how to interview and observe as a participant.

Planning—You learn how to find patterns in the behavior of a cultural group. This allows you to generalize about their behavior and predict what they might do in a given situation.

Social sensitivity—While other people's ways of doing things may be different from your own, you learn the importance of events and conditions that have contributed to this difference. You also recognize that other cultures view your ways as strange. You learn the value of behaving toward others with appropriate preparation, care, and understanding.

Accuracy in interpreting behavior—You become familiar with the range of behavior in different cultures. You learn how to look at cultural causes of behavior before assigning causes yourself.

Challenging conclusions—You learn that analyses of human behavior are open to challenge. You learn how to use new knowledge to test past conclusions.

Interpreting information—You learn how to use data collected by others, reorganizing or interpreting it to reach original conclusions.

Simplifying information—As anthropology is conducted among publics as well as about them, you learn how to simplify technical information for communication to non-technical people.

Contextualizing—Attention to details is a trait of anthropology. However, you learn that any detail might not be as important as its context, and can even be misleading when context is ignored.

Problem-solving—Often functioning within a cultural group, or acting upon culturally sensitive issues, you learn to approach problems with care. Before acting, you learn how to identify the problem, set your goals, decide upon the actions you will take, and calculate possible effects on other people.

Persuasive writing—Anthropology strives to represent the behavior of one group to another group, and is in continual need of interpretation. You learn the value of bringing someone else to your view through written argument.

Social perspective—You learn how to perceive the acts of individuals and local groups as cause and effect of larger sociocultural systems. This enables you to "act locally and think globally."

Source: John T. Omohundro, *Careers in Anthropology* (Mountain View, CA: Mayfield, 1998).

anthropology B.A. could enter with no additional training.[5] These included journalism, police work, and the travel or tour industry. They also identified twenty-eight fields the anthropology B.A. could enter if additional training, up to the M.A. or M.S. level in the appropriate discipline, was acquired. These fields included dietetics, market research, city planning, museums, personnel, and community development, to name a few.

Ten years later, two of my students conducted a survey of anthropology alumni from 32 liberal arts colleges in the northeast U.S.[6] Of the 616 respondents, 62% worked in the profit sector, 9% in the non-profit sector, and 6% in government. 16% were still in a graduate or professional school.

[5]H. Russell Bernard and Willis E. Sibley, *Anthropology and Jobs: A Guide for Undergraduates*, American Anthropological Association special publication (Washington, DC: American Anthropological Association, 1975).

[6]Lawrence W. Kratts and Clarissa Hunter, "Undergraduate Alumni Survey Results," *Anthropology Newsletter* (November 1986).

The respondents' occupations were sorted into seventeen categories. Academics accounted for 10%, some of whom were in disciplines other than anthropology, but managers ("director," "administrator," etc.) dominated at 19%. It appears that a large number of anthropology majors become actors in a bureaucracy, supervising others. Medicine, communications, and business together accounted for another 16% of respondents' current positions.

Does this range of work positions outside of anthropology, as usually conceived, signal a failure on our part to place our advisees in positions that will utilize their major? I don't think so, and neither do the alumni. 71% of the northeast alumni agreed with the statement, "my anthropology education helps me in my current work." An owner of a small business wrote, "All aspects of the [antique] business are satisfying: attending antique shows, unearthing an early item, researching its age and provenance, restoring or repairing it, and educating a potential customer about it. . . ."

Most (81%) of the alumni returning the survey claimed they were satisfied and challenged by their current work, and 74% felt their decision to major in anthropology was a good one. Some alumni waxed enthusiastic about anthropology as the foundation for a liberal arts education. A banker urged current majors, "Go for it: no one in business will ever hold a liberal arts education against you. . . . In the long run this will mark you as superior to a crowd of business students. . . ." Alumni highlighted the value in their current work of cultural relativism, examining human behavior holistically, and using qualitative research methods, all acquired in the major. A social services administrator reported, "I work as a management analyst in a county social services agency. While it is difficult to get an anthro degree recognized as relevant, the anthropological approach is, I feel, one of the best for this sort of job. I'm always translating. . . ."

More recent surveys of alumni, such as the six colleges in the North Carolina system in 1988[7] and a SUNY Plattsburgh survey in 1993,[8] produced similar results. The majority of anthropology majors are 1) glad they majored in anthropology, 2) using some or all of the skills and perspectives they acquired in the major, and 3) enjoying their work, even if few of them are hanging out shingles bearing the title "anthropologist."

Along with their satisfaction, the alumni have some complaints and some advice for current students and their teachers. Overall, alumni were disappointed with the quality and quantity of career advice they received while undergraduates. They also see now that they would have benefitted from more careful choices of electives and course work outside of anthropology.

The northeast alumni urged current students to take courses in math, statistics, communications, economics, science, and computing. This advice matches that offered by alumni from most majors, who recommend courses in

---

[7]Stanton Tefft, with Cathy Harris and Glen Godwin, "North Carolina Undergraduate Alumni Survey," *Anthropology Newsletter* (January 1988).

[8]James Armstrong, personal communication, 1993.

administration, writing, interpersonal relations, economics, accounting, and math. In our northeast survey, anthropology alumni also strongly urged students to gain as much practical experience as possible through field schools, lab and methods courses, senior theses, independent research projects, overseas study, and collaboration with professors' research.

Conclusion

The purpose of this essay has been to help anthropology teachers deal with anthro shock among their students. I advocate swift first aid with the easy answer, but it is essential to have the evidence to back up that answer. I also advocate cooperation with careers planning professionals. Anthropology offers many marketable skills, or good training for a variety of fields of work, but students, working within the world view of college life and transcript semantics, often don't know how to translate their abilities into ones the rest of the world wants.

Surveys of alumni show that they pursue many lines of work, enjoy their work, are using their anthropological perspective and skills, and are glad they majored in anthropology. Their self-descriptions in surveys suggest that they majored in anthropology because its fundamental concepts and methods for understanding human behavior matched their long-established dispositions. After college, they found satisfying employment in positions where those same dispositions—now more developed through the major—were welcome and useful. This led me to a self-discovery theory of liberal arts education. That is, college is not a place where the student, as a blank slate ready to become a cog, learns "what I need to know to get a job." Instead, college is a place where the student discovers "what I like to do" and then refines his or her ability to do it. I've discovered that many career planning professionals knew this all along.

In sum, the evidence is that anthropology students not only find meaningful work, but they can use their anthropology to get that work, and we teachers can use our anthropology to improve our career advising. Not every anthropologist feels comfortable giving career advice, for several reasons, some of which I sympathize with and some I don't. Not every student needs to rush from college to a career, either, but I have discussed here some ways to help them if they want to move along.

Postscript: Grebbleberry recovered and is now doing fine as a technical illustrator in Oregon, coupling her artistic ability to her love of archaeology.

Review Questions

1. According to Omohundro, what are the "hard" and "easy" answers to the question, "What can I do with an anthropology major?"

2. What is the difference between the way people in small-scale and complex societies make the transition into the world of work?

3. What does Omohundro mean by the term *transcultural presentation?*

4. List some of the skills acquired by undergraduate anthropology majors that are useful to employers. How can these be translated into résumé language that employers can understand?

5. According to available studies, in what job sectors do anthropology graduates most often find employment?

6. What advice do anthropology graduates have for anthropology programs and students?

Glossary

Acculturation The process that takes place when groups of individuals having different cultures come into first-hand contact, which results in change to the cultural patterns of both groups.

Action anthropology Any use of anthropological knowledge for planned change by the members of a local cultural group.

Adjustment anthropology Any use of anthropological knowledge that makes social interaction between persons who operate with different cultural codes more predictable.

Administrative anthropology The use of anthropological knowledge for planned change by those who are external to a local cultural group.

Advocate anthropology Any use of anthropological knowledge by the anthropologist to increase the power of self-determination for a particular cultural group.

Affinity A fundamental principle of relationship linking kin through marriage.

Agriculture A subsistence strategy involving intensive farming of permanent fields through the use of such means as the plow, irrigation, and fertilizer.

Allocation of resources The knowledge people use to assign rights to the ownership and use of resources.

Applied anthropology Any use of anthropological knowledge to influence social interaction, to maintain or change social institutions, or to direct the course of cultural change.

Authority The right to make and enforce public policy.

Bilateral (cognatic) descent A rule of descent relating someone to a group of consanguine kin through both males and females.

Borrowing The adoption of something new from another group. Also see *diffusion*.

Caste A form of stratification defined by unequal access to economic resources and prestige, which is acquired at birth and does not permit individuals to alter their rank.

Clan A kinship group normally comprising several lineages; its members are related by a unilineal descent rule, but it is too large to enable members to trace actual biological links to all other members.

Class A system of stratification defined by unequal access to economic resources and prestige, but permitting individuals to alter their rank.

439

Coercion   A kind of political support derived from threats, use of force, or the promise of short-term gain.

Consanguinity   The principle of relationship linking individuals by shared ancestry (blood).

Contest   A method of settling disputes requiring disputants to engage in some kind of mutual challenge such as singing (as among the Inuit).

Cosmology   A set of beliefs that defines the nature of the universe or cosmos.

Court   A formal legal institution in which at least one individual has authority to judge and is backed up by a coercive system to enforce decisions.

Cultural contact   The situation that occurs when two societies with different cultures somehow come in contact with each other.

Cultural diffusion   The passage of a cultural category, culturally defined behavior, or culturally produced artifact from one society to another through borrowing.

Cultural ecology   The study of the way people use their culture to adapt to particular environments, the effects they have on their natural surrounding, and the impact of the environment on the shape of culture, including its long-term evolution.

Cultural environment   The categories and rules people use to classify and explain their physical environment.

Cultural hybridization   The process by which a cultural custom, item, or concept is transformed to fit the cultural context of a society that borrows it.

Culture   The knowledge that is learned, shared, and used by people to interpret experience and generate behavior.

Culture shock   A form of anxiety that results from an inability to predict the behavior of others or to act appropriately in cross-cultural situations.

Descent   A rule of relationship that ties people together on the basis of reputed common ancestry.

Descent groups   Groups based on a rule of descent.

Detached observer   A researcher who adopts the strategy of detached observation, an approach to scientific inquiry stressing emotional detachment and the construction of categories by the observer in order to classify what is observed.

Diffusion   The spread of cultural traits from one society to another through a process of contact and borrowing.

Distribution   The strategies for apportioning goods and services among the members of a group.

Divination   The use of supernatural force to provide answers to questions.

Division of labor   The rules that govern the assignment of jobs to people.

Ecology   The study of the way organisms interact with each other within an environment.

Economic system   The provision of goods and services to meet biological and social wants.

Egalitarian societies   Societies that, with the exception of ranked differences between men and women and adults and children, provide all people an equal chance at economic resources and prestige. Most hunter-gatherer societies are egalitarian by this definition.

Endogamy   Marriage within a designated social unit.

Ethnocentrism   A mixture of belief and feeling that one's own way of life is desirable and actually superior to others'.

Ethnography   The task of discovering and describing a particular culture.

Exogamy   Marriage outside any designated group.

Explicit culture   The culture that people can talk about and of which they are aware. Opposite of *tacit culture*.

Extended family   A family that includes two or more married couples.

Extralegal dispute   A dispute that remains outside the process of law and develops into repeated acts of violence between groups, such as feuds and wars.

Family   A residential group composed of at least one married couple and their children.

Globalization   The process that promotes economic, political, and other cultural connections among people living all over the world.

Go-between   An individual who arranges agreements and mediates disputes.

Grammar   The categories and rules for combining vocal symbols.

Guest workers   Individuals who are given temporary visas to live and work in another country.

Horticulture   A kind of subsistence strategy involving semi-intensive, usually shifting, agricultural practices. Slash-and-burn farming is a common example of horticulture.

Hunting and gathering   A subsistence strategy involving the foraging of wild, naturally occurring foods.

Incest taboo   The cultural rule that prohibits sexual intercourse and marriage between specified classes of relatives.

Industrialism   A subsistence strategy marked by intensive, mechanized food production and elaborate distribution networks.

Inequality   A human relationship marked by differences in power, authority, prestige, and access to valued goods and services, and by the payment of deference.

Informant   A person who teaches his or her culture to an anthropologist.

Infralegal dispute   A dispute that occurs below or outside the legal process without involving regular violence.

Innovation   A recombination of concepts from two or more mental configurations into a new pattern that is qualitatively different from existing forms.

Kinship   The complex system of social relationships based on marriage (affinity) and birth (consanguinity).

Language   The system of cultural knowledge used to generate and interpret speech.

Law   The cultural knowledge that people use to settle disputes by means of agents who have recognized authority.

Leadership   The ability to influence others to act.

Legitimacy   A kind of political support based on people's positive evaluation of public policy or positive evaluation of the political structure and process that produces public policy.

Lineage   A kinship group based on a unilineal descent rule that is localized, has some corporate powers, and whose members can trace their actual relationships to each other.

Magic   Strategies people use to control supernatural power to achieve particular results.

Mana   An impersonal supernatural force inherent in nature and in people. Mana is somewhat like the concept of "luck" in U.S. culture.

Market economies   Economies in which production and exchange are motivated by market factors: price, supply, and demand. Market economies are associated with large societies where impersonal exchange is common.

Market exchange   The transfer of goods and services based on price, supply, and demand.

Marriage   The socially recognized union between two people that accords legitimate birth status rights to their children.

Matrilineal descent   A rule of descent relating a person to a group of consanguine kin on the basis of descent through females only.

Microculture   The system of knowledge shared by members of a group that is part of a larger national society or ethnic group.

Monogamy   A marriage form in which a person is allowed only one spouse at a time.

Moot   A community meeting held for the informal hearing of a dispute.

Morpheme   The smallest meaningful category in any language.

Multicultural   Literally, more than one culture. Usually applied to situations where groups with different cultural backgrounds are part of a larger social aggregate.

Mythology   Stories that reveal the religious knowledge of how things have come into being.

Naive realism   The notion that reality is much the same for all people everywhere.

Nonlinguistic symbols   Any symbols that exist outside the system of language and speech; for example, visual symbols.

Nuclear family   A family composed of a married couple and their children.

Ordeal   A supernaturally controlled, painful, or physically dangerous test, the outcome of which determines a person's guilt or innocence.

Pastoralism   A subsistence strategy based on the maintenance and use of large herds of animals.

Patrilineal descent   A rule of descent relating consanguine kin on the basis of descent through males only.

Personified supernatural force   Supernatural force inherent in supernatural beings such as goddesses, gods, spirits, and ghosts.

Phoneme   The minimal category of speech sounds that signals a difference in meaning.

Phonology   The categories and rules for forming vocal symbols.

Phratry   A group composed of two or more clans. Members acknowledge unilineal descent from a common ancestor but recognize that their relationship is distant.

Physical environment   The world as people experience it with their senses.

Policy   Any guideline that can lead directly to action.

Political system   The organization and process of making and carrying out public policy according to cultural categories and rules.

Polyandry   A form of polygamy in which a woman has two or more husbands at one time.

Polygamy   A marriage form in which a person has two or more spouses at one time. Polygyny and polyandry are both forms of polygamy.

Polygyny   A form of polygamy in which a man is married to two or more women at one time.

Prayer   A petition directed at a supernatural being or power.

Priest   A full-time religious specialist who intervenes between people and the supernatural, and who often leads a congregation at regular cyclical rites.

Production   The process of making something.

Public   The group of people a policy will affect.

Ramage   A cognatic (bilateral) descent group that is localized and holds corporate responsibility.

Rank societies   Societies stratified on the basis of prestige only.

Reciprocal exchange The transfer of goods and services between two people or groups based on their role obligations. A form of non-market exchange.

Redistribution The transfer of goods and services between a group of people and a central collecting service based on role obligation. The U.S. income tax is a good example.

Refugees People who flee their country of origin because they share a well-founded fear of persecution.

Religion The cultural knowledge of the supernatural that people use to cope with the ultimate problems of human existence.

Respondent An individual who responds to questions included on questionnaires; the subject of survey research.

Revitalization movement A deliberate, conscious effort by members of a society to construct a more satisfying culture.

Role The culturally generated behavior associated with particular statuses.

Sacrifice The giving of something of value to supernatural beings or forces.

Self-redress The actions taken by an individual who has been wronged to settle a dispute.

Semantics The categories and rules for relating vocal symbols to their referents.

Shaman A part-time religious specialist who controls supernatural power, often to cure people or affect the course of life's events.

Slash-and-burn agriculture A form of horticulture in which wild land is cleared and burned over, farmed, then permitted to lie fallow and revert to its wild state.

Social acceptance A process that involves learning about an innovation, accepting an innovation as valid, and revising one's cultural knowledge to include the innovation.

Social groups The collections of people that are organized by culturally defined rules and categories.

Social network An assortment of people with whom an individual regularly interacts but who themselves do not regularly form an organized group.

Social situation The categories and rules for arranging and interpreting the settings in which social interaction occurs.

Social stratification The ranking of people or groups based on their unequal access to valued economic resources and prestige.

Sociolinguistic rules Rules specifying the nature of the speech community, the particular speech situations within a community, and the speech acts that members use to convey their messages.

Sorcery The malevolent practice of magic.

Speech The behavior that produces meaningful vocal sounds.

Spirit possession The control of a person by a supernatural being in which the person becomes that being.

Status A culturally defined position associated with a particular social structure.

Stratified societies Societies that are at least partly organized on the principle of social stratification. Contrast with *egalitarian* and *rank societies*.

Subject The person who is observed in a social or psychological experiment.

Subsistence economies Economies that are local and that depend largely on the nonmarket mechanisms, reciprocity and redistribution, to motivate production and exchange.

Subsistence strategies Strategies used by groups of people to exploit their environment for material necessities. Hunting and gathering, horticulture, pastoralism, agriculture, and industrialism are subsistence strategies.

Supernatural Things that are beyond the natural. Anthropologists usually recognize a belief in such things as goddesses, gods, spirits, ghosts, and *mana* to be signs of supernatural belief.

Support Anything that contributes to the adoption of public policy and its enforcement.

Symbol Anything that humans can sense that is given an arbitrary relationship to its referent.

Tacit culture The shared knowledge of which people usually are unaware and do not communicate verbally.

Technology The part of a culture that involves the knowledge that people use to make and use tools and to extract and refine raw materials.

Transcendent values Values that override differences in a society and unify the group.

Transnational Literally, across national borders.

Ultimate problems Universal human problems, such as death, the explanation of evil and the meaning of life, and transcendent values that can be answered by religion.

Unit of production The group of people responsible for producing something.

Witchcraft The reputed activity of people who inherit supernatural force and use it for evil purposes.

World system The economic incorporation of different parts of the world into a system based on capitalism, not politics.

Worldview The way people characteristically look out on the universe.

Index

A

Acculturation, 383–384
Action anthropology, 383
Adaptation
   biological, 84
   cultural, 84
Adjustment anthropology, 383
Administrative anthropology, 384
Advocate anthropology, 384
Affinity, 173 (*see also* Marriage)
African hunter/gatherers, 27–34,
   89–103
Aggregate, 212
Agriculture
   definition of, 86
   horticulture as a kind of,
     124–133
   slash and burn, 127–128
AIDs, 42, 44, 161, 405
Alcoholic beverages, 126
Alliance, marriage, 188–189
Allocation of resources, 136
Amazon forest, 385–402
   management of, 124–133

Amazonian Indians, 383
Anonymity and the veil, 244
Anthropologists as expert witness,
   270
Anthropology (*see also* Cultural
   anthropology)
   academic, 383
   action, 383
   adjustment, 383
   administrative, 383
   advocate, 384
   biological, 84
   medical, 404
   uses of, 415–427
Anthropology majors, skills acquired
   by, 432–433
Applied anthropology, 79–82,
   263–271, 383
   In Malawi, 403–414
Arak (Bhil word for clan), 190
'ard (female honor), 245–246
Arrogance among the !Kung, 21–22
Aspiration, use in pronunciation,
   54
Authority, 261–262

B

Barbados, 46–51
Baseball, magic in, 310–319
Behavior, drinking, 24
Bernard, H. R., 433
Betrothal, 190–191
Bhil, 174, 300–301, 420
    marriage among, 186–193
Big man, 206–207
Bilateral descent, 214
Biological adaptation, 103
Blumer, Herbert, 13–14
Body ritual, 334–339
Bolivia, effect of cocaine on,
    156–166
Bombardier, Joseph-Armand, 381
Boreholes and the !Kung, 101–102
Borrowing, cultural, 381–382 (*see
    also* Diffusion)
Brazil, 176–185, 385–402
Bride price, 191
Bushman (*see* !Kung)

C

Career planning, 430–431
Careers
    advising about, 428–443
    in anthropology, 428–430
    of anthropology graduates, 435
    pursued by anthropology BAs,
        433–434
Cash labor, impact on kinship of, 278
Caste, 212
Caucus, 282, 288
Cell phones, was to carry, 80
Change
    among the Dobe Ju/'hoansi,
        101–102
    cultural, 381
    environmental, 104–113

Charms (*see* Fetishes)
Cherokee, 289
Chewa, 407
Chief, 278–279, 288
Child care, 176–185, 403–414
Chinese, 203–209
Civilization, disappearance of,
    104–113
Clan, 174, 189–190
Class, social, 50, 227–239
    definition of, 212
Cocaine
    in Bolivia, 156–166
    control of, 162
    impact on Indians of, 162–163
    production of, 160–161
Coercion, 261
Cognatic descent (*see* Bilateral
    descent)
Cognitive map, 13
Colonialism, impact of on rain
    forests, 134–127
Colonos (colonists in Paraguay),
    124–125, 129
Communication and language,
    53–55
Communication technology, 79–82
    forms of, 80–82
Consanguinity, 173 (*see also*
    Descent)
Consent forms, 40–41
Conservation programs, 131–132
Contests in dispute settlement, 261
Conversation and gender, 62
Conversation, styles of, 61–68
Cook, Captain James, 106
Corporate kin groups among
    Gypsies, 269
Corporations, ethnographic
    management in, 419–423
Cousin marriage, 295–296
Cosmology, 301

Courts, 261
Crack cocaine, 227–239
Cross-cultural misunderstanding, 15–22, 46–51
Cultural adaptation, 84
Cultural anthropology, 3
Cultural artifacts, 10, 12
Cultural behavior, 10,12
Cultural borrowing, 381
Cultural classification:
  of avocados, 252
  of race, 252–254
Cultural code, 84
Cultural contact, 382, 385–402
Cultural diffusion, 381
Cultural ecology, 84
Cultural environment, 85
Cultural imperialism, 374
Cultural knowledge, 11
Cultural misunderstanding, 11–12
Culture, 1–5, 420
  and adaptation, 84–85
  definition of, 1–2
  explicit, 12
  popular, 365–379
  tacit, 13
Culture, explicit, 69
Culture, tacit 69
Culture shock, 4
Curing rituals in India, 203–309

D

Dam building, 392
Dapa (Bhil word for bride price), 191
Death (*see also* Infant death)
  in Brazil, 176–185
  mothers' indifference to, 176–182
  officials' reaction to, 183–184
Deforestation
  in Paraguay, 124–133
  and the Kayapo, 385–402

Demography of the !Kung, 95
Descent
  bilateral, 174
  definition of, 173
  groups, 174
  matrilineal, 174
  patrilineal, 173, 190
Detached observation, 3, 7
Development
  and ecology, 132
  impact on forests of, 131–133
  sustainable, 126–127, 132–133
  unsustainable, 129–132
Diet selectivity of the !Kung, 93
Diffusion, cultural, 381
Disputes, 260–261
  extralegal, 260
  infralegal, 260
  legal, 260
Distribution, economic, 137
Divination, definition of, 300–301
Division of labor, 136
Dobe (*see* !Kung)
Drinking behavior, 24
Drug dealing, in Harlem, 227–239
Dyson-Hudson, Rada, 141

E

East Asia, 203–209
Easter Island, 104–113
  discovery of, 123
  subsistence patterns on, 106
Ecological resistance, 401–402
Ecology, 84–85:
  and development, 132
Economic system, 136
Economy
  definition of, 136
  formal, 227
  shadow (*see also* informal, underground), 227–239

Economies
  market, 138
  redistributive, 138
  subsistence, 138
Egalitarian society, 213
Eliade, Mircea, 325
Embera, 354
Emotional attachment, to children
    in Brazil, 176–185
Endogamy, 174
Entering the field, 36–38
Environment (*see also*
    Development, Ecology,
    Subsistence strategies)
  cultural, 84
  Kayapo relation to, 389–391
  physical, 84
Environmental degradation, on
    Easter Island, 104–113
Environmental movement, 399–401
Eskimo (*see* Inuit)
Ethical dilemmas, in research, 40
Ethnocentrism, 4
Ethnographic management, 415–427
Ethnography, 33–45
  Student, 46–51
  and culture, 7–14
  definition of, 2
  among the !Kung, 15–22
  and management, 419–423
  among prostitutes, 33–45
Ethnoscape, 376
Exchange
  definition of, 137
  market, 137, 156–166
  reciprocal, 137, 139–145
  redistributive, 144
Exogamy, 174
  village, 189
Expert witness, anthropologist as,
    270

Explicit culture, 4, 12, 69
Extended family, 174
  on Taiwan, 203–209
Extralegal disputes, 260

F

Factory work, 230
Family
  definition of, 174
  extended, 174
  nuclear, 174
  uterine, 203–209
Family loyalty, in India, 193
Famine relief program, United
    Nations, 99
Feast, among !Kung, 15–22
Female migration, 146–155
Feminal kin, 189
Fertilizer subsidies, 169
Fieldwork, 7–8, 71–72 (*see also*
    Ethnography)
  on Barbados, 46–56
  in Japan, 366–367
  among the !Kung, 15–22
  of prostitutes, 33–45
Fetishes, 315–318
Financescape, 376
Flenley, John, 108
Folk taxonomies, 252–254
  of race, 258
Foraging, 15–22, 85, 88–103
Forest
  Amazonian, 385–402
  destruction of, 109–110,125
Formal economy, 127
Forms, consent, 40–41
Franklin, Benjamin, 288
Friedl, Ernestine, 216
FUNAI (Brazilian Indian Service),
    392–393

G

Genba globalism, 376
Gender (*see also* Male dominance,
    Sex roles)
  and conversation styles, 61–68
Gender stereotypes, 68
Genderism, 63
Genetic code, 84
Gen Xers, 219
Ghosts
    Hindu beliefs in, 305
    malevolent possession by, 303–309
Gift giving, 139–145
    as academic citations, 143
    as foreign aid, 144–145
    as a way to fight, 142
Giving, meanings of, 15–22 (*see also*
    Reciprocity, Reciprocal
    exchange)
Glass ceiling, 222
Globalism, genba, 376
Globalization, 146–155, 341, 365–379:
    definition of, 341
    process of, 154–155
Go-between, 261
Goffman, Irving, 93
Grammar, 54–55
Groups
    kinship, 173
    social, 212
Group differences, explanations of,
    1–2
Guarani, 124–133
Guest workers, 342
Gypsies, American, 263–271

H

Hadza, 216–217
Hall, Edward, 13

Headman, 275
Heyerdahl, T, 382
Hicks, George, 8, 13
Hindi phonemes, 54
Hindu beliefs about ghosts, 305
Hip-hop, 365–379
    clubs, 367–369
HIV (*see* AIDS)
Honor, for men and women,
    257–258
Horticulture
    definition of, 85–86
    Guarani, 124–133
    Kayapo, 385–402
    and political structure, 277
Human nature, 279–280
Hunter, C., 434
Hunter/gatherers (*see also* hunting
    and gathering)
    political structure of, 273–277
    subsistence strategies of, 89–103
    value on equality among, 15–22
Hunting and gathering
    definition of, 85
    !Kung examples of, 15–22, 89–103,
    137
    loss of dependence on, 101–102
Hybridization, 342
Hypo-descent, 253

I

Identity, occupational, 216–217
Ideoscapes, 376
Imitative magic, 316
Incest taboo, 175
India, 1–3, 186–194, 299–305
Indian giver, 140
Indian gift, 140
Indians and cocaine production, 162
Industrialism, 86

Inequality, 212–213
Infant death, church's reaction to in Brazil, 183–184
Infanticide, passive, 179
Inflation as a result of cocaine production, 159
Informant, 3, 4 (*see also* respondent, subject of experiment)
Informants, relations with, 46–51
Infralegal dispute, 260
Inheritance, 190
Innovation, 381
Interaction, ritual nature of, 63
International Monetary Fund, 361
Inuit, 217
Iraq, 291–297
Iroquois, 205
    League of, 281–290
Islam, 240
    and the seclusion of women, 242–243

J

Japan, 365–379
Japanese Hip-hop, 365–379
Juices, kinds of, 73–77
Juicing (kind of tattooist talk), 69–78
Ju/'hoansi, Dobe, 88–103 (*see also* !Kung)

K

Kalahari desert, 89
Kanguijy (alcoholic beverage), 126
Kayapo resistance to development, 389–391
Kayapo, 385–402
    and the Brazilian government, 383–395
    and environmental groups, 383–399
Kin, feminal, 189

Kin groups, 174
King, Sarah, 108
Kinship, 172–175
    as an adaptation to agriculture, 187
    groups, 174
    impact of cash labor on, 9
    in India, 186–194
Kratts, L., 434
Kula, 142
!Kung, 15–22, 88–103, 137, 274, 276
!Kung San (*see* !Kung)
Kwakiutl potlatch, 142–143

L

Language, 4, 58
    and gender, 61–68
    and politics, 57
    resume, 434
    substantive, 263
    subsystems of, 54–65
Law, 260
    and Gypsies, 263–271
League of the Iroquois
    founding of, 283–284
    structure of, 284
    power of, 285
Legal disputes, 260
Legitimacy, 261
Leisure, amount of, 98–99
Leasurescapes, 376
Life expectancy, 178
Liminal period, 320
Liminality, 326
Lineage, 180, 189
Localization, 365, 373–376
Love, mothers for infants, 176–185

M

Magic
    in baseball, 314–319

definition of, 300
function of, 307
imitative, 316
theories of, 311
and uncertainty, 310–312
as a way to reduce anxiety, 311
in WW II, 316–317
Malawi, 167–171, 403–414
economy of, 169, 406
geography of, 406
impact of World Bank on, 170
male/female behavior, 61–68
Malinowski, Bronislaw Kaspar, 311, 319
Mana, 300
Management:
by defense, 418
ethnographic approach to, 417–426
Mantras (powerful ritual chants in India), 300
Marime (Gypsy word for pollution), 267, 270
Market
as a kind of exchange, 138
system, 138
economy, 167
Marriage
alliance, 188–189
arranged, 188–190
cousin, 295–296
definition of, 174
endogamous, 174–175
exogamous, 174–175
polyandrous, 208
polygamous, 175
polygynous, 175
Marshall Islanders, 375
Matrilineal descent, 174:
among the Chewa, 403
Mbuti (Pygmy), 261
Meaning, cultural, 12–13

Meat
distribution of, 18–19
Mediascapes, 376
Medical anthropology, definition of, 404
Men and women:, talk between, on the job, 61–68
Men's and women's roles, 245
Microculture, 3, 416
Middle East, 240–247
Midwives, 181
Migration, female, 146–155
Migrants, 344–353
and communications technology, 81–82,
Military operations, naming of, 57–60
Milk goats, introduction of in Malawi, 403–414
Miskito Indians, 114–123
Misunderstanding, cross-cultural, 27–44, 46–51
Moffatt, Michael, 431
Mongongo nuts, !Kung subsistence on, 91–93
Monogamy, 175 (*see also* Marriage)
Moot, 261
Morphemes, 55
Mortal selective neglect (*see* passive infanticide)
Mother-in-law, relations with on Taiwan, 205–206, 208
Mothering, in Brazil, 176–185
Motorcycles, in American culture, 327–328
Mukogodo, 141
Multicultural, 342
Mythology, 301

N

Nacimema, 334–339
Nadler, B., 446

Naive realism, 4, 9–10, 46, 50–51
  Tiv and American examples of,
    23–32
Nannies, 147
Narco chic (new class of Latin
    American drug barons), 157
Need, economic, 136
Nonlinguistic symbols, 55
Nuclear family, 174
Nuer, 344–353
Nutrition, 403–414

O

Oliver, Douglas, 277
Omens, among the Tiv, 16, 29
Ordeals as a way to settle disputes,
    261
Over fishing, 115
Oxen (*see also* Cattle and
    Pastoralism)
  role in feast, 15–22

P

Paraguay, 124–133
Passive infanticide, 179
Pasta (cocaine paste), 159
Pastorialism, 86
Patrilineal
  descent, 173, 190
  extended family on Taiwan,
    203–209
  systems in the Middle East,
    240–247
Patrones (Latin American land
    owners), 113
Personified supernatural force,
    300
Phonemes, 4
  definition of, 54
  Hindi example of, 54
Phonology, 54

Phratry, 174 (*see also* Descent groups)
Physical environment, 84
Pilgrimage, 320–333
  anthropology of, 323–324
Pitt-Rivers, Julian, 245
Policy, public, 261
Political
  Hierarchies, 281
  structure, 272–280
Political system, definition of, 261
Pollen, analysis of, 108, 110
Pollution, Gypsy beliefs about, 270
Polyandry, 175, 195–202 (*see
    also* Tibetan fraternal
    polyandry)
  Fraternal (definition of), 196
Polygamy, 174–175, 195, 208
Polygyny, 175, 195
Polynesia, 104–113
Popular culture, 365–379
Population density, 142
Population growth
  effects of, 111–112
  on Easter Island, 111
Potlatch, 142–143
Prayer, 300
Priests, 301
Principles of social acceptance,
    culture change, 382
Production, 136
Prostitution, 33–45, 360
Public, definition of, 261
Public policy, 261
Purdah
  in the Middle East, 240–247
  and the veil, 244
Pygmy (*see* Mbuti)

Q

Qualitative research, 417
Quechua, 157

R

Race, U.S. and Brazilian
conceptions of, 248–258
Ramage, 174 (*see also* Bilateral
descent)
Rank societies, 213
Rastafarian, 40–50
Reciprocal exchange, 137
Reciprocal gift giving, 139–145
Reciprocity, 139–145, 273–274:
definition of, 137
and risk, 273
Redistribution exchange, 137
Refugees, 342
adjustment of, 349–351
communication among, 351–352
process of becoming, 346–349
resettlement of, 344–353
Religion, 299
Resistance to subordination, 236
Resources, use of by
hunter/gatherers, 88–103
Respondent, 3
Resume language for anthropology
BAs, 434
Revitalization
definition of, 301
stages in, 301–302
Ritual, 322–323
anthropology of, 324–326
body, 334–339
in baseball, 312–314
children's, 206
curing, 303–309
definition of, 324
function of, 384
personal, 382–383
reincorporation, 320
roles, 203–209, 219, 228
of separation, 320
of women, 203–209
Religion, 299

Remlinger, Kate, 67
Respect behavior, between in-laws,
191–192
Respondent, 3
Revitalization
theory of, 301–302
Ritual
in baseball, 312–314
children's, 306
and conversation, 63
curing, 303–309
function of, 384
personal, 382–383
roles, 203–209, 210, 245
of women, 203–209
Roggeveen, Jacob, 105–107
Role, definition of, 211
Roles, of women in India, 303–309
Run for the wall, 320–333
Rynkiewich, Michael, 383

S

Sachems, 284–286
impeachment of, 286
Sacrifice, definition of, 300
Sacriscapes, 376
Sapir, Edward, 56
Sapir-Whorf hypothesis, 56
School dropouts, 230
Seafood, 114–115
Sea turtles
harpooning of, 119–120
effect on Miskito ecosystem, 121
effect on Miskito health, 121
market demand for, 116
netting of, 120
place in traditional Miskito
economy, 116
Seclusion (*see also* Purdah)
and the veil, 243
of women, 241–243

Self redress, 261

Semai, 261

Semantics, 55

Sex
  roles, 203–209

Sexual inequality, 241

Shadow economy, 227 (*see also*
  informal and underground)

Shaman, 301

Sharaf (male honor), 245

Shifting agriculture, 127–128,
  387–389

Sibley, W., 433–435

Sivai, 277

Skills acquired by anthropology BAs,
  432–433

Skinner, B. F., 310–319

Slash-and-burn agriculture, 87, 124,
  387–389 (*see also* Horticulture)

Smith, G., 382

Social acceptance of change, 382

Social class, 50, 212, 227–239

Social organization, 173–175:
  of the Kayapo, 389–391

Social role, 211

Social situation, 211–212

Social status, 211

Social stratification, 212, 278 (*see
  also* Caste, Class)

Sociolinguistic rules, 55

Sorcery, 300

Spanish Harlem, 227–239

Speech, 53

Spirit possession
  definition of, 300
  by a malevolent ghost, 303–309

Spradley, James P., 430

Standard of living, 139

States, 279

Statues on Easter Island, 106–107,
  111

Status, 125

Steadman, David, 105, 112

Story telling among the Tiv, 25

Stratified society, 127

Street culture, 232–233

Subject, 3

Subject of experiment, 3

Subsistence
  !Kung, 88–103
  patterns of on Easter Island, 106
  strategies, 85–86

Substantive law, 263

Sudan, civil war in, 347

Supernatural, 299

Supernatural force
  impersonal, 300 (*see also* mana)
  personal, 300

Support, political, 261

Sustainable development, 132–133

Symbolic interaction, premises of,
  13–14

Symbolixm, 317

Symbols, 12, 593
  nonlinguistic, 55
  vocal, 54

T

Taboo
  in baseball, 316
  incest, 175

Tacit culture, 4, 13, 69

Taiwan, 203–209

Taiwanese, 203–209

Talk, ways to, 69–70
  Juicing, 69–78

Tamoi (Guaraní headman), 127

Tattoo shop, 70–71
Tattoo talk, 69–78
Technology, 136
  Communication, 79–82
Technoscapes, 376
Teffts, S., 298
Tibet, 195–202
Tibetan fraternal polyandry
  folk explanation for, 197
  tension created by, 198
  analytical explanations of,
    198–199
Tillion, Germaine, 241
Tipo (Brazilian for racial type),
    254–256
Tiv, 23–32
Tiwi, 217
Tourism, 354–364:
  history of: 356–357
  impact of, 358–363
Trance dance, 98
Transcendent values, 299
Transnationalism, 351
Trial, of a Gypsy, 267–268
Tropical forest, subsistence in,
    124–133
Taboo, 310, 315–316,
Tourism, 342, 354–364
Transnational, forms of, 365
Turner, Victor, 325–326
Tswana, 15, 17
Tylor, Edward B., 2

U

Ultimate problems of human
  existence, 299–300
Undernourishment of children,
    403–414

Underground economy, 229–236
  (*see also* informal or shadow
  economy)
Unit of production, 137
United States
  capitol, 282–283
  frontier states, 289
Unsustainable development,
    129–132
USAID (United States Agency for
  International Development), 405
Uterine family, 203–209

V

Veil, symbolic meaning of,
    240–247
Vietnam war, 326–327
Village life, 50
Vitsa (Gypsy corporate kin group),
    264, 266
Vocal symbols, 54
Volags (voluntary agencies), 349

W

Washington concensus, 168
Wallace, A. F. C., 301
Want, economic, 136
War, civil, 347
Washo, 216
Waters, Malcolm, 374–375
Whorf, Benjamin Lee, 56
Witchcraft, 29:
  definition of, 300
Women
  community of, 207–209
  and family, 210–216
  in patrilineal systems, 203–209

Women (*continued*)
  seclusion of, 241–243 (*see also*
    Purdah)
  and work, 66–67
Women's migration
  government encouragement of,
    151
  history of, 149–150
  patterns of, 150–151
  reasons for, 152–154
  work, 215–226
Work
  as a determinate of status, 217
  Women's, 215–226
Workplace, conversation in, 61–63
World Bank, 361

World languages, 1
Worldview
  definition of, 301

X

Xingu River, 385–402

Y

Yerba mata, 125, 129
Yinger, Milton, 298

Z

Zombie, 27–28